About the Cover Image

Istanbul in the Making

Like the authors of this book, Dutch artist and photographer Martin Roemers seeks to translate global themes into human dimensions. This single image captures the boundless, almost tangible energy and tumult of Istanbul, a city of more than 10 million people and the only city in the world to connect two continents. Once the capital of three great empires—the Roman, Byzantine, and Ottoman—Istanbul (formerly named Byzantium and Constantinople) today is a leading cosmopolitan center of global civilization.

Ancillary Resource Center

for

*World in the Making:
A Global History*

BONNIE G. SMITH
MARC VAN DE MIEROOP
RICHARD VON GLAHN
KRIS LANE

Carefully scratch off the silver coating with a coin to see your personal redemption code.

This code can be used only once and cannot be shared!

If the code has been scratched off when you receive it, the code may not be valid. Once the code has been scratched off, this access card cannot be returned to the publisher. You may buy access at **www.oup.com/us/smith-world**.

The code on this card is valid for 2 years from the date of first purchase. Complete terms and conditions are available at **https://oup-arc.com.**

Access length: 6 months from redemption of the code.

Directions for registering your **Ancillary Resource Account**

Visit **www.oup.com/us/smith-world**

⬇

Click the link to upgrade your access to the student resources

⬇

Follow the on-screen instructions.

⬇

Enter your personal redemption code when prompted on the checkout screen.

⬇

For assistance with code redemption or registration for the Ancillary Resource Center, please contact customer support at **arc.support@oup.com.**

OXFORD
UNIVERSITY PRESS

World in the Making

World in the Making

A GLOBAL HISTORY

VOLUME TWO: SINCE 1300

Bonnie G. Smith
Rutgers University

Marc Van De Mieroop
Columbia University

Richard von Glahn
University of California, Los Angeles

Kris Lane
Tulane University

New York   Oxford
OXFORD UNIVERSITY PRESS

Oxford University Press is a department of the University of Oxford.
It furthers the University's objective of excellence in research, scholarship,
and education by publishing worldwide. Oxford is a registered trade mark of
Oxford University Press in the UK and certain other countries.

Published in the United States of America by Oxford University Press
198 Madison Avenue, New York, NY 10016, United States of America.

For titles covered by Section 112 of the US Higher Education
Opportunity Act, please visit www.oup.com/us/he for the latest
information about pricing and alternate formats.

Library of Congress Cataloging-in-Publication Data
Names: Smith, Bonnie G., 1940- author.
Title: World in the making : a global history / Bonnie G. Smith, Rutgers
    University, Marc Van de Mieroop, Columbia University, Richard von Glahn,
    University of California, Los Angeles, Kris Lane, Tulane University.
Description: New York : Oxford University Press, [2018] | Includes
    bibliographical references and index.
Identifiers: LCCN 2018006687| ISBN 9780190849238 (pbk. : alk. paper) | ISBN
    9780190849245 (pbk. : alk. paper) | ISBN 9780190849269 (ebook) | ISBN
    9780190849276 (ebook)
Subjects: LCSH: World history.
Classification: LCC D21 .S626 2018 | DDC 909—dc23
LC record available at https://lccn.loc.gov/2018006687

Printing number: 9 8 7 6
Printed by LSC Communications, Inc.
United States of America

Brief Contents

Contents

PART 2   Crossroads and Cultures 500–1450 C.E.

CHAPTER 14   **Collapse and Revival in Afro-Eurasia 1300–1450   488**

The Major Global Development in this Chapter: *Crisis and recovery in fourteenth- and fifteenth-century Afro-Eurasia.*

ix

PART 3   **The Early Modern World, 1450–1750**

CHAPTER 15

Empires and Alternatives in the Americas 1430–1530   530

The Major Global Development in this Chapter: *The diversity of societies and states in the Americas prior to European invasion.*

CHAPTER 17

Western Africa in the Era of the Atlantic Slave Trade 1450–1800   604

The Major Global Development in this Chapter: *The rise of the Atlantic slave trade and its impact on early modern African peoples and cultures.*

CHAPTER 18

Trade and Empire in the Indian Ocean and South Asia 1450–1750   640

The Major Global Development in this Chapter: *The Indian Ocean trading network and the impact of European intrusion on maritime and mainland South Asia.*

CHAPTER 19

Consolidation and Conflict in Europe and the Greater Mediterranean 1450–1750   678

The Major Global Development in this Chapter: *Early modern Europe's increasing competition and division in the face of Ottoman expansion.*

CHAPTER 20

Expansion and Isolation in Asia 1450–1750   720

The Major Global Development in this Chapter: *The general trend toward political and cultural consolidation in early modern Asia.*

CHAPTER 21

Transforming New Worlds: The American Colonies Mature 1600–1750   758

The Major Global Development in this Chapter: *The profound social, cultural, and environmental changes in the Americas under colonial rule.*

PART 4   The World from 1750 to the Present

CHAPTER 22

Atlantic Revolutions and the World 1750–1830   800

The Major Global Development in this Chapter: *The Atlantic revolutions and their short- and long-term significance.*

CHAPTER 23 **Industry and Everyday Life 1750–1900 838**

The Major Global Development in this Chapter: *The Industrial Revolution and its impact on societies and cultures throughout the world.*

CHAPTER 24 # Nation-States and Their Empires 1830–1900   874

The Major Global Development in this Chapter: *The rise of modern nation-states and their competition for empire.*

CHAPTER 25

Wars, Revolutions, and the Birth of Mass Society 1900–1929   914

The Major Global Development in this Chapter: *The wars and revolutions of the early twentieth century and their role in the creation of mass culture and society.*

CHAPTER 26

Global Catastrophe: The Great Depression and World War II 1929–1945   954

The Major Global Development in this Chapter: *The causes and outcomes of the Great Depression and World War II.*

CHAPTER 27

The Emergence of New Nations in a Cold War World 1945–1970　992

The Major Global Development in this Chapter: *The political transformations of the postwar world and their social and cultural consequences.*

CHAPTER 28

A New Global Age 1989 to the Present   1030

The Major Global Development in this Chapter: *The causes and consequences of intensified globalization.*

SPECIAL FEATURES

Preface

"I once met a little girl tenderly carrying a puppy in the bark [-fiber] carrying-strap that her mother used for her little sister. 'Are you stroking your baby dog?' I asked her. She solemnly replied, 'When I am big, I will kill wild pigs and monkeys; I will club them all to death when he barks!'"

The world-famous French anthropologist Claude Lévi-Strauss spent much of the mid-twentieth century scouring Brazil's backlands in search of native Americans whose cultures remained largely unchanged by contact with Europeans and others. He wanted to catalogue and analyze their unique customs, myths, and material culture before they disappeared. Made rich by global demand for coffee and other raw commodities, Brazil was rapidly industrializing, encouraging prospectors, ranchers, and homesteaders to transform what had for over ten thousand years been "Indian country."

In the late 1930s, Lévi-Strauss spent time among the Nambikwara of western Mato Grosso State, near the border with Bolivia. As he recalled in his best-selling 1955 memoir *Tristes Tropiques*: "Although the Nambikwara were easy-going, and unperturbed by the presence of an anthropologist with his notebook and camera, the work was complicated by linguistic difficulties." Long isolated, the Nambikwara spoke no Portuguese. Lévi-Strauss nevertheless learned to communicate in the Nambikwara language, such that he felt comfortable quoting the unnamed little girl with the puppy, future hunter of boars and monkeys.

Was *Tristes Tropiques* a summary of scientific observations or a personal narrative shot through with romantic views? Reflecting on these encounters in his memoir, Lévi-Strauss referred to Nambikwara territory as "the lost world," its society the least complex he had ever seen. They wore no clothes, slept on the cold ground beneath the stars, and produced no pottery, weavings, or much else beyond basic gathering and hunting tools. Lévi-Strauss concluded: "I had been looking for a society reduced to its simplest expression. That of the Nambikwara was so truly simple that all I could find in it was individual human beings."

Not long after, in 1959, Lévi-Strauss famously proposed that human societies were either "cold" or "hot," the former stuck in time or reliant on the ordering principles of origin stories whereas the latter were dynamic, always changing; in a word, history-making. The proposal spurred debate, and over the past five or six decades, scholars have almost universally rejected Lévi-Strauss's division of humanity into those who make history and those who live outside of it. Even so, the idea of "lost tribes" lives on in the popular imagination, often used as it was by Renaissance and Enlightenment thinkers as a foil against the real or perceived iniquities of "modern" societies.

World in the Making: A Global History is a textbook by four historians who assume all societies are "hot," and all people make history and always have. We feel the best way to understand the global endeavors of human beings in aggregate is to embrace change as the rule, to emphasize how all societies, all cultures, have been "making history" since the age of early hominids. The ancient concept of *Homo faber*, or humans as fundamentally makers of things—be they tools or weapons, dwellings or watercraft, nuclear bombs or iPhones—is what inspires us as world historians.

We argue in our emphasis on lives and livelihoods for a world constructed, altered, renovated, remade by ordinary people even as we acknowledge the genius of individual innovators, disruptors who broke the mold or struck out in some new direction. For us, world history is constantly exciting precisely because it is never predictable, much like the little Nambikwara girl's response to Claude Lévi-Strauss. Who knows if some other little girl in the backlands of Brazil in some earlier time broke away from her people to establish an entirely new culture dominated by woman hunters and warriors?

World in the Making is not an attempt to celebrate progress or despair over lost innocence, but rather to embrace the uncertain and jarring past. The book's Counterpoint discussions are meant in part to check our own tendency as historians to slot all the messy "stuff" of history into tidy, logical narratives. We recognize structures, some of them long-lasting, as things that humans make or construct—even as our narratives in this book are constructions—but we also marvel at history's unexpected twists; for example, when an apparently "weak" culture like that of the maroons of Suriname foiled a mighty adversary. Long-range paths may also prove surprising, as when a "great" culture like that of ancient Egypt simply did not conform to broad regional patterns.

In addition to our fascination with uncertainty and seeming chaos in the vast yet fragmentary record of our shared past, we are struck by the webs of interconnections, movements, mutual discoveries, and unexpected clashes—the crossroads where peoples meet—that also seem to define the human experience. In many cases, we are inclined to flip Lévi-Strauss's categories. We will see that an allegedly "hot" society was the one that appears to have gone cold, stuck in a mire of cherished myths, whereas the "cold" or "primitive" society adapted readily to changing conditions. Its people proved most flexible, ready to shove off for a new shore.

We may hope that the little Nambikwara girl who replied forcefully to the French anthropologist in the backlands of Brazil on a crisp morning in 1938 did not grow up to club wild pigs or monkeys, but that may be more a reflection of our tastes than of the truth about history. To survive the changing world of Brazil, that girl needed all the strength and smarts she could muster. For us, the authors of *World in the Making: A Global History*, that is "hot" stuff.

Organization

Author teams of world history textbooks typically divide the work based on geographic specialty, but we were determined to take responsibility for eras, not regions. Defining our subject matter by time period enabled us to see the connections or parallel developments that make societies part of world history—as well as the distinctive features that make them unique. Our approach also ensured a unified perspective to the many stories that each part tells. Marc Van De Mieroop covers the period from human origins to 500 C.E. (Part 1); Richard von Glahn the period 500 to 1450 (Part 2); Kris Lane the period 1450 to 1750 (Part 3); and Bonnie G. Smith the period 1750 to the present (Part 4).

Pedagogy and Features

We know from our own teaching that students need help in absorbing and making sense of information, thinking critically, and understanding that history itself is often debated and constantly revised. With these goals in mind, we bolster our narrative with a variety of learning and teaching aids, all intended to foster comprehension and analysis and to spark the historical imagination.

Part introductions provide students with an overview of the period they are about to encounter. **Chapter introductions** include "**Backstory**" sections to remind them of where they last encountered the peoples discussed in the chapter; **outlines** that preview the chapter's content; opening **vignettes** chosen to draw them into the atmosphere of the period and introduce the chapter's main themes; and **Overview Questions** that frame the main issues to consider while reading. Each major chapter section opens with a **Focus Question** intended to guide students' comprehension and—along with all three levels of questions in our book—to promote close reading and dynamic class discussion.

The **Counterpoint** section that ends each chapter breaks the grip of overgeneralization that often characterizes world history. It shows political movements, social, cultural, and economic trends, and everyday experiences that go against the grain. The counterpoint feature allows students to see and learn from historical diversity. They can get a sense that historical experience—and even our own behaviors—reveal valuable divergences from general patterns at any one time.

Making Connections, our third set of chapter questions, prompts students to think broadly about the history they have just read. It ends our chapter-closing

Review section, which incorporates as well a **timeline of important events**, a list of the **key terms** defined in our **running glossary**, and a reprise of the chapter's Overview Questions. Each chapter also includes **phonetic spellings** for many potentially unfamiliar words and a **Conclusion** that reinforces the central developments covered in the chapter. An end-of-book **Bibliography** directs students to print and online resources for further investigation.

In addition to these learning and review aids, we offer three special features in each chapter. Illustrated **Lives and Livelihoods** essays on topics ranging from the potters of antiquity to the builders of the trans-Siberian railroad allow us to provide more in-depth study of one of our key themes—namely, how people's lives intersect with larger cross-cultural interactions and global change. Our **Reading the Past** and **Seeing the Past** features, which include excerpts from written and visual primary sources, give students direct exposure to the ideas and voices of the people we are studying. They also help students build their analytical skills by modeling how historians interpret written and visual evidence.

Throughout the book we chose **images** to match as closely as we could the themes we wanted to stress. We did not conceive of the images as mere illustrations but rather as documents worthy of close historical analysis in their own right, products of the same places and times we try to evoke in the text. And our carefully developed **map program** provides sure-footed guidance to where our historical journey is taking us—a crucial necessity, since we travel to so many places not on the usual Grand Tour! In each chapter up to six **full-size maps** show major developments while up to four **"spot" maps**—small maps positioned within the discussion right where students need them—serve as immediate locators. To sum up, we wanted a complete toolbox of pedagogy and features to meet the needs of all kinds of learners.

Learning Resources for *World in the Making*

Oxford University Press offers instructors and students a comprehensive support program:

Ancillary Resource Center (ARC): This online resource center (https://arc2.oup-arc.com) is available to adopters of *World in the Making*, and includes the following:

- **Instructor's Resource Manual:** Includes, for each chapter, learning objectives, annotated chapter outline, answer guidelines for all the questions that appear in each chapter of *World in the Making*, lecture strategies, common misconceptions and difficult topics, class discussion starters, and active learning strategies.

- **Test Bank:** Includes forty questions per chapter, organized by the focus questions that frame the major subsections in each chapter.
- **PowerPoints:** Offers slides and JPEG and PDF files for all the maps and photos in the text, blank outline maps, an additional four hundred map files from *The Oxford Atlas of World History*, and approximately two thousand additional PowerPoint-based slides from OUP's Image Library, organized by themes and topics in world history.
- **Computerized Test Bank:** Includes nearly twelve hundred questions that can be customized by the instructor.
- **The World History Video Library:** Produced by Oxford University Press in collaboration with the BBC, each three- to five-minute video covers a key topic in world history, from the Buddha to the atom bomb. These videos are ideal for both classroom discussion or as online assignments.
- **Oxford First Source:** This database includes hundreds of primary source documents in world history. The documents cover a broad variety of political, economic, social, and cultural topics and represent a cross section of voices. The documents are indexed by date, author, title, and subject. Short documents (one or two pages) are presented in their entirety while longer documents have been carefully edited to highlight significant content. Each document is introduced with a short explanatory paragraph and accompanied by study questions.
- A complete **Course Management cartridge** is also available to qualified adopters. Contact your Oxford University Press sales representative for more information.
- *Sources for World in the Making:* **Volume 1: To 1500 (9780190849337):** Edited by the authors of *World in the Making* and designed specifically to complement the text, it includes over one hundred sources that give voice to both notable figures and everyday individuals. The "Contrasting Views" feature presents sources with divergent perspectives to foster comparative analysis. Only $5.00 when bundled with *World in the Making.*
- *Sources for World in the Making:* **Volume 2: Since 1300 (9780190849344):** Edited by the authors of *World in the Making* and designed specifically to complement the text, it includes over one hundred sources that give voice to both notable figures and everyday individuals. The "Contrasting Views" feature presents sources with divergent perspectives to foster comparative analysis. Only $5.00 when bundled with *World in the Making.*

- *Mapping the World: A Mapping and Coloring Book of World History:*
  This two-volume workbook includes approximately thirty-five color maps,
  each accompanied by a timeline, that chart global history from the Paleo-
  lithic to the present, as well as approximately fifty outline maps with exer-
  cises. An answer key is available to instructors. The Mapping and Coloring
  Book is free when bundled with *World in the Making*.
- **Open Access Companion Website (http://www.oup.com/us/smith-world):**
  Includes quizzes, flashcards, and web links.
- **E-Books.** Digital versions of *World in the Making* are available at many
  popular distributors, including Chegg, RedShelf, and VitalSource.

Enhanced Study Resources

Students who purchase a new copy of *World in the Making* can redeem the code that
accompanies the text to access these additional study resources, at no extra charge:

- 40 quizzes per chapter that offer an explanation and page reference for each
  question
- a study guide that provides note-taking worksheets and chapter summaries
  for each chapter
- "Mapping the World" simulations that combine audio and animated maps
  to deepen understanding of key developments in global history. Each simu-
  lation is accompanied by quiz questions.
- video quizzes that assess comprehension of key topics in world history

Students who do not buy a new copy can view a demo and purchase access to these
enhanced study resources at the Ancillary Resource Center: https://arc2.oup-arc.
com/access/smith-1e.

Bundling Options

World in the Making can be bundled at a significant discount with any of the titles
in the popular Graphic History Series, Very Short Introductions, World in a Life,
or Oxford World's Classics series, as well as other titles from the Higher Education
division world history catalog (www.oup.com/us/catalog/he). Please contact your
OUP representative for details.

Acknowledgments

The redesign and revision of *Crossroads and Cultures: A History of the World's Peoples* exemplifies the theme of its successor and the book you are about to read: *World in the Making*. It has taken a world of people with diverse perspectives and talents to craft this new edition of our text. We remain greatly indebted to the publishing team at Bedford/St. Martin's who did so much to bring the first edition of this book into being. They indeed helped us produce a new world of thinking about the global past for which we and our readers have been grateful.

We are also grateful to the editorial and management teams at Oxford University Press. They saw the potential in publishing the text in a more accessible format. The alacrity with which they executed their vision never wavered. We sincerely appreciate the support they have shown us each step of the way.

Our sincere thanks go to the following instructors, who helped us keep true to our vision of showing connections among the world's peoples and of highlighting their lives and livelihoods. The comments of these scholars and teachers often challenged us to rethink or justify our interpretations. Importantly for the integrity of the book, they always provided a check on accuracy down to the smallest detail of the vast history of world-making:

Editorial Reviewers

Kris Alexanderson, University of the Pacific

Abbe Allen, Sandhills Community College

Sara Black, Christopher Newport University

Kathy J. Callahan, Murray State University

Milton Eng, William Paterson University

Nancy Fitch, California State University

Andrei Gandila, University of Alabama in Huntsville

Steven A. Glazer, Graceland University

David Fort Godshalk, Shippensburg University

Rebecca Hayes, Northern Virginia Community College

Shawna Herzog, Washington State University

Aaron Irvin, Murray State University

Erin O'Donnell, East Stroudsburg University

Kenneth J. Orosz, Buffalo State College

Nicole Pacino, University of Alabama in Huntsville

Patrick M. Patterson, Honolulu Community College

Daniel R. Pavese, Wor-Wic Community College

Christian Peterson, Ferris State University

Nova Robinson, Seattle University

Nicholas Lee Rummell, Trident Technical College

Eric Strahorn, Florida Gulf Coast University

Bianka R. Stumpf, Central Carolina Community College

Brian Ulrich, Shippensburg University

Class testers and market development participants

Alem Abbay, Frostburg State University

Heather Abdelnur, Augusta University

Andreas Agocs, University of the Pacific

Kris Alexanderson, University of the Pacific

Stephen Auerbach, Georgia College

Tom Bobal, Adirondack Community College

Gayle K. Brunelle, California State University, Fullerton

Kathy Callahan, Murray State University

Aryendra Chakravartty, Stephen F. Austin State University

Celeste Chamberland, Roosevelt University–Chicago

Karen Christianson, Depaul University

Aimee Duchsherer, Minot State University

Peter Dykema, Arkansas Tech University–Russellville

Jennifer C. Edwards, Manhattan College

Robert Findlay, Solano Community College

Nancy Fitch, California State University, Fullerton

Arthur FitzGerald, San Jacinto College–North

Richard Forster, Hawaii Community College

Lucien Frary, Rider University

Tara Fueshko, William Paterson University

Jay Harrison, Hood College

Tim Hayburn, Rowan University–Glassboro

Michael Heil, University of Arkansas at Little Rock

Cecily Heisser, University of San Diego

Timothy Henderson, Auburn University at Montgomery

Gail Hook, George Mason University

Anne Huebel, Saginaw Valley State University

Kathryn Johnson, Northern Michigan University

Michael Johnson, University of Hawaii–Manoa

Thomas Jordan, Champlain College

David Longenbach, Penn State University–Lehigh Valley

Ann Lupo, Buffalo State College

Aran MacKinnon, South Georgia College

Joseph Marcum, Southeast Kentucky Community and Technical
  College–Middlesboro

David McCarter, Indiana State University

Ashley Moreshead, University of Central Florida

Philip Nash, Penn State University–Shenango

Kimberly Nath, University of Delaware

Lance Nolde, California State University, Los Angeles

Kenneth Orosz, Buffalo State College

Patrick Patterson, Honolulu Community College

Gregory Peek, Pennsylvania State University

David Raley, El Paso Community College–Mission Del Paso

Scott Seagle, University of Tennessee–Chattanooga

Michael Skinner, University of Hawaii at Hilo

Cynthia Smith, Honolulu Community College

Colin Snider, University of Texas at Tyler

Catherine Stearn, Eastern Kentucky University

Sylvia Taschka, Wayne State University

David Toye, Northeast State Community College

Richard Trimble, Ocean County College

Heather Wadas, Shippensburg University

Peter Wallace, Hartwick College

Gary Wolgamott, Pittsburg State University

Kirsten Ziomek, Adelphi University

Our special, heartfelt thanks go to Charles Cavaliere, executive editor at Oxford University Press, without whom this new edition would not have appeared in its fresh, updated form. Charles rethought the needs of today's students and teachers and pushed for our team to do likewise. His enthusiasm has kept the book evolving and its author team on its toes, especially as he gave us the benefit of his own erudition and wide-ranging interests. We surely join Charles in thanking editorial assistants Katie Tunkavige and Anna Fitzsimons for their invaluable help on many essential tasks—from communicating and guiding the authors' tasks to many behind-the-scenes efforts that we hardly know about. We also appreciate the schedules, supervision, and layouts senior production editor Marianne Paul juggled so efficiently and effectively. Our talented photo researcher Francelle

Carapetyan brought us unique, vivid images to bring our art program up-to-date. We appreciate that the book's content has been laid out in the appealing design of Michele Laseau, who succeeding in enhancing the authors' text. We thank this world of talented people for such skilled efforts and happy results.

World in the Making has a wealth of materials for students and teachers as resources for supporting the text. We urge our readers to benefit from the classroom experience and imagination that went into creating them. Marketing manager Braylee Cross, Hayley Ryan, and Clare Castro team have been working since the beginning to ensure that the book is in the best shape to benefit the diverse audience of users. We are deeply grateful for all the hard thinking Braylee and her team have done to advocate for the success of *World in the Making* in today's global classrooms.

Among the authors' greatest world-making experience has been their long-standing and happy relationship with brilliant editor Elizabeth M. Welch. More than a decade ago Beth brought her historical, conceptual, and publishing talent to the original *Crossroads and Cultures* just as she had so successfully guided so many other world history texts before that. We are more than ever grateful to have the privilege of once again working with the learned, witty Beth, this time at Charles Cavaliere's side, on *World in the Making*.

Finally, our students' questions and concerns have shaped much of this work, and we welcome all of our readers' suggestions, queries, and criticisms. We know that readers, like our own students, excel in spotting unintended glitches and also in providing much excellent food for thought. Please contact us with your thoughts and suggestions at our respective institutions.

Bonnie G. Smith
Marc Van De Mieroop
Richard von Glahn
Kris Lane

Maps

Studying with Maps

World history cannot be fully understood without a clear comprehension of the chronologies and parameters within which different empires, states, and peoples have changed over time. Maps facilitate this understanding by illuminating the significance of time, space, and geography in shaping a world constantly in the making.

Projection

A map *projection* portrays all or part of the earth, which is spherical, on a flat surface. All maps, therefore, include some distortion. The projections in *World in the Making* include global, continental, and regional perspectives. Special "spot maps" in each chapter depict information at a local, or even city, level.

Inset

The maps in *World in the Making* include *insets* that show cities, localities, or regions in detail.

Map Key

Maps use symbols to show the location of features and to convey information, such as the movement of commodities, ideas, or people. Each symbol is explained in the map's *key*.

Global Locator

Many of the maps in *World in the Making* include *global locators* that show the area being depicted in a larger context.

Scale Bar / Compass Rose

Every map in *World in the Making* includes a *scale bar* that shows distances in both miles and kilometers, and in some instances, in feet as well. The *compass rose,* included on most maps, shows the map's orientation.

Topography

Many maps in *World in the Making* show *relief*—the contours of the land. Topography is an important element in studying maps because the physical terrain has played a critical role in shaping human history.

Special Features

Notes on Dates and Spelling

Where necessary for clarity, we qualify dates as B.C.E. ("Before the Common Era") or C.E. ("Common Era"). The abbreviation B.C.E. refers to the same era as B.C. ("Before Christ"), just as C.E. is equivalent to A.D. (*anno Domini*, Latin for "in the year of the Lord"). In keeping with our aim to approach world history from a global, multicultural perspective, we chose these neutral abbreviations as appropriate to our enterprise. Because most readers will be more familiar with English than with metric measures, however, units of measure are given in the English system in the narrative, with metric and English measures provided on the maps.

We translate Chinese names and terms into English according to the *pinyin* system, while noting in parentheses proper names well established in English (e.g., Canton, Chiang Kai-shek). Transliteration of names and terms from the many other languages traced in our book follow the same contemporary scholarly conventions.

About the Authors

Bonnie G. Smith (AB Smith College, PhD University of Rochester) is Board of Governors Distinguished Professor of History Emerita, Rutgers University. She has taught world history to both undergraduate and graduate students and has been supported in her research through awards and fellowships from the Guggenheim Foundation, American Council of Learned Societies, National Humanities Center, Shelby Cullom Davis Center (Princeton), European Union, and American Philosophical Society. She has published books in world, European, and women's history, among the most recent *Modern Empires: A Reader* (Oxford University Press, 2017), and currently studies cultural hybridity.

Marc Van De Mieroop (PhD Yale University, 1983) is Professor of History at Columbia University. A specialist in the ancient history of the Middle East, he has published numerous books including *A History of Ancient Egypt* (Wiley-Blackwell, Oxford, 2011) and *A History of the Ancient Near East, ca. 3000–323 B.C.*, 3rd edition (Wiley-Blackwell, Oxford, 2016). His latest book is *Philosophy Before the Greeks: The Pursuit of Truth in Ancient Babylonia* (Princeton University Press, Princeton, 2015). He has received grants from the National Endowment of the Humanities, the American Council of Learned Societies, the John Simon Guggenheim Memorial Foundation, and several European institutions. He is the recipient of Columbia University's Lenfest Distinguished Faculty Award for excellence in teaching. Marc covers the period from human origins to 500 C.E. (Part 1) in *World in the Making*.

Richard von Glahn (PhD Yale University, 1983) is Professor of History at UCLA. Richard is the author of numerous books and articles on Chinese economic and social history, including *Fountain of Fortune: Money and Monetary Policy in China, 1000–1700* (University of California Press, 1996), *The Sinister Way: The Divine and the Demonic in Chinese Religious Culture* (University of California Press, 2004), and most recently *The Economic History of China from Antiquity to the Nineteenth Century* (Cambridge University Press, 2016). His research has been supported by fellowships from the National Endowment for the Humanities, the American Council of Learned Societies, and the John Simon Guggenheim Memorial Foundation. Richard is also a senior editor for the Oxford Research Encyclopedia for Asian History.

Kris Lane (PhD University of Minnesota, 1996) holds the France V. Scholes Chair in Colonial Latin American History at Tulane University in New Orleans. An award-winning teacher, he is author of *Colour of Paradise: The Emerald in the Age of Gunpowder Empires* (Yale, 2010), *Pillaging the Empire: Global Piracy on the High Seas, 1500–1750* (Routledge, 2015), and *Quito 1599: City & Colony in Transition* (University of New Mexico Press, 2002). Lane has also edited the writings of failed Spanish conquistador Bernardo de Vargas Machuca, and he has published numerous articles on the history of slavery, witchcraft, crime, and mining in early modern Spanish America. He is also the author of textbooks on Latin American history and Atlantic history. Aided by a fellowship from the John Simon Guggenheim Memorial Foundation (2015–2016), Lane is completing a book about the global consequences of a mid-seventeenth-century mint fraud at Potosí, a world-famous silver mining town high in the Andes Mountains of present-day Bolivia. Kris treats the period 1450 to 1750 (Part 3) in *World in the Making*.

World in the Making

Collapse and Revival in Afro-Eurasia 1300–1450

≡ **World in the Making** The fall of Constantinople to the Ottoman Turks in 1453 marked the end of the Byzantine Empire and heralded the coming age of gunpowder weapons. The Ottoman forces under Sultan Mehmed II breached the triple walls of Constantinople using massive cannons known as *bombards*. The Turkish cannons appear in the center of this book illustration of the siege of Constantinople, published in France in 1455.

backstory

In the fourteenth century, a number of developments threatened the connections among Afro-Eurasian societies. The collapse of the Mongol empires in China and Iran in the mid-1300s disrupted caravan traffic across Central Asia, diverting the flow of trade and travel to maritime routes across the Indian Ocean. Although the two centuries of religious wars known as the Crusades ended in 1291, they had hardened hostility between Christians and Muslims. As the power of the Christian Byzantine Empire contracted, Muslim Turkish sultanates—the Mamluk regime in Egypt and the rising Ottoman dynasty in Anatolia (modern Turkey)—gained control of the eastern Mediterranean region. Yet the Crusades and direct contact with the Mongols (subjects of Chapter 13) had also whetted European appetites for luxury and exotic goods from the Islamic world and Asia. Thus, despite challenges and obstacles, the Mediterranean remained a lively crossroads of commerce and cross-cultural exchange.

489

In August 1452, as the armies of the Ottoman sultan Mehmed II encircled Constantinople, the Byzantine emperor Constantine XI received a visit from a fellow Christian, a Hungarian engineer named Urban. Urban had applied metallurgical skills acquired at Hungary's rich iron and copper mines to the manufacture of large cannons known as *bombards*. He came to the Byzantine capital to offer his services to repel the Ottoman assault. But although Urban was a Christian, he was a businessman, too. When Constantine could not meet his price, Urban quickly left for the sultan's camp. Facing the famed triple walls of Constantinople, Mehmed promised to quadruple the salary Urban requested and to provide any materials and manpower the engineer needed.

Seven months later, in April 1453, Ottoman soldiers moved Urban's huge bronze bombards—with barrels twenty-six feet long, capable of throwing eight-hundred-pound shot—into place beneath the walls of Constantinople. Although these cumbersome cannons could fire only seven rounds a day, they battered the walls of Constantinople, which had long been considered impenetrable. After six weeks of siege the Turks breached the walls and swarmed into the city. The vastly outnumbered defenders, Emperor Constantine among them, fought to the death.

The fall of Constantinople to the Ottomans marks a turning point in world history. After perpetuating ancient Rome's heritage and glory for a thousand years, the Byzantine Empire came to an end. Islam continued to advance; in the fourteenth and fifteenth centuries, it expanded most dramatically in Africa and Asia. Italian merchants and bankers lost their dominance in the eastern Mediterranean and turned westward toward the Atlantic Ocean in search of new commercial opportunities. The bombards cast by the Hungarian engineer for the Ottoman sultan heralded a military revolution that would decisively alter the balance of power among states and transform the nature of the state itself.

The new global patterns that emerged after Constantinople changed hands had their roots in calamities of the fourteenth century. The Ottoman triumph came just as Europe was beginning to recover from the catastrophic outbreak of plague known as the Black Death. The demographic and psychological shocks of epidemic disease had severely tested Europe's political and economic institutions—indeed, even its Christian faith. The Black Death also devastated the Islamic world. Economic depression struck hard in Egypt, Syria, and Mesopotamia, the heartland of Islam. However, Europe's economy recovered more quickly.

In Asia, the fourteenth century witnessed the rise and fall of the last Mongol empire, that of Timur (also known as Tamerlane). The end of the Mongol era marked the passing of nomadic rule, the resurgence of agrarian bureaucratic states such as Ming China and the Ottoman Empire, and the shift of trade from the overland Silk Road to maritime routes across the Indian Ocean. Commerce attained unprecedented importance in many Asian societies. The flow of goods across Eurasia and Africa created new concentrations of wealth, fostered new patterns of consumption, and reshaped culture. The European Renaissance, for example, although primarily understood as a rebirth of the classical culture of Greece and Rome, also drew inspiration from the wealth of goods that poured into Italy from the Islamic world and Asia. By contrast, Japan remained isolated from this global bazaar, and this isolation contributed to the birth of Japan's distinctive national culture. For most Afro-Eurasian societies, however, the maritime world increasingly became the principal crossroads of economic and cultural exchange.

OVERVIEW QUESTIONS

The major global development in this chapter: Crisis and recovery in fourteenth- and fifteenth-century Afro-Eurasia.

As you read, consider:

1. In the century after the devastating outbreak of plague known as the Black Death, how and why did Europe's economic growth begin to surpass that of the Islamic world?

2. Did the economic revival across Eurasia after 1350 benefit the peasant populations of Europe, the Islamic world, and East Asia?

3. How did the process of conversion to Islam differ in Iran, the Ottoman Empire, West Africa, and Southeast Asia during this period?

4. What political and economic changes contributed to the rise of maritime commerce in Asia during the fourteenth and fifteenth centuries?

Fourteenth-Century Crisis and Renewal in Eurasia

FOCUS How did the Black Death affect society, the economy, and culture in Latin Christendom and the Islamic world?

No event in the fourteenth century had such profound consequences as the **Black Death** of 1347–1350. The unprecedented loss of life that resulted from this **pandemic** abruptly halted the economic expansion that had spread throughout

Black Death The catastrophic outbreak of plague that spread from the Black Sea to Europe, the Middle East, and North Africa in 1347–1350, killing a third or more of the population in afflicted areas.

Europe and the Islamic heartland in the preceding three centuries. Although the population losses were as great in the Islamic world as in Latin Christendom, the effects on society, the economy, and ideas diverged in important ways.

Largely spared the ravages of the Black Death, Asian societies and economies faced different challenges following the collapse of the Mongol empires in the fourteenth century. Expanding maritime trade and the spread of gunpowder weapons gave settled empires a decisive edge over nomadic societies, an edge that they never again relinquished. The founder of the Ming dynasty (1368–1644) in China rejected the Mongol model of "universal empire" and strove to restore a purely Chinese culture and social order. The prestige, stability, and ruling ideology of the Ming state powerfully influenced neighbors such as Korea and Vietnam—but had far less effect on Japan.

The "Great Mortality": The Black Death of 1347–1350

On the eve of the Black Death, Europe's agrarian economy already was struggling under the strain of climatic change. Around 1300 the earth experienced a shift in climate. The warm temperatures that had prevailed over most of the globe for the previous thousand years gave way to a **Little Ice Age** of colder temperatures and shorter growing seasons; it would last for much of the fourteenth century. The expansion of agriculture that had occurred in the Northern Hemisphere during the preceding three centuries came to a halt. Unlike famine, though, the Black Death pandemic struck the ruling classes as hard as the poor. Scholars estimate that the Black Death and subsequent recurrences of the pandemic killed approximately one-third of the population of Europe.

Although the catastrophic mortality (death rates) of the Black Death is beyond dispute, the causes of the pandemic remain mysterious. The Florentine poet Giovanni Boccaccio (1313–1375), an eyewitness to the "great mortality," described the appearance of apple-sized swellings, first in the groin and armpits, after which these "death-bearing plague boils" spread to "every part of the body, wherefrom the fashion of the contagion began to change into black or livid blotches . . . in some places large and sparse, and in others small and thick-sown." The spread of these swellings, Boccaccio warned, was "a very certain token of coming death."[1] The prominence of these glandular swellings, or buboes, in eyewitness accounts has led modern scholars to attribute the Black Death to bubonic plague, which is transmitted by fleas to rats and by rats to humans. The populations of western Eurasia had no previous experience of the disease, and hence no immunity to it. Outbreaks of plague continued to recur every decade or two for the next century, and intermittently thereafter.

Boccaccio and other eyewitnesses claimed that the Black Death had originated in Central Asia and traveled along overland trade routes to the Black Sea. The first outbreak among Europeans occurred in 1347 at the Genoese port of

pandemic An outbreak of epidemic disease that spreads across an entire region.

Little Ice Age Name applied by environmental historians to periods of prolonged cool weather in the temperate zones of the earth.

Caffa, on the Crimean peninsula. The Genoese seafarers then spread the plague to the seaports they visited throughout the Mediterranean. By the summer of 1350 the Black Death had devastated nearly all of Europe (see Map 14.1).

Historian William McNeill has suggested that the Black Death was a by-product of the Mongol conquests. He hypothesized that Mongol horsemen carried the plague bacillus from the remote highland forests of Southeast Asia into Central Asia, and then west to the Black Sea and east to China. The impact of the plague on China remains uncertain, however. The Mongol dynasty of Qubilai (KOO-bih-lie) Khan already was losing its hold on China in the 1330s, and by the late 1340s China was afflicted by widespread famine, banditry, and civil war. By the time the Ming dynasty took control in 1368, China's population had fallen

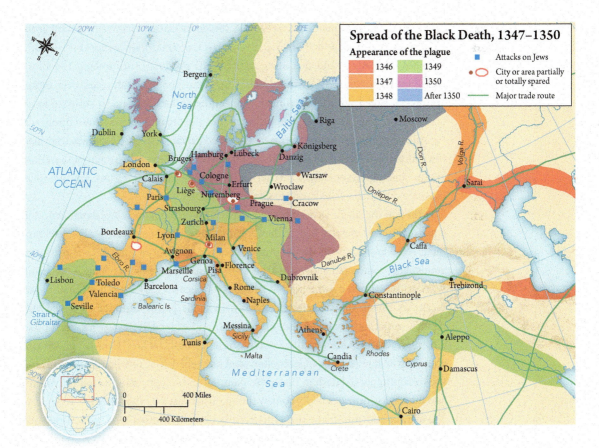

≡ **MAP 14.1   Spread of the Black Death, 1347–1350** From Caffa on the shores of the Black Sea, Genoese merchant ships unwittingly carried the plague to Constantinople and other Mediterranean ports in the summer of 1347. Over the next four years the Black Death advanced across the Mediterranean Sea and throughout central and northern Europe. Hundreds of Jewish communities were attacked or destroyed by Christians who blamed the pandemic on the Jews.

substantially. Yet Chinese sources make no mention of the specific symptoms of the Black Death, and there is no evidence of pandemic in the densely populated areas of South and Southeast Asia.

The demographic collapse resulting from the Black Death was concentrated in Europe and the Islamic lands ringing the Mediterranean. In these regions population growth halted for over a century. In the Islamic world, as in Europe, the loss of human lives and livestock seriously disrupted agriculture. While rural inhabitants flocked to the towns in search of food and work, urban residents sought refuge in the countryside from the contagion that festered in crowded cities. The scarcity of labor following the pandemic prompted a return to pastoral nomadism in many rural areas, and the urban working classes who survived benefited from rising wages. "The wages of skilled artisans, wage workers, porters, servants, stablemen, weavers, masons, construction workers, and the like have increased manyfold," wrote the Egyptian historian al-Maqrizi (al-mak-REE-zee), who served as Cairo's market inspector from 1399 to 1405. But, he added, "of this class only a few remain, since most have died."[2]

Population losses and declining agricultural production following the Black Death undermined the Mamluk (MAM-luke) sultanate, which ruled over Egypt and Syria. Faced with decreasing revenues, the sultanate tried to squeeze more taxes from urban commerce and industry. But the creation of state monopolies in the spice trade and the sugar industry throttled private enterprise and undermined the commercial vitality of Cairo and Damascus. The impoverishment of the urban artisan and merchant classes further weakened the Mamluk regime, leading to its ultimate downfall at the hands of Ottoman conquerors in 1517.

Although the Black Death afflicted Latin Christendom and the Islamic world in equal measure, their responses to the epidemic diverged in significant ways. Christians interpreted the plague as divine punishment for humanity's sins. Acts of piety and atonement proliferated, most strikingly in the form of processions of flagellants (from *flagella*, a whip used by worshippers as a form of penance), whose self-mutilation was meant to imitate the sufferings of Christ. In many places Christians blamed vulnerable minorities—such as beggars, lepers, and especially Jews—for corrupting Christian society. Although the Roman Church, kings, and local leaders condemned attacks against Jews, their appeals often went unheeded. Macabre images of death and the corruption of the flesh in European painting and sculpture in the late fourteenth and fifteenth centuries vividly convey the anguish caused by the Black Death.

Muslims did not share the Christian belief in "original sin," which deemed human beings inherently sinful, and so they did not see the plague as a divine punishment. Instead, they accepted it as an expression of God's will, and even a blessing for the faithful. Muslim cleric Ibn al-Wardi (IB-unh al-wahr-dee), who succumbed to the disease in 1349, wrote that "this plague is for Muslims a martyrdom and a

≡ **Dance of Death** The scourge of the Black Death dramatically influenced attitudes toward death in Latin Christendom. Literary and artistic works such as this woodcut of skeletons dancing on an open grave vividly portrayed the fragility of life and the dangers of untimely death. For those unprepared to face divine judgment, the ravages of disease and death were only a prelude to the everlasting torments of hell.

reward, and for the disbelievers a punishment and rebuke."[3] The flagellants' focus on atonement for sin and the scapegoating of Jews seen in Christian Europe were wholly absent in the Islamic world.

Rebuilding Societies in Western Europe 1350–1492

Just as existing religious beliefs and practices shaped Muslim and Christian responses to the plague, underlying conditions influenced political and economic recovery in the two regions. Latin Christendom recovered more quickly than

Islamic lands. In Europe, the death toll caused an acute labor shortage. Desperate to find tenants to cultivate their lands, the nobility had to offer generous concessions, such as release from labor services, that liberated the peasantry from the conditions of serfdom. The incomes of the nobility and the church declined by half or more, and many castles and monasteries fell into ruin. The shortage of labor enabled both urban artisans and rural laborers to bargain for wage increases. Many nobles, unable to find tenants, converted their agricultural land into pasture. Hundreds of villages were abandoned. In much of central Europe, cultivated land reverted back to forest.

Economic change brought with it economic conflict, and tensions between rich and poor triggered insurrections by rural peasants and the urban lower classes throughout western Europe. In England, King Richard II's attempt to shift the basis of taxation from landed wealth to a head tax on each subject incited the Peasant Revolt of 1381. Led by a radical preacher named John Ball, the rebels presented a petition to the king that went beyond repeal of the head tax to demand freedom from the tyranny of noble lords and the Christian Church:

> Henceforward, that no lord should have lordship but that there should
> be proportion between all people, saving only the lordship of the king;
> that the goods of the holy church ought not to be in the hands of men of
> religion, or parsons or vicars, or others of holy church, but these should
> have their sustenance easily and the rest of the goods be divided between
> the parishioners, ... and that there should be no villeins [peasants subject to a lord's justice] in England or any serfdom or villeinage, but all are
> to be free and of one condition.[4]

In the end the English nobles mustered militias to suppress the uprising. This success could not, however, reverse the developments that had produced the uprising in the first place. A new social order began to form, one based on private property and entrepreneurship rather than nobility and serfdom, but equally extreme in its imbalance of wealth and poverty.

Perhaps nowhere in Europe was this new social order more apparent than in Italy. In the Italian city-states, the widening gap between rich and poor was reflected in their governments, which increasingly benefited the wealthy. Over the course of the fifteenth century, the ideals and institutions of republican (representative) government on which the Italian city-states were founded steadily lost ground. A military despot wrested control of Milan in 1450. Venice's **oligarchy**—rule by an exclusive elite—strengthened its grip over the city's government and commerce. In Florence, the Medici family of bankers dominated the city's political affairs. Everywhere, financial power was increasingly aligned with political power.

oligarchy Rule by a small group of individuals or families.

In the wake of the Black Death, kings and princes suffered a drop in revenues as agricultural production fell. Yet in the long run, royal power grew at the expense of the nobility and the church. In England and France, royal governments gained new sources of income and established bureaucracies of tax collectors and administrators to manage them. The rulers of these states transformed their growing financial power into military and political strength by raising standing armies of professional soldiers and investing in new military technology. The French monarchy, for instance, capitalized on rapid innovations in gunpowder weapons to create a formidable army and to establish itself as the supreme power in continental Europe. Originally developed by the Mongols, these weapons had been introduced to Europe via the Islamic world by the middle of the fourteenth century.

The progress of the Hundred Years' War (1337–1453) between England and France reflected the changing political landscape. The war broke out over claims to territories in southwestern France and a dispute over succession to the French throne. In the early years of the conflict, the English side prevailed, thanks to the skill of its bowmen against mounted French knights. By 1400, combat between knights conducted according to elaborate rules of chivalry had yielded to new forms of warfare. Cannons, siege weapons, and, later, firearms undermined both the nobility's preeminence in war and its sense of identity and purpose. An arms race between France and its rivals led to rapid improvements in weaponry, especially the development of lighter and more mobile cannons. Ultimately the French defeated the English, but the war transformed both sides. The length of the conflict, the propaganda from both sides, and the unified effort needed to prosecute the increasingly costly war all contributed to the evolution of royal governments and the emergence of a sense of national identity.

New economic conditions contributed to the growth of monarchical power (see Map 14.2). To strengthen their control, the rulers of France, England, and Spain relied on new forms of direct taxation, as well as financing from bankers. The French monarchy levied new taxes on salt, land, and commercial transactions, wresting income from local lords and town governments. The marriage of Isabella of Castile and Ferdinand of Aragon in 1469 created a unified monarchy in Spain. This expansion of royal power in Spain depended heavily on loans from Genoese bankers. In their efforts to consolidate power, Ferdinand and Isabella, like so many rulers in world history, demanded religious conformity. In 1492 they conquered Granada, the last Muslim foothold in Spain, and ordered all Jews and Muslims to convert to Christianity or face banishment. With the *Reconquista* (Spanish for "reconquest") of Spain complete, Ferdinand and Isabella turned their crusading energies toward exploration. That same year, they sponsored the first of Christopher Columbus's momentous transatlantic voyages in pursuit of the fabled riches of China.

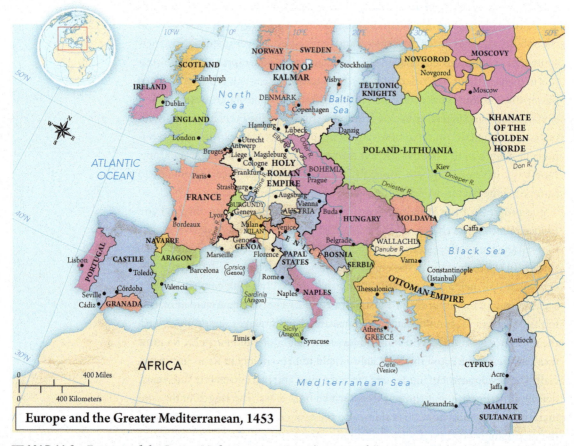

Europe and the Greater Mediterranean, 1453

≡ **MAP 14.2** **Europe and the Greater Mediterranean, 1453** The century following the Black Death witnessed the growth of royal power and territorial consolidation across Europe, most notably in England and France. But central Europe and Italy remained politically fragmented. The Ottoman conquest of Constantinople in 1453 extinguished the Byzantine Empire and sharpened the conflict between Christendom and the Islamic world in southeastern Europe.

Ming China and the New Order in East Asia 1368–1500

State building in East Asia, too, fostered the development of national states. The Yuan dynasty established in China by the Mongol khan Qubilai had foundered after his death in 1294. Qubilai's successors wrung as much tribute as they could from the Chinese population, but they neglected the infrastructure of roads, canals, and irrigation and flood-control dikes that the Chinese economy depended on. When peasant insurrections and civil wars broke out in the 1350s, the Mongol leaders abandoned China and retreated to their steppe homeland. After a protracted period of war and devastation, a Chinese general of peasant origin restored native rule, founding the Ming dynasty in 1368 (see Map 14.3).

The Ming founder, Zhu Yuanzhang (JOO yuwen-JAHNG) (r. 1368–1398)—better known by his imperial title, Hongwu (hoong-woo)—resurrected the basic Chinese institutions of civil government. But throughout his life Hongwu viewed the scholar-official class with suspicion. Born a peasant, Hongwu saw himself as a populist crusading against the snobbery and luxurious lifestyle of the rich and powerful. Once in command, he repeatedly purged high officials and exercised despotic control over his government. Hongwu reinstituted the civil service examinations system to select government officials, but he used the examinations and the state-run school system as tools of political indoctrination, establishing the teachings of twelfth-century Neo-Confucian philosopher Zhu Xi (JOO shee) as the standard for the civil service exams. Zhu shared the Neo-Confucian antipathy toward Buddhism as a foreign religion and sought to reassert the Confucian commitment to moral perfection and the betterment of society. **Neo-Confucianism** advocated a strict moral code and a patriarchal social hierarchy, and the Ming government supported it with the full force of imperial law.

The Neo-Confucian ideology of Hongwu emphasized the patriarchal authority of the lineage, and his policies deprived women of many rights, including a share in inheritance. It outlawed the remarriage of widows. By 1300 many elite families practiced foot binding, which probably originated among courtesans and entertainers. From around age six the feet of girls were tightly bound with bandages, deforming the bones and crippling them. The feet of adult women ideally were no more than three or four inches long; they were considered a mark of feminine beauty and a symbol of freedom from labor. Foot binding accompanied seclusion in the home as a sign of respectable womanhood.

Despite the strictures of patriarchal society, in the households of nonelite groups, women played an essential economic role. Women worked alongside men in rice cultivation and performed most tasks involved in textile manufacture. The spread of cotton, introduced from India in the thirteenth century, gave peasant women new economic opportunities. Most cotton was grown, ginned (removing the seeds), spun into yarn, and woven into cloth within a single household, principally by women. Confucian moralists esteemed spinning, weaving, and embroidery as "womanly work" that would promote industriousness and thrift; they became dismayed, however, when women displayed entrepreneurial skill in marketing their wares.

Hongwu rejected the Mongol model of a multiethnic empire and turned his back on the world of the steppe nomads. He located his capital at Nanjing, on the south bank of the Yangzi River, far from the Mongol frontier. Foreign embassies were welcome at the Ming court, which offered trading privileges in return for

Neo-Confucianism
The reformulation of Confucian doctrines to reassert a commitment to moral perfection and the betterment of society; dominated Chinese intellectual life and social thought from the twelfth to the twentieth century.

≡ **MAP 14.3   The Ming Empire, 1449**   After expelling the Mongols, the rulers of the Ming dynasty rebuilt the Great Wall to defend China from nomad invasions. Emperor Yongle moved the Ming capital from Nanjing to Beijing and launched expeditions commanded by his trusted aide Zheng He that voyaged throughout Southeast Asia and the Indian Ocean.

tribute and allegiance to the Chinese emperor. But Hongwu distrusted merchants as much as he did intellectuals. In 1371 he forbade Chinese merchants from engaging in overseas commerce and placed foreign traders under close government scrutiny.

Hongwu's son, the Emperor Yongle (r. 1402–1424), reversed his father's efforts to sever China from the outside world. Instead, Yongle embraced the Mongol vision of world empire and rebuilt the former Mongol capital of Dadu, creating the modern city of Beijing. Throughout his reign Yongle campaigned to subdue the Mongol tribes along the northern frontier, but with little success. He also wanted to expand southward. In 1405 he launched, as we will see, a series of naval expeditions under Admiral Zheng He (JUNG-huh), and in 1407 he invaded and conquered Vietnam (see again Map 14.3). Like his father, however, Yongle was an autocrat who promoted Neo-Confucian policies, even as he sought to reestablish some of the global connections Hongwu had tried to sever.

The Ming dynasty abandoned its designs for conquest and expansion after the death of Yongle in 1424. Yet the prestige, power, and philosophy of the Ming state continued to influence its neighbors, with the significant exception of Japan (see Counterpoint: Age of the Samurai in Japan, 1185–1450). Vietnam regained its independence from China in 1427, but under the long-lived Le dynasty (1428–1788), Vietnam retained Chinese-style bureaucratic government. The Le rulers oversaw the growth of an official class schooled in Neo-Confucianism and committed to forcing its cultural norms, kinship practices, and hostility to Buddhism on Vietnamese society as a whole. In Korea, the rulers of the new Yi dynasty (1392–1910) also embraced Neo-Confucian ideals of government. Under Yi rule the Confucian-educated elite acquired hereditary status with exclusive rights to political office. In both Vietnam and Korea, aristocratic rule and Buddhism's dominance over daily life yielded to a "Neo-Confucian revolution" modeled after Chinese political institutions and values.

Islam's New Frontiers

> ↘ **FOCUS** Why did Islam expand dramatically in the fourteenth and fifteenth centuries, and how did new Islamic societies differ from established ones?

In the fourteenth and fifteenth centuries, Islam continued to spread to new areas, including central and maritime Asia, sub-Saharan Africa, and southeastern Europe.

In the past, Muslim rule had often preceded the popular adoption of Islamic religion and culture. Yet the advance of Islam in Africa and Asia came about not through conquest, but through slow diffusion via merchants and missionaries. The universalism and egalitarianism of Islam appealed to rising merchant classes in both West Africa and maritime Asia.

During this period, Islam expanded by adapting to older ruling cultures rather than seeking to eradicate them. Timur, the last of the great nomad conquerors, and his descendants ruled not as Mongol khans but as Islamic sultans. The culture of the Central Asian states, however, remained an eclectic mix of Mongol, Turkish, and Persian traditions, in contrast to the strict adherence to Muslim law practiced under the Arab regimes of the Middle East and North Africa. This pattern of cultural adaptation was even more evident in West Africa and Southeast Asia.

Islamic Spiritual Ferment in Central Asia 1350–1500

The spread of Sufism in Central Asia between 1350 and 1500 played a significant role in the process of cultural assimilation. **Sufism**—a mystical tradition that stressed self-mastery, practical virtues, and spiritual growth through personal experience of the divine—had already emerged by 1200 as a major expression of Islamic values and social identity. Sufism appeared in many variations and readily assimilated local cultures to its beliefs and practices. In contrast to the orthodox scholars and teachers known as *ulama*, who made little effort to convert nonbelievers, Sufi preachers were inspired by missionary zeal and welcomed non-Muslims to their lodges and sermons. This made them ideal instruments for the spread of Islam to new territories.

One of Sufism's most important royal patrons was Timur (1336–1405), the last of the Mongol emperors. Born near the city of Samarkand (SAM-ar-kand) when the Mongol Ilkhanate in Iran was on the verge of collapse (see Chapter 13), Timur—himself a Turk—grew up among Mongols who practiced Islam. He rose to power in the 1370s by reuniting quarreling Mongol tribes in common pursuit of conquest.

From the early 1380s, Timur's armies relentlessly pursued campaigns of conquest, sweeping westward across Iran into Mesopotamia and Russia and eastward into India. In 1400–1401 Timur seized and razed Aleppo and Damascus, the principal Mamluk cities in Syria. Rather than trying to consolidate his rule in Syria and Anatolia (modern Turkey), however, Timur turned his attention eastward. He was preparing to march on China when he fell ill and died in 1405. Although Timur's empire quickly fragmented, his triumphs would serve as an inspiration to later empire builders, such as the Mughals in India and the Manchus

Sufism A tradition within Islam that emphasizes mystical knowledge and personal experience of the divine.

in China. Moreover, his support of Sufism would have a lasting impact, helping lay the foundation for a number of important Islamic religious movements in Central Asia.

The institutions of Timur's empire were largely modeled on the Ilkhan synthesis of Persian civil administration and Turkish-Mongol military organization. While Timur allowed local princes a degree of autonomy, he was determined to make Samarkand a grand imperial capital (see Reading the Past: A Spanish Ambassador's Description of Samarkand). The citadel and enormous bazaar built by Timur have long since perished, but surviving mosques, shrines, and tombs illuminate Timur's vision of Islamic kingship: all-powerful, urbane and cosmopolitan, and ostentatious in its display of public piety.

After Timur's death in 1405, his sons carved the empire into independent regional kingdoms. Yet Sufi brotherhoods and the veneration of Sufi saints exerted an especially strong influence over social life and religious practice in Central Asia. Timur had lavished special favor on Sufi teachers and had strategically placed the shrines of his family members next to the tombs of important Sufi leaders. The relics of Timur in Samarkand, along with the tombs of Sufi saints, attracted pilgrims from near and far.

Elsewhere in the Islamic world, a number of religious movements combined the veneration of Sufi saints and belief in miracles with unorth-

Timur Enthroned We can glean some sense of Timur's self-image from the *Book of Victories*, a chronicle of Timur's campaigns commissioned by one of his descendants in the 1480s. This scene portrays the ceremony in 1370 when Timur declared himself successor to the Chagadai khans. (The John Work Garrett Library, The Sheridan Libraries, Johns Hopkins University)

odox ideas derived from Shi'ism, the branch of Islam that maintains that only descendants of Muhammad's son-in-law Ali have a legitimate right to serve as caliph. One of the most militant and influential of these radical Islamic sects was the Safavid (SAH-fah-vid) movement founded by a Sufi preacher, Safi al-Din (SAH-fee al-dean) (1252–1334). Like other visionary teachers, Safi preached the need for a purified Islam cleansed of worldly wealth, urban luxury, and moral laxity. The Safavids roused their followers to attack Christians in the Caucasus region, but they

READING THE PAST

A Spanish Ambassador's Description of Samarkand

In September 1403, an embassy dispatched by King Henry III of Castile arrived at Samarkand in hopes of enlisting the support of Timur for a combined military campaign against the Ottomans. Seventy years old and in failing health, Timur lavishly entertained his visitors but made no response to Henry's overtures. The leader of the Spanish delegation, Ruy Gonzalez de Clavijo, left Samarkand disappointed, but his report preserves our fullest account of Timur's capital in its heyday.

The city is rather larger than Seville, but lying outside Samarkand are great numbers of houses that form extensive suburbs. These lay spread on all hands, for indeed the township is surrounded by orchards and vineyards. . . . In between these orchards pass streets with open squares; these are all densely populated, and here all kinds of goods are on sale with breadstuffs and meat. . . .

Samarkand is rich not only in foodstuffs but also in manufactures, such as factories of silk. . . . Thus trade has always been fostered by Timur with the view of making his capital the noblest of cities; and during all his conquests . . . he carried off the best men to people Samarkand, bringing thither the master-craftsmen of all nations. Thus from Damascus he carried away with him all the weavers of that city, those who worked at the silk looms; further the bow-makers who produce those cross-bows which are so famous; likewise armorers; also the craftsmen in glass and porcelain, who are known to be the best in all the world. From Turkey he had brought their gunsmiths who make the arquebus. . . . So great therefore was the population now of all nationalities gathered together in Samarkand that of men with their families the number they said must amount to 150,000 souls . . . [including] Turks, Arabs, and Moors of diverse sects, with Greek, Armenian, Roman, Jacobite [Syrian], and Nestorian Christians, besides those folk who baptize with fire in the forehead [i.e., Hindus]. . . .

The markets of Samarkand further are amply stored with merchandise imported from distant and foreign countries. . . . The goods that are imported to Samarkand from Cathay indeed are of the richest and most precious of all those brought thither from foreign parts, for the craftsmen of Cathay are reputed to be the most skillful by far beyond those of any other nation.

Source: Ruy Gonzalez de Clavijo, *Embassy to Tamerlane, 1403–1406*, trans. Guy Le Strange (London: Routledge, 1928), 285–289.

Examining the Evidence

1. What features of Timur's capital most impressed Gonzalez de Clavijo?

2. How does this account of Samarkand at its height compare with the chapter's description of Renaissance Florence?

also challenged Muslim rulers such as the Ottomans and Timur's successors. At the end of the fifteenth century, a charismatic leader, Shah Isma'il (shah IS-mah-eel), combined Safavid religious fervor with Shi'a doctrines to found a **theocracy**—a state subject to religious authority. It would rule Iran for more than two centuries and shape modern Iran's distinctive Shi'a religious culture.

Ottoman Expansion and the Fall of Constantinople 1354–1453

The spread of Islam in Central Asia would have profound consequences for the region. In the eyes of Europeans, however, the most significant—and alarming—advance was the Ottoman expansion into the Balkan territories of southeastern Europe. The Byzantine state was severely shaken by the Black Death, and in 1354 the Ottomans took advantage of this weakness to invade the Balkans. After a decisive victory in 1389, the Ottoman Empire annexed most of the Balkans except the region around Constantinople itself, reducing it to an isolated enclave.

The growing might of the Ottoman Empire stemmed from two military innovations: (1) the formation of the **janissary corps**, elite army units composed of slave soldiers, and (2) the use of massed musket fire and cannons, such as the bombards of Urban, the Hungarian engineer whom we met at the start of this chapter. In the late fourteenth century the Ottomans adopted the Mamluk practice of organizing slave armies that would be more reliably loyal to the sultan than the unruly *ghazi* ("holy warrior") bands that Osman (r. 1280–1324), the founder of the Ottoman state, had gathered as the core of his army. At first, prisoners and volunteers made up the janissary corps. Starting in 1395, however, the Ottomans imposed a form of conscription known as *devshirme* (dev-SHEER-may) on the Christian peoples of the Balkans to supplement Turkish recruits. Adolescent boys conscripted through the devshirme were taken from their families, raised as Muslims, and educated at palace schools for service in the sultan's civil administration as well as the army.

Practical concerns dictated Ottoman policies toward Christian communities. Where Christians were the majority of the population, the Ottomans could be quite tolerant. Apart

theocracy A state ruled by religious authorities.

janissary corps Slave soldiers who served as the principal armed forces of the Ottoman Empire beginning in the fifteenth century; also staffed much of the Ottoman state bureaucracy.

≡ **Ottoman Expansion, c. 1200–1453**

from the notorious devshirme slave levy, Ottoman impositions were less burdensome than the dues the Balkan peoples had owed the Byzantine emperor.
The Ottomans allowed Balkan Christians freedom to practice their religion,
and they protected the Greek Orthodox Church, which they considered in-
dispensable to maintaining social order. In Anatolia and other places where
Christians were a minority, however, the Ottomans took a much harder line. By
1500 Christian society in Anatolia had nearly vanished; most Christians had
converted to Islam.

Despite their own nomadic origins, the Ottomans regarded nomadic tribes, like
religious minorities, as a threat to stability. Many nomads were forcibly deported
and settled in the Balkans and western Anatolia, where they combined farming
with stock raising. Due to heavy taxes imposed on animal herds, nomads had to
earn additional income through transport, lumbering, and felt and carpet manufacture. Strong demand from European customers and the imperial capital of
Istanbul (the name Mehmed II gave to Constantinople) stimulated carpet weaving
by both peasants and herders.

The patriarchal family, in which the wife is subject to her husband's control, was
a pillar of Ottoman law, just as it was in Ming China. Although men usually controlled property in the form of land and houses, women acquired wealth in the
form of money, furnishings, clothes, and jewelry. Women invested in commercial
ventures, tax farming, and moneylending. Because women were secluded in the
home and veiled in public—long-established requirements to maintain family
honor and status in the central Islamic lands—women used servants and trusted
clients to help them conduct their business activities.

The final defeat of the Byzantine Empire by Ottoman armies in 1453 shocked
the Christian world. Mehmed II's capture of Constantinople also completed a radical transformation of the Ottoman enterprise. The Ottoman sultans no longer saw
themselves as roving ghazi warriors, but as monarchs with absolute authority over
a multinational empire at the crossroads of Europe and Asia. A proudly Islamic
regime, the Ottoman sultanate aspired to become the centerpiece of a broad cosmopolitan civilization spanning Europe, Asia, and Africa.

Commerce and Culture in Islamic West Africa

West African trading empires and the merchants they supported had long served
as the vanguard of Islam in sub-Saharan Africa. The Mali Empire's adoption of
Islam as its official religion in the late thirteenth century encouraged conversion
to Islam throughout the West African savanna. Islam continued to prosper despite
the collapse of Mali's political dominion in the mid-fourteenth century.

The towns of Jenne and Timbuktu, founded along the Niger River by Muslim merchants in the thirteenth century, emerged as the new crossroads of trans-Saharan trade. Jenne benefited from its access to the gold mines and rain forest products of coastal West Africa. Timbuktu's commercial prosperity rose as trade grew between West Africa and Mamluk Egypt. Islamic intellectual culture thrived among the merchant families of Timbuktu, Jenne, and other towns.

As elsewhere in the Islamic world, West African trader families readily combined religious scholarship with mercantile pursuits. Since the

≡ Timbuktu Manuscript Timbuktu became a hub of Islamic culture and intellectual life during the thirteenth and fourteenth centuries. Scholars and students assembled impressive libraries of Arabic texts, such as this Qur'an. Written mostly on paper imported from Europe, Timbuktu's manuscripts were preserved in family collections after the city's leading scholars were deported to North Africa by Moroccan invaders in 1591.

eleventh century, disciples of renowned scholars had migrated across the Sahara and founded schools and libraries. The Moroccan Muslim scholar and traveler Ibn Battuta (IB-uhn ba-TOO-tuh), who visited Mali in 1352–1353, voiced approval of the people's "eagerness to memorize the great Qur'an: they place fetters on their children if they fail to memorize it and they are not released until they do so."[5] The Muslim diplomat Hasan al-Wazzan (hah-SAHN al-wah-zan), whose *Description of Africa* (published in Italian in 1550) became a best-seller in Europe, wrote that in Timbuktu "the learned are greatly revered. Also, many book manuscripts coming from the Berber [North African] lands are sold. More profits are realized from sales of books than any other merchandise."[6]

Muslim clerics wielded considerable influence in the towns. Clerics presided over worship and festival life and governed social behavior by applying Muslim law and cultural traditions. Yet away from the towns the majority of the population remained attached to ancestral beliefs in nature spirits, especially the spirits of rivers and thunder. Healer priests, clan chiefs, and other ritual experts shared responsibility for making offerings to the spirits, providing protection from evil demons and sorcerers, and honoring the dead.

Advance of Islam in Maritime Southeast Asia

Muslim Arab merchants had dominated maritime commerce in the Indian Ocean and Southeast Asia since the seventh century. Not until the thirteenth century, however, did Islam begin to gain converts in Malaysia and the Indonesian archipelago. By 1400 Arab and Gujarati traders and Sufi teachers had spread Islam throughout maritime Asia. The dispersion of Muslim merchants took the form of a **trade diaspora**, a network of merchant settlements dispersed across foreign lands but united by common origins, religion, and language, as well as by business dealings.

Political and economic motives strongly influenced official adoption of Islam. In the first half of the fourteenth century, the Majapahit (mah-jah-PAH-hit) kingdom (1292–1528), a bastion of Hindu religion, conquered most of Java and forced many local rulers in the Indonesian archipelago to submit tribute (see Map 14.4, page 510). In response, many of these rulers adopted Islam as an act of resistance to dominance by the Majapahit kings. By 1428 the Muslim city-states of Java's north coast, buoyed by the profits of trade with China, secured their independence from Majapahit. Majapahit's dominion over the agricultural hinterland of Java lasted until 1528, when a coalition of Muslim princes forced the royal family to flee to Bali, which remains today the sole preserve of Hinduism in Southeast Asia.

Cosmopolitan port cities, with their diverse merchant communities, were natural sites for religious innovation. The spread of Islam beyond Southeast Asia's port cities, however, was slow and uneven. Because merchants and Sufi teachers played a far greater role than orthodox ulama in the spread of Islam in Southeast Asia, relatively open forms of Islam flourished. The Arab shipmaster Ibn Majid (IB-uhn maj-jid), writing in 1462, bemoaned the corruption of Islamic marriage and dietary laws among the Muslims of Melaka (mah-LAK-eh): "They have no culture at all. The infidel marries Muslim women while the Muslim takes pagans to wife.... The Muslim eats dogs for meat, for there are no food laws. They drink wine in the markets and do not treat divorce as a religious act."[7] Enforcement of Islamic law often was suspended where it conflicted with local custom. Southeast Asia never adopted some features of Middle Eastern culture often associated with Islam, such as the veiling of women.

Local pre-Islamic religious traditions persisted in Sumatra and Java long after the people accepted Islam. The most visible signs of conversion to Islam were giving up the worship of idols and the consumption of pork and adopting the practice of male circumcision. In addition, the elaborate feasting and grave

trade diaspora A network of merchants from the same city or country who live permanently in foreign lands and cooperate with one another to pursue trading opportunities.

goods, slave sacrifice, and widow sacrifice (*sati*) that normally accompanied the burials of chiefs and kings largely disappeared. Malays and Javanese readily adopted veneration of Sufi saints and habitually prayed for assistance from the spirits of deceased holy men. Muslim restrictions on women's secular and religious activities met with spirited resistance from Southeast Asian women, who were accustomed to active participation in public life. Even more than in West Africa, Islam in Southeast Asia prospered not by destroying traditions, but by assimilating them.

In regions such as West Africa and Southeast Asia, then, Islam diffused through the activities of merchants, teachers, and settlers rather than through conquest. The spread of Islam in Africa and Asia also followed the rhythms of international trade. While Europe recovered slowly from the Black Death, thriving commerce across the Indian Ocean forged new economic links among Asia, Africa, and the Mediterranean world.

The Global Bazaar

> **FOCUS** How did the pattern of international trade change during the fourteenth and fifteenth centuries, and how did these changes affect consumption and fashion tastes?

Dynastic changes, war, and the Black Death roiled the international economy in the fourteenth century. Yet the maritime world of the Indian Ocean, largely spared both pandemic and war, displayed unprecedented commercial dynamism. Pepper and cotton textiles from India, porcelain and silk from China, spices and other exotic goods from Southeast Asia, and gold, ivory, and copper from southern Africa circulated through a network of trading ports that spanned the Indian Ocean, Southeast Asia, and China. These trading centers attracted merchants and artisans from many lands, and the colorful variety of languages, dress, foods, and music that filled their streets gave them the air of a global bazaar (see Map 14.4).

The crises of the fourteenth century severely disrupted the European economy, but by 1450 Italy regained its place as the center within Latin Christendom of finance, industry, and trade. Italian production of luxury goods surpassed Islamic competitors' in both quantity and quality. Wealth poured into Italy, where it found new outlets in a culture of conspicuous consumption.

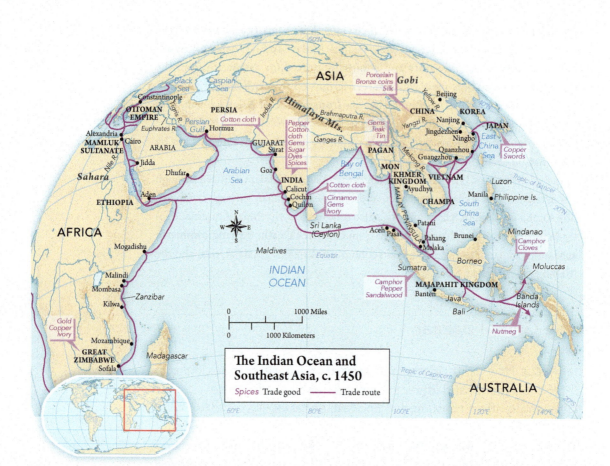

≡ **MAP 14.4** **The Indian Ocean and Southeast Asia, c. 1450** Spared the devastation of the Black Death, maritime Asia flourished in the fourteenth and fifteenth centuries. But travel across the Asian seas still had to follow the rhythms of the seasonal monsoon winds. The Islamic sultanate of Melaka on the Malay peninsula emerged as a great commercial crossroads where merchants from the Indian Ocean and the China seas gathered to trade.

Economic Prosperity and Maritime Trade in Asia 1350–1450

In Qubilai Khan's day, hostility among the Mongol khanates disrupted Central Asian caravan trade. After 1300 maritime commerce largely replaced inland trade over the ancient Silk Road. Asian merchants from India to China would seize the opportunities presented by the new emphasis on maritime trade.

In India, improvements in spinning wheels and looms, and above all the invention of block printing of fabrics in the fourteenth century, led to a revolution in cotton textile manufacture. Using block printing (carved wooden blocks covered with dye), Indian weavers produced colorful and intricately designed fabrics—later known in Europe as chintz, from the Hindi *chint* ("many-colored")—that were far cheaper than luxury textiles such as silk or velvet. Although cotton cultivation and weaving spread to Burma, Thailand, and China, Indian fabrics dominated Eurasian markets (see Lives and Livelihoods: Urban Weavers in India).

Along with textiles, India was famous for its pepper, for

Wedding Present of Chinese Porcelains Avid demand in the Muslim world stimulated development of China's renowned blue-and-white porcelains. This Persian miniature from around 1480 illustrates the story of a Chinese princess who in a gesture of diplomacy is sent to marry a Turkish nomad chieftain. The dowry that accompanies the reluctant bride includes blue-and-white porcelains and brass wares of Turkestan design.

which Europeans had acquired a taste during the age of the Crusades. Muslim merchants from Gujarat controlled both cotton and pepper exports from the cities of Calicut and Quilon (KEE-lon). By 1500 Gujarati merchants had created a far-flung trade network across the Indian Ocean from Zanzibar to Java. Gujarati *sharafs* (from the Persian word for "moneylender") and Tamil *chettis* ("traders") acted as bankers for merchants and rulers alike in nearly every Indian Ocean port.

China's ocean-going commerce also flourished in the fourteenth century. Silk had long dominated China's export trade, but by the eleventh century domestic silk-weaving was flourishing in Iran, the Byzantine Empire, and India. Instead, China retained its preeminent place in world trade by exporting porcelain, which became known as "chinaware." Much admired for their whiteness and translucency, Chinese ceramics already had become an important item of Asian maritime trade in the tenth century. In the thirteenth century, artisans at Jingdezhen (JING-deh-JUHN) in southern China perfected the techniques for making porcelain wares, which were harder and whiter than previous types of ceramics. By 1400, Jingdezhen had become the largest manufacturing city in the world, housing more than one thousand kilns with some seventy thousand craftsmen engaged in several dozen specialized tasks.

LIVES AND LIVELIHOODS

Urban Weavers in India

Industry and commerce in India, especially in textiles, grew rapidly beginning in the fourteenth century. Specialized craftsmen in towns and regional groups of merchants formed guilds that became the nuclei of new occupational castes, *jati* (JAH-tee). Ultimately these new occupational castes would join with other forces in Indian society to challenge the social inequality rooted in orthodox Hindu religion.

It was growth in market demand and technological innovations such as block printing that drove the rapid expansion of India's textile industries. Luxury fabrics such as fine silks and velvet remained largely the province of royal workshops or private patronage. Mass production of textiles, by contrast, was oriented toward the manufacture of cheaper cotton fabrics, especially colorful chintz garments. A weaver could make a woman's cotton *sari* in six or seven days, whereas a luxury garment took a month or more.

Weaving became an urban industry. It was village women who cleaned most of the cotton and spun it into yarn; they could easily combine this simple if laborious work with other domestic chores. But weaving, bleaching, and dyeing cloth were skilled tasks performed by professional urban craftsmen, or in some cases by artisans living in separate weavers' settlements in the countryside.

Increased affluence brought further social and economic differentiation to the ranks of weavers. Although guild leaders negotiated orders from merchants and princes, artisans could freely sell their own wares through urban shops and country

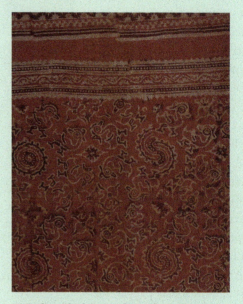

≡ Indian Block-Printed Textile, c. 1500
Block-printed textiles with elaborate designs were in great demand both in India and throughout Southeast Asia, Africa, and the Islamic world. This cotton fabric with geese, lotus flower, and rosette designs was manufactured in Gujarat in western India.

fairs. The most successful weavers became merchants and brokers, buying more looms and hiring others to work under their supervision. By the fourteenth century some weavers had begun to add the honorific title *chetti* (merchant) to their names.

The rising prosperity of weavers whetted their aspirations for social recognition. Enforcing laws governing caste purity amid the whirl and congestion of city life was far more difficult than in the villages. As a fourteenth-century poet wrote about the crowded streets of his hometown of Jaunpur in the Ganges Valley, in the city "one person's caste-mark gets stamped on another's forehead, and a brahman's holy thread will be found hanging around an untouchable's neck."[1] Brahmans objected to this erosion of caste boundaries, to little avail. Weaver guilds became influential patrons of temples and often served as trustees and accountants in charge of managing temple endowments and revenues.

In a few cases the growing economic independence of weavers and like-minded artisans prompted complete rejection of the caste hierarchy. Sufi preachers and *bhakti* (BAHK-tee)—devotional movements devoted to patron gods and goddesses—encouraged the disregard of caste distinctions in favor of a universal brotherhood of devout believers. The fifteenth-century bhakti preacher Kabir, who was strongly influenced by Sufi teachings, epitomized the new social radicalism coursing through the urban artisan classes. A weaver himself, Kabir joined the dignity of manual labor to the purity of spiritual devotion, spurning the social pretension and superficial piety of the Brahmans and Muslim clerics.

By the seventeenth century, such ideas had coalesced into a separatist religious movement, Sikhism, centered on a trinity of labor, charity, and spiritual devotion. The Sikhs, who gained a following principally among traders and artisans in the northwestern Punjab region, drew an even more explicit connection between commerce and piety. In the words of a hymn included in a sixteenth-century anthology of Sikh sacred writings,

> The true Guru [teacher] is the merchant;
> The devotees are his peddlers.
> The capital stock is the Lord's Name, and
> To enshrine the truth is to keep His account.[2]

Sikh communities spurned the distinction between pure and impure occupations. In their eyes, holiness was to be found in honest toil and personal piety, not ascetic practices, book learning, or religious rituals.

Questions to Consider

1. In what ways did the organization of textile production reinforce or challenge the prevailing social norms of Hindu society?

2. In what ways did religious ideas and movements reflect the new sense of dignity among prosperous Indian merchants and craftsmen?

For Further Information:

Ramaswamy, Vijaya. *Textiles and Weavers in Medieval South India*. Delhi: Oxford University Press, 1985.

Vanina, Eugenia. *Urban Crafts and Craftsmen in Medieval India (Thirteenth–Eighteenth Centuries)*. New Delhi: Munshiram Manoharlal, 2004.

1. Vidyapati Thakur, *Kirtilata*, quoted in Eugenia Vanina, *Urban Crafts and Craftsmen in Medieval India (Thirteenth–Eighteenth Centuries)* (New Delhi: Munshiram Manoharlal, 2004), 143.

2. *Sri Guru Granth Sahib*, trans. Gophal Singh (Delhi: Gur Das Kapur & Sons, 1960), 2:427.

The most avid consumers of Chinese porcelains were in the Islamic world, reflecting the global nature of the Chinese ceramics industry. Muslims used Chinese porcelains both as eating and drinking vessels and to decorate mosques, tombs, and other holy places. Imports of Chinese porcelain devastated local ceramic manufacturing in many parts of maritime Asia, from the Philippines to East Africa.

In mainland Southeast Asia, the shift in political power from the inland rice-growing regions toward coastal port cities reflected the new prominence of maritime trade in the region's economic life. Burma exported cotton to China as early as 1400 and became an important source of metals, gems, and teak for shipbuilding. The profits of maritime commerce fueled the emergence of Ayudhya (a-YOOD-he-ya) in Thailand as the dominant power in mainland Southeast Asia in the late fourteenth century. By 1400 Ayudhya was challenging Majapahit for control of the Southeast Asian trade routes between India and China.

China influenced patterns of international trade not only as a producer, as with ceramics, but as a market for exported goods. It was Chinese demand that drove the rapid expansion of pepper cultivation in Southeast Asia, in particular Sumatra, during the fifteenth century. In return for exports of pepper, sandalwood, tin and other metals, fine spices, and exotic products of the tropical rain forests, Southeast Asia imported cotton cloth from India and silks, porcelain, and bronze coins from China. In the wake of this trade boom, Indian and Chinese merchant communities sprouted across maritime Southeast Asia. The trade diasporas of Gujarati Muslims and Chinese from Guangzhou (Canton) and Quanzhou (CHYWAN-joe) created networks of cultural as well as economic influence, ultimately altering the balance of political power as well (see again Map 14.4).

China's Overseas Overture: The Voyages of Zheng He 1405–1433

The growth of South Asian maritime trade attracted the attention of the Chinese government, and in the early fifteenth century, the Ming dynasty in China took a more active role in maritime Southeast Asia. From the 1390s Malay princes in Sumatra appealed to the Ming court for protection against the demands of the Majapahit kings. In 1405 the Ming emperor Yongle decided to intervene by sending a naval expedition to halt the expansionist aggression of Majapahit and Ayudhya and to assert Chinese authority over the maritime realm.

Yongle entrusted the fleet to the command of his closest confidant, a young military officer named Zheng He (1371–1433). Zheng, born into a Muslim family who had served the Mongol rulers of the Yuan dynasty, was conscripted into the eunuch corps (castrated males employed as guardians of the imperial household) and placed in the retinue of the prince who would become Emperor Yongle.

For his mission to Southeast Asia, Yongle equipped Zheng He with a vast armada, a fleet of sixty-three ships manned by nearly twenty-eight thousand sailors, soldiers, and officials. Zheng's seven-masted flagship, more than four hundred feet long, was a marvel of Chinese nautical engineering. His fleet later became known as the "treasure ships" because of the cargoes of exotic goods and tribute they brought back from Southeast Asia, India, Arabia, and Africa. But Zheng's primary mission was political, not economic.

Departing in November of 1405, Zheng's fleet sailed first to Java in a show of force designed to intimidate Majapahit. He then traveled to Sumatra and Melaka and across the Indian Ocean to Ceylon and Calicut. No sooner had Zheng He returned to China in the autumn of 1407 than Yongle dispatched him on another voyage. Yongle had recently launched his invasion of Vietnam, and the purpose of the second voyage was to curtail Ayudhya's aggression and establish a Chinese presence at strategic ports such as Melaka along the Straits of Sumatra. Altogether Yongle commissioned six expeditions under Zheng He's command. During the fourth and subsequent voyages, Zheng He sailed beyond India to Arabia and down the east coast of Africa.

The projection of Chinese power over the sea lanes of maritime Asia led to far-reaching economic and political changes. The close relations Zheng He forged with rulers of port cities strengthened their political independence and promoted their commercial growth. Under the umbrella of Chinese protection, Melaka flourished as the great crossroads of Asian maritime trade.

The high cost of building and equipping the treasure ships depleted the Ming treasury, however. In 1430, Yongle's successor dispatched Zheng He on yet another voyage, his seventh. After traveling once again to Africa, Zheng died during his return home. With the passing of the renowned admiral, enthusiasm for the expeditions evaporated. Moreover, the Ming court faced a new threat: a resurgent Mongol confederation in the north. In 1449 a foolish young Ming emperor led a military campaign against the Mongols, only to be taken captive. The Ming court obtained the emperor's release by paying a huge ransom, but its strategic priorities had been completely transformed. Turning its back on the sea, the Ming state devoted its energies and revenues to rebuilding the Great Wall, much of which had crumbled to dust, as a defense against further Mongol attacks.

The shift in Chinese policy did not mean the end of Chinese involvement in maritime trade. Chinese merchants continued to pursue trading opportunities in defiance of the imperial ban on private overseas commerce. Melaka's rulers converted to Islam but welcomed merchants from every corner of Asia. The population probably reached one hundred thousand before Melaka was sacked by the Portuguese in 1511. Spurred by the growing European appetite for Asian spices, the violent intrusion of the Portuguese would transform the dynamics of maritime trade throughout Asia.

SEEING THE PAST

Leonardo da Vinci's *Virgin of the Rocks*

While living in Milan in the early 1480s, Leonardo accepted a commission to paint an altarpiece for the chapel of Milan's Confraternity of the Immaculate Conception, a branch of the Franciscan order. Leonardo's relationship with the friars proved to be stormy. His first version of the painting (now in the Louvre), reproduced here, apparently displeased his patrons and was sold to another party. Only after a fifteen-year-long dispute over the price did Leonardo finally deliver a modified version in 1508.

In portraying the biblical encounter between the child Jesus and the equally young John the Baptist during the flight to Egypt, Leonardo replaced the traditional desert setting with a landscape filled with rocks, plants, and water. Leonardo's dark grotto creates an aura of mystery and foreboding, from which the figures of Mary, Jesus, John, and the angel Uriel emerge as if in a vision. A few years before, Leonardo had written

Virgin of the Rocks, c. 1483–1486

Commerce and Culture in the Renaissance

European expansion in the late fourteenth and early fifteenth centuries was preceded and influenced by a period of dramatic change, the sweeping transformation in European culture known as the **Renaissance**. In its narrow sense *Renaissance* (French for "rebirth") refers to the revival of ancient Greek and Roman philosophy, art, and literature that originated in fourteenth-century Italy. Scholars

about "coming to the entrance of a great cavern, in front of which I stood for some time, stupefied and uncomprehending. . . . Suddenly two things arose in me, fear and desire: fear of the menacing darkness of the cavern; desire to see if there was any marvelous thing within."[1] The scene's ambiguity may have been the reason the friars rejected this version. The painting they eventually took added features such as a halo for Jesus and a cross-like staff for John that clarified their identities.

Fantastic as the scene might seem, Leonardo's meticulous renderings of rocks and plants were based on close observation of nature. Geologists have praised Leonardo's highly realistic sandstone rock formations and his precise placement of plants where they would most likely take root.

Masterpieces such as *The Virgin of the Rocks* display Leonardo's careful study of human anatomy, natural landscapes, and botany. Although he admired the perfection of nature, Leonardo also celebrated the human mind's rational and aesthetic capacities, declaring, "We by our arts may be called the grandsons of God."[2]

1. Arundel ms. (British Library), p. 115 recto, cited in Martin Kemp, *Leonardo da Vinci: The Marvelous Works of Nature and Man* (Oxford: Oxford University Press, 2006), 78.

2. John Paul Richter, ed., *The Notebooks of Leonardo da Vinci* (reprint of 1883 ed.; New York: Dover, 1970), Book IX, 328 (para. 654).

Examining the Evidence

1. How does Leonardo express the connection between John (at left) and Jesus through position, gesture, and their relationships with the figures of Mary and the angel Uriel?

2. The friars who commissioned the painting sought to celebrate the sanctity and purity of their patron, the Virgin Mary. Does this painting achieve that effect?

rediscovered classical learning and began to emulate the language and ideas of Greek and Roman philosophers and poets; these individuals became known as humanists, students of the liberal arts or humanities. The new intellectual movement of **humanism** combined classical learning with Christian piety and dedication to civic responsibilities.

At the same time, the Renaissance inaugurated dramatic changes in the self-image and lifestyle of the wealthy. The new habits of luxurious living and magnificent display diverged sharply from the Christian ethic of frugality. Innovations in material culture and aesthetic values reflected crucial changes in the Italian economy and its relationship to the international trading world of the Mediterranean and beyond.

The Black Death had hit the Italian city-states especially hard. Diminishing profits from trade with the Islamic world prompted many Italian merchants to abandon commerce in favor of banking. Squeezed out of the eastern Mediterranean by the Turks and Venetians, Genoa turned its attention westward. Genoese bankers became financiers to the kings of Spain and Portugal and supplied the funds for their initial forays into the Atlantic in search of new routes to African gold and Asian spices. European monarchs' growing reliance on professional armies, naval fleets, and gunpowder weapons also stimulated demand for banking services, forcing them to borrow money to meet the rising costs of war.

Italy became the primary producer of luxury goods for Europe, displacing the Islamic world and Asia. Before 1400, Islamic craftsmanship had far surpassed that of Latin Christendom. The upper classes of Europe paid handsome sums to obtain silk and linen fabrics, ceramics, rugs, glass, metalwork, and jewelry imported from the Mamluk Empire. "The most beautiful things in the world are found in Damascus," wrote Simone Sigoli, a Florentine who visited the city in 1386. "Such rich and noble and delicate works of every kind. . . . Really, all Christendom could be supplied for a year with the merchandise of Damascus."[8] But the Black Death, Timur's invasions, and Mamluk mismanagement devastated industry and commerce in Egypt and Syria.

Seizing the opportunity these developments created, Italian entrepreneurs first imitated and then improved on Islamic techniques and designs for making silk, tin-glazed ceramics known as *maiolica* (my-OH-lee-kah), glass, and brassware. By 1450 these Italian products had become competitive with or eclipsed imports from Egypt and Syria. Italian firms captured the major share of the international market for luxury textiles and other finished goods, and the Islamic lands were reduced to being suppliers of raw materials such as silk, cotton, and dyestuffs.

Along with Italy's ascent in finance and manufacturing came a decisive shift in attitudes toward money and its use. The older Christian ethics of frugality and

Renaissance A period of intense intellectual and artistic creativity in Europe, beginning in Italy in the fourteenth century as a revival of the classical civilization of ancient Greece and Rome.

humanism The study of the humanities (rhetoric, poetry, history, and moral philosophy), based on the works of ancient Greek and Roman writers, that provided the intellectual foundations for the Renaissance.

disdain for worldly gain gave way to prodigal spending and consumption. Much of this torrent of spending was lavished on religious art and artifacts, and the Roman papacy stood out as perhaps the most spendthrift of all. Displaying personal wealth and possessions affirmed social status and power. Civic pride and political rivalry fueled public spending to build and decorate churches and cathedrals. Rich townsmen transformed private homes into palaces, and artisans fashioned ordinary articles of everyday life—from rugs and furniture to dishes, books, and candlesticks—into works of art. Public piety blurred together with personal vanity. Spending money on religious monuments, wrote the fifteenth-century Florentine merchant Giovanni Rucellai (ROO-chel-lie) in his diary, gave him "the greatest satisfaction and the greatest pleasure, because it serves the glory of God, the honor of Florence, and my own memory."[9]

"Magnificence" became the watchword of the Renaissance. Wealthy merchants and members of the clergy portrayed themselves as patrons of culture and learning. Worldly goods gave tangible expression to spiritual refinement. The paintings of Madonnas and saints that graced Renaissance mansions were much more than objects of devotion: they were statements of cultural and social values. New commercial wealth created an expanded market for art, which was in turn shaped by the values associated with commerce.

As with Islam in West Africa, the intellectual ferment of the Renaissance was nurtured in an urban environment. Humanist scholars shunned the warrior culture of the old nobility while celebrating the civic roles and duties of townsmen, merchants, and clerics. Despite their admiration of classical civilization, the humanists did not reject Christianity. Rather, they sought to reconcile Christian faith and doctrines with classical learning. By making knowledge of Latin and Greek, history, poetry, and philosophy the mark of an educated person, the humanists transformed education and established models of schooling that would endure down to modern times.

Nowhere was the revolutionary impact of the Renaissance felt more deeply than in visual arts such as painting, sculpture, and architecture. Artists of the Renaissance exuded supreme confidence in the human capability to equal or even surpass the works of nature. The new outlook was exemplified by the development of the techniques of perspective, which artists used to convey a realistic, three-dimensional quality to physical forms, most notably the human body.

Above all, the Renaissance transformed the idea of the artist. No longer mere tradesmen, artists now were seen as possessing a special kind of genius that enabled them to express a higher understanding of beauty. In the eyes of contemporaries, no one exemplified this quality of genius more than Leonardo da Vinci

(1452–1519), who won renown as a painter, architect, sculptor, engineer, mathematician, and inventor. Leonardo spent much of his career as a civil and military engineer in the employ of the Duke of Milan, and developed ideas for flying machines, tanks, robots, and solar power that far exceeded the engineering capabilities of his time. Leonardo sought to apply his knowledge of natural science to painting, which he regarded as the most sublime art (see Seeing the Past: Leonardo da Vinci's *Virgin of the Rocks*).

The flowering of artistic creativity in the Renaissance was rooted in the rich soil of Italy's commercial wealth and nourished by the flow of goods from the Islamic world and Asia. International trade also invigorated industrial and craft production across maritime Asia and gave birth there to new patterns of material culture and consumption. In Japan, however, growing isolation from these cross-cultural interactions fostered the emergence of a national culture distinct from the Chinese traditions that dominated the rest of East Asia.

COUNTERPOINT: Age of the Samurai in Japan 1185–1450

> **FOCUS** How and why did the historical development of Japan in the fourteenth and fifteenth centuries differ from that of mainland Eurasia?

In Japan as in Europe, the term *Middle Ages* brings to mind an age of warriors, a stratified society governed by bonds of loyalty between lords and vassals. In Japan, however, the militarization of the ruling class intensified during the fourteenth and fifteenth centuries, a time when the warrior nobility of Europe was crumbling. Paradoxically, the rise of the **samurai (sah-moo-rye)** ("those who serve") warriors as masters of their own estates was accompanied by the increasing independence of peasant communities.

In contrast to the regions explored earlier in this chapter, Japan became more isolated from the wider world during this era. After the failed Mongol invasion of Japan in 1281, ties with continental Asia became increasingly frayed. Thus, many Japanese see this era as the period in which Japan's unique national identity—expressed most distinctly in the ethic of *bushidō* (boo-shee-doe), the "way of the warrior"—took its definitive form. A culture based on warriors, rather than Confucian scholars, created a different path for the development of Japanese society.

samurai Literally, "those who serve"; the hereditary warriors who dominated Japanese society and culture from the twelfth to the nineteenth century.

"The Low Overturning the High"

During the Kamakura period (1185–1333), the power of the **shogun**, or military ruler, of eastern Japan was roughly in balance with that of the imperial court and nobility at Kyoto in the west. Warriors dominated both the shogun's capital at Kamakura (near modern Tokyo) and provincial governorships, but most of the land remained in the possession of the imperial family, the nobility, and religious institutions based in Kyoto. After the collapse of the Kamakura government in 1333, Japan was wracked by civil wars. In 1336 a new dynasty of shoguns, the Ashikaga (ah-shee-KAH-gah), came to power in Kyoto. Unlike the Kamakura shoguns, the Ashikaga aspired to become national rulers. Yet not until 1392 did the Ashikaga shogunate gain uncontested political supremacy, and even then it exercised only limited control over the provinces and local samurai.

Japan, 1185–1392

In the Kamakura period, the samurai had been vassals subordinated to warrior clans to whom they owed allegiance and service. But wartime disorder and Ashikaga rule eroded the privileges and power of the noble and monastic landowners. Most of their estates fell into the hands of local samurai families.

Just as samurai were turning themselves into landowners, peasants banded together in village associations to resist demands for rents and labor service from their new samurai overlords. These village associations created their own autonomous governments to resist outside control while requiring strict conformity to the collective will of the community. As one village council declared, "Treachery, malicious gossip, or criminal acts against the village association will be punished by excommunication from the estate."[10] Outraged lords bewailed this reversal of the social hierarchy, "the low overturning the high," but found themselves powerless to check the growing independence of peasant communities.

The political strength of the peasants reflected their rising economic fortunes. Japan's agrarian economy improved substantially with the expansion of irrigated rice farming. The village displaced the manorial estate as the basic institution of rural society. Japan in the fifteenth century had little involvement in foreign trade, and there were few cities apart from the metropolis of Kyoto, which had swelled to 150,000 inhabitants by midcentury. Yet the prosperity of the agrarian economy generated considerable growth in artisan crafts and trade in local goods.

shogun The military commander who effectively exercised supreme political and military authority over Japan during the Kamakura (1185–1333), Ashikaga (1336–1573), and Tokugawa (1603–1868) shogunates.

The New Warrior Order

After the founding of the Ashikaga shogunate, provincial samurai swarmed the streets of Kyoto seeking the new rulers' patronage. In this world of "the low over-turning the high," warriors enjoyed newfound wealth while much of the old nobil-ity was reduced to abject poverty.

While derided by courtiers as uneducated and boorish, the shoguns and samurai became patrons of artists and cultural life. The breakdown of the traditional social hierarchy allowed greater intermingling among people from diverse backgrounds. The social and cultural worlds of the warriors and courtiers merged, producing new forms of social behavior and artistic expression.

In the early years of the Ashikaga shogunate, the capital remained infatuated with Chinese culture. As the fourteenth century wore on, however, this fascina-tion with China was eclipsed by new fashions drawn from both the court nobility and Kyoto's lively world of popular entertainments. Accomplishment in poetry and graceful language and manners, hallmarks of the courtier class, became part of samurai self-identity as well. A new mood of simplicity and restraint took hold, infused with the ascetic ethics of Zen Buddhism, which, as we saw in Chapter 9, stressed introspective meditation as the path to enlightenment.

The sensibility of the Ashikaga age was visible in new kinds of artistic display and performance, including poetry recitation, flower arrangement, and the com-plex rituals of the tea ceremony. A new style of theater known as *nō* reflected this fusion of courtly refinement, Zen religious sentiments, and samurai cultural tastes. Thus, the rise of warrior culture in Japan did not mean an end to sophistication and refinement. It did, however, involve a strong focus on cultural elements that were seen as distinctly Japanese.

In at least one area, developments in Japan mirrored those in other parts of the world. The warriors' dominance over Ashikaga society and culture led to a decisive shift toward patriarchal authority. Women lost rights of inheritance as warrior houses consolidated landholdings in the hands of one son who would continue the family line. The libertine sexual mores of the Japanese aristocracy depicted in Lady Murasaki's *Tale of Genji* (c. 1010) (see Chapter 12) gave way to a new emphasis on female chastity as an index of social order. The profuse output of novels, memoirs, and diaries written by court women also came to an end by 1350.

By 1400, then, the samurai had achieved political mastery in both the capital and the countryside and had eclipsed the old nobility as arbiters of cultural values. This warrior culture, which combined martial prowess with austere aesthetic tastes, stood in sharp contrast to the veneration of Confucian learning by the Chinese literati and the classical ideals and ostentatious consumption prized by the urban elite of Renaissance Italy.

Conclusion

The fourteenth century was an age of crisis across Eurasia and Africa. Population losses resulting from the Black Death devastated Christian and Muslim societies and economies. In the long run Latin Christendom fared well: the institution of serfdom largely disappeared from western Europe; new entrepreneurial energies were released; and the Italian city-states recovered their commercial vigor and stimulated economic revival in northern Europe. However, the once-great Byzantine Empire succumbed to the expanding Ottoman Empire and, under fire by Urban's cannon, came to an end in 1453. Following the Ottoman conquest, the central Islamic lands, from Egypt to Mesopotamia, never regained their former economic vitality. Still, the Muslim faith continued to spread, winning new converts in Africa, Central Asia, and Southeast Asia.

The fourteenth century also witnessed the collapse of the Mongol empires in China and Iran, followed by the rise and fall of the last of the Mongol empires, that of Timur. In China, the Ming dynasty spurned the Mongol vision of a multinational empire, instead returning to an imperial order based on an agrarian economy, bureaucratic rule, and Neo-Confucian values. New dynastic leaders in Korea and Vietnam imitated the Ming model, but in Japan the rising samurai warrior class forged a radically different set of social institutions and cultural values.

The Black Death redirected the course of European state-making. Monarchs strengthened their authority, aided by advances in military technology, mercenary armies, and fresh sources of revenue. The intensifying competition among national states would become one of the main motives for overseas exploration and expansion in the Atlantic world. At the same time, the great transformation in culture, lifestyles, and values known as the Renaissance sprang from the ruin of the Black Death.

✱ review

The major global development in this chapter: Crisis and recovery in fourteenth- and fifteenth-century Afro-Eurasia.

Important Events	
1315–1317	Great Famine in northern Europe
1325–1354	Travels of Ibn Battuta in Asia and Africa
1336–1573	Ashikaga shogunate in Japan
1337–1453	Hundred Years' War between England and France
1347–1350	Outbreak of the Black Death in Europe and the Islamic Mediterranean
c. 1351–1782	Ayudhya kingdom in Thailand
1368–1644	Ming dynasty in China
1381	Peasant Revolt in England
1392–1910	Yi dynasty in Korea
1405	Death of Timur; breakup of his empire into regional states in Iran and Central Asia
1405–1433	Chinese admiral Zheng He's expeditions in Southeast Asia and the Indian Ocean
1421	Relocation of Ming capital from Nanjing to Beijing
1428–1788	Le dynasty in Vietnam
1453	Ottoman conquest of Constantinople marks fall of the Byzantine Empire

KEY TERMS

Black Death (p. 491)
humanism (p. 518)
janissary corps (p. 505)
Little Ice Age (p. 492)
Neo-Confucianism (p. 499)

oligarchy (p. 496)
pandemic (p. 491)
Renaissance (p. 517)
samurai (p. 520)
shogun (p. 521)

Sufism (p. 502)
theocracy (p. 505)
trade diaspora (p. 508)

CHAPTER OVERVIEW QUESTIONS

1. How and why did Europe's economic growth begin to surpass that of the Islamic world in the century after the Black Death?
2. Did the economic revival across Eurasia after 1350 benefit the peasant populations of Europe, the Islamic world, and East Asia?
3. How did the process of conversion to Islam differ in Iran, the Ottoman Empire, West Africa, and Southeast Asia during this period?
4. What political and economic changes contributed to the rise of maritime commerce in Asia during the fourteenth and fifteenth centuries?

MAKING CONNECTIONS

1. What social, economic, and technological changes strengthened the power of European monarchs during the century after the Black Death?
2. How and why did the major routes and commodities of trans-Eurasian trade change after the collapse of the Mongol empires in Central Asia?
3. In what ways did the motives for conversion to Islam differ in Central Asia, sub-Saharan Africa, and the Indian Ocean during this era?
4. In this period, why did the power and status of the samurai warriors in Japan rise while those of the warrior nobility in Europe declined?

For further research into the topics covered in this chapter, see the Bibliography at the end of the book.

For additional primary sources from this period, see *Sources for World in the Making*.

PART 3

The Early Modern World, 1450–1750

☰ In this exquisite miniature painting from the 1590s, the Mughal emperor Akbar receives the Persian ambassador Sayyid Beg in 1562. The painting is an illustration commissioned for Akbar's official court history, the *Akbarnama*, and thus would have been seen and approved by the emperor himself. The meeting is emblematic of the generally amiable relationship between the Mughals and their Safavid neighbors in Iran.

Between 1450 and 1750, regional societies gave way to multiethnic empires, and horse-borne warriors gave way to cannon and long-distance sailing craft. Historians call this era "early modern" because it was marked by a shift toward centralized, bureaucratic, monetized, and technologically sophisticated states. Yet most of these "modern" states also clung to divine kingship and other remnants of the previous age, and most sought to revive and propagate older religious or philosophical traditions. Some states embraced tolerance, whereas others fought bitterly over matters of faith.

A striking novelty was the creation of permanent linkages between distant regions, most notably the Americas and the rest of the world. Early globalization accelerated changes in everything from demography to commerce to technology, allowing populations to grow and individuals to get rich. Yet globalization also enabled the spread of disease, and some innovations made warfare more deadly; early modernity did not promise longer and better lives for everyone.

Beginning around 1450, Iberians—the people of Spain and Portugal—used new ships and guns to venture into the Atlantic, where they competed in overseas colonization, trade, and conquest. They did so at the expense of millions of native peoples, first in Africa and the East Atlantic and then throughout the Americas and beyond. Other Europeans followed in the Iberians' wake, but the silver of Spanish America became the world's money.

Modernity affected Africa most deeply via the slave trade. The older flow of captive workers to the Muslim Middle East and Indian Ocean basin continued into early modern times, but it was displaced by a more urgent European demand in the Atlantic. The desire for slaves to staff distant plantations and mines fueled existing antagonisms within Africa even as it spawned new ones.

In the Indian Ocean basin a freer model of interaction developed. By 1450 Islamic merchants had come to dominate these seas by establishing trading networks from East Africa to Southeast Asia. After 1500, European interlopers discovered that in such a thriving, diverse, and politically decentralized region, they would have to compete fiercely for space. This they did, first by establishing coastal trading forts, then by moving inland.

On the Eurasian mainland, with the aid of modern firearms, powerful Ottoman, Russian, Safavid, and Mughal leaders turned from regional consolidation to imperial expansion by 1500. Unlike the Safavids and Mughals, the Ottomans sought to extend their empire overseas, taking on rivals in the Mediterranean and the Indian Ocean. Russia would venture abroad under Peter the Great.

Europe remained mostly embroiled in religious and political conflict. The religious schism known as the Protestant Reformation touched off bloody wars, and doctrinal disputes persisted. Warfare itself was transformed from knightly contests and town sieges to mass infantry mobilization and bombardment of strategic fortresses. Europe's political fractures enabled the rise of market economies, with more states sponsoring overseas colonizing ventures. New forms of government emerged, along with a questioning of ancient authorities. From this came a new science, emphasizing empirical observation and secular reasoning.

In early modern East Asia, by contrast, introversion was the rule. Although both China and Japan had strong seafaring traditions by 1450, state policies from the fifteenth to the sixteenth century discouraged external affairs. Despite official isolation, both

regions proved to be dynamic. Political consolidation and population growth were matched with a shift from tributary to money economies. In the Chinese Ming and Qing Empires, this led to a rise in demand for silver, stimulating global circulation of this mostly American-produced metal. Porcelain and silk, much of it produced by poor women working in the household, were sent abroad in exchange. With the patronage of newly wealthy merchants and bureaucrats, the arts flourished on a scale not seen before.

By 1700, the American colonies were not the neo-Europes their first colonizers had envisioned. Centuries of ethnic and cultural mixture, forced labor regimes, frontier expansion, and export-oriented economies all led to formation of distinct societies. In much of the Americas, the different outlooks of European colonizers and colonists would prove irreconcilable.

Despite these profound transformations, many people remained largely unaffected by the currents of early modernity. Most of North and South America, Polynesia, Oceania, central and southern Africa, and highland Asia remained beyond the zone of sustained contact with foreigners. New commodities and biological transfers were only beginning to be felt in many of these places at the end of the early modern era. As a result of their long isolation, inhabitants of these regions would be among the most drastically affected by modernity's next wave. ◼

Empires and Alternatives in the Americas 1430–1530

✳ backstory

By the fifteenth century the Americas had witnessed the rise and fall of numerous empires and kingdoms, including the classic Maya of Mesoamerica, the wealthy Sicán kingdom of Peru's desert coast, and the Cahokia mound builders of the Mississippi Basin. Just as these cultures faded, there emerged two new imperial states that borrowed heavily from their predecessors. The empires discussed in this chapter, the Aztec and Inca, were the largest states ever to develop in the Americas, yet they were not all-powerful. About half of all native Americans, among them the diverse peoples of North America's eastern woodlands, lived outside their realms.

≡ **World in the Making** Perched on a granite ridge high above Peru's Urubamba River, the Inca site of Machu Picchu continues to draw thousands of visitors each year. First thought to be the lost city of Vilcabamba, then a convent for Inca nuns, Machu Picchu is now believed to have been a mid-fifteenth-century palace built for the Inca emperor and his mummy cult. It was probably more a religious site than a place of rest and recreation.

In 1995, archaeologists discovered a tomb on a peak overlooking Arequipa, Peru. Inside was the mummified body of an adolescent girl placed there some five hundred years earlier. Evidence suggests she was an *aclla* (AHK-yah), or "chosen woman," selected by Inca priests from among hundreds of regional headmen's daughters. Most aclla girls became priestesses dedicated to the Inca emperor or the imperial sun cult. Others became the emperor's concubines or wives. Only the most select, like the girl discovered near Arequipa, were chosen for the "debt-payment" sacrifice, or *capacocha* (kah-pah-KOH-chah), said to be the greatest honor of all.

According to testimonies collected after the Spanish conquest of the Incas in 1532 (discussed in the next chapter), the capacocha sacrifice was a rare event preceded by rituals. First, the victim, chosen for her (and rarely, his) physical perfection, trekked to Cuzco, the Inca capital. The child's father brought gifts from his province and in turn received fine textiles from the emperor. Following an ancient Andean tradition, ties between ruler and ruled were reinforced through such acts of reciprocity. The girl, too, received skirts and shawls, along with votive objects. These adorned her in her tomb, reached after a long journey on foot from Cuzco.

As suggested by later discoveries, at tomb-side the aclla girl was probably given a beaker of maize beer. In a pouch she carried coca leaves. Coca, chewed throughout the Andes, helped fend off altitude sickness, whereas the maize beer induced sleepiness. Barely conscious of her surroundings, the girl was lowered into her grass-lined grave, and, according to the forensic anthropologists who examined her skull, struck dead with a club.

Why did the Incas sacrifice children, and why in these ways? By combining material, written, and oral evidence, scholars are beginning to solve the riddle of the Inca mountain mummies. It now appears that death, fertility, reciprocity, and imperial links to sacred landscapes were all features of the capacocha sacrifice. Although such deadly practices may challenge our ability to empathize with the leaders, if not the common folk, of this distant culture, with each new fact we learn about the child mummies, the closer we get to understanding the Inca Empire and its ruling cosmology.

The Incas and their subjects believed that death occurred as a process, and that proper death led to an elevated state of consciousness. In this altered state a person could communicate with deities directly, and in a sense join them. If the remains of such a person were carefully preserved and honored, they could act as an oracle, a conduit to the sacred realms above and below the earth. Mountains, as sources of springs and rivers, and sometimes fertilizing volcanic ash, held particular significance.

In part, it was these beliefs about landscape, death, and the afterlife that led the Incas to mummify ancestors, including their emperors, and to bury chosen young people atop mountains that marked the edges, or heights, of empire. Physically perfect noble children such as the girl found near Arequipa were thus selected to communicate with the spirit world. Their sacrifice unified the dead, the living, and the sacred mountains, and also bound together a far-flung empire that was in many ways as fragile as life itself.[1]

But this fragility was not evident to the people gathered at the capacocha sacrifice. By about 1480, more than half of all native Americans were subjects of two great empires, the Aztec in Mexico and Central America and the Inca in South America. Both empires subdued neighboring chiefdoms through a mix of violence, forced relocation, religious indoctrination, and marriage alliances. Both empires demanded allegiance in the form of tribute. Both the Aztecs and Incas were greatly feared by their millions of subjects. Perhaps surprisingly, these last great native American states would prove far more vulnerable to European invaders than their nonimperial neighbors, most of whom were gatherer-hunters and semi-sedentary villagers. Those who relied least on farming had the best chance of getting away.

OVERVIEW QUESTIONS

The major global development in this chapter: The diversity of societies and states in the Americas prior to European invasion.

As you read, consider:

1. In what ways was cultural diversity in the Americas related to environmental diversity?

2. Why was it in Mesoamerica and the Andes that large empires emerged around 1450?

3. What key ideas or practices extended beyond the limits of the great empires?

Many Native Americas

↘ **FOCUS** What factors account for the diversity of native American cultures?

Scholars once claimed that the Western Hemisphere was sparsely settled prior to the arrival of Europeans in 1492, but we now know that by then the population of the Americas had reached some sixty million or more. Although vast open spaces remained, in places the landscape was more intensively cultivated and thickly populated than western Europe (see Map 15.1). Fewer records for nonimperial groups survive than for empire builders such as the Incas and Aztecs, but scholars have recently learned much about these less-studied cultures. Outside imperial boundaries, coastal and riverside populations were densest. This was true in the Caribbean, the Amazon, Paraguay-Paraná, and Mississippi River Basins, the Pacific Northwest, and parts of North America's eastern seaboard.

Ecological diversity gave rise in part to political and cultural diversity. America's native peoples, or Amerindians, occupied two ecologically diverse continents. They also inhabited tropical, temperate, and icy environments that proved more or less suitable to settled agriculture. Some were members of egalitarian gatherer-hunter bands; others were subjects of rigidly stratified imperial states. In between were traveling bands of pilgrims led by prophets; chiefdoms based on fishing, whaling, or farming; regional confederacies of chiefdoms; and independent city-states.

Political diversity was more than matched by cultural diversity. The Aztecs and Incas spread the use of imperial dialects within their empires, but elsewhere hundreds of distinct Amerindian languages could be heard. Modes of dress and adornment were even more varied, ranging from total nudity and a few tattoos to highly elaborate ceremonial dress. Lip and ear piercing, tooth filing, and molding of the infant skull between slats of wood were but a few of the many ways human appearances were reconfigured. Architecture was just as varied, as were ceramics and other arts. In short, the Americas' extraordinary range of climates and natural resources both reflected and encouraged diverse forms of material and linguistic expression. Perhaps only in the realm of religion, where shamanism persisted, was a unifying thread to be found.

☰ **Canadian War Club** This stone war club with a fish motif was excavated from a native American tomb in coastal British Columbia, Canada, and is thought to date from around 1200 to 1400 C.E. Such items at first suggest a people at war, but this club was probably intended only for ceremonial use. Modern Tsimshian inhabitants of the region, who still rely on salmon, describe the exchange of stone clubs in their foundation myths.

Main Settlement Areas in the Americas, c. 1492

Main areas of settlement, c. 1492	
Major trade route	

Principal crops

Amaranth		Potatoes, sweet potatoes	
Beans		Quinoa	
Cacao		Squash, pumpkins, gourds	
Chilies		Sunflowers	
Cotton		Tobacco	
Maize		Tomatoes	
Manioc		Peanuts	

≡ **MAP 15.1   Main Settlement Areas in the Americas, c. 1492**   Most native Americans settled in regions that supported intensive agriculture. The trade routes shown here linked peoples from very different cultures, mostly to exchange rare items such as shells, precious stones, and tropical bird feathers, but seeds for new crops also followed these paths.

Shamanism consisted of reliance on healer-visionaries for spiritual guidance. In imperial societies shamans constituted a priestly class. Both male and female, shamans had functions ranging from fortune teller to physician, with women often acting as midwives. Still, most native American shamans were males. The role of shaman could be inherited or determined following a vision quest. This entailed a solo journey to a forest or desert region, prolonged physical suffering, and controlled use of hallucinogenic substances. In many respects Amerindian shamanism resembled shamanistic practices in Central Asia and sub-Saharan Africa.

Often labeled "witch doctors" by Christian Europeans, shamans maintained a body of esoteric knowledge that they passed along to apprentices. Some served as historians and myth keepers. Most used powerful hallucinogens to communicate with the spirits of predatory animals, which were venerated almost everywhere in the Americas. Animal spirits were regarded as the shaman's alter ego or protector, and were consulted prior to important occasions. Shamans also mastered herbal remedies for all forms of illness, including emotional disorders. These rubs, washes, and infusions were sometimes effective, as shown by modern pharmacological studies. Shamans nearly always administered them along with chants and rituals aimed at expelling evil spirits. Shamans, therefore, combined the roles of physician and religious leader, using their knowledge and power to heal both body and spirit.

The many varieties of social organization and cultural practice found in the Americas reflect both creative interactions with specific environments and the visions of individual political and religious leaders. Some Amerindian gatherer-hunters lived in swamplands and desert areas where subsistence agriculture was impossible using available technologies. Often such gathering-hunting peoples traded with—or plundered—their farming neighbors. Yet even farming peoples did not forget their past as hunters. As in other parts of the world, big-game hunting in the Americas was an esteemed, even sacred activity among urban elites.

Just as hunting remained important to farmers, agriculture could be found among some forest peoples. Women in these societies controlled most agricultural tasks and spaces, periodically making offerings to spirits associated with human fertility. Amerindian staple foods included maize, potatoes, and manioc, a lowland tropical tuber that could be ground into flour and preserved. With the ebb and flow of empires, many groups shifted from one mode of subsistence to another, from planting to gathering-hunting and back again. Some, such as the Kwakiutl (KWAH-kyu-til) of the Pacific Northwest, were surrounded by such abundant marine and forest resources that they never turned to farming. Natural abundance combined with sophisticated fishing and storage systems allowed the Kwakiutl to build a settled culture of the type normally associated with agricultural peoples.

shamanism
Widespread system
of religious belief and
healing originating in
Central Asia.

Thus, the ecological diversity of the Americas helped give rise to numerous cultures, many of which blurred the line between settled and nomadic lifestyles.

Tributes of Blood: The Aztec Empire 1325–1521

FOCUS What core features characterized Aztec life and rule?

Mesoamerica, comprised of modern southern Mexico, Guatemala, Belize, El Salvador, and western Honduras, was a land of city-states after about 800 C.E. Following the decline of Teotihuacán (tay-oh-tee-wah-KAHN) in the Mexican highlands and the classic Maya in the greater Guatemalan lowlands, few urban powers, with the possible exception of the Toltecs, managed to dominate more than a few neighbors.

This would change with the arrival in the Valley of Mexico of a band of former gatherer-hunters from a northwestern desert region they called Aztlán (ost-LAWN), or "place of cranes." As newcomers these "Aztecs," who later called themselves Mexica (meh-SHE-cah, hence "Mexico"), would suffer humiliation by powerful city-dwellers centered on Lake Texcoco, now overlain by Mexico City. The Aztecs were at first regarded as barbarians, but as with many conquering outsiders, in time they would have their revenge (see Map 15.2).

Humble Origins, Imperial Ambitions

Unlike the classic Maya of preceding centuries, the Aztecs did not develop a fully phonetic writing system. They did, however, preserve their history in a mix of oral and symbolic, usually painted or carved, forms. Aztec elders maintained chronicles of the kind historians call master narratives, or state-sponsored versions of the past meant to glorify certain individuals or policies. These narratives related foundation myths, genealogies, tales of conquest, and other important remembrances. Though biased and fragmentary, many Aztec oral narratives were preserved by young native scribes writing in Nahuatl (NAH-watt), the Aztec language, soon after the Spanish Conquest of 1519–1521 (discussed in the next chapter).

Why is it that the Spanish victors promoted rather than suppressed these narratives of Aztec glory? In one of history's many ironic twists, Spanish priests arriving in Mexico in the 1520s taught a number of noble Aztec and other Mesoamerican youths to adapt the Latin alphabet and Spanish phonetics to various local languages, most importantly Nahuatl. The Spanish hoped that stories of Aztec rule and religion, once collected and examined, would be swiftly discredited

≡ **MAP 15.2 The Aztec Empire, 1325–1521** Starting from their base in Tenochtitlán (now Mexico City), the Aztecs quickly built the most densely populated empire in the Americas. Their first objective was the Valley of Mexico itself. Although a line of kings greatly extended the empire, not all peoples fell to the Aztec war machine, including the Tlaxcalans to the east of Tenochtitlán and the Tarascans to the west. Also unconquered were the many nomadic peoples of the desert north and the farming forest peoples of the southeast.

and replaced with Western, Christian versions. Not only did this quick conversion not happen as planned, but an unintended consequence of the information-gathering campaign was to create a vast body of Mesoamerican literature written in native languages.

The Aztecs were a quick study in the production of written historical documents, and most of what we know of Aztec history relies heavily on these hybrid, sixteenth-century sources (see Seeing the Past: An Aztec Map of Tenochtitlán). Aside from interviews with the elders, several painted books, or codices, marked with precise dates, names, and other symbols, survive, along with much archaeological and artistic evidence. In combining these sources with Spanish eyewitness accounts of the conquest era, historians have assembled a substantial record of Aztec life and rule.

SEEING THE PAST

An Aztec Map of Tenochtitlán

Named for Mexico's first Spanish viceroy, the *Codex Mendoza* was painted by Aztec artists about a dozen years after the Spanish Conquest of 1519–1521. It was commissioned by the viceroy as a gift for the Holy Roman emperor and king of Spain, Charles V. After circulating among the courts of Europe, the *Codex Mendoza* landed in the Bodleian Library in Oxford, England, where it remains. Much of the document consists of tribute lists, but it also contains an illustrated history of Aztec conquests, crimes and punishments, and even a map of Tenochtitlán, the Aztec capital. This symbol-filled map is reproduced here.

According to legend, the Aztec capital came into existence when an eagle landed on a cactus in the middle of Lake Texcoco. This image, now part of the Mexican national flag, is at the center of the map. Beneath the cactus is a picture of a stone carving of a cactus fruit, a common Aztec symbol for the human heart, emblem of sacrifice. Beneath this is a third symbol labeled afterward by a Spanish scribe "Tenochtitlán."

The city, or rather its symbol, marks the meeting of four spatial quarters. In each quarter are various Aztec nobles, only one of whom, Tenochtli (labeled "Tenuch" on the map), is seated on a reed mat, the Aztec symbol of supreme authority. He was the Aztecs' first emperor; the name "Tenochtli" means "stone cactus fruit."

The lower panel depicts the Aztec conquests of their neighbors in Colhuacan and Tenayuca. Framing

Tenochtitlán, from the *Codex Mendoza*

the entire map are symbols for dates, part of an ancient Mesoamerican system of timekeeping and prophesying retained by the Aztecs. Finally, barely legible in the upper left-hand corner is the somewhat jarring signature of André Thevet, a French priest and royal cosmographer who briefly possessed the *Codex Mendoza* in the late sixteenth century.

Examining the Evidence

1. What does this map reveal about the Aztec worldview?

2. How might this document have been read by a common Aztec subject?

≡ **Lake Texcoco and Tenochtitlán, c. 1500**

The Aztecs apparently arrived in the Valley of Mexico sometime in the thirteenth century, but it was not until the early fourteenth that they established a permanent home. The most fertile sites in the valley were already occupied, but the Aztecs were not dissuaded; they had a reputation for being tough and resourceful. Heeding an omen in the form of an eagle perched on a cactus growing on a tiny island near the southwest edge of Lake Texcoco, the refugees settled there in 1325. Reclaiming land from the shallow lakebed, they founded a city called Tenochtitlán (teh-noach-teet-LAWN), or "cactus fruit place." Linked to shore by three large causeways, the city soon boasted stone palaces and temple-pyramids.

The Aztecs transformed Tenochtitlán into a formidable capital. By 1500 it was home to some two hundred thousand people, ranking alongside Nanjing and Paris among the world's most populous cities at the time. At first the Aztecs developed their city by trading military services and lake products such as reeds and fish for building materials, including stone, lime, and timber from the surrounding hillsides. They then formed marriage alliances with regional ethnic groups such as the Colhua, and by 1430 initiated imperial expansion.

Intermarriage with the Colhua, who traced their ancestry to the warrior Toltecs, lent the lowly Aztecs a new, elite cachet. At some point the Aztecs tied their religious cult, focused on the war god Huitzilopochtli (weetsy-low-POACH-tlee), or "hummingbird-on-the-left" to cults dedicated to more widely known deities, such as the water god Tlaloc. A huge, multilayered pyramid faced with carved stone and filled with rubble, now referred to by archaeologists as the Templo Mayor, or "Great Temple," but called by the Aztecs Coatepec, or "Serpent Mountain," became the centerpiece of Tenochtitlán. At its top, some twenty stories above the valley floor, sat twin temples, one dedicated to Huitzilopochtli, the other to Tlaloc. Coatepec was built to awe and intimidate. In the words of one native poet,

> Proud of itself
> Is the City of Mexico-Tenochtitlán
> Here no one fears to die in war
> This is our glory
> This is Your Command
> Oh Giver of Life

Have this in mind, oh princes
Who could conquer Tenochtitlán?
Who could shake the foundation of heaven?[2]

The Aztecs saw themselves as both stagehands and actors in a cosmic drama centered on their great capital city.

Enlarging and Supplying the Capital

With Tenochtitlán surrounded by water, subsistence and living space became serious concerns amid imperial expansion. Fortunately for the Aztecs, Lake Texcoco was shallow enough to allow an ingenious form of land reclamation called *chinampa* (chee-NAHM-pah). **Chinampas** were long, narrow terraces built by hand from dredged mud, reeds, and rocks, bordered by interwoven sticks and live trees. Chinampa construction also created canals for canoe transport. Building chinampas and massive temple-pyramids such as Coatepec without metal tools, wheeled vehicles, or draft animals required thousands of workers. Their construction, therefore, is a testimony to the Aztecs' power to command labor.

Over time, Tenochtitlán's canals accumulated algae, water lilies, and silt. Workers periodically dredged and composted this organic material to fertilize maize and other plantings on the island terraces. Established chinampa lands were eventually used for building residences, easing urban crowding. By the mid-fifteenth century the Aztecs countered problems such as chronic flooding and high salt content at their end of the lake with dikes and other public works.

Earlier, in the fourteenth century, an adjacent "twin" city called Tlatelolco (tlah-teh-LOLE-coe) had emerged alongside Tenochtitlán. Tlatelolco was the Aztec marketplace. Foods, textiles, and exotic goods were exchanged here. Cocoa beans from the hot lowlands served as currency, and products such as turquoise and quetzal feathers arrived from as far away as New Mexico and Guatemala, respectively. Though linked by trade, these distant regions fell well outside the Aztec domain. All products were transported along well-trod footpaths on the backs of human carriers. Only when they arrived on the shores of Lake Texcoco could trade goods be shuttled from place to place in canoes. Tlatelolco served as crossroads for all regional trade, with long-distance merchants, or *pochteca* (poach-TEH-cah), occupying an entire precinct.

Aztec imperial expansion began only around 1430, less than a century before the arrival of Europeans. An alliance between Tenochtitlán and the city-states of Texcoco and Tlacopan led to victory against a third, Atzcapotzalco (otts-cah-poat-SAUL-coh) (see again Map 15.2). Tensions with Atzcapotzalco extended back to the Aztecs' first arrival in the region. The Aztecs used the momentum of this victory to overtake their allies and lay the foundations of a regional, tributary empire.

chinampa A terrace for farming and house building constructed in the shallows of Mexico's Lake Texcoco by the Aztecs and their neighbors.

Within a generation they controlled the entire Valley of Mexico, exacting tribute from several million people. The Nahuatl language helped link state to subjects, although many subject groups retained local languages. These persistent forms of ethnic identification, coupled with staggering tribute demands, would eventually help bring about the end of Aztec rule.

Holy Terror: Aztec Rule, Religion, and Warfare

A series of six male rulers, or *tlatoque* (tlah-TOE-kay, singular *tlatoani*), presided over Aztec expansion. When a ruler died, his successor was chosen by a council of elders from among a handful of eligible candidates. Aztec kingship was sacred in

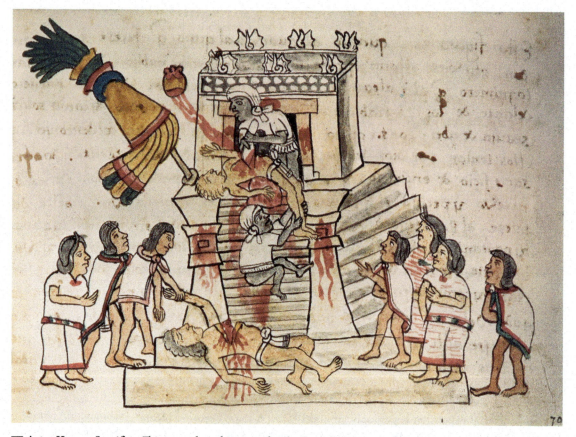

≡ **Aztec Human Sacrifice** This image dates from just after the Spanish Conquest of Mexico, but it was part of a codex about Aztec religious practices and symbols. Here a priest is removing the beating heart of a captive with a flint knife as an assistant holds his feet. The captive's bloody heart, in the form of a cactus fruit, ascends, presumably to the gods (see the same icon in Seeing the Past: An Aztec Map of Tenochtitlán, page 539). At the base of the sacrificial pyramid lies an earlier victim, apparently being taken away by noble Aztec men and women responsible for the handling of the corpse.

that each tlatoani traced his lineage back to the Toltecs. For this, the incorporation of the Colhua lineage had been essential. In keeping with this Toltec legacy, the Aztec Empire was characterized by three core features: human sacrifice, warfare, and tribute. All were linked to Aztec and broader Mesoamerican notions of cosmic order, specifically the human duty to feed the gods.

Like most Mesoamericans, the Aztecs traced not only their own but all human origins to sacrifices made by deities. In origin stories male and female gods threw themselves into fires, drew their own blood, and killed and dismembered one another, all for the good of humankind. These sacrifices were considered essential to the process of releasing and renewing the generative powers that drove the cosmos.

According to Aztec belief, humans were expected to show gratitude by following the example of their creators in an almost daily ritual cycle. Much of the sacred calendar had been inherited from older Mesoamerican cultures, but the Aztecs added many new holidays to celebrate their own special role in cosmic history. The Aztecs' focus on sacrifice also appears to have derived from their sense that secular and spiritual forces were inseparable. Affairs of state were affairs of heaven, and vice versa. Tenochtitlán was thought to be the foundation of heaven, its enormous temple-pyramids the center of human-divine affairs. Aztec priests and astrologers believed that the universe, already in its fifth incarnation after only three thousand years, was unstable, on the verge of chaos and collapse. Only human intervention in the form of sustained sacrificial ritual could stave off apocalypse.

As an antidote, the gods had given humans the "gift" of warfare. Human captives, preferably young men, were to be hunted and killed so that the release of their blood and spirits might satisfy the gods. Warrior sacrifice was so important to the Aztecs that they believed it kept the sun in motion.

Devout Aztec subjects also took part in nonlethal cosmic regeneration rituals in the form of personal bloodletting, or **autosacrifice**. According to sources, extremities and genitals were bled using thorns and stone blades, with public exhibition of suffering as important as blood loss. Blood offerings were absorbed by thin sheets of reed paper, which were burned before an altar. These bloodlettings, like captive sacrifices, emphasized the frailty of the individual, the pain of life, and indebtedness to the gods. Human blood fueled not only the Aztec realm, but the cosmos.

Given these sacrificial obligations, Aztec warfare aimed not at the annihilation but rather at live capture of enemies. Aztec combat was ideally a stylized and theatrical affair similar to royal jousts in contemporary Eurasia, with specific individuals paired for contest. Aztec warriors were noted for their fury, a trait borrowed from their patron deity, Huitzilopochtli. Chronic enemies such as the Tlaxcalans apparently learned to match the ferocious Aztec style, and some enemies, such as the Otomí, were eventually incorporated into Aztec warrior ranks.

autosacrifice The Mesoamerican practice of personal bloodletting as a means of paying debts to the gods.

Mesoamerican warriors considered death on the battlefield the highest honor. But live capture was the Aztecs' main goal, and most victims were marched naked and bound to the capital to be sacrificed. Although charged with religious meaning, Aztec warrior sacrifices were also intended to horrify enemies; visiting diplomats were made to watch them. Aztec imperial expansion depended in part on religious terror, or the ability to appear chosen by the gods for victory.

In addition to sacrificial victims, the Aztecs demanded **tribute** of conquered peoples. In addition to periodic labor drafts for public works, tribute lists included food, textiles, and craft goods for the empire's large priestly and warrior classes. Other tribute items were redistributed to favored subjects of lower status to help cement loyalties. Yet other tribute items were purely symbolic. Some new subjects were made to collect filth and inedible insects, for example, just to prove their unworthiness. As an empire that favored humiliation over co-optation and promotion of new subjects, the Aztecs faced an ever-deepening reservoir of resentment.

Daily Life Under the Aztecs

Aztec society was stratified, and Mexica nobles regarded commoners as uncouth. In between were bureaucrats, priests, district chiefs, scribes, merchants, and artisans. Although elites displayed the fruits of their subordinates' labors, most Aztec art seems to have been destined not for wealthy people's homes but for temples, tombs, and religious shrines. Despite heavy emphasis on religious ceremonies, the Aztecs also maintained a civil justice system. Quite unlike most of the world's imperial cultures, Aztec nobles sometimes received harsher punishments than commoners for similar misdeeds.

Class hierarchy was reinforced by dress and speech codes, along with many other rules and rituals. The tlatoani, for example, could not be touched or even looked in the face by any but his closest relatives, consorts, and servants. Even ranking nobles were supposed to lie face down on the ground and put dirt in their mouths before him. Nobles guarded their own rank by using a restricted form of speech. Chances for social advancement were limited, but some men gained status on the battlefield.

At the base of the social pyramid were peasants and slaves. Some peasants were ethnic Aztecs, but most belonged to city-states and clans that had been conquered after 1430. In either case, peasants' lives revolved around producing food and providing overlords with tribute goods and occasional labor. Slavery usually took the form of crisis-driven self-indenture; it was not an inherited social status. Slavery remained unimportant to the overall Aztec economy.

Merchants, particularly the mobile *pochteca* responsible for long-distance trade, occupied an unusual position. Although the pochteca sometimes accumulated

tribute Taxes paid to a state or empire, usually in the form of farm produce or artisan manufactures but sometimes also human labor or even human bodies.

great wealth, they remained resident aliens. They had no homeland, but made a good living supplying elites with exotic goods. Nonetheless, there is no evidence of complex credit instruments, industrial-style production, or real estate exchange of the sort associated with early merchant capitalism in other parts of the world at this time. The Aztec state remained tributary, the movement of goods mostly a reflection of power relations. Merchants, far from influencing politics, remained ethnic outsiders. Thus, both the Aztec economy and social structure reinforced the insularity of Aztec elites.

The life of an Aztec woman was difficult even by early modern standards. Along with water transport and other heavy household chores, maize grinding and tortilla making became the core responsibilities of most women in the Valley of Mexico, and indeed throughout Mesoamerica. Without animal- or water-driven grain mills, food preparation was an arduous, time-consuming task, particularly for the poor. Only noblewomen enjoyed broad exemption from manual work.

Sources suggest that some women assumed minor priestly roles. Others worked as surgeons and herbalists. Midwifery was also a fairly high-status, female occupation (see Lives and Livelihoods: The Aztec Midwife). These were exceptions; women's lives were mostly hard under Aztec rule. Scholars disagree, however, as to whether male political and religious leaders viewed women's duties and contributions as complementary or subordinate. Surviving texts do emphasize feminine mastery of the domestic sphere and its social value. However, this emphasis may simply reflect male desire to limit women's actions, since female reproductive capacity was also highly valued as an aid to the empire's perpetual war effort.

Indeed, Aztec society was so militarized that giving birth was referred to as "taking a captive." This comparison reflects the Aztec preoccupation with pleasing their gods: women were as much soldiers as men in the ongoing war to sustain human life. Women's roles in society were mostly domestic rather than public, but the home was a sacred space. Caring for it was equivalent to caring for a temple. Sweeping was a ritual, for example, albeit one with hygienic benefits. Hearth tending, maize grinding, spinning, and weaving were also ritualized tasks. Insufficient attention to these daily rituals put families and entire lineages at risk.

Aztec children, too, lived a scripted existence, their futures predicted at birth by astrologers. Names were derived from birthdates, and served as a public badge of fate. Sources affirm that Aztec society at all levels emphasized duty and good comportment rather than rights and individual freedom. Parents were to police their children's behavior and to help mold all youths into useful citizens. Girls and boys were assigned tasks considered appropriate for their sex well before adolescence. By age fourteen, children were engaged in adult work. One break from the chores was instruction between ages twelve and fifteen in singing and playing instruments,

LIVES AND LIVELIHOODS

The Aztec Midwife

In Aztec culture, childbirth was a sacred and ritual-ized affair. Always life-threatening for mother and child, giving birth and being born were both explic-itly compared to the battlefield experience. Aside from potential medical complications, the Aztecs considered the timing of a child's birth critical in determining her or his future. This tricky blend of physical and spiritual concerns gave rise to the respected and highly skilled livelihood of midwife. It is not entirely clear how midwives were chosen, but their work is well described in early post-conquest records, particularly the illustrated books of Aztec lore and history collectively known as the *Florentine Codex*. The following passage, translated directly from sixteenth-century Nahuatl, is one such description. Note how the midwife blends physi-cal tasks, such as supplying herbs and swaddling clothes, with shamanistic cries and speeches.

Aztec Midwife This image accompanies a description in Nahuatl, the Aztec language, of the midwife's duties written soon after the Spanish Conquest. (Firenze, Biblioteca Medicea Laurenziana, Ms. Med. Palat. 219, f. 132v. Su concessione del MiBACT)

And the midwife inquired about the fate of the baby who was born.

When the pregnant one already became aware of [pains in] her womb, when it was said that her time of death had arrived, when she wanted to give birth already, they quickly bathed her, washed her hair with soap, washed her, adorned her well. And then they arranged, they swept the house where the little woman was to suffer, where she was to perform her duty, to do her work, to give birth.

If she were a noblewoman or wealthy, she had two or three midwives. They remained by her side, awaiting her word. And when the woman became really disturbed internally,

such as drums and flutes, for cyclical religious festivals. Girls married at about age fifteen, and boys nearer twenty, a pattern roughly in accordance with most parts of the world at the time. Elder Aztec women served as matchmakers, and wedding ceremonies were elaborate, multiday affairs. Some noblemen expanded their pres-tige by retaining numerous wives and siring dozens of children.

they quickly put her in a sweat bath [a kind of sauna]. And to hasten the birth of the baby, they gave the pregnant woman cooked *ciua-patli* [literally, "woman medicine"] herb to drink.

And if she suffered much, they gave her ground opossum tail to drink, and then the baby was quickly born. [The midwife] already had all that was needed for the baby, the little rags with which the baby was received.

And when the baby had arrived on earth, the midwife shouted; she gave war cries, which meant the woman had fought a good battle, had become a brave warrior, had taken a captive, had captured a baby.

Then the midwife spoke to it. If it was a boy, she said to it: "You have come out on earth, my youngest one, my boy, my young man." If it was a girl, she said to it: "My young woman, my youngest one, noblewoman, you have suffered, you are exhausted." . . . [and to either:] "You have come to arrive on earth, where your relatives, your kin suffer fatigue and exhaustion; where it is hot, where it is cold, and where the wind blows; where there is thirst, hunger, sadness, despair, exhaustion, fatigue, pain. . . ."

And then the midwife cut the umbilical cord.

Source: Selection from the Florentine Codex in Matthew Restall, Lisa Sousa, and Kevin Terraciano, eds., *Mesoamerican Voices: Native-Language Writings from Colonial Mexico, Oaxaca, Yucatan, and Guatemala* (New York: Cambridge University Press, 2005), 216–217.

Questions to Consider

1. Why was midwifery so crucial to the Aztecs?
2. How were girls and boys addressed by the midwife, and why?

For Further Information:

Carrasco, David, and Scott Sessions. *Daily Life of the Aztecs, People of the Sun and Earth*, 2nd ed. Indianapolis: Hackett, 2008.

Clendinnen, Inga. *Aztecs: An Interpretation*. New York: Cambridge University Press, 1994.

At around harvest time in September, Aztec subjects ate maize, beans, and squash seasoned with salt and ground chili peppers. During other times of the year, and outside the chinampa zone, food could be scarce, forcing the poor to consume roasted insects, grubs, and lake scum. Certain items, such as frothed cocoa, were reserved for elites. Stored maize was used to make tortillas year-round, but two poor harvests in a row, a frequent occurrence in highland Mexico, could reduce rations considerably.

In addition to periodic droughts, Aztec subjects coped with frosts, plagues of locusts, volcanic eruptions, earthquakes, and floods. This ecological uncertainty restricted warfare to the agricultural off-season. Without large domesticated animals and metal tools, agricultural tasks throughout Mesoamerica demanded virtual armies of field laborers equipped only with fire-hardened digging sticks and obsidian or flint knives.

Animal protein was scarce, especially in urban areas where hunting opportunities were limited and few domestic animals were kept. Still, the people of Tenochtitlán raised turkeys and plump, hairless dogs (the prized Xolo breed of today). Even humble beans, when combined with maize, could constitute a complete protein, and indigenous grains such as amaranth were also nutritious. Famines still occurred, however, and one in the early 1450s led to mass migration out of the Valley of Mexico. Thousands sold themselves into slavery to avoid starvation.

The Limits of Holy Terror

As the Aztec Empire expanded, sacrificial debts became a consuming passion among pious elites. Calendars filled with sacrificial rites, and warfare was ever more geared toward satisfying a ballooning cosmic debt.

By 1500 the Aztec state had reached its height, and some scholars have argued that it had even begun to decline. Incessant captive wars and tribute demands had reached their limits, and old enemies such as the Tlaxcalans and Tarascans remained belligerent. New conquests were blocked by difficult terrain, declining tributes, and resistant locals. With available technologies, there was no place else for the empire to grow, and even with complex water works in place, agricultural productivity barely kept the people fed. Under the harsh leadership of Moctezuma II ("Angry Lord the Younger") (r. 1502–1520), the future did not look promising. Although there is no evidence to suggest the Aztec Empire was on the verge of collapse when several hundred bearded, sunburned strangers of Spanish descent appeared on Mexico's Gulf Coast shores in 1519, points of vulnerability abounded.

Tributes of Sweat: The Inca Empire 1430–1532

⬎ **FOCUS** What core features characterized Inca life and rule?

At about the same time as the Aztec expansion in southernmost North America, another great empire emerged in the central Andean highlands of South America. There is no evidence of significant contact between them. Like the Aztecs, the Incas burst out of their highland homeland in the 1430s to conquer numerous neighbors and huge swaths of territory. They demanded tribute in goods and labor, along with allegiance to an imperial religion. Also like the Aztecs, the Incas based their expansion on a centuries-long inheritance of technological, religious, and political traditions.

By 1500 the Incas ruled one of the world's most extensive, ecologically varied, and rugged land empires, stretching nearly three thousand miles along the towering Andean mountain range from the equator to central Chile. Like most empires ancient and modern, extensive holdings proved to be a mixed blessing (see Map 15.3).

From Potato Farmers to Empire Builders

Thanks to archaeological evidence and early post-conquest narratives, much is known about the rise and fall of the Inca state. Still, like the early Ottoman, Russian, and other contemporary empires, numerous mysteries remain. As in those cases, legends of the formative period in particular require skeptical analysis. The Inca case is somewhat complicated by the fact that their complex knotted-string records, or *khipus* (also *quipus*, KEY-poohs), have yet to be deciphered.

Scholars agree that the Incas emerged from among a dozen or so regional ethnic groups living in the highlands of south-central Peru between 1000 and 1400 C.E. Living as potato and maize farmers, the Incas started out as one of many similar groups of Andean mountaineers. Throughout the Andes, clans settled in fertile valleys and alongside lakes between eighty-five hundred and thirteen thousand feet above sea level. Though often graced with fertile soils, these highland areas suffered periodic frosts and droughts, despite their location within the tropics. Even more than in the Aztec realm, altitude (elevation above sea level), not latitude (distance north or south of the equator), was key.

Anthropologist John Murra described Inca land use as a "**vertical archipelago**," a stair-step system of interdependent environmental "islands." Kin groups occupying the altitudes best suited to potato and maize farming established settlements in cold uplands, where thousands of llamas and alpacas—the Americas' only large domestic animals—were herded, and also in hot lowlands, where cotton, peanuts, chilis, and the stimulant coca were grown. People, animals, and goods traveled between highland and lowland ecological zones using trails and hanging bridges.

Other Andeans inhabited Peru's desert coast, where urban civilization was nearly as old as that of ancient Egypt. Andean coast dwellers practiced large-scale irrigated agriculture, deep-sea fishing, and long-distance trade. Trading families outfitted large balsawood rafts with cotton sails and plied the Pacific as far as Guatemala. Inland trade links stretched over the Andes and into the Amazon rain forest. Along the way, coast-dwelling traders exchanged salt, seashells, beads, and copper hatchets for exotic feathers, gold dust, and pelts. The Incas would exploit all

vertical archipelago Andean system of planting crops and grazing animals at different altitudes.

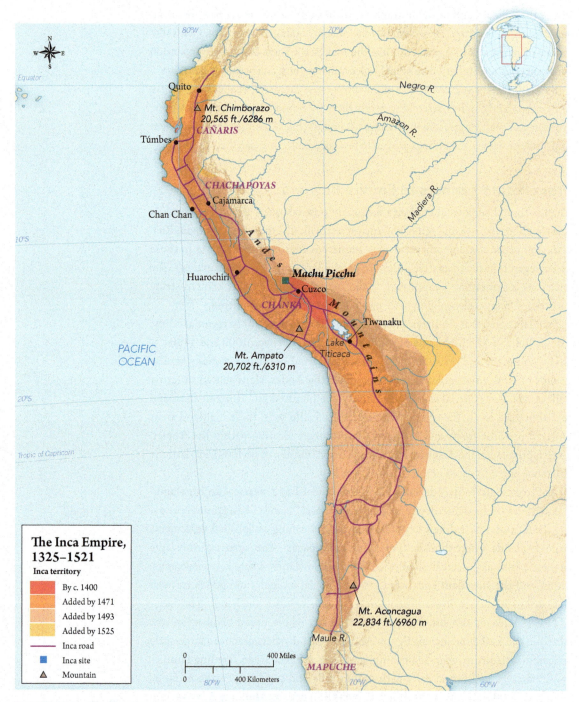

≡ MAP 15.3 The Inca Empire, 1325–1521 Starting from their base in Cuzco, high in the Andes, the Incas built the most extensive empire in the Americas, and the second most populous after that of the Aztecs. They linked it by a road system that rivaled that of the ancient Romans. Some groups, such as the Cañaris and Chachapoyas, resisted Inca domination for many years, and the Mapuche of Chile were never conquered.

of these regions and their interconnections, replacing old exchange systems and religious shrines with their own. Around 1200 C.E. they established a base near Cuzco (KOOS-coh), in Peru's highlands not far from the headwaters of the Amazon, and soon after 1400 they began their drive toward empire (see again Map 15.3).

The Great Apparatus: Inca Expansion and Religion

Cuzco, located in a narrow valley at a breathtaking altitude of over two miles above sea level, served as the Incas' political base and religious center. Like the Aztecs, the Incas saw their capital as the hub of the universe, calling it the "navel of the world." Paths and roads radiated out in all directions and tied hundreds of subsidiary shrines to the cosmically ordained center. Compared with the Aztec capital of Tenochtitlán, however, Cuzco was modest in size, perhaps home to at most fifty thousand. Still, Cuzco had the advantage of being stoutly built of hewn stone. Whereas most of Tenochtitlán's temples and palaces were dismantled following the Spanish Conquest, Cuzco's colossal stone foundations still stand.

The Incas in the early fifteenth century began conquering their neighbors. In time each emperor, or Sapa ("Unique") Inca, would seek to add more territory to the realm, called Tawantinsuyu (tuh-wahn-tin-SUE-you), or, "The Four Quarters Together." The Sapa Inca was thought to be descended from the sun and was thus regarded as the sustainer of all humanity. Devotion to local deities persisted, however, absorbed over time by the Incas in a way reminiscent of the Roman Empire's assimilation of regional deities and shrines. This religious inclusiveness helped the empire spread quickly even as the royal cult of the sun was inserted into everyday life. In a similar way, Quechua (KETCH-wah) became the Incas' official language even as local languages persisted.

Inca expansion was so rapid that the empire reached its greatest extent within a mere four generations of its founding. In semi-legendary times, Wiracocha Inca (r. 1400–1438) was said to have led an army to defeat an invading ethnic group called the Chankas near Cuzco. According to royal sagas, this victory spurred Wiracocha to defend his people further by annexing the fertile territories of other neighbors. Defense turned to offense, and thus was primed the engine of Inca expansion.

Wiracocha's successor, Pachacuti Inca Yupanki (r. 1438–1471), was more ambitious, so much so that he is widely regarded as the true founder of the Inca Empire. Archaeological evidence

Cuzco, c. 1500	
▪ Upper Cuzco	**A** Main plaza
▪ Lower Cuzco	**B** Temple of the Sun
▪ Residential Area	**C** Assembly Hall
— Road	**D** Palace of the Virgins of the Sun

≡ **Cuzco, c. 1500**

backs this claim. Pachacuti (literally "Cataclysm") took over much of what is today Peru, including many coastal oases and the powerful Chimú kingdom. Along the way, Pachacuti perfected the core strategy of Inca warfare: amassing and mobilizing such overwhelming numbers of troops and backup forces that fighting was often unnecessary.

Thousands of peasants were conscripted to bear arms, build roads, and carry food. Others herded llamas, strung bridges, and cut building stone. With each new advance, masonry forts and temples were constructed in the imperial style, leaving an indelible Inca stamp on the landscape. Even opponents such as the desert-dwelling Chimú capitulated in the face of the Inca juggernaut. Just after the Spanish Conquest, Pachacuti was remembered by female descendants:

> As [Pachacuti] Inca Yupanki remained in his city and town of Cuzco, seeing that he was lord and that he had subjugated the towns and provinces, he was very pleased. He had subjugated more and obtained much more importance than any of his ancestors. He saw the great apparatus that he had so that whenever he wanted to he could subjugate and put under his control anything else he wanted.[3]

These remembrances underscore the Sapa Inca's tremendous power.

Pachacuti's successors extended conquests southward deep into what are today Chile and Argentina, and also eastward down the slope of the Andes and into the upper Amazon Basin. It is from this last region, the quarter the Incas called Antisuyu (auntie-SUE-you), that we derive the word *Andes*. On the northern frontier, the Incas fought bitterly with Ecuadorian ethnic groups to extend Inca rule to the border of present-day Colombia (see again Map 15.3). Here the imperial Inca conquest machine met its match: many native highlanders fought to the death.

According to most sources, Inca advances into new territory were couched in the rhetoric of diplomacy. Local headmen were told they had two options: (1) to retain power by accepting Inca sovereignty and all the tributary obligations that went with it, or (2) to defy the Inca and face annihilation. Most headmen went along, particularly once word of the Incas' battlefield prowess spread. Those who did not were either killed in battle or exiled, along with their subject populations, to remote corners of the empire.

The Incas dominated agricultural peoples and their lands, but they also spread their imperial solar cult. Whatever their motives, like the Aztecs they defined domination in simple terms: tribute payment. Conquered subjects showed submission by rendering portions of their surplus production—and also labor—to the emperor. Tribute payment was a grudgingly accepted humiliation throughout the Andes, one that many hoped to shake off at the first opportunity.

Inca religion is only starting to be understood. As the chapter-opening description of child sacrifice suggests, spirit and body were deemed inseparable despite permanent loss of consciousness. Likewise, features in the landscape, ranging from springs and peaks to boulders, were thought to emit spiritual energy (see Reading the Past: An Andean Creation Story). Even human-made landforms, such as irrigation canals, were described as "alive." These sacred **wakas** (or *huacas*) received offerings in exchange for good harvests, herd growth, and other bounties.

Andeans also venerated their ancestors' corpses. As long as something tangible remained of the deceased, they were not regarded as entirely dead. It helped that the central Andes' dry climates were ideal for mummification: preservation often required little more than removal of internal organs. It would have been fairly common in Inca times to encounter a neighbor's "freeze-dried" grandparents hanging from the rafters, still regarded as involved in household affairs. Andeans sometimes carried ancestor mummies to feasts and pilgrimages as well. Thus, Inca society included both past and present generations.

The Incas harnessed these and other core Andean beliefs, yet like the Aztecs they put a unique stamp on the region they came to dominate. Though warlike, the Incas rarely sacrificed captive warriors, a ritual archaeologists now know was practiced among ancient coastal Peruvians. Cannibalism was something the Incas associated with barbaric forest dwellers. Inca stone architecture, though borrowing from older forms, is still identifiable thanks to the use of trapezoidal (flared) doors, windows, and niches (see World in the Making, page 531). Even so, the Incas' imperial sun cult proved far less durable than local religious traditions once the empire fell. And despite the Incas' rhetoric of diplomacy, most Andeans appear to have associated their rule with tyranny. Like the Aztecs, they failed to inspire loyalty in their subjects, who saw Inca government as a set of institutions designed to exploit, rather than protect, the peoples of the empire.

Daily Life Under the Incas

Inca society, like Aztec society, was stratified, with few means of upward mobility. Along with class gradations tied to occupation, the Incas divided society according to sex, age, and ethnic origin. Everyday life thus varied tremendously among the Inca's millions of subjects, although the peasant majority probably had much in common with farming folk the world over. Seasonal work stints for the empire were a burden for men, whereas women labored to maintain households. Unlike that of the Aztec, the Inca legal system appears to have been harder on commoners than nobles. Exemplary elite behavior was expected, but not so rigidly enforced.

At the pinnacle of society was the Sapa Inca himself, the "son of the Sun." He was also believed to be the greatest warrior in the world, and everyone who came

waka A sacred place or thing in Andean culture.

READING THE PAST

An Andean Creation Story

The small Peruvian town of Huarochirí (wahr-oh-chee-REE), located in the high Andes east of Lima, was the target of a Spanish idolatry investigation at the end of the sixteenth century. The Spanish conquest of the Incas had little effect on the everyday life of Andean peasants, and many clung tenaciously to their religious beliefs. In Huarochirí, Spanish attempts to replace these beliefs with Western, Christian ones produced written testimonies from village elders in phonetically rendered Quechua, the most commonly spoken language in the Inca Empire. Like the Aztec codices, the resulting documents—aimed at eradicating the beliefs they describe—have unwittingly provided modern researchers with a rare window on a lost mental world. The passage here, translated directly from Quechua to English, relates an Andean myth that newly arrived or converted Christians considered a variation on the biblical story of Noah and the Great Flood. In the Christian story, God, angered by the wickedness of man, resolves to send a flood to destroy the earth. He spares only Noah, whom he instructs to build an ark in which Noah, his family, and a pair of every animal are to be saved from the Great Flood.

In ancient times, this world wanted to come to an end. A llama buck, aware that the ocean was about to overflow, was behaving like somebody who's deep in sadness. Even though its owner let it rest in a patch of excellent pasture, it cried and said, "In, in," and wouldn't eat. The llama's owner got really angry, and he threw a cob from some maize he had just eaten at the llama. "Eat, dog! This is some fine grass I'm letting you rest in!" he said. Then that llama began speaking like a human being. "You simpleton, whatever could you be thinking about? Soon, in five days, the ocean will overflow. It's a certainty. And the whole world will come to an end," it said. The man got good and scared. "What's going to happen to us? Where can we go to save ourselves?" he said. The llama replied, "Let's go to Villca Coto mountain. There we'll be

before him was obliged to bear a symbolic burden, such as a load of cloth or large water vessel. Only the Inca's female companions had intimate contact with him. Although the ideal royal couple according to Inca mythology was a sibling pair, in fact dozens of wives and concubines assured that there would be heirs. Unlike monarchs in Europe and parts of Africa, the Sapa Incas did not practice primogeniture, or the automatic inheritance of an estate or title by the eldest son. Neither did they leave succession to a group of elders, the method preferred by the Aztecs.

saved. Take along five days' food for yourself." So the man went out from there in a great hurry, and himself carried both the llama buck and its load. When they arrived at Villca Coto mountain, all sorts of animals had already filled it up: pumas, foxes, guanacos [wild relatives of the llama], condors, all kinds of animals in great numbers. And as soon as that man had arrived there, the ocean overflowed. They stayed there huddling tightly together. The waters covered all those mountains and it was only Villca Coto mountain, or rather its very peak, that was not covered by the water. Water soaked the

fox's tail. That's how it turned black. Five days later, the waters descended and began to dry up. The drying waters caused the ocean to retreat all the way down again and exterminate all the people. Afterward, that man began to multiply once more. That's the reason there are people until today.

[The scribe who recorded this tale, an Andean converted by Spanish missionaries, then adds this comment:] Regarding this story, we Christians believe it refers to the time of the Flood. But they [non-Christian Andeans] believe it was Villca Coto mountain that saved them.

Source: Excerpt from *The Huarochirí Manuscript: A Testament of Ancient and Colonial Andean Religion,* trans. and ed. Frank Salomon and George L. Urioste (Austin: University of Texas Press, 1991), 51–52.

Examining the Evidence

1. What do the similarities and differences between the Andean and Judeo-Christian flood stories suggest?

2. What do the differences between them reveal?

For Further Reading:

Spalding, Karen. *Huarochirí: An Andean Society under Inca and Spanish Rule.* Stanford, CA: Stanford University Press, 1988.

Urton, Gary. *Inca Myths.* Austin: University of Texas Press, 1999.

Violent succession struggles predictably ensued. Though barred from the role of Inca themselves, ambitious noblewomen exercised considerable behind-the-scenes power over imperial succession.

Just beneath the Inca imperial line were Cuzco-based nobles, identifiable by their huge ear spools and finely woven tunics. Rather like their Aztec counterparts, they spoke a dialect of the royal language forbidden among commoners. Among this elite class were decorated generals and hereditary lords of prominent clans.

Often drawn from these and slightly lower noble ranks was a class of priests and astrologers who maintained temples and shrines.

Many noblewomen and girls deemed physically perfect, like the sacrificial victim described at the start of this chapter, were also selected for religious seclusion. Seclusion was not always permanent, because some of these women were groomed for marriage to the Inca. Still more noblewomen, mostly wives and widows, maintained the urban households and country estates of the Incas, dead and alive.

Next came bureaucrats, military leaders, and provincial headmen. Bureaucrats kept track of tribute obligations, communal work schedules, and land appropriations. Following conquest, up to two-thirds of productive land was set aside in the name of the ruling Inca and the cult of the sun. Bureaucrats negotiated with headmen as to which lands these would be, and how and when subjects would be put to work on behalf of their new rulers. If negotiations failed, the military was called in for a show of force. Lower-ranking Inca military men, like bureaucrats, faced service at the hostile fringes of empire. They had little beyond the weak hold of local power to look forward to. As a result, in sharp distinction with the Aztecs, death in battle was not regarded as a glorious sacrifice among the Incas. Furthermore, many officers were themselves provincial in origin and thus had little hope of promotion to friendlier districts closer to the imperial core.

The Inca and his retinue employed numerous artisans, mostly conquered provincials. Such specialists included architects, record keepers, civil engineers, metalworkers, weavers, potters, and many others. Unlike the Aztecs, the Incas did not tolerate free traders, instead choosing to manage the distribution of goods and services as a means of exercising state power. Partly as a result, market-oriented slavery appears not to have existed under the Incas, although some conquered young men and women spared from death or exile worked as personal servants. Most Inca subjects were peasants belonging to kin groups whose lives revolved around agriculture and rotational labor obligations. For them, the rigors

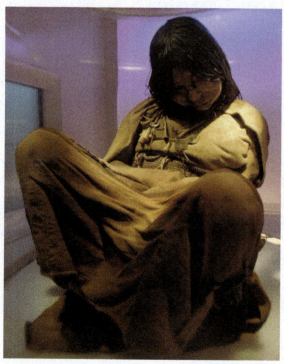

≡ **Inca Mummy** The Incas did not sacrifice humans as often as the Aztecs did, but headmen in newly conquered regions were sometimes required to give up young sons or daughters for live burial on high mountains. Such sacrifices were known as capacocha, or "debt payment." The victims, including this adolescent girl found in a shallow tomb atop twenty-thousand-foot Mount Lullaillaco in the Argentine Andes, died of exposure after the long climb, but the Incas believed them to remain semiconscious and in communication with the spirit world.

of everyday life far outweighed the extra demands of Inca rule. Only in the case of recently conquered groups, or those caught in the midst of a regional rebellion or succession conflict, was this not true. Even then, subsistence remained the average Andean's most pressing concern.

Artisans produced remarkable textiles, metalwork, and pottery, but the empire's most visible achievements were in the fields of architecture and civil engineering. The Incas' extensive road systems, irrigation works, and monumental temples were unmatched by any ancient American society. No one else moved or carved such large stones or ruled such a vast area. Linking coast, highlands, and jungle, the Incas' roads covered nearly ten thousand miles. Many road sections were paved with stones, and some were hewn into near-vertical mountainsides by hand. Grass weavers spanned gorges with hanging bridges strong enough to sustain trains of pack llamas. These engineering marvels enabled the Incas to communicate and move troops and supplies with amazing speed, yet they also served the important religious function of facilitating pilgrimages and royal processions. Massive irrigation works and stone foundations, though highly practical, were similarly charged with religious power. Thus, the Inca infrastructure not only played an important practical role in imperial government, but it also expressed the Incas' belief in the connection between their own rule and the cosmic order.

The Incas appropriated Andean metalworking techniques, which were much older and more developed than those of Mesoamerica. Metal forging was as much a religious as an artistic exercise in the Andes, and metals themselves were regarded as semi-divine. Gold was associated with the sun in Inca cosmology, and by extension with the Sapa Inca and his solar cult. Silver was associated with the moon and with several mother goddesses and Inca queens and princesses. Copper and bronze, considered less divine than gold and silver, were put to more practical uses.

Another ancient Andean tradition inherited by the Incas was weaving. Inca cotton and alpaca-fiber textiles were of extraordinary quality, and cloth became the coin of the realm. Following Andean norms of reciprocity, cooperative regional lords were rewarded by the Incas with gifts of blankets and ponchos, which they could then redistribute among their subjects. Unlike some earlier

≡ **Inca Road** Stretching nearly ten thousand miles across mountains, plains, deserts, and rain forests, the Inca Royal Road held one of the world's most rugged and extensive empires together. Using braided fiber bridges to span chasms and establishing inns and forts along the road, the Incas handily moved troops, supplies, and information across vast distances. The Royal Road had the unintentional consequence of aiding penetration of the empire by Spanish conquistadors on horseback.

coastal traditions, Inca design favored geometric forms over representations of humans, animals, or deities. Fiber from the vicuña, a wild relative of the llama, was reserved for the Sapa Inca. Some women became master weavers, but throughout most of the Inca Empire men wove fibers that had been spun into thread by women, a gendered task division later reinforced by the Spanish.

With such an emphasis on textiles, it may come as no surprise that the Incas maintained a record-keeping system using knotted strings. Something like an accounting device in its most basic form, the **khipu** enabled bureaucrats to keep track of tributes, troop movements, ritual cycles, and other important matters. Like bronze metallurgy, the khipu predates the Inca Empire, but it served the empire well. Although its capabilities as a means of data management are a subject of intense debate, the khipu was sufficiently effective to remain in use for several centuries under Spanish rule, long after alphabetic writing was introduced.

Throughout the Andes, women occupied a distinct sphere from that of men, but not a subordinate one. For example, sources suggest that although the majority of Andeans living under Inca rule were patrilineal, or male-centered, in their succession preferences, power frequently landed in the hands of sisters and daughters of headmen. Inca descendants described a world in which both sexes participated equally in complementary agricultural tasks, and also in contests against neighboring clans. Women exempted from rotational labor duties handled local exchanges of food and craft goods. Women's fertility was respected, but never equated with warfare, as in Aztec society. Interestingly, Andean childbirth was almost regarded as a nonevent, and rarely involved midwives.

As in most early modern societies, parents treated Inca children much like miniature adults, and dressed them accordingly. Parents educated children by defining roles and duties early, using routine chores deemed appropriate to one's sex and status as the primary means of education. Girls and boys also participated in most work projects. The expectation of all children was not to change society but to reproduce and maintain it through balanced relations with deities and neighbors. Contact with the Inca himself was an extremely remote possibility for most children living in the empire. A rare exception was capacocha sacrificial victims, such as the headman's daughter described at the opening of this chapter.

khipu Knotted cotton or alpaca-fiber strings used by the Incas and other Andeans to record tributes, troop numbers, and possibly narratives of events.

Just as maize was native to highland Mesoamerica and served as the base for urban development, the potato was the indigenous staple of the central Andes. A hearty, high-yield tuber with many varieties, the potato could be roasted, stewed, or naturally freeze-dried and stored for long periods. Maize could also be stored dry or toasted, but among Andeans it was generally reserved for beer making. Along with maize, many lowland dwellers subsisted on manioc, peanuts, beans, and chili peppers.

Andean pastoralism played a critical role in Inca expansion. Domesticated animals included the llama, alpaca, and guinea pig. Llamas, in addition to carrying loads, were sometimes eaten, and alpacas provided warm cloth fiber. Slaughter of domestic animals, including fertilizer-producing guinea pigs, usually accompanied ritual occasions such as weddings or harvest festivals. The average Andean diet was overwhelmingly vegetarian. Nevertheless, a common component of Inca trail food was *charqui* (hence "jerky"), bits of dried and salted llama flesh. Llamas and alpacas were never milked. Like many other peoples, Andeans restricted consumption of and even contact with certain animal fluids and body parts.

The high Inca heartland, though fertile, was prone to droughts and frosts. The warmer coast was susceptible to periodic floods. Only by developing food storage techniques and exploiting numerous microenvironments were the Incas and their subjects able to weather such events. Added to these cyclical catastrophes were volcanic eruptions, earthquakes, mudslides, tsunamis, and plagues of locusts. Still, the overall record suggests that subsistence under the Incas, thanks to the "vertical archipelago," was much less precarious than under the Aztecs.

The Great Apparatus Breaks Down

Inca expansion derived from a blend of religious and secular impulses. As in Aztec Mexico, religious demands seem to have grown more and more urgent, possibly even destabilizing the empire by the time of the last Sapa Inca. As emperors died, their mummy cults required extravagant maintenance. The most eminent of mummies in effect tied up huge tracts of land. Logically, if vainly, successive emperors strove to make sure their mummy cults would be provided for in equal or better fashion. Each hoped his legacy might outshine that of his predecessor. Given the extraordinary precedent set by Pachacuti Inca, some scholars have argued that excessive mummy veneration effectively undermined the Inca Empire.

Too, as with the Aztecs, rapid growth by violent means sowed seeds of discontent. On the eve of the Spanish arrival both empires appear to have been contracting rather than expanding, with rebellion the order of the day. The Incas had never done well against lowland forest peoples, and some such enemies kept up chronic raiding activities. Highlanders such as the Cañaris of Ecuador and the Chachapoyas of northern Peru had cost the Incas dearly in their conquest, only just completed in 1525 after more than thirty years. Like the Tlaxcalans of Mexico, both of these recently conquered groups would ally with Spanish invaders in hopes of establishing their independence once and for all.

The Inca state was demanding of its subjects, and enemy frontiers abounded. Yet it seems the Incas' worst enemies were ultimately themselves. A nonviolent means of royal succession had never been established. This was good for the empire in that capable rather than simply hereditary rulers could emerge, but bad in that the position of Sapa Inca was always up for grabs. In calmer times, defense against outside challengers would not have been difficult, but the Spanish had the good fortune to arrive in the midst of a civil war between two rivals to the throne, Huascar and Atawallpa (also "Atahualpa"). By 1532 Atawallpa defeated his half-brother, only to fall prey to a small number of foreign interlopers.

COUNTERPOINT: The Peoples of North America's Eastern Woodlands 1450–1530

FOCUS How did the Eastern Woodlanders' experience differ from life under the Aztecs and Incas?

By 1450 several million people inhabited North America's eastern woodlands. Forests provided raw materials for building as well as habitat for game. Trees also yielded nuts and fruits and served as fertilizer for crops when burned. The great mound-building cultures of the Mississippi Basin had faded by this time, their inhabitants having returned to less urban, more egalitarian ways of life. Villages headed by elected chiefs were typical (see Map 15.4).

Most of what we know about native eastern North Americans at this time derives from contact-era (1492–1750) European documents, plus archaeological studies. Although less is known about them than about the Aztecs or Incas, it appears that Eastern Woodlands peoples faced significant changes in politics and everyday life just prior to European arrival. Climate change may have been one important factor spurring conflict and consolidation.

Eastern Woodlands peoples were like the Aztecs in at least one sense. Most were maize farmers who engaged in seasonal warfare followed by captive sacrifice. According to archaeological evidence, both maize planting and warrior sacrifice spread into the region from Mesoamerica around the time of the Toltecs (800–1100 C.E.). The century prior to European contact appears to have been marked by rapid population growth, increased warfare, and political reorganization. Multi-settlement alliances or leagues, such as the Powhatan Confederacy of tidewater Virginia, were relatively new. Some confederacies were formed for temporary defensive purposes, and others were primarily religious. Some villages housed over two thousand inhabitants, and confederacies counted up to twenty thousand or more. As in the Andes, clan divisions were common, but population densities were lower.

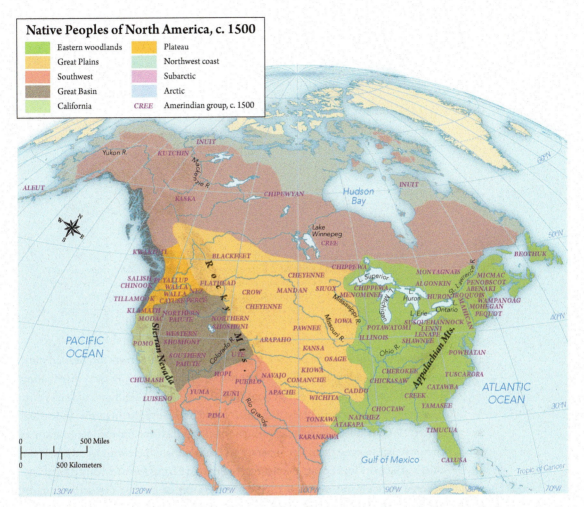

Native Peoples of North America, c. 1500

Eastern woodlands	Plateau
Great Plains	Northwest coast
Southwest	Subarctic
Great Basin	Arctic
California	CREE Amerindian group, c. 1500

≡ **MAP 15.4   Native Peoples of North America, c. 1500**   To the north of Mesoamerica, hundreds of native American groups, most of them organized as chiefdoms, flourished in a wide array of climate zones, from the coldest Arctic wilderness to the hottest subtropical deserts. Populations were highest where maize and other crops could be grown, as in the Mississippi Valley, Great Lakes, and eastern woodlands regions.

Smaller gathering-hunting groups occupied more challenging landscapes, yet thanks to their varied diet, they seem to have suffered fewer vitamin and mineral deficiencies than settled maize eaters. Even maize farmers, however, were generally taller than their European (or Mesoamerican) contemporaries. Throughout the eastern forests, including the Great Lakes region, metallurgy was limited to hammering native copper. Copper was regarded as a sacred substance associated with chiefly power. Beads made from polished seashells, or **wampum**, were similarly prized.

wampum Beads made of seashells; used in eastern North America as currency and to secure alliances.

≡ **Huron Wampum Belt** For many Eastern Woodlands peoples such as the Huron, seashells like the New England quahog (a variety of clam) were sacred trade goods. Shell beads, or *wampum*, were woven into ceremonial belts whose geometrical designs and color schemes represented clans and sometimes treaties between larger groups. The linked-hands motif in this belt suggests a treaty or covenant.

Chiefs, usually warriors or shamans elected by popular agreement, headed most Eastern Woodlands groups. They retained power, however, only by redistributing goods such as surplus food or war booty; generosity was the hallmark of leadership. Few chiefdoms were hereditary, and chiefs could be deposed at any time. Individual Eastern Woodlanders, particularly young men, yearned for independence even as circumstances forced them to cooperate and subordinate their wills to others. If the chief's generosity was a centripetal force, egalitarian desires formed a centrifugal one.

Some agricultural peoples, such as the Huron of central Ontario, Canada, had male chiefs or headmen but were organized matrilineally. This meant that society was built around clans of mothers, daughters, and sisters. Matrilineal clans occupied **longhouses**, or wooden multifamily residential buildings. Elder women consulted with chiefs, and all women played a part in urging men to war. Agriculture was a strictly female preserve among the Huron, closely linked to human fertility. Huron men handled risky activities such as hunting, warfare, and tree felling. Their sphere of influence lay largely outside the village. Men's exploits abroad, including adolescent vision quests, conferred status. Among all Eastern Woodlanders, public speech making was as prized among adult men as martial expertise. Only the most esteemed men participated in councils.

Children's lives were difficult among Eastern Woodlanders (keeping in mind that this was true of early modern childhood generally). Due to a multitude of

longhouse A wooden communal dwelling typical of Eastern Woodlands peoples.

vermin and pathogens, inadequate nutrition, smoky residences, and hazards of war and accident, relatively few children survived to adulthood. Partly for these reasons, Eastern Woodlands cultures discouraged severe discipline for children, instead allowing them much freedom.

Playtime ended early, however, as children were schooled before puberty in their respective arts and responsibilities. Girls learned to farm and cook, boys to hunt and make war. Soon after puberty young people began to "try out" mates until a suitable match was found. Though this and the seemingly casual practice of divorce among Eastern Woodlanders were considered scandalous by early modern European standards, stable monogamy prevailed.

Warfare was endemic throughout the eastern woodlands in the summer season, when subsistence itself was less of a battle. In form, these wars resembled blood feuds, or vengeance cycles. According to European witnesses, wars among the Iroquois, Mahicans, and others were spawned by some long-forgotten crime, such as the rape or murder of a clan member. As such, they were not struggles over land, but rather male contests intended to prove courage and preserve honor.

Warfare closely resembled hunting in that successful warriors were expected to ambush and capture their equivalents from the opposite camp. These unlucky individuals were then brought to the captor's longhouse for an excruciating ordeal, nearly always followed by slaughter and ritual consumption. (Female and child captives, by contrast, were "adopted" as replacements for lost kin.) The religious significance of captive sacrifice among Eastern Woodlanders has been less clearly explained than that of the Aztecs, but it seems to have been tied to subsistence anxieties.

Eastern Woodlands religions varied, but there were commonalities. Beyond the realm of everyday life was a complex spirit world. Matrilineal societies such as the Huron traced their origins to a female spirit whose grandsons invented the essential techniques of civilized life. The sky itself was often more important than the sun or moon in Eastern Woodlands mythologies, and climatic events were associated with bird spirits, such as the thunderbird.

Like Andean peoples, many Eastern Woodlanders believed that material things such as boulders, islands, and personal charms contained life essences, or "souls." Traders and warriors, in particular, took time to please spirits and "recharge" protective amulets with offerings and incantations. Periodic feasts were also imbued with spiritual energy. On the whole, religious life was an everyday affair, not an institutionalized one. Instead of priesthoods, liturgies, and temples, most Eastern Woodlands peoples relied on elders and shamans to maintain traditions and remind juniors of core beliefs.

Most Eastern Woodlanders did not regard death as a positive transition. They believed that souls lived on indefinitely and migrated to a new home, usually a recognizable ethnic village located in the western distance. Even dogs' souls migrated, as did those of wild animals. The problem with this later existence was that it was unsatisfying. Dead souls were said to haunt the living, complaining of hunger and other insatiable desires. The Huron sought to keep their dead ancestors together and send them off well through elaborate burial rituals, but it was understood that ultimately little could be done for them.

Conclusion

By the time Europeans entered the Caribbean Sea in 1492, the Americas were home to over 60 million people. Throughout the Western Hemisphere, native American life was vibrant and complex, divided by language, customs, and sometimes geographical barriers, but also linked by religion, trade, and war. Cities, pilgrimage sites, mountain passes, and waterways served as crossroads for the exchange of goods and ideas, often between widely dispersed peoples. Another uniting factor was the underlying religious tradition of shamanism.

The many resources available in the highland tropics of Mesoamerica and the Andes Mountains promoted settled agriculture, urbanization, and eventually empire building. Drawing on the traditions of ancestors, imperial peoples such as the Aztecs and Incas built formidable capitals, road systems, and irrigation works. As the Inca capacocha and Aztec warrior sacrifices suggest, these empires were driven to expand at least as much by religious beliefs as by material desires. In part as a result of religious demands, both empires were in crisis by the first decades of the sixteenth century, when Europeans possessing steel-edged weapons, firearms, and other technological advantages first encountered them. Other native peoples, such as North America's Eastern Woodlanders, built chiefdoms and confederacies rather than empires, and to some degree these looser structures would prove more resilient in the face of European invasion.

✳ review

The major global development in this chapter: The diversity of societies and states in the Americas prior to European invasion.

Important Events	
c. 900–1600	Late Woodland period of dispersed farming and hunting
c. 1200	Incas move into Cuzco region
c. 1270	Aztecs settle in Valley of Mexico
c. 1320	Aztecs ally with Colhua
c. 1325	Tenochtitlán founded at Lake Texcoco's edge
c. 1437	Incas defeat Chankas
c. 1440–1471	Sapa Inca Pachacuti expands empire into Ecuador and Bolivia
1450–1451	Great famine in Valley of Mexico
1471–1493	Incas conquer northern Chile and Argentina
1487–1502	Aztecs dedicate Coatepec (Templo Mayor) and expand sacrificial wars
1493–1525	Incas conquer northern Peru and highland Ecuador
1502–1519	Reign of Moctezuma II, conquered by Spanish
1525–1532	Inca succession war, followed by arrival of the Spanish
c. 1570	Formation of Huron Confederacy north of Lake Ontario and of Iroquois League south of Lake Ontario

KEY TERMS

autosacrifice (p. 543)
chinampa (p. 541)
khipu (p. 558)

longhouse (p. 562)
shamanism (p. 536)
tribute (p. 544)

vertical archipelago (p. 549)
waka (p. 553)
wampum (p. 561)

CHAPTER OVERVIEW QUESTIONS

1. In what ways was cultural diversity in the Americas related to environmental diversity?
2. Why was it in Mesoamerica and the Andes that large empires emerged in around 1450?

3. What key ideas or practices extended beyond the limits of the great empires?

MAKING CONNECTIONS

1. Compare the Aztec and Inca Empires with the Ming (see Chapter 14). What features did they share? What features set them apart?
2. How did Aztec and Inca sacrificial rituals differ, and why?

3. What were the main causes of warfare among native American peoples prior to the arrival of Europeans?

For further research into the topics covered in this chapter, see the Bibliography at the end of the book. For additional primary sources from this period, see *Sources for World in the Making*.

16

The Rise of an Atlantic World 1450–1600

☰ **World in the Making** Painted on calfskins, portolan ("port finder") charts were used by mariners in the Mediterranean and North Atlantic beginning in the late fourteenth century. After Columbus's momentous transatlantic voyage in 1492, portolan charts began to depict new European discoveries in the Americas with great accuracy. This 1500 map by Juan de la Cosa, who sailed with Columbus, is the earliest such chart.

✴ backstory

By the mid-1400s, some 60 million people inhabited the Americas, about half of them subjects of the Aztec and Inca Empires (see Chapter 15). These empires relied on far-flung tribute networks and drew from diverse cultural traditions even as they spread their own religious practices and imperial languages. Outside the Aztec and Inca realms, smaller states and chiefdoms occupied much of the hemisphere. Conflict between groups, whether in Peru, Brazil, Mexico, or eastern North America, was frequent.

The inhabitants of western Eurasia and North Africa were slowly recovering from the Black Death of 1347–1350 (see Chapter 14). Weakened nobilities and rebounding populations stimulated trade, political consolidation, and the adoption of new technologies for war and transport. The long-distance trade in luxury goods also recovered, but by the early 1400s the rise of the Ottoman Empire in the eastern Mediterranean intensified competition and limited western European access to overland routes such as the Silk Road.

Malintzin (mah-LEEN-tseen) was only a girl when she was traded away around 1510 to serve a noble family in what is today the state of Tabasco, Mexico. She herself was a noble, a native speaker of the Aztec language, Nahuatl (NAH-watt). Malintzin's new masters were Chontal Maya speakers, and soon she learned this language.

Throughout Malintzin's servitude in Tabasco, stories circulated there and in the neighboring Yucatan peninsula of bearded strangers. One day in the year 1519, vessels filled with such men arrived in Tabasco. The Tabascans attacked a party that came ashore, but they were defeated. In exchange for peace, they offered the strangers gold and feather work, and also several servant girls, among them Malintzin. When asked through an interpreter where the gold had come from, the Tabascans said "Mexico."

The strangers' interpreter was a Spanish castaway, Jerónimo de Aguilar, who had lived several years in the Yucatan, recently ransomed by his countrymen. Aguilar soon discovered that Malintzin knew the language of Aztec Mexico. The strangers' leader, Hernando Cortés, took a special interest in her for this reason, but he also considered her the most beautiful and intelligent of the captives.

Twice given away now, Malintzin joined the foreigners in their floating homes. Heading west, they reached an island where Cortés ordered a party ashore to make contact with villagers and, through them, to speak with traveling Aztec representatives. Only Nahuatl was spoken.

Suddenly the bilingual Malintzin was thrust into a role of global significance. She passed along in Nahuatl the words Aguilar gave her in Chontal Mayan. Then she did the reverse when the Aztec ambassadors replied. Aguilar made sense of the Mayan replies for Cortés, who was already planning a march on the Aztec capital. From here until the end of the conquest campaigns in 1521, Malintzin served as Cortés's key to Aztec Mexico.

In modern Mexican mythology Malintzin, or Malinche (mah-LEEN-cheh), is regarded as a traitor, a collaborator, even a harlot. But these characterizations are anachronistic and unfair. Malintzin was not seen as a traitor in her own day, even by the Aztecs. In their paintings of the conquest, early Nahuatl-speaking artists often placed Malintzin at the center, poised and confident.

But why had Europeans like Cortés suddenly arrived in Malintzin's world? In part it was because wealth-seeking Iberians (inhabitants of the peninsula occupied by Spain and Portugal) had long begun charting the Atlantic. Over time they developed the technologies needed to navigate open seas, exploring first the west coast of Africa and then crossing the ocean itself. Flush with capital, Italian bankers helped fund these enterprises.

The resulting Iberian encounter with the Americas was an accident of monumental significance. In quest of legendary Asian riches, Christopher Columbus and his successors landed instead in the previously isolated regions they called the New World. It was new to them, of course, but not so to native Americans like Malintzin. Cultural misunderstandings, political divisions among indigenous peoples, and European firearms aided conquest and settlement, but germs made the biggest difference.

These germs were part of what historian Alfred Crosby dubbed "the Columbian Exchange," the first major biological relinking of the earth since the continents had drifted apart in prehistoric times. Although Europeans brought deadly diseases to the Americas, they also brought animals for transport, plowing, and consumption. Another effect of this global exchange was rapid population growth in parts of the world where American crops such as potatoes and maize took root. European expansion made the Atlantic a global crossroads, the center of a new pattern of exchange affecting the entire world.

Finally, we should not make the mistake of assuming that Europeans met no significant resistance in the Americas. As we shall see in the Counterpoint that concludes this chapter, one group of native Americans who successfully fought off European conquest, in part by adopting the horse and turning it against their oppressors, were the Mapuche of Chile.

OVERVIEW QUESTIONS

The major global development in this chapter: European expansion across the Atlantic and its profound consequences for societies and cultures worldwide.

As you read, consider:

1. What were the main biological and environmental consequences of European expansion to the Atlantic after 1492?

2. What roles did misunderstanding and chance play in the conquests of the Aztecs and Incas?

3. How did Eurasian demand for silver and sugar help bring about the creation of a linked Atlantic world?

Guns, Sails, and Compasses: Europeans Venture Abroad

↘ FOCUS Why and how did Europeans begin to cross unknown seas in the fifteenth century?

Nordic and southern European mariners had long been venturing out to sea, testing winds and currents as they founded colonies and connected markets. Some shared information, but as in the Mediterranean, colonizing distant lands was a competitive process. In the fifteenth century tiny Portugal forged the world's first truly global maritime empire. Neighboring Spain followed, spurred on by Christopher Columbus and a crusading spirit.

Motives for Exploration

Early modern Europeans sought to accumulate wealth, gain power against their rivals, and spread Christianity. Commerce was a core motive for expansion, as European merchants found themselves starved for gold and silver, which they needed to purchase Asian spices, silks, gems, and other luxuries. In part because of Europe's relative poverty, ambitious monarchs and princes adopted violent means to extend their dominions overseas and to increase their tax and tribute incomes. Finally, Europe's many Christian missionaries hoped to spread their religion throughout the globe. These motives would shape encounters between Europeans and native Americans.

"Gold is most excellent," wrote Christopher Columbus in a letter to the king and queen of Spain. "Gold constitutes treasure, and anyone who has it can do whatever he likes in the world."[1] Columbus was a native of the Italian city-state of Genoa, and Genoese merchants had long traded for gold in North Africa. African gold lubricated Mediterranean and European trade, but population growth, commercial expansion, and competition among Christian and Islamic states strained supplies. It was thus the well-placed Portuguese, who established a North African foothold in Morocco in 1415, who first sought direct access to African gold (see Map 16.2, pages 576–577).

Italian merchants made some of their greatest profits on spices. Since most spices came from the tropical margins of Asia, they rose considerably in value as they passed through the hands of mostly Islamic middlemen in the Indian Ocean and eastern Mediterranean. Indian pepper and Indonesian nutmeg were but a few of the many desired condiments that Portuguese and other European merchants hoped to purchase more cheaply by sailing directly to the source. This entailed either circumnavigating Africa or finding a western passage to the Pacific.

Slaves were also prized throughout the Mediterranean basin, and demand for them grew with the expansion of commercial agriculture and the rise of wealthy merchant families. Prices also rose as source regions near the Black Sea were cut off after 1453 by the Ottomans. As the word *slave* suggests, many captives came from the Slavic regions of eastern Europe. Others were prisoners of war. In part to meet growing Christian European demand, sub-Saharan Africans were transported to North African ports by caravan. As with gold, southern European merchants sought captives by sailing directly to West Africa.

Sugar, another commodity in high demand in Europe, required large investments in land, labor, and machinery. Produced mostly by enslaved workers on eastern Atlantic islands such as Portuguese Madeira by the mid-fifteenth century, cane sugar increasingly became common as both a sweetener and preservative. As sugar took the place of honey in Old World cuisines, few consumers pondered its growing connection to overseas enslavement. In time, European demand for sugar would lead to the establishment of the Atlantic slave trade and the forced migration of millions of Africans to the Americas.

Technologies of Exploration

As they set sail for new horizons, Europeans employed innovations in three technological spheres: gun making, shipbuilding, and navigation. First was firearms manufacture. Gunpowder, a Chinese invention, had been known since at least the ninth century C.E. Chinese artisans made rockets and bombs, but it was early modern Europeans who developed gunpowder and gun making to their greatest destructive effect.

Europeans had also borrowed Chinese papermaking and movable type technologies, and by 1500 they published treatises detailing the casting and operation of cannon. Soon, crude handguns and later muskets transformed field warfare, first in Europe, then worldwide. As gun and powder technologies improved, contingents of musketeers replaced archers, crossbowmen, and other foot soldiers.

The second key technological leap was in ship construction. Although small, swift-sailing vessels traversed the medieval Mediterranean, long-distance carriers were cumbersome and even dangerous when overloaded. The Roman-style galley was a fighting vessel propelled by captive oarsmen with occasional help from sails. Galleys functioned best where seas were calm, distances short, and prisoners plentiful. Something else was needed for the rougher waters and longer voyages common in the North Atlantic. Here, shipwrights combined more rigid North Sea

Portuguese Ship The Portuguese were the first Europeans to develop ocean-going ships for extended, return voyages. Initially they combined rigid hull designs from the Atlantic with maneuverable triangular sails of Arabic origin to build caravels, but these small vessels had limited cargo space and were vulnerable to attack. This evocative image from a contemporary manuscript shows Vasco da Gama's flagship, the *St. Gabriel*, on its way to India in 1497–1498 with every stitch of canvas out. For such long trips the Portuguese chose to sacrifice the maneuverability of the caravel in favor of maximizing sail surface and relying on trade winds. The resulting ships, which could carry up to 1200 tons of cargo and were built like floating fortresses, are known as "carracks." Portugal's national symbol until recent times, the red cross of the Order of Christ, identified such ships as Portuguese. (The Art Archive/Science Academy Lisbon/ Gianni Dagli Orti.)

hull designs and square sail rigs with some of the defensive features of the galley. They also borrowed the galley's triangular or lateen sails, which in turn had been adapted from the Arabian dhows (dowz) of the Indian Ocean.

The resulting hybrid vessels, including the caravel used by ocean-crossing mariners such as Columbus, proved greater than the sum of their parts. Although slow and unwieldy by modern standards, these late-fifteenth-century European ships were the world's most durable and maneuverable means of heavy transport to date. Later modified into galleons, frigates, and clippers, they would serve as the basic models for virtually all European carriers and warships until the advent of steam technology in the early nineteenth century.

European navigational innovations also propelled overseas expansion. Cosmographers believed the world to be spherical by Columbus's time, but finding one's way from port to port beyond sight of land was still a source of worry. One aid was the magnetic compass, like gunpowder and printing a fairly ancient Chinese invention developed in a novel way by Europeans. We know from travelers' accounts that sailors in the Indian Ocean also used compasses, but rarely in combination with portolan ("port finder") sea charts, which contained detailed compass bearings and harbor descriptions (see again the chapter-opening illustration). Charts and compasses together changed European navigators' perceptions of what had formerly been trackless seas.

Another borrowed instrument, apparently Arabic in origin, was the astrolabe. A calculator of latitude (one's location north or south of the equator), it proved even more critical for long-distance maritime travel than the compass. Precise knowledge of latitude was essential for early modern sailors in particular since longitude, a more complicated east–west calculation, was hard to determine until the mid-eighteenth century.

Thus armed with an impressive ensemble of borrowed and modified tools, weapons, and sailing vessels, Europeans were poised to venture out into unknown worlds. Add the recent development of the printing press, and they were also able to publicize their journeys in new if not altogether honest ways.

Portugal Takes the Lead

Why did tiny Portugal, one of Europe's least populated kingdoms, lead the way in overseas expansion? A look at key factors helps solve this puzzle. First, Portugal was an ancient maritime crossroads straddling two commercial spheres, the Mediterranean and northeast Atlantic (see Map 16.1). Coastal shipping had grown efficient while overland transport remained slow and costly. Well before 1400, merchants from as far away as Venice and Stockholm put in at Lisbon, the Portuguese capital, to break up their journeys. Commercial competition was fostered by Portugal's kings, and along with money and goods, important shipbuilding and sailing knowledge was exchanged. Capital, in the form of money, ships, and goods, accumulated in the hands of merchant clans, many of them foreign.

Other factors besides accumulating capital pushed the Portuguese abroad. By the 1430s, fishermen regularly ventured far out into the Atlantic in pursuit of better catches. Moreover, arable land in Portugal became scarce as populations grew, rendering overseas colonization more attractive. Also, religious and strategic concerns drove Portuguese nobles to capture the Islamic port city of Ceuta (SYOO-tah), on Morocco's Mediterranean coast, in 1415. Thus, the push of limited resources at home and the pull of opportunities abroad stimulated Portuguese expansion.

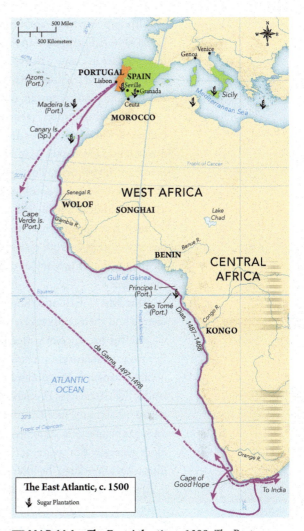

≡ **MAP 16.1   The East Atlantic, c. 1500** The Portuguese were the first Europeans to seek a sea route to Asia, and they did so by making their way south along the Atlantic coast of Africa. The diseases of tropical Africa limited Portuguese colonization to a few fortified enclaves, but they established lucrative settlement colonies in the eastern Atlantic island chains of the Azores, Madeiras, and Cape Verdes, along with the wet tropical island of São Tomé in the Gulf of Guinea. By 1500 the Portuguese had discovered that the fastest way to round the tip of Africa was to follow the prevailing winds and currents that swept to the west of the African coast before turning southeast.

With support from ambitious nobles such as Prince Henry "the Navigator" (1394–1460), Portuguese and foreign investors pooled capital and invested it in new technologies to create a network of settlement colonies and *feitorias* (fay-toe-REE-ahs), or fortified trading posts. Some invested in overseas plantations in the eastern Atlantic and Mediterranean, others in the gold and slave trades of West Africa.

The Portuguese soon learned to navigate the West African coast. By 1430 they had come upon the Azores and Madeiras, uninhabited island chains in the eastern Atlantic (see again Map 16.1). With incentives from the Crown and Italian merchant investment, Portuguese settlers colonized and farmed these islands. The Canaries, farther south, were different. These rugged volcanic islands posed distinct political and moral challenges from their inhabitants: chiefdoms descended from pre-Islamic Moroccan immigrants. "They go about naked without any clothes," wrote one Portuguese chronicler, "and have little shame at it; for they make a mockery of clothes, saying they are but sacks in which men put themselves."[2]

What was to be done? Should the inhabitants of the Canary Islands be conquered and their lands taken over by Europeans, and if so, by what right, and by whom? The presence of indigenous Canarians in fact spurred competition among European adventurers, including Spanish missionaries and French and Portuguese nobles. Spanish nobles under Isabella and Ferdinand ultimately won title to the islands. The Guanches (HWAN-chehs), as the Europeans called the largest group of native inhabitants, faced annihilation. Survivors were enslaved and made to work on sugar plantations. In many ways, the Canarian experience foretold Iberian, and more generally European, actions in the Americas. When they stood in the way of European ambitions, the interests of indigenous peoples counted for little.

Always in search of gold, which the eastern Atlantic islands lacked, and spurred on by Prince Henry, the Portuguese in 1444 reached the mouth of the Senegal River. Here the Portuguese traded warhorses for gold dust with representatives of the Muslim Wolof kingdoms. They also traded, and on a few occasions raided, for slaves. The victims of these 1440s raids and exchanges were the first Africans to be shipped en masse across Atlantic waters. Most ended up in the households and workshops of Lisbon.

The Portuguese reached the kingdom of Benin in the 1480s, when they also began settling the offshore islands of Príncipe and São Tomé. Some captives from Benin were forced to plant and refine sugar on São Tomé. The slave-staffed sugar plantation, which would define life in much of the American tropics from the fifteenth to nineteenth centuries, found a prototype here off central Africa just before Columbus's famous voyages.

feitoria A Portuguese overseas trading post, usually fortified.

By 1488, Bartolomeu Dias rounded Africa's Cape of Good Hope, and ten years later, Vasco da Gama became the first European to reach India by sea. When Christopher Columbus proposed a westward route to "the Indies," the Portuguese king, on the advice of his cosmographers, declined. Columbus's calculations were in doubt, as was the need for an alternative. Once in the Indian Ocean, the Portuguese used their sturdy ships and superior firepower to capture more than a dozen ports by 1510. The emphasis on ports reflected Portuguese ambitions. They sought to dominate the existing maritime Asian trade, not to establish a colonial land empire. Thus, as we shall see, Portuguese and Spanish expansion would take different forms.

New Crossroads, First Encounters: The European Voyages of Discovery 1492–1521

FOCUS What were the main sources of conflict between Europeans and native Americans in the first decades after contact?

Portugal's Spanish neighbors were equally interested in overseas expansion, but by Columbus's time they lagged far behind. Like Portugal, Spain had competent sailors and shipbuilders, and some families were tied to the early African trade. What would distinguish Spain's overseas enterprises from Portugal's, however, was a tendency to acquire large landmasses by force, colonize them with large numbers of settlers, and force Catholicism on all inhabitants. In part this pattern derived from the centuries-long Christian Reconquest of the Iberian peninsula that ended with the defeat of the Muslim caliphate of Granada in January 1492. As if fated, it was at Ferdinand and Isabella's military encampment at Granada that Columbus received his license to sail across the Atlantic.

Christopher Columbus in a New World

Christopher Columbus, born in Genoa in 1451, came of age in the profit-seeking East Atlantic world centered on Lisbon. Columbus married Felipa de Perestrelo, a Portuguese noblewoman, but did not settle down. Instead, he sailed on Portuguese ships bound for West Africa, England, and even Iceland. He became obsessed with sailing west to China and Japan, which he had read about in the account of Marco Polo. Around 1485 Columbus left for Spain, where he eventually won the sponsorship of Isabella and Ferdinand. By 1492 he was off to cross the Atlantic in search of the successors of Qubilai Khan, China's famed thirteenth-century Mongol ruler.

≡ **MAP 16.2** **European Voyages of Discovery, c. 1420–1600** In a remarkably short time, the Portuguese and Spanish went from exploring the eastern Atlantic to circumnavigating the globe. Christopher Columbus's first Spanish-sponsored voyage across the Atlantic in 1492 and Vasco da Gama's Portuguese-sponsored trip to India in 1497–1498 heightened the competition, and by 1519 Ferdinand

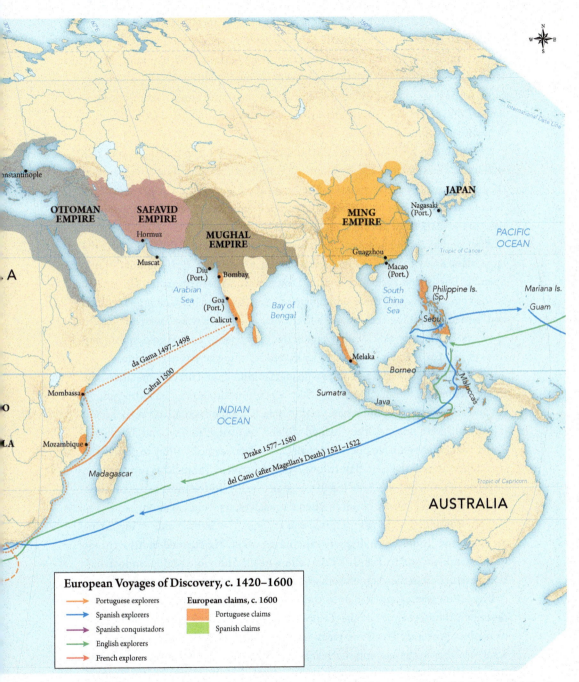

European Voyages of Discovery, c. 1420–1600

→ Portuguese explorers

→ Spanish explorers

→ Spanish conquistadors

→ English explorers

→ French explorers

European claims, c. 1600

Portuguese claims

Spanish claims

Magellan, a Portuguese navigator sailing for the Spanish, set out to circle the globe by rounding South America and crossing the Pacific. Magellan was killed in the Philippines, but some of his crew survived to return to Spain in 1522. It was not until the 1577–1580 voyage of the English privateer Francis Drake, led by a kidnapped Portuguese pilot, that another European circumnavigated the globe.

On October 12, 1492, barely a month after leaving his last stop in the Canary Islands, Columbus and his mostly Spanish crew made contact with the native Taino (tah-EE-no) inhabitants of Guanahani, one of the smaller Bahama Islands. Unable to communicate with them, Columbus imagined himself somewhere near Japan, or at least "east of India." He christened the island San Salvador, or "Holy Savior," and called the native Bahamians and all other indigenous peoples he subsequently encountered "Indians" (see Map 16.2).

Remarking in his journal that the "Indians" he met in the Bahamas were tall, well built, scantily clad, and ignorant of iron weapons, Columbus proposed that they would make excellent slaves. They reminded him of the Canary Islanders. True to his word, Columbus eventually shipped some five hundred Caribbean natives to the markets of Seville.

After landfall in the Bahamas, Columbus sailed southwest to Cuba, then east to the large island known locally as Haiti. He renamed it "Española" ("Hispaniola," "Little Spain" in English) and began looking for a town site to settle in the name of his queen. In the course of this and three subsequent voyages, Christopher Columbus claimed and named everything and everyone that came into his view for his royal Spanish sponsors. In his logbook, Columbus reiterated his hopes of finding gold, spices, and news of "the Great Khan." He died in 1506, still believing he was near China.

For the diverse American peoples who met Columbus and his crewmembers, the foreigners provoked mixed feelings. They brought useful goods, including hatchets and sewing needles, but when their demands for food, gold, and sexual companionship were not met, they turned violent, torturing, raping, and murdering native islanders at will. No one, least of all Columbus, seemed willing to punish the newcomers or rein them in. Before long, some frustrated Taino hosts returned the violence in kind, but this only led to vengeance raids. In the most extreme cases, native women killed their children, then themselves, to avoid violation.

As he continued looking for China, and for gold, Columbus came to regard his arrival in the "Indies" as a divinely sanctioned event. He claimed in his writings that the Indians, particularly his Taino allies, needed him for religious indoctrination, instruction in the ways of work and trade, and physical protection.

Protection was essential due to the presence of "evil" Indians, as Columbus described them, enemies of the Taino. The word *Caribbean* derives from Carib, or *caribe*, apparently an ethnic term. Groups of so-called Caribs did inhabit the smaller islands to the east and south of Borinquen, the large island renamed Puerto Rico by the Spanish. Although culturally similar to the Taino, these Caribs were said to have a particularly bad habit: they ate human flesh.

"Man-eating" natives were a predictable New World wonder, the sort of marvel medieval travelers had described for sensation-hungry readers. Columbus happily played along. It appears he blended the Latin *canis* (dog) and local ethnic name *caribe* to produce a new word: *canibal*, or "cannibal." *Carib* and *cannibal* soon became interchangeable terms in the lexicon of Spanish conquest, and the image of the cannibal stuck fast in the European imagination. Indeed, almost as quickly as news of the Indies reached Europe, printers rushed to illustrate the alleged atrocities of the Caribbean "dog-people."

Scholars disagree as to whether the so-called Caribs practiced cannibalism. What mattered for Columbus and his followers was that their allies, the "good Indians," said they did. With such a legal pretext (the eating of human flesh being regarded as a clear violation of natural law in the Western tradition), the newcomers could claim to be serving a necessary police role. They alone could adequately "protect" and "punish"—that is, take over Western-style functions of government in the "New World."

Spanish sovereignty in the Americas required more legal support. Even before the voyages of Columbus, Portugal's overseas interests had clashed with Spain's. With the pope's mediation, in 1494 the Spanish and Portuguese split the world into two zones of influence. According to the Treaty of Tordesillas, the Spanish were to rule everyone living 370 leagues (roughly 1110 miles) or more west of the Canaries. Africa, Asia, and eventually Brazil, which was not known to Europeans until 1500, fell to the Portuguese (see again Map 16.2).

Why was the Roman Catholic pope involved in an agreement of this kind? First, fifteenth-century Europeans regarded his authority as above that of secular rulers. More important, however, was the matter of spreading the Christian gospel, a job Columbus himself embraced. Iberian monarchs, as pious Catholics, promised to sponsor the conversion of everyone their subjects encountered abroad and also to continue the medieval fight against "infidels." Commerce may have supplied the initial and most powerful motive for overseas expansion, but a drive for religious and cultural hegemony soon played an important part in European colonization.

≡ **Dog-Faced Cannibals** European readers of chivalry tales and travel accounts expected the American "New World" to yield fantastic and horrible creatures. Early news from the Caribbean and Brazil suggested the existence of humans with doglike, omnivorous appetites, seeming to confirm the alleged observations of Marco Polo and other medieval travelers. In this 1527 woodcut, a German artist fused Weimaraner-like dogs' heads with naked German butchers, one with a raised steel cleaver, to represent native Americans. Since this image predates the Spanish conquest of the Incas by five years, the horned llama-like animal at lower left is of special interest.

From Independence to Servitude: The Encomienda System

Although missionaries were present in the Caribbean from the 1490s, early Spanish colonization was mostly a mad dash for gold and slaves. Settlers had little interest in working the land, preferring instead to live off native American slaves and tribute payers. As news of massive abuse and alarming death rates reached Spain, Queen Isabella demanded an end to Amerindian slavery. After 1503 only violent rebels and alleged cannibals were to be enslaved.

Would the Taino then be free in exchange for accepting Catholicism and Spanish protection against the Caribs? No, in large part because their labor was thought necessary to mine gold, which Spain's monarchs desperately wanted. Compromise came in the form of the *encomienda* system. Native villages were entrusted to Spaniards in a manner resembling medieval European feudalism: village farming folk were to offer labor and surplus produce to their "lord" in exchange for military protection. Chiefs served as middlemen. The Spanish *encomenderos* who received these fiefdoms were self-styled men-at-arms, and from their ranks would come the conquerors of the mainland.

Indians deemed good and faithful subjects paid tributes to their encomendero, or "trustee," as he was called, in local goods, twice a year. Adult men were also required to work for the encomendero from time to time. For his part, the encomendero was to protect his tributaries from outside attack and ensure their conversion to Christianity. However reciprocal in theory, the encomienda system was in fact used mostly to round up workers for the gold mines. It looked like slavery to the few Spanish critics who denounced it, and even more so to the many thousands of native peoples who suffered under it.

One Spanish critic was Bartolomé de Las Casas, a Hispaniola encomendero's son turned Dominican priest who became the leading defender of native American rights in early modern times. Through constant pleading at court, and in university debates and publications, Las Casas helped to suppress the indigenous slave trade and restrict the encomienda system by the early 1540s. For the Tainos, the reforms came too late. By 1510 there were only a few hundred encomienda subjects whereas a decade before there had been hundreds of thousands. By almost any measure, the Columbian era in the Caribbean was a disaster.

Columbus's Successors

Columbus's accomplishments spawned dozens of like-minded expeditions (see again Map 16.2). These included the four voyages of Amerigo Vespucci (1497–1504), a Florentine merchant for whom the continents of the Western

encomienda A feudal-style grant of a native American village to a conquistador or other Spaniard.

Hemisphere would later be named. Vespucci won fame as a publicist of the new lands and peoples that Europeans were encountering throughout the American tropics. Vespucci soon realized that the Americas were not part of Asia. This did not, however, prevent him from embracing other European preconceptions. In relating his voyages to Brazil, Vespucci calmly described the roasting and eating of human flesh among the local inhabitants. His reports only added to the European fixation on native American cannibalism.

Other voyages included those of Juan de Solís and Ferdinand Magellan. Both were Portuguese explorers sailing for Spain, and both, like Columbus, sought a westward route to Asia. Solís sailed up the Río de la Plata estuary near modern Buenos Aires in 1516, but was captured and killed in a skirmish with local inhabitants. Magellan learned details of the Argentine coast from survivors of the Solís expedition, then organized a much more ambitious voyage to the Moluccas, or Maluku, in what is today Indonesia. The epic journey that followed, arguably one of the boldest ever undertaken, was recorded by the Venetian Antonio de Pigafetta.

Of the five ships that left Spain in 1519, two were wrecked before Magellan reached the straits at the southern tip of South America that still bear his name. When food ran short, crewmembers shot and salted penguins and sea lions. Encounters with the native inhabitants of Tierra del Fuego and the neighboring mainland were brief and hostile. Always the good publicist, Pigafetta described encounters with primitive giants, giving rise to the legend of Patagonia, or "the land of Big Foot."

Once in the Pacific, Magellan sailed northwest to Guam, in the Mariana Islands. The four-month ocean crossing had left the crew malnourished; many died from the effects of scurvy, a disease caused by lack of vitamin C. Magellan then sailed to the Philippine island of Sebu, where he became embroiled in a dispute between local chieftains. Alarmed to find Muslim merchants active in the region, Magellan sought to create an alliance with new converts to Christianity through a show of force. Instead, he and forty crew members were killed. Only one vessel escaped, returning to Spain in 1522 by following the new Portuguese sailing route through the Indian and Atlantic oceans. For the first time in recorded history, the world had been circumnavigated (see again Map 16.2).

Meanwhile, in the Caribbean, Spanish colonists became disillusioned with the fabled "West Indies" of Columbus. Unhappiest of all were the newest immigrants, desperate young men with dreams of gold. They fanned out across the Caribbean in search of new sources of wealth, both human and metallic. Most failed, and many died, but some eventually found what they sought: fabled continental empires rich beyond belief.

Columbian Exchange Historian Alfred Crosby's term for the movement of American plants, animals, and germs to the rest of the world and vice versa.

The Columbian Exchange

In a landmark 1972 book, historian Alfred Crosby argued that the most significant consequences of 1492 were biological.[3] What Crosby called the **Columbian Exchange** referred to the massive interoceanic transfer of animals (including humans), plants, and diseases that followed in Columbus's wake. Many of these transfers, such as the introduction of rats and smallpox to the Americas, were unintentional. Yet all had profound consequences.

Since European explorers circled the globe shortly after Columbus's time, this process of biological exchange was a worldwide phenomenon. Indigenous cuisines, farming practices, and transportation modes were changed, sometimes for the better. Northern European populations, for example, grew rapidly thanks to Andean potatoes, which thrived in cool, wet climates. South and Southeast Asian cuisines were altered by the introduction of American capsicum peppers and peanuts, which flourished in the Old World tropics.

But European livestock also rapidly altered landscapes, sometimes with catastrophic consequences. In the worst case, the highlands of central Mexico were reduced to deserts following the introduction of sheep in the sixteenth century. Lacking predators, and having access to vast new pastures, their populations exploded. Similar processes of environmental transformation were later repeated in Australia, New Zealand, Argentina, and the western United States.

As in the case of ship-borne rats, many unwanted exchanges took place as well. Worst among these were diseases, mostly caused by viruses, bacteria, and blood parasites, introduced to previously unexposed hosts. In Africa and Eurasia the repeated spread of diseases such as smallpox, measles, and mumps had allowed people over time to develop immunity against these and other pathogens. As seen in Chapter 14, pandemics of plague could still be devastating, but never to the extent that they would be in long-isolated regions overseas. The peoples of the Americas, Australia, and Polynesia

≡ **Maize** Perhaps the most globally transformative native American crop (vying with the potato), maize was first domesticated in highland Mexico some 7000 years ago. This 1542 German depiction is the most accurate to survive from the first decades after maize was introduced to Europe. Similar varieties soon transformed global dietary patterns, particularly in sub-Saharan Africa. Some cultures adopted maize only as livestock feed.

proved tragically vulnerable in this regard; they suffered what was probably the worst demographic collapse in history.

Germs, coupled with colonialism, killed tens of millions. Evidence suggests that throughout the Americas and Pacific Islands, indigenous populations declined by almost 90 percent within a century. Recovery and acquired immunity came slowly. With the introduction of malaria, yellow fever, and other mosquito-borne blood parasites, America's lowland tropics became especially deadly. On the plus side, world food exchanges spurred population growth in Europe, Africa, and Asia, and contributed to the rebound of the Americas. Overall, the spread of American crops boosted world population significantly before the end of early modern times. The peoples of the Americas, however, paid a steep price for the Columbian Exchange.

Spanish Conquests in the Americas 1519–1600

> ⬇ **FOCUS** What factors enabled the Spanish to conquer the Aztec and Inca Empires?

Two men disappointed by the Caribbean islands were Hernando Cortés and Francisco Pizarro. Cortés gained fame after 1521 as conqueror of the Aztecs, and Pizarro after 1532 as conqueror of the Incas. Their experiences on the American mainland gave rise to the almost mythical Spanish-American livelihood of **conquistador**, or conqueror. Like Columbus, neither man acted alone, but both altered the course of global history.

The Fall of Aztec Mexico

As we saw in Chapter 15, the people known as Aztecs called themselves Mexica (meh-SHEE-cah). By the time Spaniards reached them in the late 1510s, the Mexica ruled much of Mesoamerica, often by terror. Cortés would soon discover, however, that the Aztec Empire was vulnerable.

A brash and ambitious leader, Hernando Cortés left his base in southern Cuba after a dispute with his sponsor, the governor. In Yucatan, as we have seen, he found an extraordinarily valuable translator in Malintzin. By September of 1519 Cortés set out for the interior from the new town of Veracruz on Mexico's Gulf coast. With him were Malintzin and several hundred horses and well-armed men, accompanied by fighting dogs. After attacking both Aztec allies and enemies, the

conquistador Spanish for "conqueror," a new livelihood in the Americas after Columbus.

Cortés's Invasion
of the Aztec Empire,
1519-1521

Aztec Empire, 1519
Cortés's original route, 1519
Cortés's retreat, 1520
Cortés's return route, 1520–1521

0   100 Miles
0   100 Kilometers

≡ **Cortés's Invasion of the Aztec Empire,**
1519–1521

Spanish and several thousand new allies entered Tenochtitlán in November 1519 as guests of the emperor, Moteuczoma, or "Moctezuma," II.

Shortly after being treated to a feast by the curious and gracious Moctezuma, Cortés and his followers managed to seize the unsuspecting emperor. Fearful for their ruler's life, the Aztec people, now leaderless, faced great uncertainty. Cortés ordered that anyone who opposed the Spanish and their allies would be publicly cut to pieces and fed to the dogs. Treachery, terror, and seizure of indigenous leaders were in fact stock tactics developed by Spanish conquistadors in the Caribbean. These tactics proved even more effective against mainland imperial peoples who depended on divine kings. Attached to their subsistence plots, settled farmers had nowhere to run.

There followed several months of looting and destruction, punctuated by battles and skirmishes. Some who resented the Aztecs supported the Spanish, most significantly the Tlaxcalans, but others resisted violently. Soon unfamiliar diseases such as smallpox and influenza swept through Tenochtitlán and the entire Valley of Mexico, decimating a vast and densely populated region already facing food shortages. Ironically, the people who would give the world maize, tomatoes, chocolate, vanilla, and a thousand other life-sustaining and pleasurable foods were now receiving only the deadliest ingredients of the Columbian Exchange: viruses and bacteria. Cortés ordered that images of the Virgin Mary be placed atop Aztec temples to assert the power of the invaders' Christian deities.

While Cortés went to negotiate with soldiers sent by Cuba's governor to arrest him in early 1520, the Spaniards left behind in Tenochtitlán provoked a siege by massacring Aztec nobles. Rushing to the city with Cuban recruits whom he had just won over, Cortés reached his comrades only to be trapped by the Aztec warriors. The desperate Spaniards brought out the captive emperor, Moctezuma, in hopes of calming tempers, but he was killed in a hail of stones. The besieged Spanish tried to flee Tenochtitlán but were quickly pinned down on one of the city's three narrow causeways. Cortés and others escaped at the head of the pack, but many other Spaniards, about half the total number, fell into Aztec hands. According to Aztec accounts, when the city's male warriors fell dead or exhausted, women warriors took over, attacking with equal vigor (see Reading the Past: Tlatelolcan Elders Recall the Conquest of Mexico).

READING THE PAST

Tlatelolcan Elders Recall the Conquest of Mexico

In what would become New Spain, or colonial Mexico, Spanish missionaries quickly introduced European-style writing systems. Indigenous scribes picked them up within a few decades of the conquest, rendering Nahuatl, Maya, and other local languages in a Latinate script with Spanish phonetics. Formal documents, including histories and sermons, were produced in this manner, but also interviews, myths, genealogies, criminal testimonies, and a host of everyday transactions. The following excerpt is a direct English translation of a Nahuatl document from about 1540 relating the conquest of both Tenochtitlán and its "twin city," Tlatelolco. The Tlatelolcan elders relating the story to junior scribes apparently witnessed and participated in the events in question.

"And when they reached Yacocolco here, Spaniards were captured on the Tlilhuacan [tleel-WALK-on]

road, as well as all the people from the various altepetl [allied city-states]. Two thousand died there, and the Tlatelolcans were exclusively responsible for it. At this time we Tlatelolcans set up skull racks; skull racks were in three places. One was in the temple courtyard at Tlillan, where the heads of our [present] lords [the Spaniards] were strung; the second was in Yacocolco, where the heads of our lords [the Spaniards] were strung, along with the heads of two horses; the third place was in Çacatla, facing the Cihuateocalli [see-wah-tayoh-CAH-yee] [Woman-Temple]. It was the exclusive accomplishment of the Tlatelolcans. After this they drove us from there and reached the marketplace. That was when the great Tlatelolcan warriors were entirely vanquished. With that the fighting stopped once and for all. That was when the Tlatelolcan women all let loose, fighting, striking people, taking captives. They put on warriors' devices, all raising their skirts so that they could give pursuit."

Source: James Lockhart, ed. and trans., *We People Here: Nahuatl Accounts of the Conquest of Mexico* (Berkeley: University of California Press, 1993), 265–267.

Examining the Evidence

1. What does this document tell us about Aztec political identity during the conquest?

2. What does it tell us about military culture and gender roles?

Cortés and his bedraggled Spanish forces eventually regrouped with aid from the Tlaxcalans, their staunchest allies, but it was over a year before Tenochtitlán and its twin city of Tlatelolco fell. Cut off from the mainland, the Aztecs faced starvation, then attack by land and water. Cortés ordered thirteen small, European-style sailing vessels built on the shores of Lake Texcoco, and armed with cannon these helped pound remaining Aztec warrior contingents in canoes. By August 1521 Cortés and his men and allies had forced the Aztecs to retreat to Tlatelolco. Both cities were then occupied and pillaged.

Soon after, a successor emperor to Moctezuma was killed for allegedly hiding booty, prompting dissatisfied conquistadors to fan out across Mesoamerica in search of riches and other empires. The self-promoting Cortés traveled to Spain to consolidate his gains, but found little support from the emperor Charles V. Conquest of the Aztec center had been difficult, and at the fringes conquest carried on. Far more difficult would be winning the hearts and minds of millions of former Aztec subjects now anxious to assert their own agendas. This would be the long story of colonial Mexico, a "New Spain" so unlike its Iberian namesake.

The Fall of Inca Peru

When Francisco Pizarro left Panama City in 1522 in search of "Pirú," a mythical chieftain, he had no idea that events high in the Andes would conspire to favor his dream of repeating the success of Cortés. But as with Cortés and his many companions and aides, an empire—even with guns, germs, and steel on one's side—could not be toppled overnight.

In fact it took a decade of reconnaissance and failure before Pizarro at last marched into Peru. In the meantime he had acquired Quechua translators immersed in Castilian Spanish; a small army of men with horses, armor, and state-of-the-art weapons; and a license from Charles V. By late 1532, when Pizarro's forces began marching across a coastal desert reminiscent of southern Spain, Peru at last seemed ripe for the taking.

Tawantinsuyu (tah-wahn-tin-SUE-you), as the Incas called their empire, faced crisis in 1532. A succession battle had recently been won by Atawallpa (also Atahualpa). According to eyewitness accounts, when Pizarro and his 168 men climbed into the Andes to meet Atawallpa in the city of Cajamarca, the new Sapa Inca was flush with victory. Atawallpa seemed invulnerable, and apparently intended, rather like Moctezuma in Mexico, to draft the foreigners into his service. In November 1532 Pizarro and

≡ Pizarro's Invasion of the Inca Empire, 1531–1533

his men captured Atawallpa in an act reminiscent of Cortés's seizure of Moctezuma. Humiliated, Atawallpa was held hostage for nearly a year as his subjects scrambled to collect enough gold and silver to free him. The Incas possessed far more precious metals than the Aztecs, and the ransom they offered was staggering. Suddenly Pizarro and his followers were rich beyond their wildest dreams.

Thus "Peru" became synonymous with great wealth among Europeans, an association soon reinforced by the discovery of immensely rich silver mines. Despite the ransom, however, Atawallpa was killed on Pizarro's orders in 1533. The treachery was complete, and by 1534 Tawantinsuyu was in Spanish hands.

The Conquest: Myths and Realities

How did a small number of Spanish men topple two of the world's largest empires? Some biologists and anthropologists have claimed that these great, isolated indigenous empires faced inevitable defeat because they lacked iron, sufficient protein, draft animals, wheeled vehicles, writing, acquired immunity to numerous pathogens, and other advantages. Historians have long puzzled over this riddle, too, but more with an eye on human actors and the timing of events.

For their part, the conquistadors and their Spanish contemporaries regarded these victories as the will of their Christian God. Spain's enemies—and internal critics such as Las Casas—emphasized the conquistadors' "sins" of treachery, cruelty, lust, and greed. By the nineteenth century, historians less interested in judging the Spanish focused on individual leadership. They emphasized the intelligence and tenacity of Cortés and Pizarro, and the apparent weakness and indecisiveness of their adversaries, Moctezuma and Atawallpa.

Pizarro Meets Atawallpa Throughout colonial times native and European artists depicted the day in 1532 when Inca emperor Atawallpa met Francisco Pizarro. This is the first known image of the Peruvian encounter, a woodcut accompanying an eyewitness account published in Seville, Spain, in 1534. It depicts Atawallpa on a litter holding up what is probably the prayer book given him by the priest Vicente de Valverde, also pictured. Pizarro stands back with his fellow Spaniards, armed but not poised to attack. In the distance is a European-style castle presumably meant to stand for an Inca city. Notably absent is the native Andean interpreter whom we know only by his Christian name, "Little Philip."

Recently, historians have focused on other causal factors. These include the importance of indigenous allies and interpreters; the conquistadors' accumulated experience as "Indian fighters" in the Caribbean; imperial politics and the timing of Spanish arrival; indigenous adaptation to Spanish fighting methods; contrasting

SEEING THE PAST

Malintzin and the Meeting Between Moctezuma and Cortés

This image, taken from the early post-conquest document known as the *Florentine Codex*, was created by an indigenous Mexican artist who had been exposed to European prints and paintings while being schooled by Spanish friars. In it, Malintzin translates the words between Aztec emperor Moctezuma and Hernando Cortés at their first momentous meeting.

Examining the Evidence

1. How does this drawing reflect the indigenous artist's instruction by Spanish friars?

2. To what extent is it a reflection of Malintzin's perceived importance in the conquest of Mexico?

Malintzin Interprets for Cortés and Moctezuma
(The Granger Collection, New York.)

goals of warfare; and of course, the introduction of novel weapons, animals, and diseases. Most historians agree that the conquests resulted from the convergence of these many variables—a number of them, such as the appearance of the able translator Malintzin, unpredictable (see Seeing the Past: Malintzin and the Meeting Between Moctezuma and Cortés).

Were indigenous peoples overawed by Spanish horses and technology, and did they view the newcomers as gods? Much evidence suggests the answer is "no." As this quote from a Spanish soldier who participated in the conquest of Mexico suggests, Aztec warriors adapted rapidly to the threat of cannon and armored opponents on horseback:

> One day an Indian I saw in combat with a mounted horseman struck the horse in the chest, cutting through to the inside and killing the horse on the spot. On the same day I saw another Indian give a horse a sword thrust in the neck that laid the horse dead at his feet. . . . Among them are extraordinary brave men who face death with absolute determination.[4]

The evidence from Inca Peru barely differs. After the capture of Atawallpa in 1532, Andean warriors avoided open field engagements where they might be run down by mounted Spaniards, preferring instead to ambush their enemies as they crossed rivers and traveled through narrow canyons. Simple stones and slingshots proved a surprising match for guns and steel swords in these conditions. Rebellions and raids continued for decades in the Mexican and Peruvian backcountry, but the Spanish conquest of the Aztec and Inca imperial cores was sealed by those empires' own former subjects: although they did not know what was in store for them, most were anxious for something different.

A New Empire in the Americas: New Spain and Peru 1535–1600

FOCUS Why was the discovery of silver in Spanish America so important in the course of world history?

Soon after conquest, Spanish settlers penetrated deep into the Americas, transforming the world's largest overseas land empire into the world's greatest source of precious metals. Spain's monarchs in turn used this mineral bounty to pursue their ambitions in Europe and beyond. Merchants used it to link the world economy. But for the millions of native Americans subjected to Spanish rule, life would revolve around negotiating a measure of freedom within an imperial system at least as taxing as those of the Aztecs and Incas.

American Silver and the Global Economy

In 1545 an indigenous prospector found silver ore on a high, red mountain in what is today Bolivia. The Cerro Rico, or "Rich Hill," of Potosí (poh-toe-SEE) turned out to be the most concentrated silver deposit ever discovered (see Map 16.3). This

European Claims in the Americas, c. 1600

European claims, c. 1600

- 🟩 Spanish
- 🟧 Portuguese
- 1492   Date of conquest or settlement
- ⊕   Headquarters of the Inquisition

Major economic activities

- 🗡 Brazilwood   🏺 Silver
- 🟨 Gold   ⬇ Sugar Plantation
- 💧 Mercury   🟩 Emeralds
- ◯ Pearls

≡ **MAP 16.3   European Claims in the Americas, c. 1600** Beginning in the 1510s, the Spanish used bases in Cuba and on the Isthmus of Panama to launch the conquests of the Aztec and Inca Empires. In search of similar empires, Spanish explorers drove deep into the interiors of North and South America; by the 1540s they had penetrated the U.S. Southwest and South America's Río de la Plata basin, and made their way down the Amazon. Other conquests in Central America, northwest Mexico, and New Granada led to the creation of a vast Spanish-American Empire, under the twin capitals of Mexico City and Lima. Portuguese Brazil, by contrast, consisted of only a few small settlements along the Atlantic coast, but by 1600 it was the world leader in sugar production, increasingly dependent on the labor of enslaved Africans.

and related silver discoveries in early Spanish America transformed not only life in the colonies, but the global economy. As we will see in subsequent chapters, in regions as distant as China and South Asia, American silver affected people's livelihoods in profound ways. Even before Potosí, silver mines had been located in Mexico, and new finds followed. Mexican districts such as Zacatecas (zah-cah-TAY-cus) and Guanajuato (hwan-uh-WAH-toe) were expanding by the 1550s and would continue to drive Mexico's economy for centuries.

Although the Spanish adopted Old World techniques of tunneling and refining, the silver boom also spurred technical innovations. Chief among these was the use of mercury to separate silver from crushed ore. Amalgamation, as this process is known, was practiced in antiquity, but it was Bartolomé de Medina, a merchant working in Mexico in the mid-1550s, who patented a refining process suitable for New World environments. Medina's invention revolutionized Spanish-American silver mining even as it spread one of the world's most persistent toxins, mercury.

Amalgamation was implemented in Potosí after 1572. Although Spain itself produced mercury, New World sources had been sought since conquest. Before long, the mine owners' dreams came true: in highland Peru the mercury mines of Huancavelica (wan-kah-bell-EE-cah) were discovered in 1564. Thus the Spanish paired Andean mercury with Andean silver, sparking an enormous boom in production. Potosí yielded tens of millions of ounces of silver annually by the 1580s.

Even with abundant mercury, silver production remained costly. Unlike gold panning, underground mining required massive investment. Water-powered ore-processing mills, first developed in Germany, were among the world's most complex machines at the time, and mercury remained expensive despite Spanish price controls. Less often calculated, although well known even in the sixteenth century, were the environmental and health costs of mercury pollution. Soils, rivers, and refinery workers' clothing were saturated with mercury, leading to neurological disorders and birth defects. "Trembling like someone with mercury poisoning" became a common colonial metaphor for fright, akin to "shaking like a leaf."

More costly than mercury and machines was labor. Mining was hard and deadly work, attracting few volunteers. African slaves supplemented the workforce in boomtowns such as Zacatecas and Potosí, but Spanish-American silver mines came to rely mostly on native American draft and wage workers. The draft, or *mita* (MEE-tah) as it was called in the Andes, entailed a year of service in Potosí, Huancavelica, or some other mining center, followed by six years of work in one's own home region, usually in subsistence farming or herding. In Mexico the Spanish implemented a similar system called *repartimiento* (reh-par-tee-MYEN-toe). Drafted indigenous laborers received a small wage and rations during their work

mita A Spanish revival of the Inca draft labor system.

repartimiento An allotment of indigenous laborers in colonial Mexico, similar to the Andean mita.

The Rich Mountain of Potosí This c. 1603 image of Potosí's famous Cerro Rico shows not only the legendary red mountain with its silver veins but also workers, most of them native Andeans, refining silver by mercury amalgamation, and antlike llamas carrying ore down the mountain. The ore-crushing mill in the foreground is powered by a stream of water supplied by canals coming down from artificial reservoirs built high in a neighboring mountain range.

stints, but given the danger of these jobs and the high cost of living in mining towns, the mita and repartimiento severely disrupted indigenous lifeways. Many considered draft work a death sentence.

Potosí boomed in the first years of the mita, but heightened demand for mine laborers in this remote and unhealthy site only worsened an already dramatic indigenous demographic collapse. Most eligible workers who remained in the region learned to avoid the most dangerous tasks, and many sold whatever they could to pay a cash fee for exemption. Mine owners were forced to pay wages to stay in business.

American Silver and Everyday Life

The silver bonanza of the sixteenth century altered many livelihoods. In the Spanish colonies, everything from ranch work to church building was connected in one way or another to the flow of silver. Dependent miners living in towns such as Potosí and Zacatecas spurred merchants and landowners to expand their inventories, crops, and livestock herds. Mule-drivers, weavers, tanners, and other specialists came to rely on the mines' productivity for their sustenance. In town centers, indigenous market women carved out a lucrative space as well. Silver production even drove Spanish missionaries to intensify conversion efforts. Worldwide, Spanish-American silver funded the expansion of the Catholic Church.

Whereas most indigenous peoples adapted to Spanish laws and civic traditions and even tolerated the oppressive obligations of mine work, they usually resisted total conversion to Catholicism. Confident in the universality of their religion, European missionaries expected indigenous populations to accept Christianity as they themselves understood it. When they did not, conversion turned to coercion. Soon after military conquest, priests and Church officials used violent means to advance their project.

Native Americans were not the only victims of religious intolerance. Offices of the **Inquisition**, a branch of the Catholic Church dedicated to enforcing orthodox beliefs and practices, were established in Mexico City and Lima in 1570–1571 and Cartagena in 1610. Their purpose was to punish alleged deviants and heretics among the Spanish settlers and people of African descent. In the indigenous majority (soon exempted from prosecution by the Inquisition due to their newness to the faith), complete conversion was limited by long-held beliefs. Most native American converts adopted the Christian God, his holy intermediaries, and saints on their own terms, as new additions to an already crowded pantheon. Missionary priests became pessimistic and often angry with this half-hearted Catholicism, although some realized that conversion was a slow process requiring that they themselves achieve a better understanding of would-be converts.

It was only after some priests learned to speak indigenous languages fluently that Europeans began to transform native cosmologies. One way around conflicting beliefs was to ignore elders and focus conversion efforts on native youths, particularly boys. Upon maturity, they would be exemplary believers, leaders in the new faith. Many such boys were removed from their parents' custody, taught to read and write, and ordered to collect myths and sagas. These stories were then altered by European priests to match Christian history and beliefs.

The missionaries had less success with women. Despite the burdens of colonialism, indigenous women continued teaching their children the old ways while

Inquisition A branch of the Catholic Church established to enforce orthodoxy.

also pressing for social recognition within the new order. Some, like Malintzin, refashioned themselves as something in between Spanish and indigenous, often bearing **mestizo** (meh-STEE-soh) or mixed-heritage children. But the persistence of indigenous language and lifeways was due mostly to humble indigenous women, unsung keepers of the hearth. Despite Spanish determination to remake the Americas to serve European interests and ambitions, diverse indigenous cultures would continue to shape colonial society.

Brazil by Accident: The Portuguese in the Americas 1500–1600

> ↘ **FOCUS** How and why did early Portuguese Brazil develop differently from Spanish America?

The Portuguese followed a distinct path in colonizing Brazil. The trend in the century after contact in 1500 was from benign neglect and small-scale trade with indigenous coast-dwellers toward a more formal royal presence and settled plantation agriculture, mostly concentrated along the northeast coast. By 1600, Brazil was the world's largest sugar producer. It also became the prime destination for sub-Saharan African slaves. A key stimulus for this shift was French encroachment in Brazil. The arrival of French traders and religious refugees forced the Portuguese to briefly take their eyes off India.

Native Encounters and Foreign Competitors

It was on the way to India in early 1500 that Pedro Álvares Cabral and his fleet were blown westward from Cape Verde, in West Africa. Toward the end of April the fleet sighted land, which the captain dubbed the "Island of the True Cross." The landmass was later found not to be an island, but rather part of the continent of South America. The huge eastern portion of the continent claimed by Portugal under the 1494 Treaty of Tordesillas would later be called Brazil (see again Map 16.3).

Brazil was initially of little interest to Portugal. Without gold or some other lucrative export, there seemed to be no point in colonizing this distant land. Brazil's one obvious resource, and what earned it its name, was brazilwood, a tree with a deep-red, pithy heart. Portuguese traders, soon followed by French competitors, set up posts all along Brazil's vast coast to barter with indigenous Tupi speakers for precut, red-hearted logs.

mestizo A person of mixed European and native American ancestry.

Brazilwood was shipped to Europe, where dye was extracted and sold at profit. Native Brazilians willingly participated in this trade because it brought them tangible benefits: metal hatchets, knives, sewing needles, and other utilitarian items, along with beads, bells, and other adornments. For some, it also brought military alliances against traditional enemies. In several places Portuguese *degredados*, or criminal castaways, survived exile and married into eminent indigenous families, becoming translators and commercial middlemen.

French competition for control of Brazil and its dyewood pressed the Portuguese to assert their claims more forcefully. A fleet of warships was sent from Lisbon in 1532 to protect Portuguese traders and to punish French interlopers. Land claims were also reorganized. After 1534 Brazil was carved into fifteen proprietary colonies, granted to courtiers by King Manoel. Brazil's new "lords" were expected to organize defense against French and indigenous enemies.

With few exceptions, the Brazilian proprietary colonies failed; the French were still a menace, and native Brazilians, not Portuguese colonists, had the run of the land. In 1549 the Crown tried another strategy: Salvador, a defensible hamlet located at the tip of a wide bay in northeastern Brazil, was made the royal capital and seat of a governor-general. Jesuit missionaries also arrived. They soon set out to convert tens of thousands of native, Tupi-speaking allies to Roman Catholicism.

The French did not easily give up on their Brazilian enterprise, and in fact redoubled their efforts at midcentury. In 1555 they established a new colony in Guanabara Bay, near modern Rio de Janeiro (see again Map 16.3). The colony's leader, however, could not sort out disputes between Catholics like himself and numerous Protestant refugees, or Huguenots. Divided by religion, like France itself at the time (as we will see in Chapter 19), the French colony was doomed. The Portuguese drove out Catholics and Protestants alike by 1567. As for indigenous enemies, Portuguese wars and slaving expeditions were just beginning.

Bitter Sugar: Slavery and the Plantation Complex in the Early Atlantic World 1530–1600

A search for precious metals and gems came up short after the capital of Salvador was established in 1549, but the Portuguese found other ways beyond brazilwood to profit from the colony. On Brazil's northeast coast, sugar cane was planted as early as the 1530s. By 1570, Brazil was the world's number one sugar producer. Cane sugar was Brazil's answer to Spanish-American silver, but like silver, sugar had a cost. First indigenous, then African, slaves were made to do the burdensome work required to produce it (see Lives and Livelihoods: Atlantic Sugar Producers).

LIVES AND LIVELIHOODS

Atlantic Sugar Producers

≡ **Sugar Plantations** Enslaved sugar-makers worked not only in fields but also in powerful mills and refining furnaces. Men, women, and children were all involved. This 1662 Dutch image of Pernambuco, Brazil, depicts enslaved sugar refinery and transport workers during the intense harvest period when the mills ran all night. The Dutch controlled Pernambuco and its sugar plantations from 1630 to 1654. (Courtesy of the John Carter Brown Library at Brown University.)

Found in countless foods and beverages, and now a major global source of biofuels, cane sugar was once a rare commodity. Introduced to the Mediterranean by Muslim traders and colonists in the eighth or ninth century C.E., sugar was at first a medicine and high-status condiment. Its source, sugar cane, a tall, thick grass, was eventually planted in Egypt, Sicily, Cyprus, and southern Iberia, and by at least the fourteenth century was processed not only by Muslims but also by Christian landowners in southern Spain and Portugal. Though later associated exclusively with slavery, sugar making in this era was done by a mixed free and enslaved labor force. Before long, women joined men in both cane fields and processing plants.

Sugar cane is so tough that considerable energy is required to extract maximum juice. Efficient presses were thus a technical hurdle for commercial producers. Like silver refining, sugar making required technical expertise and a complex sequence of chemical processes that allowed for few errors. Specialists were required to design and build ever larger and more powerful machines, which were among the most complex mechanical apparatus known at the time.

Animals such as oxen were often used for power, but waterwheels were preferred for their greater efficiency. In the generally dry and sometimes frost-prone Mediterranean basin, access to warm, well-watered plains and consistently flowing millstreams was severely limited. Bounded by ecological and capital constraints, mill ownership remained a dream of most sugar producers. This soon proved equally true in the

Atlantic islands and Brazil. For their part, millworkers, particularly the women and sometimes children who fed canes through the rollers, faced loss of limbs and sometimes death. "And in these Mills," wrote English visitor Richard Flecknoe in 1654, "the work of immediately applying the canes to the Mill being so perilous [that] if through drowsiness or heedlessness a finger's end be but engaged between the posts, their whole body inevitably follows."[1]

Rendering the precious juice into white crystal sugar was also difficult and labor intensive. Workers had to boil the juice in huge copper vats, then reduce it in a series of smaller vats into a concentrated syrup they poured into molds to crystallize. Women were usually in charge of whitening the resulting brown sugar loaves with wet clay and removing them from the molds and packing them for shipment. European consumers considered white sugar purer than brown, "purged" of imperfections. Each phase of the process required skill and close monitoring, and fires had to be stoked throughout the night. Sugar making thus produced a number of task-specific livelihoods, such as purger (purifier), mold-maker, and crating supervisor. Given its complexity, high capital investment, and careful attention to timing, sugar making has been described as an early modern precursor of industrial, or factory, production. However labeled, sugar work was monotonous and occasionally deadly.

Europeans' taste for sugar grew slowly at first, but by 1600, sugar was an ordinary ingredient in many foods. Its association with slavery also gradually increased. Numerous slaves labored in the early cane fields and mills of the East Atlantic islands of Madeira and the Canaries, but the pattern replicated in the Americas—predominantly African slaves manning large plantations—appeared first on the Portuguese island of São Tomé, off equatorial West Africa. By 1550, the so-called plantation complex was established in the Spanish Caribbean and Brazil. In the Americas, as in the Canaries, with the decimation of local cultures, indigenous slavery gave way to African slavery.

Questions to Consider:

1. How did the rise of Atlantic sugar affect the global economy?
2. How did it transform livelihoods?

For Further Information:

Mintz, Sidney W. *Sweetness and Power.* New York: Viking, 1985.

Schwartz, Stuart B., ed. *Tropical Babylons: Sugar and the Making of the Atlantic World, 1450–1680.* Chapel Hill: University of North Carolina Press, 2004.

1. E. Bradford Burns, ed., *A Documentary History of Brazil* (New York: Alfred A. Knopf, 1966), 82.

Sugar growers near Salvador competed with their counterparts in Pernambuco, one of the few surviving proprietary colonies. Each region vied for the greater share of total output, with Pernambuco usually ahead. Native Brazilian slaves were exploited in large numbers in both regions, but well before 1600 Portuguese planters turned to Africa for still more enslaved laborers. Indigenous workers died from disease and abuse, as happened in the early Spanish Caribbean, and were also prone to run away to the interior. As will be seen in greater detail in the next chapter, the Portuguese responded by importing millions of enslaved Africans from western or Atlantic Africa.

Though more resistant to Old World diseases than their native American co-workers, many Africans died in the cane fields of Brazil, literally worked to death. Instead of moderating workloads, improving nutrition and medical care, and encouraging family formation, Portuguese masters opted to exhaust the labor power of their slaves, the vast majority of them young men. The reason was as logical as it was cold-hearted: having direct access to more captives at relatively low cost, sugar planters "used up" laborers much like mine owners did mita workers in Peru. Even when female slaves were introduced and families formed, high child mortality rates discouraged reproduction. Brazil would subsequently become so dependent on Africa for labor that by the time the slave trade ended in the nineteenth century over 40 percent of all slaves transported across the Atlantic had landed in this single destination.

COUNTERPOINT: The Mapuche of Chile: Native America's Indomitable State

⌄ **FOCUS** How did the Mapuche of Chile manage to resist European conquest?

The climate of southern Chile, a land of rugged coasts and dense forests, is wet and cool. Gently rolling hills are interspersed with picturesque lakes, rivers, and volcanoes. Near the coast is a temperate rain forest. Fish and wildlife are abundant. Towering araucaria pines yield nuts rich in fat and protein, and wild berries abound in the thickets. This is the homeland of the Mapuche (mah-POOH-cheh), or Araucanians (a term derived from the Bay of Arauco), one of the Americas' most resilient native cultures. Across nearly five centuries, they successfully resisted attempted conquests by the Incas, the Spanish, and the Chilean nation-state.

Today, more than five hundred years after Columbus, the Mapuche, half a million strong, are still proclaiming their independence. It was only in the 1880s that Chilean armed forces managed to partially subdue the Mapuche using modern weapons. But what of colonial times, the era of the conquistadors? There was substantial gold in the Mapuche heartland, yet the Spanish failed to conquer them despite knowing this since the time of Pizarro. Why?

The Mapuche of Chile, c. 1550

A Culture of Warfare

Successful Mapuche resistance owed much to cultural patterns. As poets, ex-captives, and Mapuche commentators themselves noted, this was a fiercely independent people raised to fight. The Mapuche reared boys for a life of warfare, apparently before as well as after Spanish arrival in the region. Girls were raised to produce and store the food surpluses needed for the war effort. Despite arriving with horses, steel-edged weapons, and firearms, the Spanish fared little better than the Incas against the native Chileans.

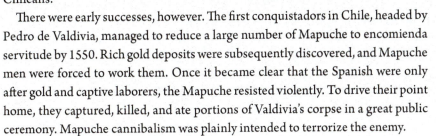

≡ The Mapuche of Chile, c. 1550

There were early successes, however. The first conquistadors in Chile, headed by Pedro de Valdivia, managed to reduce a large number of Mapuche to encomienda servitude by 1550. Rich gold deposits were subsequently discovered, and Mapuche men were forced to work them. Once it became clear that the Spanish were only after gold and captive laborers, the Mapuche resisted violently. To drive their point home, they captured, killed, and ate portions of Valdivia's corpse in a great public ceremony. Mapuche cannibalism was plainly intended to terrorize the enemy.

Uprisings Against the Spanish

What followed was a general uprising lasting from 1553 to 1557. Raids on Spanish settlements continued until 1598, when the Mapuche captured and ate yet another governor, Martín García de Loyola. This incident was followed by a mass uprising in 1599. It was a resounding success. No Spanish town remained south of the Biobío River after 1600, and Spanish attempts to reconquer the Mapuche and occupy their lands failed throughout the colonial period.

≡ **Mapuche Man and Woman**   The Mapuche peoples of Chile proved as resistant to the Spanish as they had been to the Incas. Hostilities began in 1549, and by 1599 Mapuche warriors had destroyed all inland Spanish settlements south of the Biobío River. This image, painted by a Spanish priest who fled the Mapuche in 1600, depicts a Mapuche woman with her spinning equipment and trademark horned hairstyle. To the left is the great Mapuche leader Lautaro, who led the first uprisings. As is evident, the Mapuche adopted Spanish-style helmets and body armor, which they fashioned from the raw hides of introduced cattle. Like the Plains peoples of North America, the Mapuche also adopted the horse to great effect.   (Courtesy of the University of Oviedo Library, Spain.)

What factors besides a culture of warfare allowed the Mapuche to succeed when so many other native American cultures fell to European invaders? As in North America's Great Plains, the introduction of horses by the Spanish enhanced Mapuche warrior mobility. Steel-edged weapons and guns were also captured and adopted. Further, the Mapuche "Columbian Exchange" included adopting Old World foods and animals such as wheat, apples, chickens, and pigs, markedly increasing their subsistence base.

Despite their new mounts and weapons, Chile's native warriors did not alter their style of warfare. Rather than face the better-armed Spanish on the open field, the Mapuche preferred night attacks, long-distance raiding, captive-taking, and other tactics later termed *guerrilla*, or "little war," by the Spanish. Long bamboo lances remained the weapon of choice, and Mapuche men continued to fight barefoot. Alliances were another key to success. The great uprising of 1599 linked culturally related neighbors in a confederacy that the Spanish termed "the Indomitable State."

Mapuche resistance turned southern Chile into a permanent frontier of Spanish South America. The Mapuche, though still frequently at war with their European neighbors, had proved the fact of their independence. Throughout the Spanish world, they became legendary. Only in the late nineteenth century was a tenuous peace established with the Chilean government. Like many treaties between nation-states and indigenous peoples, this peace brought not integration but marginalization and poverty. As a result, the Mapuche are still fighting.

Conclusion

The first wave of European overseas expansion in the Americas was deeply transformative, and would not be repeated in Africa, Asia, or Oceania for several centuries. Hundreds of isolated cultures were brought into contact with one another, often for the first time. European farmers and ranchers migrated to new landscapes, which they and their plants, livestock, and germs quickly transformed. Millions of sub-Saharan Africans, most of them captive laborers, joined a fast-emerging Atlantic, and soon globally integrated, world.

Spearheading this transformation were the uniquely positioned and highly motivated Portuguese, armed and outfitted to undertake risky voyages of reconnaissance and chart new routes to commercial success abroad. Although most interested in material gain, the Portuguese also promoted a militant Christianity while establishing a global network of trading posts. In Brazil they took another tack, establishing hundreds of slave-staffed sugar plantations.

Early modern Spaniards sought the same gold, spices, sugar, and slaves that motivated their Portuguese neighbors, but after encountering the Americas, they turned away from trading posts in favor of territorial conquest. Those they defeated were forced to extract wealth and accept conversion to the Catholic faith. Ironic as it may seem, it was imperial peoples such as the Aztecs and Incas who proved most vulnerable to the Spanish onslaught, and more especially to foreign disease. Mobile, scattered cultures such as the Mapuche of Chile proved far more resistant. Even at the margins, however, violent conquest and the beginnings of the Atlantic slave trade transformed livelihoods for millions. Some individuals swept up in the early phases of colonial encounter and the Columbian Exchange, such as Malintzin, found advantages and even a means to social gain. Countless others found themselves reduced to servitude in an emerging Atlantic world defined by race as much as by wealth or ancestry. This new order forged in the Americas would soon affect much of western Africa.

✴ review

The major global development in this chapter: European expansion across the Atlantic and its profound consequences for societies and cultures worldwide.

Important Events	
1441	First sub-Saharan Africans captured and taken by ship to Portugal
1492	Fall of Granada and expulsion of Jews in Spain; Columbus reaches America
1494	Treaty of Tordesillas divides known world between Portugal and Spain
1498	Vasco da Gama becomes first European to reach India by sea
1500	Portuguese reach Brazil
1519–1521	Spanish conquest of Aztec Mexico
1519–1522	Magellan's ship circumnavigates the globe
1532–1536	Spanish conquest of Inca Peru
1545	Discovery of silver deposits at Potosí
1549	Portuguese establish royal capital of Salvador; first Jesuits arrive in Brazil
1555	French establish colony in Brazil's Guanabara Bay
1564	Discovery of mercury mines in Huancavelica, Peru
1567	Portuguese drive French from Brazil
1570–1571	Inquisition established in Lima and Mexico City
1572	Mita labor draft and mercury amalgamation formalized in Potosí
1592	Potosí reaches peak production
1599	Great Mapuche uprising in Chile

KEY TERMS

Columbian Exchange (p. 582)   feitoria (p. 574)   mita (p. 591)
conquistador (p. 583)   Inquisition (p. 593)   repartimiento (p. 591)
encomienda (p. 580)   mestizo (p. 594)

CHAPTER OVERVIEW QUESTIONS

1. What were the main biological and environmental consequences of European expansion into the Atlantic after 1492?
2. What roles did misunderstanding and chance play in the conquests of the Aztecs and Incas?

3. How did Eurasian demand for silver and sugar help bring about the creation of a linked Atlantic world?

MAKING CONNECTIONS

1. How did Spanish and Portuguese imperial aims differ from those of the Incas and Aztecs (see Chapter 15)?
2. How would you compare the Spanish conquest of Mexico with the Ottoman conquest of Constantinople discussed in Chapter 14?

3. What role did European consumers play in the rise of the American plantation complex?
4. How did global demand for silver affect the lives of ordinary people in the Spanish colonies?

For further research into the topics covered in this chapter, see the Bibliography at the end of the book. For additional primary sources from this period, see *Sources of World in the Making*.

Western Africa in the Era of the Atlantic Slave Trade 1450–1800

≡ **World in the Making** This dramatic brass plaque depicts the oba, or king, of Benin in a royal procession, probably in the sixteenth century. He is seated side-saddle on a seemingly overburdened horse, probably imported and sold to him by Portuguese traders. The larger attendants to each side shade the monarch while the smaller ones hold his staff and other regal paraphernalia. Above, as if walking behind, are two armed guards. (Image copyright © The Metropolitan Museum of Art. Image source: Art Resource, NY)

✴ backstory

Prior to 1450, the lives of most western Africans focused on hoe agriculture, supplementary herding and hunting, and in some places mining and metallurgy. Chiefdoms were the dominant political form throughout the region, from the southern fringes of Morocco to the interior of Angola, although several expansive kingdoms rose and fell along the Niger and Volta Rivers, notably Old Ghana, which thrived from about 300 to 1000, and most recently, as the early modern period dawned, Mali, which flourished from about 1200 to 1400.

Trade in many commodities stretched over vast distances, often monopolized by extended families or ethnic groups. Muslim traders were dominant along the southern margins of the Sahara Desert after about 1000 C.E. Some western African merchants traded slaves across the Sahara to the Mediterranean basin, and others raided vulnerable villages for captives, some of whom were sent as far away as the Red Sea and Indian Ocean. Islam predominated by 1450 along many trade routes into the savanna, or grasslands, but most western Africans retained local religious beliefs.

605

In 1594 a youth was captured in West Central Africa. The Portuguese, who controlled the Atlantic port of Luanda, where the young captive was taken, called this region Angola, a corruption of the Kimbundu term for "blacksmith." The young man was branded, examined like a beast, and sold; he was also, in the words of his captors, "a black." In Luanda, the captive was housed in a stifling barracks with others, whose words, looks, hairstyles, and "country marks," or ritual scars, were unfamiliar.

Eventually, Roman Catholic priests who had just established a mission in Luanda appeared and spoke to the captives in mostly unintelligible words. After several weeks, each captive was sprinkled with water and given a lump of salt on the tongue. Then names were assigned. The young man was now called "Domingo." Once in the Americas, scribes recorded his name as "Domingo Angola, black slave."

Domingo was one of the lucky ones. He survived the barracks and then the grueling two-month voyage, or "middle passage," to Cartagena de Indias, on the Caribbean coast of present-day Colombia. More than one in five died during these ordeals. Once ashore, Domingo Angola was washed, oiled, examined for signs of contagious illness, and fed maize gruel and tough, salted beef.

Domingo was sent to Panama, where he was sold to a merchant traveling to Quito, high in the Andes Mountains. There, in 1595, he was sold again to two merchants heading to the silver-mining town of Potosí, several thousand miles to the south. On the way, Domingo fell ill while waiting for a ship on the Pacific coast and had to be treated. In Potosí at last, he was sold yet again. He had not yet turned nineteen.[1]

Meanwhile, back in Angola, a story arose about men and women such as Domingo who had been sent across the sea. People began to imagine that they were being captured to feed a distant race of cannibals. These "people eaters," red in color, lived somewhere beyond the sunset, on the far side of an enormous lake, and there they butchered ordinary Angolans. Human blood was their wine, brains their cheese, and roasted and ground long-bones their gunpowder. The red people—the sunburned Portuguese—were devotees of Mwene Puto, God of the Dead. How else to explain the massive, ceaseless traffic in souls, what Angolans called the "way of death"?[2]

African diaspora
The global dispersal, mostly through the Atlantic slave trade, of African peoples.

Domingo's long journey from Africa to South America was not unusual, and in fact he would have met many other Angolans arriving in Potosí via Buenos Aires. Victims of the Atlantic slave trade were constantly on the move, and slave mobility diminished only with the rise of plantation agriculture in the seventeenth and eighteenth centuries. Shuffling of ethnic groups was typical of the Atlantic slave trade and what historians call the **African diaspora**, or "great scattering" of sub-Saharan

African peoples. As we will see in the next chapter, millions of slaves were sent across the Indian Ocean from East Africa as well. This chapter focuses on western or "Atlantic" Africa, a vast portion of the continent that geographers normally split into two parts: West and West Central Africa (see Map 17.1, page 608).

Although slavery and slave trading were practiced in western Africa prior to the arrival of Europeans, both institutions changed dramatically as a result of the surge in European demand for African slaves coinciding with colonization of the Americas. New patterns of behavior emerged. African warriors and mercenaries focused more on kidnapping their neighbors in order to trade them to foreign slavers for weapons, stimulants, and luxury goods; coastal farmers abandoned lands vulnerable to raiders; formerly protective customs were called into question; and Islam and Christianity made new inroads. We now know that even inland cultures such as the Batwa, or Pygmies, of the Congo rainforest were affected by the slave trade. They were driven deeper into the forest as other internal migrants, forced to move by slavers, expanded their farms and pasturelands. There, as we will see in the Counterpoint to this chapter, the Pygmies forged a lifestyle far different from that of their settled neighbors.

OVERVIEW QUESTIONS

The major global development in this chapter: The rise of the Atlantic slave trade and its impact on early modern African peoples and cultures.

As you read, consider:

1. How did ecological diversity in western Africa relate to cultural developments?

2. What tied western Africa to other parts of the world prior to the arrival of Europeans along Atlantic shores?

3. How did the Atlantic slave trade arise, and how was it sustained?

Many Western Africas

⬇ **FOCUS** What range of livelihoods, cultural practices, and political arrangements typified western Africa in early modern times?

The African continent was home to an estimated one hundred million people at the time of Columbus's 1492 voyage. About fifty million people inhabited West

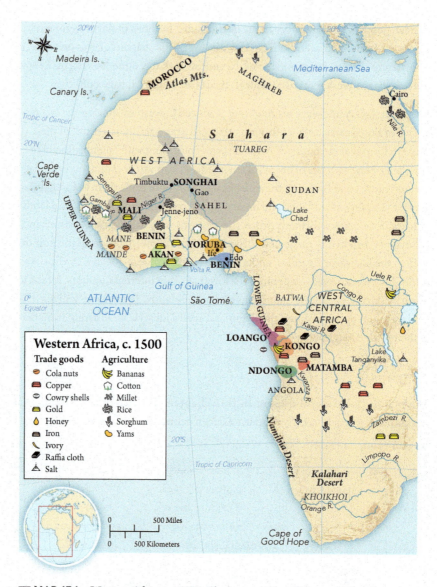

≡ **MAP 17.1   Western Africa, c. 1500** The huge regions of West and West Central Africa were of key importance to early modern global history as sources of both luxury commodities and enslaved immigrants. But western Africa was also marked by substantial internal dynamism. The Songhai Empire on the middle Niger rose to prominence about the time of Columbus. Large kingdoms and city-states also flourished on the Volta and lower Niger Rivers and near the mouth of the Congo (Zaire). Rainforests and deserts were home to gatherer-hunters such as the Batwa (Pygmies) and Khoikhoi.

and West Central Africa, what we refer to here as "western Africa." Western Africa thus had a population comparable to that of all the Americas at that time. It contained several dozen tributary states, along with numerous permanent agricultural and mobile, warrior-headed chiefdoms. There were also pastoral or herding groups, trading peoples, fishing folk, and bands of desert and rainforest gatherer-hunters. The array of livelihoods was wide, yet most western Africans lived as hoe agriculturalists, primarily cultivators of rice, sorghum, millet, and cotton (see Map 17.1).

Religious ideas and practices varied, but most Africans south of the Sahara placed great emphasis on fertility. Fertility rituals were integral to everyday life; some entailed animal sacrifice, and others, rarely, human sacrifice. Also as in many other early modern societies, discord, illness, and material hardship were often thought to be the products of witchcraft. Islam, introduced by long-distance traders and warriors after the seventh century C.E., became dominant in the dry *sahel* (from the Arabic for "shore") and savanna, or grassland, regions just south of the Sahara, and along the rim of the Indian Ocean. Christian and Jewish communities were limited to tiny pockets in the northeastern Horn and along the Maghreb, or Mediterranean coast. Over two thousand languages were spoken on the continent, most of them derived from four roots. All told, Africa's cultural and linguistic diversity easily exceeded that of Europe in the era of Columbus.

Even where Islam predominated, local notions of the spirit world survived. Most western Africans believed in a creator deity, and everyday ritual tended to emphasize communication with ancestor spirits, who helped placate other forces. Animal and plant spirits were considered especially potent.

Places were also sacred. Rather like Andean *wakas*, western African **génies** (JEHN-ees) could be features in the landscape: boulders, springs, rivers, lakes, and groves. Trees were revered among peoples living along the southern margins of the savanna, and villagers built alongside patches of old-growth forest. Through periodic animal sacrifice, western Africans sought the patronage of tree spirits, since they were most rooted in the land.

Western Africa fell entirely within the lowland tropics and was thus subject to many endemic diseases and pests. The deadly falciparum variety of malaria and other serious mosquito-borne fevers attacked humans in the hot lowlands, and the tsetse fly, carrier of the fatal trypanosomiasis virus, limited livestock grazing and horse breeding. Droughts could be severe and prolonged in some regions, spurring migration and warfare. Western Africans nevertheless adapted to these and other environmental challenges, in the case of malaria developing at least some immunity against the disease.

génie A sacred site or feature in the West African landscape.

husbandry Human intervention in the breeding of animals.

paramount chief A chief who presided over several headmen and controlled a large area.

In the arid north, beasts of burden included camels, donkeys, and horses. Cattle were also kept in the interior highlands and far south, where they were safe from tsetse flies. Arabian warhorses were greatly prized, and were traded among kingdoms and chiefdoms along the southern margins of the Sahara. They were most valued where fly-borne disease made breeding impossible. Other domestic animals included goats, swine, guinea fowl, sheep, and dogs. In general, animal **husbandry**, as in greater Eurasia, was far more developed in western Africa than in the Americas. There were also more large wild mammals in sub-Saharan Africa than in any other part of the world, and these featured prominently in regional cosmologies.

Mining and metalsmithing technologies were also highly developed. Throughout West and West Central Africa, copper-based metallurgy had grown complex by 1500. Goldsmithing was also advanced, though less widespread. This was in part because African gold was being increasingly drawn away by trade to the Mediterranean Sea and Indian Ocean. To a large extent, western Eurasia's "bullion famine" spurred European expansion into Africa.

Africans had long been great producers and consumers of iron. Whether in Mali or Angola, African ironmongers were not simply artisans but also shaman-like figures and even **paramount chiefs**—heads of village clans. African metalsmiths produced substantial tools, ornaments, and works of art. They made the iron hoes most people tended crops with, and some items were traded in bulk over vast distances.

Africa's internal trade mostly redistributed basic commodities. Those who mined or collected salt, for example, usually bartered it for other necessities such as cloth. Saharan salt was an essential dietary supplement throughout the vast West African interior. Similarly, manufactured goods such as agricultural tools were traded for food, textiles, and livestock, but bits of gold, copper, and iron also served as currency. Another key trade good was the cola nut, the sharing of which cemented social relations in much of West Africa.

☰ **A Young Woman from West Africa** Since at least medieval times, West African women surprised outside visitors with their independence, visibility, and political influence, in both Islamic and non-Islamic societies. This drawing by an English artist during a slave-trading voyage to West Africa around 1775 depicts a young woman with elaborately braided hair, pearl earrings, and a choker strung with coral or large stones. It is possible that she is a member of an elite family given these proudly displayed ornaments.

Copper and bronze bracelets were prized by some of western Africa's coastal peoples, and eventually they were standardized into currency called *manillas* (mah-KNEE-lahs). In some areas seashells such as the cowry functioned in the same way. The desire for cotton textiles from India fueled Africa's west coast demand for shell and copper-bronze currency, which in time would also contribute to the expansion of the Atlantic slave trade. Africa's east coast, meanwhile, remained integrated into the vast and mostly separate Indian Ocean trade circuit, as we will see in Chapter 18.

African societies linked by trade were sometimes also bound by politics. A shared desire to both expand household units and improve security led many Africans to form confederations and conglomerates. Like the confederacies of eastern North America (discussed in Chapter 15), some of these alliances had a religious core, but just as often they were spurred by ecological stresses such as droughts. Political flux caused ethnic and other identity markers to blend and blur as groups merged and adopted each other's languages, cosmologies, farming techniques, and modes of dress and adornment.

Nevertheless, as in the Americas, intergroup conflict was common in western Africa prior to the arrival of Europeans. Expansionist, tributary empires such as Mali and Songhai made lifelong enemies. The motives of African warfare varied, usually centering on the control of resources, and especially people, sometimes as slaves put to work on agricultural estates. European trading and political meddling on Africa's Atlantic coast would spawn or exacerbate conflicts that would reverberate deep within the continent. Full-blown imperialism would come much later, with the development of new technologies and antimalarial drugs, but it would benefit in part from this earlier political disruption.

Landlords and Strangers: Peoples and States in West Africa

⬇️ **FOCUS** What economic, social, and political patterns characterized early modern West Africa?

West Africans in the period following 700 C.E. faced radical new developments. Two catalysts for change were the introduction and spread of Islam after the eighth century and a long dry period lasting from roughly 1100 to 1500 C.E. At least one historian has characterized human relations in this era in terms of "landlords" and "strangers," a reference to the tendency toward small agricultural communities offering hospitality to travelers and craft specialists.[3] In return, these "strangers"—traders, blacksmiths, tanners, bards, and clerics—offered goods and services. The model "landlord" was an esteemed personage capable of ensuring the security and prosperity of numerous dependents and affiliates, usually conceived of as members of an extended family.

Empire Builders and Traders

The late medieval dry period also witnessed the rise of mounted warriors. On the banks of the middle and upper Niger River rose the kingdoms of Mali and Songhai, both linked to the Mediterranean world via the caravan terminus of Timbuktu (see again Map 17.1). Both empires were headed by devout, locally born Muslim rulers. One, Mansa Musa (*mansa* meaning "conqueror") of Mali, made the pilgrimage to Mecca in 1325. Musa spent so much gold during a stop in Cairo that his visit became legend.

It was gold that put sub-Saharan Africa on the minds—and maps—of European and Middle Eastern traders and monarchs. West African mines were worked by farming peoples who paid tribute in gold dust unearthed in the fallow (inactive) season (see Lives and Livelihoods: West Africa's Gold Miners). In general, land was a less-prized commodity than labor in West Africa. Prestige derived not from ownership of farmland or mines but from control over productive people, some of whom were enslaved. Captive-taking was thus integral to warfare. Like the seasonal production of gold, the seasonal production of slaves would vastly expand once Europeans arrived on Atlantic shores.

With the exception, as we will see, of the Songhai Empire, West African politics in this period was mostly confederated. Dozens of paramount chiefs or regional kings relied on tributaries and enslaved laborers for their power, wealth, and sustenance. Most common was the rise of charismatic and aggressive rulers, with few bureaucrats and judges. Rulers typically extended their authority by offering to protect agricultural groups from raiders. Some coastal rice growers in Upper Guinea drifted in and out of regional alliances, depending on political and environmental conditions. Alliances did not always spare them from disaster. Still, as actors in the Columbian Exchange, enslaved rice farmers from this region transferred techniques and perhaps grains to the plantations of North and South America.

From Western Sudan to Lower Guinea, town-sized units predominated, many of them walled. Archaeologists are still discovering traces of these enclosures, some of which housed thousands of inhabitants. As in medieval Europe, even when they shared a language, walled cities in neighboring territories could be fiercely competitive.

Dating to the first centuries C.E., West Africa was also home to sizable kingdoms. Old Ghana flourished from about 300 to 1000 C.E., followed by Mali, which thrived from about 1200 to 1400. From about the time of Columbus, the Songhai Empire, centered at Gao, rose to prominence under Sunni Ali (r. 1464–1492). Similar to the mansas of Mali, Sunni Ali was a conqueror, employing mounted lancers and squads of boatmen to great effect. Sunni Ali's successor, Muhammad Touré, extended Songhai's rule even farther. At his zenith Touré, who took the title *askiya* (AH-skee-yah), or hereditary lord, and later *caliph*, or supreme lord, controlled a huge portion of West Africa (see again Map 17.1).

The wealth and power of Songhai derived from the merchant crossroads cities of the middle Niger: Jenne, Gao, and Timbuktu. Here gold, salt, and forest products from the south such as cola nuts and raffia palm fiber were exchanged, along with other commodities. Slaves, many of them taken in Songhai's wars of expansion, were also traded to distant buyers. Stately Timbuktu, meanwhile, retained its reputation as a major market for books and a center of Islamic teachings.

Touré's successors were less aggressive than he, and as Songhai's power waned in the sixteenth century, the empire fell victim to mounted raiders from distant Morocco. With alarming audacity, and greatly aided by their state-of-the-art firearms and swift mounts, the Moroccans (among them hundreds of exiled Spanish Muslims, or Moriscos) captured the cities of Gao and Timbuktu in 1591. As their victory texts attest, these conquistadors took home stunning quantities of gold and a number of slaves. Yet unlike their Spanish and Portuguese contemporaries in the Americas, they failed to hold on to their conquest. The mighty Sahara proved a more formidable barrier than the Atlantic Ocean. After the fall of Songhai there emerged a dynasty of Moroccan princes, the Sa'dis, who were in turn crushed by new, local waves of warfare in the late seventeenth and early eighteenth centuries. Most fell victim to the Sahara's best-known nomads, the Tuareg (TWAH-regh).

Sculptors and Priest-Kings

Farther south, near the mouth of the Niger River, was the rainforest kingdom of Benin, with its capital at Edo. Under King Ewuare (EH-woo-AH-reh) (r. c. 1450–1480), Benin reached the height of its power in the mid-fifteenth century, subjecting many towns and chiefdoms to tributary status. Benin grew wealthy in part by exporting cloth made by women in tributary villages. This trade expanded with the arrival of Portuguese coastal traders around 1500, revitalizing Benin's power. Some of the most accomplished sculptors in African history worked under King Ewuare and his successors, producing cast brass portraits of Benin royalty, prominent warriors, and even newly arrived Europeans. This was but one of the many

LIVES AND LIVELIHOODS

West Africa's Gold Miners

≡ **Implements of the Gold Trade** West Africa was long legendary for its gold, which was first traded across the Sahara and later to Europeans arriving along the Atlantic coast. In the Akan region of present-day Ghana, gold dust circulated as currency, with portions measured by merchants in a hanging balance against tiny, fancifully designed brass weights. Gold dust was stored in brass boxes and dished out with decorated brass spoons. Smaller exchanges employed cowry shells, brought to Atlantic Africa from the Maldive Islands in the Indian Ocean.

and around streams flowing down from eroded mountain ranges. Sources describing West African gold mining in early modern times are rare, but anecdotal descriptions combined with somewhat later eyewitness accounts suggest that women did many of the most strenuous tasks. The Scottish traveler Mungo Park described non-enslaved West African women miners among the Mande of the upper Niger in the 1790s as follows:

About the beginning of December, when the harvest is over, and the streams and torrents have greatly sub-

Until 1650, gold was a more valuable West African export than slaves, and it remained highly significant for many years afterward. The mines and their workers, some of whom were enslaved, remained in the control of local kings whose agents then traded gold to long-distance merchants with ties to Europeans on the coast. Gold diggings were concentrated along the upper reaches of the Senegal, Niger, and Volta Rivers, mostly in

sided, the Mansa, or chief of the town, appoints a day to begin *sanoo koo*, "gold washing"; and the women are sure to have themselves in readiness by the time appointed.... On the morning of their departure, a bullock is killed for the first day's entertainment, and a number of prayers and charms are used to ensure success; for a failure on that day is thought a bad omen.... The washing of the sands of the streams is by far the easiest way of obtaining the gold dust, but in most places the sands have been so narrowly searched before that unless the stream takes some new course, the gold is found but in small quantities. While some of the party are busied in washing the sands, others employ themselves farther up the torrent, where the rapidity of the stream has carried away all the clay, sand, etc., and left nothing but small pebbles. The search among these is a very troublesome task. I have seen women who have had the skin worn off the tops of their fingers in this employment. Sometimes, however, they are rewarded by finding pieces [nuggets] of gold, which they call *sanoo birro*, "gold stones," that amply repay them for their trouble. A woman and her daughter, inhabitants of Kamalia, found in one day two pieces of this kind.

Mande men, according to Park, participated in excavating deep pits in gold-bearing hills "in the height of the dry season," producing clay and other sediments "for the women to wash; for though the pit is dug by the men, the gold is always washed by the women, who are accustomed from their infancy to a similar operation, in separating the husks of corn from the meal." To be efficient, panning required intense concentration and careful eye-hand coordination, and use of several pans to collect concentrates. This skill was appreciated, as Park explains: "Some women, by long practice, become so well acquainted with the nature of the sand, and the mode of washing it, that they will collect gold where others cannot find a single particle." Gold dust was then stored in quills (the hollow shafts of bird feathers) plugged with cotton, says Park, "and the washers are fond of displaying a number of these quills in their hair."

Source: Mungo Park, *Travels in the Interior Districts of Africa,* ed. Kate Ferguson Masters (Durham, NC: Duke University Press, 2000), 264–267.

Questions to Consider

1. Why was West African gold mining seasonal?

2. How were tasks divided between men and women, and why?

3. Was gold washing demeaning labor, or could it be a source of pride?

For Further Information:

Philip D. Curtin, *Economic Change in Precolonial Africa: Senegambia in the Era of the Slave Trade.* Madison: University of Wisconsin Press, 1975.

SEEING THE PAST

Art of the Slave Trade: A Benin Bronze Plaque

Copper and bronze metallurgy were advanced arts in western Africa long before the arrival of Europeans. Metal sculpture in the form of lifelike busts, historical plaques, and complex representations of deities was most developed in western Nigeria and the kingdom of Benin. Realistic representations of elite men and women appear to have served a commemorative function, as did relief-sculpted plaques depicting kings, chiefs, and warlords in full regalia. Beginning in the 1500s, sculptors in Benin and neighboring lands began to depict Portuguese slave traders and missionaries, bearded men with helmets, heavy robes, and trade goods, including primitive muskets. This plaque depicts Portuguese slavers with a cargo of *manillas*, the bronze bracelets that served as currency in the slave trade until the mid-nineteenth century.

Examining the Evidence

1. How were Portuguese newcomers incorporated into this traditional Benin art form?

2. How might this bronze representation of foreigners and their trade goods been a commentary on the slave trade?

Plaque of Portuguese Traders with Manillas
(Image copyright © The Metropolitan Museum of Art. Image source: Art Resource, NY)

livelihoods afforded by urban living (see Seeing the Past: Art of the Slave Trade: A Benin Bronze Plaque).

Just west of Benin were city-states ruled by ethnic Yoruba clans. At their core was the city of Ife (EE-feh), founded in around 1000 c.e. Ife metalsmiths and sculptors were as accomplished as those of Benin, and their large cast works have been hailed as inimitable. Yoruba political leaders, called *obas*, performed a mix of political and religious duties. Most of these priest-kings were men, but a significant number were women. One of the oba's main functions was to negotiate with ancestor deities thought to govern everyday life. Some slaves taken from this region to the Americas appear to have masked ancestor worship behind the Roman Catholic cult of saints.

Urban life also matured along the banks of the lower Volta River, in what is today Ghana. Here Akan peoples had formed city-states, mostly by controlling regional gold mines and trading networks. The Akan initially focused on transporting gold and cola nuts to the drier north, where these commodities found a ready market among the imperial societies of the middle Niger. With the arrival of Europeans on the Atlantic coast in the late fifteenth century, however, many Akan traders turned toward the south. Throughout early modern times, women held great power in Akan polities, and matrilineal inheritance was standard. Even in patrilineal empires such as Mali and Songhai, women could wield considerable power, especially in matters of succession.

Land of the Blacksmith Kings: West Central Africa

⬂ **FOCUS** What economic, social, and political patterns characterized early modern West Central Africa?

Human interaction in West Central Africa, called by some historians "land of the blacksmith kings," was in part defined by control of copper and iron deposits. As in West Africa, however, the vast majority of people practiced subsistence agriculture, limited to hoe tilling because the tsetse fly eliminated livestock capable of pulling plows. For this reason, few people other than gatherer-hunters such as the Pygmies inhabited Africa's great equatorial forest. Most preferred to farm the savanna and fish along the Atlantic coast and major riverbanks.

The Congo (Zaire) River basin, second only to the Amazon in terms of forest cover, was of central importance to human history in West Central Africa. Although patterns of belief and material culture varied, most people spoke derivations of Western Bantu. Islam was known in some areas but remained marginal in influence. Most inhabitants of West Central Africa lived in matrilineal or patrilineal kin-based villages, a small minority of them under paramount chiefs. In all, the region was marked by a cultural coherence similar to that of Mesoamerica (discussed in Chapter 15).

oba A priest-king or queen of the Yoruba culture (modern southern Nigeria).

manikongo A "blacksmith" king of Kongo.

Farmers and Traders

The hoe-agriculturalists who formed the vast majority of West Central Africans grew millet and sorghum, complemented by yams and bananas in certain areas. Bananas, a crop introduced to the region some time before 1000 C.E., enabled farmers to exploit the forest's edge more effectively and devote more energy to textile making and other activities. Some forested areas were too wet for staple crops but still offered game, medicinal plants, and other products. Pygmy forest dwellers, for example, traded honey, ivory, and wild animal skins to farming neighbors for iron points and food items. Tsetse flies and other pests limited the development of animal husbandry in West Central Africa, except in the drier south.

Wherever they lived, West Central Africans, like Europeans and Asians, embraced native American crops in the centuries following Columbus's voyages. Maize became a staple throughout Central Africa, along with cassava (manioc), peanuts, chili peppers, beans, squash, and tobacco. Peanuts, probably introduced by the Portuguese from Brazil soon after 1500, were locally called *nguba* (NGOO-bah), from which the American term "goober peas" derives.

As the introduction of American crops demonstrates, West Central Africa may have had less direct ties to global trade than coastal West Africa, but it was part of the system. Likewise, Africa's internal trade networks were vital to West Central African life. As in West Africa, salt was traded along with foods, textiles, metal goods, and other items. Raffia palm fiber was used to manufacture cloth, and coastal lagoons were exploited for cowry shells for trade.

Throughout the region political power became increasingly associated with control of trade goods and trade routes. For example, around 1300 two kingdoms arose above and below the Malebo Pool alongside the Congo River. This was the first major portage site for all traders moving between the coast and interior. The kings of Loango, living above the falls but also controlling access to the Atlantic coast, taxed trade and also drew legitimacy from their role as caretakers of an ancient religious shrine. Below the falls and to the south, in Kongo—a kingdom misnamed by the Portuguese after the title of its warlords, the **manikongos** (mah-nee-CONE-goes)—leaders came to power in part by monopolizing copper deposits and also access to cowry shells, the region's main currency.

Smiths and Kings

As in West Africa, power also derived from the mystique surrounding metallurgy. The introduction of ironworking to the

Kongo Territory, c. 1500

0   180 Miles

0   180 Kilometers

LOANGO

Loango

Malebo Pool

Congo R.

Kasai R.

Kwango R.

Kwanza R.

Mpinda 1501

KONGO

Mbanza (São Salvador)

Luanda

MATAMBA

NDONGO

Kwanza R.

■ Portuguese fort, with date of occupation

≡ **Kongo Territory, c. 1500**

region sometime early in the Common Era had made the majority of farmers dependent on smiths for hoes, blades, and other implements. Making the most of this reliance, some blacksmiths became kings. By 1500, Kongo commanded an area stretching inland from the right bank of the Congo River south and east some 185 miles, absorbing numerous villages, slaves, and tributaries along the way. A few small kingdoms existed to the north and east, often with copper deposits serving as their lifeblood. These kingdoms eventually challenged Kongo directly, in part because they were subjected to Kongo slave-raiding. In what is today Angola, just north of the Kwanza River, there emerged in the sixteenth century the Ndongo (NDOAN-go) kingdom. Just northeast of Ndongo lay the Matamba kingdom. Initially tributaries of Kongo, the people of Matamba shifted their relations in favor of Ndongo as Portuguese influence there grew in the sixteenth century. By 1600, the Portuguese held forts deep in Ndongo country, using them to procure slaves from farther inland.

Less is known about the peoples of the more isolated and forested middle Congo basin, but archaeologists have recently shown that large chiefdoms were being consolidated there as early as the thir-

☰ Mbundu Blacksmiths This late-seventeenth-century watercolor depicts a Mbundu blacksmith and assistant at work. As the assistant operates the typical African bellows with rods attached to airbags, the master smith hammers a crescent-shaped iron blade on an anvil. Other blades, including what may be a sickle or hoe, lie on the ground to the left of the anvil. In the background a curious audience looks on.

teenth century, and they lasted into early modern times. Here, innovations in sword manufacture seem to have enabled some chiefs to monopolize trade along Congo River tributaries. Like elites everywhere, these chiefs considered themselves the spiritual kin of predatory lords of the animal kingdom, in this case the leopard and eagle.

We know less about women's livelihoods than men's, but it appears that in early modern West Central Africa, as in many preindustrial societies, women tended to work mostly at domestic tasks such as child rearing, food preparation, and other aspects of household management. Men were frequently engaged in hunting, herding, trade, and warfare, so women's responsibilities often extended to agriculture. In many places, women planted yams in hard soils by slicing through the crust with machetes made by village men. Almost everywhere, women tended the food crops and men cleared forest.

Strangers in Ships: Gold, Slavery, and the Portuguese

FOCUS How did the early Portuguese slave trade in western Africa function?

As we saw in Chapter 16, the Portuguese arrived in western Africa soon after 1400 in search of gold and a sea route to India. For over a century they were the only significant European presence in the region. During that time, Portuguese explorers, merchants, missionaries, and even criminal castaways established *feitorias*, or fortified trading posts, and offshore island settlements. There were no great marches to the interior, no conquests of existing empires. Instead, the Portuguese focused on extracting Africa's famed wealth in gold, ivory, and slaves through intermediaries. In a pattern repeated in Asia, the Portuguese dominated maritime trade.

From Voyages of Reconnaissance to Trading Forts 1415–1650

On the Gambia River the Portuguese sought the gold of Mali, at this time an empire in decline but still powerful in the interior (see again Map 17.1). The warring states of the region were happy to trade gold for horses, and chronic conflicts yielded a surplus of captives. With explicit backing from the pope, Portuguese merchants readily accepted African slaves as payment. Once in Portuguese hands, healthy young males were reduced to an accounting unit, the **peça** (PEH-sah), literally "piece." Women, children, the disabled, and the elderly were discounted in terms of fractions of a peça.

African enslavement of fellow Africans was widespread before the arrival of Europeans, and the daily experience of slavery was no doubt unpleasant. What differed with the arrival of the Portuguese in the fifteenth century was a new insistence on innate African inferiority—in a word, racism—and with it a closing of traditional avenues of reentry into free society, if not for oneself, then for one's children, such as faithful service, or in Islamic societies, religious conversion. The Portuguese followed the pope's decree that enslaved sub-Saharan Africans be converted to Catholicism, but they also adopted an unstated policy that regarded black Africans as "slaves by nature." To sidestep the paradox of African spiritual equality and alleged "beastly" inferiority, the Portuguese claimed that they sold only captives taken in "just war." Many such slaves were sold, like young Domingo Angola, to the Spanish, who took the Portuguese sellers at their word (see Reading the Past: Alonso de Sandoval, "General Points Relating to Slavery").

peça Portuguese for "piece," used to describe enslaved Africans as units of labor.

Yet African slaves were in less demand than gold prior to American colonization. Word of goldfields in the African interior encouraged the Portuguese to continue their dogged search for the yellow metal. By 1471 caravels reached West Africa's so-called Gold Coast, and in 1482 the Portuguese established a feitoria in present-day Ghana. São Jorge da Mina, which served for over a century as Portugal's major West African gold and slaving fort.

After 1500, as slave markets in Spanish America and Brazil emerged, new trading posts were established all along the West African coast. It so happened that invasions of Mande and Mane (MAH-nay) peoples into modern Guinea, Liberia, Sierra Leone, and Ivory Coast in the fifteenth and sixteenth centuries produced yet more captives through the seventeenth century (see Map 17.2). The Portuguese continued to trade copper, iron, textiles, horses, and occasionally guns for gold, ivory, and a local spice called malaguetta pepper, but by the early 1500s the shift toward slave trading was evident.

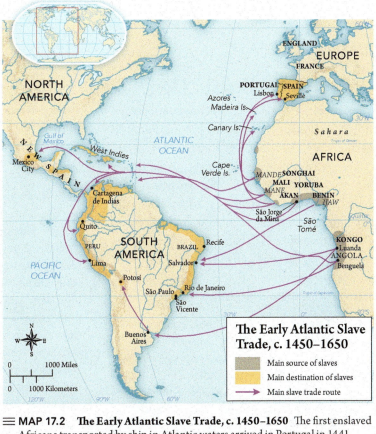

≡ MAP 17.2 The Early Atlantic Slave Trade, c. 1450–1650 The first enslaved Africans transported by ship in Atlantic waters arrived in Portugal in 1441. The Portuguese won a monopoly on African coastal trade from the pope, and until 1500, they shipped most enslaved African captives to the eastern Atlantic islands, where plantations were booming by the 1450s. Soon after 1500, Portuguese slave traders took captives first to the Spanish Caribbean (West Indies), then to the mainland colonies of New Spain and Peru. Claimed by the Portuguese in 1500, Brazil was initially a minor destination for enslaved Africans, but this changed by about 1570, when the colony's sugar production ballooned. Another early Atlantic route took slaves south to Buenos Aires, where they were marched overland to the rich city of Potosí.

The Portuguese were both extractors and transporters of wealth. They ferried luxury goods such as cola nuts and textiles, as well as slaves, between existing African trade zones. As we will see, a similar pattern developed in Asia. Virtually everywhere the Portuguese anchored their stout vessels, Africans found that they benefited as much from access to the foreigners' shipping, which was relatively secure and efficient, as from their goods. Many competing coastal lords

READING THE PAST

Alonso de Sandoval, "General Points Relating to Slavery"

Alonso de Sandoval (1577–c.1650) was a Jesuit priest born in Seville, Spain, and raised in Lima, Peru. He spent most of his adult life administering sacraments to enslaved Africans arriving at the Caribbean port city of Cartagena de Indias, in present-day Colombia. In 1627 he published a book titled *On Restoring Ethiopian Salvation*. In it, he focused on cultural aspects of sub-Saharan African societies as he understood them, all with the aim of preaching to Africans more effectively, but he also discussed the Atlantic slave trade and its justifications:

> The debate among scholars on how to justify the arduous and difficult business of slavery has perplexed me for a long time. I could have given up on explaining it and just ignored it in this book. However, I am determined to discuss it, although I will leave the final justification of slavery to legal

and ecclesiastical authorities. . . . I will only mention here what I have learned after many years of working in this ministry. The readers can formulate their own ideas on the justice of this issue. . . .

A short story helps me explain how to morally justify black slavery. I was once consulted by a captain who owned slave ships that had made many voyages to these places. He had enriched himself through the slave trade, and his conscience was burdened with concern over how these slaves had fallen into his hands. His concern is not surprising, because he also told me that one of their kings imprisoned anyone who angered him in order to sell them as slaves to the Spaniards. So in this region, people are enslaved if they anger the king. . . .

There is a more standard way in which slaves are traded and later shipped in fleets of ships to the Indies. Near Luanda are some black merchants called

made the most of these new trade ties, often to the detriment of more isolated and vulnerable neighbors.

At times commerce with the Portuguese upended a region's balance of power, touching off a series of interior conflicts. Some such conflicts were ignited by Portuguese convicts who established marriage alliances with local chiefdoms. As seen in Chapter 16 in the case of Brazil, this was the Portuguese plan, to drop expendable subjects like seeds along the world's coasts. Some took root, learned local languages, and built trading posts. In several West African coastal enclaves, mulatto or "Eurafrican" communities developed. These mixed communities were nominally Catholic, but culturally blended.

After 1510, the Portuguese moved eastward. Here among the Niger delta's tidal flats and mangroves, Ijaw (EE-jaw) boatmen were willing to trade an adult male captive for fewer than a dozen copper manillas. Rates of exchange soon moderated, *pombeiros* worth a thousand pesos. They travel inland eighty leagues [c. 250 miles], bringing porters with them to carry trade goods. They meet in great markets where merchants gather together to sell slaves. These merchants travel 200 or 300 leagues [c. 650–1000 miles] to sell blacks from many different kingdoms to various merchants or *pombeiros*. The *pombeiros* buy the slaves and transport them to the coast. They must report to their masters how many died on the road. They do this by bringing back the hands of the dead, a stinking, horrific sight. . . .

I have spent a great deal of time discussing this subject because slaves are captured in many different ways, and this disturbs the slave traders' consciences. One slave trader freely told me that he felt guilty about how the slaves he had bought in Guinea had come to be enslaved. Another slave trader, who had bought 300 slaves on foot, expressed the same concerns, adding that half the wars fought between blacks would not take place if the Spanish [or more likely, Portuguese] did not go there to buy slaves. . . . The evidence, along with the moral justifications argued by scholars, is the best we can do to carefully address this irredeemable situation and the very difficult business of the slave trade.

Source: Alonso de Sandoval, *Treatise on Slavery,* ed. and trans. Nicole Von Germeten (Indianapolis: Hackett, 2008), 50–55.

Examining the Evidence

1. Who was Alonso de Sandoval, and why did he write this passage?

2. How does Sandoval try to justify African enslavement?

3. Are Africans themselves involved in this discussion?

but overall, Portuguese demand for slaves was met by other captive-producing zones. What historians call the "Nigerian diaspora" mostly developed later in this region, in the seventeenth and eighteenth centuries. By then rival Dutch and English slavers had established their own posts (see Map 17.4, page 628). After 1650 this region was known simply as the Slave Coast.

Portuguese Strategy in the Kingdom of Kongo

Portuguese interest in Atlantic Africa shifted southeastward after 1500, based in part on alliances with the kingdom of Kongo. Within West Central Africa, cycles of trade, war, and drought influenced relationships with outsiders. Once again, local nobles forced the Portuguese to follow local rules. Still, whereas Portuguese slavers were to be largely displaced by northern Europeans in West Africa by 1650, in the southern portion of the continent they held on. As a result, the fortunes of

Kongo and Angola became ever more intimately entwined with those of Brazil, on the other side of the Atlantic.

Portuguese religious initiatives in Africa had long been split between attacks on Muslim kingdoms in the far north, epitomized by the 1415 conquest of Ceuta in Morocco (see Chapter 16), and more peaceful, although scattered and inconsistent, missionary efforts in the south. Portuguese missionaries rarely survived in the tropical interior, where malaria and other diseases took a heavy toll. Thus scores of Franciscans, Jesuits, and others died denouncing the persistent **fetishism** (roughly, "idolatry") of their local hosts. The obvious solution was to train African priests, and for a time this option was sponsored by the Portuguese royal family.

In the early sixteenth century, African priests were trained in Lisbon, Coimbra, and even in Rome. African seminaries also were established in the Cape Verde Islands and on the island of São Tomé. Despite promising beginnings, however, sharp opposition came from an increasingly racist Portuguese clergy. Emerging colonial racial hierarchies trumped the universal ideal of spiritual equality. An African clergy could also subvert the slave trade and other such commercial projects. Already in decline before 1600, the African seminaries languished in the seventeenth and early eighteenth centuries. Only with the Enlightenment-inspired reforms of the later eighteenth century (discussed in Chapter 22) were African novices again encouraged to become priests beyond the parish level.

This did not mean that Christianity had no impact on early modern Atlantic Africa. Aside from the offshore islands, in Kongo and Angola, Christianity played a critical historical role. Beginning in the 1480s, the Portuguese applied their usual blend of trade, military alliances, and religious proselytizing to carve out a niche in West Central Africa. By 1491 they had converted much of the Kongo aristocracy to Roman Catholicism. Key among the converts was the paramount chief's son, Nzinga Mbemba, who later ruled as Afonso I (r. 1506–1543).

Afonso's conversion was apparently genuine. He learned to read, studied theology, and renamed Mbanza, the capital city, São Salvador ("Holy Savior"). One of his sons became a priest in Lisbon and returned to Kongo following consecration in Rome. He was one of the earliest exemplars of western African clergy.

Ultimately, however, Christianity, like copper, tended to be monopolized by Kongo's elites; the peasant and craft worker majority was virtually ignored. Most Kongolese commoners recognized deities called **kitomi** (key-TOE-mee), each looked after by a local (non-Catholic) priest. Meanwhile, Portuguese military aid buttressed Kongo politically while fueling the slave trade.

Here, as elsewhere in Africa, the slave trade, though it offered considerable gains, also exacerbated existing dangers and conflicts and created new ones. King Afonso

fetishism The derogatory term used by Europeans to describe western African use of religious objects.

kitomi Deities attended by Kongo priests prior to the arrival of Christian Europeans.

wrote to the king of Portugal in 1526, complaining that "every day the merchants carry away our people, sons of our soil and sons of our nobles and vassals, and our relatives, whom thieves and people of bad conscience kidnap and sell to obtain the coveted things and trade goods of that [Portuguese] Kingdom."[4] Even in its earliest days, the slave trade in West Central Africa was taking on a life of its own.

pombeiro A slave-trade middleman in the West Central African interior.

As a result of Kongo's slaving-based alliance with the Portuguese, King Afonso's successors faced growing opposition. The kingdom of Kongo finally collapsed in 1569. São Salvador was sacked, and its Christian nobles were humiliated and sold into slavery in the interior. Lisbon responded to the fall of its staunchest African ally with troops. The monarchy was restored in 1574. In exchange, Kongo traders called *pombeiros* (pohm-BEH-rohs) supplied their Portuguese saviors with slaves. The process of propping up regimes in exchange for captives was to continue throughout the long history of the slave trade.

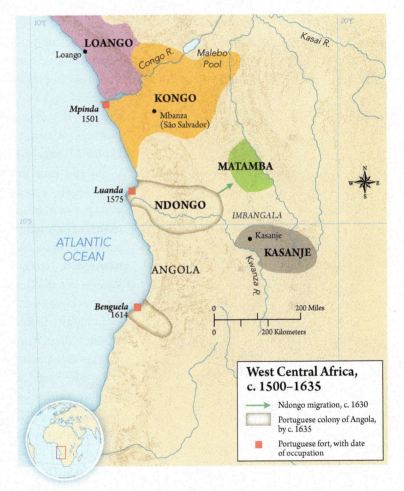

Portuguese Strategy in Angola

A second pillar of Portuguese strategy in West Central Africa was maintaining a permanent military colony in Angola, home of the young man whose story began this chapter. Beginning with the port city of Luanda, Angola was to become one of the largest and longest-lived clearinghouses for the Atlantic slave trade (see Map 17.3). It was perhaps here more than

≡ **MAP 17.3   West Central Africa, c. 1500–1635** No African region was more affected by European interlopers in early modern times than West Central Africa, the Atlantic world's main source of enslaved captives, nearly all of them shipped abroad by the Portuguese. Peoples of the interior suffered periodic slave raids as the Portuguese extended their networks south to Benguela. Some refugees migrated eastward, only to encounter new enemies—most of them allies of the Portuguese.

anywhere else in Africa that the Portuguese, aided again by droughts and other factors, managed to radically alter local livelihoods.

Evidence suggests that the early Angolan slave trade ballooned as a result of a severe and prolonged drought affecting the interior in the 1590s. The drought uprooted villagers already weakened by slave-raiding, and these luckless refugees in turn were preyed upon by still more aggressive warrior-bandits calling themselves Imbangala. The Imbangala, organized around secret military societies, soon became slaving allies of the Portuguese. These were probably Domingo Angola's captors.

Employing terrifying tactics, including human sacrifice and—allegedly—cannibalism, Imbangala raiders threatened to snuff out the Ndongo kingdom. That Ndongo survived at all depended on the creativity and wile of a powerful woman, Queen Nzinga (r. 1624–1663). Queen Nzinga sought to thwart the Imbangala by allying with their sometime business partners, the Portuguese. In Luanda she was baptized "Dona Ana," or "Queen Ann."

Queen Nzinga promised to supply slaves to her new friends, only to discover that the Portuguese had little authority over the Imbangala. Their warriors continued to attack the Ndongo, who were forced to move to a new homeland, in Matamba. From this newer, more secure base Queen Nzinga built her own slaving and trading state. When the Dutch occupied Luanda in the 1640s, the queen adapted, trading slaves to them in exchange for immunity. Before her death at the age of eighty-one, Queen Nzinga reestablished ties with the Portuguese, who again controlled the coast in the 1650s.

≡ **Queen Nzinga's Baptism** Here the same late-seventeenth-century artist who painted the Mbundu blacksmiths (see page 619) portrays the baptism of the central African Queen Nzinga. Queen Nzinga's Catholic baptism did not prevent her from making alliances with non-Catholics, both African and European, in long and violent struggles with neighbors and the Portuguese in her district of Matamba, Angola. Some witnesses say she was attended by dozens of male servants dressed as concubines.

To the south and west, meanwhile, Imbangala warriors helped establish the kingdom of Kasanje (see again Map 17.3). After 1630, Kasanje merchant-warriors operated as slavers and middlemen, procuring captives from the east. Farther south, other warriors began to interact with Portuguese settlers around the Atlantic port of Benguela. By the later seventeenth century Benguela rivaled Luanda.

Overall, West Central Africa, mostly Kongo and Angola, supplied over five million, or nearly half of the slaves sent to the Americas between 1519 and 1867. The victims were overwhelmingly poor millet and sorghum farmers struggling to eke out a living in a drought-prone and war-torn region. At least two-thirds of all African captives sent across the Atlantic were men, a significant number of them boys. Into the vortex were thrust young men such as Domingo Angola, who was sent all the way to the Andean boomtown of Potosí.

Northern Europeans and the Expansion of the Atlantic Slave Trade 1600–1800

⬎ FOCUS What were the major changes in the Atlantic slave trade after 1600?

Other Europeans had vied for a share of the Portuguese Atlantic slave trade since the mid-sixteenth century, including the English corsair Francis Drake, but it was only after 1600 that competition exploded. First the French, then the English, Dutch, Danish, and other northern Europeans forcibly displaced Portuguese traders all along the western shores of Africa. Others set up competing posts nearby. By 1650, the Portuguese struggled to maintain a significant presence even in West Central Africa. They began to supplement western African slaves with captives trans-shipped from their outposts in the Indian Ocean, primarily Mozambique (see Map 17.4).

The slave trade was logistically complex, requiring thorough documentation. This has allowed historians to cross-check multiple documents for numbers of slaves boarded, origin place-names, and age or sex groupings. These sources, a bland accounting of mass death and suffering, suggest that volume grew slowly, expanding gradually after 1650 and very rapidly only after 1750. The British, despite profiting greatly from the slave trade in western Africa through the 1790s, when volume peaked, suddenly reversed policy under pressure from abolitionists in 1807. After 1808, the British Navy helped suppress the Atlantic slave trade until it was abolished by treaty in 1850. Despite these measures, contraband slaving continued, mostly between Angola and Brazil.

The Rise and Fall of Monopoly Trading Companies

Following the example of the Spanish and Portuguese, northern European participation in the Atlantic slave trade grew in tandem with colonization efforts in the Americas. Tobacco-producing Caribbean islands such as Barbados and Martinique and mainland North American regions such as Virginia and the Carolinas were initially staffed with indentured, or contracted, European servants and only a small number of African slaves. As sugar cultivation increased in the

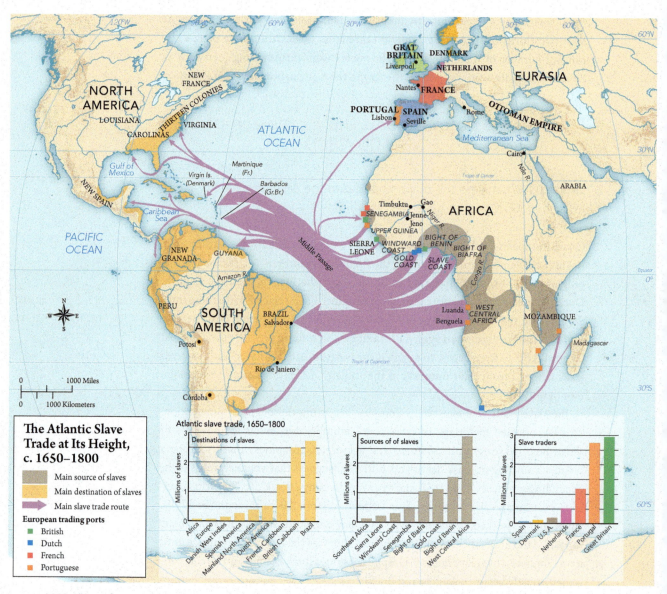

The Atlantic Slave Trade at Its Height, c. 1650–1800

Main source of slaves

Main destination of slaves

Main slave trade route

European trading ports
- British
- Dutch
- French
- Portuguese

Atlantic slave trade, 1650–1800

Destinations of slaves

Sources of of slaves

Slave traders

≡ **MAP 17.4** **The Atlantic Slave Trade at Its Height, c. 1650–1800** The Atlantic slave trade grew dramatically after 1650. New slaving nations included the Netherlands, England, France, and Denmark, all of which had colonies in the Caribbean and on the North American mainland that relied on plantation agriculture. The regions from which enslaved Africans came also shifted. West Central Africa remained a major source region, but the Upper Guinea Coast was increasingly overshadowed by the so-called Slave Coast located between the Bight of Benin and the Bight of Biafra.

Caribbean after 1650 and tobacco took off in Virginia, however, planters shifted to African slavery. This had been their wish, as their documents attest, and a declining supply of poor European contract laborers accelerated the trend.

For historians of the North Atlantic, this transition from indentured servitude to African slavery has raised questions about the origins of American racism. In sum, can modern notions of racial difference be traced to early modern American slavery and the Atlantic slave trade? Some scholars have argued that racist ideologies grew mostly *after* this shift from European to African labor. Before that, they argue, "white" and "black" workers were treated by masters and overseers with equal cruelty. In Virginia and Barbados during the early to mid-1600s, for instance, black and white indentured servants labored alongside each other, experiencing equal exploitation and limited legal protection. Scholars working in a broader historical context, however—one that takes into account Spanish, Portuguese, Dutch, and Italian experiences in the Atlantic, Mediterranean, and beyond—have been less convinced by this assertion. They argue that while racist notions hardened with the expansion of slavery in the Caribbean and North America after 1650—and grew harder still following the Scientific Revolution with its emphasis on biological classification—European views of sub-Saharan Africans had never been positive. Put another way, racism was more a cause of slavery than a result.

Portuguese slavers suffered losses, but proved resilient. As we have seen, the Portuguese had spent several centuries establishing the financial instruments and supply networks necessary to run such a complex and risky business. To compete, northern Europeans established state-subsidized monopoly trading companies. The highly belligerent Dutch West India Company was founded in 1621 to attack Spanish and Portuguese colonial outposts and take over Iberian commercial interests

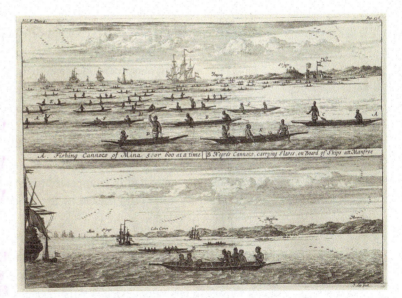

≡ **Filling the Slave Ships** The upper half of this 1732 engraving by Dutch artist Johannes Kip shows West African fishermen in canoes off the coast of present-day Ghana, with the old Portuguese fortress of São Jorge da Mina in the distance. The lower half shows slaves being ferried to a Dutch ship in a somewhat longer canoe, with a string of other European slave-trading forts in the distance. Slave ships often cruised African coasts for several months, acquiring a diverse range of captives before crossing the Atlantic.

in the Atlantic. Several slaving forts in western Africa were eventually seized. São Jorge da Mina fell in 1638, and Luanda, Angola, in 1641. Although these colonial outposts were returned in subsequent decades, the era of Portuguese dominance was over.

The French, whose early overseas activities had been stunted by the religious wars described in Chapter 20, organized a monopoly trading company in 1664 to supply their growing Caribbean market. The English, fresh from their own civil conflicts, formed the Royal African Company in 1672. By 1700, the French and English were fighting bitterly to supply not only their own colonial holdings but also the lucrative Spanish-American market. Dutch slavers also competed, supplying slaves to the Spanish up to the 1730s. Spanish-Americans, unlike other colonists, paid for slaves with gold and silver. Danish slavers also competed by the 1670s, when they established sugar plantations in the Virgin Islands.

The company model did not last. By 1725, most of the northern European monopoly slaving companies had failed. Stuck with costly forts, salaried officers, and state-mandated obligations, they were too inflexible and inefficient to survive. Thus the French, English, and Dutch resorted to a Portuguese-style system, in which private merchants, often related to one another, pooled capital to finance individual voyages. Like their Mediterranean predecessors in Venice, Genoa, and elsewhere, the trade in slaves was but one of many overlapping ventures for most of these investors. Their profits, usually averaging 10 percent or so, were reinvested in land, light industry, and other endeavors. In time, investors had little to do with the organization of slaving voyages. Nonetheless, the profits slavery produced would help fuel Europe's economic growth and development.

How the Mature Slave Trade Functioned

The slave trade proved most lucrative when European investors cut every corner. Profit margins consistently trumped humanitarian concerns. By the late seventeenth century, ships were packed tightly, food and water rationed sparingly, and crews kept as small as possible. Unlike other shipping ventures at this time, the value of the captives far exceeded the costs of ship and crew. In part this was a reflection of the risks involved.

Risks and uncertainties abounded in the slave trade. Despite a growing number of European forts along Africa's Atlantic coast, slavers were on their own in collecting captives. In short, the system was much more open and African-dominated than has generally been acknowledged. Ships spent an average of three months cruising coasts and estuaries in search of African middlemen willing to trade captives for commodities. By the late seventeenth century, competition was on the rise, affecting supply and thus price. Violence, mostly in the form of slave uprisings and hostile attacks by fellow Europeans, was a constant concern.

European ship captains in charge of the African leg of the trip hoped to receive a bounty of 2 to 5 percent on all surviving slaves. Somewhat like modern human traffickers, they were betting their lives on a relatively small fortune. As we saw with regard to Portuguese missionaries, western Africa was notoriously unhealthy for "unseasoned" Europeans, due mostly to endemic falciparum malaria, and as many as one in ten ship captains died before leaving the African coast for the Americas. Few who survived repeated the trip. Ships' doctors had scant remedies even for common ailments such as dysentery, which also afflicted slaves and crewmembers. When not ill themselves, doctors inspected slaves before embarkation, hoping to head off premature death or the spread of disease aboard ship and thereby to protect the investment.

The trade was also complicated in that few northern European products appealed to African consumers. More than anything, Africans wanted colorful cotton fabrics from India to supplement their own products. Thus northern Europeans followed the Portuguese example yet again by importing huge quantities of cotton cloth from South Asia, cowry shells from the Indian Ocean, and iron, brass, and copper from parts of Europe, particularly Spain and Sweden. Other tastes were introduced by Europeans. By 1700, American plantation commodities such as rum and tobacco were being exchanged for slaves in significant quantities. Thus, the Atlantic slave trade was a global concern.

Sources indicate that chiefs and kings throughout western Africa augmented their prestige by accumulating and redistributing commodities procured through the slave trade. The captives they sent abroad were not their kin, and western Africans appear to have had no sense of the overall magnitude of this commerce in human bodies. There were few internal brakes on captive-taking besides the diminishing pool of victims and shifting political ambitions; the African desire to hold dependents to boost prestige and provide domestic labor meshed with European demands. Along these lines, whereas female war captives might be absorbed into elite households, men and boys were generally considered dangerous elements and happily gotten rid of. It so happened that European planters and mine owners in the colonies valued men over women. Thus, however immoral and disruptive of African life it appears in retrospect, the slave trade probably seemed at the time to be mutually beneficial for European buyers and African sellers. Only the slaves themselves felt otherwise.

The Middle Passage

It is difficult to imagine the suffering endured by the more than twelve million African captives forced to cross the Atlantic Ocean. The ordeal itself has come to be known as the **Middle Passage** (see again Map 17.4). As noted at the opening of this chapter, some West Central Africans imagined the slavers' ships to be floating slaughterhouses crossing a great lake or river to satisfy white cannibals inhabiting a distant, sterile land. Portuguese sailors unambiguously dubbed them "death ships" or "floating tombs." Perhaps troubled by this sense of damnation, Portuguese priests baptized as many slaves as they could before departure.

Northern Europeans, increasingly in charge of the slave trade after 1650, took a more dispassionate approach. Slaves, as far as they were concerned, were a sort of highly valued livestock requiring efficient but impersonal handling. Put another way, the care and feeding of slaves were treated as pragmatic matters of health, not faith. Rations were the subsistence minimum of maize, rice, or millet gruel, with a bit of fish or dried meat added from time to time. Men, women, and children were assigned separate quarters. Women were given a cotton cloth for a wrap, whereas men were often kept naked, both to save money and to discourage rebellion by adding to their humiliation. Exercise was required on deck in the form of dancing to drums during daylight hours. Like cattle, slaves were showered with seawater before the nighttime lockdown. The hold, ventilated on most ships after initial experiences with mass suffocation and heatstroke, was periodically splashed with vinegar.

Despite these measures, slave mortality on the one- to three-month voyage across the Atlantic was high. On average, between 10 and 20 percent of slaves did not survive. This high mortality rate is all the more alarming in that these slaves had been selected for their relative good health in the first place, leaving countless other captives behind to perish in makeshift barracks, dungeons, and coastal agricultural plots. Many more died soon after landing in the Americas, often from dysentery. Some who were emotionally overwhelmed committed suicide along the way by hurling themselves into the ocean or strangling themselves in their chains. A few enraged men managed to kill a crewmember or even a captain before being executed. Slaves from different regions had trouble communicating, and thus successful slave mutinies remained rare.

The conditions of the Middle Passage worsened over time. In the name of increased efficiency, the situation below decks went from crowded to crammed between the seventeenth and eighteenth centuries. On average, crews of 30 to 40 common sailors oversaw 200 to 300 slaves in around 1700, whereas the same number oversaw 300 to 400 slaves after 1750. These are only averages; even in the 1620s, some ships carried 600 or more slaves.

Although some Iberian clergymen protested the horrors of this crossing as early as the sixteenth century, it took the eighteenth-century deterioration of conditions aboard slave ships to awaken the conscience of participating nations. In England, most importantly, African survivors of the Middle Passage such as Olaudah

Middle Passage The Atlantic crossing made by slaves taken from Africa to the Americas.

Equiano (c. 1745–1797) testified before Parliament by the late eighteenth century. "Permit me, with the greatest deference and respect," Equiano began his 1789 autobiography, "to lay at your feet the following genuine Narrative, the chief design of which is to excite in your august assemblies a sense of compassion for the miseries which the Slave-Trade has entailed on my unfortunate countrymen."[5] Such testimonies, backed by the pleas of prominent Quakers and other religious figures, were finally heard. Abolition of the Atlantic slave trade, first enforced by the British in 1808, would come much more easily than abolition of slavery itself.

Volume of the Slave Trade

It is important to note that the trans-Saharan and East African slave trades preceded the Atlantic one discussed here, and that these trades continued throughout early modern times. In fact, the volume of the Atlantic trade appears to have eclipsed these other avenues to foreign captivity only after 1600. That said, the Atlantic slave trade ultimately constituted the greatest forced migration in early modern world history. Compared with the roughly 2 million mostly free European migrants who made their way to all parts of the Americas between the voyage of Columbus in 1492 and the British abolition of the slave trade in 1808, the number of enslaved Africans to cross the Atlantic and survive is astounding—between 10 and 12 million.

Also astounding is the fact that the vast majority of these Africans arrived in the last half century of the "legal" slave trade, that is, after 1750. Up until 1650 a

≡ **Olaudah Equiano** Olaudah Equiano, whose slave name was Gustavus Vassa, became a celebrity critic of the Atlantic slave trade in the late eighteenth century after writing a memoir of his experiences as a slave and free man of color in Africa, North America, the Caribbean, and Europe.

total of approximately 710,000 slaves had been taken to American markets, most of them to Spanish America (262,700). Brazil was the next largest destination, absorbing about a quarter of a million slaves to that date. São Tomé, the sugar island in the Gulf of Guinea, and Europe (mostly Iberia) absorbed about 95,000 and 112,000 slaves, respectively. Madeira and the Canaries imported about 25,000 African slaves, and the English and French West Indies, 21,000 and 2500, respectively. The average annual volume for the period up to 1650 was approximately 7500 slaves per year.

The second (1650–1750) and third (1750–1850) stages of the Atlantic slave trade witnessed enormous growth. By 1675, nearly 15,000 slaves were being carried to the colonies annually, and by 1700 nearly 30,000. The total volume of the trade between 1700 and 1750 was double that of the previous fifty years, bringing some 2.5 million slaves to the Americas. The trade nearly doubled yet again between 1750 and 1800, when some 4 million Africans were transported. By this time the effect of the Atlantic slave trade on western African societies was considerable. The trade was restricted by the British after 1808, but slavers still managed to move some 3 million slaves, mostly to Brazil, and to a lesser extent Cuba and the United States, by 1850. Northern U.S. shipbuilders were key suppliers to Brazilian slavers to the very end.

It appears that in the first three centuries of the Atlantic slave trade most African captives came from the coastal hinterland. This changed only after about 1750, when colonial demand began to outstrip local sources of supply. Thereafter, slaves were brought to the coast from increasingly distant interior regions. In West Africa this amounted to something of an inversion of the caravan trading routes fanning out from the Niger River basin, but in West Central Africa entirely new trails and trade circuits were formed. Also, whereas war captives and drought refugees had been the main victims in the past, now random kidnapping and slave-raiding became widespread.

COUNTERPOINT: The Pygmies of Central Africa

FOCUS How did the Pygmies' rainforest world differ from the better-known environment of savannas and farms?

As in the Americas, certain forest, desert, and other margin-dwelling peoples of Africa appear to have remained largely immune to the effects of European conquest, colonization, and trade. But such seeming immunity is difficult to gauge, especially since we now know some margin-dwelling groups once thought to be naturally isolated were in fact refugees from conquest and slaving wars. Many were driven from the more accessible regions where they had once hunted or otherwise exploited nature to survive. Distinct cultures such as the Batwa (BAH-twah), a major Pygmy group of the great Congo rainforest, and the Khoikhoi (COY-coy) and other tribespeople of southern Africa's Kalahari Desert, were until only recently thought to have been unaffected by outsiders before the nineteenth century.

Recent scholarship, and most surviving gatherer-hunters themselves, suggest otherwise.

Life in the Congo Rainforest

Still, for the Pygmies, as for many of the world's tropical forest peoples, life has long been distinct from that of settled agriculturalists. Even now, Pygmies live by exploiting the natural forest around them, unaided by manufactured goods. These forests, marked by rugged terrain and washed

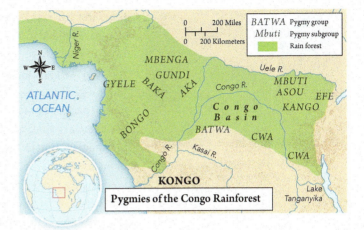

Pygmies of the Congo Rainforest

≡ **Pygmies of the Congo Rainforest**

by superabundant rains, make agriculture and herding impossible. Short of cutting down huge swaths of trees, which in this region often leads to massive soil erosion, neither can be practiced. This is not to say space is limited. Indeed, the Congo River basin is home to the world's second-largest rainforest, after that of the Amazon in South America; it is vast. As in the Amazon, most forest animals are modest in size, with the important exception of the African elephant, which early modern Pygmies occasionally hunted for food and tusks.

Until recent times, most Pygmies were gatherer-hunters. Their superior tracking abilities, limited material possessions, and knowledge of useful forest products such as leaves for dwellings and natural toxins for bow hunting allowed them to retreat in times of external threats such as war. Herding and farming Bantu-speaking and Sudanic neighbors were at a disadvantage in Pygmy country, which seems to have prevented Pygmy militarization or formation of defensive confederacies. The Congo rainforest is also attractive in that it is much less affected by malarial mosquitoes than the surrounding farmland. In recent times only a few Pygmy groups, such as the much-studied Mbuti (M-BOOH-tee), have remained separate enough from neighboring farmers and herders to retain their short stature and other distinct characteristics. The Pygmies' highly distinctive singing style and instrumentation, most of it Mbuti, have become famous with the rise of world music.

Everyday Pygmy life has been examined in most detail by anthropologists, who have emphasized differences between Pygmy and neighboring Bantu rituals. Whereas Bantu speakers have venerated dead ancestors in a way that has deeply affected their long-term settlement patterns, warfare, and kin groupings, the Pygmies have long preferred to "let go" of their dead—to move on, as it were.

Modern-Day Pygmies Here Baka Pygmies of Cameroon and the Central African Republic hunt in the Congo rainforest using nets, sticks, and vines. The woman also carries a machete for butchering the catch and a basket for the meat.

Similarly, whereas Bantu coming-of-age rituals such as circumcision have tended to be elaborate and essential to social reproduction, Pygmies have traditionally marked few distinct phases in life. Most important, the Pygmies have venerated the forest itself as a life-giving spirit, whereas outsiders have treated it as a threatening space and potential source of evil. Has it always been so?

Legendary since ancient Egyptian times for their small, reed-like bodies, simple lifestyles, good-natured humor, and melodious music, the Pygmies have long been held up as the perfect counterpoint to urban civilization and its discontents. It is only recently that the Pygmies and other nonsedentary peoples like them have been treated historically, as makers rather than "non-actors" or victims of history. The absence of written records produced by the Pygmies themselves has made this task difficult, but anthropologists, historians, linguists, and archaeologists working together have made considerable headway.

Pygmy-Bantu Relations

It seems that sometime after 1500, the introduction of iron tools and banana cultivation to the central African interior began to alter settlement patterns and overall demography. This change placed Pygmies and Bantu neighbors in closer proximity, as more and more forest was cut for planting and Bantu moved into Pygmy territory. Bantu speakers, some of them refugees from areas attacked by slavers or afflicted by drought, appear to have displaced some Pygmy groups and to have intermarried with others. They seem to have adopted a variety of Pygmy religious beliefs, although Bantu languages mostly displaced original Pygmy ones. Also after 1500, American crops such as peanuts and manioc began to alter sedentary life at the forest's edge, leading to still more interaction, not all of it peaceful, between the Pygmies and their neighbors. Pygmies adopted American capsicum peppers as an everyday spice.

Were the Pygmies driven from the rainforest's edge into its heart by the slave trade? Perhaps in some places, yes, but the evidence is clearer for increased interaction with Bantu migrants. Early effects of globalization on Pygmy life are more easily tracked in terms of foods adopted as a result of the Columbian Exchange. Despite these exchanges and conflicts, the Pygmies have managed to retain a distinct identity that is as intertwined with the rhythms of the forest as it is with the rhythms of settled agriculture.

Although the story of the Pygmies' survival is not as dramatic as that of the Mapuche of Chile (see Chapter 16), their culture's richness and resilience serve as testaments to their peoples' imagination, will, and ingenuity. Their adaptation to the rainforest—probably in part a result of early modern historical stresses, which pushed them farther into the forest—reminds us of a shared human tendency to make the most of a given ecological setting, but also that the distinction between civilized and "primitive" lifestyles is a false one, or at least socially constructed.

Conclusion

Western African societies grew and changed according to the rhythms of planting, harvest, trade, and war, and these rhythms continued to define everyday life in early modern times. Droughts, diseases, and pests made subsistence more challenging in sub-Saharan Africa than in most parts of the world, yet people adapted and formed chiefdoms, kingdoms, and empires, often underpinned, at least symbolically, by the control of iron and other metals. Iron tools helped farmers clear forest and till hard soils.

Islam influenced African society and politics across a broad belt south of the Sahara and along the shores of the Indian Ocean, but even this powerful religious tradition was to a degree absorbed by local cultures. Most western African states and chiefdoms were not influenced by Christian missionaries until the late nineteenth century. It was malaria, a disease against which many sub-Saharan Africans had at least some acquired immunity, that proved to be the continent's best defense.

But Africa possessed commodities demanded by outsiders, and despite their failure to penetrate the interior in early modern times, it was these outsiders, first among them the seaborne Portuguese, who set the early modern phase of western African history in motion. The Portuguese came looking for gold in the mid-fifteenth century, and once they discovered the dangers of malaria, they stuck to the coast and offshore islands to trade through intermediaries, including coastal chiefs and kings. First they traded for gold, but very soon for war captives. In return, the Portuguese brought horses, cloth, wine, metal goods, and guns. Local chiefs became powerful by allying with the newcomers, and they expanded their trading and raiding ventures deep into the continental interior. Thus began a symbiotic relationship, copied and expanded by the English, Dutch, French, and other northern Europeans, that swelled over four centuries to supply the Americas with some 12 million enslaved African laborers, the largest forced migration in world history. Among these millions of captives, most of whose names we shall never know, was young Domingo Angola, a West Central African teenager caught up in a widening global web of trade, conquest, and religious conversion.

✶ review

The major global development in this chapter: The rise of the Atlantic slave trade and its impact on early modern African peoples and cultures.

Important Events	
c. 1100–1500	Extended dry period in West Africa prompts migrations
c. 1450	Kingdom of Benin reaches height of its power
1464–1492	Reign of Sunni Ali in the Songhai Empire
1482	Portuguese establish trading fort of São Jorge da Mina (Ghana)
1506–1543	Reign of Afonso I (Nzinga Mbemba) of kingdom of Kongo
1569	Collapse of kingdom of Kongo
1574	Portuguese-aided restoration of kingdom of Kongo
1591	Moroccan raiders conquer Songhai Empire
1621	Formation of Dutch West India Company
1624–1663	Reign of Queen Nzinga in the Ndongo kingdom of Angola
1638–1641	Dutch seize São Jorge da Mina and Luanda
1672	Formation of English Royal African Company
1750–1800	Atlantic slave trade reaches highest volume
1807	British declare Atlantic slave trade illegal

KEY TERMS

African diaspora (p. 606)
fetishism (p. 624)
génie (p. 609)
husbandry (p. 610)

kitomi (p. 624)
manikongo (p. 618)
Middle Passage (p. 632)
oba (p. 617)

paramount chief (p. 610)
peça (p. 620)
pombeiro (p. 625)

CHAPTER OVERVIEW QUESTIONS

1. How did ecological diversity in western Africa relate to cultural developments?
2. What tied western Africa to other parts of the world prior to the arrival of Europeans along Atlantic shores?
3. How did the Atlantic slave trade arise, and how was it sustained?

MAKING CONNECTIONS

1. How does the Moroccan conquest of Songhai compare with the Spanish conquest of the Aztecs (see Chapter 16)?
2. How did gender roles differ between the kingdoms of West Africa and those of North America's Eastern Woodlands (see Chapter 15)?
3. How did the Portuguese experience in Africa differ from events in Brazil (see Chapter 16)?
4. How did growing European competition for enslaved Africans alter the nature of enslavement and trade in Africa itself?

For further research into the topics covered in this chapter, see the Bibliography at the end of the book. For additional primary sources from this period, see *Sources for World in the Making.*

Trade and Empire in the Indian Ocean and South Asia 1450–1750

backstory

For centuries before the rise of the Atlantic system (see Chapter 16), the vast Indian Ocean basin thrived as a religious and commercial crossroads. Powered by the annual monsoon wind cycle, traders, mainly Muslim, developed a flourishing commerce over thousands of miles in such luxury goods as spices, gems, and precious metals. The network included the trading enclaves of East Africa and Arabia and the many ports of South and Southeast Asia. Ideas, religious traditions—notably Islam—and pilgrimages moved along the same routes. The vast majority of the region's many millions of inhabitants were peasant farmers, many of them dependent on rice agriculture.

≡ **World in the Making** In this exquisite miniature painting from the 1590s, the Mughal emperor Akbar receives the Persian ambassador Sayyid Beg in 1562. The painting is an illustration commissioned for Akbar's official court history, the *Akbarnama*, and thus would have been seen and approved by the emperor himself. The meeting is emblematic of the generally amiable relationship between the Mughals and their Safavid neighbors in Iran.

Born to Persian immigrants in the Afghan city of Kandahar, Princess Mihr un-nisa (meer oon-NEE-sah), known to history as Nur Jahan, or "Light of the World," married the Mughal emperor Jahangir (jah-hahn-GEER) in 1611, at the age of thirty-four. As the emperor turned to science and the arts, as well as to his addictions to wine and opium, Nur Jahan assumed the ruler's duties throughout the last decade of her husband's life, which ended in 1627. She had coins struck in her name, and most importantly, she made certain that a daughter from an earlier marriage and her brother's daughter both wed likely heirs to the Mughal throne.

As her husband withdrew from worldly affairs, Nur Jahan actively engaged them. After a visit from the English ambassador in 1613, she developed a keen interest in European textiles. She established domestic industries in cloth manufacture and jewelry making and developed an export trade in indigo dye. Indigo from her farms was shipped to Portuguese and English trading forts along India's west coast, and then sent to Europe.

In 1614, Nur Jahan arranged for her niece to marry Jahangir's favorite son, Prince Khurram, known after he became emperor as Shah Jahan. The niece, who took the title Mumtaz Mahal, died in 1631 while bearing her fourteenth child. Heartbroken, Shah Jahan went into mourning and commissioned a mausoleum for Mumtaz in the city of Agra. This graceful structure of white marble is known as the Taj Mahal.

Nur Jahan attended court and rode horses proudly in public without her husband. Such conduct was not considered inappropriate for a woman of her status in her time. Like other South Asian noblewomen, Nur Jahan expressed her rank through public piety, commissioning religious buildings and elaborate gardens, several of which survive. She played an active and sometimes controversial role in politics until her death in 1644.

For most of the early modern period the lands surrounding the Indian Ocean remained in the hands of powerful local rulers, as exemplified by Nur Jahan. Some, like her, engaged in maritime trade. Trade on the Indian Ocean followed the **monsoons**, alternating dry and humid winds generated by the seasonal heating and cooling of air masses over Asia. To exploit these winds, Arab sailors developed swift, triangular-rigged vessels that carried them to and from East Africa. Southeast Asian sailors developed other vessel types influenced by Chinese shipbuilders. Large populations, a wide array of luxury trade goods, and religious pilgrimage sites such as Mecca and Benares, made this area a vibrant saltwater crossroads.

India, with its huge, mostly Hindu population, lay at the center of the basin's trading system. India's black pepper was world-famous, as were its diamonds, but it was

monsoon A wind system that influences large climatic regions such as the Indian Ocean basin and reverses direction seasonally.

India's cotton fabrics that were most profitable. Gold from sub-Saharan Africa and later silver from the Americas lubricated Indian Ocean trade. Nur Jahan minted rupees in American silver and African gold.

American silver was first brought by the Portuguese, who arrived in the region with three main goals: to monopolize the spice trade to Europe, to take over key shipping lanes, and to fight the expansion of Islam and spread Christianity instead. For a time they succeeded with goals one and two, but the third proved impossible—in part because Portuguese arrival coincided with the emergence of Eurasia's so-called gunpowder empires, most famously the Mughals, Safavids, and Ottomans.[1] Some historians also apply the term "gunpowder empire" to the Portuguese and other Europeans who took their powerful weapons abroad in the name of commerce and Christianity. Control of the sea paid off, and with the decline of the Muslim gunpowder empires in the eighteenth century, Europeans—primarily the English and the Dutch—gained control of Indian Ocean shores.

OVERVIEW QUESTIONS

The major global development in this chapter: The Indian Ocean trading network and the impact of European intrusion on maritime and mainland South Asia.

As you read, consider:

1. What environmental, religious, and political factors enabled trading enclaves to flourish in the Indian Ocean basin?

2. How did the rise and fall of India's land empires reflect larger regional trends?

3. How did Europeans insert themselves into the Indian Ocean trading network, and what changes did they bring about?

Trading Cities and Inland Networks: East Africa

FOCUS How did Swahili Coast traders link the East African interior to the Indian Ocean basin?

The history of early modern East Africa is best understood in terms of linkages among Indian Ocean traders from as far away as China and the cities and peoples of the African interior. Brokering Africa's ties to Asia were merchant families and princes clustered in port towns and cities stretching from Ethiopia in the northeast to Mozambique in the southeast.

By 1500, Muslims predominated in these East African trading ports. Some were descendants of early Persian, Arabian, and South Asian overseas traders and missionaries, but most were native Africans, mostly Bantu speakers. Swahili, still spoken throughout this region, is a Bantu language laced with Arabic terms. In early modern times, scribes recorded transactions in Swahili using Arabic script. Thus, the society and culture of East African trading ports blended African and Asian elements, reflecting the economic connections between the two regions.

Portuguese and Ottoman traders arrived in these ports around 1500, but neither managed to control more than a few of them at a time. Dutch, French, and English merchants arrived in the seventeenth century, but they, too, failed to monopolize East African trade. Offshore, the French established a minor presence on Madagascar and then on much smaller Réunion, but neither island had been vital to the ancient monsoon trading circuit. As free from each other as they were from outsiders, the hundred-odd ports of East Africa's Swahili Coast remained largely independent until the imperial scramble of the late nineteenth century (discussed in Chapter 24).

Port Towns and Beginnings

The East African coast had served as a regional crossroads for more than a thousand years. Archaeologists have determined that Muslim trader-missionaries had reached many East African port towns by the eighth century C.E., soon after the founding of Islam. Seaborne trade in ivory, gold, and ceramics dated back to classical antiquity. Early modern East African traders continued this commerce, bringing luxury goods from Central, South, and even East Asia to the coast in exchange for Africa's treasured raw materials. Traders also exchanged slaves for luxuries, but the scale of the Indian Ocean slave trade seems to have remained small in this period.

By modern standards, most East African trading ports were towns. The largest, such as Kilwa, Sofala, Malindi, and Mombasa, had perhaps ten thousand inhabitants at their height. Most towns were much smaller, home to only several hundred permanent residents. Quelimane (keh-lee-MAH-neh) and Mogadishu fell somewhere in between, with a few thousand inhabitants. Nearly all of the region's cities were walled, but only the most opulent had mosques of stone or coral block rather than adobe. Merchants occupied house blocks clustered within each city's walls.

In exchange for tributes, local princes protected merchant families, negotiating with inland chiefdoms for trade goods and subsistence items.

Indian Ocean Connections

East African traders exported elephant tusks and gold in exchange for South Asian cloth, much of it from Cambay in the Gujarat region of northwest India (see Map 18.1). They also imported Persian and even Chinese ceramics, along with spices, tobacco (after 1500), and many other items. African ivory was prized

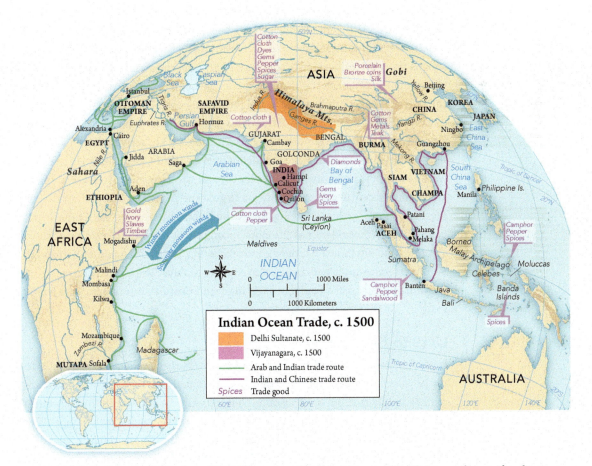

≡ **MAP 18.1   Indian Ocean Trade, c. 1500** Often manned by East African and South Asian sailors, swift-sailing Arab dhows carried traders, pilgrims, and luxury goods all over the Indian Ocean. Farther east, Chinese junks plied the warm waters of Southeast Asia, trading porcelain and silk for spices and aromatic woods. The two trade circuits overlapped, and interactions were largely peaceful, both circuits benefiting from the markets of opulent land empires such as southern India's Vijayanagara and sponsoring city-states such as Melaka.

throughout Asia for its soft texture, and African gold, mostly from the southern interior, was in high demand as currency. In much of India, women brought dowries of gold when they married, displaying it in the form of fine jewelry. As we have seen in previous chapters, African gold was an essential world currency prior to European expansion into the Americas.

Most goods were carried in **dhows** (dowz), swift, single-decked ships with triangular sails and about two hundred tons' capacity. Traders used smaller vessels and dugout canoes to navigate rivers such as the Zambezi and to ferry goods through the treacherous coral reefs that lay between East Africa's towns.

Despite the value of most Indian Ocean trade goods, shippers traveled only lightly armed. Although piracy had long been known, and was even expected in waters such as India's Malabar Coast, violent theft at sea seems to have become a serious threat to Indian Ocean commerce only after the arrival of the Portuguese, who sought to establish trading monopolies through brute force. Their actions in turn encouraged contraband trade and the fencing of stolen goods.

Chinese maritime visits to East Africa, though memorable, were few. As we saw in Chapter 14, the famous Ming admiral Zheng He arrived first in Malindi in the late 1410s, and then at Mogadishu in the early 1430s. Zheng He's vessels were enormous, more than double the size of the largest Portuguese ships to arrive about a century later. In addition to gold and ivory, the Ming admiral filled his ample holds with local items, including a veritable zoo for the Chinese emperor. There is no evidence of attempts to conquer or to establish trading posts or colonies, and afterward Chinese goods came to East Africa again only through Southeast Asian intermediaries, often Muslim Malays. The Chinese retreat from the Indian Ocean left a void that early modern European interlopers were happy to fill.

Links to the Interior

Less often described than East Africa's ties to overseas merchants were its links to the African interior. Each port's hinterland was small, but coastal towns and cities did not simply face outward, as once believed. Almost all Swahili town-dwellers relied on nearby agricultural plots for survival, and many traded with independent cattle herders. Swahili elites owned slaves purchased from the interior, who produced food for both their masters and themselves. The African products in greatest demand overseas, however, came from the more densely populated southern interior.

This was most true of gold dust, traded northward from the mouth of the Zambezi River (see again Map 18.1). Its main sources lay in the Mutapa kingdom (formerly

dhow A small sailing vessel with triangular rigs used in monsoon trade to East Africa.

Great Zimbabwe), located on the Zimbabwe Plateau. Here, as in parts of contemporary West Africa, men and women panned for gold in the agricultural off-season. A few mines went underground. It appears that an annual average of about a ton of gold entered the Indian Ocean trade circuit during the sixteenth century.

Ivory was a different sort of product; collecting it required the hunting and slaughter of wild animals. Although modern demand for ivory has led to the extinction of elephants in parts of Africa, it appears that most of the tusks fed into the early modern Indian Ocean circuit were a byprod-

Exchanger of Cambay In this early-sixteenth-century watercolor, apparently by a self-taught Portuguese artist, a merchant in Cambay, on India's northwest coast, collects and changes gold, silver, and other coins of many mint marks and denominations. A tiny balance hangs behind him on one side, and a strongbox seems to float in midair on the other. To the right, people of many faiths, clothing styles, and colors come to seek his services. At least two are women bearing gold coins.

uct of subsistence hunting. Hunters went out only seasonally, and without firearms. Bringing down an adult elephant with spears and longbows was extremely dangerous, and the compensation was not attractive enough to make it a livelihood. Aside from the dangers of ivory procurement, interior peoples such as the Shona speakers of the Mutapa kingdom were not easily pressured into market exchanges of any kind. With no particular need for Asian products, they carried ivory and gold to the seaports at their leisure.

By 1500 trade was thriving between East Africa and partners in the Indian Ocean basin. The arrival of the Portuguese at about that time would disrupt that valuable balance. With nothing to offer the well-off merchants of East Africa, India, and the Arabian Sea region, the Portuguese turned to force. Using their guns, stout vessels, and Mediterranean fort-building techniques, they sought to profit from the Indian Ocean trade by impeding it—that is, by enforcing monopolies on certain items and taking over vital ports. Ultimately this worked better in India than elsewhere, but the Portuguese tried desperately to gain control of East African trade, and even to penetrate the continent's southeast interior in search of Mutapa's gold. Although they failed to conquer Mutapa, the Portuguese traded with its rulers and gained control of gold exports. As they had done in western Africa, in East Africa the Portuguese concentrated fortified posts, or *feitorias*, which they established at Mozambique, Sofala, and Mombasa. The Dutch and English would soon follow.

Trade and Empire in South Asia

> ⬊ **FOCUS** What factors account for the fall of Vijayanagara and the rise of the Mughals?

As in East Africa, dozens of independent trading enclaves in South Asia prospered in early modern times. Many coastal cities and their hinterlands were subject to Muslim sultans or Hindu princes, most of whom drew their sustenance from the merchants they protected. Trading populations were larger than those of East Africa and more diverse. Religious minorities included Jains, Jews, Parsis (Zoroastrians), and Christians. As densely packed commercial crossroads, India's port cities maintained close ties to the subcontinent's rich interior, at this time home to two major empires. One was in ascendance, the Muslim Mughal Empire in the north, and the other in decline, the Hindu kingdom of Vijayanagara (vizh-ah-ya-na-GAR-ah) in the south (see again Map 18.1).

Vijayanagara's Rise and Fall 1336–1565

Vijayanagara grew into an empire around 1500, only to disintegrate due to internal factionalism and external, mostly northern Muslim (although not Mughal) attacks. Because of its swift demise and the near-total loss of its written records, Vijayanagara remains one of the most enigmatic empires of the early modern period. With Muslim kingdoms dominating much of the subcontinent by the time the Portuguese arrived around 1500, Hindu Vijayanagara appears to have been something of an anachronism. Like the contemporary Aztec and Inca Empires of the Americas, Vijayanagara was neither a gunpowder empire nor an early modern, bureaucratic state. Massive stone temples and lively artistic works hint at great opulence and power, but the nature of daily life for commoners remains obscure, although it has been reconstructed in part by archaeological work and from the observations of early European visitors.

Literally, "city of triumph," the kingdom of Vijayanagara was said to have been founded by two brothers in 1336. They chose the town site of Hampi, in the southern interior, to revive a purist version of the Hindu state. According to legend, the brothers had been captured in northern frontier wars and forced to convert to Islam in Delhi, but once back in their homeland they renounced that faith and sought the advice of Hindu Brahmans. Hundreds of temples were built along the Tungabadhra River gorge to venerate the state's patron deity, Virupaksha (vee-rooh-PAHK-shah), among others. By 1370, the empire covered most of southern India, with the exception of Malabar in the far southwest.

Whereas Muslim and Christian rulers were generally regarded as pragmatic "warriors of the faith," Hindu rulers were often seen as divine kings. Their most important duties involved performing the sacred rituals believed to sustain their kingdoms. Whether in Vijayanagara or in distant Bali in Southeast Asia, Hindu kingship relied on theatricality and symbolism quite removed from the everyday

≡ **Hampi** This is an aerial view of part of Hampi, ancient capital of the Hindu kingdom of Vijayanagara in south-central India. The main temple rises in the smoky distance, marking the end of a long ceremonial promenade fronted by stone structures. The Tungabhadra River winds alongside, and all around are hills strewn with granite boulders, giving the city a primeval, almost timeless feel. Hampi fell to northern invaders in 1565.

concerns of imperial administration. Hindu kings participated in warfare and other serious matters, but their lives were mostly scripted by traditional sacred texts. Their societies believed that they would ensure prosperity in peacetime and victory in war by properly enacting their roles.

Life in Vijayanagara cycled between a peaceful period, when the king resided in the capital and carried out rituals, and a campaign season, when the king and his retinue traveled the empire battling with neighboring states and principalities. Like so much under Hindu rule, even victory on the field was scripted, and the warring season itself served as a reenactment of legendary battles. Each campaign started with a festival reaffirming the king's divinity. Although he was renowned for his piety, it was his martial prowess that most set him apart from mere mortals. He was the exemplar of the **Kshatriya** (K-SHAH-tree-yah), or warrior **caste**, not the technically higher ranking **Brahman**, or priestly caste.

Celebratory temple inscriptions record the names and deeds of many monarchs, but thanks to the records of foreign visitors the Vijayanagara king we know most about was Krishna Deva Raya (r. 1509–1529). Portuguese merchants and ambassadors traveled to his court on several occasions, and all were stunned by the monarch's wealth and pomp. At his height, Krishna Deva Raya controlled most of India south of the Krishna River. Most Indian diamonds were mined nearby, providing a significant source of state revenue. But it was the constant flow of tribute from the *rajas*, the subject princes, that built his "city of triumph." Imperial demand drove the rajas to trade their products for Indian Ocean luxuries such as African gold and ivory. The king sat upon a diamond-studded throne, and two hundred subject princes attended him constantly at court. Each wore a gold ankle bracelet to indicate his willingness to die on the king's behalf.

Krishna Deva Raya welcomed the Portuguese following their 1510 conquest of Muslim-held Goa (GO-ah), a port on India's west coast that would become the keystone of Portugal's overseas empire. His armies required warhorses in the tens of thousands, and an arrangement with the Portuguese would give him easier access to horses from Arabia and Iraq. As they had done in western Africa, the Portuguese happily served as horse-traders to conquering non-Christian kings in exchange for access to local goods. Krishna Deva Raya used the imported mounts to extend Vijayanagara's borders north and south, and the Portuguese sent home some of the largest diamonds yet seen in Europe.

Vijayanagara shared some features with the roughly contemporaneous Aztec and Inca states—it was a tributary empire built on a combination of military force

Kshatriya A member of the warrior caste in Hindu societies.

caste A hereditary social class separated from others in Hindu societies.

Brahman A member of the priestly caste in Hindu societies.

and religious charisma. Subject princes were required to maintain armies and give surpluses to their king at periodic festivals; material display reaffirmed the king's divinity. Proper subordination of the rajas was equally important. Krishna Deva Raya was said to require so much gold from certain rajas that they were forced to sponsor pirates to generate revenue. Most tribute, however, came from the sale of farm products, cloth, and diamonds.

Above the rajas, Krishna Deva Raya appointed district administrators called *nayaks*. These were usually relatives, and each oversaw several lesser kingdoms. The system was intended to both replicate and feed the center, with each raja and nayak sponsoring temple construction and revenue-generating projects. Large-scale irrigation works improved agricultural yields, and at bridge crossings and city gates, officials taxed goods in transit. The demands of the city and empire placed great pressure on southern India's forests and wetlands, and increased diamond mining sped deforestation and erosion of riverbanks. Environmental consequences of expansion were noted but were not, as far as we know, a major cause of decline.

Dependent as it was on trade, the expansion of Vijayanagara required a policy of religious tolerance similar to that later practiced by the Mughals. Jain merchants and minor princes were vital subjects since they helped link Vijayanagara to the world beyond India. Brahmanic or priestly law largely restricted Hindu trade to the land, whereas Jains could freely go abroad. Muslim coastal merchants were also allowed into the imperial fold, as they had far greater access than the Jains to luxury imports and warhorses. They had their own residential quarter in the capital city of Hampi. The early Portuguese policy in India was to exploit niches in this preexisting trade system—not to conquer Vijayanagara, but simply to drive out competing Muslim merchants.

Though connected to the outside world mainly through the luxury goods trade, the empire's economy was based on rice cultivation. While kings and Brahmans reenacted the lives of the gods, most of Vijayanagara's subjects toiled their lives away as rice farmers. Around 1522 the Portuguese visitor Domingos Paes (see Reading the Past: Portuguese Report of a Vijayanagara Festival) described work on a huge, stone-reinforced reservoir: "In the tank I saw so many people at work that there must have been fifteen or twenty thousand men, looking like ants, so that you could not see the ground on which they walked."[2]

Vijayanagara's rice fed its people, but it was also exported. Special varieties were shipped as far abroad as Hormuz, on the Persian Gulf, and Aden, at the mouth of the Red Sea. More common rice varieties, along with sugar and some spices, provisioned the merchants of many Indian Ocean ports, including those of East

READING THE PAST

Portuguese Report of a Vijayanagara Festival

The Portuguese merchant Domingos Paes (PAH-ish) visited Vijayanagara in 1520 with a larger diplomatic and commercial mission sent from Goa, the Portuguese trading post on India's southwest coast. Paes's report of the capital of Hampi and King Krishna Deva Raya's court, apparently written for Portugal's official chronicler back in Lisbon, is among the richest to survive. Paes describes a portion of a multiday festival that served to glorify the king and reaffirm the hierarchy of the state but also to reenact cosmic battles:

At three o'clock in the afternoon everyone comes to the palace. They do not admit everyone at once (they allowed us to go into the open part that is between the gates), but there go inside only the wrestlers and dancing-women, and the elephants, which go with their trappings and decorations, those that sit on them being armed with shields and javelins, and wearing quilted tunics. As soon as these are inside they range themselves around the arena, each one in his or her place. . . . Many other people are then at the entrance gate opposite to the building, namely Brahmins, and the sons of the king's favorites, and their relations; all these noble youths who serve before the king. The officers of the household go about keeping order amongst all the people, and keep each one in his or her own place. . . .

The king sits dressed in white clothes all covered with [embroidery of] golden roses and wearing his jewels—he wears a quantity of these white garments, and I always saw him so dressed—and around him stand his pages with his betel [to

Africa and Gujarat. It was through the sale of rice abroad that many subject princes obtained African gold for their king, with annual payments said to be in the thousands of pounds each by the time of Krishna Deva Raya.

Following Krishna Deva Raya's death in 1529, Vijayanagara fell victim first to internal succession rivalries, and then to Muslim aggressors. In 1565, under King Ramaraja, a coalition of formerly subject sultans defeated the royal army. Hampi, the capital city, was sacked, plundered, and abandoned; it was an overgrown ruin by 1568. Remnant Hindu principalities survived in the southeast but eventually fell to the expansionist Mughals. By the seventeenth century only a few Hindu states remained around the fringes of South Asia, including remote Nepal. The Hindu principalities of Malabar, meanwhile, fell increasingly into the hands of Europeans and Muslim Gujarati merchants. Still, the memory of chew], and his sword, and the other things which are his insignia of state. . . . As soon as the king is seated, the captains who waited outside make their entrance, each one by himself, attended by his chief people. . . . As soon as the nobles have finished entering, the captains of the troops approach with shields and spears, and afterwards the captains of archers. . . . As soon as these soldiers have all taken their places the women begin to dance. . . . Who can fitly describe to you the great riches these women carry on their persons?— collars of gold with so many diamonds and rubies

and pearls, bracelets also on their arms and upper arms, girdles below, and of necessity anklets on their feet. . . .

Then the wrestlers begin their play. Their wrestling does not seem like ours, but there are blows [given], so severe as to break teeth, and put out eyes, and disfigure faces, so much so that here and there men are carried off speechless by their friends; they give one another fine falls, too. They have their captains and judges who are there to put each one on equal footing in the field, and also to award the honors to him who wins.

Source: Robert Sewell, *A Forgotten Empire (Vijayanagar): A Contribution to the History of India* (London: Sonnenschein, 1900), 268–271.

Examining the Evidence

1. What does the selection suggest with regard to social hierarchy and prescribed gender roles in Vijayanagara?

2. How does this description of divine kingship compare with, for example, the Incas (see chapter 15)?

Vijayanagara's greatness and wealth lived on, to be revived much later by Hindu nationalists.

The Power of the Mughals

Another empire was expanding rapidly in India's north as Vijayanagara crumbled in the south. Beginning around 1500, under a Timurid (from Timur, the famed fourteenth-century Central Asian ruler discussed in Chapter 14) Muslim warlord named Babur (the "Tiger," r. 1500–1530), the Mughal Empire emerged as the most powerful, wealthy, and populous state yet seen in South Asia. By the time of Nur Jahan in the early 1600s, the Mughals (literally "Mongols," the great fourteenth-century emperors from whom the Mughals descended) had over 120 million subjects, a population comparable only to that of Ming China.

Accumulating wealth from plunder and tribute and employing newly introduced gunpowder weapons and swift warhorses to terrifying effect, the Mughals subdued dozens of Hindu and Muslim principalities as they pushed southward (see Map 18.2). Like many early modern empire builders, the Mughals were outsiders who adapted to local cultural traditions to establish and maintain legitimacy.

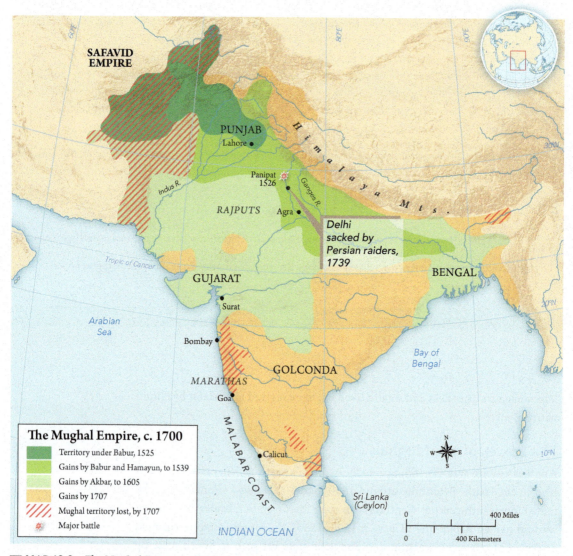

The Mughal Empire, c. 1700

- ▨ Territory under Babur, 1525
- ▨ Gains by Babur and Hamayun, to 1539
- ▨ Gains by Akbar, to 1605
- ▨ Gains by 1707
- ▧ Mughal territory lost, by 1707
- ✳ Major battle

≡ **MAP 18.2   The Mughal Empire, c. 1700**   Descendants of mounted Central Asian raiders, the Mughals expanded their control over the Indian subcontinent after 1500 with devastating, gunpowder-backed force followed by ethnic and religious accommodation. By 1700, the empire was approaching its greatest extent, after which rebellions and invasions began to force it to contract.

In terms of Indian Ocean commerce, their rapid rise drove up demand for luxury imports, and, as in the case of Nur Jahan, some high-ranking Mughal nobles invested directly in exports of items such as indigo and gems.

Despite rule by Muslim overlords, most South Asians remained Hindus in early modern times, but those who converted to Islam enjoyed some benefits. Initially, conversion to Islam brought tax exemptions, but these were suspended in the late sixteenth century under Emperor Akbar. As we will see, during and after his reign, lasting fusions between Hinduism and Islam emerged in various parts of the subcontinent.

Like its religion, South Asia's dynamic economy was little changed after conquest. Under Mughal rule, South Asia's legendary textiles, grains, spices, gems, and many other products continued to find buyers worldwide. Truly new markets for Indian goods emerged in the Americas and parts of sub-Saharan Africa, supplied by Portuguese and other European shippers. Lacking commodities Indians wanted, European traders paid for South Asia's goods in hard cash. As a result, India, like China, enjoyed a consistently favorable balance of trade throughout early modern times. Along with funding armies, this wealth from abroad fueled construction, especially of religious buildings. With royal sponsorship like that of Nur Jahan, many of India's most iconic structures, such as the Taj Mahal and Red Fort, were built along the Ganges River plain.

True to the Timurid heritage it shared with its Safavid Persian and Ottoman Turkish neighbors (discussed in the next chapter), Mughal rule in India was marked by both extraordinary court opulence and near-constant power struggles and rebellions. Indeed, factionalism and succession crises eventually led to Mughal decline. Soon after 1700, this decline in central authority left Mughal India vulnerable to European as well as Persian imperial designs. Persian raiders sacked the capital of Delhi in 1739, and by 1763 the English East India Company won rights to tax former Mughal subjects in the province of Bengal, effectively exercising sovereignty in the Indian interior. Despite these reversals of fortune, life for the bulk of South Asia's millions of poor farmers and artisans scarcely changed.

Gunpowder Weapons and Imperial Consolidation 1500–1763

The emperor, or "Mughal," Babur spent most of his life defeating Afghan warlords. Horses and archers were still critical in these early victories, as was Babur's charismatic leadership, but by the 1510s some of the emperor's forces were using matchlock guns in battle. By the 1526 Battle of Panipat, outside Delhi, Babur's armies had perfected the use of cannons (see again Map 18.2). As Babur recalled nonchalantly in his memoir, the *Baburnama*: "Mustafa the artilleryman fired some good shots from the mortars mounted on carts to the left of the center [flank]."[3] Some sixteen thousand men were said to have died in this battle, and Babur celebrated by plundering the city of Agra. In 1527, although hugely outnumbered by a Hindu Rajput alliance of some eighty thousand cavalry and five hundred armored war elephants, Babur and his army won handily. Gunpowder weapons continued to prove decisive as Babur and his successors drove south.

Humayun, as Babur's son was known, took over the emerging Mughal Empire at his father's death in 1530, but he suffered setbacks. In 1535, he employed Ottoman military engineers and Portuguese gunners to attack the kingdom of Gujarat, a major textile exporter facing the Arabian Sea, but sources say his crippling addiction to opium cost valuable time, forcing a withdrawal of troops. In the course of this ill-fated adventure, an Afghan warlord rose from the ashes to reconquer almost everything Babur had won in the north. Humayun went into exile in Safavid Persia, but he returned to India aided by gun-toting Safavid forces. By 1555, Humayun had used this expanded firepower to regain his father's conquests, only to die in 1556 after hitting his head on the stairs of his library. Councilors decided the next Mughal would be Humayun's twelve-year-old son, Akbar.

India's historic role as an interfaith crossroads was only heightened during the long reign of Akbar (literally "the Great," r. 1556–1605). Though founded by Timurid horsemen who regarded themselves as warriors of the Islamic faith in the Sunni tradition, by the time of Akbar a quick succession of marriages had linked Shi'ite Safavid and Hindu royalty to the central Mughal line. For over a century Persian remained the language of the court, and relations with the Safavids were friendly. Most notable, however, was the steady "Indianization" of the Mughal emperors themselves. The wealth and diversity of the subcontinent, not to mention the beauty and charm of Hindu Rajput princesses, absorbed them. Akbar was no exception: his son Jahangir, the next emperor, was born to a Hindu princess.

This process of absorption was accelerated by Akbar's eclectic personality. Fascinated with everything from yogic asceticism to the fire worship of India's Parsi, or Zoroastrian, minority, by the 1570s Akbar began formulating his own hybrid religion. It was a variety of emperor worship forced mostly upon high-ranking subjects. Somewhat like the early modern Inca and Japanese royal cults that tied the ruling house to the sun, Akbar's cult emphasized his own divine solar radiance. Staunch Muslim advisers rebelled against this seeming heresy in 1579, but Akbar successfully repressed them. In the end, Akbar's faith won few lasting converts—and left visiting Jesuit missionaries scratching their heads—yet its mere existence demonstrated an enduring Mughal tendency toward accommodation of religious difference.

Despite his eclecticism and toleration, Akbar clung to core Timurid cultural traditions, such as moving his court and all its attendant wealth and servants from one grand campsite to another. He was said to travel with no fewer than one hundred thousand attendants. He also never gave up his attachment to gunpowder warfare. Recalcitrant regional lords such as the Rajput Hindu prince Udai Singh defied Akbar's authority in the 1560s, only to suffer the young emperor's wrath. A protracted 1567 siege of the fortified city of Chitor ended with the deaths of some twenty-five thousand defenders and their families. Akbar himself shot the commander of the city's defenses dead with a musket, and his massive siege cannons, plus the planting of explosive mines, brought down its formidable stone walls. A similar siege in 1569 employed even larger guns, hauled into position by elephants and teams of oxen. Few princes challenged Akbar's authority after these devastating demonstrations of Mughal firepower.

By the end of Akbar's reign, the Mughal Empire stretched from Afghanistan to Bengal, and south to about the latitude of Bombay (today Mumbai; see again Map 18.2). Emperor Jahangir (r. 1605–1627) was far less ambitious than his father Akbar, and as we saw in the opening paragraphs to this chapter, his addictions and interests led him to hand power to his favored wife, Nur Jahan, an effective administrator and business woman but not a conqueror. Jahangir's reign was nevertheless significant. A devoted patron of the arts and an amateur poet, Jahangir took Mughal court splendor to new heights (see Seeing the Past: Reflections of the Divine in a Mughal Emerald). His illustrated memoir, the *Jahangirnama*, is a candid description of life at the top of one of the early modern world's most populous and wealthy empires.

New conquests under Shah Jahan (r. 1628–1658) and Aurangzeb (aw-WRONG-zeb) (r. 1658–1707) carried the empire south almost to the tip of the subcontinent. These rulers had made few innovations in gunpowder warfare; as in the days of Babur, religion was as important a factor in imperial expansion as technology. Shah Jahan was an observant but tolerant Muslim, whereas Aurangzeb was a true holy warrior who called for a return to orthodoxy. Aurangzeb's religious fervor was a major force in the last phase of Mughal expansion.

The emperor's main foe was Prince Shivaji (c. 1640–1680), leader of the Hindu Marathas of India's far southwest. Aurangzeb employed European gunners, whose state-of-the-art weapons helped him capture several of Shivaji's forts, but he mostly relied on muskets, cannons, and other weapons designed and cast in India. Large swivel guns were mounted on camels, a useful adaptation. For his part, Shivaji

SEEING THE PAST

Reflections of the Divine in a Mughal Emerald

In the seventeenth century, foreign visitors repeatedly claimed that the Mughal court was the richest in the world. The Mughal emperor and his family wore delicately tailored silk garments and other luxurious clothes, dripping with jewels. Many great stones, such as the one pictured here, have survived in museums or private collections. Fabulous gemstones weighing hundreds of carats were routinely exchanged and given as gifts to important visitors, loyal subjects, and favored heirs.

India's early modern rulers had direct access to precious metals, diamonds, rubies, and pearls, but emeralds—especially prized because green was the color of Islam—were hard to come by. Old mines in Egypt had long since played out, and sources in Afghanistan and Pakistan remained unknown, or at least untapped. Emeralds were found, however, in faraway New Granada, the Spanish American colony now roughly comprised by the Republic of Colombia. Beginning in the late sixteenth century, Spanish mine owners traded emeralds dug from the high Andes to Spanish and Portuguese merchants with ties to Goa, Portugal's most important trading post in India. From there, merchants traded the stones inland to intermediaries and even to

Mughal Emerald

the Mughal emperor himself. Once in the hands of the renowned artisans of the world's most opulent court, raw Colombian emeralds were faceted, tumbled, and carved into a wide variety of royal jewels. Some were carefully inscribed with Arabic verses from the Qur'an or special prayers. The one pictured here contains a Shi'a prayer praising the Twelve Imams. It was meant to be sewn into a ritual garment, prayer-side in, as a protective amulet.

Examining the Evidence

1. How does this precious object reflect patterns of early modern globalization?

2. Why would the royal owner commission a religious object of such magnificence?

was never able to field more than a few hundred musketeers, relying instead on swift mounts and guerrilla raids. Despite a major offensive sent by Aurangzeb after Shivaji's death, the Marathas bounced back within a few decades and won recognition of their homeland.

Only under Aurangzeb's successor, Muhammad (r. 1720–1739), did Mughal stagnation and contraction set in. Rebellions by overtaxed peasants and nobles alike sapped the empire's overstretched resources, and Muhammad's guns proved increasingly outmoded. Europeans were by this time shifting to lighter and more mobile artillery, but the Mughals were casting larger and ever-more-unwieldy cannons. A cannon said to be capable of shooting one-hundred-pound balls, dubbed "Fort Opener," was so heavy it had to be pulled by four elephants and thousands of oxen. Most of the time, it remained stuck in the mud between siege targets. Muhammad Shah finally lost Delhi and the great Mughal treasury to Iran's Nadir Shah, successor to the Safavids, in 1739. The empire fell into disarray until the reign of Shah Alam II, who took the throne in 1759, only to fall under British influence in 1763. He ruled as a puppet of English East India Company until 1806.

Typical of early modern empire builders, the Mughals shifted between peaceful pragmatism and deadly force. They made alliances with subject peoples, offering them a share of power and the right to carry on established livelihoods. When not engaged in wars of expansion, emperors such as Akbar and Shah Jahan mediated disputes, expanded palace structures, and organized tribute collection. Elite tax-collectors and administrators called *zamindars* (SAW-mean-dars) lived off their shares of tribute, ruling like chiefs over zones called *parganas*, similar to the Ottoman *timars* (discussed in the next chapter). Somewhat medieval in structure, this sort of decentralized rule bred corruption, which in turn led to waves of modernizing reform.

As in the similarly populous and cash-hungry empire of Ming China, Mughal tax reform moved toward a centralized money economy (India's rulers had long enjoyed the privilege of minting gold, silver, and copper coins), stimulating both rural and urban markets. By Akbar's time, most taxes were paid in cash. Meanwhile, European merchants, ever anxious for Indian commodities, reluctantly supplied their South Asian counterparts with precious metals. As in China, this boost to the Mughal money supply was critical, since India had few precious metals mines of its own. The influx of cash, mostly Spanish-American silver pesos, continued even after the 1739 Persian sack of Delhi, but it was arguably a mixed blessing. As in contemporary China, and indeed in Spain itself, the heightened commercial activity and massive influx of bullion did not beget modern industrialization in

India. Instead, it bred increased state belligerence and court grandeur. In a sense, the old "Mongolian" notions of governance were simply magnified, financed in a new, more efficient way. Even gunpowder weapons became little more than objects of show.

Everyday Life in the Mughal Empire

Despite its Islamic core and general policy of religious toleration, Mughal India remained sharply divided by status, or caste, as well as other types of social distinctions. India's caste divisions, like the so-called estates of Europe (nobility, clergy, and commoners), were thought to be derived from a divine order, or hierarchy, and could scarcely be challenged. Women's lives were circumscribed in virtually all but regal and wealthy merchant circles. The Hindu practice of **sati**, in which widows committed suicide by throwing themselves onto their husbands' funeral pyres, continued under Islamic rule, although there is much debate about its frequency. Akbar opposed the practice, but he did not ban it. Polygamy, sanctioned by Islam and embraced by Akbar and other rulers, was practiced by any man who could afford to support what amounted to multiple households.

Lower-caste folk, meanwhile, suffered regardless of gender. Worst off were the so-called Untouchables, who were relegated to disposing of human waste, animal carcasses, and other jobs requiring the handling of filth. Like those in many other parts of the early modern world, Mughal elites defined their own dignity most clearly by denying it to those around them—all the while displaying their innate goodness and superiority through ritualized, ostentatious acts of charity.

Most Mughal subjects were subsistence farmers, many of them tied to landlords through tributary and other customary obligations. The Mughal state thrived mostly by inserting itself into existing tributary structures, not by reordering local economies. Problems arose when Mughal rulers raised tax quotas sharply, or when droughts, floods, and other natural disasters upset the cycle of agricultural production. Unlike the Ming and Qing Chinese, or even the Spanish in Mexico, the Mughals devoted very little of their tremendous wealth to dams, aqueducts, and other public works projects. What was new, or modern, was that paper-pushing bureaucrats recorded farmers' tax assessments.

sati The ancient Indian practice of ritual suicide by widows.

Even in good times, most South Asians lived on only a small daily ration of rice or millet, seasoned with ginger or cumin and—lightly—salt, an expensive state-monopoly item. Some fruits, such as mangoes, were seasonally available, but protein sources were limited. Even in times of bounty, religious dietary restrictions

☰ **Building a Palace** This Mughal miniature from the 1590s is quite unusual in depicting ordinary working folk, along with a pair of animal helpers. Men of several colors, ages, and states of dress engage in heavy labor, transporting and lifting stones, beams, and mortar; splitting planks; setting stones; and plastering domes. Several women are sifting sand or preparing mortar, and at center right are two well-dressed men who appear to be architects or inspectors. Two similar inspectors appear in the upper right, and only in the upper left corner do we glimpse the elite palace inhabitants, seemingly oblivious to the goings-on below.

kept most people thin. After centuries of deforestation, people used animal dung as cooking fuel. Intensive agriculture using animal-drawn plows and irrigation works was widespread, but mass famines occurred frequently. The Columbian Exchange was marginally helpful. After about 1600, American maize and tobacco were planted, along with the capsicum peppers that came to spice up many South Asian dishes. Maize spurred population growth in some parts of India, whereas tobacco probably shortened some people's lives. Most tobacco was produced as a cash crop for elite consumption.

India's cities grew rapidly in Mughal times, in part due to stress-induced migration. Nine urban centers—among them Agra, Delhi, and Lahore—exceeded two hundred thousand inhabitants before 1700. After Akbar's rule, the shift to tax collection in cash was a major stimulus to urban growth and dynamism. Even small towns bustled with commercial activity as the economy became more monetized, and all urban centers formed nuclei of artisan production.

Several South Asian coastal and riverside cities produced abundant cotton and silk textiles. They usually followed the putting-out, or piecework, system, in which merchants "put out" raw materials to artisans working from home. As in China and northern Europe, women formed the backbone of this industry, not so much in weaving but rather in the physically harder tasks of fiber cleaning and spinning. Other, mostly male artisans specialized in woodworking, leather making, blacksmithing, and gem cutting. Perhaps the most visible artisanal legacy from Mughal times was in architecture. Highly skilled stonemasons produced Akbar's majestic Red Fort and Shah Jahan's inimitable Taj Mahal.

Some men found employment in the shipyards of Surat, Calicut, and the Bay of Bengal, and others set sail with their seasonal cargoes of export goods and pilgrims. Gujarati Muslim merchants were dominant in the Arabian Sea even after the arrival of Europeans, but Hindus, Jains, and members of other faiths also participated. Unlike the Ottomans, the Mughals never developed a navy, despite their control of maritime Gujarat since Akbar's conquest of the region in 1572 (see again Map 18.2). On land, by contrast, the empire's military absorbed thousands of men. Frontier wars with fellow Muslims and southern Hindus were nearly constant. Christian Europeans were mostly seen as tangential commercial allies, technical advisers, and arms suppliers.

In the northwestern Punjab region an internal challenge emerged, this time mounted by leaders of a relatively new religious sect, Sikhism. Sikhism was something of a hybrid between Islam and Hinduism, but it tended more toward the latter and thus found deeper support among Hindu princes than among Islamic ones. Merchants and artisans were particularly attracted to the faith's recognition of hard work and abstinence (as we saw in Chapter 14). Peasant and

artisan followers of Guru Gobind
Singh (1666–1708) rebelled in 1710,
and their plundering raids reached
Delhi. The rebellion was violently
quashed by Shah Farrukhsiyar (far-
ROOK-see-yar) (r. 1713–1720) in
1715, but sporadic raids and uprisings continued until the end of the
eighteenth century, when the Sikhs
at last established a separate state.

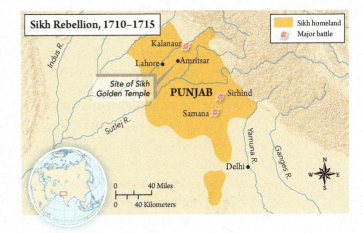

≡ **Sikh Rebellion, 1710–1715**

In sum, the mighty Mughals ruled
over the richest and most populous of
Eurasia's early modern Islamic empires, and theirs remained by far the
most culturally diverse. Mounted warriors used guns to crush or intimidate
neighbors in new and terrifying ways, quickly absorbing huge swaths of terrain
and millions of subject peoples. Yet generally, the resulting rule was neither intolerant nor authoritarian. As long as they paid cash tributes, regions could preserve their religious diversity and a degree of autonomy. Problems arose with
imperial overstretch, succession crises, and excessive taxation. Rebels, particularly non-Muslim ones, increasingly shook imperial foundations. More subtle
but ultimately more serious were the inroads made by European commercial
agents, in particular those of Britain's East India Company. These men, from
Connecticut-born clerk Elihu Yale to governor-general Robert Clive, formed
the spearhead of a new imperialism.

European Interlopers

⤵ **FOCUS** What factors enabled Europeans to take over key Indian
Ocean trade networks?

Direct trade for Indian luxuries had been a dream of Europeans since the days of
Marco Polo. Unfortunately, as the Portuguese explorer Vasco da Gama and his
followers quickly discovered, Europeans had little that appealed to South Asians.
With the exception of certain types of guns and clocks, the Portuguese had no
products that could not be had in some form already, often more cheaply, and guns
would soon be copied. Like Portugal, India was an ancient crossroads, but it was
far larger and richer, and vastly more productive. Complex trade circuits had long

linked India's rich interior and bustling ports to the wider world. In such a crowded marketplace, only silver and gold found universal acceptance because they functioned as money. Frustrated, the Portuguese turned to piracy, financing their first voyages by plunder rather than trade.

Portuguese Conquistadors 1500–1600

As would prove true in China, only precious metals opened India's doors of trade to newcomers. Even with powerful guns and swift ships on their side, the vastly outnumbered Portuguese had no choice but to part with their hard-won African gold and Spanish-American silver. They were fortunate in that silver soon arrived in quantity through Portugal's growing Atlantic trade with the Spanish, particularly after 1550. Profits made in the slave trade were routinely reinvested in spices and other goods from India. Meanwhile, the security of all exchanges was guaranteed with brute force, and in some places, such as Goa in India and Melaka in Malaysia, outright conquest.

Genuine Portuguese conquests in Asia were few but significant. Crown-sponsored conquistadors focused on strategic sites for their fortified trading posts, mostly traditional mercantile crossroads and shipping straits not effectively controlled by local princes. These *feitorias* resembled those already established along the western coast of Africa, but most proved far more expensive and difficult to maintain. The Indian Ocean's sea traffic was huge, and competition was fierce.

The Portuguese grand plan—never realized—was to monopolize all trade in the Indian Ocean by extracting tolls and tariffs from local traders, regardless of political allegiance. For a time they sold shipping licenses. If traders failed to produce such licenses when passing through Portuguese-controlled ports, their goods were confiscated. On top of this, they had to pay duties.

Within a half-century of da Gama's 1498 voyage to India the Portuguese controlled access to the Persian Gulf, Red Sea, South China Sea, and Atlantic Ocean, along with many major coastal trading enclaves (see Map 18.3). Being so few in a region of millions, the Portuguese strategy was pragmatic. By tapping existing trade networks and setting up feitorias, they could efficiently collect spices and textiles, along with what were essentially extortion payments. Friends would be given silver, enemies lead. The method worked as long as the Portuguese faced no competition and remained unified.

Despite early Ottoman attacks, serious competitors would not arrive until about 1600. Portuguese unity was another matter. Given the distance to Lisbon, it proved impossible to enforce consistent policy in dealing with Indian Ocean merchants and princes. Ironically, it was "friendly" local merchants, rajas, and

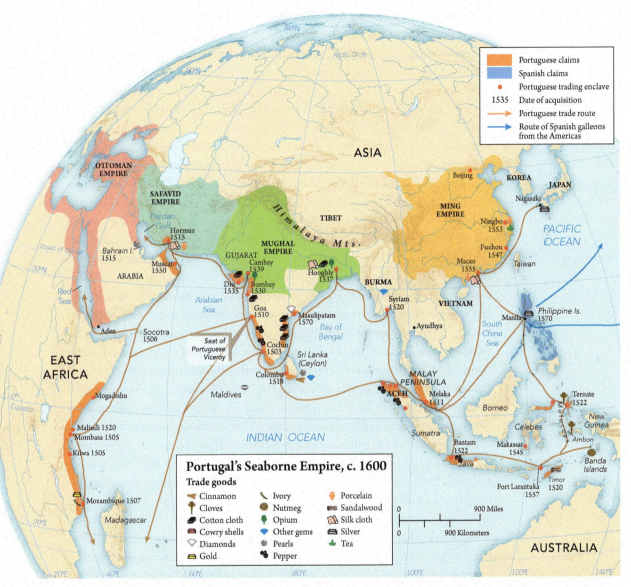

ASIA

PACIFIC OCEAN

Portuguese claims
Spanish claims
Portuguese trading enclave
1535   Date of acquisition
Portuguese trade route
Route of Spanish galleons from the Americas

Portugal's Seaborne Empire, c. 1600
Trade goods

Cinnamon
Cloves
Cotton cloth
Cowry shells
Diamonds
Gold

Ivory
Nutmeg
Opium
Other gems
Pearls
Pepper

Porcelain
Sandalwood
Silk cloth
Silver
Tea

≡ **MAP 18.3   Portugal's Seaborne Empire, c. 1600**   With their castle-like sailing vessels and potent gunpowder weapons, the Portuguese inserted themselves violently into the greater Indian Ocean basin beginning in 1498. From their stronghold in Goa, they monopolized regional and export trade in luxury goods, either by shipping these items themselves or by forcing others to purchase licenses. After 1580, the Portuguese were under Spanish rule, which linked the lucrative Asian trade routes to New World silver arriving in the Philippines.

sultans—Arab, Hindu, and otherwise—who benefited most from Portuguese sponsorship and protection. As in western Africa, for several centuries the Portuguese unwittingly did as much to facilitate local aspirations as to real-ize their own. What they grandly called the "State of India," *Estado da Índia,* gradually proved more "Indian" than Portuguese, though for a short time it was highly profitable to the Crown.

Portugal's grand religious project was similarly absorbed. In 1498 Vasco da Gama expressed confidence in the spread of Roman Catholicism to East Africa: "On Easter day the Moors [Muslims] we had taken captive told us that in the town of Malindi [a Swahili port on the coast of Kenya] there were four vessels belonging to Christians from India, and if we should like to convey them there they would give us Christian pilots, and everything else we might need, including meats, water, wood, and other things."[4] Da Gama wrongly took this to mean that there was a preexisting Christian base or network in the region upon which the Catholic Portuguese could build. Ultimately, Portuguese efforts to convert the many peoples of the Indian Ocean basin failed even more miserably than in Atlantic Africa, though not for lack of trying. Francis Xavier, an early Jesuit missionary (see Chapter 19), worked tirelessly and died an optimist. Whereas he focused on converting slaves and lower-caste people, others sought to bend the will of monarchs such as Akbar, hoping they would set an example. Small Christian communities formed at Goa and other strongholds, but everywhere they went, Portuguese missionaries faced literally millions of hostile Muslims and perhaps equal or greater numbers of uninterested Hindus, Buddhists, Confucianists, Jains, Parsis, Sikhs, Jews, and others. In short, Christianity, at least in the form presented by the Portuguese, did not appeal to the vast majority of people inhabiting the Indian Ocean basin. As we will see in Chapter 20, only in Japan, the Philippines, East Timor, and other select areas, mostly in the western Pacific, did early modern Catholic missionaries strike a chord.

Despite the failure of Christian missionary efforts, trade was brisk. The so-called *carreira da Índia* (cah-HEY-rah dah EENDJ-yah), or India voyage, became legendary in Portuguese culture. Even on successful trips, death rates on this annual sail between Lisbon and Goa were high due to poor sanitation, prolonged vitamin C deprivation, questionable medical therapies, and other health challenges. Also, although early modern navigators were arguably more adept than medieval ones, shipwrecks plagued the India voyage. Unlike local dhows, sixteenth- and seventeenth-century Portuguese vessels were huge, round-hulled, and built for cargo rather than speed or maneuverability, and foundered due to overloading. The coral reefs of southeast Africa became a notorious graveyard of the carreira.

By the later sixteenth century, Portuguese monopolies had weakened. With so much wealth at stake and so few enforcers on hand, corruption and contraband flourished. Shipwrecks and piracy became more frequent, as did competition from better-armed northern Europeans. As Luiz Vaz de Camões (cah-MOYSH), veteran of adventures in the East Indies, composed the triumphant poem that would become Portugal's national epic, *The Lusíads*, Portugal was on the eve of losing not only its heirless king but also its hard-won conquests in the Indian Ocean. It was the Spanish under Philip II who would offer the first humiliation. Shortly after, Spain's sworn enemies, the Dutch, would deal the Portuguese a series of crushing blows.

The Dutch and English East India Companies 1600–1750

As Portuguese fortunes declined and Mughal expansion continued toward the turn of the seventeenth century, South Asia's overseas trade underwent reorganization. This shift involved many players, including the familiar Gujarati merchants, the increasingly powerful Ottomans, Persia's expanding Safavids, and others. But ultimately it was Dutch and English newcomers, and to a lesser extent the French, who would have the greatest long-term impact. All formed powerful **trading companies** in the seventeenth and eighteenth centuries, each backed by state-of-the-art cannons and first-rate sailing ships.

Despite these important changes, it would be highly misleading to project the later imperial holdings of these foreigners back onto the seventeenth and early eighteenth centuries. Only the Dutch came close to establishing a genuine "Indian Ocean Empire" during early modern times. Meanwhile, East Africans, South and Southeast Asians, and other native peoples of the Indian Ocean continued to act independently, in their own interests. It was the sudden, unexpected collapse of the Mughals and other gunpowder-fueled Asian states in the later eighteenth century that allowed Europeans to conquer large landmasses and to plant colonies of the sort long since established in the Americas.

The Dutch East India Company, known by its Dutch acronym VOC, was founded in 1602. The company aimed to use ships, arms, and Spanish-American silver to displace the Portuguese as Europe's principal suppliers of spices and other exotic Asian goods. Though not officially a state enterprise, the Dutch East India Company counted many ranking statesmen among its principal investors, and its actions abroad were as belligerent as those of any imperial army or navy. In the course of almost two centuries, the VOC extended Dutch influence from South Africa to Japan. Its most lasting achievement was the conquest of Java, base for the vast Dutch colony of Indonesia.

Although they never drove the Portuguese from Goa, the Dutch displaced their Iberian rivals nearly everywhere else. Their greatest early successes were in southern India and Java, followed by Sri Lanka (Ceylon), Bengal, Melaka, and Japan (see Map 18.4). In Southeast Asia conquest was followed with enslavement and eventually plantation agriculture of the sort established by the Spanish and Portuguese in the Americas. The VOC also imposed this sequence on Ceylon (see Lives and Livelihoods: Cinnamon Harvesters in Ceylon).

trading companies Private corporations licensed by early modern European states to monopolize Asian and other overseas trades.

LIVES AND LIVELIHOODS

Cinnamon Harvesters in Ceylon

Long before the arrival of Europeans in 1506, the island of Sri Lanka, or Ceylon (its colonial name), was world-renowned for its cinnamon exports. This wet, tropical island off India's southeast tip, largely under control of competing Buddhist kings, was also famous for its sapphires, rubies, pearls, and domesticated elephants. Like India's pepper and Southeast Asia's cloves, mace, and nutmeg, Ceylonese cinnamon fetched extraordinary prices throughout Eurasia and parts of Africa where it was used as a condiment, preservative, and even medicine. As late as 1685 a Portuguese observer noted, "Every year a great number of vessels arrive from Persia, Arabia, the Red Sea, the Malabar Coast [of India], China, Bengal, and Europe to fetch cinnamon." Attempts to transplant the spice elsewhere, including Brazil, all failed, and early conquistador claims of finding cinnamon in Ecuador's eastern jungles proved false. As part of the Columbian Exchange, Ceylonese cinnamon became an ingredient in hot chocolate, a beverage developed in colonial Mexico that took Europe by storm.

The spice grew wild in forests belonging to the kingdom of Kandy, in Ceylon's southwest highlands. In 1517, the Portuguese struck a deal that allowed them to use and fortify the port of Colombo to monopolize cinnamon exports in exchange for cloth, metal ware, and military assistance against rivals. The Portuguese did not engage directly in cinnamon production, but rather traded for it with the king and certain nobles. The king and his nobles in turn collected cinnamon as a tribute item produced on feudal-type estates called *parawenia*. A special caste of male workers known as *chalias* was responsible for planting, harvesting, slicing, drying, and packaging Ceylon's most prized crop. The chalias were not enslaved, but rather served as dependents of the king and various noblemen and military officers in exchange for use rights to land for subsistence farming in the off-season, plus rations of rice and occasionally a cash wage.

Cinnamon is derived from the shaved and dried inner bark of the small *Cinamomum verum* tree, a variety of laurel. Although the spice can be harvested wild, Ceylon's chalias pruned, transplanted, and even planted the trees by seed in order to maximize output and improve quality. At harvest time the chalias cut ripe cinnamon trees and then removed the bark to meet quotas set by the king and other estate holders.

Next came peeling, the key process, and the one for which the chalias were best known. As a seventeenth-century Portuguese writer described them, "These cinnamon peelers carry in their girdle a small hooked knife as a mark of their occupation." Working in pairs, one chalia made two lengthwise incisions on the ripe sticks using his hooked knife and carefully removed the resulting half-cylindrical strips of bark. His companion then used other tools to separate a gray outer bark from the thin, cream-colored inner bark. The inner bark was then left to dry, curling, thickening, and turning brown as it oxidized. The chalias then packaged the resulting "cinnamon sticks" black pepper for long sea voyages to help draw out moisture.

We have no documents written by the chalias to give us a sense of their views, but we do know that a leader of a 1609 rebellion against the Portuguese was a member of this caste and the son of a cinnamon cutter. Tapping into local discontent, the Dutch East India Company (VOC) displaced the Portuguese in 1658 after making an alliance with the king of Kandy. Once established on the island, the Dutch shifted to direct planting and harvesting, using enslaved laborers and totally monopolizing trade in cinnamon in order to maximize profits. The king was reduced to the status of client. Dutch work demands were rigorous and punishments harsh for even light offenses. Dissatisfaction with the VOC ran deep. The British took over Ceylon in 1796 following the collapse of the VOC, but their management of the cinnamon economy was not as careful, and both price and quality fell. Ceylon's export sector would be revived after 1800 with the introduction of American tropical crops adapted by British botanists: cinchona (quinine), cacao, and rubber.

≡ **Harvesting Cinnamon** This engraving, based on a simpler one from 1672, depicts cinnamon harvesters in Ceylon (Sri Lanka). The Portuguese were the first Europeans to attempt to monopolize the global export of this spice, but local kings were difficult to conquer and control. Only in the later seventeenth century did the Dutch manage to establish plantation-type production, with the final product, the now familiar cinnamon sticks, monopolized by the Dutch East India Company (VOC).

in cloth-covered bundles weighing about one hundred pounds. These were given to overlords; the king of Kandy alone was said to demand over five hundred tons each year. Cinnamon was often bundled with

Questions to Consider

1. How was cinnamon grown, harvested, and prepared for export?

2. How did cinnamon harvesting fit into traditional, precolonial landholding and labor systems?

3. How did Dutch rule change the lives and livelihoods of cinnamon harvesters?

For Further Information:

Valentijn, François. *Description of Ceylon.* Edited by Sinnappah Arasaratnam. London: Hakluyt Society, 1978.

Winius, George D. *The Fatal History of Portuguese Ceylon* New York: Cambridge University Press, 1971.

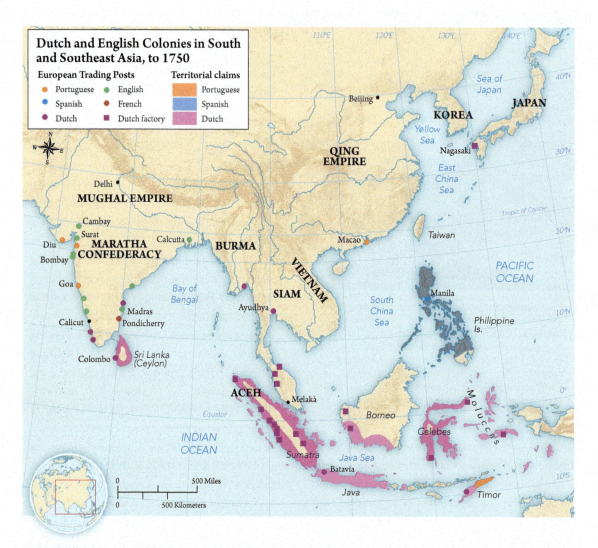

≡ **MAP 18.4   Dutch and English Colonies in South and Southeast Asia, to 1750** Although the Portuguese remained active in the Indian Ocean basin and South China Sea until the twentieth century, after 1600 the Dutch and English had largely displaced them. The East India Companies of these two countries sought to conquer and defend key trading enclaves, both against each other and against the later-arriving French.

The monopolistic mentality of contemporary Europe drove Dutch aggression: profits were ensured not by free trade but by absolute control over the flow of commodities and the money to pay for them. The VOC began by monopolizing spices. After seizing the pepper-growing region of southern Sumatra, the VOC turned to the riskier business of establishing plantations to grow coffee and other tropical cash crops. Like the Portuguese before them, the Dutch devoted at least as much cargo space to interregional trade as to exports. Thus clever local traders and many thousands of Chinese merchants benefited from the Dutch determination to monopolize trade.

The VOC, like other Indian Ocean traders, relied on Spanish-American silver to lubricate commerce. Between 1600 and 1648, when these rival empires were at war, some silver was plundered from the Spanish in the Caribbean by Dutch pirates, but most was extracted through trade, both official and contraband. Recent research has revealed the importance of illegal Dutch slave traders in Buenos Aires after a major peace agreement was signed with Spain in 1648. The silver of Potosí in this case bypassed Europe entirely to go to Dutch trading posts in India, Southeast Asia, and China. Mexican silver, meanwhile, flowed out of Dutch Caribbean ports such as Curaçao, through Amsterdam, and into the holds of outbound company ships. Trade in Manila extracted still more Spanish silver. Though ever more divided in its political loyalties, the world was becoming ever more unified in its monetary system.

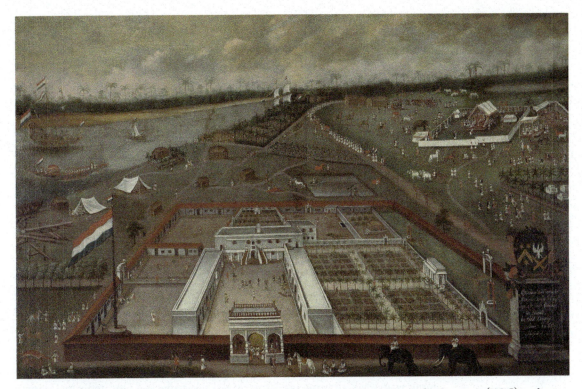

☰ **Dutch Headquarters in Bengal** This painting from 1665 depicts the Dutch East India Company (VOC) trading fort at Hugly, on the banks of the Ganges River in the Indian province of Bengal. As they did elsewhere along the rim of the rich and populous Indian Ocean basin, the Dutch sought to establish exclusive control over specific commodities, usually after driving out the Portuguese. In Bengal, the main export items were fine cotton print fabrics, which, along with a variety of products already circulating in the region, they traded mostly for Spanish-American silver.

Compared with the VOC, the English East India Company (EIC), founded two years earlier in 1600, had more modest aims and much less capital. Nevertheless, it used force and a royal charter to displace the Portuguese in several strategic ports, especially around the Arabian peninsula and on the coasts of India. Given England's internal problems in the seventeenth century (discussed in the next chapter), progress was slow and uneven. Only in the late seventeenth century did English traders in India begin to amass considerable fortunes, mostly by exporting spices, gems, and cloth from their modest fortresses at Surat, Bombay, Madras, and Calcutta (see again Map 18.4). Like the VOC, however, the EIC grew increasingly powerful over time, eventually taking on an imperial role.

COUNTERPOINT: Aceh: Fighting Back in Southeast Asia

⬊ **FOCUS** Why was the tiny sultanate of Aceh able to hold out against European interlopers in early modern times?

The province and city of Aceh (AH-cheh), at the northwest tip of the island of Sumatra in Indonesia, was transformed but not conquered in early modern times. Like many trading enclaves linked by the Indian Ocean's monsoon winds, Aceh was a Muslim sultanate that lived by exchanging the produce of its interior, in this case black pepper, for commodities supplied by other, distant kingdoms. Aceh's rulers participated directly in trade, dictating its terms and enjoying many of its benefits. Yet unlike most such enclaves, which fell like dominoes to European interlopers, Aceh held out. For many reasons, but perhaps most importantly a new-found religious fervor, the Acehnese defeated many would-be conquistadors.

The Differing Fortunes of Aceh and Melaka

Aceh's rulers were probably related to those of the less fortunate Malay trading city of Melaka. Melaka was a former fishing village with a fine natural harbor and strategic location on the east end of the narrow Melaka Strait. It was said to have been founded by a Hindu prince who converted to Islam in around 1420. Melaka's rulers forged profitable alliances to regions as far away as China, but ties to the interior were weak, drawing predators. Melaka was attacked repeatedly by Javanese sultans, and in the end it fell to Portuguese cannons in 1511. Although Melakan forces had guns and fought valiantly against the Europeans, when the tide turned they found themselves without a backcountry into which they might flee and reorganize. The Dutch followed in 1641, displacing the Portuguese.

Unlike Melaka, Aceh's influence reached deep into the interior and across hundreds of miles of coast. After defeating Portuguese invaders in 1518, Aceh emerged as one of the most assertive seaborne Islamic states in the entire Indian Ocean, tapping military aid from the distant Ottomans and shipping considerable quantities of pepper to the Mediterranean via the Red Sea. But Aceh's repeated efforts to conquer Portuguese-controlled Melaka failed, and by the late seventeenth century the kingdom declined. Still, it was not until the nineteenth century that the Dutch reduced Aceh to colonial status.

Aceh, "the Veranda of Mecca"

Aceh's early modern history has been gleaned from several outside sources, and also local, sometimes official, chronicles, including epic poems written in Malay and Acehnese in the sixteenth and seventeenth centuries to celebrate the deeds of its sultans. Although poets tended to exaggerate the greatness of their patrons and to conflate or compress events, the epics express Acehnese Islamic pride, mostly as the region's bulwark against

Aceh

the militant Christian Portuguese. Ottoman, Portuguese, Dutch, and English sources note that Aceh was a great meeting place for Southeast Asian pilgrims on their way to Mecca, and it came to be known as *Serambi Mekkah*, the Veranda of Mecca.

Despite its intensely Islamic identity, Acehnese culture respected female independence. Women controlled and inherited nearly all property, from houses to rice fields, and at marriage men moved to their wives' households. Men in fact spent much of their time away on business or engaged in religious study, leaving women in charge of most everyday life. Pre-Islamic kin structures governed daily affairs, while *ulama*, or religious scholars, oversaw matters of business and state. Criminal cases reveal that local custom could override Islamic prescriptions, especially when it came to capital punishment. The result was a somewhat mild, woman-friendly Southeast Asian blend of secular and religious life reminiscent of West Africa.

Aceh was immediately recognized as a powerful state by northern European visitors in the early seventeenth century. The first Dutch envoys were jailed from 1599 to 1601 for mishandling court etiquette, but soon after, English visitors representing Queen Elizabeth I and the newly chartered East India Company made a better impression. Of particular interest to the Acehnese shah was Dutch and English hostility to Portugal, which also sent ambassadors. Playing competing Europeans off one another soon became a profitable game. And the Europeans were by no means alone—sizable trading and diplomatic missions arrived in Aceh from eastern and western India, Burma, and Siam. Sultan Iskandar Muda used English and Dutch traders to drive the Gujaratis out of the pepper trade in the 1610s, only to force the Europeans out of it in the 1620s. He continued to ship pepper to Red Sea intermediaries, but steadily lost out to both English and Dutch merchants, who turned to other Southeast Asian sources.

Aceh's decline has been traditionally associated with the rise of female sultans in the seventeenth century, much as occurred in the Ottoman Empire at about the same time (as we will see in Chapter 19). Sultana Taj al-Alam Safiyat al-Din Shah ruled from 1641 to 1675. She was the daughter of the renowned conqueror Iskandar Muda Shah (r. 1607–1636), but her politics focused mostly on domestic affairs, in part because Aceh was in a period of restructuring after her father's failed 1629 attack on Portuguese Melaka. Like her counterparts in Istanbul and Agra, Safiyat al-Din was a great patron of artists and scholars. Under her sponsorship, Acehnese displaced Malay as the language of state and the arts.

Safiyat al-Din was succeeded by three more sultanas, the last of whom was deposed following a 1699 decree, or **fatwa**, from Mecca declaring women unfit to serve as sultans. Careful reading of sources suggests that female sultans were not the cause of Aceh's declining power in the region, but rather a symptom of a general shift toward the Malay style of divine kingship. Even in decline, Aceh held out throughout early modern times and beyond against European attempts to subject it to colonial rule.

Conclusion

Thanks to reliable monsoon winds, the vast Indian Ocean basin had long been interconnected by ties of trade and religion, and this general pattern continued throughout early modern times. The region's countless farmers depended as they had for millennia on the monsoon rains.

Change came, however, with the rise of gunpowder-fueled empires both on land and at sea. Beginning about 1500, seaborne Europeans forcibly took over key ports and began taxing the trade of others, while Islamic warriors on horseback blasted resistant sultans and rajas into tribute-paying submission in South Asia. Smaller sultanates and kingdoms also adopted gunpowder weapons after 1500, both to defend themselves against invaders and to attack weaker neighbors. Although such armed conflict could be deadly or at least disrupt everyday life, for most ordinary people in the long run it meant a rise in tribute demands, and

fatwa A decree issued by Islamic religious officials.

in some places a turn to forced cultivation of export products such as cinnamon or pepper.

Despite the advances of belligerent Islamic and Christian empires throughout the Indian Ocean, most inhabitants did not convert. Religious tolerance had long been the rule in this region, and although the Portuguese were driven by an almost crusading fervor to spread Catholicism, in the end they were forced to deal with Hindus, Buddhists, Jews, and Muslims to make a profit. Later Europeans, most of them Protestants, scarcely bothered to proselytize prior to modern times, choosing instead to offer themselves as religiously neutral intermediaries.

The Mughals, like the kings of Vijayanagara before them, followed a tradition of divinely aloof religious tolerance, although conversion to the state faith had its benefits, particularly in trade. As with Christianity, Islamic practices varied greatly throughout this vast region, and these differences were visible in customs of female mobility, dress, and access to positions of power. Nur Jahan represented a temporary period of Mughal openness to feminine power and public expression, and Aceh's "Sultanate of the Women" represented another in Southeast Asia.

Europeans adapted to local cultures of trade when using force was impractical. For most of the early modern period, they had no choice, at least outside their tiny, fortressed towns. Only with the decline of great land empires such as that of the Mughals in the eighteenth century did this begin to change. Though it happened much more slowly than in contemporary Latin America or western Africa, by the end of the early modern period European imperial designs had begun to alter established lifeways throughout the Indian Ocean basin. Expansion into the interior, first by overseas trading companies such as the English East India Company and the Dutch VOC, would grow in the nineteenth century into full-blown imperialism. Only a few outliers, such as the Muslim revivalist sultanate of Aceh, managed to hold out, and even their time would come.

✳ review

The major global development in this chapter: The Indian Ocean trading network and the impact of European intrusion on maritime and mainland South Asia.

Important Events	
1336–1565	Vijayanagara kingdom in southern India
1498	Vasco da Gama reaches India
1500–1763	Mughal Empire in South Asia
1509–1529	Reign of Krishna Deva Raya of Vijayanagara
1510	Portuguese conquest of Goa, India
1511	Portuguese conquest of Melaka
1517	Portuguese establish fort in Sri Lanka (Ceylon)
1526	Battle of Panipat led by Mughal emperor Babur
1530	Consolidation of Aceh under Sultan Ali Mughayat Shah
1556–1605	Reign of Mughal emperor Akbar
1567	Akbar's siege of Chitor
1600	English East India Company founded in London
1602	Dutch East India Company (VOC) founded in Amsterdam
1605–1627	Reign of Mughal emperor Jahangir
1641	Dutch take Melaka from Portuguese
1641–1699	"Sultanate of Women" in Aceh
1658	Dutch drive Portuguese from Ceylon
1701	William Kidd hanged in London for piracy
1739	Persian raiders under Nadir Shah sack Delhi
1764	English East India Company controls Bengal

KEY TERMS

Brahman (p. 650)
caste (p. 650)
dhow (p. 646)

fatwa (p. 674)
Kshatriya (p. 650)
monsoon (p. 642)

sati (p. 660)
trading companies (p. 667)

CHAPTER OVERVIEW QUESTIONS

1. What environmental, religious, and political factors enabled trading enclaves to flourish in the Indian Ocean basin?
2. How did the rise and fall of India's land empires reflect larger regional trends?
3. How did Europeans insert themselves into the Indian Ocean trading network, and what changes did they bring about?

MAKING CONNECTIONS

1. In what ways did Indian Ocean trade differ from the contemporary Atlantic slave trade (see Chapter 17)? What role did Africa play in each?
2. How did traditional kingdoms such as Vijayanagara differ from those of the Americas prior to the Spanish conquest (see Chapter 15)?

For further research into the topics covered in this chapter, see the Bibliography at the end of the book. For additional primary sources from this period, see *Sources for World in the Making.*

Consolidation and Conflict in Europe and the Greater Mediterranean 1450–1750

≡ **World in the Making** Court artists painted this 1588 Ottoman miniature to illustrate Suleiman the Magnificent's 1526 victory over Christian forces at the Battle of Mohacs, which left Hungary without a monarch and divided between the Habsburg and Ottoman Empires. Traditional cavalry forces face off in the left foreground, but most prominent is the sultan himself in the upper right, on a white horse just behind a line of large Ottoman cannon.

✷ backstory

Europe and the greater Mediterranean basin gradually recovered from the devastating Black Death of 1347–1350 (see Chapter 14), but the inhabitants of this geographically divided region faced many challenges at the start of the early modern period. Christian Europeans grew increasingly intolerant of religious diversity. In the most extreme case, Iberian Muslims and Jews were forced to convert to Catholicism or leave the peninsula after 1492, prompting a great diaspora, or scattering, largely into Morocco and Ottoman lands, but also into Italy, France, and northern Europe. Resource-poor and avid for Asian trade goods and precious metals, western Europeans raced to develop new technologies of war and long-distance transport to compete with one another as well as with non-Europeans abroad. In contrast, the Muslim Ottomans of the eastern Mediterranean had been expanding their tributary land empire since the fourteenth century. By the later fifteenth century they would take to the sea to extend their conquests into the Mediterranean and the Indian Ocean.

In 1590, a clerk working in the Spanish city of Seville named Miguel de Cervantes applied for a colonial service job in South America. Such assignments usually went to applicants with noble connections, but Cervantes hoped his military service would compensate. He had been wounded in the Battle of Lepanto in 1571, fighting against the Ottomans. He had also been held captive in Algiers by North Africa's Barbary pirates. Despite all of this, he was turned down.

Before employment in Seville, Cervantes had tried writing, publishing a modestly successful novel in 1585. Spanish literature was booming. The novels, plays, and poems of Spain's "Golden Century" fed on the changes resulting from overseas colonization and religious upheavals. Playwrights and poets rewrote the conquests of the Aztecs and Incas as tragedies, and one writer, "El Inca" Garcilaso de la Vega, son of a Spanish conquistador and an Inca princess, thrilled readers with tales of a vanished Inca paradise. He based his best-selling *Royal Commentaries of the Incas* on stories told by his mother in Cuzco.

Cervantes never crossed the Atlantic, but he found plenty to inspire him in the vibrant crossroads city of Seville, Spain's largest. Yet as Cervantes's 1605 masterpiece, *Don Quixote*, revealed, it was the author's experiences as a prisoner in Algiers that most prepared him to bridge cultures and upend literary conventions. Although regarded as the quintessential Spanish novel—set in the Spanish countryside—*Don Quixote* includes many passages relating the travails of forced converts to Christianity from Islam and renegade Christians living in North Africa, risking their lives to find love or maintain family fortunes. Cervantes died in 1616, in the midst of a brief truce between Spain and its greatest rival of the day, the emerging Dutch Republic. "El Inca" Garcilaso died the same year.

Europe and the greater Mediterranean were home to diverse peoples who had long been linked together. Yet this dynamic region was increasingly divided by political, religious, and ethnic conflict. Christians fought Jews and Muslims, and, in the movements known as the Protestant and Catholic Reformations, one another. Emerging national identities hardened, even as trade increased. Christian Europe viewed Ottoman expansion with alarm, and fear of growing Muslim power contributed to rising tension and conflict between Christians and Muslims. Piracy flourished, and war raged from the Low Countries to the Balkans, eventually engulfing nearly all of Europe by 1618. In the course of the Thirty Years' War that followed, Catholics and Protestants slaughtered each other by the tens of thousands. Economic woes compounded the chaos, exacerbated by a drop in silver revenues from the mines of Spanish America. Prolonged cold weather led to a cycle of failed harvests. Amid growing anxiety, rebellions broke out from Scotland to the Persian frontier.

Out of this period of instability, which some historians have labeled the "seventeenth-century crisis," came profound innovations in science, government, and the economy. The combination of growing religious skepticism, deep interest in the physical world sparked by overseas discoveries, and new optical technologies led a small cluster of European intellectuals to turn to scientific inquiry, initiating what later would be hailed as a "scientific revolution." Political innovations included absolutism and constitutionalism, two novel approaches to monarchy. Nearly all of Europe's competing states engaged in overseas expansion, using the Atlantic as a gateway to the wider world. With the support of their governments, merchants and investors in western Europe challenged the global claims of the Spanish and Portuguese.

Christian European overseas expansion was driven in part by the rise of the Ottoman Empire. The Ottoman realm, which by 1550 straddled Europe, the Middle East, North Africa, Arabia, and parts of Central Asia, was strategically located between three vast and ancient maritime trade zones. No early modern European state approached the Ottomans' size, military might, or cultural and religious diversity, and no contemporary Islamic empire did as much to offset rising Christian European sea power. The Ottomans were arguably the most versatile of the early modern "gunpowder empires."

OVERVIEW QUESTIONS

The major global development in this chapter: Early modern Europe's increasing competition and division in the face of Ottoman expansion.

As you read, consider:

1. To what degree was religious diversity embraced or rejected in early modern Europe and the greater Mediterranean, and why?

2. How did Christian Europe's gunpowder-fueled empires compare with that of the Ottomans?

3. What accounts for the rise of science and capitalism in early modern western Europe?

The Power of the Ottoman Empire 1453–1750

FOCUS What factors explain the rise of the vast Ottoman Empire and its centuries-long endurance?

Founded by Turkic warriors in the early fourteenth century, the Ottoman Empire grew rapidly after its stunning 1453 capture of the Byzantine capital, Constantinople (see Chapter 14). As in Mughal India, gunpowder weapons introduced by

Christian Europeans sped the Ottomans' rise and helped them push deep into Europe as well as the Middle East and North Africa. The Ottomans also took to the sea, challenging the Venetians, Habsburgs, and other contenders in the Mediterranean, as well as the Portuguese in the Indian Ocean. But it was arguably clever governance, minimal trade restrictions, and religious tolerance, not gunpowder weapons or naval proficiency, that permitted this most durable of Islamic empires to survive until the early twentieth century.

Tools of Empire

As we saw in Chapter 14, Mehmed II's conquest in 1453 of Constantinople not only shocked the Christian world but also marked a dramatic shift in the Ottoman enterprise. The sultans no longer viewed themselves as the roving holy warriors of Osman's day. Instead, they assumed the identity of Islamic rulers with supreme authority over a multinational empire at the crossroads of Europe and Asia.

To maintain control over the provinces, the Ottomans drew on the janissary corps, elite infantry and bureaucrats loyal to the sultan. Within a century of the capture of Constantinople, the janissaries were recruited through the ***devshirme*** (dev-SHEER-may), the conscription of Christian youths from eastern Europe. Chosen for their good looks and fine physiques, these boys were converted to Islam and sent to farms to learn Turkish and to build up their bodies. The most promising were sent to Istanbul to learn Ottoman military, religious, and administrative techniques. Trained in Ottoman ways, educated in the use of advanced weaponry, and shorn of family connections, the young men recruited through the devshirme were thus prepared to serve as janissaries wholly beholden to the sultan. In later years the janissaries would challenge the sultan's power, but for much of the early modern era, they extended and supported Ottoman rule. A few rose to the rank of Grand Vizier (roughly, "Prime Minister").

The ***timar*** system of land grants given in compensation for military service was another means to manage the provinces while ensuring that armed forces remained powerful. It was similar to Mughal India's *parganas* and Spanish America's *encomiendas* in that all three imperial systems rewarded frontier warriors while preventing them from becoming independent aristocrats. Sultans snatched timars and gave them to others when their holders failed to serve in ongoing wars, an incentive to keep fighting. Even in times of stability, the timars were referred to as "the fruits of war." Timar-holders turned new territories into provinces. Able administrators were rewarded with governorships. Although the timar and devshirme systems changed over time, it was these early innovations in frontier governance and

devshirme
The Ottomans' conscription of Christian male youths from eastern Europe to serve in the military or administration.

timar A land grant given in compensation for military service by the Ottoman sultan to a soldier.

military recruitment that stabilized Ottoman rule in the face of succession crises, regional rebellions, and other shocks.

Expansion and Consolidation

Mehmed II's 1453 capture of Constantinople earned him the nickname "Conqueror." By 1464, Mehmed had added Athens, Serbia, and Bosnia to the Ottoman domain, and by 1475, the Golden Horde khanate was paying tribute to the Ottomans (see Map 19.1). In the Mediterranean, Venice suddenly faced a genuine rival, and the Genoese were driven from their trading posts in the Black Sea. In 1480 the Ottomans attacked Otranto, in southern Italy, and in 1488 they struck

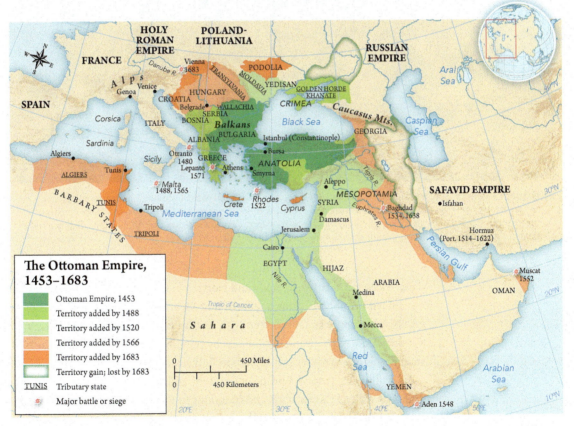

≡ **MAP 19.1   The Ottoman Empire, 1453–1683**   In early modern times the Ottomans developed one of the world's most extensive and lasting empires. What held their hugely diverse empire together was its flexible bureaucratic structure, which frequently rewarded faithful conquered subjects and allowed loose tributary arrangements at the fringes. The Ottomans struggled most on the eastern frontier with the Shi'ite Safavids and in the northwest against the Habsburg Holy Roman Empire and other Christian kingdoms.

≡ **Istanbul's Skyline** When the former Constantinople became the capital of the Ottoman Empire, its rulers and court patrons soon transformed its architecture and overall skyline. The domes in the foreground make up part of the formerly Christian basilica Hagia Sophia, which was transformed into a mosque after 1453. In the distance rises Istanbul's imposing Blue Mosque, built between 1609 and 1616 for Sultan Ahmed I.

Malta, a key island between Sicily and North Africa. Meanwhile Constantinople, now named Istanbul, became a reflection of Mehmed's power, and also his piety. The city's horizon was soon dotted with hundreds of domes and minarets. With over one hundred thousand inhabitants by the time of the sultan's death in 1481, Istanbul was one of the largest capitals in Eurasia.

The Ottomans turned European artillery and janissary fighters on Islamic neighbors such as the Safavids and Mamluks in Syria and Egypt. Under Selim I (r. 1512–1520), called "the Grim," both were overwhelmed, although the Safavids would continue to challenge Ottoman power. Ottoman influence now touched the shores of the Indian Ocean, where Selim and the Ottomans challenged Portuguese expansion. The Muslim holy cities of Medina and Mecca became Ottoman protectorates, a boon for the state's religious reputation.

Christian Europe again felt the sting of Ottoman artillery under Selim's successor, Suleiman (soo-lay-MAHN) (r. 1520–1566), called "the Magnificent." Suleiman immediately captured Belgrade and Rhodes. Belgrade gave Suleiman near-total control of eastern Europe, and Rhodes gave him effective rule over the eastern Mediterranean. In the western Mediterranean, the sultan supported Muslim pirates such as the Barbarossa brothers of Algiers, who targeted Europeans and held Christian captives for ransom (see Counterpoint: The Barbary Pirates). In 1565 the Ottomans laid siege to Malta. Though unsuccessful, this huge expedition displayed "the Great Turk's" naval capacity.

As the siege of Malta attested, Suleiman was determined to challenge the Habsburgs, as was his successor, Selim II (r. 1566–1574). But the Ottomans were dealt a terrible blow in 1571 when Habsburg forces sponsored by Spain's Catholic king Philip II (r. 1556–1598) overpowered Selim's navy at the Battle of Lepanto off the Greek coast (see again Map 19.1). Some six thousand janissaries faced off against over twenty thousand European recruits, among them the future author of *Don Quixote*. The Christians prevailed, and widely commemorated their victory.

Although the Battle of Lepanto marked the waning of Ottoman sea supremacy, Selim II's will was not broken. His forces captured Tunis and Cyprus, and the navy was quickly rebuilt. A poet praised the sultan's vision:

If it were not for the body of Sultan Selim,
This generous king, this source of happiness
The enemy would have occupied
The country from one end to the other
God would not have helped us.
Neither would he have granted us conquest.[1]

Battle with the Habsburgs reached a crescendo with the 1683 siege of Vienna. Ottoman gun technology had kept pace with that of western Europe, and some observers claimed that Ottoman muskets in fact had better range and accuracy than those used by Vienna's defenders. Heavy siege artillery was not deployed as effectively as against Safavid Persia, however, and this may have proved a fatal mistake. Ottoman attempts to mine Vienna's walls failed just as tens of thousands of allies led by the Polish king arrived to save the day for the Habsburgs. At least fifteen thousand Ottoman troops were killed. Never again would the Ottomans pose a serious threat to Christian Europe.

To the east, war with Persia occupied the sultans' attention throughout the sixteenth century. Since 1500, Safavid shahs had incited rebellions against

Ottoman rule in outlying provinces, denouncing its Sunni leadership as corrupt. The Ottomans responded by persecuting both rebels and innocents caught in between. Under Suleiman, campaigns against the Safavids in the 1530s and 1540s were mostly successful thanks to new guns, but reversals were common. As one Ottoman eyewitness put it in the 1550s, "The territories called Persia are much less fertile than our country; and further, it is the custom of the inhabitants, when their land is invaded, to lay waste and burn everything, and so force the enemy to retire through lack of food."[2] The Safavids were just far enough away, making intermediate cities such as Baghdad the key battlegrounds.

Beginning in the late 1570s, Murad III exploited Safavid political instability to expand Ottoman influence beyond the frontier established by Suleiman. By 1590, the Ottomans controlled Mesopotamia and were a firm presence in the Caucasus region. Still, the empire was rocked in the decades around 1600 by price inflation caused by a massive influx of Spanish-American silver, which flowed into the empire from Europe in exchange for Ottoman silks and spices. Ottoman attempts to fix prices and debase coins only worsened the problem, and troops facing food shortages and poor pay rioted.

Some historians have argued that the Ottoman Empire was in decline following the reign of Suleiman the Magnificent. Like Habsburg Spain, also said to be in decline despite its size and wealth, Ottoman efforts to conquer new lands increasingly ended in stalemate. The crushing weight of military expenses forced sultans and viziers to make humiliating concessions. Losses to the Safavids were worst, amounting to a total reversal of Murad III's gains. Frontier setbacks were not always evident from the center. Istanbul, with some four hundred thousand inhabitants by this time, was by far Eurasia's largest city.

Murad IV (r. 1623–1640) managed to recapture Baghdad, but a succession crisis ensued. Only after 1648 was the matter settled, with seven-year-old Mehmed IV (r. 1648–1687) on the throne. A child emperor required interim rule by regency, and in this case Mehmed's mother, Turhan, took control after fighting off challenges from other powerful women at court whose sons claimed a right to the throne. As a result of this direct feminine management of the Ottoman Empire, analogous to that of much tinier Aceh in these years (see Chapter 18), Turhan's regency has been called "the Sultanate of the Women."

Ottoman court women had long been a powerful political force despite their strict seclusion from society. First, succession politics dictated control over the sultan's sexual life. Women dominated this arena as early as the mid-sixteenth century. It was not seductive young wives and concubines who counted most, but rather elder women, particularly the Queen Mother. Second, much like Nur Jahan in Mughal India, powerful Ottoman women were patrons of the arts and of pious works, and they figured prominently in royal rituals. The sultan was the ultimate patriarch, but it was his family that constituted the model of Ottoman society. Documents reveal that the royal harem, source of lurid speculation by Europeans, was in fact a sacred, familial space, more haven than prison.

Daily Life in the Ottoman Empire

Most Ottoman subjects were rural peasants and herders. Urban society, by contrast, was hierarchical, divided by occupation. Beneath the Osman royal family was the *askeri* (AS-keh-ree), or "military" class, which was tax-exempt and dependent on the sultan. In addition to military leaders, the askeri included bureaucrats and *ulama*, religious scholars versed in canon law. Whereas the Safavids considered religious authorities superior to the shahs, the Ottoman sultans only took the advice of their chief ulama. Beneath the askeri was a much broader class of taxpayers called *reaya* (RAH-ya), or "the flock." The reaya included everyone from common laborers to merchants. Thanks to an Ottoman tradition of meritocracy and inclusion, provincial members of the lower classes could gain status through education or military service.

In the countryside, farmers' and pastoralists' lives revolved around cycles of planting and harvest, seasonal movement of animal herds, and the rhythms of commerce and religious observance. Some men were drafted into military service, leaving women to manage households, herds, and farms. Women in both rural and urban contexts also engaged in export crafts such as silk weaving, carpet making, and ceramic manufacture. Thus, even rural life in the Ottoman Empire was shaped by the larger forces of international trade and the demands of the Ottoman military.

More mobile by far were merchants. The rich merchants of trading crossroads such as Aleppo, Damascus, Smyrna, and Cairo profited from their access to Asian and African luxuries. Ottoman trade taxes were relatively low, and the empire rarely resorted to the burdensome wartime demands made by European states on

≡ **Istanbul Street Scene** This rare sixteenth-century Ottoman street scene depicts men and women exchanging a variety of goods—flowers, almonds, ducks, bread—near the famous bazaar of Istanbul, formerly Constantinople. The exchanges take place next to the Column of Constantine, a relic of Roman rule under the city's namesake emperor.

LIVES AND LIVELIHOODS

Ottoman Coffeehouse Owners and Patrons

An institution of modern life in much of the world today, the coffeehouse, or café, originated at the southern fringes of the Ottoman Empire around 1450. The coffee bean, harvested from a small tree that scientists would later call *Coffea arabica*, had long been roasted, ground, and brewed in the Ethiopian and Somalian highlands of East Africa. At some point, coffee was transplanted to the highlands of the Yemen, just across the Red Sea at the southern tip of the Arabian peninsula (see again Map 19.1). Here members of Sufi Muslim brotherhoods adopted coffee drinking to aid them in their all-night meditations and chants. Merchants sailing north on the Red Sea carried the new habit-forming beverage to Cairo and Istanbul. From here it spread quickly throughout the entire Mediterranean commercial world. By the late seventeenth century, there were coffeehouses in all the major cities of western Europe. By the early eighteenth century, coffee itself was planted in the tropical Americas.

Despite coffee's sobering effects, many *imams*, or religious scholars, were initially skeptical of its propriety. The word coffee apparently derives from *qahwa*, one of several Arabic terms for wine. Imams used this word since the beverage altered consciousness in a noticeable, if not necessarily debilitating, way. Eventually, coffee was decreed an acceptable drink in accordance with scripture, and was widely consumed during fasts such as Ramadan. Both men and women were allowed to

≡ **Ottoman Coffeehouse** This late-sixteenth-century miniature depicts a packed Ottoman coffeehouse. The patrons and serving staff all appear to be male, but they represent many classes and age groups, and possibly several religious traditions. When rebellions or other political troubles brewed, coffeehouses were a source of concern for Ottoman authorities. (CBL T 439.9)

drink coffee, but several *fatwas*, or religious prohibitions, were issued against female coffee vendors in the early sixteenth century. As a result, both public coffee consumption and sale became male preserves.

Coffee's troubles were far from over. If coffee itself was declared wholesome, the places where it was commonly consumed were not. Coffeehouses, sometimes run by non-Muslims, proliferated in major market cities such as Cairo by the early 1500s, drawing hordes of lower-class traders, artisans, and even slaves. Unable to suppress the café even at the core of empire, Ottoman religious leaders simply denounced them as dens of vice. Female musicians played and danced scandalously in some, conservative clerics argued, while others abided homosexual prostitution. Some coffeehouses served as well-known hangouts for opium and hashish addicts, further tainting their reputation. Then came tobacco smoking, introduced from the Americas by European merchants in the early seventeenth century.

As later proved true in Europe, there were other reasons to fear the coffeehouse. Ottoman officials suspected the cafés as hotbeds of insurrection and treason. Still, they proved impossible to suppress, and coffee vendors sprang back into action when authorities closed them down. The Ottomans finally relented, deciding that the coffeehouse was an ideal place to gauge popular reactions to state policy and to plant spies. In an era before restaurants, and in a religious climate hostile to alcohol and hence taverns, the coffeehouse met a variety of social needs. It was first a place where traveling merchants far from the comforts of home could exchange information, buy their associates a few rounds of coffee, and perhaps relax with a game of backgammon and a water-cooled smoke. For men of the working class, the coffeehouse became a place of rest and collegiality, and occasionally of political ferment.

Questions to Consider

1. How did Islamic clerics' attitude toward coffee change? What factors might account for this shift?
2. How and why did the Ottoman state come to accept the coffeehouse as a social institution?

For Further Information:

Hattox, Ralph. *Coffee and Coffee Houses: The Origins of a Social Beverage in the Medieval Near East.* Seattle: University of Washington Press, 1985.

Schivelbusch, Wolfgang. *Tastes of Paradise: A Social History of Spices, Stimulants, and Intoxicants.* Translated by David Jacobson. New York: Vintage, 1993.

their merchant communities. On the flip side, the Ottoman state invested little in trading infrastructure beyond maintenance of **caravanserais**, or travelers' lodges located along trade routes.

Recent research has revealed that ordinary women under Ottoman rule, much like court women, enjoyed more power than previously thought. Women had rights to their own property and investments, fully protected by shari'a, or Islamic law, before, during, and after marriage. This was, however, a rigidly patriarchal society. Women were expected to marry, and when they did they had few legal rights in relation to their husbands, who were permitted multiple wives and could divorce them at any time. Although women were treated as inferiors under Ottoman rule, they had greater access to divorce than women in most early modern European societies.

Although devoutly Muslim at its core, the Ottoman state, with some forty million subjects by the mid-seventeenth century, was tolerant of religious diversity. Imperial policies reflected a practical desire to gain the cooperation of diverse subjects, a particular challenge in frontier districts such as Cyprus and the Balkans. Converts to Islam gained tax benefits, but punitive measures to force subjects to convert to the state religion were never used.

Many Jews in the Ottoman Empire maintained their religious independence. Some Jewish communities were centuries old and had local roots, but many more came as *Sephardim*, refugees from Iberian expulsions after 1492. Sephardic physicians, merchants, and tax collectors were a common sight in Istanbul, and by the later sixteenth century many Ottoman towns had Jewish communities. Members of the Jewish Mendes family served as merchants, bankers, and advisers to the sultan.

Incorporative and flexible, the Ottoman state proved one of the most durable in world history. Gunpowder weapons, though important, were most critical in the early phases of expansion. Individual rulers varied in terms of aptitude and ambition, but the state itself held firm. Fierce allegiance to Sunni Islam and control of its key shrines lent the Ottomans religious clout, yet their system of governance did not persecute non-Muslims. Shi'ite Muslims, by contrast, were considered heretics, and this religious schism fueled a lasting rivalry with neighboring Persia.

Finally, in the realm of commerce, merchants and trade guilds existed in several Ottoman cities, notably Aleppo, but overseas ventures and entrepreneurial activities remained limited (see Lives and Livelihoods: Ottoman Coffeehouse Owners and Patrons). The state placed minimal restrictions on trade and provided some infrastructure in the form of caravanserais, but there was no policy equivalent to Iberian support of overseas commerce in the form of trading forts and convoys.

caravanserai
A roadside inn for merchants on the Silk Road and other overland trade routes.

In this regard the Ottoman Empire was profoundly different from the rising "merchant empires" of western Europe, where an increasingly global and highly competitive mercantile capitalism hitched state interests directly to those of bankers and merchants.

Europe Divided 1500–1650

➘ **FOCUS** What sparked division in Europe after 1500, and why did this trend persist?

Europe in the age of Ottoman ascendancy was diverse, fractured, and dynamic. By 1500, commerce and literacy were rising, populations were growing, and craftsmen were perfecting technologies of warfare, manufacture, and navigation. Publishers capitalized on demand for fiction long before Cervantes, but they also made available new thoughts on religion and science plus translations of classical works. Thus, the growth of literacy helped unsettle old notions of time, space, and human potential. A less visible transformation was taking place in the countryside, where traditional relationships tying peasants to feudal lords were replaced with commercial ones. Most notable in western Europe, especially in England, this shift entailed a rise in renting, sharecropping, and wage work, a proliferation of market-oriented farms owned by urban elites, and the privatization of lands formerly enjoyed as common resources. Peasants displaced by this capitalist restructuring of the countryside increasingly filled Europe's cities. Some went overseas to try their luck in the colonies.

Everyday Life in Early Modern Europe

Historians estimate that Europe in 1492 had a population of about seventy million, or slightly more than the population of the Americas at Columbus's arrival. By 1550, Europe counted some eighty-five million inhabitants, and it was still growing rapidly. This population increase was mostly due to reduced mortality rather than increased births. Unlike larger Ming China and Mughal India, Europe's high growth rate was not sustained. A series of epidemics and climatic events beginning in around 1600, coupled with the effects of the Thirty Years' War (1618–1648) and other conflicts, led to population stagnancy and even decline. Europe's population in 1630 was below eighty million, and would not reach one hundred million until just before 1700.

The Columbian Exchange was largely responsible for the sixteenth-century population increase, as American crops altered European diets after 1500. Maize,

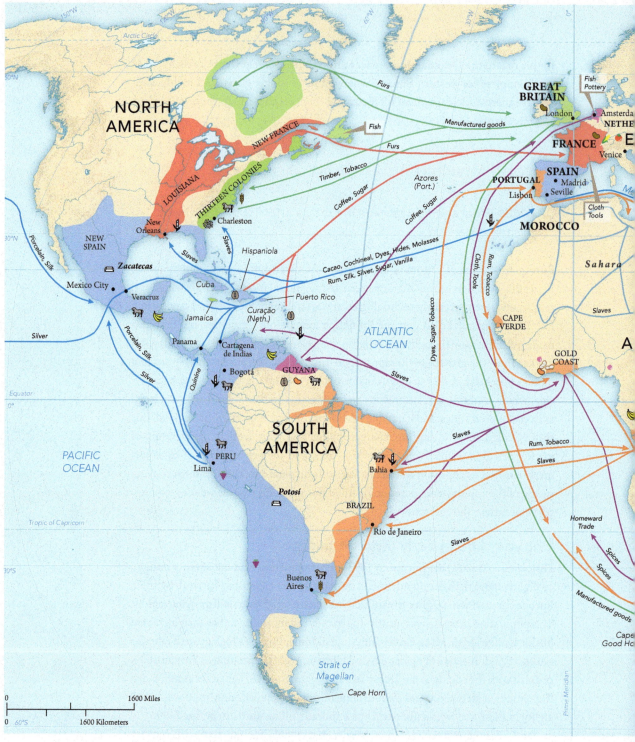

NORTH AMERICA

NEW FRANCE

LOUISIANA

THIRTEEN COLONIES

New Orleans

Charleston

NEW SPAIN

Zacatecas

Mexico City

Veracruz

Jamaica

Cuba

Hispaniola

Curaçao (Neth.)

Puerto Rico

Panama

Cartagena de Indias

Bogotá

GUYANA

SOUTH AMERICA

Lima

PERU

Potosí

Bahia

BRAZIL

Rio de Janeiro

Buenos Aires

PACIFIC OCEAN

Equator

Tropic of Capricorn

Strait of Magellan

Cape Horn

ATLANTIC OCEAN

Furs

Fish

Manufactured goods

Timber, Tobacco

Furs

Coffee, Sugar

Azores (Port.)

Coffee, Sugar

Slaves

Slaves

Slaves

Cacao, Cochineal, Dyes, Hides, Molasses

Rum, Silk, Silver, Sugar, Vanilla

Porcelain, Silk

Silver

Porcelain, Silk

Silver

Quinine

Slaves

Slaves

Slaves

Slaves

Slaves

Slaves

Rum, Tobacco

Rum, Tobacco

Cloth, Tools

Dyes, Sugar, Tobacco

Homeward Trade

Spices

Spices

Manufactured goods

Cape of Good Hope

Prime Meridian

GREAT BRITAIN

London

Fish Pottery

Amsterdam

NETHE

FRANCE

Venice

PORTUGAL

Lisbon

SPAIN

Madrid

Seville

Cloth Tools

MOROCCO

Sahara

CAPE VERDE

GOLD COAST

A

Slaves

Cloth, Tools

0   1600 Miles

0   60°S   1600 Kilometers

≡ **MAP 19.2   World Trade, c. 1720**

Europeans revolutionized global trade through maritime expansion and competition.
Overland trade continued apace, but it was European seaborne merchants who were
most responsible for bringing exotic goods to Europe, Africa, and the Americas, and for

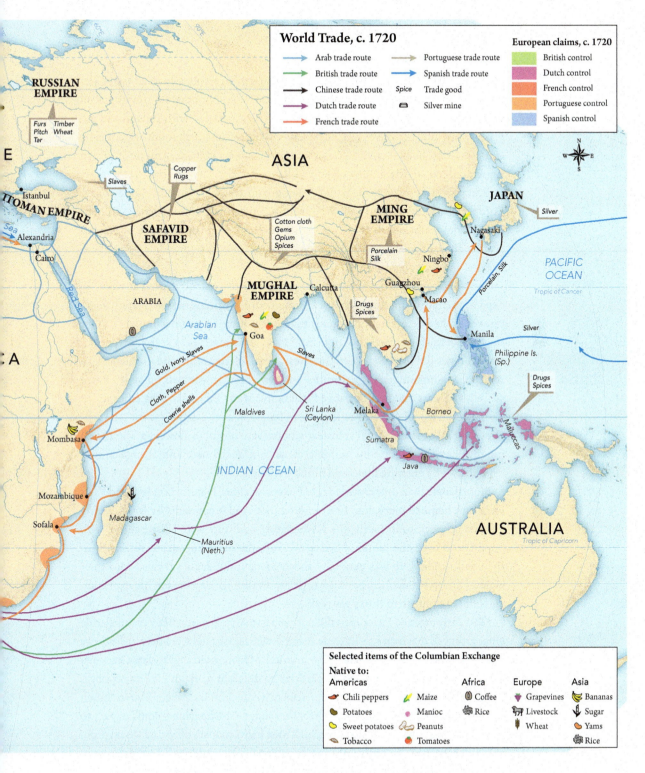

World Trade, c. 1720

European claims, c. 1720

Arab trade route
Portuguese trade route
British trade route
Spanish trade route
Chinese trade route
Spice Trade good
Dutch trade route
Silver mine
French trade route

British control
Dutch control
French control
Portuguese control
Spanish control

RUSSIAN EMPIRE

Furs Timber
Pitch Wheat
Tar

ASIA

OTTOMAN EMPIRE

Istanbul

Slaves

Copper
Rugs

JAPAN

Silver

Alexandria

Cairo

Red Sea

SAFAVID EMPIRE

MING EMPIRE

Nagasaki

PACIFIC OCEAN

Tropic of Cancer

Cotton cloth
Gems
Opium
Spices

Porcelain
Silk

Ningbo

ARABIA

Arabian Sea

MUGHAL EMPIRE

Calcutta

Guagzhou

Macao

Porcelain, Silk

Goa

Drugs
Spices

Manila

Silver

Gold, Ivory, Slaves

Slaves

Philippine Is.
(Sp.)

Cloth, Pepper

Maldives

Sri Lanka
(Ceylon)

Melaka

Borneo

Drugs
Spices

Cowrie shells

Sumatra

Moluccas

Mombasa

INDIAN OCEAN

Java

Mozambique

Madagascar

Sofala

Mauritius
(Neth.)

AUSTRALIA

Tropic of Capricorn

Selected items of the Columbian Exchange
Native to:

Americas		Africa	Europe	Asia
Chili peppers	Maize	Coffee	Grapevines	Bananas
Potatoes	Manioc	Rice	Livestock	Sugar
Sweet potatoes	Peanuts		Wheat	Yams
Tobacco	Tomatoes			Rice

transporting tropical plantation products and precious metals to the rest of the world.
The Atlantic slave trade was just one sector of Europe's increasingly global and deeply
interconnected trading sphere.

potatoes, tomatoes, capsicum peppers, and many other foods reordered tastes and needs. In some cases this sped population growth, and in others it simply spiced up an otherwise bland diet. Potatoes came to be associated with Ireland and paprika with Hungary and Spain, but these and other American foods were widely embraced and helped spur a sophisticated consumer culture. American-grown sugar, tobacco, and later chocolate, vanilla, and coffee also figured prominently in Europe's taste revolution, as did Asian-grown tea and a host of exotic spices. Europeans also demanded new drugs such as opium and quinine bark, and merchants who trafficked in these and other tropical goods often made enormous profits. Thus, Europe's new connection with the Americas altered its population, culture, and economy (see Map 19.2).

The rise of commercial farming and peasant displacement, as well as overseas expansion, transformed ecosystems. Throughout Europe forest was cleared. Some princes limited deforestation, usually to preserve hunting grounds rather than for the good of the forest itself, but peasants still entered reserves in search of fuel and timber. Laws did little to relieve the stress, turning environmental problems into social ones. Shipbuilders, metalsmiths, and construction workers consumed forest as well, and wars and fires destroyed still more. Many European port cities relied on imported wood, sometimes looking as far afield as the Americas for new supplies. Not all environmental transformations were negative, however. The Dutch improved transportation by building canals and reclaimed land for agriculture from the sea by erecting dikes and filling wetlands.

More people than ever crowded into European cities. Naples, London, and Paris were each home to more than two hundred thousand inhabitants by 1600. Nearly a dozen other cities in Iberia, the Netherlands, and Italy were close behind, with populations over one hundred thousand. Still, the most Europeans remained in the countryside. Life was generally short. Some individuals survived into their eighties and even nineties, but high infant mortality yielded overall life expectancies of only eighteen to thirty-six years.

Most early modern Europeans did not rush to marry, nor were they compelled to enter arranged marriages, as in some Asian societies. Women were between twenty and twenty-five, on average, when they married. Men married slightly later, between twenty-three and twenty-seven, in part due to itinerant work and military obligations. Relatively few children were born out of wedlock, at least according to church records, but many were conceived before marriage. Most partners could expect to be widowed within twenty years, in which time half a couple's offspring would probably also have died. Moreover, one in ten women died in childbirth. In Europe, as in much of the world at this time, the prospect of death was never far away.

Protestant and Catholic Reformations

Like Islam, Christianity had long been subject to disagreements and schisms. Yet the critiques of Roman Catholicism presented by several sixteenth-century northern European theologians marked the deepest split thus far. Catholic reformers beginning with the German monk Martin Luther argued that the church had so deviated from early Christian teachings that only radical reform could save it. For such reformers, the corruption and worldliness of the church were symptoms of a much deeper problem. In their view, the church had drifted into doctrinal and theological error. Inspired by a newfound faith in the individual rooted in Renaissance humanism (see Chapter 14), Luther and his followers emphasized the individual's ability to interpret scripture and communicate directly with God, without the intercession of priests. Although this opposition to Church teachings was theological, its implications were political. Outraged Catholic officials branded Luther and his followers Protestant (or protesting) heretics, and much of Europe entered a century of conflict fueled by religious hatred (see Map 19.3).

In 1517 Luther circulated "Ninety-Five Theses"—propositions for academic debate—in which he charged that church policy encouraged priests to ignore their parishioners, keep concubines, and concentrate on money-grubbing. Worse, according to Luther, the church had corrupted Christian teachings on sin and forgiveness by inventing Purgatory, a spiritual holding pen where the deceased were purged of their sins before entering Heaven. Luther denounced the widespread sale of **indulgences**, written receipts that promised the payer early release from Purgatory, as a fraud. Such teachings appealed to oppressed German peasants, many of whom took up arms in a 1525 rebellion. A social conservative, Luther withheld support from the uprising, but the revolutionary potential of Protestant Christianity was now revealed.

Church fathers ordered Luther defrocked and excommunicated. He responded by breaking away to form his own "Lutheran" church. Critiques similar to Luther's came from the Swiss Protestant Ulrich Zwingli in 1523 and France's John Calvin in 1537. By the 1550s, Protestantism was widespread in northern Europe, and its democratic and antiauthoritarian undercurrents soon yielded radical political results. Still, most Europeans remained Catholic, revealing a deep, conservative countercurrent. Despite this conservatism, Catholicism, too, would be transformed.

Another schism occurred in 1534 when England's King Henry VIII declared his nation Protestant. Although Henry broke with the church for personal and political reasons rather than theological ones (the king wanted a divorce that the pope refused to grant), Anglican Protestantism became the new state religion. Critics were silenced by Henry's execution of England's most prominent Catholic intellectual,

indulgence In early modern Europe, a note sold by the Catholic Church to speed a soul's exit from Purgatory.

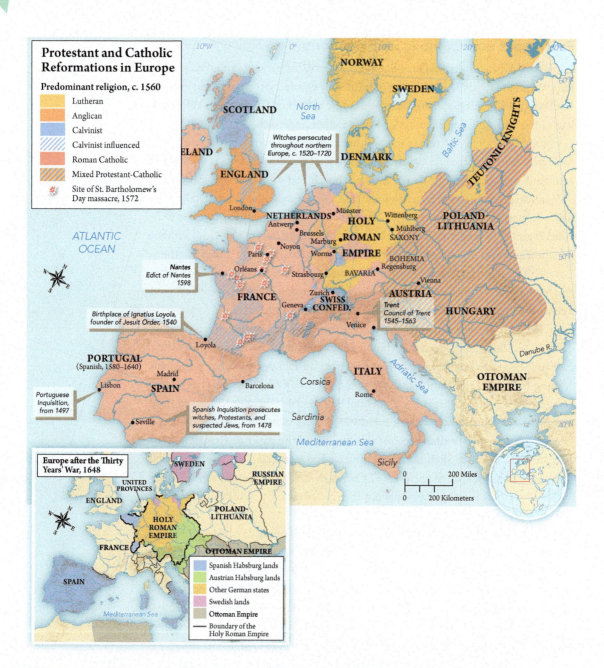

MAP 19.3 Protestant and Catholic Reformations in Europe What Protestants called the Reformation was a fundamental questioning of Roman Catholic doctrine and practice. The dispute quickly produced violence and led some kingdoms, such as England, to break entirely from papal authority. France dissolved into civil war, and Spain and Portugal used their Inquisitions to persecute Protestants as heretics. A Catholic Reformation sought to reform and strengthen the church, but conflict continued to bubble up, leading soon after 1600 to the disastrous Thirty Years' War.

Sir Thomas More, author of *Utopia* (1517). As elsewhere in Europe, however, this early break with Rome hardly marked the end of Catholicism in England.

The Catholic Church's leaders responded to Protestantism in disbelief, then vengeful anger. Some among the outraged Catholic majority launched strong but peaceful assaults. In Spain, for example, Ignatius of Loyola in 1534 founded a new religious order. Approved by the pope in 1540, the Society of Jesus, or Jesuits, soon became the Catholic Church's greatest educators and wealthiest property managers. More important for global history, they served as missionaries to head off Protestant initiatives overseas. Within a few decades of Loyola's founding of the order, Jesuit preachers were in Brazil, West Africa, Ceylon, and Japan (see Seeing the Past: Gift Clocks for the Emperors of China). Others won back converts in central Europe on the eve of the Thirty Years' War.

In the face of the Protestant challenge, some church officials called for self-examination, and even the pope agreed that the church needed to clarify its mission. The Council of Trent (1545–1563) yielded a new charter for the Roman Catholic Church. Far from offering compromises, however, Trent reaffirmed conservatism. Purgatory and indulgences were not eliminated, nor was priestly celibacy. Sacraments such as marriage were reinforced and sexual behavior more circumscribed than before. The church also policed ideas and banned books. Cervantes was fortunate to have only one sentence of *Don Quixote* removed. In some places, such as the staunchly Catholic Iberian world, the Holy Office of the Inquisition acted as enforcer of the new precepts, rooting out and punishing alleged deviance. Historians have shown that ordinary Catholics could be skeptical of the church's dogmatic claims, but much of what we know about these freethinkers comes from their Inquisition trial records.

In the wake of Trent, France's Catholics fiercely persecuted Calvinist Protestants, or Huguenots. This culminated in the Saint Bartholomew's Day massacre of 1572, in which tens of thousands of Huguenots were slaughtered (see again Map 19.3). Just back from America, horrified Huguenot Jean de Léry wrote that "civilized" French Christians had proved themselves far more barbaric than Brazil's Tupinamba cannibals, who at least killed according to rigid honor codes. Hostilities ended only in 1598 when the French king Henry IV signed the Edict of Nantes granting Protestants freedom to practice their religion. It helped that Henry IV was a former Protestant, but the Huguenots' troubles were not over.

Imperial Spain and Its Challenges

With fractured kingdoms and duchies the rule in early modern Europe, unified Spain proved an exception. Largely financed by the wealth of their numerous

SEEING THE PAST

Gift Clocks for the Emperors of China

With the exception of raw silver, China had little need of products introduced by Europeans hoping to trade for silk, porcelain, and eventually, tea. This presented a great problem for merchants short of silver, but it also challenged early modern European missionaries. The first Jesuits arrived in China in the 1550s, barely a decade after the pope's formal recognition of their order. They spent their first years trying to win poor converts inhabiting cities along the South China Sea, but by the 1580s some Jesuit priests, such as the Italian Matteo Ricci, began working their way toward Beijing. Given China's huge population, it made sense to try to convert those at the top of the social order in hopes that they would mandate the conversion of their many millions of subjects. Chinese eunuchs, courtiers, and princes were not easily swayed even by the most sophisticated philosophical arguments, but they were almost universally fascinated by advances in Western science and technology.

Courting the Qing: European Gift Clocks in the Forbidden City

Aware of this, Ricci developed a special program of "Christian science," attempting to link Western cartography, optics, metallurgy, and clockmaking to notions of divine order. He carried a European clock to Beijing in hopes of wowing the emperor

overseas colonies, Spain's Catholic Habsburg monarchs sought to consolidate their gains in Europe, and more importantly, to challenge the much larger and more powerful Ottoman Empire to the east. As we have seen, the fight against the "Great Turk," to use the language of the day, forever altered the lives of veterans such as Miguel de Cervantes.

Philip II came to the throne of Spain in 1556, when his father, Holy Roman Emperor Charles V (r. 1516–1556), abdicated. The title of "Emperor" passed to Ferdinand, Charles's brother, but Philip inherited extensive holdings of his own. Taken together, his kingdoms were much larger and richer than his uncle's.

in 1601, and it proved a big hit. A Chinese chronicle from 1603 records the event as follows: "In the twenty-eighth year of the reign of Wanli of the Ming dynasty, the great Westerner Li Madou [Matteo Ricci] presented a self-sounding bell, a mysterious and unknown art. The great bell sounds the hours, at midday, one sound."[3]

The Chinese were relatively uninterested in Western notions of timekeeping itself because they had their own means and units of measurement. Instead, the Chinese admired the clocks for their intricate and mechanical construction and welcomed them as "high-tech" status symbols. The Jesuits were for many years allowed special access to the Forbidden City, the Ming and Qing imperial palace in Beijing, primarily as clock repairmen. Their efforts to link clockwork to godliness in a Christian sense failed, but they did eventually spawn royal workshops that were capable of producing elaborate if not particularly accurate timepieces. Under Qing rule, the Royal Office of Clock Manufacture opened in 1723. By this time, advances in English clock- and watchmaking coincided with increased British interest in China, leading to a new wave of gift timepieces meant to win favor at court. Those shown here are on display in the Forbidden City's Palace Museum. Gifts from a range of Western ambassadors, they reveal European states' centuries-long effort to curry favor with the Chinese Empire.

Examining the Evidence

1. Why might European missionaries such as Ricci think that bringing clocks to China would aid conversion efforts?
2. How did Chinese appreciation of these clocks reflect cultural differences between them and Europeans?

Source: Catherine Pagani, *Eastern Magnificence and Western Ingenuity: Clocks of Late Imperial China* (Ann Arbor: University of Michigan Press, 2001).

Indeed, by 1598, the year of his death, Philip II ruled the world's first empire "upon which the sun never set." The distant Philippines were named for him in 1565. Still, governing a global empire brought more burden than pleasure. A forceful but pious monarch, Spain's so-called Prudent King would die doubting his own salvation.

One of Philip's first concerns, inherited from his father, was centralization in Spain. Castile and Aragon had been nominally united with the marriage of Isabella and Ferdinand in 1469, but local nobles and cities such as Barcelona continued to challenge royal authority. Charles's attempts to assert his will had sparked

armada A fleet of warships; usually used in reference to the Spanish naval fleet defeated by England in 1588.

rebellions in the 1520s, and regional resentments continued to fester throughout the period of overseas expansion. Philip responded in part by turning Madrid, formerly a dusty medieval crossroads in central Castile, into a world-class capital. The capital's building boom was funded by American treasure. Palaces, churches, monasteries, and residential structures proliferated, prompting envious neighbors to joke that the Spanish had discovered a magic formula for turning silver into stone.

Thanks to New World treasure, Spain had become Europe's most formidable state by the second half of the sixteenth century. Among other successes, Philip's forces had beaten, as we have seen, the Ottoman navy at Lepanto in 1571. Philip's biggest setback was the revolt of the Netherlands, a religiously divided region inherited from his father. The so-called Dutch Revolt, which began in 1566, taxed Iberian resources severely before its end in 1648. This was a war the Spanish lost, despite enormous effort.

Two other key events in Philip II's reign were the assumption of the Portuguese throne in 1580 and the 1588 attempt to invade England by sea. Both had global significance. Portugal's King Sebastian died without an heir in 1578, and the subsequent succession crisis ended only when Philip, whose mother was Isabella of Portugal, stepped in to take the crown. Philip's move required an armed invasion, and the Portuguese always regarded Spanish rule, which lasted from 1580 until 1640, as unlawful. In global terms, Spanish-Portuguese union meant that one monarch now ruled a substantial portion of Europe, much of the Americas, and dozens of Asian and African ports, islands, and sea routes. No European challenger was even close.

Philip knew this, and he assumed his good fortune was a reflection of divine will. Irritated by English harassment of the Spanish in the Americas and by English aid to the Dutch rebels, and determined to bring England back into the Catholic fold, Philip decided to launch an invasion of the British Isles. Such an undertaking would require an enormous concentration of military resources, and as at Lepanto, the stakes were correspondingly huge.

The Spanish **Armada** of 1588, the largest and most expensive naval force assembled up to that time, appears in retrospect to have been a folly. Neither side regarded the invasion as foolish at the time, however, and ultimately it was defeated

≡ **Route of the Spanish Armada, 1588**

due to a host of factors, only some of them within Spanish control. The Spanish stockpiled supplies for years, and even Cervantes took part, as a clerk charged with cataloguing food stores. When it came time to fight, English defenders such as the pirate Francis Drake, aided by Dutch allies, were critical; they knew the English Channel and understood Spanish tactics and technology. English guns were also powerful, carefully placed, and well manned. Aiding this defense were harsh weather, contrary winds, poorly mounted cannon, and other complications. Spanish luck went from bad to worse.

Ships not sunk by English and Dutch artillery were battered by waves and drawn off course by fierce gusts. The Spanish fleet scattered, and the remaining vessels were forced to sail north around Scotland to avoid capture. Here in the North Atlantic, Spanish sailors died by the hundreds of hunger and exposure. Some survivors were captured off the coast of Ireland. The English, hardly the sea power they would later become, were jubilant. Subjects of the fiercely Protestant Elizabeth I had proved that mighty Philip and his great armada were not invincible after all.

Spain's misfortunes compounded in the wake of the armada disaster, and although the world's most extensive empire was hardly crumbling, Philip II's successors faced a potent new competitor in the form of the breakaway Dutch Republic. The Dutch projected their power overseas beginning in the 1590s, and by 1640 the Dutch East and West India companies took over many of the key trading posts held by the joint Spanish-Portuguese Empire from the Caribbean islands to Japan. Beginning in 1630, the West India Company occupied northeastern Brazil. What the Dutch did not know was that at precisely this time the main sources of Spanish wealth, the great silver mines of Potosí in present-day Bolivia, were petering out. Declining silver revenues combined with other chance factors sparked what has become known as "the seventeenth-century crisis" (see Figure 19.1).

The Seventeenth-Century Crisis

Few topics have generated as much debate among historians as the seventeenth-century crisis, a series of events and trends affecting much of Europe and the Mediterranean basin between 1600 and 1660. Some scholars have even claimed that no general crisis occurred, only a cluster of

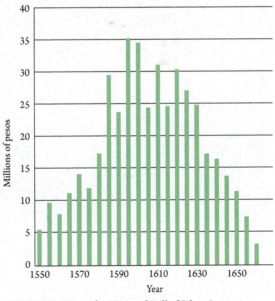

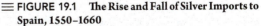

≡ FIGURE 19.1   The Rise and Fall of Silver Imports to Spain, 1550–1660

unrelated catastrophes. In any case, Europe's post-1660 rebound and push toward global maritime dominance seems remarkable. How did one of the world's most politically divided, religiously intolerant, and economically fractured regions give rise, in a relatively short time, to secular models of government, rational scientific inquiry, and financial capitalism, all hallmarks of modernity?

Historians focus on different causes, depending on their interpretive bent. Political and military historians focus on the "modern" horrors and early nationalism of the Thirty Years' War. Here, unlike in Asia and North Africa, gunpowder led to the dissolution rather than consolidation of empires. Economic historians focus on the shifting influx of American silver and its effects on food and other commodity prices. Some argue that inflated prices and economic depression had both negative and positive effects, sparking riots while prompting technical and financial innovations. Still other historians, informed by modern scientific techniques, focus on climate, analyzing ice cores and tree rings, along with traditional historical sources, to document the extent of the so-called Little Ice Age, which, as we will see, enveloped Europe from about 1550 to 1700. In the end it is hard to say which of these factors was most responsible for either the widespread turmoil or the swift turnaround that followed, but most historians agree that something transformative had occurred.

In the midst of a twelve-year truce between the Spanish and Dutch, the Thirty Years' War (1618–1648) broke out in central Europe. This conflict pitted Christian factions against one another in a civil and international war that radically reshaped Europe's borders. The Thirty Years' War was devastating for civilians. Caught in the crossfire, they were forced to support occupying troops, only to be massacred for doing so when the tide turned and the other side's troops moved in.

In essence, the Thirty Years' War was over the internal

The Thirty Years' War Dutch artist Jan Maertszen de Jonghe depicts the horrors of the battlefield in this 1634 rendering of the 1627 Battle of Dirschau, near Gdansk, Poland. The battle pitted Swedish king Gustav II, whose slain body appears in the foreground, against Polish-Lithuanian forces led by General Stanislaw Koniecpolski, shown here astride a chestnut horse. Soldiers and horses lie dead or wounded, but later in the Thirty Years' War, it was civilian casualties that reached levels not seen before in Europe.

politics of the Holy Roman Empire in central Europe (see again Map 19.3). This was really only a loose confederacy, since near-autonomy had been ceded to many Lutheran and Calvinist principalities and duchies. Inhabitants of these Protestant enclaves rightly feared a more assertive Catholic emperor. Emperor Ferdinand II was such a person, an ambitious, Jesuit-educated militant. When Ferdinand started to re-Catholicize central Europe, the various enemies of the Habsburgs sent aid, then joined the fray.

Before the war ended, several German and Bohemian princes, the kings of Denmark, Poland, and Sweden, plus the English, French, Dutch, and finally the Spanish had all been drawn into the conflict. Contemporary engravings and paintings from its last phase depict the full range of human cruelty, a reminder, like the Saint Bartholomew's Day massacre, that Europeans were capable of horrendous savagery. At war's end at least a third of the population of Germany had died, and the region's infrastructure lay in ruins. From population decline to decreased agricultural production, the war was a manifestation of the seventeenth-century crisis.

It was also enormously costly in terms of money, the supply of which was shifting. Economic historians have found that throughout Europe prices rose even as demand fell. In one interpretation, an overabundance of silver in the late sixteenth century drove prices up, after which a sequence of plagues, droughts, wars, and other disasters killed off both consumers and suppliers of basic goods throughout Europe, leading to depression. A sustained drop in silver income beginning in around 1600 made hard money scarce when it was already overvalued, forcing many people to resort to barter. Thus, the fabulous wealth of the Americas proved both a blessing and a curse, shifting the global balance of power in Europe's favor at the same time that it led to economic volatility.

Hard times for most could be good for some, and it appears that the Dutch fared rather well, particularly in comparison with the Spanish and Portuguese. The Netherlands' unique mix of financial capitalism, religious toleration, and overseas conquest seemed to offset many of the difficulties faced by other states (see Reading the Past: An Exiled European Muslim Visits the Netherlands). The Dutch East India Company's spice-island takeovers in Southeast Asia were key, as seen in Chapter 18, but Dutch pirates, many sponsored by the West India Company, were also busy capturing Spanish silver fleets in the Caribbean.

Historians have long suggested that the climatic change known as the Little Ice Age may have spurred rebellion and even war during the seventeenth century, but only recently have enough data been assembled to model the century's weather cycles. It now appears that four of the five coldest summers ever recorded in the Northern Hemisphere occurred in the seventeenth century, and

READING THE PAST

An Exiled European Muslim Visits the Netherlands

After an Ottoman-supported rebellion in Andalusia lasting from 1569 to 1571, Spain's remaining forced converts from Islam, or Moriscos, faced increasing persecution. Many fled to Morocco, Algeria, and other havens in North Africa, especially during a last wave of expulsions ordered by Philip III from 1609 to 1614. Among the refugees was Ahmad Ibn Qasim Al-Hajari, born with the Spanish surname Bejarano around 1569, apparently in the village of Hornachos, Extremadura, not far from the birthplaces of Francisco Pizarro and Hernando Cortés. Al-Hajari went on to become a major spokesman for the Morisco community in exile, and he wrote and traveled widely. His best-known work, composed and circulated in both Arabic and Spanish, is called *The Supporter of Religion Against the Infidels* (c.1637). In it, Al-Hajari describes his visit to the Netherlands:

About the Netherlands: You should know that I set out for that country deliberately, although it lies farther from our own country than France. But a man should seek protection from others or from himself, and after I had experienced the way French sailors were treating Muslims, I said: I will not return to my country in one of those ships, but I will go to the country of the Netherlanders, because they do not harm Muslims but treat them well. . . .

After I reached the City of Amsterdam, I marveled at the beauty of its architecture and the style of its buildings, its cleanness and the great number of its inhabitants. Its population was almost like that of the City of Paris in France. There is no city in the world with so many ships as it has! One says that the total number of its ships, including the smaller and the bigger ones, is 6,000. As for the houses, each of these is painted and decorated

that global volcanic activity was probably a major contributor to the cooldown. Global cooling shortened growing seasons just as Europeans were pushing into more marginal lands. In alpine valleys, for example, peasants and herders were driven from their homes by advancing glaciers. Unprecedented droughts ravaged traditionally wet regions such as Scotland in the 1630s and 1640s, fueling violent uprisings.

The Little Ice Age affected regions far beyond European borders. The worst drought in five hundred years was recorded on the Yangzi River between 1641 and 1644, probably contributing to the 1644 fall of the Ming dynasty in China (discussed in Chapter 20). Ottoman territories were also hit: Egypt's Nile River fell to with marvelous colors from top to bottom. Not one resembles another in the art of its painting. All the streets are made of paved stones.

I met someone who had seen the lands of the East, the lands of the Slavonians, Rome and other countries of the world. He told me that he had never seen a city so nicely decorated.

One should know that the Netherlands consists of seventeen islands, all of which used to belong to the Sultan of Al-Andalus [i.e., the king of Spain]. At a certain time, a man appeared in those lands who was held as a great scholar by them, called Luther, as well as another scholar called Calvin. Each of them wrote his view of the corruption and deviation from the religion of our lord Jesus and the Gospel that had come about in the religion of the Christians. They said the popes in Rome misled the people by worshiping idols and by the additions they introduced into the faith by forbidding priests and monks to marry, and many other things. All the people of the Netherlands—I mean, of the Seven Islands—embraced this doctrine and they rose up against their sultan until today. The people of the Sultanate of the English also follow this doctrine. There are also many of them in France. Their scholars warn them against the popes and the worshiping of idols. They tell them they should not hate Muslims because they are the Sword of God on His earth against the worshipers of idols.

Source: Ahmad Ibn Qasim Al-Hajari, *The Supporter of Religion Against the Infidel,* ed. and trans. P. S. Van Koningsveld, Q. Al-Samarrai, and G. A. Wiegers (Madrid: Consejo Superior de Investigaciones Científicas, 1997), 194–195.

Examining the Evidence

1. What aspects of the Netherlands most impress al-Hajari?

2. How clear is al-Hajari's understanding of the Protestant Reformation?

its lowest recorded levels between 1640 and 1643. Troops on the Persian frontier rebelled when their pay in silver coin proved insufficient to buy food.

Within Europe, the seventeenth-century crisis gained more sinister social dimensions with the rise of witchcraft trials and Inquisition prosecutions. In Protestant Europe, thousands of women were executed for alleged acts of sorcery, and in Catholic Spain and its colonies an unprecedented number of Jews were killed by order of the Inquisition between 1637 and 1649. It is difficult to know why these repressive outbursts occurred in the midst of war, famine, and other problems, but the tendency to scapegoat vulnerable persons in uncertain times has been documented elsewhere. More positive outcomes of the seventeenth-century crisis included scientific discoveries and novel political ideas that eventually took on global importance.

European Innovations in Science and Government 1550–1750

⬊ **FOCUS** What factors enabled European scientific and political innovations in the early modern period?

In the aftermath of the religious wars, a new wave of political consolidation occurred in northern and central Europe in the form of absolutist and constitutionalist monarchies. Many of these states, like their Spanish, Portuguese, and Dutch predecessors, expanded overseas. Global expansion entailed great risks and huge defense costs, so in addition to building professional navies, states created licensing agencies and sponsored monopoly trading companies. Financial innovations included stock markets and double-entry accounting, essential ingredients of modern capitalism. Also emerging from divided Europe was the "scientific revolution." Although restricted for many years to a handful of theorists and experimenters, Europe's embrace of science was to prove globally significant.

The Scientific Revolution

As with the "seventeenth-century crisis," historians have long debated whether or not Europe experienced a "scientific revolution" in the early modern era. Skeptics argue that the innovations of the period were too restricted to educated elites to justify the term *revolution*. In contrast, proponents describe a shift in worldview that resonated beyond the small circle of "scientific rebels."

Call it what we may, European intellectuals after about 1550 challenged received wisdom and employed mathematical formulas and empirical (observable) data in an effort to discover the rules by which nature operated. Inductive and deductive reasoning were guiding principles in their efforts. Inductive reasoning—deriving general principles from empirical evidence—was most clearly articulated by the Englishman Sir Francis Bacon. Its complement, deductive reasoning—the process of reasoning from a self-evident general principle to a specific fact—was the contribution of French mathematician René Descartes. The search for universal rules led some to explain the motions of the cosmos. Since this was akin to describing "Heaven" in a secular way, many churchmen bristled.

The first breakthroughs were made by a Polish monk, Nicolaus Copernicus. Copernicus was the first to systematically question the ancient Ptolemaic model, which was geocentric, or earth-centered. Copernicus's observations of conflicted with **geocentrism**, suggesting instead that the stars and planets, including the earth, revolved around the sun. Fearing ridicule, Copernicus did not publish his *On the Revolutions of the Heavenly Spheres* until 1543, the year of his death. Following Copernicus, the Danish astronomer Tycho Brahe compiled a wealth of "eyeball" data. This data was precise enough to help the German Johannes Kepler work out a heliocentric, or sun-centered, model in which the planets circled the sun in elliptical orbits.

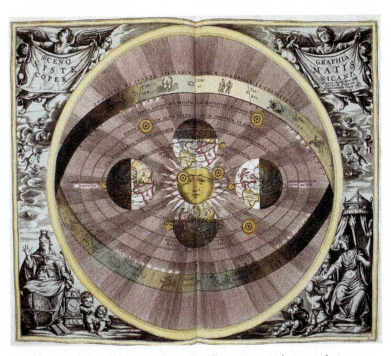

≡ **The Copernican Universe** The earth still appears quite large in relation to other planets in this 1660 rendering of a heliocentric, or sun-centered, cosmos, but the breakthrough initiated by Nicolaus Copernicus in 1543 is fully evident.

Europe's most probing minds were open to **heliocentrism**, and some went on to risk their lives to advance the project. In works such as *The Advancement of Learning* (1605), Sir Francis Bacon attacked reliance on ancient writers and supported the scientific method based on inductive reasoning and empirical experimentation. Bacon had his critics, but he was shielded from persecution by the Protestant English state. By contrast, the Italian scientist Galileo Galilei is best remembered for his insistence, against an unforgiving Catholic Church, that nature was governed by mathematical laws. Although the Inquisition placed Galileo under house arrest, his use of new, high-grade telescopes to observe the moons of Jupiter furthered the cause of heliocentrism and challenged reliance on received wisdom.

Deviations between Kepler's model and empirical observations were worked out by the English scientist Isaac Newton. The elliptical planetary orbits discovered by Kepler, Newton argued through word and formula in *Principia Mathematica* (*Mathematical Principles*, 1687), resulted from the laws of motion, including the principle of gravity, which explained the forces that controlled the movement not

geocentrism The ancient belief that the earth is the center of the universe.

heliocentrism The early modern discovery that the sun is the center of our solar system.

only of planets but of objects on earth. The whole universe was brought together in one system. Whereas Copernicus had feared publishing his findings in his lifetime, Newton faced a receptive audience. His synthesis would prevail until the twentieth century.

Other Europeans were testing boundaries in distant corners of the world. In the last years of the sixteenth century the Italian Jesuit Matteo Ricci stunned the Ming court with his knowledge of mechanics and mathematics. The Spanish-American metallurgist and parish priest Alvaro Alonso Barba went further, challenging received wisdom through experimentation in his 1627 treatise, *The Art of Metals*. Here in the silver mines of Potosí (Bolivia), Barba was sufficiently informed to comment on Galileo's 1610 publication, *Sidereus Nuncius* (*The Starry Messenger*).

The Emergence of Capitalism

Historians differ as to how modern **capitalism**—an economic system in which private parties make their goods and services available on an open market and seek to exploit market conditions to profit from their activities—came about. But most agree that in early modern Europe there were two overlapping stages: first commercial, and later industrial. Large trading companies such as the Dutch VOC were essential to the commercial stage of capitalism. They spread risk by selling shares while also exploiting extensive communications and transportation networks. The VOC and English EIC operated on a huge scale, spawning numerous subsidiary businesses, from banks to insurance companies to stock exchanges. Thus, financial innovation tied even ordinary Europeans to global expansion.

In the countryside, mechanical and transport innovations yielded productivity gains that outpaced population growth, especially in northwestern Europe. The arrival of potatoes and other New World crops boosted yields and filled peasant bellies. American sugar was increasingly used to preserve fruits through the long winter. Better food security enabled some peasants to sell their surplus labor for cash wages. Wages made peasants small-scale consumers, a new kind of market participant.

More dependable food supplies came with a social cost, however, first felt by English peasants. Only landowners with secure titles to their property could take advantage of the new crops to practice commercial farming. Rich landowners therefore "enclosed" the land—that is, consolidated their holdings—and got Parliament to give them title to the common lands that in the past had been open to all. Land enclosure turned tenant farmers and sharecroppers into landless farm laborers. Many moved to the cities to seek work.

capitalism In early modern Europe, a new way of conducting business by pooling money, goods, and labor to make a profit.

Cities were home to merchants, or burghers, as well as to wage workers. The burghers, or **bourgeoisie**, grew to compete with the old nobility, particularly in England, the Netherlands, and parts of France, Germany, and Italy, as consumers of luxury goods. Especially after 1660 their economic power boosted their political power.

Europe's manufacturing sector was also transformed by commercial capitalism. Beginning in the late Middle Ages, rising demand for textiles led to expanded production of woolen and linen fabrics. The major growth of the cloth industries took place in northern Europe beginning in the sixteenth century, when Spanish-American silver flowed through Spain to France, England, and Holland, despite ongoing conflicts. Asians did not much care for Europe's products, but colonists did. Millions of bolts of Dutch and French linens, as well as English woolens, were sent across the Atlantic, and even the Pacific, to Spanish and Portuguese colonies. Global interdependence grew ever tighter through the circulation of fabrics and silver. Europe's textile manufacturers demanded Spanish-American and Brazilian dyes, and profits from international trade were then reinvested in more land for flax growing, larger weaving shops, and wages for more workers. With the application of scientific principles and innovative mechanical apparatus by the early eighteenth century, the stage was set for the emergence of industrial capitalism in England (discussed in Chapter 23).

England's commercial leadership in the eighteenth century originated in seventeenth-century mercantilism. **Mercantilism** was a system of economic regulations aimed at increasing the power of the state. It rested on the general premise that a nation's power and wealth were determined by its supply of precious metals, which were to be acquired by increasing exports and reducing imports to achieve domestic self-sufficiency. What distinguished English mercantilism was the notion that government economic regulations should serve private interests as well as the public needs of the state. For example, the Navigation Acts of the seventeenth century required that English goods be transported in English ships and restricted colonial exports to raw materials, enriching English merchants and manufacturers as well as the Crown.

New Political Models: Absolutism and Constitutionalism

Two new state forms arose in Europe after the Thirty Years' War: absolutism and constitutionalism. As the Habsburgs fell into decline, challengers sought to fill the void, including the commercially savvy Dutch, but it was the French under King Louis XIV who emerged preeminent. Not far behind were the English, who despite a midcentury civil war consolidated control over the British Isles and many overseas possessions by the early eighteenth century. As imperial rivals, Britain

bourgeoisie In early modern Europe, a new class of burghers, or urban-dwelling merchants.

mercantilism A system of economic regulations aimed at increasing the power of the state.

and France developed distinct systems of governance later copied and modified by others. The monarchs of England found themselves restricted by elected parliaments, whereas those of France sought absolute authority and claimed quasi-divinity. Despite their differences, the British and French created the largest and widest-ranging navies yet seen in world history.

Although Spain's Philip II and other Habsburgs had acted in autocratic and grandiose ways since the mid-sixteenth century, no European monarch matched the heady blend of state drama and personal charisma of France's Louis XIV (r. 1643–1715). The "Sun-King," as he came to be known, personified the absolutist ruler who shared power with no one. Louis XIV spent much of his long reign centralizing state authority in order to make France a global contender. Though successful in the short run, Louis's form of **absolutism**—propped up by rising taxes and contempt for the masses—sowed the seeds of its own destruction.

Louis XIV was enthroned as a five-year-old, and his mother, Anne of Austria, and her Italian-born adviser and rumored lover, Cardinal Mazarin, ruled in his name. Under the regency, resistance emerged in the form of the *Fronde*, a five-year period of instability from 1648 to 1653 that grew from a regional tax revolt into a potential civil war. Critics coined the term *Fronde*, French for a child's slingshot, to signify that the revolts were mere child's play. In fact, they threatened the Crown. Historians of the seventeenth-century crisis have often linked the uprisings to climate change, agricultural stresses, and price fluctuations. Whatever the Fronde's causes, nobles and district courts, or *parlements* (PARLE-mohn), asserted their power against the regency. In the end, the revolt was put down, and when Mazarin died in 1661, Louis XIV assumed total control.

Louis XIV spent the next decades taming nobles and potential religious opponents through patronage and punishment. His rule was authoritarian and intolerant of religious difference. After persecuting nonconformist Catholics in the 1660s, Louis exiled the country's remaining Huguenots, French Protestants whose protection had been guaranteed by Henry IV. Absolutism was extended to the press as well, with pro-state propaganda and harsh censorship the order of the day.

French absolutism also required loyal crown officers, called *intendants* (ON-tohn-don). These officials governed districts, or departments, in the king's name, administering justice, collecting taxes, and organizing defense. Loyal bureaucrats also included high-ranking commoners such as Jean-Baptiste Colbert, Louis's minister of finance. Colbert also oversaw naval and overseas trade affairs, managing French expansion in the Caribbean and North America. As the Ottomans had already shown, rewarding merit-worthy commoners with high office was as important to early modern government as containing the

absolutism A political theory holding that all power should be vested in one ruler; also such a system of government.

aspirations of high nobles. Building an overseas empire greatly expanded the scope of patronage politics.

More than any other early European monarch, Louis XIV arranged court life to serve as a sort of state theater. The king was allegedly divine, and physical proximity to him was regarded as both desirable and dangerous. A constant stream of propaganda in the form of poems, processions, statues, and medals celebrated the greatness of the monarch. "The state?" Louis asked rhetorically. "It is I."

To house his bulging court, which included mobs of fawning nobles, Louis XIV ordered thousands of artisans and laborers to construct a palace befitting his magnificence. Built between 1662 and 1685, Versailles, just outside Paris, was hardly the pleasure dome outsiders imagined it to be. And it was far less opulent than the palace of Louis's near contemporary, Mughal emperor Shah Jahan. Yet Versailles set a new model for European court grandeur.

Tax increases helped to cover the costs of building and maintaining Versailles, but more costly by far were the armed forces. Naval construction boomed under Colbert's direction, and the professionalization and reorganization of land forces was even more extensive. By 1700 France, a country of some twenty million people, could field three hundred thousand soldiers. This was more than ten times the number of soldiers in England, a country with about half of France's total population.

Louis used his military primarily to confront the Habsburgs, although his aggression upset many others, including the English, Swedes, and Dutch. First were incursions into the Spanish Netherlands in the 1660s and 1670s, then into Germany in the 1680s and 1690s. Both conflicts ended with only minor gains for France, but Louis was feared enough to be dubbed the "Christian Turk." Meanwhile, the Crown sponsored French trading companies that sought to penetrate the markets of Africa, the Middle East, India, and Southeast Asia.

≡ **Palace of Versailles** In this 1668 aerial view of Versailles, painter Pierre Patel seeks to encompass the full splendor of French king Louis XIV's famous palace and retreat. Begun in 1661, Versailles instantly became a symbol of absolutist power, a virtual city unto itself. Many early modern rulers ordered the construction or expansion of similarly opulent structures, such as the Ottomans' Topkapi Palace in Istanbul and the Mughals' Red Fort complex in Delhi.

Most important in global terms was the War of the Spanish Succession (1701–1714). This conflict proved disastrous for the French because most of Europe allied against them, fearing the consequences of French control over Spanish territories. It ended with France forced to cede exclusive trading privileges with Spanish America to the English (see Map 19.4). Military service, meanwhile, became standard for French commoners, along with high taxes and periodic food shortages. Absolutism was good for centralizing authority, but not, as it would turn out, for keeping the peace.

The turmoil of seventeenth-century Europe resulted in both absolute monarchy and an alternative: **constitutionalism**. This form of government requires rulers to share power with representative bodies, or parliaments. In England, birthplace of constitutionalism, taxation was always at issue, but so were religious freedom and class representation.

Constitutions were charters guaranteeing subjects certain rights, but which subjects and what rights? For a time, it was mostly elites whose interests won out. Indeed, far from being democratically elected representatives of the popular classes, members of the constitutionalist parliament—whether in England, Holland, or Poland—were generally landlords and merchants. Some were prominent clergymen. None were artisans or peasants.

English constitutionalism did not emerge peacefully. Instead, when in 1641 King Charles I (r. 1625–1649) challenged England's centuries-old Parliament of wealthy property owners, he met a resistance so violent it cost him his life. Charles's timing, as historians of the seventeenth-century crisis have pointed out, could not have been worse: thousands were starving after a sequence of failed harvests. Outraged subjects decided that if the king was judged to be acting out-of-bounds, he should go.

England's showdown with the king had a long backstory. Charles had distrusted Parliament from the beginning and refused to call it into session throughout the 1630s. Unconventional taxes and religious edicts eroded the king's support in England and provoked a rebellion in Scotland. Parliament was called in 1640 to meet this last crisis, but representatives surprised the monarch by demanding sweeping reforms. Many Protestants felt that the king supported Catholicism, the religion of his French wife, and the most radical among them, the Puritans, pushed hardest for checks on royal power. Charles reacted with force, touching off the English Civil War of 1642 to 1646.

After intense fighting, the Puritan faction under Oliver Cromwell emerged victorious. Cromwell and his Puritan supporters took over Parliament and brought Charles to trial. The king was convicted of tyranny and executed in 1649.

Cromwell, who styled himself "Lord Protector," proved instead to be a dictator. Dissenters were crushed, and Cromwellian forces subjugated Scotland and Ireland with terror and mass displacement. Overseas conflicts with the Dutch and French

constitutionalism An early modern system of government based on a written charter defining a power-sharing arrangement between a monarch and representative bodies, or parliaments.

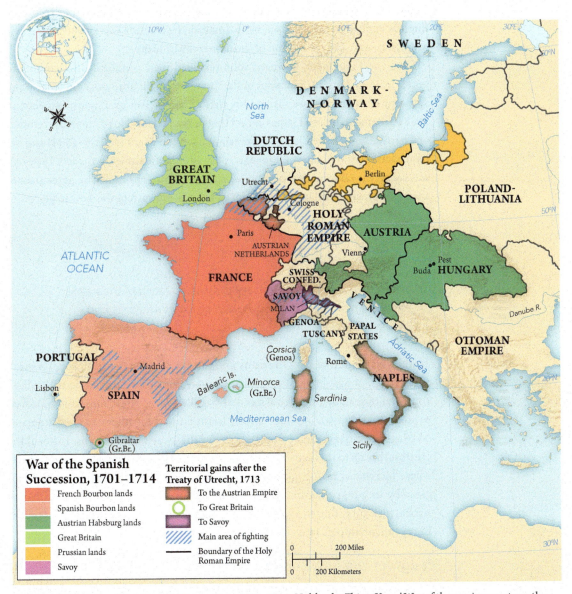

≡ **MAP 19.4   War of the Spanish Succession, 1701–1714** Unlike the Thirty Years' War of the previous century, the War of the Spanish Succession was openly understood to be a global power contest rather than a conflict over religious faith. With the Ottomans, Iberians, and even the Dutch in decline, the main contestants were Great Britain and France. Great Britain and its allies won the war, but in the Treaty of Utrecht they allowed the French prince to take the throne as Philip V in exchange for a monopoly on the slave trade to Spanish America and other concessions, such as the strategic Mediterranean post of Gibraltar and the island of Minorca.

resulted in few victories and expanded taxes. When Cromwell died in 1658, few English subjects mourned his passing. Instead, the reaction was a sweeping revival of Anglicanism and restoration of the monarchy in 1660.

King and Parliament, however, soon resumed their conflicts. After coming to power in 1685, James II ran afoul of Parliament with his absolutist tendencies and apparent desire to impose his and his wife's Catholicism on English subjects. In 1688 Parliament deposed James, an act that proved far less bloody than the removal of Charles I, and invited James's Protestant daughter Mary (r. 1689–1694) and her Dutch husband, William of Orange (r. 1689–1702), to assume the throne. The event was called the Glorious Revolution because the monarchs signed an agreement to share power with Parliament. A model constitutional system was now in place.

COUNTERPOINT: The Barbary Pirates

FOCUS Why were the Barbary pirates of North Africa able to thrive from 1500 to 1800 despite Ottoman and European overseas expansion?

To the vast empire of the Ottomans and the fractured states of Europe, Africa's north coast, or Maghreb, offers a dual counterpoint. The early modern Maghreb consisted of sea-hugging city-states and tribal enclaves stretching from Morocco to present-day Libya. Although fiercely Islamic and sympathetic to the Ottomans, no Maghribi city ever fell completely under the sway of the sultans. Instead, the greatest threats to this centerless region's autonomy came from Christian Europe, whose merchants had long traveled to Africa in pursuit of slaves and gold. Energized by its gunpowder-fueled 1492 conquest of Granada, Spain invaded North Africa with fury, but struggled to hold onto a few rocky outposts. Subsequent European interlopers fared little better.

Reign of the Sea Bandits

After 1500, sea banditry flourished along what Europeans called the Berber, or Barbary, Coast. Early pirate leaders included Oruç and Hayreddin Barbarossa, Greek brothers who settled in Algiers and ruled it from 1516 to 1546. The Barbarossa (Italian for "red beard") brothers were already famous for their raids on the coast of Italy. They briefly combined forces with neighboring Tunis to launch attacks and share out booty, but regional jealousies prevailed and the cities again competed. The raiders focused on capturing merchant vessels at sea, but what made the Barbarossas household names were their audacious land attacks and kidnappings.

Hayreddin later strengthened ties to the Ottomans, but he remained independent of the sultan's orders.

As Ottoman sea power declined after 1580 and Atlantic shipping ballooned, other pirate bases sprang up along the west coast of Morocco. Key after 1600 was the tiny city of Salé (sah-LAY), whose pirate attacks on Spanish and Portuguese shipping were financed and sometimes manned by

The Barbary Coast, c. 1560

exiled Iberian Jews and Muslims. Aside from these vengeful European "renegades," as they were called, a number of Morocco's own seafaring Berber tribes engaged in piracy and extortion. Countless young men came of age beneath the pirate flag.

By the time Miguel de Cervantes was held captive in Algiers in the late 1570s, Maghribi hostage trafficking and extortion rackets formed a sophisticated business. The pirates used swift sailing vessels and state-of-the-art European guns to steal money and merchandise, but mostly they kidnapped Christian Europeans, preferably men and women of high status. Some hostages were mistreated and forced to do hard labor, but as Cervantes describes in *Don Quixote*, most were allowed to send letters to relatives on the other side of the Mediterranean requesting ransoms. Barbary Coast extortion also included selling safe passage to European shippers—that is, promising *not* to kidnap them or steal their merchandise in exchange for money, arms, and shipbuilding materials.

Northern European merchants struck many such deals, and at first Protestant newcomers were particularly welcomed given their access to advanced weapons and shared hatred of Catholic Iberians. Still, failure to pay for protection led to harsh reprisals. Some pirates raided as far away as the English Channel in the early 1600s, and before long thousands of northern Europeans languished, like the Spaniard Cervantes before them, in the jails of Algiers, Tunis, and Tripoli.

The Barbary Wars

Although internal divisions and poor leadership among Maghribi sovereigns became more evident over time, it was sustained rivalry among the Europeans that prevented any coordinated attack on the Barbary pirates until the early nineteenth

☰ Ransoming Christians Unlike in the Americas, where piracy also thrived in the early modern period, the Barbary pirates of Africa's north coast specialized in kidnapping and extortion. The ransom of Christian captives held in cities such as Algiers and Tunis was organized by Catholic religious orders, who collected sums from as far away as Spanish America to free men and women whose relatives could produce no ransom. This seventeenth-century European engraving depicts Catholic priests heroically carrying ransom money, while Christian prisoners appear as cruelly mistreated victims cowering behind their Muslim captors.

century. Only then, when merchants from the fledgling United States rejected demands for protection money, did the Barbary pirates see a reversal in fortune. In a pet project of President Thomas Jefferson, the United States won the support of traditional European powers, most significantly the French, to bomb the Barbary pirates into submission. The so-called Barbary Wars' unexpected result was near-total French takeover of North Africa, which ended only in the 1960s.

Conclusion

Fueled by gunpowder, silver, and religious fervor, Europe and the Mediterranean basin exploded after 1500 as the world's most belligerent region, but it was also the most commercially dynamic. Relative resource poverty compelled Europeans to trade with one another, but regional identities, exacerbated by religious differences, led them to fight as often as they cooperated. This trend only continued as nationalist loyalties were hardened by the rise of Protestantism.

By contrast, in these years the Sunni Muslim Ottomans built a vast land empire encompassing eastern Europe, Southwest Asia, Egypt, and much of Arabia. They did so with force, but also by cleverly integrating new subjects into the ranks of government and the armed forces. Ottoman pragmatism favored religious tolerance. The Ottoman world became a haven for many of Europe's persecuted Jews, and conquered Christians were not forced to convert to Islam. Chronic wars with the Habsburgs and Safavids provided opportunities for social advancement, but they also absorbed state resources, eventually bogging the empire down.

A battered Europe emerged from its seventeenth-century crisis to begin a new phase of national division. There also emerged three globally significant trends: a new science based on direct observation and experimentation, an increasingly capitalist economy, and centralized government. As modern as this sounds, Europeans still saw the quest for wealth and power as a zero-sum game, in which gain by one side meant loss by the others, driving them to seek resource monopolies and lay claim to ever more distant lands and peoples.

Former Barbary captive Miguel de Cervantes of Spain could hardly have known what lay ahead for Europe and the greater Mediterranean, but his vision of a newly interconnected world continued to inspire his imagination. In the opening to the second part of *Don Quixote*, published in 1615, Cervantes jokingly claimed that he had received a letter from the Chinese emperor inviting him to establish a Spanish school at court for which his "world-famous" novel would be the main text. Cervantes claimed that he had declined the offer only because he was ill and could not afford the trip.

✳ review

The major global development in this chapter: Early modern Europe's increasing competition and division in the face of Ottoman expansion.

	Important Events
1453	Ottoman conquest of Constantinople
1492	Spanish take Granada, expel Jews
1517	Martin Luther disseminates "Ninety-Five Theses," sparking the Protestant Reformation
1520–1566	Reign of Ottoman emperor Suleiman
1540	Ignatius Loyola founds the new Catholic order of the Jesuits
1543	Nicolaus Copernicus, *On the Revolutions of the Heavenly Spheres*
1545–1563	Council of Trent
1571	Battle of Lepanto
1572	St. Bartholomew's Day massacre
1580	Philip II of Spain takes over Portuguese Empire
1598	Edict of Nantes ends French Religious War
1618–1648	Thirty Years' War
1640	Portugal wins independence from Spain
1642–1646	English Civil War
1643–1715	Reign of Louis XIV of France
1683	Ottomans defeated in Vienna by Polish-Austrian alliance
1687	Isaac Newton, *Principia Mathematica*
1688	Glorious Revolution in England
1701–1714	War of the Spanish Succession

KEY TERMS

absolutism (p. 710)
armada (p. 700)
bourgeoisie (p. 709)
capitalism (p. 708)

caravanserai (p. 690)
constitutionalism (p. 712)
devshirme (p. 682)
geocentrism (p. 707)

heliocentrism (p. 707)
indulgence (p. 695)
mercantilism (p. 709)
timar (p. 682)

CHAPTER OVERVIEW QUESTIONS

1. To what degree was religious diversity embraced or rejected in early modern Europe and the greater Mediterranean, and why?

2. How did Christian Europe's gunpowder-fueled empires compare with that of the Ottomans?
3. What accounts for the rise of science and capitalism in early modern western Europe?

MAKING CONNECTIONS

1. How did battles for control of the Mediterranean compare with those for control of Indian Ocean trade (see Chapter 18)?
2. How globally important was the Protestant Reformation?

3. In what ways were the Barbary pirates similar to the Atlantic slave traders (see Chapter 17)? How were they different?

For further research into the topics covered in this chapter, see the Bibliography at the end of the book. For additional primary sources from this period, see *Sources for World in the Making*.

20

Expansion and Isolation in Asia 1450–1750

≡ **World in the Making** This life-size portrait from Beijing's Palace Museum depicts China's Emperor Qianlong (1711–1799) at a grand old age. The use of perspective—the illusion of three-dimensional space— reflects the influence of European Jesuit artists who resided at court after the early seventeenth century, but the emperor's pose reflects a Chinese taste for a more statuelike representation of imperial power. His elaborate silk garments and pearl-encrusted headgear and necklace suggest the wealth of the Qing treasury, which despite massive expenditures and waste, boasted a huge surplus in silver for much of the emperor's reign.

backstory

By the fifteenth century, Russia had shaken off Mongol rule and was beginning to expand from its base in Moscow. Russian expansion would eventually lead to conflict with China, which by the fifteenth century was by far the world's most populous state. Self-sufficient, widely literate, and technically sophisticated, China vied with Europe for supremacy in both practical and theoretical sciences. As we saw in Chapter 14, the Ming dynasty had also become a global power capable of mounting long-distance sea voyages, yet by the 1430s its rulers had chosen to withdraw and focus on consolidating internal affairs. By contrast, Japan was deeply fractured in the fifteenth century, its many districts and several islands subject to feuding warlords. Korea, though less densely populated than either of its neighbors east or west, was relatively unified under the Yi dynasty, which came to power in the late fourteenth century. In mainland Southeast Asia, several Buddhist kingdoms were by this time undergoing a major reconfiguration. Neo-Confucianism was on the rise in Vietnam. The Philippine Islands, meanwhile, remained politically and ethnically diverse, in part due to their complex geography.

Wang Yangming (1472–1529) had trouble on his hands. As governor of China's Jiangxi Province, he had to collect taxes and keep the peace for his Ming overlords. Wang had risen through the ranks of the civil service through a mix of intelligence, connections, and ambition. Now he was faced with a rebellious prince, Zhu Chen-hao, and his followers. Acting as general, Wang successfully attacked the rebels with every weapon at hand, including bronze cannon probably copied from the Portuguese. More important than the suppression of the rebellion was the aftermath. Wang chose not to terrorize the populace as his predecessors might have, but instead moved quickly to rebuild, pardoning many rebels and winning their loyalty to the Ming emperor.

Wang Yangming's effective governorship won praise, but he was better known as a philosopher. Wang was among the most renowned **Neo-Confucianists** of early modern China. As described in Chapter 14, the philosophical movement known as Neo-Confucianism revived an ancient tradition. The fifth-century B.C.E. Chinese philosopher Kongzi (Latinized as "Confucius") envisioned the ideal earthly society as a mirror of divine harmony. Although he prescribed ancestor worship, Confucius developed a system of ethics rather than a formal religion. Education and scientific experimentation were highly valued, but so was submission to social superiors. Some of Confucius's ideas were elaborated by his fourth-century B.C.E. successor, Mengzi, or Mencius, whose commentaries inspired Wang Yangming.

As the Jiangxi episode suggested, Wang was as much a man of action as he was a scholar. In fact, Wang saw no clear distinction between his military and intellectual lives, arguing that only by doing could one learn. In addition to challenging scholarly reflection in matters of policy, Wang argued that individuals possessed an innate sense of right and wrong, something akin to the Western notion of conscience. Some scholars have argued that at least one result of the diffusion of Wang's teachings was a heightened sense among Chinese elites of the worthiness of the individual.

Neo-Confucianism
The revival of Confucius's ancient philosophy stressing agrarian life, harmony between ruler and ruled, and respect for elders and ancestors.

Neo-Confucianists sought to restore order to societies they felt had descended into chaos. For Wang, putting Ming society back on track required forceful action. Other Neo-Confucianists favored reflection, but Wang's activism struck the right chord in early sixteenth-century China, and was widely promoted by educators, first in China and later in Korea and Vietnam. Japan borrowed more selectively from Neo-Confucianism. When blended with Buddhist beliefs already rooted in all these regions, Neo-Confucianism emerged as a religion of state. A foundation for many legal as well as moral principles, it helped hold together millions of ethnically diverse and socially divided people. In other parts of Asia, however, religion fueled division and conflict. The Philippines were a battleground between recent converts to Islam and Roman Catholicism, and Russia was defining itself as a revived Byzantium, expanding frontiers across Asia in the name of Orthodox Christianity.

Change swept Asia in early modern times, sometimes provoked by foreigners, but mostly resulting from internal developments. The overall trend was toward political consolidation under powerful dynasties. These centralizing governments sought to suppress dissent, encourage religious unity, and expand at the expense of weaker neighbors, often using new military technologies to achieve this end. Whole new classes of bureaucrats and merchants flourished, and with them came wider literacy in vernacular languages, support of the arts, and conspicuous consumption. Despite some punishing episodes of war, rebellion, and natural disaster, the early modern period in East Asia was arguably more peaceful than in most of Europe, the Middle East, or Africa. It was an era of steady population growth, commercial expansion, political consolidation, and cultural florescence.

OVERVIEW QUESTIONS

The major global development in this chapter: The general trend toward political and cultural consolidation in early modern Asia.

As you read, consider:

1. What factors led to imperial consolidation in Russia and China? Who were the new rulers, and what were the sources of their legitimacy?

2. Why was isolation more common in these empires than overseas engagement, and what were some of the benefits and drawbacks of isolation?

3. In what ways did early modern Asians transform their environments, and why?

Straddling Eurasia: Rise of the Russian Empire 1462–1725

FOCUS What prompted Russian territorial expansion?

Beginning in 1462, Moscow-based princes combined new weapons technology with bureaucratic innovations to expand their holdings. By the time Tsar Peter the Great died in 1725, the Russian Empire encompassed a huge swath of northern Asia, stretching from the Baltic to the Pacific (see Map 20.1).

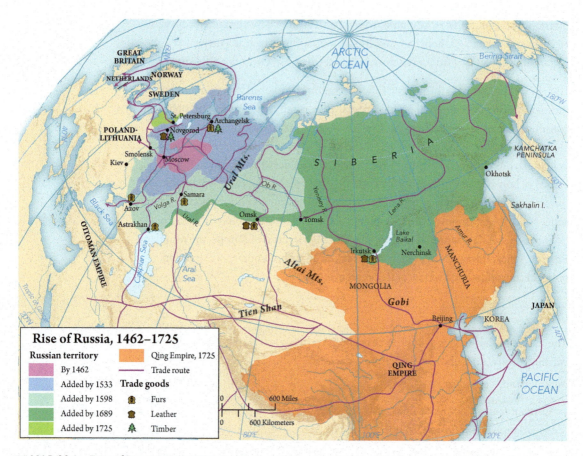

≡ **MAP 20.1** **Rise of Russia, 1462–1725** Beginning with the consolidation of Muscovy in the mid-fifteenth century, Russia grew steadily to become one of the world's largest—albeit least densely populated—land empires.

serf A dependent agricultural laborer attached to a property and treated much like a slave.

Russian imperialism was conservative, with Russian Orthodoxy, the state religion, serving as a kind of nationalist "glue" throughout early modern times. Religious and cultural unity, plus a tendency toward isolation, inhibited efforts at social and agricultural reform. Although Peter the Great would end his reign by copying elements of western European governance and science, Russia remained an essentially tributary, agricultural regime until the nineteenth century. Military reforms were Peter's most modern legacy. Although a modest merchant class had long existed in cities such as Moscow and Novgorod, the majority of Russians remained **serfs**, bound peasants with little more freedom than slaves.

Consolidation in Muscovite Russia

After the fall of Constantinople in 1453, some Russian Christians prophesied that the principality of Muscovy was to be the new Byzantium, and Moscow the "third Rome." The Russian Orthodox Church was fiercely anti-Catholic and frequently energized by apocalyptic visionaries. These visionaries inspired the grand princes who ruled Moscow following the Black Death, and each seemed more determined than the last to expand both Muscovy and the Orthodox Church's domain. As the early modern period progressed, the Ottomans and their allies threatened Russia in the south, and the Poles, Lithuanians, and Swedes periodically threatened in the west. The eastern Tatars, though in decline after Timur (see Chapter 14), also menaced.

Russia took shape under Moscow's grand prince, Ivan III (r. 1462–1505), nicknamed "the Great." Under Ivan the Great, the Muscovites expanded northward, tying landlocked Muscovy to the commercially vibrant Baltic Sea region. By the later sixteenth century, Russian monarchs allowed English, Dutch, and other non-Catholic European merchants to settle and trade in the capital. These merchants sought to circumvent the Ottomans and other intermediaries to purchase East and South Asian fabrics and spices. Alliances with foreign merchants gave Muscovite rulers access to artillery, muskets, and other Western gunpowder technologies in exchange for furs and Asian textiles. These new weapons in turn fueled Russian imperial expansion, mostly across the steppes to the east and south (see again Map 20.1).

Russia's next great ruler, and first tsar (literally, "Caesar"), was Ivan IV (r. 1533–1584), "the Terrible." Although remembered mostly for bizarre behavior in his later years, Ivan IV was an effective monarch. In addition to conquering cities in the distant territories of the Golden Horde in the 1550s and acquiring fur-producing territories in Siberia, Ivan IV also reformed the Muscovite bureaucracy, judiciary, and treasury. The church, always at the heart of Russian politics, was also reorganized and partly subordinated to the state.

Ivan earned his nickname beginning in the 1560s when he established a personal fiefdom called the *oprichnina* (oh-preech-NEE-nah), which, like the Ottoman *timar* and *devshirme* systems, helped to break the power of nobles and replace them with dependent state servants. This abrupt political shuffling crippled commercial cities such as Novgorod, however, and generally threw the empire into disarray. Meanwhile, wars begun in 1558 with Poland and Sweden went badly for Ivan's outgunned forces. Things went no better on the southern front, and in 1571 Moscow fell to the eastern Tatars. Psychologically unstable during his last decade, Ivan died of a stroke in 1584. Thanks in part to Ivan's personal disintegration, which included his killing of the heir apparent, Russia descended into chaos after Ivan's death. Historians call the subsequent three decades Russia's "Time of Troubles."

The Time of Troubles (1584–1613) was punctuated by succession crises, but it was also an era of famine, disease, military defeat, and social unrest, akin to Europe's "seventeenth-century crisis." Exploiting the dynastic chaos, the king of Poland and Lithuania tried to place his son on the Russian throne. The prospect of a Catholic ruler sparked Russia's first massive peasant rebellion, which ended with the humiliating occupation of Moscow by Polish forces. In 1613 an army of nobles, townspeople, and peasants drove out the intruders and put on the throne a nobleman, Michael Romanov (r. 1613–1645), founder of Russia's last royal line.

The Romanovs' New Frontiers

The Romanovs rebuilt Muscovy and "rebooted" empire. Starting at seven million in 1600, Russia's population doubled by 1700. Impressive as this growth was, all of Russia's inhabitants could have fit into a small corner of China. Further, they looked more to leadership from the church, which had regained authority, than from the crown.

Tsar Peter the Great (r. 1689–1725) faced a powerful and insubordinate church. He responded by prosecuting wandering preachers as enemies of the state. But what made Peter "great" was not his harsh dealings with the church but his push to make Russia a competitor on par with western European nation-states. To this end, he stoked expansionist conflicts, imported arms and military experts, built a navy, and professionalized the armed forces. The Imperial Russian Army soon became world class, but at great cost to taxpayers.

Peter, a man of formidable size and boundless energy, is often remembered for his attempts to Westernize Russia, to purge it of "backward" characteristics. Boyars, or nobles, were ordered to shave their beards and change their dress, and all courtiers were required to learn French. A new capital, St. Petersburg, was built in the French style, complete with a summer palace inspired by Louis XIV's Versailles. But the empire's destiny lay in Asia.

Russian expansion across Asia was not only a military process. The growth of the fur trade reverberated through the ecosystems of Siberia, and settling the steppes of the south and east entailed wrenching social change and transformation of the landscape. As frontier forts and agricultural and ranching colonization advanced, indigenous nomads were massacred, driven out, incorporated into trade or tributary networks, or forced to convert to Christianity. The steppe frontier was a haven for fugitives, too, including a number of runaway serfs.

Foreign merchants now entered Moscow from many quarters, including the Middle East and South Asia, yet the government granted only limited access to Russian urban markets and even less to interior supply regions. Russian merchants thus retained control of imperial commerce despite limited access to credit and precious metals. They used distant ports such as Archangel, on the White Sea, to trade leather and other goods with the English and Dutch. Furs were traded to Europe, and also to the Ottoman and Persian Empires. By the time of Peter the Great, England depended on Russian timber, which it paid for with gold (coming mostly from Brazil by this time, as we will see in the next chapter).

The Russian Empire, in sum, drew from a blend of religious self-confidence, demographic growth, commercial links, and

Peter the Great A giant of Russian history, the Romanov tsar Peter the Great spent much of his adult life trying to modernize and expand his vast realm, which spanned the Eurasian continent. He is shown here, tall in the saddle and supremely confident, at the 1709 Battle of Poltava (in present-day Ukraine), where he and his army defeated Sweden's King Charles XII. The artist depicts Peter as blessed by an angel, whereas King Charles was forced to seek refuge with the Ottomans.

the personal ambitions of its Moscow-based tsars. More gunpowder empire than modern state, Russia nevertheless grew to encompass more terrain than any other Eurasian state in its time, despite its sparse population. Repression of the serf majority, however, would spark a new wave of rebellions before the end of the eighteenth century.

China from Ming to Qing Rule 1500–1800

FOCUS How did the shift to a silver cash economy transform Chinese government and society?

By 1500, thanks to several millennia of intensive agriculture and a tradition of vast public works projects, China was home to at least 110 million people, almost twice as many as Europe. Moreover, China under the Ming dynasty (1368–1644) was virtually self-sufficient. Rice and other foodstuffs, along with livestock and manufactured goods, were transported and redistributed throughout the empire by way of canals, roads, and fortified posts that had been constructed by drafted peasant laborers over the centuries.

Only silver was in short supply as Ming rulers shifted China's economy from copper or bronze currency and simple barter to silver money exchanges, especially after 1550. Commercialization and a "hard money" economy necessitated links to the outside world. China's surplus of silk, in demand abroad since antiquity, made exports profitable. Fine porcelain and lacquer wares also brought in foreign exchange, as would tea later on. Western ideas and technologies arrived with Christian missionaries in the mid-sixteenth century, but they barely influenced Chinese culture. China, a technologically advanced and literate society, wanted only silver from the West.

The final century of Ming rule, from about 1540 to 1644, witnessed a commercial revival and improvement in standards of living. It also saw the return of mounted enemies in the north, the Manchu. And, despite the prosperity, there were no guarantees against the famine and disease that had plagued previous centuries. China's bureaucracy, though efficient by world standards, was inadequate to the task of mass relief. Peasant families could at best hope for community cooperation in hard times.

Late Ming Imperial Demands and Private Trade

The most important emperor of late Ming times was Wanli (r. 1573–1620). Wanli was not known for being in touch with his subjects, yet one of his policies had global implications. Wanli ordered many of China's taxes collected in silver rather than in the form of labor service, rice, or other trade goods. The shift to hard currency eased price standardization across the empire. This was the "Single Whip Law" of 1581, so named since it bundled various taxes into one stinging payment.

Given China's immense population, demand for silver soared. Portuguese and Chinese merchants first imported Japanese silver, but the Chinese soon focused on Manila, the Philippine capital, where they exchanged silk, porcelain, and other goods for Spanish-American silver coming from Mexico (see Map 20.3, page 749). Thanks to Wanli, a Chinese commercial colony emerged in Manila.

The Manila trade was profitable for both Spanish and Chinese merchants. The annual trans-Pacific voyages of the "Manila galleons" that left Acapulco, Mexico, each year loaded with the silver of Potosí (Bolivia), Zacatecas (Mexico), and other American mining centers, continued through the early nineteenth century. Still more Spanish-American silver reached China from the West, traveling through Europe, the Middle East, and the Indian Ocean basin to ports such as Macao and Guangzhou (Canton). Since China, compared with Europe or India, valued silver at a relatively higher rate than gold, profit could be made in almost any exchange.

How China absorbed so many tons of silver without dramatic price inflation remains a matter of scholarly debate. One outlet was government spending, for by the early seventeenth century Ming rulers were outfitting costly armies. Defense against Manchu and other northern raiders grew increasingly expensive, but in the end proved ineffectual. Were fluctuations in silver income to blame for Ming decline?

Echoing historians of the seventeenth-century crisis in Europe, scholars long claimed that a dip in silver revenues after 1630 rendered the Ming almost defenseless. More recent research, however, suggests no such dip occurred; silver kept pouring in through the 1640s. Other factors must have trumped imperial budget issues. Meanwhile, private merchants who supplied the military profited handsomely from China's silver-based economy, as did those who exported silk to Manila. Only in the nineteenth century would China's vast silver holdings begin to flow outward in exchange for opium and other imports.

Trade to the outside world stimulated China's economy in several ways, especially in the coastal regions around Nanjing and Canton. Men labored on in rice fields since taxes in the form of raw commodities were still required despite growing monetization. Women, however, were increasingly drawn into the production of silk thread and finished textiles for export. Women did most spinning and weaving in their own households as piecework. This yielded essential household income but also added to an already burdensome workload. Although Chinese women worked for men, much like Dutch and Irish women in the linen industry, they were now key suppliers to the global commercial economy (see Lives and Livelihoods: Silk Weavers in China). After silk, China's most admired product was its porcelain, known as "chinaware" in the West (see Seeing the Past: Blue-on-White: Ming Export Porcelain).

LIVES AND LIVELIHOODS

Silk Weavers in China

Silk production, or sericulture, dates back several thousand years in China, but export volume grew most dramatically in early modern times, beginning with the late Ming. It was stimulated in particular by the massive influx of Spanish American silver after 1581. Most Chinese silk producers were concentrated in the southeast, especially along the lower Yangzi River (see again Map 20.2). Imperial factories were established under the Ming in Nanjing and Beijing, but most tasks were spread among peasants who worked at home at specific tasks assigned by private merchants. The merchants paid peasants for their mulberry leaves, cocoons, spun fiber, and finished fabrics.

Silk fiber is spun from the cocoons of the silkworm, produced by the worms' digestion of large quantities of mulberry leaves. The worms are fragile creatures susceptible to diseases and in need of constant supervision and feeding. Since they were tended in environments susceptible to drastic temperature changes, the worms' welfare was a constant source of worry.

≡ **Chinese Silk Weaving** This rare detail from a Ming ceramic vase shows a group of Chinese women weaving silk on a complex loom. Both highly technical and vast in scale, Chinese silk production was unmatched in early modern times.

Manchu Expansion and the Rise of the Qing Empire

China in the last years of Ming rule faced crisis. Severe droughts crippled the north from 1641 to 1644, but other factors also accelerated imperial decline. Court intrigues created a vacuum of leadership just as Manchu raids grew most threatening, draining resources as early as the 1620s. The Manchu reduced Korea to tributary status in 1637, and by 1642 they reached Shandong Province.

Rather like the linen industry in early modern Holland and Ireland, silk production in Ming and Qing China was extremely labor intensive and largely dependent on women. Caring for silkworms was added to a host of domestic and agricultural tasks, and spinning, which had to be finished rapidly before the cocoons rotted, was often done late into the night. Many households stopped interacting with neighbors entirely until silk season had passed, so intense and delicate was the work. Still, silk making was attractive to peasants since it allowed them to enter the market economy at greater advantage than with food products, which were heavy and susceptible to spoilage or consumption by rodents and other vermin. Because the industry itself was not taxed, many peasants planted mulberry bushes and tended cocoons in order to meet the emperor's silver cash tax demands.

Commercial producers eventually developed large reeling machines operated by men, but in early modern times most reeling was done by women on small hand-turned devices. Some peasants also wove textiles, but often not those who produced the raw fiber. With time, like European linen manufacture, Chinese silk production became a highly capitalized industry.

Questions to Consider

1. From its origins as an ancient Chinese art, how did silk manufacture change in early modern times?
2. How did silk weaving differ from sugar making in the Americas (Chapter 16's Lives and Livelihoods) or gold mining in West Africa (Chapter 17's Lives and Livelihoods)?

For Further Reading:

Vainker, S. J. *Chinese Silk: A Cultural History.* New Brunswick: Rutgers University Press, 2004.

Min-hsiung, Shih. *The Silk Industry in Ch'ing China.* Translated by E-tu Zen Sun. Ann Arbor: University of Michigan, 1976.

But it was a local rebel, Li Zicheng, who facilitated the Manchu capture of Beijing in 1644. As the capital fell to Li, both the Ming emperor and his wife committed suicide. To rid the capital of the rebels, a Ming official sought Manchu aid. The Manchus seized the moment and occupied the capital. Calling themselves the Qing, or "Pure," dynasty, the Manchus assumed the role of ruling minority (see Map 20.2).

SEEING THE PAST

Blue-on-White: Ming Export Porcelain

Before industrialization, China's artisans produced a vast range of consumer goods, from ordinary metal nails to fine silk textiles. After silk, China was most renowned for its porcelain, a special variety of clay pottery fired to the point that it was transformed into glass. The center of this artisanal industry was (and remains) Jingdezhen (JING-deh-juhn), in eastern Jiangxi Province. The combination of properly mixed kaolin clay and high heat made it possible for artisans, mostly men, to fashion durable vessels, plates, and other items of extraordinary thinness. Over many centuries Chinese painters and calligraphers developed a range of styles and techniques for decorating porcelain, including the application of cobalt pigments that emerged from the kiln in stark blue contrast to the white base. The Ming developed this "blue-on-white" product specifically for export, first to the Muslim world and later to regions throughout the globe. Like the example shown here from about 1600, many blue-on-white porcelain products were decorated with Western and other foreign images, including monograms and pictures of the Virgin Mary.

Ming Blue-on-White Export Porcelain Like the example shown here from about 1600, many blue-on-white porcelain products were decorated with Western and other foreign images, including monograms and pictures of the Virgin Mary.

Porcelain making continued throughout the Qing period, as well, but with a shift toward individual artistic virtuosity rather than mass, anonymous production.

Examining the Evidence

1. How did Chinese artisans adapt their product to match the tastes of foreigner buyers?

2. Compare this Ming plate of around 1600 with the example on p. 844 of "Wedgwood blue" china created in industrializing Britain around two centuries later. What aesthetic and physical qualities were the British manufacturers seeking to duplicate, and why?

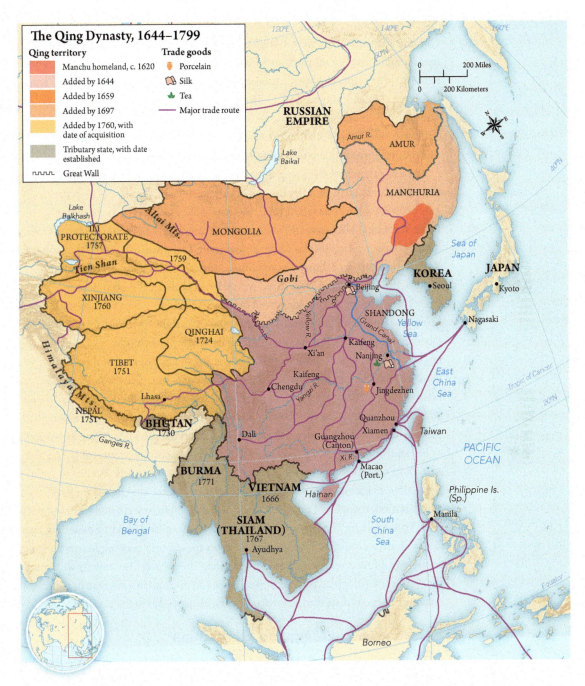

The Qing Dynasty, 1644–1799

Qing territory

- Manchu homeland, c. 1620
- Added by 1644
- Added by 1659
- Added by 1697
- Added by 1760, with date of acquisition
- Tributary state, with date established
- Great Wall

Trade goods

- Porcelain
- Silk
- Tea
- Major trade route

RUSSIAN EMPIRE

Lake Baikal

Amur R.

AMUR

MANCHURIA

Lake Balkhash

Altai Mts.

ILI PROTECTORATE 1757

MONGOLIA

1759

Tien Shan

Gobi

XINJIANG 1760

QINGHAI 1724

Yellow R.

Beijing

SHANDONG

Grand Canal

Yellow Sea

KOREA
Seoul

JAPAN
Kyoto

Nagasaki

Sea of Japan

TIBET 1751

Himalaya Mts.

Xi'an

Kaifeng

Nanjing

Kaifeng

Chengdu

Yangzi R.

Jingdezhen

East China Sea

Tropic of Cancer

Lhasa

NEPAL 1751

BHUTAN 1730

Ganges R.

Dali

Quanzhou
Xiamen

Guangzhou (Canton)

Xi R.

Macao (Port.)

Taiwan

PACIFIC OCEAN

BURMA 1771

VIETNAM 1666

Hainan

SIAM (THAILAND) 1767

Ayudhya

South China Sea

Manila

Philippine Is. (Sp.)

Bay of Bengal

Borneo

Equator

0   200 Miles
0   200 Kilometers

≡ **MAP 20.2 The Qing Dynasty, 1644–1799** The Qing were mounted outsiders who developed a vast Asian empire, first by toppling the Ming dynasty to their south in 1644, and then by annexing interior regions one by one through the eighteenth century. Although conquered regions such as Tibet and Mongolia were extensive, most Qing subjects lived in the former Ming core, home to the world's largest concentration of people.

The transition to Qing rule after 1644 proved surprisingly smooth, and most Chinese subjects' lives were barely changed. Although the new Qing emperors maintained a distinct ethnic identity and dealt harshly with dissenters, they tended to improve on rather than revolutionize Chinese patterns of governance. As a result, the empire quickly rebounded. Under Qing rule, Western gunpowder technology was so fully embraced that it enabled the conquest of much of Mongolia, Tibet, and the Amur River basin (claimed by Russia) by the 1750s. Tributaries from these distant provinces trekked to Beijing to pay homage to the "pure" emperor.

The ascendancy of the Qing dynasty (1644–1911) was cemented by Emperor Kangxi's accession in 1661. By the end of his rule in 1722, China was an expansionist empire. Mongolia, annexed in 1697, was a base for this project, and a buffer against Peter the Great's Russia. By 1700 much of mainland Southeast Asia, formerly defiant, paid tribute to the Qing emperor in exchange for political autonomy. Kangxi's successors followed his example, and by 1751 Tibet and Nepal fell to the Qing. Chinese colonists were lured west with tax breaks and homesteads.

By the 1750s, under the long-lived emperor Qianlong (chee-YEN-loong), China seemed to be reaching the limits of its military capability. Victory against southern Siberian peoples demonstrated Qing military might, but trouble was brewing, and not just at the fringes. Rebellions rocked the entire realm. Subjects in the core districts grew restless, and guerrilla warfare and massacres of ethnic Chinese colonists became constant features of frontier life. Qianlong clung to power until 1796, and despite ballooning war costs, the emperor's reign had boasted some of the biggest treasury surpluses in early modern history. The silver of the Americas had funded Qing expansion.

Expanding trade and population growth altered China's environment in the Ming and Qing eras. Devastating floods were frequent, but their relationship to human rather than divine action was rarely explored except by a few alert public works officials. Deforestation, though not in itself a cause of floods, often exacerbated them. As peasants cleared land for planting and cut forests for firewood and building materials, rainfall catchment diminished. Rains swept away exposed soil, creating massive erosion upstream and river sedimentation downstream. The problem became so widespread that Chinese territorial expansion and colonization in Qing times were in part aimed at resettling peasants displaced by environmental catastrophes in the heartland.

Everyday Life in Ming and Qing China

Ming intellectuals were annoyed by China's shift to commercialism. As in many traditional societies (except Islamic ones), merchants and traders were an almost suspect class, esteemed only slightly above actors and musicians. Chinese society as defined by Confucius emphasized production over exchange, the countryside over the city, and continuity over change or mobility. The ideal was a linked grouping of agriculturally self-sufficient provincial units overseen by patriarchs. These units were to be connected not by trade, but by a merit-based governing hierarchy headed by a divine monarch.

Within this model, even peasant self-sufficiency was expected. Relying on the market was a signal of distress. Men were supposed to farm and women were supposed to spin and weave, both remaining in their home villages and pro-

≡ **Chinese Beggars** Although most early modern Chinese artists depicted idealized things of beauty, such as rugged landscapes and fanciful creatures in flight, some turned their attention to ordinary people. This c. 1500 Ming image depicts two wandering beggars, one apparently talking to himself and the other brandishing a serpent, presumably his helper at winning alms from curious or terrified passersby.

ducing only for their own consumption. Surpluses, a divine gift to the pious and industrious, were not to be sold but rather offered to the emperor to express fealty and submission. Bureaucrats and scholars, who lived from these surpluses, kept track of them on paper.

Such was the ideal Neo-Confucian society. As we have seen, however, hard times proved frequent in early modern China: droughts, floods, plagues, and even pirates took their toll. Peasants suffered most, especially those driven to frontier lands. Natural disasters, along with increasing state demands for cash taxes, compelled many to migrate and sell their labor to whoever could pay. Evidence suggests that many couples practiced birth control to avoid the financial pressure of additional children.

Meanwhile, landlords and merchants were getting rich through market exchange. The social inequity resulting from this process was in part what bothered Chinese traditionalist intellectuals. What struck them as worse, however, was the market economy's tendency to reward nonproductive and even dishonest behavior. It was the appearance of the uppity rich, not the miserably poor, that most bothered the educated old guard.

The Flourishing of Art and Culture

As in Golden Age Spain, the arts and literature thrived in China despite political decline. This seeming paradox was due in part to the patronage of merchants who had made fortunes in the economic upswing, but it was also a function of the surplus of unemployed, literate civil servants. Literacy grew in the late Ming era, and with it came mass distribution of books, many on science. Novels and plays were also hugely popular. The 1610 play *The Lute* included woodblock prints of scenes for those unable to see a live performance. Some writers narrated travel adventures in the interior for curious urban readers.

In the years around 1600, foreign visitors, notably the Italian Jesuit Matteo Ricci in 1601, impressed the Chinese court with their scientific knowledge, though not with their religion. When he was not fixing European clocks brought as gifts for the emperor (see page 698), Ricci translated Confucius for a Western audience and composed religious tracts in court Chinese. As in Mughal India, Jesuit court visitors influenced painting styles, particularly royal portraiture. The Jesuits remained important at court through the Qing era, but ultimately they won few converts to Christianity.

Japan in Transition 1540–1750

⬇ **FOCUS** How did self-isolation affect Japan?

daimyo A regional lord in feudal and early modern Japan.

samurai The hereditary warrior who dominated Japanese society and culture from the twelfth to the nineteenth century.

shogun The supreme military commander in Japan, who also took political control.

Located in the North Pacific Ocean, Japan was isolated from the rest of the world for most of the early modern period. A brief opening in the sixteenth century allowed foreign ideas and technologies to enter and permitted a large but ineffectual invasion of Korea. Soon after 1600, however, Japan's leaders enforced seclusion and, like their neighbors in China, consolidated power internally. Japan would not be reopened for over two centuries.

Most inhabitants of the three major islands, Honshu, Kyushu, and Shikoku, were peasants, nearly all of them subjects of regional lords, called **daimyo**. Above Japan's rice-farming peasant majority were warriors called **samurais**, some of them mercenaries and others permanent employees of powerful daimyo. Above the daimyo a group of generals, including the top-ranking **shogun**, jockeyed to become Japan's supreme ruler. By 1600 the royal family had been reduced to ceremonial figureheads. In the peace that came with closure, Japan's population expanded and the arts flourished.

Rise of the Tokugawa Shogunate and the Unification of Japan

As we saw in Chapter 14, Japan's so-called golden age of the eleventh and twelfth centuries was followed by a breakdown of central authority and a rise in competing military factions. This chaotic period, heyday of the samurai warriors, lasted several centuries. The daimyo sometimes succeeded in bringing a measure of order to their domains, but no one daimyo family could establish predominance over others.

At the end of the sixteenth century, several generals sought to quell civil war and to unify Japan. One such general, Toyotomi Hideyoshi (1535–1598), not only conquered his rivals but, with the Kyoto emperor's permission, assumed the role of top shogun. After Hideyoshi died, Tokugawa Ieyasu (1542–1616) seized control. Assuming the title of shogun in 1603, he declared that thereafter rulership was hereditary. The Tokugawa (TOH-koo-GAH-wah) Shogunate would endure until 1867.

With the shoguns in charge of Japan's core districts, regional lords were forced to accept allegiance to the emerging unified state or face its growing might. Most submitted, and peace ensued. Peasant rebellions occurred periodically, sometimes led by disgruntled samurais, but the state's adoption of Neo-Confucian ideals similar to those embraced in China and Korea stressed duty and hierarchy over rights and individual freedom. Most Japanese accepted the benefits of peace and worked within their assigned roles.

≡ **Tokugawa Japan**

Hideyoshi's rule had been notable for two things: tolerating Iberian Christian missionaries and launching two invasions of Korea in 1593 and 1597. Ieyasu soon reversed course, however, banning missionaries and making peace with Korea. Contact with foreigners, particularly Europeans—called *nanban*, or "southern barbarians," a reference to their arrival from southern seas—was restricted after 1614 to the island of Deshima, near Nagasaki. Foreign families were not permitted to reside on Japanese soil, and by the 1630s all missionaries and traders had been expelled but one Dutch merchant. A representative of the Dutch East India Company, he was forbidden to discuss religion. Chinese bachelor merchants residing in Nagasaki were treated with similar suspicion.

Was seclusion a response to Christianity? Not entirely, but it played a role. It was not the foreignness of the nanbans' religion that worried the shoguns, but rather

nanban A Japanese term for "southern barbarians," or Europeans; also applies to hybrid European-Japanese artistic style.

its believers' insistence that it was the one true religion. Japan was religiously pluralistic. One could follow imported Confucian principles, for example, yet also be a Buddhist. Taoist ideas and rituals were also widespread. Beyond this, most Japanese venerated nature spirits according to Shinto traditions.

Strictly monotheistic, focused on eternal salvation rather than everyday behavior, and fully understood only by foreign specialists, Christianity looked subversive. Priests and followers were executed in waves from 1597 to the late 1630s, when a Christian-led rebellion was suppressed. Then, the shoguns ordered unrepentant priests and converts publicly beheaded, boiled, or crucified. The only remnants of Catholicism to survive were scattered names of priests and saints, most of them venerated in older Japanese fashion by isolated peasants and fishing folk.

Harsh as it was, the shoguns considered their repression of Christianity a political rather than religious action. Stories of Spain's lightning-fast conquests in the distant Americas and nearby Philippines had long circulated in Japan, and Dutch and English merchants played up alleged Spanish cruelties. Portugal's violent actions in India, Africa, and Southeast Asia were also well known, suggesting to Japan's rulers that Catholic missionaries, particularly Iberians, were a spearhead for conquest. Indiscreet Spanish visitors suggested as much in the 1590s, confirming Japanese fears.

Following Christian suppression in the 1630s, the shoguns controlled the interior by forcing subordinate lords to maintain households in the new capital of Edo (modern Tokyo). Wives and children lived in the city and its growing suburbs as virtual hostages, and the daimyo themselves had to rotate in and out of the capital at least every other year. A new version of court life was one result of this shifting center, and with it grew both a vibrant capital city and a complex road and inn system lacing Japan together. With Edo's primacy, Osaka became a major marketplace. Kyoto thrived as a cultural center.

Only in the north was there anything like imperial expansion after the failed invasions of Korea. Japanese merchants had long traded with the Ainu of Hokkaido. The Ainu (EYE-new), whose men sported tattoos and long beards, descended from Siberians and probably also Austronesian islanders. The Japanese considered them barbarians, and the Ainu considered the Japanese treacherous. By 1650 Japanese trading families had colonized southernmost Hokkaido, but pressures on the Ainu sparked rebellion. The Tokugawa state was reluctant to waste money invading and fortifying Hokkaido, but it did claim the island as Japanese territory. Only when the Russians threatened in the late eighteenth century to annex Ainu-inhabited islands farther north did the Japanese back their claims with force. Ainu culture was violently suppressed, but survives to the present day.

Everyday Life and Culture in Tokugawa Japan

Japan's population grew from about ten million in 1600 to nearly thirty million in 1700, when it stabilized. This rapid growth was made possible by relative peace, but expansion and integration of the rice economy contributed as well. Rice's high yields encouraged creation of even the smallest irrigated fields, and some daimyo were skillful marketers of their tributaries' main product. Most rice was sold in cities and to elites, while peasants ate a healthier diet of mixed grains, vegetables, and soy products. Urban-rural reciprocity was key, and processed human excrement collected in cities and villages was the main fertilizer. As surprising as it may seem, Japan's system of waste collection and recycling was the most hygienic and efficient in the world. Whole guilds were dedicated to the collection and marketing of what in the West was regarded as dangerous filth. The water supply of Edo, with over half a million people by the eighteenth century, was cleaner and more reliable than that of London. Thus, this system improved overall human health as it created connections between urban and rural Japanese.

New strains of rice introduced from Southeast Asia also allowed farmers to extend cultivation. By contrast, American crops such as maize and peanuts were not embraced in Japan as they were in China. Only sweet potatoes were appreciated, and they saved millions of lives during times of famine. As elsewhere, agricultural expansion and diversification in Japan also had negative ecological consequences. Leaders recognized that deforestation intensified floods, and they responded to this problem efficiently, organizing workers to replant depleted woodlands by the eighteenth century.

Shoguns kept daimyos in check after 1615 by permitting only one castle in each domain, and sharply limiting expansion, but peace encouraged other forms of private construction. Like agriculture, Japan's construction boom took a toll on forests, as did increased shipbuilding. Vulnerability to earthquakes gave rise to building codes and design innovations. Hence, in agriculture and construction the leaders of Tokugawa Japan demonstrated the power of centralized government, limiting growth, regulating construction, and shaping the connections between their subjects.

Although most Tokugawa subjects remained peasants, a leisure class also emerged, mostly concentrated in Kyoto. Merchants imported raw silk from China, which Japanese artisans processed and wove. Other imports included sandalwood, sugar, and spices from Southeast Asia. Consumption of fine fabrics and other

☰ **Kyoto Festival** This c. 1750 painting of a festival in Kyoto depicts not only the daimyo, or local lord, and his ox-drawn cart and procession of armed samurai, but also daily goings-on about town. Many people seem to be engaged in conversation indoors, although they are quite visible thanks to open screens, allowing them to view the procession. Near the top of the panel, women and children stroll toward what appears to be a recitation. The use of patterned gold clouds to fill in empty spaces was a convention of early modern Japanese art, and here it adds a fog-like layer to the painting's depth.

products by the wealthy expanded the artisan sector, but did not spark industrialization. There was simply not a large enough wage-earning consumer class in Japan to sustain industrial production. Instead, the trend was toward high-quality "boutique" goods such as samurai swords and ceremonial kimonos, rather than mass-produced consumer goods.

One precursor to modern Japanese industrialization did appear in the production of cotton cloth. Most traditional peasant clothing prior to the sixteenth century had been made from hemp fiber, and only through trade with Korea and China had cotton come to figure in Japan's economy. Initially, cotton was in demand among sixteenth-century samurai warriors, who used it for clothing, lining for armor, and fuses for guns. Fishing folk also consumed cotton sailcloth. Trade restrictions stimulated internal production of cotton textiles to such a degree that it reached near-industrial levels by the eighteenth century.

Japanese commoners got by on a diet mostly of grain porridges. They consumed little meat and no milk or cheese, and away from coastal areas where seafood and fish could be harvested, most protein came from beans and soy products such as tofu. Fruits, vegetables, herbs, grasses, fungi, insects, and larvae were roasted or pickled for consumption in winter or in lean times. Tobacco, an American crop, grew popular under Tokugawa rule. It was smoked by men and women of all classes in tiny clay pipes, serving a social function much like the sharing of tea. When tea was too expensive, as it often was, common folk drank boiled water, which was at least safe. In all, the peasant diet in Tokugawa Japan, though short of protein, was as nourishing as that of western Europe at the same time.

Women of every class faced obstacles to freedom in Japan's male-dominated and often misogynist society. Most were expected to marry at an early age and spend their lives serving their husbands, children, and in-laws. Still, as in other traditional societies, there were openings for female self-expression and even access to power in Tokugawa Japan. At court, noblewomen exercised considerable influence over succession and the everyday maintenance of proper decorum, and in the peasant sphere women managed household affairs, particularly when men were away on military duty or business. Widows could become quite powerful, especially those managing the affairs of dead merchant husbands.

Emergence of a National Culture

With the growth of cities and rise of a leisure class, Japanese literature and painting flourished, along with flower arranging, puppet theater, board games, and music. The writer Ihara Saikaku (EH-hah-rah sigh-kah-KOO) grew popular at the end of the seventeenth century with his tales contrasting elite and working-class life. Saikaku idealized homosexual relations between senior and junior samurais, and also those among actors and their patrons, mostly wealthy townsmen. In "The Great Mirror of Male Love," Saikaku described most of these relationships as temporary, consensual, and often purchased. More than a hint of misogyny pervades the writings of Saikaku, but that sentiment is less evident in his "Life of an Amorous Woman" and other stories relating the adventures of courtesans and female prostitutes.

In Edo, Kyoto, and especially the rice-trading city of Osaka, entertainments were many and varied. Daimyo and samurai landlords came to Osaka to exchange their rice tributes for money, which they then spent locally or in Edo, where they had to pay obeisance to the emperor. Regional elites' frequent visits to these two cities helped make them economic and cultural crossroads for Japan as a whole. Many samurais moved to these cities permanently as their rural estates diminished in size across generations. Social tension arose as the old warrior class tried to adapt to urban life, but fortunately, there was much to distract them. Some worked for little compensation as teachers or policemen, but the wealthier samurais found time for the theater, musical concerts, and poetry readings. **Sumo** wrestling matches were popular among many urbanites, as were board games, the tea ceremony, calligraphy, bonsai cultivation, and landscaping. More costly pursuits such as gambling, drinking, and sexual diversions were restricted to the so-called Licensed Quarters of the major cities.

Early modern European visitors, especially Catholic priests, found the general Japanese tolerance of prostitution, female impersonation, and homosexuality shocking, but they made little effort to understand Japanese cultural attitudes about sex and shame. Prostitution often was degrading to women and in some places approached the level of sex slavery. Still, there were groups of female escorts such as the geisha whom outsiders mistook for prostitutes. The **geisha** were indentured servants who made their living as private entertainers to the wealthiest merchants and landowners visiting or inhabiting cities. Geisha dress, makeup, and comportment were all highly ritualized and distinctive. Although the geisha had control over their adult sexual lives, their first coital experience, or "deflowering," was sold to the highest bidder. Many young male prostitutes also acted as female impersonators in kabuki theater.

Kabuki was a popular form of theater that first appeared in Kyoto in 1603 as a way to advertise a number of female prostitutes. Subsequent shows caused such violence among potential customers that the Tokugawa government allowed only men to perform. As these female impersonators became associated with male prostitution, the state established official theaters that punished actors and patrons who engaged in sexual relations. By the eighteenth century, kabuki performances had become so "sanitized" that they included moralizing Neo-Confucian speeches. Even so, playwrights such as Chikamatsu Monzaemon (1653–1724) retained ribald humor amid lessons in correct behavior. At the other end of the spectrum was the somber tradition of Noh theater, associated with Buddhist tales and Shinto shrines.

sumo A Japanese professional wrestler known for his heft.

geisha A professional female entertainer in Tokugawa Japan.

kabuki A popular Japanese theater known for bawdy humor and female impersonation.

Poetry flourished as never before during the era of seclusion, and poets such as the itinerant and prolific Matsuo Bashō (1644–1684) were widely read. Here is a sample of his work:

On my way through Nagoya, where crazy Chikusai is said to have practiced quackery and poetry, I wrote:

With a bit of madness in me,
Which is poetry,
I plod along like Chikusai
Among the wails of the wind.
Sleeping on a grass pillow
I hear now and then
The nocturnal bark of a dog
In the passing rain.[1]

Despite isolation, Japan was among the world's most literate societies in early modern times. By 1700 there were some fifteen hundred publishers active between Edo, Kyoto, and Osaka, publishing at least seventy-three hundred titles. Books were sold or rented in both city and countryside. Early forms of comic books were circulating by the eighteenth century, the most popular ones resembling today's pulp fiction. Most books were published on woodblock presses despite the fact that movable type was known from both mainland Asian and European sources—another example of the fact that early modern Japan, like China, had little need of the West.

≡ **Kabuki Theater** Tokugawa Japan's ribald kabuki theater tradition became wildly popular in major cities after 1600. Kabuki actors were initially prostitutes, first young women and then young men, but objections from the samurai led by 1670 to the creation of a class of older men licensed to act in drag. In this c. 1680 screen painting by Hishikawa Moronobu, actors, costume designers, makeup artists, washerwomen, and stagehands all appear to be absorbed in their own little worlds. The painting seems to confirm early modern Japan's inward gaze and cultural and material self-sufficiency.

yangban The noble class in early modern Korea.

Korea, a Land in Between 1392–1750

FOCUS How did life for common folk in early modern Korea differ from life in China or Japan?

The Korean peninsula falls between China and Japan, with the Yellow Sea to the west and the Sea of Japan to the east. In 1392 Korea came to be ruled by the Yi (or Choson) dynasty, which remained in power until 1910. Though unified since the late seventh century, the Korean peninsula developed its distinctive culture primarily during Yi times, partly in response to Chinese and Japanese invasions. Korea had long been influenced by China, and had likewise served as a conduit linking the Asian mainland to Japan. The guiding principles of the early Choson state were drawn from the work of Confucius, as in contemporary China and Japan, and grafted onto a society that mostly practiced Buddhism. Still, Koreans regarded themselves as a distinct and autonomous people, unified by a language and culture.

Capital and Countryside

It was under the first Yi ruler that Seoul, then known as Hanyang, became Korea's capital. Following Chinese principles of geomancy, the city site, backed by mountains and spread along the Han River plains, was considered blessed. Successive rulers drafted nearby peasants to expand the city and add to its grandeur. By 1450 Hanyang boasted substantial royal palaces, bureaucratic buildings, markets, and schools.

Choson leaders asserted central power by reducing Buddhist temples and monasteries. Temple lands were confiscated and distributed to loyal officials. A kind of Neo-Confucian constitution was drafted advocating more radical state takeover and redistribution of land to peasants, but nobles balked and tenant farming persisted. Early modern Korea's government mirrored China's in some ways, but a difference was the prominence of a noble class, the **yangban**. Yangban elites staffed high councils and regional governorships. A uniquely Korean institution known as the Samsa, a kind of academic oversight committee, had power even over the king, acting as a moral police force. Official historians, also drawn from the educated noble class,

Choson Korea

CHINA

KOREA

Sea of Japan

Yalu R.

Hanyang (Seoul)

Han R.

Yellow Sea

Korea Strait

JAPAN

0   90 Miles
0   90 Kilometers

→ Japanese invasions, 1592, 1597
→ Manchu invasions, 1627, 1637

≡ **Choson Korea**

were allowed to write what they observed, keeping their work secret from the king. But most Korean bureaucrats were selected via Chinese-style civil service examinations. The pressure was so great that some enterprising students hid tightly rolled crib-notes in their nostrils. Military service proved unpopular, partly because it was associated with slavery, and enrollment in school won exemption.

Korea's needed defense apparatus was formed when the nobles' private forces were consolidated into a national, standing army by the mid-fifteenth century. Professional military men took exams, and peasants were drafted to serve in frontier outposts. The Jurchen and other horse warriors periodically threatened Korea's northern provinces, but many chieftains were co-opted by the Choson state in the fifteenth century. Another defense strategy was to settle the northern frontier with land-hungry peasants from the south.

≡ **Social Order in Early Modern Korea** Korean life under the Yi dynasty was marked by sharp class divisions, with a large portion of the poorer country folk living as slaves. This eighteenth-century painting on silk shows a notable individual on promenade, elaborately dressed, shaded, and otherwise attended, as more humble figures kneel in submission in the foreground. The broad-brimmed black hats and flowing garments were typical of high-ranking Koreans.

After these early initiatives, defense became less of a concern, and the general devaluing of military service left Korea vulnerable by the time the Japanese invaded in 1593 and 1597. Despite their massive forces and lightning speed, the Japanese under Shogun Hideyoshi were soon driven out with aid from Ming China. The Manchus were not so easily subdued, however. They invaded Korea in 1627 and 1636, rendering it a tributary by 1637. Still, Korea retained considerable autonomy.

Korea exported ginseng, furs, and a few other items to China in exchange for silk and porcelain, but its overseas trade was limited, and few Korean merchants ventured beyond Japan or the nearby Ryukyu Islands, especially Okinawa. Korean merchants in the south complained of Japanese pirates, the same ones who menaced China from the thirteenth to seventeenth century. The Choson government attempted to suppress the pirates, but Japan's fractured political system and occasional sponsorship of the pirates rendered this fruitless.

Everyday Life in Choson Korea

Most Koreans under Yi rule were rice farmers. Wet-field rice cultivation expanded dramatically in the south beginning in the fifteenth century thanks to government initiatives and adaptation of Chinese techniques. Southern populations grew accordingly. Population estimates are debated, but it appears that Korea grew from about five million inhabitants in 1450 to some ten million by 1600. In colder and drier parts of the peninsula, especially in the far north, peasants relied on millet and barley. As in Japan, these healthy grains were widely disdained as hardship rations. Soybeans were later planted, adding a new source of protein. Koreans also exploited seacoasts and rivers for mollusks and fish, and some raised pigs and other livestock. Vegetables such as cabbage were pickled for winter consumption, spiced by the eighteenth century with capsicum peppers introduced from the Americas.

Ordinary folk did not obsess over genealogies as much as the noble yangban class did, but their mating customs could still be rigid. Some marriages were arranged, occasionally between young children. Women appear to have lost considerable autonomy with the rise of Neo-Confucianism, and widows were even presented with a knife with which to kill themselves should they be sexually violated or otherwise dishonored. According to some sources, Korean women more often used their suicide knives to kill attackers. Female entertainers, or **kisaeng**—like their Japanese counterparts, the geisha—were sometimes able to accumulate capital and achieve literary fame.

Teachers in Choson Korea took on the moral advisory role played by priests or imams in early modern Christian or Islamic societies, and in the seventeenth century Neo-Confucian scholars, following the lead of China's Wang Yangming, attempted to reform Korean society and government. Education was highly valued, and literacy widespread (see Reading the Past: Scenes from the Daily Life of a Korean Queen). It was in the Choson era that Korean students became outspoken critics of the state, launching a number of mass protests in the late seventeenth and early eighteenth centuries. Despite the ruling class's attachment to Neo-Confucian philosophy and suppression of Buddhist monasteries, popular religious ideas persisted, especially in the countryside. Alongside some Buddhist beliefs, mountain deities and sacred stones or trees were venerated, and shamanism was practiced for divination and healing. Many healing shamans were women.

kisaeng A geisha-like female entertainer in early modern Korea.

READING THE PAST

Scenes from the Daily Life of a Korean Queen

The following selection is taken from the diary of Lady Hong (1735–1815), a queen during Korea's long Yi dynasty. Unlike most male authors of the time, who wrote in Chinese (in part to show off their education, much as many European men at this time wrote in Latin rather than their own vernaculars), Lady Hong wrote in the Korean script. She also devoted great attention to the details of everyday life, including close observations of individual emotions. After stating that she began to write her memoirs at the urging of a nephew, Lady Hong describes her birth and early upbringing:

> I was born during the reign of King Yongjo, at noon on 6 August 1735, at my mother's family's home in Kop'yong-dong, Pangsongbang. One night, before I was born, my father had dreamed of a black dragon coiled around the rafters of my mother's room, but the birth of a daughter did not seem to fit the portent of his dream.
>
> My paternal grandfather, Lord Chong-hon, came to look at me, and took an immediate fancy to me, declaring, "Although it is a girl, this is no ordinary child!" As I grew up, he became so fond of me that he was reluctant to let me leave his lap. He would say jokingly, "This girl is quite a little lady already, so she is sure to grow up quickly!"
>
> The womenfolk of our family were all connected with the most respected clans of the day. My mother came from the Yi family—an upright clan. My father's eldest sister was married to a famous magistrate; while his second sister was a daughter-in-law of Prince Ch'ong-nung; and his youngest sister was a daughter-in-law of the minister of the board of civil office. Despite these connections, they were not haughty or extravagant, as is so often the case. When the family gathered together on festival days, my mother always treated the elder members with respect, and greeted the younger ones with a kind smile and an affectionate word. Father's second brother's wife was likewise virtuous, and her esteem for my mother was exceeded only by that for her mother-in-law. She was an outstanding woman—noble-minded and well educated. She was very fond of me; taught me my Korean alphabet and instructed me in a wide range of subjects. I loved her like a mother and indeed my mother used to say I had grown too close to her.

Source: Lady Hong, *Memoirs of a Korean Queen*, ed. and trans. Choe-Wall Yangh-hi (London: KPI, 1985), 1–4.

Examining the Evidence

1. In what ways do these passages reveal Neo-Confucian values?

2. What do these passages tell us about gender roles in a Neo-Confucian court society?

Choson Korea appears unique among early modern states in that it was both ethnically homogeneous and heavily reliant on slave labor. Korea's enslaved population, perhaps as much as 30 percent of the total by 1550, appears to have emerged as a result of several factors: debt peonage (self-sale due to famine or debt) and penal servitude (punishment for crimes, including rebellion). Debt peonage and penal servitude were not unusual in the early modern world, and both could be found in neighboring China. What made slavery different in Korea was that the legal status of the enslaved, once proclaimed, was likely to be inherited for many generations. Self-purchase was extremely difficult, and slave owners clung to their chattels tenaciously. Korea's rigid social structure, far more hierarchical than neighboring China's or Japan's, only reinforced perpetual bondage. Moralists criticized slavery as early as the seventeenth century, but it was not until forced contact with outsiders after 1876 that the institution died out. Korea's last slaves were freed only in 1894.

Consolidation in Mainland Southeast Asia 1500–1750

➘ **FOCUS** What trends did mainland Southeast Asia share with China, Korea, Japan, and Russia?

Mainland Southeast Asia, encompassing the modern nations of Burma (Myanmar), Thailand, Cambodia, Laos, and Vietnam, followed a path more like that of China than of the Southeast Asian islands discussed in Chapter 18. Overall trends on the mainland included political consolidation, mostly by Buddhist kings; growth of large, tribute-paying populations due to intensive wet rice cultivation; and a shift toward cash crops such as sugar for export. Unlike the diverse islands of Indonesia and the Philippines, which fell increasingly into the hands of European interlopers (see Counterpoint: "Spiritual Conquest" in the Philippines), mainland Southeast Asia in early modern times experienced gunpowder-fueled, dynastic state-building.

Political Consolidation

The mainland Southeast Asian kingdoms in place by 1700 formed the basis for the nation-states of today. As happened in Muscovite Russia, access to European guns enabled some emerging dynasties to expand in the sixteenth and seventeenth centuries. Another catalyst for change was the rapid growth of global maritime trade (see Map 20.3). Overseas commerce transformed not only traditional maritime hubs such as Melaka and Aceh, as seen in Chapter 18, but also Pegu in Burma,

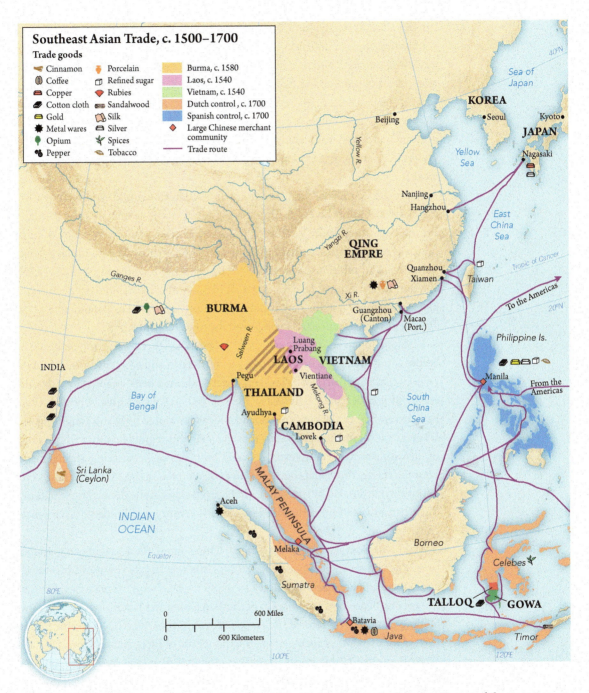

Southeast Asian Trade, c. 1500–1700

Trade goods

Cinnamon	Porcelain
Coffee	Refined sugar
Copper	Rubies
Cotton cloth	Sandalwood
Gold	Silk
Metal wares	Silver
Opium	Spices
Pepper	Tobacco

Burma, c. 1580
Laos, c. 1540
Vietnam, c. 1540
Dutch control, c. 1700
Spanish control, c. 1700
Large Chinese merchant community
Trade route

≡ **MAP 20.3   Southeast Asian Trade, c. 1500–1700**   Maritime trade between the Indian Ocean and the western Pacific went back thousands of years, but it grew exponentially in volume and value after 1500, when Europeans arrived with gunpowder weapons and Spanish-American silver, eager to carve out trading enclaves and establish monopolies on key commodities such as pepper and opium.

Ayudhya (or Ayutthaya) in Thailand, and Lovek (near modern Phnom Penh) in Cambodia. Here Buddhist kings used trade revenues to enhance their realms by attracting scholars, building libraries and monasteries, and constructing temples and images of the Buddha. Some saw themselves as incarnations of the Buddhist ideal of the universal king. Funded in part by trade, a massive bronze Buddha and supporting temple complex were built in the city of Luang Prabang, in Laos, beginning in 1512. A solid gold Buddha was also commissioned. Such costly religious monuments, as seen elsewhere, are a reminder of early modern devotion and wealth.

A notable example of mainland Southeast Asian state-building driven by commercial wealth and access to European gunpowder weapons arose in southern Burma beginning in the 1530s. Portuguese mercenaries aided a regional king's takeover of the commercial city of Pegu, and a new, Pegu-based Buddhist dynasty with imperial ambitions soon emerged. Under King Bayinnaung (r. 1551–1581) the Burmese expanded into Thailand and Laos. After building many pagodas, or ceremonial towers, in his new conquests, admirers referred to Bayinnaung as the "Victor of Ten Directions." He preferred the title "King of Kings."

Vietnam followed a different path, largely due to Chinese influence. Even before Ming expansion southward in the fourteenth and early fifteenth centuries, Neo-Confucian principles of law and governance had been adopted by Vietnamese royalty under the Le dynasty (1428–1788). Yet, like Korea, whose nobility had also embraced the kinds of reformist ideas promoted by Wang Yangming, the Chinese veneer in Vietnam barely masked a vibrant regional culture whose sense of identity was never in question. China brokered power-sharing arrangements between the northern and southern halves of Vietnam in the 1520s, but new, competitive dynasties, led by the Trinh and Nguyen clans, were already in the making. Their battles lasted until the late seventeenth century and hindered Vietnamese consolidation.

Mainland Southeast Asia resembled China more than neighboring islands in another sense: high overall population. This was largely the result of wet-rice agriculture and acquired immunity to many lowland tropical maladies. Massive water-control projects reminiscent of those in China and Japan allowed Vietnam's feuding clans to field tens of thousands of troops by 1700. Rice-rich Burma was even more populous, capable of fielding hundreds of thousands of troops as early as 1650. Unlike China, most of the kingdoms of mainland Southeast Asia collected tribute in the form of rice and goods rather than silver throughout the early modern period.

Commercial Trends

Exports from mainland Southeast Asia were not monopolized by Europeans, and in fact many commodities found their principal markets in China and Japan. Sugar cane originated in Southeast Asia, but refined sugar found no market until the late seventeenth century, when growers in Vietnam, Cambodia, and Thailand adopted Chinese milling technology and began to export their product northward. Only Taiwan competed with these regions for the Japanese "sweet" market. Tobacco, introduced from Mexico via Manila, joined betel leaves (traditionally wrapped around areca nuts) as a popular stimulant throughout the region by the seventeenth century. Other drugs had more profound consequences. The Dutch were the first to push the sale of opium from India in the 1680s (initially as a tobacco additive), and it soon created a class of addicts willing to pay any amount of silver cash for it.

Imports to mainland Southeast Asia consisted primarily of cloth from India, an old "monsoon circuit" trade good that fostered resident communities of merchants, most of them Muslims, from as far away as Gujarat, in the Arabian Sea. Chinese merchants brought cloth, too, along with metal wares, porcelain, and a wide range of goods acquired through interregional trade. On the whole, the Chinese were more competitive and successful middlemen in mainland Southeast Asia than Europeans in early modern times.

Interregional commerce and urbanization enabled many Southeast Asian women to engage in trade as well, a pattern that fit well with the general regional tendency toward female independence noted in Chapter 18. The wives and concubines of long-distance merchants not only carried on important business transactions on land, they traveled with their husbands and lovers at sea. Some Southeast Asian women were autonomous intermediaries for European merchants, most famously Soet Pegu, a Burmese woman who lived in the Thai capital of Ayudhya. She was the principal broker for the Dutch in Thailand (then known as Siam) for many years beginning in the 1640s.

The global financial crisis of the seventeenth century, coupled with regional wars, epidemics, and droughts, left mainland Southeast Asia in a weakened state. Burma contracted considerably, as did neighboring Siam. Laos survived as a separate kingdom only due to its isolation from these two neighbors, and it became even more inward-looking. Cambodia was similarly introverted under Khmer rule, and Vietnam suffered a severe decline. Mainland Southeast Asia submitted to paying tribute to China's Qing emperors in the course of the eighteenth century. In spite of the trend toward contraction, however, the region remained nearly impervious to European designs.

COUNTERPOINT: "Spiritual Conquest" in the Philippines

FOCUS In contrast to the general trend of political consolidation in early modern Asia, why did the Philippines fall to a European colonizing power?

The Philippine Islands are a large volcanic chain in the tropical waters of the western Pacific (see Map 20.4). Like most Southeast Asian islands, the Philippines were settled by ancient Austronesian mariners. With the exception of a few small Islamic sultanates in the southern islands, the Philippines at the dawn of early modern times had no dynastic rulers or overarching religious or ethical traditions to unify

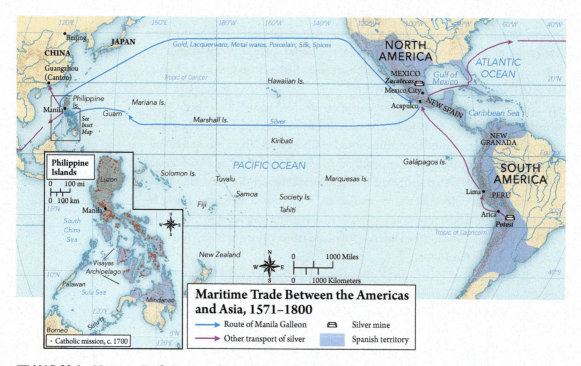

≡ **MAP 20.4   Maritime Trade Between the Americas and Asia, 1571–1800**   One of the most notable changes in the early modern period was the permanent linking of East Asia and the Americas through the so-called Manila galleon. Although only a few of these lumbering Spanish ships traversed the vast Pacific each year after 1571, they brought millions of ounces of silver to Manila, where the silver was exchanged for Chinese silk, porcelain, and many other commodities. These luxury goods were then shipped east to Mexico. Some were sold in Spanish America, but most were reshipped to Spain for consumption or resale.

its population. Over one hundred languages were spoken throughout the archipelago, and material culture differed from one river valley or island to the next.

Kin-based political units rarely exceeded two thousand members, and most were mutually hostile. The islands' total population was probably between one and two million in 1500, and acquired immunity to Old World diseases appears to have been robust, certainly superior to that of Europeans who came later. As in most of Southeast Asia, women in the Philippines were relatively powerful and autonomous in politics, business, and domestic affairs. Both slavery and long-distance trade were established institutions, and some Filipinos used a writing system on bamboo slats, now lost.

Filipino traders sailing large outrigger vessels maintained contact with the East and Southeast Asian mainland, as well as with southern Japan, and Chinese merchants had long operated small trading posts in the Philippines, including one at Manila on the northern island of Luzon. Filipino exports included sugar and cotton, along with a bit of gold panned from mountain streams. Imports included metal goods, porcelain, spices, and textiles. Most Filipinos mixed farming with fishing and the raising of small livestock, mostly pigs and chickens.

Arrival of the Spanish

Filipino life was forever altered when Spanish conquistadors arrived from Mexico in 1565. By 1571 the Spanish had made Manila their capital city: a base for trade with China and a springboard for regional conquest. Shipyards were established at nearby Cavite to outfit the great galleons sent annually to Acapulco (see again Map 20.4). Conquest was difficult in such a divided region, but these same divisions prevented a unified effort to repulse the Spanish. European invaders managed to gradually dominate many regions of the Philippines by making alliances with local chieftains in exchange for gifts and favors. Where local headmen resisted, obedient substitutes were found and placed in power.

Early Spanish colonists feverishly searched for gold, pearls, and other exportable commodities, but their hopes fizzled before the end of the sixteenth century. There was ultimately little to collect in the way of marketable tribute, and the small enclave around Manila became, rather like a contemporary Portuguese outpost, the exclusive preserve of Spanish merchants, soldiers, and missionaries. A few bureaucrats eventually followed, linking Manila to its official capital in faraway Mexico City.

Outside Manila's Spanish core a substantial Chinese merchant community formed, and many of its residents converted to Catholicism and intermarried with local Filipino elites. In the end it was Catholic priests arriving on the annual ships from Mexico who proved responsible for what has come to be known as the "spiritual conquest" of the Philippines. As a result of lax crown oversight, the absence of precious minerals or other high-value exports, and general Filipino receptiveness to Roman Catholicism, before the end of early modern times a fairly small number of highly energetic priests managed to transform much of the archipelago into a veritable theocracy (a state ruled by religious authority), amassing huge amounts of territory and much political power in the process.

Missionaries from several Catholic orders learned to preach in Tagalog, the language of the greater Manila area, as well as a few other regional languages. Lack of standardized languages and writing systems complicated missionary efforts in some places, as did the racist refusal to train an indigenous clergy, yet the absence of a region-wide state religion or code of ethics similar to Buddhism or Confucianism probably eased acceptance of Catholicism's universalist claims. Indigenous religion persisted, however. In time, Spanish and Mexican missionaries established hundreds of rural churches and frontier missions, most of them concentrated in the northern islands but some stretching south through the Visayas archipelago and into northern Mindanao.

≡ **An Elite Filipino Couple** This rare image from about 1600 shows a Filipino husband and wife with the local label of Tagalog. Although Filipinos spoke many languages and practiced many religions, the Tagalog language was the one chosen by Spanish priests for evangelization. Alongside Spanish, it became the islands' official language. The couple shown here displays dress and grooming similar to those of Malay elites living throughout Southeast Asia. The man holds the hilt of a kris dagger, a symbol of high status, while his wife stands draped in the finest Chinese silk.

The Limits of "Spiritual Conquest"

Southern Mindanao and the Sulu Islands remained staunchly Muslim, however, and hence enemy territory in the Spanish view. Periodic battles pitted self-styled crusading Spaniards against the so-called Moors of this region, and some missionaries related harrowing stories of martyrdom and captivity among "pirate infidels" reminiscent of accounts from North Africa's Barbary Coast (discussed in Chapter 19). Indeed, hundreds of letters to Spain's kings and to the pope describe these mostly fruitless struggles.

Other threats to Christian hegemony came from bands of headhunters inhabiting the mountainous interior of Luzon and smaller islands, but despite these challenges, the Philippines emerged from early modern times deeply transformed, in some ways more like Latin America than any other part of Asia. It would ironically be Filipino youths such as José Rizal, trained by the Jesuit and Franciscan successors of these early missionaries, who would lead the struggle to end Spanish colonialism at the last years of the nineteenth century.

Conclusion

China, Japan, Korea, and mainland Southeast Asia were home to a large portion of the world's peoples in early modern times. Russia was, by contrast, vast but thinly populated. In all cases, however, the most notable trend in northern and eastern Asia was toward internal political consolidation. The Philippines, though relatively populous, proved to be an exception, falling with relative ease into the hands of Spanish invaders. Outside Orthodox Russia and the Buddhist regions of Southeast Asia, Neo-Confucian principles of agrarian order and paternalistic harmony guided imperial consolidation. Despite some shocks in the seventeenth century, steady population growth and relative peace in China, Japan, and Korea seemed only to reinforce Confucius's ideal notions of educated self-sufficiency and limited need for foreign trade.

Internal changes, however, particularly in China, profoundly affected the rest of the world, and some regional political trends were accelerated by foreign imports such as gunpowder weapons. Wang Yangming, whose story began this chapter, was just one of many new imperial officials to use these deadly tools of power. Western weapons also aided Burmese and later Qing overland expansion in a way reminiscent of the Islamic "gunpowder empires" discussed in Chapters 18 and 19. Global trade also proved susceptible to East Asia's centralizing early modern policies. China's shift to a silver-based currency in the sixteenth century reordered world trade patterns. Suddenly, the Americas, Europe, and many Asian neighbors found themselves revolving in an increasingly tight, China-centered orbit. Virtually overnight, the village of Manila became one of the world's most vibrant trading crossroads. Manila was also an outlying colony, as will be seen in the next chapter, of an increasingly powerful Spanish America. It was only in the nineteenth century that many parts of East and Southeast Asia began to experience the types of outside domination long experienced by these colonies.

✳ review

The major global development in this chapter: The general trend toward political and cultural consolidation in early modern Asia.

Important Events	
1392–1910	Yi dynasty established in Korea
1543	Portuguese reach Japan
1555–1581	Expansion of Burma under King Bayinnaung
1565	Spanish conquest of Philippines begins
1571	Manila becomes Philippine capital and key Pacific trading post
1581	Chinese Ming emperor Wanli issues Single Whip Law
1584–1613	Time of Troubles in Russia
1597–1630s	Persecution of Japanese Christians
1601	Matteo Ricci demonstrates Western technology in Ming court
1602–1867	Tokugawa Shogunate in Japan
1614	Japanese contact with foreigners restricted
1627, 1636	Manchu invasions of Korea
1644	Manchu invasion of Beijing; Ming dynasty replaced by Qing
1661–1722	Qing expansion under Emperor Kangxi
1689–1725	Russian imperial expansion under Tsar Peter the Great
1751	Qing annexation of Tibet

KEY TERMS

daimyo (p. 736)
geisha (p. 742)
kabuki (p. 742)
kisaeng (p. 746)

nanban (p. 737)
Neo-Confucianism (p. 722)
samurai (p. 736)
serf (p. 724)

shogun (p. 736)
sumo (p. 742)
yangban (p. 744)

CHAPTER OVERVIEW QUESTIONS

1. What factors led to imperial consolidation in Russia and China? Who were the new rulers, and what were the sources of their legitimacy?
2. Why was isolation more common in these empires than overseas engagement, and what were some of the benefits and drawbacks of isolation?

3. In what ways did early modern Asians transform their environments, and why?

MAKING CONNECTIONS

1. How did imperial Russia's rise compare with that of the Ottomans or Habsburgs (see Chapter 19)?
2. How did China under the Ming and Qing compare with the other most populous early modern empire, Mughal India (see Chapter 18)?

3. How did Iberian missionaries' efforts in the Philippines compare with those in western Africa (see Chapter 17)?

For further research into the topics covered in this chapter, see the Bibliography at the end of the book. For additional primary sources from this period, see *Sources for World in the Making*.

Transforming New Worlds: The American Colonies Mature 1600–1750

≡ **World in the Making** Scenes of everyday life in eighteenth-century Brazil are extremely rare, but fortunately an Italian military engineer known in Portuguese as Carlos Julião chose to depict enslaved and free people of color in Salvador da Bahia, Rio de Janeiro, and the diamond diggings of northern Minas Gerais during several tours of duty. This image of a free woman of color in the diamond town of Tejuco, home of Chica da Silva (whose story opens this chapter), suggests that she is attracting the romantic attention of a bespectacled Portuguese immigrant. Both are clothed with a mix of fine Asian and European fabrics, testament to the wealth of the diamond diggings. Opulence, violence, and the constant mixing of peoples were core features of life on Brazil's colonial mining frontier.

✳ backstory

As we saw in Chapter 16, the Americas were transformed in early modern times, emerging as a global crossroads whose products, including silver, sugar, and tobacco, would change the world. The wealth of the Americas would be extracted at incalculable cost. By 1600 millions of native Americans had died from the effects of conquest, overwork, and epidemic disease. As a result, the Spanish and Portuguese enslaved West and West Central Africans and brought them to work the plantations and mines. Livestock imported from Europe roamed far and wide in the Americas, transforming the landscape and displacing native species.

Born of an enslaved African mother and a Portuguese father in the Brazilian diamond-mining camp of Tejuco, Chica da Silva, "the slave who became queen," has long fired the imagination. In 1753, when Chica was about twenty, she was purchased by a royal contractor from Portugal. Before long, Chica became his mistress and the talk of Tejuco. Freed soon after her purchase, Chica established her own opulent household and went on to bear her former master thirteen children. He lavished upon Chica and her children gifts, fine clothing, a large townhouse, and country estates. Together, the couple owned hundreds of slaves. When Chica went down the street with her bright silk gowns and retinue of servants, people made way.

Visitors from Portugal were scandalized that an illegitimate "half-breed" woman could flaunt such extravagance. Indeed, laws forbade such public display by persons of "free-colored" status. In Brazil's diamond and gold districts, however, such laws seemed made to be broken. After her death, storytellers surmised that Chica da Silva used cruelty and promiscuity to advance her wealth and status. According to them, Chica da Silva was a kind of Brazilian archetype: the sexually insatiable and power-hungry *mulata* (mulatto).

Historian Júnia Furtado has challenged this view of Chica. First, Furtado asks, how could a woman who bore thirteen children in fifteen years have been a seductress? Second, Chica was hardly unique: of 510 family residences in Tejuco, 197 were headed by free women of color, several of them recent slaves like Chica. Moreover, records show that Chica da Silva closely attended to matters of propriety: she had her children educated and used much of her fortune to fund religious causes. She was essentially a typical elite "Portuguese" woman who happened to live in an atypical, racially mixed, mining frontier world.

The story of Chica da Silva highlights several features of colonial life in the Americas. First, most colonies were based on the forced labor of people of color to produce raw materials. Second, the proximity of peoples of different colors, or "races," led to racial mingling and new avenues for social advancement. For some, new populations of mixed heritage upset notions of racial purity, ethnicity, hierarchy, and propriety. For others, breeding across color lines was a natural consequence of proximity. Although the abuses of colonialism can hardly be overstated, the life of Chica da Silva embodies the complexities and contradictions of colonial life in the Americas.

Such changes were taking place throughout the hemisphere. Despite its slower start, Portuguese Brazil came to resemble Spanish Mexico and Peru after 1695, when gold and diamonds were discovered in the interior. The slave-based sugar and tobacco economy of Brazil's northeast declined and then rebounded. Despite early failures, planters from northern European countries developed Caribbean island and mainland colonies such as Barbados and Virginia to compete with Spanish and

Portuguese colonies in the export of sugar and tobacco. Northern European masters differed in using indentured servants, poor women and men from their own countries who contracted terms of servitude in exchange for passage to the Americas. However, most **indenture** terms were short, usually three years, and before long their masters reinvested the capital accumulated from their labors in African slavery.

In the far north, Europeans competed with indigenous groups for access to furs, timber, agricultural land, fish, and other natural resources. These European colonists, like their counterparts in the tropics, kept slaves, but they did not rely on them for subsistence or export products. To the chagrin of all northern Europeans, gold and silver were nowhere to be found, and a water passage to China was similarly elusive. The colonists would have to make do with less glamorous exports, such as salted cod and timber.

OVERVIEW QUESTIONS

The major global development in this chapter: The profound social, cultural, and environmental changes in the Americas under colonial rule.

As you read, consider:

1. How did the production of silver, gold, and other commodities shape colonial American societies?

2. How and where did northern Europeans insert themselves into territories claimed by Spain and Portugal?

3. How did racial divisions and mixtures compare across the Americas by the mid-eighteenth century?

The World That Silver Made: Spanish America 1570–1750

↘ FOCUS How did mineral wealth steer the development of Spanish America?

As we saw in Chapter 16, the Spanish moved quickly to consolidate their American colonies following the discovery of precious metals. Their two great bases were the viceregal capitals of Lima and Mexico City, and although much territory remained in indigenous hands, the Spanish empire in America was vast. A colonial bureaucracy and various arms of the Catholic Church were firmly in place by 1570, occupying stone buildings as imposing as many in Europe. Armed fleets hauled tons of gold and

indenture A labor system in which Europeans contracted for several years of unpaid labor in exchange for free passage across the Atlantic and housing.

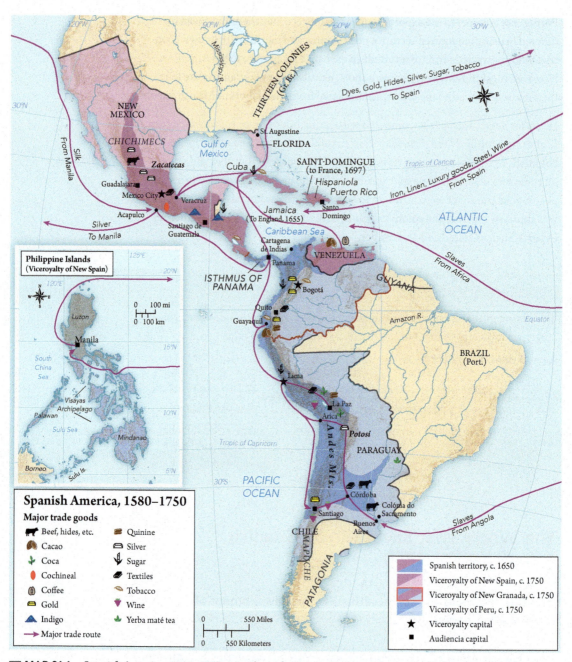

≡ **MAP 21.1**   **Spanish America, 1580–1750**   In early modern times Spain was the most significant power in the Americas. Although Dutch, English, and French competitors gained ground in North America and the Caribbean after 1600, and the Portuguese finally moved to expand Brazil after 1700, during this period Spanish America, divided into three viceroyalties by 1750, remained the richest and most densely populated region in the Western Hemisphere by far. Meanwhile, the distant Philippines, governed from Mexico City, served as both a trade node with East Asia and a base for missionary expansion.

silver to Europe and Asia each year, returning with a wide array of luxury goods, including Chinese silk and Dutch linen. Pirates constantly menaced this rich transoceanic commerce (see Map 21.1).

Gold and silver also financed the purchase of slaves, and soon people of African descent were found throughout Spanish America. Slaves mined the gold of New Granada (Colombia) and minted the silver coins of Potosí. Young Domingo Angola, whose story opened Chapter 17, was one of many such uprooted Africans. Offsetting the climb in African-descended populations was the decline of the indigenous population. From a total of some forty million in 1500, the number of native Americans living within the sphere of Spanish dominance fell to less than five million by 1600. Epidemic disease was the main culprit, but harsh labor conditions, displacement, and physical abuse accelerated decline. Although some recovery was evident by the mid-eighteenth century, native populations in the former Inca and Aztec realms never returned to precontact levels.

Governing and Profiting from the Colonies

The Spanish crown developed many institutions for colonial governance. Some, such as the appeals court, or *audiencia*, were based on Spanish models; others were American innovations. Bureaucratization drew upon Spain's emerging class of university-trained lawyers. These lawyers often clashed with the conquistadors and their offspring.

Colonial provinces were headed by crown-appointed governors or magistrates, and clusters of these provinces made up audiencia jurisdictions. Few subjects' legal appeals went beyond these courts, and indigenous groups quickly learned to use the audiencias to their advantage in disputes with Spanish landlords and mine owners. The viceroys of Mexico, Peru, and later New Granada and the Río de la Plata mostly oversaw defense and crown income, and stood in symbolically for the distant king.

The cities of Santo Domingo, Mexico City, Lima, Bogotá, and Buenos Aires became capitals of vast districts, but even small provincial towns exerted power over the surrounding countryside. As in Spain, town councils were the basic unit of governance throughout Spanish America.

Legally, the colonies were divided between a "republic of Indians" and a "republic of Spaniards." This divided system was created not out of fears of racial mixing, which occurred anyway, but rather to shelter and thus more efficiently exploit Spanish America's indigenous population. In short, the king wanted to keep the number of officially registered "Indians" high, since only they were subject to tribute payment and labor drafts. Native Americans under Spanish rule were legally bound to villages, and indigenous headmen collected tributes twice a year and organized labor pools.

Spain's transoceanic mail service was slow but surprisingly reliable once the annual fleet system was in place after the mid-sixteenth century. Word of trouble in the

audiencia The high appeals court in Spanish America.

≡ **Mexico City's Plaza Mayor** Mexico City's *plaza mayor*, or great square, painted here in 1695, served as the city's main marketplace, exposition grounds, and social crucible. It was a place to see and be seen. In this anonymous painting one gets a sense of the size and grandeur of New Spain's capital at its height, although nature's wrath is on the horizon in the form of Popocatépetl, a huge, active volcano, spewing ash ominously into the darkened sky.

colonies—or new mineral finds—always reached the king, and his decrees and tax demands always made the return trip. Thanks to this complex bureaucracy and regular transportation system, Spain's many distant colonies felt connected to the motherland.

Early Spanish conquistadors and settlers were an ambitious lot, and they quickly fanned out over an enormous area in search of gold, silver, and other commodities. In addition to mines, they gained title to land and encomiendas, or access to the labor and tribute of native Americans. These royal grants enabled some Spaniards to develop large landed estates and cattle ranches. Beef, tallow, and hides were consumed in great quantities in regional capitals and mining towns such as Potosí and Zacatecas. In seventeenth-century Mexico a "mining-ranching complex" developed, tying distant regions together. Most silver was ultimately exported, but many other commodities were produced for the internal market.

Spanish America was unusual among early modern overseas colonies in that its economy was both export-oriented and self-sufficient from an early stage. Only luxury goods such as fine textiles and iron and steel items were not produced locally. Why a local iron industry did not develop might seem strange since iron deposits were available, but the short answer is silver. Spanish-American merchants simply had so much silver to export that they struggled to find enough imports to balance the trade. Spanish authorities outlawed local iron production to protect merchant interests.

Crown and merchant interests focused primarily on the silver mining industry. Spain's kings relied on silver taxes, especially the so-called *quinto real*, or "royal fifth," of the silver mined. Collection of this and other taxes increasingly fell into private hands. The crown also rented out the mercury monopoly, which was crucial in processing silver. Subcontracting these duties bred corruption, and by 1600 crown control of mining and silver exports became weak. By the 1640s contraband trade was also flourishing, especially around Buenos Aires and along Caribbean shores, where newly arrived slaves and luxury merchandise were traded for silver ingots and "pieces of eight," all tax-free.

Despite a growing culture of corruption and tax evasion, some mine owners followed the rules. One who stood out was Antonio López de Quiroga, who used his profits from selling silver to the mint in Potosí to buy up abandoned mines, hire the most skilled workers available, and employ innovations such as black-powder blasting. By the 1670s, López de Quiroga was the local equivalent of a billionaire, a major benefactor of churches, and even a sponsor of lowland conquest expeditions. Similar stories were repeated in the mines of Mexico.

As we saw in Chapter 19, Spain's Habsburg monarchs and ministers envisioned the colonial economy as a closed mercantile system, intended to benefit the mother country through taxation while enabling subjects of varying status to seek and consolidate wealth (although not to gain crown-challenging titles of nobility).

≡ **Spanish "Piece of Eight"** This *peso de a ocho*, or "piece of eight," was minted in the famous silver mining city of Potosí in 1688, during the reign of the last Habsburg king, Charles II. In addition to the coin maker's initials, "VR," the piece of eight bears symbols of Spain's overseas empire, including the Pillars of Hercules (the Strait of Gibraltar) and the great waves of the "Ocean Sea," or the Atlantic. "Plus Ultra," or "Further Beyond," the motto of Spain's first Habsburg king and Holy Roman Emperor Charles V, became the motto of empire as well. The Spanish piece of eight served for several centuries as the standard world currency.

No foreigners were supposed to trade with the American colonies except through approved monopoly holders based in Seville. These monopolists also controlled (theoretically) all trade through Acapulco to Manila and back. Although this closed-system ideal was realized to a surprising degree given the great distances involved, it soon fell prey to individual wiles and corrupt cartels as Spain itself fell into decline under a succession of weak kings after Philip II (r. 1556–1598). Only after 1700, with the rise of the Bourbon dynasty, did the crown manage to reassert itself forcefully in colonial economic affairs. As we will see in the next chapter, widespread rebellion would follow.

Everyday Life in Spanish America

As the colonies matured, Spain's diverse American subjects found new possibilities for social and material improvement, but they also faced many constraints. Life spans in colonial Spanish America were similar to those of contemporary Europe for elites, but as we have seen, they were considerably shorter for people of indigenous and African descent. Medical care was more an art than a science, and epidemics, particularly of smallpox, hit everyone. Slaves, criminals, and draftees with smallpox scars on their faces appear frequently in documents. They were the lucky ones, the survivors.

Many of the regions settled by the Spanish were prone to earthquakes, volcanic eruptions, and landslides, which were widely regarded as judgments of God. When in 1661 a volcano dumped several feet of ash on Quito, now the capital of Ecuador, Catholic priests ordered that an image of the Virgin Mary be paraded through the streets until the eruption ceased. Such religiosity was manifest in many aspects of colonial Spanish-American society, including art and literature, and it helped shape local norms of gender and race relations. In fact, Catholicism came to serve as a common cultural touchstone, connecting the members of a diverse society.

Unlike parts of English, French, and Dutch America, as we will see, Spanish America was never intended as a refuge for religious dissenters. From the beginning the region was a Roman Catholic domain. Even recent converts to Christianity were not allowed to emigrate for fear of allowing Judaism or Islam into the colonies. Spain's Romas, or gypsies, were likewise banned due to their alleged fondness for fortune telling and witchcraft. Still, some recent converts and Romas, along with miscellaneous "unorthodox" foreigners from Portugal, France, Italy, Germany, the Low Countries, and even Greece, managed to sneak aboard Indies-bound ships leaving Seville. In the colonies, the beginning of the Inquisition after 1570, plus waves of anti-idolatry campaigns after 1560, soon led to persecution of nonconformists.

How did the mass of subject peoples, most of them indigenous peasants and enslaved Africans, respond to these demands for spiritual conformity? Faced with threats and punishments from priests and officials, along with the persuasive efforts of missionaries, most native and African-descended subjects at least nominally accepted Catholicism. What soon emerged, however, was a complex fusion of Catholic practices with a more secretive, underground world of non-Christian cults, shamanistic healing practices, and witchcraft. Scholars have learned much about these alternative religious spheres in recent years from Inquisition and anti-idolatry records, and some have sought to trace their roots to parts of Africa and elsewhere.

According to Christian scripture, all human beings were redeemable in the creator's eyes, regardless of sex, age, status, color, or birthplace. Thus, many church leaders believed that non-Western habits such as nudity and even cannibalism could be reformed and did not justify permanent discrimination. It was on such grounds that Spanish priests such as Bartolomé de Las Casas had argued so successfully against Amerindian slavery (see Chapter 16).

By contrast, African slavery was hardly debated by Spanish priests and theologians. Some church leaders even sought to justify it. Settlers, particularly those in need of workers, were inclined to view both native Americans and Africans as inferior and uneducable; such racist views suited their interests. For its part, the Spanish crown sought protection of subject Amerindians not so much for reasons of faith, but because natives paid their tributes in silver. Slaves, being outside the tributary economy, were left mostly to their own devices, although Spanish law contained some protections, certainly more than those developed by later colonists such as the Dutch, French, and English.

By the seventeenth century, Spanish America was molded by a variety of forces. But it was only biology—some would say the law of human attraction—that subverted the system. To start, a surplus of male European settlers in the early years quickly led to *mestizaje* (mess-tee-ZAH-hey), Spanish for "mixture," and a significant mixed-heritage population. In some places it was indigenous women, ranging in status from servants such as Malintzin to Aztec and Inca princesses, who gave birth to a new generation of *mestizos*, as mixed-blood offspring were called. In other cases it was enslaved or free women of African descent who bore **mulatto** children to Spanish colonizers. There were many examples resembling Brazil's Chica da Silva throughout Spanish America, though none so rich or famous. Indigenous women also had children by African men, and countless other "mixtures" occurred in the course of three centuries of colonial rule.

mestizaje Spanish for "mixture," referring to racial blending of any type.

mestizo Spanish for "mixed," or offspring of Europeans and native Americans.

mulatto Offspring of Europeans and Africans.

SEEING THE PAST

Gentlemen of Esmeraldas

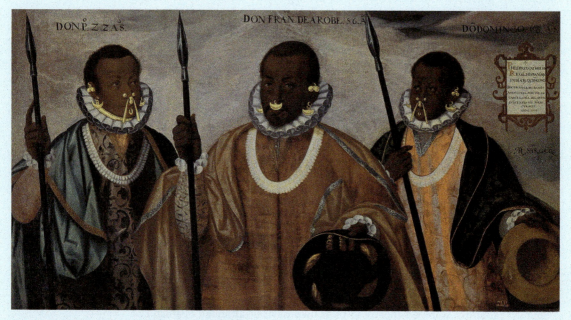

Andrés Sánchez Gallque, *Gentlemen of Esmeraldas*

To attribute all this to the power of physical attraction would be an oversimplification. Some relationships across color lines were forced and criminal, others merely fleeting, and still others were permanent and even church-sanctioned. Though some bureaucrats and bishops might have wished it so, neither state nor church outlawed interracial marriage in colonial Spanish America. Only marriage across huge status gaps, as, say, between a nobleman and a slave, was forbidden. By 1750 Spanish-American society was so "mixed" that the term *casta*, or "caste," formerly applied by the Portuguese in India, was adopted to categorize the bewildering range of socioracial types. Hundreds of paintings depict the various unions and offspring comprising Spanish America's so-called *sistema de castas*, or "system of castes" (see Seeing the Past: *Gentlemen of Esmeraldas*).

In 1599 Andrés Sánchez Gallque, an indigenous artist from Quito, the former Inca capital, painted a group portrait of three men who had climbed up from the Pacific coast province of Esmeraldas to sign a treaty with the colonial government. The three men, Don Francisco de Arobe and his two sons, Pedro and Domingo, were maroons, descendants of escaped slaves who swam ashore following a shipwreck in the 1540s. They were in Quito to sign a treaty agreeing not to ally with pirates. The Spanish honorific title "Don" was used for all three men since they were recognized as indigenous chiefs. As it happened, Don Francisco de Arobe was the son of an African man and a native woman from Nicaragua. Other Esmeraldas maroons had intermarried with local indigenous inhabitants.

In exchange for agreeing to defend the coast against intruders, the Arobes were sent to a professional tailor in Quito and given a wide variety of luxury textiles, including ponchos and capes made from Chinese silk brought to Acapulco by the Manila galleon. The maroon leaders also received linen ruff collars from Holland and iron spearheads, probably from the Basque region of northern Spain. Their own adornments included shell necklaces and gold facial jewelry typical of South America's northwest Pacific coast. The painting was sent to Philip III as a memento of peace. It is now housed in Madrid's Museo de América.

Examining the Evidence

1. What might these men's wide array of adornments symbolize?

2. What image does Sánchez Gallque seem to wish to convey to the king of Spain?

Source: Kris Lane, *Quito 1599: City and Colony in Transition* (Albuquerque: University of New Mexico Press, 2002).

Women's experiences varied more by social class than color. Many Spanish-American women were widowed at a relatively young age, which gave some a boost in terms of economic security and independence. Despite a generally stifling patriarchal culture, Spanish inheritance law was relatively generous to women. The wives of merchants, in particular, frequently found themselves in charge of substantial enterprises and estates, with much freedom to administer them. More significantly, widows wielded influence over their children's marriage choices. When children married well, estates could be combined and expanded, cementing a family's fortunes in the face of uncertainty. Such was the story of the family of Simón Bolívar, whose story opens the next chapter. Among his ancestors, it was women who made many of the most important choices.

≡ **Peruvian Blacksmiths** Although all iron and steel were imported by privileged wholesalers to the Spanish-American colonies, it was local blacksmiths who fashioned these raw materials into horseshoes, hinges, nails, tools, and many other items. In this mid-eighteenth-century watercolor from the Pacific-coast city of Trujillo, Peru, a man and woman work together to forge tools. By this time, nearly all artisans were of indigenous, African, or mixed background, since hand labor was generally disdained by those claiming to be of pure European stock. This pair appears to be of mestizo, or mixed Spanish and indigenous, heritage.

Poor women in Spanish America had other worries. Most were engaged in market-oriented activity, even if they lived in the countryside. Weaving, spinning, and pottery-making were often female tasks. Urban women of poor to middling status were usually either servants or vendors, with some working alongside artisan husbands as cobblers, tanners, tailors, cigar-rollers, and even blacksmiths. Along with their burdensome duties as wet nurses, cooks, and cleaners, female domestic servants and slaves were also hired out, handing over the wages to their masters. Despite harsh conditions, access to markets meant access to cash, allowing some socially marginalized urban women, for example indigenous and mixed-race women in Potosí, to accumulate capital.

In a different category altogether were Catholic nuns. Most were wealthy, but some were of humble background, including women born out of wedlock. Every Spanish-American city had at least one convent, and often half a dozen or more. Inside lived not only the nuns themselves, but their female servants and slaves. Lima, for example, in 1630 counted over 1366 nuns served by 899 female African slaves out of a total city population of about forty thousand. Convents also served as shelters for widows and women facing hardships, and as reformatories for those accused of prostitution and minor crime. Though confining, Spanish-American nunneries occasionally nurtured female intellectuals and mystics of great renown, such as St. Rose of Lima (1586–1617) and Juana Inés de la Cruz (1651–1595). Famous for her biting wit, de la Cruz even took on the misogynist ways of Mexican society in verse:

> Who would have the greatest blame
> In an errant love affair,
> She who falls to him who begs

Or he who plays the beggar?
Or who should be more guilty
Though each is evil-doing,
She who sins for pay,
Or he who pays for sinning?[1]

Gold, Diamonds, and the Transformation of Brazil 1695–1800

FOCUS How was Brazil transformed by the mining boom of the eighteenth century?

Beginning in around 1695, the coastal, sugar-based export economy of Portuguese Brazil began to change, sparked by the discovery of gold and diamonds in Brazil's south-central highlands. What followed was the greatest bonanza in world history prior to California's gold rush. The consequences were profound and lasting. First, over half a million Portuguese immigrants flowed into Brazil between 1700 and 1800. Second, the African slave trade was expanded. Third, the Portuguese crown elevated Brazil to the status of viceroyalty in 1720. Finally, Brazil's center shifted southward, away from the sugar zone of the northeast. Rio de Janeiro became Brazil's new capital in 1763 (see Map 21.2). On a global scale, Brazilian gold's importance briefly rivaled that of Spanish-American silver, flowing through Lisbon and into allied England, helping to finance the early stages of the Industrial Revolution.

Boom Times for Colonial Brazil

In the mid-1690s, a mulatto aide traveling with Brazilian slave hunters discovered gold in the highlands northeast of São Paulo. By 1800 Brazil had exported between 2.5 and 4.5 million pounds of gold, and several million carats of raw diamonds. Up to this time diamonds had come almost entirely from India, and gold from West Africa and Spanish America. Soon after 1700, a district capital was set up in the town of Ouro Preto (OR-ooh PREH-too), or "Black Gold," and the region was dubbed Minas Gerais (MEAN-us jheh-HICE), or "General Mines." Prospectors and slaves flowed into Minas Gerais in droves, among them Chica da Silva's African mother and Portuguese father. Hordes of merchants came close on their heels.

Unlike the silver mines of Spanish America, Brazil's gold and diamond mines were almost all of the surface, or "placer," variety. Wherever gold and diamonds

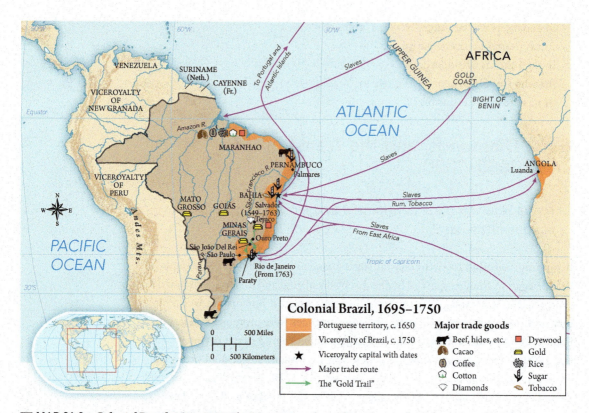

≡ **MAP 21.2   Colonial Brazil, 1695–1750** The Portuguese colony of Brazil was radically transformed after the discovery of gold and diamonds in the southern highlands around 1695. Gold-seeking colonists rushed in by the tens of thousands from Portugal, the Azores, and elsewhere in the empire, and the Atlantic slave trade, once focused on the sugar-producing northeast, shifted south to Rio de Janeiro and expanded rapidly.

were found, teams of enslaved workers, mostly young African-born men, excavated riverbanks while others panned or redirected streams to get at gravel beds and sandbars. Early commentators described this work as hellishly hard, exacerbated by severe food shortages.

Environmental consequences followed. Historians estimate that Brazilian gold miners overturned tens of thousands of square miles of topsoil to a depth of at least one and a half feet, resulting in massive erosion. Deforested regions were invaded by inedible grasses and weeds. Laws from as early as the 1720s mandated forest conservation, but these decrees were not observed. Deforestation to support farming and the raising of livestock to feed the miners went even further, forever transforming the Brazilian highlands.

As happened in Spain soon after the discovery of Potosí and other major silver mines in Spanish America, a wave of emigration swept Portugal following the

Brazilian bonanza of 1695. Never a populous country, Portugal could ill afford the loss of tens of thousands of residents, especially young, able-bodied men. So many Portuguese men came to Minas Gerais in the first years after 1700 that a minor war broke out between them and the **creole** "Paulistas," or residents of São Paulo, who had discovered the mines. Crown authorities sided with the newcomers, and eventually established order by sending in troops.

The Atlantic slave trade expanded dramatically in response to the Brazilian bonanza. Unlike in Mexico and Peru, where most mine work was carried out by indigenous draft and later mestizo or mulatto wage workers, in the goldfields of Brazil, whose indigenous populations had been nearly wiped out, African slavery quickly became the only form of labor employed. The few women to enter Minas Gerais in the early years of the rush were also primarily enslaved Africans, and they were in such high demand that most became the prized concubines of Portuguese men. Some were rented out as prostitutes in exchange for gold dust and diamonds. One such woman gave birth to Chica da Silva. Thus, the discovery of gold and diamonds in Brazil drew millions of migrants, some voluntary but many more forced, to the Americas.

The Portuguese crown took an immediate interest in the Brazilian gold rush, establishing a taxation and monopoly trade system similar to that developed by the Spanish in Mexico and Peru. Gold taxes, the same "royal fifth" demanded by the Spanish crown, were collected at specified sites, and all trade was directed along royal, stone-paved roads complete with official stations where mule-loads were inspected and taxed. The "gold trail" eventually terminated in Rio de Janeiro, changing the city's destiny (see again Map 21.2). Rio became capital of the viceroyalty of Brazil in 1763.

≣ **Brazilian Diamond Diggers** Images of colonial mineworkers in the Americas are rare. Fortunately, the Italian military engineer Carlos Julião sought to depict the labors of Brazil's enslaved and mostly African-born diamond workers in Minas Gerais in the eighteenth century, precisely when Chica da Silva was the richest woman in the district and her common-law husband was possibly the wealthiest man in Portugal. The workers here are searching through diamond-bearing gravel under close surveillance (although the first overseer appears to be napping). Despite the surveillance, many slaves managed to hide diamonds, trading them later for food, clothing, alcohol, or cash.

creole A European born in the Americas and his or her descendants.

As in Spanish America, royal control over mining districts was tenuous, and smuggling, particularly of diamonds, soon became a huge problem. Official control centered on the town of Tejuco (today's Diamantina) and was headed by royal contractors from Portugal, such as Chica da Silva's common-law husband. Although the diamond mines were closely monitored and slaves were subjected to physical inspections, there were always ways of hiding and trading stones. As an incentive to be honest and work hard, slaves were promised instant freedom if they found diamonds above a very large size, but few were so lucky.

Much more often, enslaved diamond miners traded small stones to corrupt bureaucrats and merchants for cash. Slaves in the gold mines did the same. Wealth thus accumulated was then used to purchase the workers' freedom or the freedom of their children. One of the ironies of the Brazilian gold and diamond mines was that although the work itself was more dangerous than that of the cane fields and sugar mills of the northeast, the odds of obtaining freedom were considerably higher. Knowing that enslaved Africans outnumbered them by a huge margin here in the mountainous backlands, Portuguese masters and crown officials accepted a measure of secret trade and self-purchase.

Everyday Life in Golden-Age Brazil

With slavery so central to Brazil's colonial economy, it is no surprise that this institution deeply influenced society. At first indigenous and then African cultural elements fused with Portuguese imports to create a new, hybrid culture. Only certain elites proved resistant to this hybridization, doing their best to mimic metropolitan styles and ideas. Some members of this elite class, such as the Portuguese diamond contractor who purchased Chica da Silva, embraced "Afro-Brazil" in a more literal sense, by forming families of mixed ancestry. Other Brazilians practiced Catholicism while seeking the aid of folk healers, clairvoyants, and other officially illegal religious figures, many of them of African ancestry.

As in Spanish America, Brazil's colonial authorities worried about the presence of Judaism and people of Jewish ancestry. In the colony's early years some New Christians, or forced converts, had been allowed to immigrate. By the 1590s, some of these settlers were discovered to be secretly practicing Judaic rituals. Infrequent visits by the Inquisition, which never set up a permanent tribunal in Brazil, uncovered evidence of "heresy," or at least unorthodox religious practices (such as kosher food preparation), but few were prosecuted. Brazil's Jewish community became more evident during the 1630–1654 Dutch occupation of Pernambuco in northeast Brazil. Under the Dutch, Brazil's Jews were allowed to build a synagogue and practice their religion openly. When the Portuguese regained control of the northeast in 1654, several Jewish planter families relocated to Dutch Suriname, where they set up slave-staffed plantations (see Counterpoint: The Maroons of Suriname).

The Inquisition also persecuted secret Jews in Minas Gerais in the early eighteenth century, in part to confiscate their valuable estates and stocks of merchandise. Poor Brazilians were targeted, too, however, especially Afro-Brazilian religious practitioners. None were burned, but many were publicly shamed, exiled, or sentenced to galley service. Usually denounced as "fetishists," devil-worshippers, and witches, these specialists maintained certain African religious traditions, usually blended with Catholicism and native American shamanism. Often, Catholic saints were used to mask male and female West African deities, as later happened in Cuba and Saint-Domingue (Haiti). In other cases, religious brotherhoods combined West Central African spirit possession with Catholic Christianity. These brotherhoods, often devoted to black saints such as St. Benedict the Moor and St. Efigenia, were common throughout Brazil, but were especially powerful in Minas Gerais, where the missionary orders were banned for fiscal reasons.

Even before the discovery of gold, Brazil hosted the largest communities of **maroons** in the Western Hemisphere. By 1650 the maroon (from the Spanish term *cimarrón*, meaning "runaway") community of Palmares, really a confederation of a dozen fugitive villages, was home to some ten thousand or more ex-slaves and their descendants. Despite numerous military campaigns organized by planters in coordination with slave hunters, Palmares was broken up only in 1694. With the development of Minas Gerais, dozens of new maroon villages popped up in the gold-rich backcountry.

As in Spanish America, it was in the cities most affected by the great mining boom—and by sugar wealth—that Brazilian material culture grew most opulent. Churches modeled after European ones, such as those in Salvador in the northeast and Rio de Janeiro in the south, testify to the piety of both elites and poor religious brotherhoods. Even more stunning and original are the many churches and chapels of Minas Gerais, stretching from lonely Tejuco to São João del Rei (see again Map 21.2). Many of these structures were designed, built, and decorated by slaves and their descendants. In Tejuco, several were commissioned by Chica da Silva.

As the case of Chica da Silva illustrates, people of mixed heritage rose to prominent positions in Brazil, particularly in frontier districts. Arguably the colony's greatest artistic genius was the sculptor and architect Francisco Lisboa, like Chica the child of an enslaved African mother and free Portuguese father. Popularly known as Aleijadinho, or "Little Cripple" (due to leprosy), Lisboa was among the most original architects and sculptors of his era, carving fantastic soapstone façades with chisels strapped to the stumps of his hands.

maroon In the seventeenth and eighteenth centuries, a runaway slave and his or her descendants.

Brazil's gold rush ended by 1800, but by this time the northeastern sugar industry was undergoing a revival, along with tobacco, rice, cotton, and other cash crops. Portuguese officials had begun encouraging diversification and experimentation. The vast Amazon basin was now being explored as a potential source of minerals, cacao, medicinal barks, and other export commodities. Coffee, which would later become Brazil's prime export, was also experimentally planted, at first in the north. In export agriculture, Brazil's greatest competitors were in the Caribbean.

Bitter Sugar, Part Two: Slavery and Colonialism in the Caribbean 1625–1750

FOCUS How did sugar production and slavery mold Caribbean societies?

When the Dutch captured Pernambuco in 1630, they were most interested in sugar. How had the Portuguese managed to produce so much of it so cheaply? What the Dutch discovered was northeast Brazil's peculiar blend of loamy tropical soils, high-technology mills, and slave labor. By the time the Dutch abandoned Brazil in 1654, they had learned all they needed to know about sugar production.

English and French visitors had also taken notes as they displaced the Spanish in parts of the Caribbean, such as Jamaica and western Hispaniola (later known as Saint-Domingue, then Haiti). Techniques of sugar manufacture were copied, and from the mid-seventeenth century onward the story of the Caribbean was but the story of sugar and slavery, continued. After Brazil, this island region was the largest destination for enslaved Africans brought across the Atlantic—over one-third of the total (see Map 21.3).

Pirates and Planters

Development in the Caribbean was slow and not very methodical. Throughout the sixteenth century, French, English, and Dutch traders challenged Spanish monopolies while corsairs preyed on ships and lightly defended towns. One of the most famous corsairs was Sir Francis Drake, who plundered Spanish vessels and ports as he circumnavigated the globe in the late 1570s. Drake also dabbled in the contraband slave trade, but the grateful English crown looked the other way to award him a knighthood. Only in around 1600 did northern Europeans

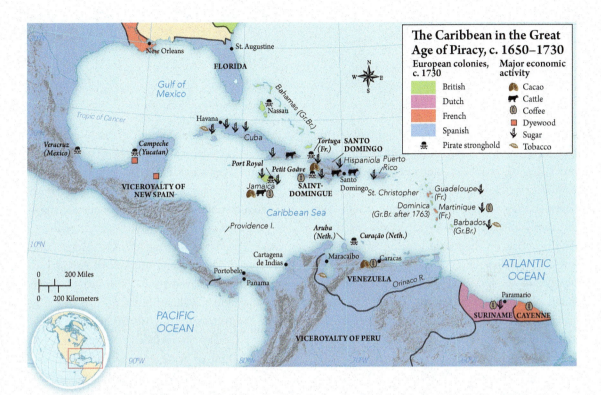

≡ **MAP 21.3** **The Caribbean, c. 1650–1730** It was in the Caribbean that Spain's exclusive claims on American territory and trade were first challenged. Soon after 1500, the French, English, and Dutch started to raid Spanish ships and periodically sack such key ports as Santo Domingo, Cartagena de Indias, Veracruz, and Havana. By 1600, these same foreign challengers began to establish lasting colonies, often in marginal places not settled by the Spanish or deemed too expensive to defend.

begin to establish permanent Caribbean colonies. The Dutch focused on small islands such as Curaçao and St. Christopher. The English followed on tiny Providence Island off the coast of modern Nicaragua. The French focused on western Hispaniola and Tortuga, a small island just offshore to the north. All these efforts combined experimental plantations, usually to grow tobacco or sugar, with contraband trade and piracy (see Lives and Livelihoods: Caribbean Buccaneers).

Spanish retaliation was fierce at first, but declined rapidly after 1648. The deepening seventeenth-century crisis rendered defense expenditures prohibitive. A massive English attack on Santo Domingo was successfully repulsed in 1655, but Jamaica was seized. The Spanish had largely ignored the island since it lacked gold. Within a decade Port Royal, opposite Kingston Harbor on Jamaica's south coast, was a major base for contraband traders and buccaneers,

buccaneer A Caribbean-based pirate of the seventeenth century.

LIVES AND LIVELIHOODS

Caribbean Buccaneers

Atlantic colonization schemes and wars gave rise to a new social type in the seventeenth century: the **buccaneer**, or Caribbean pirate. Privately financed sea raiders sailing under French, English, or Dutch commissions were active from the early 1500s, but it was only in the mid-1600s that locally based sea bandits acting on their own became an endemic problem. Some used French trading posts like Tortuga Island north of St. Domingue (Haiti) or the Dutch island of Curaçao off the coast of Venezuela, but after 1655 Port Royal, Jamaica, became the greatest of all buccaneer bases (see again Map 21.3). The party ended when the city slid into the ocean in a 1692 earthquake. Some survivors sought to regroup in the Indian Ocean, especially on Madagascar.

The first buccaneers were northern European indentured servants and war veterans, many of whom were sent to the Caribbean sugar islands to meet the labor needs of planters. Either by escape or having served out their terms, these indentures took to living off the land in St. Domingue shooting wild cattle and roasting their meat on crude barbecues, or *boucans*. Known by 1650 as *boucaniers* in French, and buccaneers in English, the hunters began to organize raids on straggling merchant vessels in dugout canoes. Their guerrilla tactics and expert marksmanship made them difficult to counter. Some, such as the Welshman Henry Morgan, made deals to share booty with colonial governors in exchange for legal protection, and later joined the colonial service. Others, such as François L'Ollonais,

were unattached terrors of the Spanish Main. L'Ollonais was said to have carved the heart from a living victim and taken a bite. Piracy was about booty, not terror, however, and Spanish ships and towns, since they often contained silver and other portable treasures, were the main objects of buccaneer desire.

Once a raid was carried off, the pirates rendezvoused in the bars and brothels of Port Royal, whose markets thrived from the influx of stolen goods and money. When the buccaneers began in the late 1660s to attack English, French, and Dutch ships with the ferocity formerly reserved for Spanish ones, the hunters became the hunted. Antipiracy laws from as early as the 1670s led to arrests and hangings, and by 1680 many buccaneers fled to the Pacific and Indian Oceans. A group of pirates who set out from the Virginia coast in the early 1680s returned to the Chesapeake with treasure stolen along the coast of Peru only to land in jail and have their booty confiscated by royal officials. A portion of their loot was used to found the College of William & Mary in 1693.

At about the same time, a new pirate base was created on the island of Madagascar, which no Europeans had successfully colonized. From here buccaneers sailed north to stalk Muslim vessels traveling from India to the Arabian peninsula. The capture of several rich prizes by Henry Avery and other famous pirates in the 1690s led the English to send pirate hunters, among them the former buccaneer William Kidd. Kidd reverted to piratical activity off the coast of India, and was eventually arrested and jailed in New England before being sent to London for execution in 1701. After a break during the War of the Spanish Succession (1701–1714), which absorbed many buccaneers as privateers and even navy men, the war on Caribbean piracy returned in force, prosecuted mostly by the English Admiralty.

In the midst of England's war on piracy emerged some of the greatest figures of the era, among them Bartholomew Roberts. "Black Bart," as he was sometimes known, was one of the first pirates to prey on Portuguese ships carrying gold and diamonds to Europe from Brazil. When killed by English pirate hunters off the coast of Ghana in 1722 he was wearing a diamond-studded gold cross taken near

"Black Bart" The great age of maritime commerce also gave rise to the great age of piracy, an activity that peaked between 1660 and 1730. Among the most successful pirates was Bartholomew "Black Bart" Roberts, shown here near the African port of Whydah, where he captured and ransomed a number of English slave ships. Roberts was killed in 1722 in an engagement with the English Royal Navy near present-day Gabon. There followed a new and long-lasting era of policing the sea.

Rio. By about 1725 the last wave of Anglo-American pirates, including the only known female pirate duo of Ann Bonny and Mary Read, was squelched.

Questions to Consider:

1. What factors made buccaneer society possible in the seventeenth-century Caribbean?
2. What trends led to the sudden demise of the buccaneers' livelihood?

For Further Information:

Earle, Peter. *The Pirate Wars.* Boston: St. Martin's Griffin, 2006.

Lane, Kris. *Pillaging the Empire: Piracy on the High Seas, 1500–1750.* New York: Routledge, 2015.

among them Henry Morgan. Morgan and his followers sacked Panama City in 1671, striking another major blow against the Spanish. Jamaican planters, meanwhile, began to build a slave-staffed sugar economy in the interior. The French islands of Martinique, Guadeloupe, and Saint-Domingue followed a similar path.

The English colony of Barbados was a surprising success. A small and virtually uninhabited island at the easternmost edge of the Caribbean, Barbados had been of no interest to the Spanish and Portuguese. The first English settlers came to plant tobacco around 1625. In time, capital accumulated from tobacco, along with advice and capital lent by Dutch refugees from Brazil, led the colony's planters to shift to sugar. Indentured servitude gave way to African slavery, and with slavery came rebellions. Even so, by the 1680s Barbados was a major world exporter of high-quality sugar, a position it held through the eighteenth century. Barbados showed that the Brazilian plantation model could transform even the smallest tropical island into a veritable gold mine.

As slavery and sugar-growing expanded on other Caribbean islands and parts of the mainland (especially Dutch Suriname), non-Iberian colonists began to surpass their predecessors in overall exports. In the course of the eighteenth century, the English, Dutch, and French embraced slavery on a scale and with an intensity not seen in Spanish America or Brazil. Slave codes grew increasingly harsh, and punishments cruel. Planters, preachers, and governors expressed virtually no interest in protecting slaves' families or dignity, much less their souls. By 1750 the planters of Jamaica routinely tortured, raped, and otherwise terrorized enslaved Africans. They themselves admitted it, and wrote that such harsh measures were necessary to quell rebellion while maximizing production. Visitors to eighteenth-century Suriname described public executions as run-of-the-mill events, and those who visited Saint-Domingue wrote of sugar production on a vast, industrial scale. Slaves were consumed like so much timber.

The Rise of Caribbean Slave Societies

Whereas Brazilian planters used cheaper, enslaved native American workers as a bridge to mass African slavery, French, Dutch, and English planters in the Caribbean used indentured European servants. Throughout the seventeenth century thousands of poor servants and convicts staffed tobacco and sugar plantations alongside growing numbers of Africans and their descendants. If they survived the harsh conditions of the tropics, these servants could expect freedom within three to seven years. Many did not live to see that day, but the profits accumulated during these few years enabled plantation owners to purchase a permanently enslaved workforce. Scholars remain divided as to whether indentured Europeans were treated as badly as enslaved Africans.

By the early eighteenth century, Caribbean plantation society had begun to mature. Great houses in the European style dotted many islands, and slave communities grew into neo-African villages. Churches in these often Protestant lands were far more modest than in Catholic Brazil, however, and represented several denominations. African religious traditions flourished, often with little influence from the colonizers' faiths. In Jamaica and Saint-Domingue, the constant influx of African-born slaves, coupled with general European disdain for slaves' spiritual lives, led to the formation of new, hybrid religious traditions, called Obeah and Vodoun (or Voodoo), respectively.

A great difference that did exist between Brazil and the Caribbean sugar colonies lay in the realms of racial mixture and shared religious traditions. European men routinely kept African and mulatto mistresses, as in Minas Gerais and other parts of Brazil, but they were usually loath to recognize their children, much less educate them in Europe and incorporate them into high society. Treated as a dirty secret and even a petty crime, racial mixture soon gave rise to sharply graded color categories quite distinct from Spanish America's fluid sistema de castas. As for religion, Europeans showed nothing but contempt for "Obeah men" and "Voodoo priestesses," treating them as frauds and quacks. Partly as a result, some of these new religious leaders, male and female, played key roles in slave uprisings.

As in Brazil, *marronage*, or slave flight, was common throughout the Caribbean. Refuges for long-term runaways proved scarce on smaller, low-lying islands such as Barbados and Curaçao, but larger and more rugged islands such as Jamaica, Dominica, and Saint Domingue abounded with possibilities for safe haven. Here in rugged highlands such as Jamaica's Blue Mountains, maroons were so successful they were able to negotiate treaties with planters and colonial officials. Jamaican maroon leaders such as Nanny and Cudjoe were folk heroes to the enslaved and a constant thorn in the side of the British.

Sugar production provided significant capital gains and, like Brazilian gold, probably helped to spark England's industrialization. Yet slavery of such horrific cruelty and scale also sowed the seeds of its own destruction. Slave traders responded to ratcheting Caribbean demand by packing their ships ever more tightly, turning slaving itself into an increasingly predatory exercise in more and more regions of Africa. Some slaves were brought from as far away as the Indian Ocean island of Madagascar. By the late eighteenth century, white abolitionists at last began to join the long-ignored chorus of African and

African-American voices against this enormous crime against humanity in the name of profit. For the first time, English tea drinkers thought twice before sweetening their brew.

Growth and Change in British and French North America 1607–1750

⬎ **FOCUS** How did European relations with native peoples differ in the British and French colonies of North America?

European colonization of North America followed a different path than that of Spanish America or Brazil. There were, however, similarities: plantations developed, missionaries preached, people bred or married across color lines, and in places slave labor came to dominate. But overall, nontropical, Atlantic North America was characterized by a slow advance of European settler families practicing subsistence agriculture, livestock-raising, fishing, and commerce according to Old World norms. Eastern North America, both French and English, was to become, in the words of historian Alfred Crosby, a "neo-Europe" (see Map 21.4). Indigenous peoples, unlike in Spanish and Portuguese America where they had been absorbed and forcibly converted, were mostly driven from their lands or annihilated.

Experiments in Commercial Colonialism

French, Dutch, and English colonization of eastern North America took root in the first decades of the seventeenth century. English Jamestown was founded on Virginia's Powhatan River (renamed "James" after the king) in 1607 and French Quebec, on Canada's St. Lawrence, in 1608. Henry Hudson, an employee of the Dutch East India Company, began reconnoitering the river that took his name in 1609. Once it was clear that the Hudson River did not lead to the Pacific Ocean, a Dutch fur-trading post was established in 1618. As early as 1605 French Huguenots (or Protestant refugees) had also begun farming the coast of Maine and Nova Scotia, which they called Acadia.

Mariners such as Hudson continued searching in vain for a **northwest passage** to China. Others probed the soils of Newfoundland for signs of gold or silver. The survival of the earliest colonies in the tiny, fortified enclaves of "New France," "New Netherland," and "Virginia" depended on alliances with indigenous inhabitants. At the same time, all three European competitors were preoccupied with each other's designs on the region, a source of lasting conflict. Moreover, everyone

northwest passage
Searched-for sea route to Asia via North America.

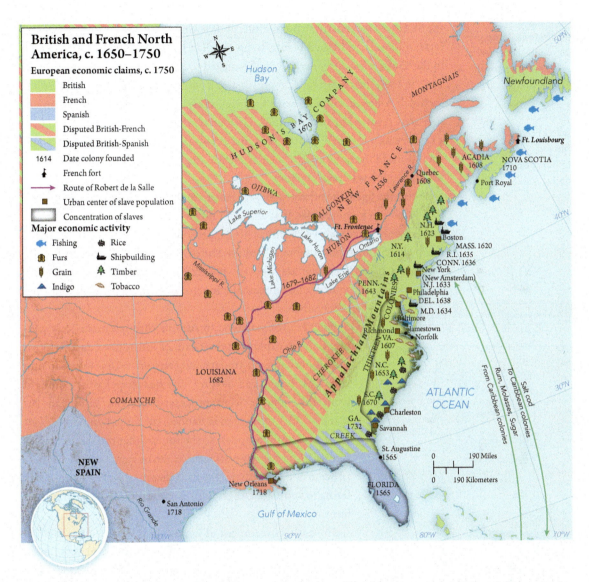

≡ MAP 21.4 British and French North America, c. 1650–1750 Although its export commodities paled in comparison with Spanish-American silver, Brazilian gold, and Caribbean sugar, British and French North America developed an increasingly powerful economy between 1650 and 1750. By 1700 its south produced substantial exports on slave-staffed plantations, and its north blended extraction of forest and marine products with commerce and re-export of Caribbean-derived rum.

worried about the Spanish, who had violently driven the French from Florida and the Dutch from Venezuela.

New France, first governed by Samuel de Champlain, marked France's renewed effort to colonize the Americas. Jacques Cartier and other mariners had explored

joint-stock company
A colonial commercial venture with a royal charter and private shareholders.

métis French for "mixed," or offspring of Europeans and native Americans.

the St. Lawrence shortly after Columbus's time, and French colonists had planted forts in Florida and Brazil before being expelled by the Spanish and Portuguese in the 1560s. Only after France itself returned to calm, after the religious wars of 1562 to 1598 (discussed in Chapter 19), was a permanent colony deemed feasible. In North America, conflicts with the English broke out by the 1610s and 1620s; they were resolved by treaty in 1632. Quebec would subsequently survive for over a century as a fortified trading post funded by absentee investors. Military alliances with indigenous groups such as the Montagnais and Huron proved critical throughout New France's history.

Unlike the Spanish and Portuguese, French, English, and Dutch colonizers created **joint-stock companies** that attracted investors in the mother country and took on a financial and even political life of their own. Amsterdam's stock market was by far Europe's most vibrant, and the Dutch VOC was considered the shining model of such enterprises, because it successfully combined commercial, military, and diplomatic functions to turn a private profit from colonialism.

New France managed to survive through many long winters only by exploiting the chain of indigenous and **métis**, or mixed-heritage, fur traders and trappers extending deep into the Great Lakes and beyond. The beaver pelts they brought from the interior were processed for the European hat market. Only these men in canoes, the famed *coureurs de bois* ("runners of the woods," as the independent fur traders were known), and a few Jesuits went much beyond the fort. Settlers concentrated mostly in the St. Lawrence valley, eking out a living in subsistence agriculture supplemented by fishing and hunting.

The early government of Jamestown, Virginia, funded like New France by a group of absentee investors, blended business and military models. This proved to be a bad idea. Despite high hopes, the Virginia Company experiment failed disastrously, and it was nearly abandoned after only a few years. Men such as John Smith, though in some ways capable leaders, could not keep restless fellow settlers from antagonizing local indigenous groups belonging to a confederacy headed by the chieftain Powhatan. The settler-soldiers refused to farm, and theft of indigenous food stores led to reprisals, spawning decades-long cycles of vengeance. Tsenacommocah

≡ **Chesapeake Bay, c. 1650–1700**

(sen-uh-COMB-uh-cuh), as Powhatan's subjects called the Chesapeake Bay region, was not easily conquered, and indigenous attacks in the 1620s nearly wiped out the first English settlers' plantations.

Eventually, English settlers got the upper hand and began profiting from tobacco exports. Although enslaved Africans arrived as early as 1619, initially indentured English servants were the primary source of labor. Soil exhaustion was rapid, causing the tobacco frontier to sweep inland toward the Appalachian Mountains and southward into North Carolina. Soaring demand for land to cultivate tobacco prompted Indian attacks and culminated in a settler rebellion led by Nathaniel Bacon in 1676. Bacon and some five hundred followers ran Virginia's governor out of Jamestown for allegedly dealing too kindly with native groups. Although colonial authorities rejected Bacon's calls to uproot the Indians, English policy turned sharply toward "removal." As Indians were forced westward, indentured servitude and small plots gave way to African slavery and large plantations.

The stony region dubbed New England, initially settled by religious dissenters called Puritans, followed a distinct trajectory. Soon after arriving more or less by accident in Plymouth, Massachusetts, in 1620 the first "pilgrims," as they called themselves, faced the problem of establishing a working relationship with indigenous peoples in a land of limited agricultural and commercial potential. The colony was sponsored by the Virginia Company, but in 1629 a new corporation, the Massachusetts Bay Company, was chartered by prominent Puritans in England.

Elder churchmen latched onto the rights of self-governance entailed by this charter, and Boston emerged as capital of the deeply religious Massachusetts Bay colony. As in cold New France, survival was a challenge. Servants suffered most in the first hard years; indigenous peoples were largely ignored.

Religious and labor discipline led to some success for early New Englanders, but both also bred division. Dissenters fled southward to found Rhode Island and

≡ **Pilgrims Set Sail on the *Mayflower*** In this iconic seventeenth-century woodcut, a trio of English separatists leaves the temporary refuge of Leiden, a major Dutch university town, to sail to North America on the *Mayflower*. The Pilgrims, as they came to be known, hoped to found a colony in Virginia territory, but after landing by accident on the coast of Massachusetts in 1620, they chose to stay.

Connecticut; others were punished internally. Expansion of subsistence farms throughout the region yielded surplus wheat and other grains, and cod fishing in the Newfoundland Banks grew ever more important, as did whaling. Colonial authorities signed treaties with compliant indigenous neighbors; those who resisted faced enslavement or death. The Puritans were not pacifists, and like Samuel de Champlain and John Smith, they used firearms to terrorizing effect. They also had no qualms about enslaving war captives. As in Virginia, missionary efforts were few, perhaps in part because of emerging English notions of individual religious freedom, but also because of racism. The general pattern of European-indigenous relations in New England, as it would eventually be throughout British North America, was total displacement.

Newfoundland and Nova Scotia were chartered for commercial reasons in the 1620s, the latter disputed with the French for over a century. Proprietary colonies soon followed to the south of New England. Court favorites were given vast tracts of American lands in exchange for promises to defend and develop them as havens for settlers and for the export of raw materials to benefit the mother country. These proprietary colonies later yielded states such as Pennsylvania, Delaware, and Maryland. In 1664, the English captured Dutch New Amsterdam, a fur-trading post established in 1625 and increasingly a site of contraband trade; they renamed it New York. By 1700, England dominated eastern North America from Newfoundland to the Carolinas. Religiously diverse, British North America lacked an overarching structure of governance. In this the English differed from the bureaucratic and centralizing Spanish.

By the early eighteenth century, Virginia, Maryland, the Carolinas, and England's other mid-Atlantic and southern colonies were home to huge, export-oriented plantations. Planters focused first on tobacco, then rice, indigo, and other cash crops. More like the Caribbean and parts of Iberian America than New France or New England, the mid-Atlantic and southeast colonies grew quickly into slave-based societies. The region's trade was dominated by port towns such as Norfolk, Baltimore, and Charleston, their vast hinterlands dotted with great plantation houses and substantial slave quarters. Pockets of indigenous resistance could still be found in the eighteenth century, but native groups wishing to remain independent were increasingly forced westward beyond the Appalachian Mountains. Their place was taken by growing numbers of poor white settlers.

The northeast seaboard colonies, including the thriving port of New York, followed a different, less export-oriented path, although mercantile connections to the Caribbean and other primary goods-producing regions were strong. Rum distilling and re-export became a major New England industry, alongside shipbuilding and fishing. All of these businesses connected north-eastern British America to the Atlantic slave trade, and bulk items such as salt cod soon became central to the diet of enslaved Africans in Jamaica. Perhaps most significant compared with Spanish and Portuguese America was the great freedom to trade with foreigners that English colonists generally enjoyed. This was not legal, but as Chapter 23 will show, England failed to enforce its colonial trading policies until after 1750. When it finally did so, it provoked violent rebellion.

Everyday Life in the Northern Colonies

Given the long winters and relative isolation of the St. Lawrence River basin, life for early French Canadians was both difficult and lonely. Food stores were a major concern, and settlers relied on a blend of native generosity and annual supply ships from France. Thousands of colonists were sent to develop the land, along with soldiers to guard against English or Indian attacks. The result was the militarization of the backcountry, displacing and massacring native groups in a way reminiscent of England's uncompromising "removal" policy.

Jesuit missionaries set out to convert these embattled, indigenous inhabitants to Roman Catholicism. The priests, few in number, concentrated on large semi-sedentary groups such as the Huron, Algonkin, and Ojibwa. Sometimes the missionaries learned local languages, made friends with prominent chieftains or their sons, and found success. At other times, their failures ended in their deaths, memorialized by their brethren as religious martyrdom. French Jesuits did not give up on North American Indians, in any case, and eventually worked their way from the Great Lakes down the Mississippi basin. Military explorers followed, including the nobleman Robert de la Salle, who in 1682 claimed the lower Mississippi, which he called Louisiana, for King Louis XIV (see again Map 21.4).

Life in the American backcountry claimed by France was in many ways dominated by native peoples, a frontier arrangement historian Richard White has labeled "the middle ground." Here at the edge of imperial control indigenous Americans, métis fur traders, and European missionaries, soldiers, and homesteaders all found themselves interdependent. Not everyone found this arrangement to their liking, least of all crown representatives, but on the frontier the social divisions of race, religion, gender, and culture were blurred or overlooked (see Reading the Past: A Swedish Traveler's Description of Quebec). Put another way, "the middle ground" was the most egalitarian space in the early modern Americas. Like Chica da Silva's

READING THE PAST

A Swedish Traveler's Description of Quebec

Pehr ("Peter") Kalm was a Swedish naturalist who visited Canada around 1749. In the following passages, translated from the Swedish in the 1770s, Kalm describes the inhabitants of the Christian Huron village of Lorette, just outside the capital of French Canada, Québec City.

August the 12th. This afternoon I and my servant went out of town, to stay in the country for a couple of days that I might have more leisure to examine the plants that grow in the woods here, and the state of the country. In order to proceed the better, the governor-general had sent for an Indian from Lorette to show us the way, and teach us what use they make of the spontaneous plants hereabouts. This Indian was an Englishman by birth, taken by the Indians thirty years ago, when he was a boy, and adopted by them, according to their custom, instead of a relation of theirs killed by the enemy. Since that time he constantly stayed with them, became a Roman Catholic and married an Indian woman: he dresses like an Indian, speaks English and French, and many of the Indian languages. In the wars between the French and English, in this country [a reference to chronic conflicts preceding the Seven Years' War], the French Indians have made many prisoners of both sexes in the English plantations [i.e., farms], adopted them afterwards, and they married with people of the Indian nations. From hence the Indian blood in Canada is much mixed with European blood, and a great part of the Indians now living owe their origin to Europe. It is likewise remarkable that a great part of the people they had taken during the war and incorporated with their nations, especially the young people, did not choose to return to their native country, though their parents and nearest relations came to them and endeavored to persuade them to it, and though it was in their power to do it. The licentious life led by the Indians pleased them better than that of their European relations; they dressed like the Indians and regulated all their affairs in their way. It is therefore difficult to distinguish them except by their color, which is somewhat whiter than that of the Indians. There are likewise examples of some Frenchmen going amongst the Indians and following their way of life. There is on the contrary scarce one instance of an Indian's adopting the European customs.

Source: Peter Kalm, *Travels into North America*, trans. John Reinhold Forster (London: 1771), 3:184.

Examining the Evidence

1. How does Kalm assess the "cultural divide" and racial mixture in French Canada?

2. What made Indian customs preferable to European ones in this region, according to Kalm?

fluid world in backcountry Brazil, the possibilities could be astonishing, at least in the eyes of outsiders.

Unlike in Spanish or Portuguese America, sexual relations across color lines were relatively rare in British North America, except in frontier outposts. In part, this was a result of demography: European men and women migrated to the eastern seaboard in close to equal numbers over time, and indigenous peoples were relatively few and were rarely incorporated into settler society. When racial mixture occurred, it was most commonly the result of illicit relations between white men and enslaved women of African descent. Such relations, which according to surviving documents were more often forced than consensual or long-term, were most common in the plantation districts of the Chesapeake and Carolina Low Country. Still, some mixed-race children were born in northern cities such as New York and Boston, where slaves and free people of color could be found in close proximity to whites. Throughout the British colonies, blatantly racist "antimiscegenation" laws dating to the seventeenth century also discouraged black-white unions, because these were thought to undermine the social hierarchy. Racial codes and covenants were most rigidly enforced in regions highly dependent on African slavery, namely the mid-Atlantic and southeast. Still, as Virginia planter and future U.S. president Thomas Jefferson's long-term, child-producing relationship with his slave, Sally Hemings, demonstrates, human urges and affinities could override even the strictest social taboos and legal codes.

Slavery existed in New France, but on a small scale. A few Africans could be found in growing towns such as Montreal, but most slaves were indigenous war captives used for household labor. In early New England, enslaved Africans and a few indigenous slaves served in similar roles, and also in artisan workshops and on board ships. Thousands of enslaved Africans lived and worked in the bustling shops and port facilities of New York City by the early eighteenth century, and many more lived and worked on farms in rural Pennsylvania. Slave rebellions were relatively rare in these regions, although the slaves of New York were highly outspoken and sometimes alarmed city authorities. Slave resistance mostly consisted of work stoppages, tool breaking, truancy, and other "passive" means. Faced with racist exclusion, small black religious communities, mostly of the Anglican, Methodist, and Baptist denominations, eventually formed.

Even more distinct slave cultures emerged in regions where Africans predominated, from Maryland to Georgia. Here plantation life took on some of the features of the English Caribbean, with large numbers of enslaved Africans and their descendants concentrated in prison-like barracks within view of great plantation houses. As archaeologists and historians are increasingly discovering, enslaved Africans had a thriving religious and material world of their own, one that contrasted sharply to the tidy, well-heeled world of the English planter families who claimed lordship over them. African religious practices, while muted by comparison with those of the Caribbean or Brazil, were widely known and respected among the enslaved population. Secret shamanistic and medicinal practices were also common. Whites appear to have known virtually nothing about the slaves' hidden culture.

Violent rebellions and mass marronage along the Atlantic seaboard were rare in comparison with the Caribbean or even Brazil. There were simply far more whites who could be mustered to put down an uprising in Virginia or North Carolina than in Jamaica or Barbados, where slaves outnumbered white settlers by huge margins. Geography limited marronage as well. The mountains were distant and inhabited by Indians. During winter, maroons could be more easily tracked by hunters due to diminished forest cover, and they were hard-pressed to find food in the wild. Some slaves ran away to cities, and even to Spanish Florida, but it was nearly impossible to form lasting maroon communities. Unlike Spanish and Portuguese America, slaves' legal access to freedom through self-purchase or emancipation was severely limited, as was access to the religion of the planters. Only in places such as South Carolina were concentrations of recently arrived Africans great enough to create the kinds of "neo-Africas" found in much of Brazil and the Caribbean. Thus, while societies throughout the Americas included a mixture of Europeans, Africans, and indigenous Americans, the relationships among these groups and the hybrid cultures that emerged varied from region to region, depending on local conditions and the goals and beliefs of the colonizers.

COUNTERPOINT: The Maroons of Suriname

FOCUS How did the runaway slaves of Dutch Suriname create a lasting independent state of their own?

In defiance of slavery on plantations and in mines, fugitive Africans and their descendants established free, or "maroon," communities throughout the Americas. Slaves escaped brutal conditions in Hispaniola, Puerto Rico, Cuba, and Panama. Others fled into the hills east and southwest of Mexico City. Still others found refuge in backcountry Venezuela, Colombia, Ecuador, Peru, and Bolivia. Slaves in Portuguese Brazil did likewise, forming in the hills of Alagoas, a small province of northeastern Brazil, the largest maroon confederacy in history: the Quilombo (key-LOAM-boh) of Palmares. Similar maroon settlements emerged in English Jamaica, as well as French Saint-Domingue, Guadeloupe, and Martinique. But it was in the small colony of Dutch Suriname on South America's northern coast that African and African-American fugitives established the Americas' most resilient and distinctive maroon culture.

From Persecution to Freedom

Dutch and Portuguese Jewish planters ejected from Brazil after 1654 brought enslaved Africans to Suriname to grow and process sugar cane. By the 1660s, dozens of plantations dotted the banks of the Saramaka, Suriname, and Marowijne Rivers. Faced not only with intensive, uncompensated labor in the hot sun but also with physical and psychological torture, many of the enslaved escaped upriver into dense forests once inhabited by Carib and Arawakan-speaking indigenous peoples. Sheltered by cataracts, rapids, and winding tributaries, dozens and then hundreds of runaways settled beyond the reach of planters and colonial authorities. If captured, the maroons, male and female, faced dismemberment and public execution, tactics of terror meant to dissuade those on the plantations from fleeing.

By 1700 Suriname's maroons had formed several independent chiefdoms, each augmenting its numbers through periodic raids on the plantations downriver. Women were especially prized. Within a few decades the maroons numbered in the thousands. Taking advantage of the rugged geography of the Suriname interior and adapting to its challenging environment, the maroons carved out a "neo-Africa" in the backlands. After numerous failed expeditions to capture and re-enslave the maroons, plantation owners sought peace in the 1740s, only to return with even larger and better-armed expeditions after 1750. The maroons remained resolute and eventually won freedom from the Dutch government, which sent them arms and other trade goods to keep peace. As early as the late eighteenth century a few maroon groups allowed small numbers of Christian missionaries to visit them, but the missionaries won few converts and most of them soon died of malaria and other tropical diseases.

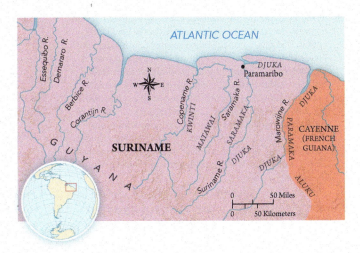

≡ **The Maroons of Suriname**

A Rebel Negro armed & on his guard.

London: Published Decr 2^d 1794 by J. Johnson, St Pauls Church Yard.

Maroon of Suriname The largest and best-armed maroon communities in the Americas emerged in the backlands of Dutch Suriname, on the north coast of South America. Here escaped slaves armed themselves by raiding coastal plantations. Their raids sparked reprisals, which included full-blown wars by the later eighteenth century. A soldier in these wars, John Gabriel Stedman, wrote a sympathetic account of the struggles of slaves and maroons in Suriname that became evidence used by the emerging abolitionist cause in England. Engraver Francesco Bartolozzi followed Stedman's descriptions to depict this maroon warrior on the march, stolen gun in hand and death—or slain enemies—literally at his feet.

Suriname's Distinctive Maroon Culture

Six major maroon groups, the Saramaka, Djuka, Aluku, Paramaka, Matawai, and Kwinti, continue to live in Suriname and neighboring French Guiana, and many retain, thanks to vibrant oral traditions, substantial memories of the period of slavery and the punishing wars the planters prosecuted against them. Some maroon descendants began writing histories of these events as early as the 1880s. Others have moved in the decades following Suriname's independence from the Dutch in 1975 to the coastal capital of Paramaribo or even to Dutch cities such as Amsterdam and Leiden. Maroon culture nevertheless remains very much alive.

Maroon culture in Suriname, built around matrilineal villages, was so striking to early outside visitors that they assumed its rituals and complex artistic traditions to be direct transfers from some part of western Africa. The distinctive architecture, decorative patterns, textile traditions, and musical styles all hark back to Africa. Anthropologists looked for specific links in African art, language, and religion, but found no single traceable root—only broad associations and isolated words. Anthropologists Richard and Sally Price have argued that Suriname's distinctive maroon culture was something new, a product of resistance to colonialism. By combining archival and anthropological research they have shown how strands of western African thought and practice converged with the contingencies of fugitive life at the margins of a European-dominated plantation society. To survive, runaway Africans and their descendants learned to select the best local forest products such as wood for canoes and thatch for roofs, then planted known, imported crops such as bananas and plantains, as well as local ones like maize. Through raids and treaties they obtained cooking pots, textiles, and other manufactured goods, all of which they combined, then decorated, to create a new and distinctive material culture.

Descendants of the original maroon elders have preserved and passed along memories of the long-past horrors and escape from slavery, as in the following passage, recited by the Saramakan leader Lántifáya and recorded by Richard Price in 1978:

> In slavery, there was hardly anything to eat. It was at the place called Providence Plantation. They whipped you till your ass was burning. Then they would give you a bit of plain rice in a calabash [bowl made from the fruit of a tropical American tree]. (That's what we've heard.) And the gods told them that this is no way for human beings to live. They would help them. Let each person go where he could. So they ran.[2]

Conclusion

The colonial Americas underwent the deepest alterations of the world's regions in early modern times, environmentally and socially. Mining of precious metals for export to Europe and Asia drove the Spanish and Portuguese deep into the interior, transforming vast landscapes and giving rise to new social and economic relations. Autonomous indigenous groups, followed later by enslaved Africans, were driven farther inland as they searched for refuge. Punishing forms of labor persisted through the eighteenth century, but indigenous populations began to recover from disease shocks. In the lawless mining frontier of Brazil, racial mixing proved a pragmatic response to demographic realities, challenging notions of propriety and permissiveness.

More rigidly racist social orders developed in the French, Dutch, and English Caribbean and along the eastern seaboard of North America. That a successful and publicly recognized woman of color such as Chica da Silva could have emerged in Jamaica or Virginia is virtually unimaginable. The intense religiosity of the seventeenth and early eighteenth centuries, manifested in both Spanish-American Catholicism and English Puritanism, faded only slowly and left a long-lasting legacy. American dependence on slavery and other forms of forced labor would also die a lingering death. In these and other key ways, the Americas and their European motherlands grew steadily and irreconcilably apart.

✳ review

The major global development in this chapter: The profound social, cultural, and environmental changes in the Americas under colonial rule.

Important Events	
1570	Spanish galleons begin annual service linking Acapulco to Manila
1607	English establish colony at Jamestown, Virginia
1608	French establish colony at Quebec City
1618	Dutch establish colony of New Netherland on upper Hudson River
1625	Dutch settle New Amsterdam on Manhattan Island; English establish colony on Barbados
1630	Dutch capture northeast Brazil
1654	Portuguese drive Dutch from Brazil; some colonists move to Suriname
1655	English seize Jamaica from the Spanish
1664	English take New Amsterdam from Dutch, rename it New York
1671	Henry Morgan's buccaneers sack Panama City
1676	Bacon's Rebellion in Virginia
1694	Great Brazilian maroon community of Palmares destroyed
1695–1800	Discovery in Brazilian interior of gold and diamonds inaugurates Brazil's "gold rush"
1701–1714	War of the Spanish Succession
1720	Brazil elevated to status of viceroyalty
1763	Rio de Janeiro elevated to status of capital of Brazil

KEY TERMS

audiencia (p. 763)
buccaneer (p. 777)
creole (p. 773)
indenture (p. 761)

joint-stock company (p. 784)
mestizaje (p. 767)
mestizo (p. 767)
métis (p. 784)

mulatto (p. 767)
maroon (p. 775)
northwest passage (p. 782)

CHAPTER OVERVIEW QUESTIONS

1. How did the production of silver, gold, and other commodities shape colonial American societies?
2. How and where did northern Europeans insert themselves into territories claimed by Spain and Portugal?

3. How did racial divisions and mixtures compare across the Americas by the mid-eighteenth century?

MAKING CONNECTIONS

1. How did Spanish America's imperial bureaucracy compare with those of the Ottomans and other "gunpowder empires" discussed in Chapters 18 to 20?
2. How did the labor systems of the American colonies compare with those of western Eurasia (see Chapter 19)? With those of Russian and East Asia (see Chapter 20)?

3. What role did religious diversity play in colonial American life compared with contemporary South and Southeast Asia (see Chapter 18)?
4. In what ways did economic developments in colonial Brazil differ from developments in Spanish America?

For further research into the topics covered in this chapter, see the Bibliography at the end of the book. For additional primary sources from this period, see *Sources for World in the Making.*

PART 4

The World from 1750 to the Present

≡ After World War II, colonized peoples created independent nations, sometimes wrenching freedom through armed struggle and bloodshed. Ghanaians celebrated their achievement of nationhood in 1957 with festive ceremonies, including lavish dress such as that worn by this young girl. She adorns her body with a headdress and a salute to independence on her skin along with white ceremonial body markings. Others wore clothing printed with images of new political leaders—a clear sign of this next stage of world-making.

Many of the trends of the early modern period continued after 1750. Global connections continued to intensify, and science and technology advanced at an ever faster pace. As part of their growing competition for land, natural resources, and the control of populations, governments armed themselves with more destructive weaponry. The accelerating rate of change in technology, population growth, consumerism, and the introduction of new livelihoods and forms of government marks the shift from early modern times to what historians call the late modern era, the period from about 1750 to the present.

The great empires of the early modern period—the Qing, Mughal, Ottoman, and Spanish—faced challenges as the modern period opened. Many of these challenges arose from the outside forces, but these empires also faced problems within their borders, such as the enormous costs of military supremacy, religious dissent, natural disasters, and the social changes that accompanied modernity. The Qing, Mughal, Ottoman, and Spanish Empires would all disappear in the late modern period.

Lives and livelihoods were transformed as mechanical power came to substitute for human power in the Industrial Revolution, which began around 1750 in western Europe and spread throughout the globe. Newly created factory work moved production out of the home, and a variety of other new occupations connected with the rise of industry developed. Still, agriculture remained a primary form of work for the vast majority of people until well into the twentieth century. Indeed, modern industry did not displace older ways of doing things all at once. Slavery in fact gave a crucial boost to industrial growth by providing raw materials and food for industrial workers. Although a declining labor system, slavery has remained a livelihood down to the present. Women in the workforce often held the worst jobs and were paid less than men even for equivalent tasks.

Emboldened by new wealth and industrial technology, a cluster of European states, eventually joined by Japan and the United States, built cohesive, effective governments with modern military capabilities and mass armies. During this period, most of them developed constitutional governments based on the rule of law and the explicit elaboration of the rights of citizens. Constitutional government and legal rights were often gained through revolutions or other dramatic changes in rulership, but these states were backed by unified citizens. Historians characterize such states as "nation-states." As they became stronger because of their citizen support, the rising nation-states sought to extend their power through what is known as the "new imperialism." Unlike the expansionists of the early modern period, new imperialists had the "tools of empire" to take over the institutions and economies of other parts of the world more completely. Late modernity saw the imperial nations try to dominate Africa, Asia, and other parts of the world both economically and politically.

Competition and conflict among these imperial nations intensified, as did organized resistance to their rule. In the twentieth century the imperial powers waged two horrific wars—World Wars I and II—in the course of which tens of millions of people died. Eventually, colonized people took advantage of the war-weakened imperialists, winning their freedom and setting up independent states after World War II ended in 1945. The rest of the twentieth century down to the present has been a story of these nation-states asserting their place in the modern world.

Recent modern history is filled with the struggles involved in asserting this independence, first under the conditions of the Cold War between the Soviet Union and United States that followed

World War II, and then during the period of U.S. dominance after 1989. Genocide, civil war, poverty, and an unprecedented migration of peoples globally have characterized human life in the past few decades. Terrorism, the pollution of the earth's atmosphere, and the spread of deadly diseases are also part of our most recent history.

Nonetheless, the world's peoples have attempted to create new forms of world governance to eliminate the worst abuses of modern life.

Writers and artists have innovatively explored modernity's difficulties. Historians and philosophers have also analyzed the consequences of growing military power on the one hand and life-enhancing developments such as medical breakthroughs and the communications revolution on the other. Many of these thinkers believe that there is no alternative to deliberate study of the past as the basis for informed decisions on how we continue to make our world. ■

Atlantic Revolutions and the World 1750–1830

≡ **World in the Making** Simón Bolívar, the "Liberator," traveled the Atlantic world, gaining inspiration from the Enlightenment and revolutionary events. On his return to South America, he helped spearhead the movement for independence there. No democrat, Bolivar learned from hard experience that success demanded support from South America's rich variety of slaves and other workers.

✳ backstory

Rising global trade and maturing slave systems brought wealth to merchants and landowners in many parts of the world during the seventeenth and eighteenth centuries. Emboldened by this newfound wealth, they joined bureaucrats and aristocrats in the struggle for more influence, not only in the great land-based empires such as the Qing, Mughal, and Ottoman states but also in some of the small states of Europe. Except for Spain, these small European states had developed overseas coastal trading posts, which after several centuries they hoped to exploit more efficiently and turn into true empires. They had also built their military capability and gained administrative experience as they fought one another for greater global influence. Maintaining this influence was costly, however. Simultaneously the Scientific Revolution (see Chapter 19) and the beginnings of a movement to think more rationally about government were causing some critics in Europe to question the traditional political and social order.

Simón Bolívar (1783–1830) began life as the privileged son of a family that in the sixteenth century had settled in Caracas, a city in Spanish-controlled South America. His early years were full of personal loss: his father died when he was three, his mother when he was five, and his grandfather, who cared for him after his mother's death, when he was six. Bolívar's extended family sent him to military school and then to Spain to study—typical training for prominent "creoles," as South Americans of European descent were called. Following the death of his young wife, the grieving Bolívar traveled to Paris, where his life changed: he saw the military hero Napoleon crown himself emperor in 1804 and witnessed crowds fill the streets of the capital with joy. "That moment, I tell you, made me think of the slavery of my country and of the glory that would come to the person who liberated it," he later wrote.[1] After a visit to the newly independent United States, Bolívar returned to Caracas in 1807, determined to free his homeland from the oppressions of Spanish rule. He, too, took up arms, leading military campaigns, which along with popular uprisings eventually ousted Spain's government from much of Latin America. For his revolutionary leadership, contemporaries gave him the title "Liberator."

The creation of independent states in Latin America was part of a powerful upheaval in the Atlantic world. North American colonists successfully fought a war of independence against Britain in 1776. The French rose up in 1789 against a monarchy that had bankrupted itself, ironically in part by giving military support to the American rebels. In 1791 a massive slave revolt erupted in the prosperous French sugar colony of Saint-Domingue, leading to the creation of the independent state of Haiti. The independence of Latin American states was globally inspirational. The English poet Lord Byron named his yacht *Bolivar* and in the 1820s went off to liberate Greece from the Ottomans.

These upheavals were connected with a transformation of thought and everyday life in the West called "the Enlightenment." Traders in Asia, Africa, and the Americas had brought ideas and goods to Europe. The arrival of new products such as sugar, coffee, and cotton textiles freed many Europeans' lives from their former limits, and this newfound abundance led to new thinking. Both ordinary people and the upper classes proposed changing society. Ideas from Enlightenment thinkers and global contact affected North American politicians, Caribbean activists, and creole reformers like Simón Bolívar, transforming them into revolutionaries. The impulse for change extended beyond the Atlantic world. In Ottoman-controlled Egypt, French revolutionary forces under the command of Napoleon Bonaparte invaded, claiming to bring new political ideas of liberty. A determined leader, Muhammad Ali, helped drive out the French and then promoted reform himself. Thus, global connections of different kinds played a key role in creating the conditions that sparked the development of new ideas and in providing pathways for the spread of those ideas.

By 1830, when the revolutionary tide in Latin America ended, the map of the world had changed, but that change came at a great cost. Alongside the birth of new nations and a growing belief in political reform, there had been widespread hardship and destruction. Soldiers died by the hundreds of thousands; civilians also perished because political and social change set them against one another. The breakdown of established kingdoms was the work of the warriors, the masses, and determined leaders, but this age of revolution crushed many. Napoleon Bonaparte was condemned to exile, and even so privileged a revolutionary as Bolívar died of utter exhaustion in 1830 just as the new nations of Latin America began their independent existence.

OVERVIEW QUESTIONS

The major global development in this chapter: The Atlantic revolutions and their short- and long-term significance.

As you read, consider:

1. What role did the Scientific Revolution and expanding global contacts play in the cultural and social movement known as the Enlightenment?

2. Why did prosperous and poor people alike join revolutions in the Americas and in France?

3. Why were the Atlantic revolutions so influential, even to the present day?

The Promise of Enlightenment

FOCUS What were the major ideas of the Enlightenment and their impacts?

Europeans in the eighteenth century had a great deal to think about. The scientific revolution had challenged traditional views of nature and offered a new methodology for uncovering nature's laws. Reports from around the world on foreign customs, ways of conducting government, alternative techniques in agriculture, and trade practices fueled discussion worldwide but especially among Europeans. Moreover, participation in this intellectual ferment was not limited to the political and social elite. As literacy, already advanced in Chinese and Japanese cities, spread in Europe, ever more people were caught up in the debate over social, political, and economic change. These wide-ranging reconsiderations are collectively called the Enlightenment.

A New World of Ideas

Some Enlightenment writers hammered away at the abuses of monarchies and proposed representative rule based on the consent of the governed—a proposal that later became the foundation of many states. The will of a monarch is not the best basis for government, English philosopher John Locke wrote late in the seventeenth century. Rather, he maintained, governments should be established rationally, by mutual consent of the governed. The idea of compact or **contract government** grew from Locke's philosophy that people were born free, equal, and rational, and that natural rights, including personal freedoms, were basic to all humans. In Locke's view, governments were formed when people made the rational choice to give up a measure of freedom and create institutions that could guarantee natural rights and protect everyone's property. If a government failed to fulfill these purposes, the people had the right to replace it. Locke's ideas justified the situation in seventeenth-century England, where citizens and the Parliament had twice ousted their king.

In contrast to Locke, French writers Voltaire and Baron Louis Montesquieu criticized their own society's religious and political abuses by referring to practices in China and elsewhere beyond Europe. They set their widely read writings in faraway lands or used wise foreigners to show Europe's backwardness. A wealthy trained jurist, Montesquieu in *The Persian Letters* (1721) featured a Persian ruler visiting Europe and writing back home of the strange goings-on. The continent was full of magicians, Montesquieu's hero reports, such as those who could turn wine and wafers into flesh—a mocking reference to the Christian sacrament of communion. Voltaire, a successful author thrown several times into jail for insulting the authorities, portrayed worthy young men cruelly treated by priests and kings in his rollicking novels *Zadig* (1747) and *Candide* (1759). Voltaire asked for a society based on merit, not on aristocracy of birth: "There is nothing in Asia that resembles the European nobility: nowhere in the Orient does one find an order of citizens distinct from all the rest . . . solely by their birth."[2] Voltaire did not have the story quite right, but other Enlightenment thinkers joined his call for reason, hard work, and opportunity in both economic life and politics.

Swiss-born Jean-Jacques Rousseau took up the theme of freedom and opportunity in many influential writings. In *The Social Contract* (1762) he claimed that "man

contract government
A political theory that views government as stemming from the people, who agree to surrender a measure of personal freedom in return for a government that guarantees protection of citizens' rights and property.

is born free," but because of despotic government "he is everywhere in chains." As for the process of shaping the modern citizen, Rousseau's best-selling novel *Emile* (1762) describes the ways in which a young boy is educated to develop many practical skills. Instead of learning through rote memory, as was common, Emile masters such skills as carpentry and medicine by actually working at them, and he spends much time outdoors, getting in touch with nature by living away from corrupt civilization. Like China's Kangxi emperor (the fourth of the Qing dynasty), whom Enlightenment thinkers held up as a model, Emile becomes a polymath—that is, someone with a knowledge of many subjects and numerous skills, especially those that could earn him a livelihood. Emile thus becomes a responsible citizen who can fend for himself following natural laws, not despotically imposed ones.

Enlightenment thinkers also rethought the economy. In 1776, Scottish philosopher Adam Smith published one of the most influential Enlightenment documents, *On the Wealth of Nations*. Citing China as an important example throughout, Smith proposed to free the economy from government monopolies and mercantilist regulations. This idea of **laissez faire** (French for "let alone") became part of the theory called **liberalism**, which endorsed economic and personal freedom guaranteed by the rule of law. Smith saw trade as benefiting an individual's character because it required cooperation with others in the process of exchanging goods. The virtues created by trade were more desirable than the military swaggering and confrontation of aristocratic lives, and he continually stressed that alongside individualism there needed to be concern for the well-being of the community as a whole. Slavery, he argued, was inefficient and ought to be done away with. Still other Enlightenment writers said that a middle-class way of life promoted sensibility, love of family, thrift, and hard work—again, in stark contrast to the promiscuous and spendthrift habits these reformers saw in the nobility.

Enlightenment thinkers explicitly drew on the knowledge acquired through global economic connections. Such connections also made it possible for Enlightenment ideas to spread around the world. Some Japanese thinkers and officials wanted to learn about recent Western breakthroughs in practical subjects as well as scientific practices based on rational observation and deduction. Chinese scholars, though not directly influenced by Enlightenment thought, were reflecting on issues of good government and the capacities of the individual within the imperial system. Future nation builders in the North American colonies—Benjamin Franklin, John Adams, and Thomas Jefferson—were steeped in both the practical and political sides of the Enlightenment, running businesses, designing buildings, conducting scientific experiments, and writing political documents.

Enlightenment thought reached many in Western society—high and low, male and female. Population growth in cities such as Paris opened neighborhoods and

laissez faire
An economic doctrine that advocates freeing economies from government intervention and control.

liberalism
A political ideology that emphasizes free trade, individual rights, and the rule of law to protect rights as the best means for promoting social and economic improvement.

public sphere
A cultural and political environment that emerged during the Enlightenment, where members of society gathered to discuss issues of the day.

work life, allowing new ideas to flourish. Women of the wealthier classes conducted salons—that is, meetings in their homes devoted to discussing the latest books and findings. German Jewish women, often kept at a distance from Christians, made a name for themselves by forming such groups. Along with coffeehouses in European and colonial cities, modeled on those in the Ottoman Empire, salons created a **public sphere** in which people could meet outside court circles to talk about current affairs. Together with the new public libraries, reading groups, and scientific clubs that dotted the Atlantic world, they built new community bonds and laid the groundwork for responsible citizenship. Instead of a monarchical government single-handedly determining thought and policy, ordinary people in Europe and its colonies, relying on knowledge gained from public discussion, could express their opinions on the course of events and thereby undermine government censorship.

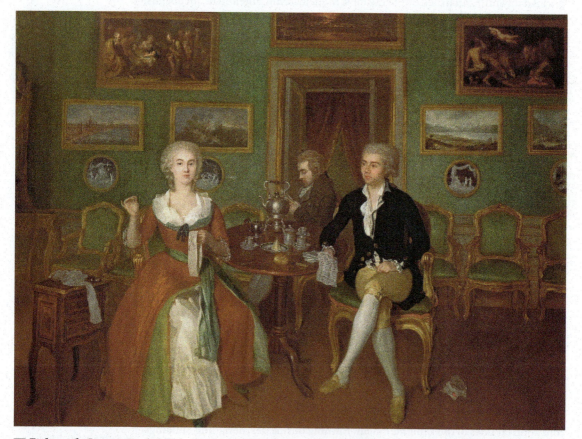

≡ **Eighteenth-Century English Drawing Room**   When drinking their tea imported from Asia, middle- and upper-class Europeans aimed for elegance, inspired by Asian tea rituals. They used porcelain, whose production European manufacturers had recently figured out, and wore sparkling white muslin, probably imported from India, which produced high-quality cloth that Europeans valued above cotton from anywhere else.

The ideals of the Enlightenment were well represented in the *Encyclopedia* (1751–1772) of France's Denis Diderot. This celebrated work contained dozens of technical drawings of practical machinery that could advance prosperity. The *Encyclopedia* described the freedoms and rights nature endowed on *all* people, not just aristocrats. Like Rousseau, Diderot maintained that in a natural state all people were born free and equal. French writer Olympe de Gouges further proposed that there was no difference among people of different skin colors. "How are the Whites different from [the Black] race? . . . Why do blonds not claim superiority over brunettes?" she asked in her "Reflections on Negroes" (1788). "Like all the different types of animals, plants, and minerals that nature has produced, people's color also varies."[3] Essayists in the *Encyclopedia* added that women too were born free and endowed with natural rights.

Many of the working people of Europe's growing towns and cities responded enthusiastically to the ideas set forth by Enlightenment philosophers such as Voltaire and Rousseau. The French glassworker Jacques Ménétra, for example, acquired and also distributed these new antireligious and egalitarian ideas as he moved from city to town and village, installing glass windows. With some religious schooling and then an apprenticeship in his trade, Ménétra, like his fellow journeymen artisans, led this kind of mobile life as a young man before establishing his own shop in Paris. During his travels, he provided news of the Parisian thinkers to artisans along his route. Young journeymen like Ménétra helped make the Enlightenment an affair not only of the well-born but also of many average people.

Enlightenment and the Old Order

Despite its critique of monarchs, church officials, and the aristocracy, "Enlightenment" was a watchword of some of Europe's most powerful rulers. "Enlightened" rulers came to sense that more rational government could actually strengthen their regimes, for example by increasing governmental efficiency and tax revenues. Instead of touting his divine legacy, Prussian king Frederick the Great (r. 1740–1786) called a ruler someone who would "work efficiently for the good of the state" rather than "live in lazy luxury, enriching himself by the labor of the people."[4] A musician and poet, Frederick studied several languages, collected Chinese porcelain, and advocated toleration. For him, Enlightenment made monarchs stronger. Spreading to Russia, the Enlightenment moved Catherine the Great (r. 1762–1796) to sponsor the writing of a dictionary of the Russian language, to correspond with learned thinkers such as Diderot, and to work to improve the education of girls. Additionally, Catherine's goal was to put a stop to aristocrats' "idle time spent in luxury and other vices corrupting to the morals," as she put it, and instead transform the nobility into active and informed administrators of her far-flung empire and its diverse peoples (see Seeing the Past: Portrait of Catherine the Great).[5]

SEEING THE PAST

Portrait of Catherine the Great

Catherine the Great was a monarch of towering ability and ambition. Although her regime was known for smashing peasant uprisings and territorial conquests, it also promoted the arts and knowledge. Catherine commissioned the first dictionary of the Russian language and communicated with the greatest thinkers of the Enlightenment. While sponsoring education, she tried to reform her government to increase its power. In this regard, Enlightenment was not just about the fine arts but also about generally raising the economic and political profile of the monarchy through rationally devised policies.

Enlightenment thinkers often referred to the excellent customs and the rational policies of non-Western monarchs of their day—especially those in China—but also prized classical Greece and Rome for their democratic and republican forms of government. For this image, a skilled Parisian craftsperson of the 1760s chose Minerva—Roman goddess of both war and wisdom—as the figure

Catherine the Great as the Roman Goddess Minerva
(Hillwood Estate, Museum & Gardens;
Photo by Ed Owen.)

closest to the celebrated Catherine. The luxurious detail on this round box assures us that it was destined for an aristocratic palace, perhaps that of the monarch herself.

Examining the Evidence

1. What does this depiction of the empress as Minerva tell you about the society over which Catherine ruled?

2. How does this image of leadership compare with others you have seen, including those of U.S. presidents? How do you account for the differences? For the similarities?

The Spanish monarchy in the eighteenth century likewise instituted a series of policy changes called the Bourbon Reforms, named after the ruling "Bourbon" family of monarchs. They aimed to make the monarchy financially sound by taxing the colonies more efficiently. Spain's rulers also attempted to limit the church's independence. Often opposing slavery and promoting better treatment of native peoples, the Jesuit order, for instance, had many followers in Spain's "New World" empire. Thus the order was an alternate source of allegiance: the monarchy outlawed it.

Leaders of the Spanish colonies adopted many Enlightenment ideas, including scientific farming and improvements in mining—subjects dear to forward-looking thinkers who read the *Encyclopedia*. In Mexico, reformers saw the education of each woman as central to building responsible government. As one journalist put it, under a mother's care the young citizen "grows, is nourished, and acquires his first notions of Good and Evil. [Therefore] women have even more reason to be enlightened than men."[6] In this view, motherhood was not a simple biological act but a livelihood critical to a strong national life.

European prosperity depended on the productivity of slaves in the colonies, and wealthy slave owners used Enlightenment fascination with nature to devise scientific explanations justifying the oppressive system. Though many Enlightenment thinkers such as Olympe de Gouges wanted equality for "noble savages," in slave owners' minds Africans were by nature inferior and thus rightly subject to exploitation. Scientists captured Africans for study and judged racial inferiority to be a "scientific fact." Others justified race-based slavery in terms of character: blacks were, one British observer explained, "conceited, proud, indolent and very artful" in contrast to the egalitarian and hard-working European.[7] Thus, some strands of Enlightenment thought helped buyers and sellers of Africans and native Americans argue that slavery was useful and rational, especially because slaves could produce wealth and help society as a whole make progress.

Popular Revolts in an Age of Enlightenment

Popular uprisings in many parts of the world, including in slave societies, showed the need for improved government. In Russia, people throughout society came to protest serfdom's irrationality and unfairness. In 1773 the discontent of many serfs crystallized around Emel'ian Ivanovich Pugachev, once an officer in the Russian army, who claimed to be Peter III, the dead husband of Catherine. Tens of thousands of peasants, joined by rebellious workers, serf soldiers in Catherine's overworked armies, and Muslim minorities rose up, calling for the restoration of

Pugachev Uprising in Russia, 1773

Pugachev, alias Peter, to the throne. Promised great riches for their support, serfs plundered noble estates and killed aristocrats. They justified revolt in slogans and songs: "O woe to us slaves living for the masters. . . . how shameful and insulting / That another who is not worthy to be equal with us / Has so many of us in his power."[8] The rebellion was put down only with difficulty. Once Catherine's forces captured Pugachev, they cut off his arms and legs, then his head, and finally hacked his body to pieces—just punishment, nobles believed, for the crimes of this "monster" against the monarchy and upper classes.

Uprisings among the urban poor, farmworkers, and slaves also occurred in the Caribbean and other parts of the Western Hemisphere. Slaves fled their masters to Maroon communities far from plantations. Native peoples in Latin America protested harsh conditions, which only grew worse with Spain's demand for more revenue. Some envisioned the complete expulsion of the Spaniards or the overthrow of the wealthy creoles, who owned estates and plantations. Between 1742 and 1783, several different groups in Peru attempted to restore Inca power and end the tax burden inflicted by the Bourbon Reforms. Backed by his determined, talented wife Michaela Bastida, charismatic trader and wealthy landowner Tupac Amaru II (TOO-pack a-MAH-roo), an indigenous leader who took his name from the Inca leader of the late sixteenth century, led tens of thousands against corrupt government. Eventually captured by Spanish authorities, Tupac Amaru II had his tongue cut out, was drawn and quartered by four horses, and finally was beheaded—after first watching the execution of his family. Rebellions continued amid the complexities of Enlightenment.

Revolution in North America

FOCUS What factors lay behind the war between North American colonists and Great Britain?

The Atlantic world was part of a global trading network. A Boston newspaper in the 1720s advertised the sale of Moroccan leather, Indian chintz and muslin fabrics, South American mahogany, and Asian tea. The global livelihoods of merchants, fishermen, and sailors enabled the British colonies to grow prosperous and cosmopolitan, engaged in all facets of Enlightenment and commercial growth.

The British Empire and the Colonial Crisis 1764–1775

In the eighteenth century European states waged increasingly costly wars to boost global power. The expense of the Seven Years' War of 1756–1763 was enormous as Europeans also fought to gain influence in South Asia, the Philippines, the Caribbean, and North America. Ultimately beating both the French and the Spanish, Britain received all of French Canada and Florida at the end of the war (see Map 22.1). It wanted higher colonial taxation to recoup its expenses and pay the costs of administering its empire.

In 1764 the British Parliament raised taxes on molasses with the Sugar Act, on printed material and legal documents with the Stamp Act (1765), and on useful commodities such as paper, glass, and paint with the Townshend Acts (1767)—all of them important to colonists' everyday lives. Tapping England's own history of revolution and the new political theories, colonial activists protested, insisting that if they were going to be taxed, they needed direct representation in the English Parliament. This argument followed Locke's theory of the social contract: a government where citizens were not represented had no right to take their property in taxes. With a literacy rate of 70 percent among men and 40 percent among women in the North American colonies, new ideas about government and reports of British misdeeds spread easily.

The Birth of the United States 1775–1789

When yet another tax was placed on prized imported tea, a group of Bostonians, disguised as native Americans, dumped a load of tea into the harbor in December 1773. The British government responded to the "Boston Tea Party" by closing the seaport's thriving harbor. As tensions escalated, colonial representatives gathered for an all-colony Continental Congress that resulted in a coordinated boycott of British goods. In April 1775 artisans and farmers in Lexington and Concord fought British troops sent to confiscate a stockpile of ammunition from rebellious colonists. On July 4, 1776, the Continental Congress issued its "Declaration of Independence," a short, dramatic document written largely by Thomas Jefferson that aimed—like the Enlightenment itself—to convert its readers to the side of reason in matters of government. The Declaration argued that the monarchy was tyrannical and had forfeited its right to rule. It went on to articulate an Enlightenment doctrine of rights—the famous rights of "life, liberty, and the pursuit of happiness." Some of the rebel colonists likened themselves to "slaves" lacking individual freedom, drawing a parallel—even though some of them, including Thomas Jefferson, were slave owners—with slave rebels across the Western world.

≡ MAP 22.1   Colonial Crisis and Revolution in North America, 1754–1789 The Seven Years' War left Great Britain with a hefty war debt and the threat of Native American clashes. To prevent the latter, the Proclamation of 1763 forbade colonists' settlement west of the Appalachians. Taxation to fund the debt affected all colonists, from northern merchants to owners of southern plantations, sparking resistance until the British surrender at Yorktown in 1781.

The British sent a powerful army and navy to defeat the colonists, while colonists engaged in war both against the British and viciously among themselves. As British forces burned coastal towns and occupied New York, Philadelphia, and other crucial centers of commerce and government, George Washington headed the Continental Army, which lacked clothing, food, pay, and efficient recruiting. In the background, revolutionaries and loyalists burned one another's property and otherwise inflicted horrific damage on neighbors holding opposite views. Even so, against large British armies in battle formation, the colonists proved effective at guerrilla warfare, sniping with bows and arrows if they lacked guns. Others joined in: colonial women fed armies in their vicinity, knitted and sewed clothing, and cared for the wounded. Critical help arrived from countries interested in blocking British expansionism, foremost among these France but also Spain and the Netherlands. Substantial assistance from the French under the Marquis de Lafayette ultimately brought the British to surrender at Yorktown in 1781 (see again Map 22.1).

Growing immigration had made the United States ethnically diverse well before its founding. Uprisings and disputes over trade and taxation followed the 1781 victory, showing that a strong **federation**, or union of states, was needed. The Articles of Confederation, drawn up in 1777 as a provisional constitution, proved weak because they gave the central government few powers. A "frail and tottering edifice seems ready to fall upon our heads and crush us beneath its ruins," Alexander Hamilton, Washington's trusted aide, warned.[9] In 1787, a Constitutional Convention met in Philadelphia to draft a new constitution. Two-thirds of the delegates were educated lawyers, many of them versed in Enlightenment thought, but some had humble beginnings, including a delegate from Connecticut who had worked as a shoemaker before becoming a merchant. Most, however, were men of property: George Washington, who presided over the meeting, not only had a substantial plantation (like others in the group) but also was the owner and manager of his wife's hundreds of slaves.

The Constitution enshrined the contract theory of government from the Enlightenment with its opening words: "We the people of the United States in order to form a more perfect union . . . ." The document also reflected a primary motive of these well-off founders in creating a strong government: to protect the right to private property. What, however, should the Constitution say about slaves, individuals who were themselves property? Should slavery be acknowledged, as many of the representatives from the southern states wanted, or should it be abolished, as major participants such as Alexander Hamilton of New York believed? Born in the Caribbean of a poor family, Hamilton's job as a bookkeeper while still a young

federation A union of equal and sovereign states rather than a thoroughly integrated nation.

teenager gave him valuable connections with merchant families in North America; they helped him relocate to New York City, where he attended Columbia College and then studied law. His roots in the Caribbean made Hamilton abhor the slave system. "The existence of slavery," he wrote, "makes us fancy many things that are founded neither in reason or experience."[10]

Hamilton lost this argument. The new Constitution, formally adopted in 1789, echoed the aims of the revolution and the rights of individuals—except slaves and women. It fostered commerce and the spirit of industry by providing stable laws.

Samuel Jennings, *Liberty Displaying the Arts and Sciences* **(1792)** This painting shows Liberty displaying Enlightenment accomplishments in the arts and sciences to freed slaves. Although across the West, Liberty was usually depicted as a woman, the principles of equal citizenship expressed in the Constitution and the Declaration of Independence did not apply to women, African Americans, or native Americans. (The Library Company of Philadelphia)

Its banking structure promised reliability in the international credit markets, and it advanced U.S. involvement with the global economy by lifting restrictions on commerce and business life. The political rights given to the minority—the enfranchised white men—by the U.S. Constitution and by state law inspired this burst of activity, innovation, and enterprise. To achieve the Constitution, the founders, as men of the Enlightenment, negotiated, made concessions, and came to hard-fought agreements. The U.S. Constitution thus became a monument to consensus politics and to the form of government called a **republic**. Given the heated disputes, George Washington wrote to the Marquis de Lafayette in France that achieving the document was "little short of a miracle."

The French Revolution and the Napoleonic Empire

> ↘ **FOCUS** What changes emerged from the French Revolution and Napoleon's reign?

In 1780, on the eve of victory in its War of Independence, the fledgling United States had only about 2.7 million people, but its triumph had a powerful impact on the far larger population in Europe. "The [French] nation has been awakened by our revolution," Ambassador Thomas Jefferson wrote in 1788 to President George Washington, "they feel their strength, they are enlightened."[11] More directly, the cost of French participation in global warfare with Britain, including the North American War of Independence, hastened the collapse of the monarchy. France's taxation policy put the cost of warfare on the poor and exempted the wealthy from paying their share. In 1789, less than a decade after the victory at Yorktown, the French people took matters into their own hands, ultimately ousting the king and launching a republic. The French Revolution resonated far and wide, and under the French conqueror Napoleon Bonaparte, revolutionary principles advanced across Europe and beyond, even as Europe's monarchs struggled to halt the march of "liberty, equality, fraternity."

From Monarchy to Republic 1789–1792

Having borrowed recklessly (as had his predecessors) to pursue wars and princely living, the French monarch Louis XVI (r. 1774–1793) in 1787 was met with a firm "no" when he asked for more loans from bankers and financial help from the aristocracy. The king was forced to summon the Estates General—a representative

republic A political system in which the interests of all citizens are represented in the government.

body that had not met since 1614—to the palace at Versailles to bail out the government. Members of the Estates General arrived at their meeting in May 1789, carrying lists of grievances from people of all occupations and walks of life.

Competing agendas converged at the meeting of the Estates General: those of the monarchy to repair its finances; those of the nobility to take power from the king; and those of the common people, who at the time were suffering from crop failures, heavy taxation, governmental restraints on trade, and a slowdown in business because of bad harvests. The meeting quickly broke down when representatives of the middle classes and common people left the general meeting. They were joined by sympathetic, reform-minded aristocrats and clergymen such as Abbé Sieyès, who asked what this mass of commoners meant to the kingdom. "Everything," he responded to his own question. "What has it been until now in the political order? Nothing."[12] This varied group of representatives declared itself a National Assembly of "citizens" of France, not the lowly subjects of a king.

Soon much of France was overwhelmed by enthusiasm for this new government based on citizen consent. On July 14, 1789, crowds in Paris stormed the Bastille, a notorious prison where people could be incarcerated simply at the king's orders. The liberation of the Bastille by the people of Paris so symbolized the French Revolution that it became France's national holiday, just as the Declaration of Independence on July 4 eventually made that Independence Day in the United States.

In its first years, Enlightenment principles and strong citizen protest motivated the legislators of the National Assembly, who like U.S. revolutionary leaders were mostly from the propertied classes. With peasants rioting in the countryside against the unfair rule of aristocratic landowners, in August 1789 the nobility surrendered its privileges, such as its exemption from taxation. Later that month the National Assembly issued the "Declaration of the Rights of Man and of the Citizen," an announcement of the basic rights possessed by each citizen, including rights to free speech, to property ownership, and to safety from arbitrary acts of the state. In 1791, Olympe de Gouges issued a "Declaration of the Rights of Woman and the Female Citizen," declaring, "Woman is born free and lives equal to man in her rights."

In October 1789, the market women of Paris, protesting the soaring cost of food, marched to the palace of Versailles and captured the royal family, bringing it to live "with the people" in the city and thus showing that monarchs existed to serve the people. The government passed laws reducing the power of the clergy and abolishing the guild system and other institutions that slowed trade. Suddenly people could pursue the jobs they wanted on their own terms outside guild restrictions. Enthusiastic demonstrations by newly empowered citizens helped make the liberal Enlightenment program of freedom for the person and for trade a reality.

≡ **Women's March to Versailles** Although the French Revolution began with the ceremonial meeting of the Estates General, people from many livelihoods soon joined in. In October 1789, the market women of the city marched to the royal palace at Versailles, returning the monarch to the city of Paris, where they could keep an eye on him.

These early acts of the French Revolution stirred the hearts and minds of many. Women petitioned for a range of rights, and for a time the power of the husband over his wife was eliminated. Across the English Channel, poet William Wordsworth captured the rush of youthful belief that through newly active citizens the world would be reborn: "Bliss was it in that dawn to be alive, / But to be young was very heaven!" The Declaration of the Rights of Man and of the Citizen inspired the addition of a Bill of Rights to the U.S. Constitution, which outlined the essential rights, such as freedom of speech, that the government could never overthrow. English author Mary Wollstonecraft penned *A Vindication of the Rights of Man* (1790) in defense of the revolution.

Two years later Wollstonecraft followed up with *A Vindication of the Rights of Woman* (1792), a globally influential work that saw men's privileges over women as similar to the French aristocracy's privileges over the peasantry. Wollstonecraft wrote from bitter experience. Born into a well-to-do family, her brother not only inherited most of the family estate but also took his sisters' inheritances for himself. Destitute, they had to earn a living without having been trained to do so. Wollstonecraft first became a governess and then a journalist, whose classic works protested that the legal privileges of men allowed them to impoverish women. Wollstonecraft's book was evidence for Mirza Abu Talib Khan's *Vindication of the Liberties of the Asiatic Women* (1801). A well-traveled Indian official, he claimed that women in Asia had complete control over family funds whereas European women were left utterly without resources.

War, Terror, and Resistance 1792–1799

As revolutionary fervor spread across national borders, in the spring of 1792 the royal houses of Austria and Prussia declared war on France. Wartime brought to power the lawyer Maximilien Robespierre, who became convinced that it was time to do away with the monarchy and to establish a republic. Patriotic holidays to replace religious ones, dishes with revolutionary slogans, and new laws making the family more egalitarian turned the country upside down. Workshops were set up for the unemployed to earn a living by making war goods, and all citizens were urged to help the war effort. In 1793 both King Louis XVI and Queen Marie Antoinette were executed by guillotine—an "enlightened" mode of execution because it killed swiftly and reduced suffering. France prepared for total transformation.

Claiming that there could be no rights in wartime, Robespierre and the newly created Committee of Public Safety stamped out free speech, squashed the women's clubs aiming to gain the rights of citizenship, and executed people such as Olympe de Gouges. This was the Terror, during which the government murdered people from all classes and livelihoods—from the highest to the lowest—because enemies of the republic, the government claimed, lurked on all rungs of the social ladder. To justify its actions, the Committee of Public Safety turned to Rousseau's idea of the **general will**. Rousseau's interpretation of the social contract maintained that once agreement among citizens had created a state, that state acted with a higher wisdom with which truly loyal citizens could not disagree, especially in wartime. The "general will" or collective spirit justified the Terror's mass executions and the suspension of individual rights and even free thought. The concept was one of the French Revolution's most powerful revolutionary legacies, enacted

general will The political concept that once agreement among citizens creates a state, that state is endowed with a higher wisdom about policies with which virtuous citizens could not disagree.

not only by totalitarian regimes in the twentieth century but even by democracies during times of stress.

By 1794, largely because the war was turning in France's favor, moderate politicians regained public support and overthrew Robespierre's faction. Simultaneously, France's revolutionary armies went on the offensive, spreading the idea of rights, constitutions, and republicanism to countries across Europe. These citizen-soldiers believed in republican government, especially the upward mobility in the revolutionary army. A newly minted officer, the young Napoleon Bonaparte (1769–1821), seized the opportunity.

Napoleon's Reign 1799–1815

Bonaparte, born into a modest Corsican family, became commander-in-chief of the French revolutionary army in Italy at the age of twenty-seven. A student of Enlightenment thought and an avid reader of history, Napoleon entered the army just as its aristocratic officers were fleeing the revolution by moving to other countries. Rising to power through the ranks, he attempted the conquest of Egypt in 1798 but escaped the country as he began to lose the campaign. Returning to France, Napoleon took advantage of the turbulent political scene to seize power, crowning himself emperor in 1804. "As in Rome, it took a dictator to save the Republic,"[13] Napoleon said.

Yet Napoleon solidified many revolutionary changes, notably those concerning citizenship and the right to private property, as outlined in the Code Napoleon (1803–1804), a new set of basic laws. The Code set rules for property, ending restrictions on sales of the nobility's land and establishing rules for assets such as bonds, stocks, and mortgages. The Code advanced prosperity by providing secure laws for commercial, industrial, and agricultural livelihoods; Napoleon's founding of national schools for teachers, engineers, and the military served this end too. In the realm of family law, however, the Code reversed gains made by women during the revolution by making the wages and other property of married women the legal property of their husbands and by not allowing them to be guardians of their own children. Financial impoverishment gave women no choices in life but to remain loyal wives—principles that Napoleon's triumphant armies spread through Europe and that encouraged imitators around the world. He thus enforced Rousseau's idea that women should raise the next generation of citizens but not be equal citizens themselves.

Maintaining loyalty by keeping the nation at war and plundering other countries, Napoleon launched successful wars against Spain, the German states, and Italy (see Map 22.2). Then, in 1812, he made a disastrous attempt to invade and conquer Russia. The Russian army, the Russian people, and deadly winter conditions combined to deal him a catastrophic defeat. A coalition of German, Russian, Austrian, and British forces defeated Napoleon in Paris in 1814 and then definitively at Waterloo in 1815.

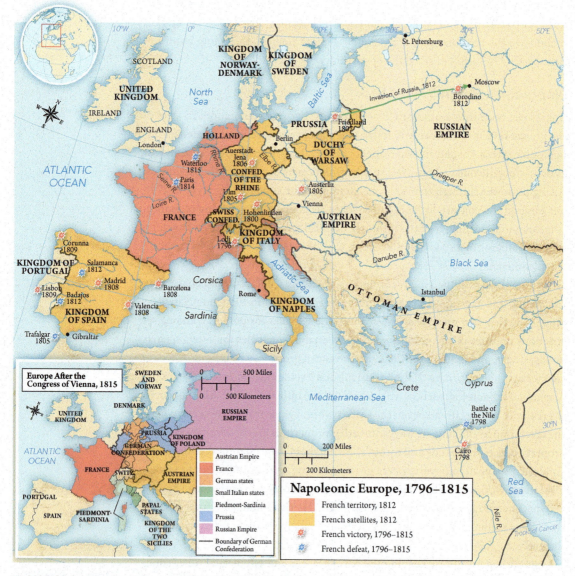

≡ **MAP 22.2 Napoleonic Europe, 1796–1815** Napoleon's Europe was tumultuous and bloody until 1815, when the allied forces of Austria, Prussia, Russia, and Great Britain finally defeated the French emperor's "Grand Army." French forces brought revolutionary ideas and aroused national feeling but suffered from imperial overreach; victors redrew the political map of Europe to ensure a balance of power.

At the Congress of Vienna (1814–1815), the coalition resettled the boundaries of European states in hopes of blocking further reforms (see again Map 22.2). It was far too late to stamp out the principles of constitutional government and natural rights, however. Monarchs (including France's) restored to their thrones in 1815 found limitations on their powers. Moreover, Napoleon's military campaigns spread principles of rights and citizenship and lodged them in people's minds around the world.

Muhammad Ali and the Revolutionary Spirit in Egypt

Despite Napoleon's ultimate defeat, the revolutionary legacy fomented reform activity for more rational government not only across Europe but also outside it. When the French revolutionary armies under Napoleon invaded Egypt in 1798, they faced the forces of the Ottoman Empire, whose administration, like that of other great land-based empires, was in decline. From time to time a modernizing sultan came to power hoping to enact reforms, but the entrenched powers of the janissaries (elite troops) and ulamas (learned Muslim authorities) usually put a stop to such efforts. The similarly entrenched Mamluk (MAM-luke) military force that ran the Egyptian government increasingly alienated landlords and other elites with its violence and demands for more taxes.

To some among these elites, the Atlantic revolutions provided a wealth of ideas for reform. Napoleon entered the country accompanied by a huge team of doctors, artists, scientists, and other learned men armed with proposals for more enlightened rule. Amid combined resistance from local Mamluk leaders, Ottomans, and British, the French army departed Egypt, leaving behind rising interest in European ideas, political innovation, and technology.

Muhammad Ali (1769–1849) was a prime student of "enlightened" ways. An officer in the Ottoman forces, Muhammad Ali had worked his way up the military ranks during the anti-French campaign. Born in the Ottoman Balkans (present-day Albania), Muhammad Ali began his career as a merchant before the Ottoman army drafted him as part of the Albanian quota of young men owed to the Ottomans. Muhammad Ali's rise to power was based on military accomplishments and on the negotiating skills he learned as a merchant. As a politician he exchanged favors with ordinary people and persuaded wealthy traders and soldiers alike to support his ouster of the hated Mamluks.

Appointed viceroy in 1805, Muhammad Ali set out to modernize Egypt, hiring French and other European administrators, technicians, and military men to advise him. Illiterate until he was forty-seven, he had many works translated into Arabic, the translations being read to him as they progressed. One major work, a translation of Italian political theorist Machiavelli's *The Prince*, he cut short

≣ **Napoleon Celebrates the Birthday of Muhammad** Napoleon's invasion of Egypt simultaneously brutalized and tried to accommodate Egyptians. The French army ransacked homes and public buildings, but some Egyptians welcomed the books and scientific drawings Napoleon made available to them in the name of Enlightenment.

because the message was "commonplace," Muhammad Ali reportedly announced. "I see clearly that I have nothing to learn from Machiavelli. I know many more tricks than he knew."[14] He advanced economic specialization in the country, sponsoring the large-scale production of cotton by several hundred thousand slaves while discouraging agriculture that was not for the market. Centralization of government, founding of public schools, improved transportation, and tighter bureaucratic control of Islam rounded out Muhammad Ali's reforms. His death in 1849 left his dream to make Egypt fully independent of the Ottomans unfulfilled, but he remained for many the founder of modern Egypt.

Revolution Continued in the Western Hemisphere

⬎ **FOCUS** What were the motives and methods of revolutionaries in the Caribbean and Latin America?

Such was the strength of late eighteenth-century global contacts that news of the French and American Revolutions quickly spread to other parts of the Atlantic world. In the Western Hemisphere, revolutions broke out on the island of Hispaniola, motivating slave revolts elsewhere and arousing fear among whites. In Latin America, rebellion erupted not only among slaves and oppressed workers but also among middle- and upper-class creoles such as Simón Bolívar who wanted independence from Spain and Portugal. The Napoleonic Wars disturbed global trade, adding further to discontent and swelling the calls for political change.

Revolution in Haiti 1791–1804

News of the French Revolution spread to the Caribbean island of Hispaniola, where the sugar plantations and coffee farms enriched merchants, plantation owners, and sugar refiners—whites and free blacks alike. The western part of the island was the French colony of Saint-Domingue (san-doe-MANGH, modern Haiti). The eastern part of Hispaniola was Santo Domingo (modern Dominican Republic), a colony of Spain. Saint-Domingue was the wealthiest colony in the region, in part because the newly independent United States could now purchase sugar from French rather than British plantations, and it did so from Saint-Domingue. Merchants in France poured vast sums into expanding production to reap profits there.

Caribbean slaves lived and died under inhumane conditions. The hot, humid climate made work punishing and kept their life span short. Some committed suicide; women used plant medicines to induce abortions and prevent bearing children who would live in misery. Slaves also developed community bonds to sustain them. The spirit of community and resistance arose from the daily trade of vegetables grown by the slaves in their small garden plots, from the use of a common language made up of French and various African dialects, and from joint participation in Vodoun and other religious traditions among slaves on the islands.

Solidarity and suffering made the Caribbean ripe for revolution. Slave uprisings took place regularly, and, as we saw in Chapter 21, individual slaves escaped into the forests and hills to create new maroon communities, some of which wrested independence from Spain. Added to this, the Caribbean—like the entire Atlantic region—was a crossroads of ideas. Among those ideas were freedom and human rights, circulating not only among African and North American slaves but also among the several thousand free blacks and mulattos in Haiti, who constituted some 30 percent of the slave owners in the region. When whites passed legislation discriminating against them, these successful black landowners and traders lobbied politicians in Paris for equality. The outbreak of the French Revolution in 1789 made their demands grow louder. "You must return to these oppressed citizens," a group of free blacks entreated the National Assembly in October 1789, "the rights that have been unjustly stripped from them." As one free black put it in 1790, all were "more committed than ever to uphold [our rights] with the last drop of our blood."[15]

Rumors that French revolutionaries had freed them spread among the slaves, and in 1791 an organized slave uprising erupted in Saint-Domingue (see Map 22.3). From a cluster of leaders, the free black Pierre-Dominique Toussaint Louverture (too-SAN loo-ver-CHURE) emerged as the most able military commander. The slave revolt moved from success to success, and in 1794, against the wishes of plantation owners and merchants—both black and white—the French revolutionary government formally declared that blacks had rights equal to those of whites. Toussaint, himself a former slave and one grateful to France for its support of black equality, joined the French in driving back the British and Spanish, who had intervened in hopes of conquering the French portion of the island for themselves. When black plantation owners refused to cooperate politically or economically with ex-slaves, civil war broke out. In 1800 Toussaint overcame this too and issued a series of stiff reforms. Although slaves were free, they were to return to the sugar plantations, Toussaint

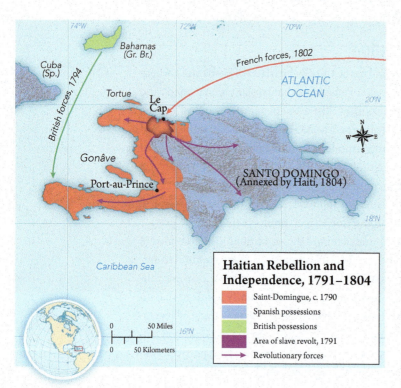

Haitian Rebellion and Independence, 1791–1804

- Saint-Domingue, c. 1790
- Spanish possessions
- British possessions
- Area of slave revolt, 1791
- Revolutionary forces

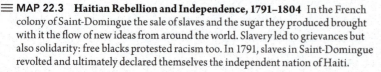

≡ **MAP 22.3   Haitian Rebellion and Independence, 1791–1804** In the French colony of Saint-Domingue the sale of slaves and the sugar they produced brought with it the flow of new ideas from around the world. Slavery led to grievances but also solidarity: free blacks protested racism too. In 1791, slaves in Saint-Domingue revolted and ultimately declared themselves the independent nation of Haiti.

legislated, and for their work they would receive a quarter of the profit from sugar production. The owners would receive another fourth, and the government would receive half.

By this time, however, Napoleon had come to power in France. Answering the appeal of Saint-Domingue plantation owners—who wanted far more profit than 25 percent—he determined to "pursue the rebels without mercy [and] flush them out," thereby regaining the upper hand in the colony.[16] The campaign led to the capture of Toussaint, who died in jail in 1803. All blacks now united against any French takeover, as the invading army suffered huge losses—some fifty thousand of an army of fifty-eight thousand—many of them from yellow fever. On January 1, 1804, the black generals who defeated the French proclaimed the independent republic of Haiti.

Revolutions in Latin America, 1810–1830

The thirst for change gripped people in other empires. In Spain's Latin American empire discontent among artisans, agricultural workers, and slaves, along with rivalries among creoles and Spanish-born officials sent from the homeland, erupted after the Napoleonic conquest of the Iberian peninsula in 1808. "It is now time to overthrow the [Spanish] yoke," a group of rebels in La Paz (capital of Bolivia today) declared in 1809. "It is now time to declare the principle of liberty in these miserable colonies."[17] This spirit swept the Spanish lands, as the government back home in Europe crumbled.

When Napoleon invaded Spain and Portugal in 1807, he sent the ruling dynasties packing to give his own family control. The Portuguese monarch fled to Brazil in hopes of ruling the empire from the colonies, while in Spain the monarch was replaced by Napoleon's brother Joseph. Guerrilla warfare erupted against the French while Spanish activists also organized **juntas** (HUN-tahs), or ruling councils, around the country despite French rule. In 1808, a national junta unveiled a broad program of reform. In the Spanish colonies, political confusion set in. Like imperial rulers elsewhere, the Spanish kings had come to treat their colonies as

≡ **Toussaint Louverture** In 1791, Toussaint Louverture, a freed slave and slave owner, joined a slave revolt that erupted in Saint-Domingue, France's prosperous Caribbean sugar colony. Louverture, shown here in his general's uniform, possessed strong military skills and soon became the leader of the Haitian Revolution, writing the constitution of the fledgling nation.

junta A ruling council.

cash cows, milking them dry to pay for a lavish way of life in Europe. In the disorder brought on by the Napoleonic invasions, reform-minded colonial leaders saw an opportunity to end these heavy burdens by ousting Spain entirely.

The Napoleonic Wars opened up the possibility of transformative change. Because Spain was allied with Britain in the wars against Napoleon, people in the Spanish colonies had new contacts and new opportunities. Like Britain, Spain had formerly tried to prevent its colonies from manufacturing their own goods or trading directly with other countries. All goods were to be carried in Spanish vessels. Trade-minded local creoles resented these restrictions, as well as the privileged place of Spanish traders and the monopoly on good jobs enjoyed by Spanish aristocrats. The wars threw open ports to British vessels carrying both new ideas and new products. Mule drivers, parish priests, and market people also spread global news, alerting neighborhoods in distant towns to the possibility for change. Aspiring leaders saw a situation full of potential. Their struggles for independence would last until 1830 (see Map 22.4).

Reformers and rebels sprang into action throughout Latin America. In the lucrative colony of Mexico, Father Miguel Hidalgo, a Mexican priest trained in Enlightenment thought by the Jesuits and exiled by the Spanish to a rural parish because of his ideas, opened a campaign against colonial rule in 1810. His soldiers were his parishioners, most of them native American day laborers for the Spanish and creoles. The collapse of silver mining and the soaring prices of food made them desperate. Hidalgo's army swelled to some sixty thousand fighters, who hoped to get paid or fed as they fought. The average fighter, in the opinion of the Mexican viceroy however, was a "robber, assassin, and libertine."[18] Hidalgo's followers, motivated in fact by outrage at the poverty and oppression, slaughtered Spaniards, creoles, and anyone else who stood in their path.

Father Hidalgo was captured and executed in 1811, but other armies appeared under the leadership of mulattos, mestizos (mixed-blood people of native American and European ancestry), and well-born creoles, who wanted the Spanish out and opportunity reborn. The Spanish, however, were able to turn other native Americans, slaves, and mestizos against creole-led armies by pointing out that creoles owned the exploitative large farms. By 1815 the Spanish had put an end to this first stage of the Mexican drive for independence and had executed its leaders—adding to the hatred of colonialism that many felt.

Amid ongoing attacks from bandits and personal armies, discontented creoles set aside their prejudices to unite with the native masses. They developed an effective nationalist sensibility, accepting the idea to distinguish *all* those inhabitants of Mexico born in the New World—the *Americanos*—from those born in Spain.

MAP 22.4 Revolutions in Latin America, 1810–1830 As revolution rolled across the Atlantic world, colonial subjects in Latin America were equally roused to prolonged and wide-ranging struggles for independence from Spain. People from many walks of life and ethnicities as well as soldiers from different parts of the world were all motivated by the potential for revolutionary transformation.

Continued guerrilla fighting eroded the institutions of Spanish rule in Mexico, but the decisive move came when the creole leader Augustin de Iturbide (ee-tur-BEE-deh) allied his forces with Vicente Guerrero (goo-RER-eh), a leader of the popular armies, himself a mestizo. Iturbide had once served the Spanish as an army officer, winning battles and collecting tribute for the government, but his creole birth blocked his advance. Resentment of unearned Spanish privilege made him a natural ally of people who were also held back by what the Spanish saw as low birth—that is, native American, black, mestizo, or mulatto. Iturbide's and Guerrero's forces reached an agreement for a constitutional monarchy independent of Spain. In 1821, the three hundredth anniversary of the Spanish conquest of Mexico, Iturbide entered Mexico City as Spanish rule disintegrated. Still, the start of Father Hidalgo's uprising of the common people on September 16, 1810, not this event, came to mark Mexico's Day of Independence.

Across South America similar independent rebel armies sprang up, most of them controlled by a local strongman, or *caudillo* (kauh-DEE-yoh), who was able to raise armies from people of all classes and ethnicities. While keeping peace locally, the *caudillos* had as many problems getting along with one another as they did enduring Spanish rule. One quality these creoles shared, however, was their contempt for native Americans, Africans, mulattos, and mestizos. Simón Bolívar mustered caudillo support to liberate Venezuela in 1811, but at the time he firmly believed that slavery could be maintained in the fight for national independence.

Nonetheless, with the Spanish monarch's return to power after the defeat of Napoleon in 1815, it became clear that creoles in Latin America needed to ally themselves with oppressed workers, agricultural laborers, and the *llaneros* (yah-NEH-rows), or local cowboys, of all races (see Lives and Livelihoods: The Cowboy Way of Life). Allying with the llaneros, Bolívar called for the forging of a Gran Colombia—a united nation like the United States, composed of all lands liberated from the foreign-born Spanish. Spanish oppression, the appeal to all "Americans," and the help of black troops enabled Bolívar to take Bogotá, Caracas, and Quito by 1822. In the meantime Argentinean general José de San Martin conquered Buenos Aires, western Argentina, and Chile, moving into Peru in 1818. His armies bogged down in Peru, however, leaving the final task of ousting the Spanish to Bolívar, whose armies finally took Lima in 1823 and upper Peru or Bolivia in 1825 (see again Map 22.4). Both San Martin and Bolívar had originally seen no conflict between their own freedom and the existence of slavery, but as the need for slave support became obvious, Bolívar declared it "madness that a revolution for liberty should try to maintain slavery."[19] Many liberation leaders thus promised and awarded slave soldiers their emancipation, either immediately as a way of attracting fighters or after the wars as a reward for victory.

Brazil gained its independence from Portugal more tranquilly and with little change in the social situation: slavery and the bureaucracy alike were left intact. The ruling family, safe in Brazil, was summoned back to Portugal at the end of the Napoleonic Wars, but the king left his son Pedro behind in the capital of Rio de Janeiro. Pedro proceeded to cooperate with business and other leaders and in 1822 declared Brazil independent of Portugal and made himself king. With the masses set against Portuguese foreigners, there was widespread rejoicing at independence even without major social change. A frontier society like the United States, Brazil beckoned entrepreneurs, adventurers, and exiles from around the world as a land of opportunity.

In general, however, the new Latin American countries had been so devastated by years of exploitation, misrule, banditry, and armed uprising that except in Brazil, economies lay in shambles. Instead of effecting social reform that would have encouraged economic initiative, most new governments worked to ensure creole dominance, often refusing the promised slave emancipation. In 1799 a Spanish bishop-elect had noted the "great conflict of interests and the hostility which invariably prevails between those who have nothing and those who have everything."[20] Independence did not transform this situation, and thus the grass-roots forces that would have promoted innovation and increased activity were thwarted.

New Ideologies and Revolutionary Legacies

Despite the failure of the revolutions in the Americas and Europe to bring full and free citizenship to slaves, women, and a range of other oppressed peoples, they nonetheless inspired hopes for the economic opportunity and personal freedom that define the term *liberalism*. Inspired by Enlightenment principles, revolutionaries sought to create centralized nation-states ruled under a constitution instead of arbitrary rulings by monarchs and aristocrats. In the early days of both the North American and French republics, this faith in a unified nation of like-minded peoples, which came to be known as **nationalism**, went hand in hand with liberalism. The unified rule of law under a single nation, as embodied in the U.S. Constitution and the Declaration of the Rights of Man, would guarantee constitutional rights and economic growth through free trade. Latin American leaders such as Bolívar had much less faith in all the people of the nation being ready for participation in government.

Complicating ideas of nationalism, opponents of the new governments of the United States and France believed that time-honored monarchical traditions were a better guarantee of a peaceful society than constitutions and republics. Such thought was called **conservatism**, and many prominent conservatives, appalled

nationalism A belief in the importance of one's nation, stemming from its unique laws, language, traditions, and history.

conservatism A political philosophy emphasizing the continuation of traditional institutions and opposition to sudden change in the established order.

LIVES AND LIVELIHOODS

The Cowboy Way of Life

One of the most important livelihoods in the Western Hemisphere was that of cowboys or cattle hunters. Called *gauchos* in Argentina, *llaneros* in Venezuela and Colombia, and *vaqueros* in Mexico, cowboys rode the prairies rounding up the wild horses and cattle that grazed there. They created their livelihood, for only after 1494 when Columbus first introduced cattle into the Caribbean did cattle spread across both North and South America. As the livestock multiplied, cowboys hunted down the wild animals and slaughtered them. Cowboys developed an entire range of skills, making lassos, for example, from horses' tails. Their most lucrative products were animal hides and byproducts such as leather and tallow for candle making.

These herdsmen, similar to those on the Asian steppes, were usually nomadic. Living as far as possible from cities and the centers of government,

Gauchos Like cowboys, their North American counterparts, gauchos prided themselves on skills with wild horses and other animals. In this etching, a gaucho hurls a rope with an attached ball to capture a rhea by entangling its legs in the rope. As South America developed economically, the gaucho came to symbolize its independent spirit.

romanticism
A European philosophical and artistic movement of the late eighteenth and early nineteenth centuries that valued feeling over reason and glorified traditional customs, nature, and the imagination.

by the violence and bloodshed of the French Revolution, argued the case for tradition, continuity, and gradual reform based on practical experience. Among them, Edmund Burke of England attacked Enlightenment ideas of a social contract, citizenship, and newfangled constitutions as destructive to the wisdom of the ages.

Like conservatism, **romanticism**—a philosophical and artistic movement that glorified nature, emotion, and the imagination—emerged partly in reaction to the Enlightenment's reliance on reason, especially after the violent excesses of the French Revolution. Closely related to early nationalism, romanticism was also a response to the political turmoil of the Napoleonic Wars. Thus arose a romantic nationalism, especially in territories such as the German states. Romantic nationalists they aimed to keep their independence and to escape government regulation, which increased under the Bourbon Reforms. Cowboys in all areas usually refused to ride mares, deeming it unmanly, and generally prided themselves on maintaining the rough, masculine ways of frontiersmen. Enterprising landowners, however, set up vast ranches and challenged the claims of the gauchos, llaneros, and vaqueros, who saw wild horses as their own.

Settled ranchers hired their own cattle tenders and then encouraged the government to see the independent cowboys as "cattle rustlers" and thieves.

Their independent way of life eventually led nation builders to mythologize gauchos, llaneros, and other cowboys as symbols of freedom for the nation as a whole. Their experience with horses and survival skills made them valuable fighters on both sides in the wars for Latin American independence.

Questions to Consider

1. For what reasons would some gauchos and llaneros ally themselves with upper-class creoles in the Latin American independence movements?
2. Why have cowboys become such icons in both North and South America?

For Further Information:

Loy, R. Philip. *Westerns and American Culture, 1930–1955.* 2001.
Oliven, Ruben George. *Tradition Matters: Modern Gaucho Identity in Brazil.* 1996.
Reding, Nick. *The Last Cowboys at the End of the World: The Last Gauchos of Patagonia.* 2001.
Slatta, Richard W. *Gauchos and the Vanishing Frontier.* 1983.

revered language and traditions as sources of a common feeling among peoples. "Perfect laws are the beautiful and free forms of the interior life of a nation," wrote one German jurist, criticizing reformers' desire to take the Napoleonic Code as a model for change. For him, the Napoleonic Code had come neither "out of the life of the German nation" nor from its ancient past and shared cultural experience.[21]

To make the revolutionary legacy more complicated yet, Napoleon Bonaparte and Simón Bolívar ultimately became romantic heroes to rich and poor alike, even though they represented Enlightenment ideals of social mobility and economic modernizing. "My wife and I," said one distillery worker in southern France in 1822, "have the emperor in our guts."[22] The many poets, musicians, and artists influenced by romanticism earned their livelihoods not only by glorifying feelings instead of reason but by spreading the myth of Napoleon and Simón Bolívar as superhuman rulers who overcame horrific obstacles to become conquerors. These powerful, if conflicting, ideas—liberalism, nationalism, conservatism, and romanticism—resonated down through the next centuries, shaping both local and global politics.

COUNTERPOINT: Religious Revival in a Secular Age

FOCUS What trends in Enlightenment and revolutionary society did religious revival challenge?

In the influential cases of France and the United States, the principle of a secular state—one tied to no particular religion—flourished, supported by the Enlightenment idea that reason rather than faith should determine social, political, and economic regulations. The French under Robespierre devised national festivals to substitute for religious holidays and even converted churches into "temples of reason." Yet secularism did not prevail everywhere. In Europe and North America, great surges of religious fervor took hold of people's daily lives, and in the Arabian peninsula reformers sought to restore Muslims to the fundamental teachings of Islam. Perhaps most consequentially, Muslim *jihadis* overthrew centuries-old kingdoms in West Africa, transforming these societies into massive slave-holding Islamic states.

Christianity's Great Awakening

The spirit of Christian revival first took shape in Prussia, where Lutherans had called for a renewal of faith in the late seventeenth century. As Protestant revival spread across the European continent, people joined new evangelical churches, most of them focused on sharpening the inward experience of faith. In the middle of the eighteenth century, a wave of revivals that historians term the "Great Awakening" took place throughout Britain and the North American colonies. Emotional orators such as the English preachers John Wesley and George Whitefield roused the faithful to join new communities of faith such as Methodism, the evangelical Protestant church founded by Wesley and characterized by active concern with social welfare and public morals. Some observers were appalled by the sight of worshippers literally weeping at the perils of damnation, finding the scene "horrible beyond expression."[23] Nonetheless, in the middle colonies of British North

READING THE PAST

Phillis Wheatley, "On Being Brought from Africa to America"

Born in Senegal in 1853, Phillis Wheatley was seven when she was sold into slavery to a Boston family, who educated her along with their children. Wheatley published celebrated poetry while a slave, becoming a sensation in New England and even traveling to England in 1773. A voyager to three continents, Wheatley was a true child of the Atlantic world. This poem, written while she was a teenager, contains a host of ideas and images about slavery. As you read, consider why this short verse might pose problems for some modern readers.

> 'Twas mercy brought me from my Pagan land,
> Taught my benighted soul to understand
> That there's a God, that there's a Saviour too:
> Once I redemption neither sought now knew,
> Some view our sable race with scornful eye,
> "Their colour is a diabolic die."
> Remember, Christians, Negroes, black as Cain,
> May be refin'd, and join th' angelic train.

Examining the Evidence

1. In what ways does this poem reflect Enlightenment thought?

2. How does it relate to the Great Awakening?

3. Which ideas in the poem might present-day critics condemn? Which ideas might they praise?

America alone, some 550 new Protestant congregations were organized between 1740 and 1770.

African American slaves were also fervent believers, finding in religion evidence of their humanity (see Reading the Past: Phillis Wheatley, "On Being Brought from Africa to America"). Religion later provided arguments for an end to slavery as part of a rising democratic impulse among people who together addressed their comments directly and emotionally to God. Beginning around 1800, the United States experienced a Second Great Awakening in the face of the growth of science, rationalism, and emotional coldness in the old churches. Despite religious enthusiasm, governments such as that of the United States declined to proclaim an official faith because of their people's religious diversity and because of Enlightenment thinkers' suspicion of churches as institutions.

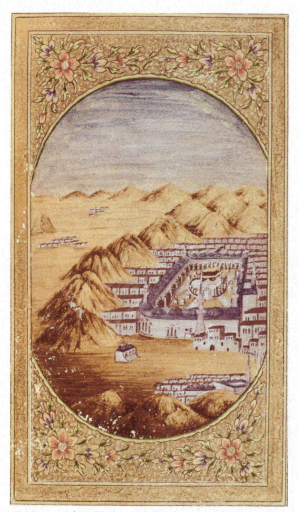

≡ **Mecca and Wahhabism** Wahhabis fought for a purified Islamic faith and an end to "superstitious" beliefs. Because the pilgrimage to Mecca was one of the five "pillars" of the faith, Mecca itself, depicted here, remained a center of religious devotion that grew in importance as Islam spread around the world.

Government and Religion Allied

In some instances, ties between government and religion became stronger, not weaker. In the Arabian peninsula an eighteenth-century religious reformer, Muhammad ibn Abd al-Wahhabi developed a strong alliance with Muhammad ibn Sa'ud, the head of a small market town. Ibn Abd al-Wahhabi called on Muslims to return to the tenets of Islam, most importantly the worship of the single god, Allah. At the time, people worshipped local fortune tellers and healers as well as graves, rocks, and trees. Thus, in one way Wahhabi revival aimed to rid Islam of its superstitions and superstitious leaders.

One traveler found Arabs "so negligent of religion" that they were "generally considered infidels." Ibn Abd al-Wahhabi got help in his quest to return Arabs to the basic principles of Islam from the house of Sa'ud, the town's leading family. Unity of worship would come with political unity, led in ibn Abd al-Wahhabi's mind by the Sa'uds. They would unite the various tribes under a purified Islamic practice, realizing al-Wahhabi's belief that "Arab" meant Muslim.[24]

Finally, Muslims carried out *jihad* across West Africa in the eighteenth and nineteenth centuries. Overturning what they saw as corrupt governments, some of them Muslim, jihadist leaders sought to restore purity in behavior and thought and to eliminate greed, vanity, and other attitudes that contradicted Islamic values. Jihad was thus both a political and an individual struggle, which in the late eighteenth and early nineteenth centuries entailed the overthrow of a false Islam for a true one—in this case, an Islam in which practicing Muslims were not sold into slavery while false believers were at risk. At the turn of the century, jihadi leader Uthman dan Fodio (1754–1817) was successful in establishing new purified religious governments that built slave enclaves and that ended the rule of nonbelievers. As conquered nonbelievers were enslaved, the slave population soared to the point that more slaves lived in West Africa than in either Brazil or North America.

The powerful jihadist revolution in West Africa forms a counter-point to the secularly based political revolutions in other parts of the Atlantic world. Yet, it also shows that Africans too were on the march against corrupt political rule.

Conclusion

This period saw widespread challenges to centuries-old empires in the Americas, Europe, the Caribbean, West Asia, Africa, and Egypt. The most direct of these challenges came from the popular uprisings known as the Atlantic revolutions. In these revolutions, state power and rigid social structures impinged on people's lives by promoting high taxes and controlling commerce. Deepening poverty and frustrated ambition afflicted ordinary folk, whether in France or in Peru, causing both riots and political activism. These economic conditions awakened some revolutionaries. Others were inspired to push for political reform by Enlightenment ideas about government based on individual rights and the rational rule of law rather than on inherited privilege and notions of a divine order. Simón Bolívar

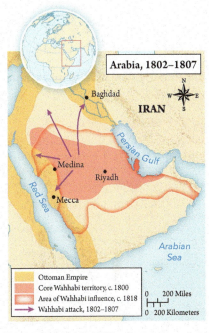

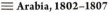
Arabia, 1802–1807

was one such secular-minded revolutionary and state-builder. Other political actors, such as the Sa'ud family of the Arabian peninsula and jihadis in West Africa, drew on religious fervor in their state-building, forming a counterpoint to the general trend.

Independence in the Western Hemisphere affected the entire world. As frontier societies, North American and Latin American countries served as magnets for European investment and for people searching for better livelihoods. Still, count-less people of all classes and ethnicities who participated in the uprisings in the Atlantic world benefited not at all or in the most limited way. Slavery remained entrenched and even expanded in some countries; women, free blacks, and other people of color were usually disqualified from participating in politics. As repre-sentative government developed, it too was uneven, especially in Latin America, where a creole elite dominated the new nations.

These political revolutions nonetheless formed a platform for further social and economic change, and we remember them for their powerful and enduring influence. In the short term, the revolutions created conditions for heightened manufacturing and eventually the Industrial Revolution. In the long term, they gave citizens confidence to use their freedom. "It is harder to release a nation from servitude than to enslave a free nation," Bolívar had written, quoting the Enlight-enment author Montesquieu, and in this respect the age of revolutions nurtured aspirations and opened up opportunities.[25]

✳ review

The major global development in this chapter: The Atlantic revolutions and their short- and long-term significance.

Important Events	
1751–1772	Publication of the *Encyclopedia*
1762	Jean-Jacques Rousseau publishes *The Social Contract* and *Emile*
1775–1781	Revolution in North America
1776	Adam Smith, *The Wealth of Nations*
1789	U.S. Constitution formally adopted; revolution begins in France
1791	Revolution begins in Haiti
1792	France declared a republic; Mary Wollstonecraft writes *A Vindication of the Rights of Woman*
1799	Napoleon comes to power
1804	Haiti becomes independent from France
1811	Simón Bolívar first takes up arms against Spain
1815	Napoleon is defeated at Waterloo; Congress of Vienna resettles the boundaries of European states
1816	Argentina becomes independent from Spain
1817	Chile becomes independent from Spain
1821	Mexico and Peru become independent from Spain
1822	Brazil becomes independent from Portugal
1825	Bolivia becomes independent from Spain

KEY TERMS

conservatism (p. 829)

contract government (p. 804)

federation (p. 813)

general will (p. 818)

junta (p. 825)

laissez faire (p. 805)

liberalism (p. 805)

nationalism (p. 829)

public sphere (p. 806)

republic (p. 815)

romanticism (p. 830)

CHAPTER OVERVIEW QUESTIONS

1. What role did the scientific revolution and expanding global contacts play in the cultural and social movement known as the Enlightenment?

2. Why did prosperous and poor people alike join revolutions in the Americas and in France?

3. Why were the Atlantic revolutions so influential, even to the present day?

MAKING CONNECTIONS

1. What was the relationship between the Enlightenment and the political revolutions of the late eighteenth and early nineteenth centuries?

2. What are the common challenges that centuries-old empires faced during this period?

3. What makes Napoleon a significant historical figure?

4. Why was there so much bloodshed in the various efforts to achieve political and social change?

For further research into the topics covered in this chapter, see the Bibliography at the end of the book. For additional primary sources from this period, see *Sources for World in the Making*.

23

Industry and Everyday Life
1750–1900

≡ **World in the Making** An artist from an elite samurai family, Kiyochika Kobayashi was so fascinated by technology and industry that in 1879 he placed a train front and center in this moonlit scene set in Takanawa Ushimachi, just outside of Tokyo. Earlier portrayed as a slum called Oxtown with garbage strewn about its roads, Takanawa Ushimachi became alluring to this artist, thanks to the arrival of the railroad. Kiyochika also introduced such elements as clocks, cameras, electric lighting, and the massive cannons churned out by industry. (Santa Barbara Museum of Art, Gift of Dr. and Mrs. Roland A. Way, 1984.31.5.)

✳ backstory

As we saw in Chapter 22, between 1750 and 1830 popular uprisings led to a revolutionary wave across the Atlantic world. Throwing off old political systems, revolutionaries also aimed to unchain their economies by eliminating stifling restrictions on manufacturing and commerce imposed by guilds and governments. Free global trade advanced further with the end of British control of the United States and Spanish control of much of Latin America. During the same period, slavery came under attack as an immoral institution that denied human beings equal rights and prevented a free labor force from developing. As Enlightenment ideas for good government flourished, reformers pushed to replace traditional aristocratic and monarchical privileges with rational codes of law. Free trade and free labor, promoted by enlightened laws and policies, helped bring dramatic changes to the global economy, most notably the unparalleled increase in productivity called the Industrial Revolution.

As a seven-year-old in 1799, Robert Blincoe started working in a cotton mill outside the town of Nottingham, in central England. Robert was an orphan, and with others from his London orphanage he was sent to the mill. Orphans were to contribute to England's prosperity, but it was not certain that Robert would even survive to adulthood. As his group reached the mill, he heard onlookers in the town mutter, "God help the poor wretches."[1] Robert soon found out why. He watched as his fellow child workers wasted away from the long hours and meager food, and he looked on as the orphan Mary Richards was caught up in the machinery: he "heard the bones of her arms, legs, thighs, etc successively snap . . . her head appeared dashed to pieces, . . . her blood thrown about like water from a twirled mop."[2] Older workers tortured small Robert, pouring hot tar into a blazing metal bowl and placing it on his head until his hair came off and his scalp was burned. Only when Robert reached age twenty-one, his entire body scarred for life from beatings, was he released from his grim "apprenticeship."

Robert Blincoe was a survivor of the Industrial Revolution—a change in the production of goods that substituted mechanical force for human energy. Beginning in Britain around 1750, European factories churned out machine-made products that came to replace more expensive artisanal goods. Agriculture continued to dominate the world economy, but in the twentieth century, industry would outstrip agriculture as the leading economic sector.

Industrialization transformed the livelihoods of tens of millions of people in the nineteenth century. Its course was ragged, offering both danger and advantage. Some like Robert Blincoe were driven into factories where conditions were often hazardous and even criminal. The efficient new weaving machines gave jobs to some, but they impoverished artisans, such as the Indian and European handloom weavers who continued to follow traditional manufacturing methods. Industry influenced agriculture, as factories consumed more raw materials and as the growing number of workers in cities depended for their food on distant farmers, many of them slaves or indentured workers. With the global spread of industry, cultural life echoed the transformation, as writers, musicians, painters, and thinkers depicted their new societies. Whether a region had comparatively few factories, as in India and South America, or a dense network of them, as in Britain, patterns of work and everyday life changed—and not always for the better, as Robert Blincoe's case shows.

OVERVIEW QUESTIONS

The major global development in this chapter: The Industrial Revolution and its impact on societies and cultures throughout the world.

As you read, consider:

1. In what ways did the Industrial Revolution change people's work lives and ideas?

2. How did the Industrial Revolution benefit people, and what problems did it create?

3. How and where did industrial production develop, and how did it affect society and politics?

The Industrial Revolution Begins 1750–1830

FOCUS What were the main causes of the Industrial Revolution?

The **Industrial Revolution** unfolded first in Britain and western Europe, eventually tipping the balance of global power in favor of the West. Although Britain led in industry, the economies of Qing (ching) China and India were larger until almost 1900, when Britain surpassed them in overall productivity. A burning question for historians is how, in a climate of worldwide industriousness, Britain had come to the forefront of the great industrial transformation.

The Global Roots of Industrialization

Industrialization took place amid a worldwide surge in productive activity sometimes called the "Industrious Revolution." Industriousness rose, as people worked longer hours and tinkered to find new ways to make goods, developing thousands of new inventions in the process. In Qing China from the mid-1650s to 1800, productivity increased along with population, which soared from 160 million people in 1700 to 350 million in 1800. The dynamic economy improved many people's lifestyles and life expectancy and encouraged people to work harder to acquire the new products constantly entering the market. Chinese life expectancy increased to the range of thirty-four to thirty-nine years, longer than almost anywhere else in the world, including western Europe, where in 1800 it was thirty in France and thirty-five in Britain. Crops from the Western Hemisphere helped raise the standard of living wherever they were imported and grown, and awareness of such popular Chinese products as cotton textiles and porcelain spread through international trade. Silver

Industrial Revolution
A change in the production of goods that substituted mechanical power for human energy, beginning around 1750 in Britain and western Europe; it vastly increased the world's productivity.

flowed into China as Europeans purchased its highly desirable goods. As the nine-teenth century opened, Qing China was the most prosperous country on earth.

Europe, in contrast, produced little that was attractive to foreign buyers, and in the seventeenth century warfare, epidemics, and famine reduced its population from eighty-five million to eighty million. After 1700, however, Europe's population surged like that of China, more than doubling by 1800, thanks to global trade that introduced nutritious foods and useful know-how. Population growth put pressure on British energy resources, especially fuel and food. With their populations rising rapidly, both Britain and China faced the limits of artisanal productivity and natural resources. The Industrial Revolution allowed the British to surpass those limits (see Map 23.1).

Great Britain: A Culture of Experimentation

Why did the Industrial Revolution happen in Britain first? After all, many regions have the coal, iron deposits, and other resources that went into creating the first modern machines. It was not just resources, however, that propelled Britain to the industrial forefront. The Scientific Revolution had fostered both new reliance on direct observation and deep curiosity about the world. The British and other Europeans traveled the globe, which exposed them to technological developments from other societies. From China, for example, they learned about such imple-ments as seed drills and winnowing machines to process grain. The widely read *Encyclopedia*, composed in France during the Enlightenment, featured mechanical designs from around the world, making them available to networks of tinkerers and experimenters. The massive expansion in productivity was initially not about theoretical science, but about Britain's practical culture of trial and error.

Curious British artisans and industrious craftspeople worked to supply the surg-ing population, to meet the shortage in energy due to declining wood supplies, and to devise products that the world might want to buy. "The age," wrote critic Samuel Johnson, "is running mad after innovation."[3] From aristocrats to artisans, the British latched onto news of successful experiments both at home and abroad. They tinkered with air pumps, clocks, and telescopes. European craftspeople worked hard to copy the new goods imported from China, India, and other coun-tries. From the sixteenth century on, for example, European consumers bought hundreds of thousands of foreign porcelain pieces, leading would-be manufactur-ers in the Netherlands, France, and the German states to try to figure out the pro-cess of porcelain production. They finally succeeded early in the 1700s. Despite inventive activity across Europe, it was England that pulled ahead.

One English innovator who stands out is Josiah Wedgwood (1730–1795), founder of the Wedgwood dishware firm that still exists. Wedgwood developed a range of new processes, colors, and designs, making his business a model for large-scale

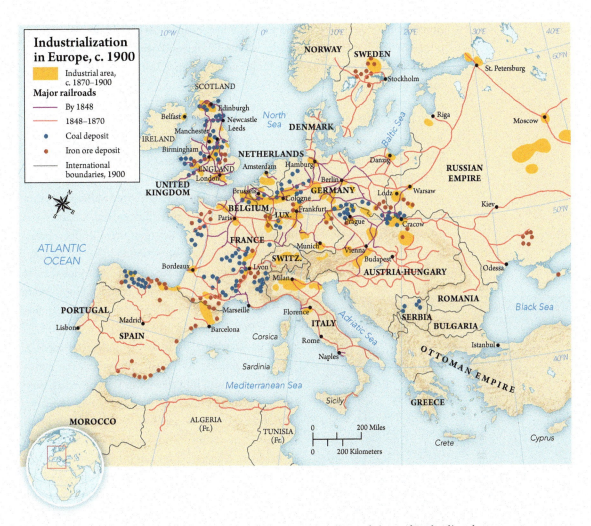

Industrialization in Europe, c. 1900

▮	Industrial area, c. 1870–1900

Major railroads

——	By 1848
——	1848–1870
●	Coal deposit
●	Iron ore deposit
——	International boundaries, 1900

≡ **MAP 23.1   Industrialization in Europe, c. 1900** Beginning in the workshops of England's tinkerers, industrialization spread across western Europe to Germany and then to Russia. The presence of raw materials such as coal and iron ore sparked industrial development, albeit unevenly, but so did curiosity and inventiveness. Sweden, for example, lacks mineral resources, so its people harnessed water power to develop electricity.

production. He grew up in a family that produced rough, traditional kinds of pottery on a very small scale. As a poor, younger son with an inquisitive mind, he used his bent for experimentation to devise many types of ceramics. Helped by his wife and by the personal funds she invested in the company, Wedgwood kept meticulous records of his five thousand experiments with "china" (so called because Chinese porcelain set the standard for ceramic production). His agents searched the world for the right grade of clay to compete with Asian products, and he copied Asian designs unashamedly. In Wedgwood, the distinctive British culture of artisanal experimentation came together with the inspiration provided by global connections; the result was industrial innovation. Wedgwood's vast fortune and spirit of experimentation passed down to his grandson Charles Darwin, who proposed the theory of evolution.

World Trade and the Rise of Industry

As population rose across many parts of the globe and as nations fought wars worldwide over trade, global shipping increased to supply people at home and transport far-flung armies and navies. Improved shipping brought grain from North America, wood from Canada and Russia, cotton from Egypt and the United States, and eventually meat from Australia to wherever industrial growth occurred. Imports and Europe's own produce fed urban workers. Commodities such as tea, coffee, chocolate, and opium derivatives, which the lower classes were coming to use in the nineteenth century, helped them endure the rigors of industry. Thus, dense global trade networks and raw materials produced by workers from around the world were critical to the Industrial Revolution and urban growth.

Slaves were also crucial to industrial success. Eleven million Africans captured on the continent were sold into slavery in the Americas, raising capital to invest in commerce and industry. Slaves worldwide produced agricultural products such as sugar and rice that enriched global traders. Cheaper foodstuffs cut the expenses of factory owners, who justified low wages by pointing to workers' decreasing costs for their everyday needs. To clothe their slaves, plantation owners bought inexpensive factory-made textiles pumped out by British machines, though the rising number of slaves in West Africa also produced textiles for nearby markets. In the northern United States, slave ironworkers were put to work building metallurgical businesses, and across the Western Hemisphere slaves' skills played a crucial role in producing copper and tin as well as cotton and dyes for factory use worldwide. Had free labor alone been used in these processes, some historians believe, the higher cost of raw materials and

≡ **Wedgwood China** Josiah Wedgwood, the eighteenth-century English potter-turned-industrialist who founded a company still prosperous today, worked day and night to figure out the ingredients, formulas, and processes necessary to make "china"—that is, inexpensive, heat-resistant dishware patterned after China's renowned but costly and fragile porcelain. Wedgwood copied designs from around the world to brighten his dishware, but he is best known for his "Wedgwood blue" products, which were directly inspired by China's famed blue-and-white patterns.

food would have slowed development of global trade and the pace of experiments with factories and machines.

The Technology of Industry

Technology was a final ingredient in the effort to meet the needs of a growing and increasingly interconnected population. In the eighteenth century, British inventors devised tools such as the flying shuttle (1733) to speed the weaving of textiles by individuals working at home. This, in turn, led to improvements in spinning to meet the increased demand for thread created by speedier weaving. The spinning jenny, invented about 1765 by craftsman James Hargreaves, allowed an individual worker, using just the power of her hand, to spin not one bobbin of thread, but up to 120 at once. At about the same time, Richard Arkwright and partners invented the water frame, another kind of spinning machine that used water power. When hand-driven spinning machines could be linked to a central power source such as water, many could be placed in a single building. Thus, the world's first factories arose from the pressure to increase production of English cloth for the growing global market.

Still another, even more important breakthrough arose when steam engines were harnessed to both spinning and weaving machines. Steam engines could power a vast number of machines, which drew more people out of home textile production and into factories. It was a pivotal piece of technology not just for textiles, but for the Industrial Revolution as a whole. Steam engines were used first in the gold and silver mining industry, then in textile production, and finally in driving trains and steamboats. The steam engine had been invented earlier in China, and was used there and elsewhere to pump water from mines. In 1765, James Watt, a Scottish craftsman, figured out how to make the steam engine more practical, fuel-efficient, and powerful—"cheap as well as good" was how he put it.[4] In 1814, British engineer George Stephenson placed the machine in a carriage on rails, inventing the locomotive. The first steam-powered ship crossed the Atlantic soon after, in 1819.

The **interchangeability of parts** was another critical aspect of the Industrial Revolution. The many wars fought for global trade and influence in the eighteenth and early nineteenth centuries produced rising demand for weapons. By 1790 French gunsmith Honoré Blanc, experimenting with tools and gauges, had produced guns with fully interchangeable parts. This lowered the cost per weapon and made repair possible for merchants and soldiers based in any part of the world. The goal was to "assure uniformity [of output], acceleration of work, and economy of price," as a government official put it in 1781.[5] The idea of interchangeability in weaponry and machinery was crucial to the unfolding Industrial Revolution.

interchangeability of parts A late-eighteenth-century technological breakthrough in which machine and implement parts were standardized, allowing for mass production and easy repair.

Industrialization After 1830

⬊ **FOCUS** How did industrialization spread, and what steps did nations and manufacturers take to meet its challenges?

One striking feature of industrialization is its unstoppable spread within countries, across regions, and around the world despite resistance to it from threatened workers and fearful rulers. Industrialization brings ongoing efficiencies, which have proven important to meet the needs of a growing global population. From its birth in England and western Europe, entrepreneurs across the continent advanced the industrial system, as did innovators in the United States. Outside of Europe and the United States, thorough industrialization generally did not develop until the twentieth century. Even though industry developed unevenly in different places, it affected the wider world by increasing demand for raw materials and creating new livelihoods.

Industrial Innovation Gathers Speed

The nineteenth century was one of widespread industrial, technological, and commercial innovation (see Map 23.2). Steam engines moved inexpensive manufactured goods on a growing network of railroads and shipping lanes, creating a host of new jobs outside of factory work (see Lives and Livelihoods: Builders of the Trans-Siberian Railroad).

Although craftsmen-tinkerers created the first machines, such as the spinning jenny and water frame, sophisticated engineers were more critical to later revolutionary technologies. In 1885 the German engineer Karl Benz devised a gasoline engine, and six years later France's Armand Peugeot constructed the first automobile. Benz produced his first car two years later in 1893. After 1880, electricity became more available, providing power to light everything from private homes to government office buildings. The Eiffel Tower in Paris, constructed for the International Exhibit of 1889 and for decades the tallest structure in the world, was a monument to the age's engineering wizardry; visitors rode to its summit in electric elevators, its electric lights ablaze.

To fuel this explosive growth, the leading industrial nations mined and produced massive quantities of coal, iron, and steel during the second half of the century. Output by the major European iron producers increased from eleven million to twenty-three million tons in the 1870s and 1880s alone. Steel output grew even more impressively in the same decades, from half a million to eleven million tons. Manufacturers used the metal to build more than one hundred thousand locomotives that pulled trains, transporting two billion people annually.

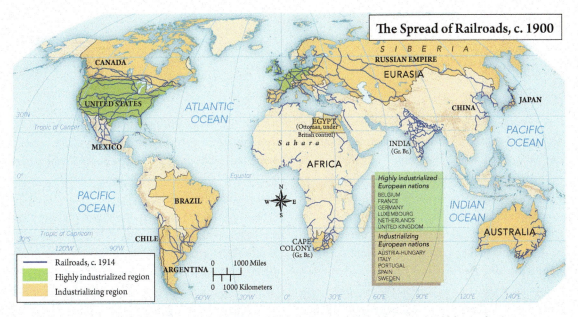

The Spread of Railroads, c. 1900

Railroads, c. 1914
Highly industrialized region
Industrializing region

Highly industrialized European nations
BELGIUM
FRANCE
GERMANY
LUXEMBOURG
NETHERLANDS
UNITED KINGDOM

Industrializing European nations
AUSTRIA-HUNGARY
ITALY
PORTUGAL
SPAIN
SWEDEN

≡ **MAP 23.2   The Spread of Railroads, c. 1900** The spread of railroads throughout the world fostered industrialization because it required tracks, engines and railroad cars, and railway stations, which were increasingly made of iron, steel, and glass. Railroads generated economic growth beyond the building of trains and tracks, however. Entire cities grew up around railroad hubs, which attracted new migrants—not just hard-working builders but also professionals and service workers—to fill the needs of the growing population.

Historians sometimes contrast two periods of the Industrial Revolution. In the first, in the eighteenth and early nineteenth centuries, innovations in textile machinery powered by steam energy predominated. The second, in the later nineteenth century, concentrated on heavy industrial products and electrical and oil power. This was the pattern in Britain, but industrialization was never so neat elsewhere: textile factories and blast furnaces were built simultaneously, and small workshops grew faster than the number of factories. Livelihoods pursued at home—called **outwork**—persisted in garment making, metalwork, and such "finishing trades" as metal polishing. In fact, factory production fostered "industriousness" more than ever, and factory, small workshop, and home enterprise have coexisted ever since.

Industrial innovations in machinery and chemicals also transformed agriculture. Chemical fertilizers boosted crop yields, and reapers and threshers mechanized harvesting. In the 1870s, Sweden produced a cream separator, a first step toward mechanizing dairy farming. Wire fencing and barbed wire replaced more labor-intensive wooden fencing and stone walls, allowing large-scale cattle-raising. Refrigerated railroad cars and steamships, developed between the 1840s and 1870 in several countries, allowed fruits, vegetables, dairy products, and meat to be transported without spoiling, increasing the size and diversity of the urban food supply.

outwork A method of manufacturing in which raw or semifinished materials are distributed to households where they are further processed or completed.

LIVES AND LIVELIHOODS

Builders of the Trans-Siberian Railroad

Axes, saws, and wheelbarrows—these were the tools that built the greatest railway project ever undertaken. Stretching across Siberia from Moscow in the west to Vladivostok on the Sea of Japan (see again Map 23.2), the scale of the trans-Siberian railroad was enormous by any measure: miles laid (fifty-seven hundred), earth moved (one hundred million cubic yards), rail installed (more than one hundred million tons), and bridges and tunnels constructed (sixty miles). Because this remote wilderness lacked roads, the endeavor was difficult and expensive. Except for lumber, all supplies needed to be transported. Cut stone for bridge supports and gravel for the railbed came from quarries sometimes hundreds of miles away. Ships carried steel parts for bridges thousands of miles across the seas, from Odessa on the Black Sea to Vladivostok. In winter horse-drawn sleds and in summer horse-drawn wagons transported material to the work sites. Cut through forests, blasted through rock, raised over rivers and swampy lands, the project was completed in nine sections over thirteen years from 1891 to 1904.

Hundreds of thousands of manual laborers did the work. At the height of its construction, the trans-Siberian employed as many as ninety thousand workers on each of its original nine sections. Many were recruited by contractors who scoured Russian cities and villages for hefty men. Prisoners and soldiers were forced to work on the project.

Around the large work sites, the army and police stood guard to prevent disruption as the grueling, dangerous labor progressed. The government set up state liquor stores near work camps to appease laborers in their off-hours.

Getting the job done quickly and cheaply was the government's top priority. Worker safety was of little concern, and casualties were many among the unskilled workforce. Cutting through forests to lay rail and dynamiting through hills to construct

≡ **Convict Railroad Workers in Siberia, 1895** The tsarist government of Russia mobilized hundreds of thousands of workers to build the trans-Siberian railroad, the main line of which took thirteen years (1891–1904) to complete. Convicts provided essential manpower, and this image shows their housing and living conditions. The labor entailed moving mountains of soil and rock and bringing in lumber and iron track, all without benefit of machinery and in the harsh Siberian climate.

tunnels took thousands of lives. The anonymous dead lived on only in poetry:

> The way is straight, the embankment narrow,
> Telegraph poles, rails, bridges,
> And everywhere on both sides are Russian bones—...
> Brothers! You remember our reward!
> Fated to be strewn in the earth.[1]

The only apparent safety precaution was forbidding prisoners to work with explosives.

Minister of Finance Sergei Witte maintained that the railroad would make Russia the dominant global market in the world: "The silk, tea, and fur trade for Europe, and the manufacturing and other trade for the Far East, will likely be concentrated in Moscow, which will become the hub of the world's transit movement," he predicted.[2] Long after the line's completion, the trans-Siberian railroad provided good jobs for railway workers in Siberia. In settlements along the rail line, business thrived, and cities such as Novosibirsk provided scores of new opportunities for service workers supporting railroad personnel.

The trans-Siberian railroad did indeed transform the livelihoods of the empire as a whole. The government sent some five million peasants from western Russia to Siberia between 1890 and 1914. The massive migration was intended to extend Russian power across the empire's vast expanse. The government designated millions of acres of land—populated at the time by nomadic Asian foragers and herders—for Russian, Ukrainian, and Belorussian settlers. Russian bureaucrats hoped that as the peasants intermingled with indigenous peoples, the non-Russian ethnic groups would become "Russianized" even as they lost hunting lands and pasturage that were the basis of their livelihoods. The population of Siberia soared with the influx of farmers. Russia would never be the same.

Questions to Consider

1. What jobs were needed to construct the trans-Siberian railroad, and how were workers treated?

2. How did the railroad affect livelihoods other than those directly connected with its construction?

3. How would you balance the human costs of building the railroad with the human opportunities it created?

4. What changes did the trans-Siberian railroad bring to Russia?

1. Nicholai Nekrasov, quoted in J. N. Westwood, *A History of the Russian Railways* (London: George Allen and Unwin, 1964), 33.

2. Quoted in Stephen G. Marks, *Road to Power: The Trans-Siberian Railroad and the Colonization of Asian Russia, 1850–1917* (London: I. B. Tauris, 1991), 117.

Challenges to British Dominance

Other countries began to narrow Britain's industrial advantage. The United States industrialized rapidly after its Civil War (discussed in Chapter 24) ended in 1865, and Japan joined in after 1870. Argentina, Brazil, Chile, and Mexico gained industries at varying rates between 1870 and 1914, producing textiles, beer, soap, cigarettes, and an array of other products. In Argentina, the introduction of cigarette-rolling machinery allowed the National Tobacco Company's twenty-eight hundred workers to turn out four hundred thousand cigarettes per day by the end of the 1890s. In the same decade, its leading textile company produced 1.6 million yards of cloth annually. Industry—if not full-scale industrialization—circled the globe.

Two countries in particular began to surpass Britain in research, technical education, innovation, and growth rates: Germany and the United States. Germany's burst of industrial energy occurred after its states unified as a result of the Franco-Prussian War of 1870–1871 (discussed in Chapter 24). At the time, Germany took the French territories of Alsace and Lorraine with their textile industries, mineral deposits, and metallurgical factories. Investing heavily in research, German businesses began to mass-produce goods such as railroad stock and weapons and spent as much money on education as on its military, helping Germany's electrical and chemical engineering capabilities soar.

After its Civil War, the United States began to exploit its vast natural resources intensively, including coal, ores, gold, and oil. The value of U.S. industrial goods vaulted from $5 billion in 1880 to $13 billion in 1900. Whereas German accomplishments relied heavily on state promotion of industrial efforts, U.S. growth depended on innovative individuals, such as Andrew Carnegie in iron and steel and John D. Rockefeller in oil. As the nineteenth century came to a close, Britain struggled to keep ahead of its industrial competitors.

Industrialization in Japan

Between 1750 and 1850 merchants, peasant producers, artisans, and even samurai warriors laid the foundation for Japan's industrialization. They engaged in brisk commerce, especially with the Asian mainland. Japan exported its sophisticated pottery—some two million pieces to Southeast Asia alone in the first decade of the nineteenth century—and it imported books, clocks, and small precision implements, especially from China. Trade within Japan increased too. Businessmen and farmers produced sake, silk, paper, and other commodities for internal consumption. Japan's roads were clogged with traffic in people and goods (see Seeing the Past: Japan's Industrious Society). The samurais—the traditional warrior class—were what we might describe as underemployed after two centuries of peace under the Tokugawa Shogunate (see Chapter 20). To occupy their time, some samurais studied the new findings in science and engineering coming from China and Europe and experimented with electricity or created important devices such as thermometers that helped improve silkworm breeding. Merchants were also an economic force. As in Europe, they supplied peasant families with looms and other machines for spinning and weaving at home. The inventive Japanese were more than ready to take advantage of Western machinery when the opportunity arose.

Japanese innovators craved Western-style mass production, beginning with textiles, guns, railroads, and steamships. It had become clear that, as one Japanese administrator wrote in 1868, "machinery is the basis of wealth."[6] Already, Western ships seeking access to Japanese ports and trade had flaunted the power of their own industries. In 1853 U.S. Commodore Matthew Perry steamed into Edo (now Tokyo) Bay and demanded diplomatic negotiations with the emperor. Some samurais urged resistance, but senior officials knew how defenseless the city would be against naval bombardment. The next year Perry signed an agreement on behalf of the United States under which Japan would open its ports on a regular basis.

Both individual Japanese people and the government were motivated in good part by the desire to learn the skills that would allow them to protect Japan through industrial prosperity and military strength. Inventors adapted European mechanical designs, using the country's wealth of skilled workers to make everything from steam engines to telegraph machines. The state sent delegations to Europe and the United States with the goal of "swiftly seizing upon the strengths of the Western industrial arts," as the minister of industry wrote in 1873.[7] By the early 1870s the reformed central government known as the Meiji Restoration (see Chapter 24) had overseen the laying of thousands of miles of railroad and telegraph lines, and by the early twentieth century the country had some thirty-two thousand factories, many of them small; fifty-four hundred steam engines; and twenty-seven hundred machines run by electricity. Japan industrialized using an effective mixture of state, local, and individual initiatives based on a foundation of industriousness. This combination eventually led to Japan's central role in the world economy.

Economic Crises and Solutions

Even as some nations industrialized, the process brought uneven prosperity to the world and seesawing booms and busts, especially in the second half of the nineteenth century. Because global trade bound industrialized western Europe to international markets, a recession—by today's definition, a period of negative economic growth lasting six months or longer—could simultaneously affect the economies of such diverse regions as Germany, Australia, South Africa, California, Argentina, Canada, and the West Indies. At the time, economists, industrialists, and government officials did not clearly understand the workings of industrial and

SEEING THE PAST

Japan's Industrious Society

Famed Japanese artist Ando Hiroshige (1797–1858) is best known for his prints of nature and for his several series about work life in early-nineteenth-century Japan. In these works, Hiroshige combined his great printmaking skills with knowledge of Dutch and other Western art. The exchange went both ways, as Western artists borrowed from Hiroshige in return. Impressionists were especially drawn to his focus on daily life and his vibrant use of color. Later, Hiroshige's serial method and drawing technique influenced the creators of comic strips.

Hiroshige depicted the many livelihoods of Japan in some of his works. In particular he showed commercial life on the road to Edo (now Tokyo), the capital of Japan, before it industrialized. The road is clogged with busy people loaded with goods and supplies, demonstrating the "industrious" economies that laid the essential groundwork for full industrialization.

Hiroshige, *Nihon-bashi*, from the series *Fifty-Three Stations on the Tokaido* (Road to Tokyo)

Examining the Evidence

1. What attitude toward work comes through in this print?

2. How does it contrast with the attitude displayed in the document on page 866 by Mexican women workers?

interconnected economies. When a stubborn recession struck in the 1870s, lasting in some places for decades, they were stunned.

One reason for the recession of the 1870s was the skyrocketing start-up costs of new enterprises. Compared to steel and iron factories, the earliest textile mills had required little capital. After midcentury, industries became what modern economists call capital-intensive rather than labor-intensive: to grow, companies had to buy expensive machinery, not just hire more workers. This was especially true in developing countries such as those in Latin America, where the need to import machinery and hire foreign technicians added to costs.

Second, increased productivity in both agriculture and industry led to rapid price declines. Improved transportation allowed the expanding production of meat and grain in the United States, Australia, and Argentina to reach distant global markets rapidly, driving down prices. Wheat, for example, dropped to one-third its 1870 price by the 1890s. Consumers, however, did not always benefit from this persistent decrease in prices, or deflation, because employers slashed wages and unemployment rose during economic downturns. When this occurred, consumers just stopped purchasing manufactured goods, driving the economy further downward.

≡ **Industrializing Japan, c. 1870–1900**

Thus, a third major reason for the recession was underconsumption of manufactured products. Industrialists had made their fortunes by emphasizing production, not consumption. "Let the producers be many," went a Japanese saying, "and the consumers be few."[8] This attitude was disastrous because many goods were not sold, and the result was that prices for raw materials collapsed globally. People lost their land, jobs, and businesses.

In response to these conditions, governments around the world took action to boost consumption and control markets and prices. New laws protected innovation through more secure patents and spurred development of the limited-liability corporation, which protected investors from personal responsibility, or liability, for a firm's debt. **Limited liability** greatly increased investor confidence in financing business ventures. As prices fell in the 1870s and 1880s, governments broke any commitments they had made to free trade. They imposed tariffs (taxes) on imported agricultural and manufactured goods to boost sales of domestic products. Latin American countries levied tariffs that were some five times those in Europe. Without this protection from cheap European goods, a Mexican official predicted, new industries would "be annihilated by foreign competition."[9]

limited liability Legal protection for investors from personal responsibility for a firm's finances.

Business people also took steps to end the economic turmoil. They advanced the development of **stock markets**, which financed the growth of industry by selling shares or part ownership in companies to individual shareholders. In an international economy linked by telegraph, telephone, railways, and steamships, the London Stock Exchange was a center of this financial activity. At the same time, firms in single industries banded together in **cartels** to control prices and competition. One German coal cartel founded in 1893 dominated more than 95 percent of coal production in Germany. Thus, business owners deliberately blocked open competition to ensure profitability and economic stability.

Another way to address the economic crisis was to add managerial expertise. In the late 1800s, industrialists began to hire others to run their increasingly complex day-to-day operations—a revolutionary change in business practices. A generation and more earlier, factory owners such as Richard Arkwright had been directly involved in every aspect of the business and often ran their firms through trial and error. Now, separate managers specializing in sales and distribution, finance, or purchasing made decisions. The rise of the manager was part of the emergence of a "white-collar" service sector of office workers, with managers (generally male) at the high end of the pay scale and secretaries, file clerks, and typists (increasingly female) at the low end. Armies of white-collar employees channeled the flow of information to guide industry.

A final solution to the economic crisis was the development of consumer capitalism, to remedy the underconsumption of manufactured goods at the heart of the recession. The principal institution for boosting consumption was the department store, which daring entrepreneurs founded after midcentury to promote sales. Department stores gathered an impressive variety of goods in one place, in imitation of the Middle Eastern bazaar and the large Asian merchant houses, and they eventually replaced many of the single-item stores to which people were accustomed. Buenos Aires alone had seven major department stores, among them Gath y Chaves (GOT e shah-VEZ), which by 1900 had grown to occupy a multistoried building of thirteen-thousand-plus square feet, and which tripled its space five years later. From the Mitsui family in Tokyo to the Bloomingdales in New York, entrepreneurs set up institutions for mass consumerism.

Just as factories led workers to greater productivity, these modern palaces aimed to stimulate more consumer purchases. Luxury items like plush rugs and ornate draperies spilled over railings in glamorous disarray. Shoppers no longer bargained over prices; instead they reacted to sales, a new marketing technique that could incite a buying frenzy. Department stores also launched their own brands: Gath y Chaves began a line of ready-to-wear clothing, recognizing that busy urban workers no longer had time to make their own. Stores hired attractive salesgirls,

stock market A site for buying and selling financial interests, or stock, in businesses; examples include the London and Hong Kong stock exchanges.

cartel A group of independent business organizations in a single industry formed to control production and prices.

another variety of service worker, to lure customers to buy. Shopping was not only an urban phenomenon: glossy mail-order catalogues from the Bon Marché in Paris and Sears, Roebuck in the United States arrived regularly in rural areas to help farmers buy the products of industry. Department stores encouraged urban and rural shoppers alike to participate in the global, industrial marketplace.

The Industrial Revolution and the World

> ↘ **FOCUS** How did industrialization affect societies in China, South and West Asia, and Africa?

Industrialized Western nations pulled ahead of the once-dominant economies of China, India, and the Ottoman Empire, despite the real wealth that some local merchants, landowners, and entrepreneurs created for themselves. Like Japan, other nations in the early nineteenth century were often unwilling to trade with Europe, which was widely seen as both uncivilized and a source of inferior goods. Even an English man, commenting on the high quality of a shawl from India, agreed: "I have never seen a European shawl I would use, even if it were given to me as a present."[10] This attitude led Europeans and Americans alike to use threats of violence to open foreign markets because their productivity demanded outlets for manufactured goods, their factories needed raw materials, and their industrial workers depended on foreign food and stimulants.

≣ **Gath y Chaves Department Store** The first department stores, such as this one in Buenos Aires, Argentina, were built to resemble palaces and present the possibility of luxury to everyone. By assembling an array of goods once sold in individual small stores, the department store was revolutionary because it focused on increasing consumption rather than driving production, as industry had done. The first department stores were the direct ancestors of today's megastores and Internet shopping.

The Slow Disintegration of Qing China

A prime example was Qing China—the wealthiest and most productive country in the world on the eve of the Industrial Revolution—which enjoyed prosperity because of the silver flooding in to buy its cottons, porcelains, and other coveted items (see Map 23.3). Revolutionary upheavals in the Americas and the Napoleonic Wars in Europe suddenly stopped the flow of silver and curtailed trade, eating away at the

Qing China, 1830–1911

- Qing Empire, 1911
- Territory ceded to Russia, by 1911
- Area of Taiping Rebellion, c. 1840–1864
- Main area of porcelain production

Major trade goods
- Cotton cloth
- Iron products
- Porcelain
- Tea

Railroads, by 1911
- Chinese
- Russian
- British
- Japanese
- French
- German

- British attacks of the First Opium War, 1839–1842
- Treaty port, opened 1842
- Treaty port, opened 1858–1911

≡ **MAP 23.3   Qing China, 1830–1911**   Qing officials knew that opium was dragging China's people into addiction, but the resulting Opium War with Britain to restrict the supply only made matters worse. Led by the British, Europeans forced open Chinese ports, destroyed historic Chinese cities, and helped create uprisings such as the Taiping Rebellion.

source of China's wealth and strangling job opportunities. On world markets, imitation European goods began to compete with Chinese products, and social unrest erupted among the affected workers. Commercial rivalry soon turned to war.

Europeans had grown dependent on a variety of products from India and China, especially tea. The five chests of tea Europeans had purchased annually in the 1680s had soared to more than twenty-three million pounds annually by 1800. With nothing to sell in exchange, this meant a severe trade imbalance for Europe, whose cheap but inferior textiles were rejected by Chinese consumers. By the 1820s, however, the British had found something the Chinese would buy—opium. Grown in British-controlled India, opium was smuggled into China, where it was illegal. So great was the demand for the illegal drug in China that even after

buying tea the British smugglers turned a handsome profit. China's big payout in silver for illegal drugs caused a drain on its economy; Chinese officials also worried about growing addiction. A Chinese government official commanded the British to surrender their opium, as the British government sent a fleet to China to keep the illegal drug market open.

In the Opium War (1839–1842) that followed, Western firepower won decisive victories, and with the 1842 Treaty of Nanjing, China agreed to pay the British an indemnity (or fine), allow British diplomats access to the country, open five ports to trade, and reduce tariffs. While illegal opium made fortunes for British merchants, the Opium War made life difficult for Chinese workers. During the conflict, many lost their jobs, while a severe postwar depression was compounded by floods and famines between 1846 and 1848. In the late 1840s peasant religious leader Hong Xiuquan (hung she-o-chew-on) built a following among the underemployed and unemployed. Hong had failed to get the career he desperately wanted—a place in the prestigious Chinese civil service. As Hong failed successive attempts to pass the required exam, he fell feverishly ill and had religious visions that convinced him he was the brother of Jesus.

≡ **Weighing Opium in India** Opium grown in India went mostly to the Chinese market, though some found its way to Europe through Middle Eastern middlemen. Opium cured headaches, sleeplessness, and general aches and pains, but consumers in both Asia and Europe also welcomed the euphoric feeling of well-being the drug created. Many people became addicted, among them such famous Western artists as novelist Sir Walter Scott, poet Elizabeth Barrett Browning, and composer Hector Berlioz. British merchants and the British government, however, were concerned not with addiction but with sales and profits.

By 1850, Hong's preaching of his version of Christianity had attracted some twenty thousand disciples. Hong's social message promised a better future: he promoted work for all, equality of the sexes, and communal living, which appealed to hard-pressed ordinary people. It emphasized industriousness: "The diligent husbandman will be rewarded and the idle husbandman punished."[11] Like some of the Christian missionaries now entering China, Hong asked his followers to give up alcohol and opium and reject oppressive customs such as foot binding as first steps toward a perfect society—the Heavenly Kingdom of Peace, or Taiping Tianguo. His armies of rebels set off across the country, ultimately gathering millions more adherents (see again Map 23.3). To most Chinese, economic distress was evidence that their rulers had lost "the Mandate of Heaven"—that is, their political legitimacy. The Taiping Rebellion accelerated the crisis of the Qing government, already weakened by the Opium War. At this critical juncture, however, the movement's leaders began to quarrel among themselves and adopt a lavish lifestyle, which weakened the rebellion. The imperial militia, aided by U.S. military know-how, ultimately defeated the Taiping in 1864. Hong himself died that year in the final siege of Nanjing. In the end, some sixty million Chinese died in the slaughter.

The lesson learned by some intellectuals and officials was the value of Westernization, by which they meant modernizing the military, promoting technological education, and expanding industrialization. This led in the 1870s to the opening of mines and the development of textile industries, railroads, and the telegraph. However, the Dowager Empress Cixi, who had seized power during the uprising, zigzagged between maintaining imperial control of the government and modernization projects. It was unclear which impulse would triumph.

Competition in West and South Asia

By this time the Ottoman Empire was the longest lived modern empire. It had profited from wide-ranging trade as well as its extensive system of textile manufacture—one so far-reaching that Europeans, Africans, and Asians had long coveted its silks, dyes, fine cottons, and woven rugs. Western industrialization changed the balance of trade. As prices for textiles and thread dropped, artisans spinning and weaving at home suffered, working longer hours just to earn a living wage. Textile manufacturing had traditionally been done in the home during winter to provide income during the agricultural off-season. These artisanal ways persisted, but in the last third of the nineteenth century some carpet factories were established across the Ottoman lands. Young unmarried girls, who were less expensive to hire than men and worked for just three or four years (that is, long enough to earn a dowry to attract a husband), replaced lifelong artisans. The Industrial Revolution left many Ottoman subjects, in the words of a British traveler, "ragged beyond belief."[12]

Although the Industrial Revolution hurt craftworkers globally, it boosted the fortunes of other workers. After 1815, the ruler of Egypt, Muhammad Ali, set his subjects to mastering the industry's "strange machinery," and he eventually exempted workers in silk factories from service in the army.[13] Ottoman merchants prospered, as did owners of large estates who could send cotton and other agricultural products to markets around the world on railroads and steamships. New jobs opened up: in 1911 there were thirteen thousand railroad workers in the empire, and thousands more had helped construct the lines. In the Ottoman Empire, regional rulers such as Muhammad Ali who recognized the need for modern skills founded engineering schools and expanded technical education. The Industrial Revolution opened opportunities for some even as it made life more difficult for others.

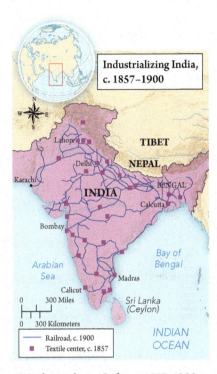

When Europe's cheap, lower-quality textiles flooded world markets, including those of the Indian subcontinent, the cut-rate competition hurt India's skilled spinners, weavers, and dyers. Furthermore, Britain taxed the textiles Indian craftsmen produced, tilting the economic playing field in favor of British goods. Even so, as in the Ottoman Empire, some in India's lively commercial economy adapted well. In Bengal between the

≡ Industrializing India, c. 1857–1900

1830s and 1860s, entrepreneur Dwarkanath Tagore teamed up with British engineers and officials to found raw silk firms, coal mines, steamship companies, and an array of other businesses that made his family fabulously wealthy. India's first textile factory opened in Bombay in 1853, and by 1914 India had the fourth-largest textile industry and the fourth-longest railway system in the world. Yet the coming of industry hurt artisanal families, sending many to farm in the countryside and others to the new jute factories (where jute, a native plant fiber, was processed into rugs, baskets, and other consumer items). As a result, some in India grew more rural as the West became more urban.

Besides textiles, India exported such manufactures as iron, steel, and jute products. Entrepreneurs such as Jamsetji Tata competed globally, founding a dynasty based first in textiles, then in iron and steel, and continuing in the twentieth century with airplanes and software. Yet British officials and merchants filled their pockets by imposing high taxes and taking more than their share of the region's prosperity. Moreover, although the British improved the Indian infrastructure—building the rail system, for example—the benefits of such improvements made it easier to extract and then sell India's agricultural goods on the world market to the profit of the very few.

A New Course for Africa

Industrialization had long-term consequences for Africa as well. During the nineteenth century, the Atlantic slave trade declined due to mounting protests against slavery and the growth of more profitable economic activities. As Denmark (1803) and Britain (1807) abolished the international slave trade, power in West Africa shifted to Muslim jihadis there who would not deal with European slavers, overthrew those rulers who did, and themselves built huge plantations in West Africa.

Since the Enlightenment, abolitionists had called for an end to the slave trade and to slavery itself. The antislavery message, crafted by blacks themselves and by white religious leaders, invoked Christian morality and the ideas of natural rights that had shaped the revolutions in the Atlantic world. In England, former slaves were eloquent participants in the antislavery movement, which expanded in the early nineteenth century to include international conferences. As the trade in humans was progressively outlawed, abolitionists worked to end slavery completely, a goal achieved in the Western Hemisphere in 1888 when Brazil became the last country in the Americas to outlaw it. Even after 1888, however, slavery continued in many parts of the world, including Africa and Asia (see Map 23.4).

The rationale for ending slavery had an economic dimension, and many merchants, financiers, and workers supported the abolitionist movement. The price of slaves had risen during the eighteenth century, so the use of slaves became more expensive. Some plantation owners recognized that it was more profitable if Africans worked in Africa to produce raw materials such as palm oil and cotton. Factory workers supported abolition because they regarded slaves as cheap competition in the labor market. Free labor became a widely accepted ideology in industrial areas.

The decline of profits from the Atlantic slave trade threw some African elites into economic crisis. Many quickly adapted, simply moving the slave trade south to supply markets in Brazil. Slavers arriving in some African ports learned to load ships and depart in some one hundred minutes to escape British surveillance. In the course of the nineteenth century, even as Europeans worked to abolish the trade, approximately 3.5 million slaves were taken from West Africa alone to sell in the Atlantic world and as large a stock was enslaved to work on African plantations, making goods for local markets but also providing raw materials for global manufacturing. The jihadi rulers expanded slavery within West Africa, waging war and kidnapping to capture non-Muslim or non-observant Muslim slaves for their own use. For fear of enslavement, "One could not go to another town's sector of the market without being led by an armed elder," one Nigerian man recalled.[14]

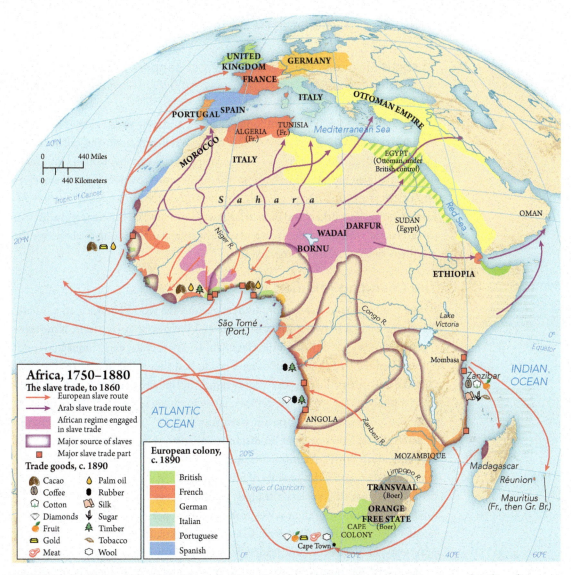

Legend contents:

Africa, 1750–1880
The slave trade, to 1860
→ European slave route
→ Arab slave trade route
African regime engaged in slave trade
Major source of slaves
■ Major slave trade part

Trade goods, c. 1890
🫘 Cacao   🝧 Palm oil
☕ Coffee   ● Rubber
Cotton   Silk
▽ Diamonds   ↓ Sugar
Fruit   ♣ Timber
Gold   Tobacco
Meat   Wool

European colony, c. 1890
British
French
German
Italian
Portuguese
Spanish

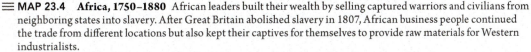

≡ **MAP 23.4   Africa, 1750–1880** African leaders built their wealth by selling captured warriors and civilians from neighboring states into slavery. After Great Britain abolished slavery in 1807, African business people continued the trade from different locations but also kept their captives for themselves to provide raw materials for Western industrialists.

Many historians believe that the expansion of slavery to profit from commodities for industrialization condemned Africa to underdevelopment. West Africa, one British traveler noted in the 1830s, "is disorganized, and except in the immediate vicinity of the towns, the land lies waste and uncultivated."[15] Industrialization had far-reaching consequences worldwide.

Industry and Society

FOCUS How did industrialization affect people's everyday lives and livelihoods?

Where industry took hold, livelihoods changed and new social classes emerged. In industrialized cities, people were less and less self-sufficient, and old social arrangements declined. At first, the two growing social groups, workers and manufacturers, lived side by side because the first factory owners were themselves often modest artisans who personally put their inventions to work. As industry advanced, however, workers and industrialists were divided into increasingly distinct social classes, with manufacturers and wealthy merchants coming to challenge the privileges of entrenched aristocracies.

The Changing Middle Class

Before the Industrial Revolution, traders around the world had formed a middle class, sandwiched between the aristocrats and the peasants and serfs. Now most factory owners joined this middle class. Unlike aristocrats, early industrial innovators often led frugal lives full of hard work, and they tried to ensure that their children and others did too. The Tagore family in India thrived on its efforts, leading Dwarkanath Tagore's son to refuse charity to a beggar-priest: "I shan't give you money . . . you are able to work, and earn your bread."[16] While early businessmen directed the factories or went on distant sales trips, their wives often tended the accounts, dealt with subcontractors, supervised workers (especially if they were female), and organized shipments of finished goods. As manufacturers grew prosperous, they became society's leaders, building large houses, consuming a few luxuries, and removing their wives from factory supervision. These middle-class women lived what historians term a "cult of domesticity" that signaled a family's prosperity. Modern economic leaders have collectively been called the *bourgeoisie*, a French term for the middle-class groups at the center of the Industrial Revolution.

With the march of industry, public monies often funded increasingly costly scientific research, as part of the state's commitment to building national wealth. The middle class grew to include professionals with empirical knowledge beneficial to industrial society, such as doctors, lawyers, professors, and journalists—all of whom drew on the scientific method and objective analysis in their work.

Prosperous men of the evolving middle class founded a range of societies and clubs to create solidarity and foster the exchange of knowledge. In Japan in 1876, the city fathers of Kanazawa opened an industrial museum to spread technical knowledge among the public. Wealthy citizens around the world worked to improve city life. "Reserve large areas for football, hockey, and parks," Indian industrialist Jamsetji Tata advised urban renovators. "Earmark areas for Hindu temples, Mohammedan mosques, and Christian churches."[17]

Well-to-do women banded together to provide baby clothes for newborn children and other goods to impoverished workers. Indian reformer Savithribai Phule, married at age nine, joined her husband in aiding the lowest-caste "Untouchables," despite mounting criticism and threats of violence against her. She founded schools for the girls of the Untouchable caste, claiming to feel "immeasurably happy" with her volunteer work.[18] As industrialization and rapid urban growth disturbed centuries-old ways of life, these institutions, in the words of one English official, promoted "the protection of their [industrialists'] property" by reducing worker misery and uniting the middle classes against those with "anti-social and revolutionary principles."[19]

≡ **An East Indian Middle-Class Family** Sometime in the late nineteenth century, this middle-class family donned their best clothes and sat for this formal portrait. The father may have worked for the British government or been an independent merchant or factory owner. This family wore fashionable Western clothing, although some of the women adapted their outfits by adding elements of the traditional sari to their dress.

The New Working Class

While the middle classes enjoyed increased comfort and prosperity, industrial workers led lives governed by the machine, the factory whistle, and eventually the time clock of the office or department store. Initially, many industrial workers, whether in the United States, Japan, Britain, or Argentina, were young, unmarried women whose families no longer needed them on farms, which now took fewer hands to run. Factories were magnets, offering steady wages and, often, supervised living quarters. Women and children were paid less than men, reducing labor costs but providing jobs far preferable to round-the-clock domestic service as maids. After her husband died in 1910, the Mexican widow Marcela Bernal del Viuda de Torres left her young sons to live with relatives and took her two daughters to Mexico City to find work for all three in its thriving factories. As Marcella said when explaining the move to her daughters, "I'm sure not going to let you end up as maids."[20]

The worker's day was often long, grueling, and unsafe, as Robert Blincoe witnessed firsthand. In 1844 England limited women's work to twelve hours per day, but in Japan men and women worked fourteen to seventeen hours a day even late in

Kinder, die vor Ort geschafft werden

≡ **Child Labor in Britain** Although the exploitation of children is still a feature of industrialization, the use of child labor by early industrialists was especially harsh, as this late-nineteenth-century illustration of children at work in the mines demonstrates. After these children were lowered side by side into claustrophobic conditions, they faced the rough job of physically hauling carts of coal out of the mines through narrow passageways. Like their adult counterparts, they suffered from coal dust and extremes of heat and cold. After parliamentary hearings on mine work, children's work and that of women who worked in and near the mines were regulated.

the century. Machines lacked even minimal safety features, leading to amputated limbs, punctured eyes, torn-off scalps, and other crippling injuries. A Japanese observer described cotton workers in urban factories as "pale and exhausted with faces like invalids" and "young girls with the lifeblood sucked out of them."[21]

Workers' health deteriorated in many cities: the lure of industrial work swelled urban populations to the breaking point and made cities, as one critic put it, "a too fertile source of disease."[22] There was not enough housing, and sanitary facilities were almost nonexistent. Europe's cities were usually surrounded by medieval walls, which limited their natural expansion, and humid factories nurtured disease. Epidemics of tuberculosis, pneumonia, and deadly cholera erupted, as happened, for example, in the camps housing thousands of Indian railroad builders. In its early days, industry's human costs were clear.

Many people resisted the introduction of labor-saving machines that threatened their livelihoods. Some handicraft workers—notably the Luddites (named after their leader, Ned Ludd)—attacked whole factories in northern England in 1812 and smashed the menacing new machines. In the countryside, day laborers left threatening notes for those who introduced threshing machines: "[W]e will burn down your barns and you in them this is the last notis."[23] The British government mobilized its armies, executing many and sending large numbers to populate Australia and New Zealand—which industrialized in turn.

Under the older values of city life, artisans mutually supported one another, but as rural folk migrated to cities in search of industrial jobs, workers were often strangers to one another. Between 1820 and 1840 the Russian government of Poland deemed that Lodz would become a textile center, for example, and thousands of migrant workers from the countryside quickly moved there. Chinese migrated to the Caribbean to service the sugar industry, and South Asians took their commercial and other skills to East Africa. Single young people or migrating widows in India lived beyond the reach of their families and community networks. Prostitution soared, along with sexually transmitted diseases and illegitimacy. Thus social connections in local communities broke down, as did the sense of rural time. No longer did sunrise and sunset determine the beginning and end of the workday. Now the clock set the hours for work, as factory whistles signaled the start of the workday, while stopwatches timed the pace of work. Industrialists imposed heavy fines on anyone late by even a minute. With alcohol a prominent feature of life in a world where there was no safe water or milk supply, however, drunkenness sometimes undermined the strict discipline industrialists hoped to impose.

The Sexual Division of Labor

Industrialists and manufacturers followed the tradition of dividing work along gender lines; the division was generally arbitrary. In some factory towns the weavers were all men, and women performed some processes in finishing the woven cloth. In other places, women tended the looms, and men only repaired and maintained the machines. Women's work in factories, even though it might be identical to men's, was said to require less skill; it always received lower pay. Men dreaded the introduction of women into a factory, which could signal that the owner intended to save on wages by cutting men's jobs. Whereas a husband's independent identity as handloom weaver or shoemaker was a proud if threatened one, his wife or daughters often became factory workers, earning the extra income that financed his independence.

The majority of women, both unmarried and married, worked to support their families or themselves. Factory owners and supervisors often demanded sexual favors from women as the price of employment. "Even the decent jobs, for example, those in banks," one Russian woman complained, "are rarely available unless one first grants favors to the director, the manager, or some other individual."[24] It was normal for supervisors to select one favorite woman, take her as a mistress, and then fire her once he tired of the relationship. Domestic service, which expanded with the rising prosperity of the middle class, saw many a housemaid fall victim to fathers and sons in middle-class families. If these sexual relations became known, the women would be fired, and pregnant servants quickly lost their jobs. This is why Marcela de Torres feared for her daughters.

The new white-collar sector advanced the sexual division of labor. Cost-conscious employers looking for workers with mathematical, reading, and writing skills gladly offered jobs to women. Since respectable lower-middle-class women had few other employment options, businesses in the service sector, as in the factories, paid women much less than men for the same work. All sectors of the industrial economy perpetuated the idea that women were simply worth less than men and should receive lower wages (see Reading the Past: Mexican Women on Strike).

READING THE PAST

Mexican Women on Strike

As industrialization progressed, factory workers increasingly responded to the harsh conditions of industrialization by organizing unions and banding together to strike. They directed their demands to factory owners and government officials, and they sought support from their fellow citizens. For instance, in 1881, women cigarette workers in Mexico City wrote a letter to a magazine for elite women in which they suggested that poverty might lead them to prostitution. At the same time, women cigar workers posted this placard around Mexico City to explain their strike against the factory owners.

Oppression by the Capitalist!

Until October 2, 1881, we used to make 2185 cigars for four reales [Mexican money], and now they have increased the number of cigars and lowered our salary. On October 3, 1881, through the mediation of El Congreso Obrero [The Congress of Workers], we agreed to make 2304 cigars for four reales. It is not possible for us to make more. We have to work from six in the morning until nine at night. . . . We don't have one hour left to take care of our domestic chores, and not a minute for education. The capitalists are suffocating us. In spite of such hard work, we still live in great poverty. What are our brother-workers going to do? What are the representatives of the Mexican press going to do? We need protection, protection for working women!

Source: Susie S. Porter, *Working Women in Mexico City: Public Discourses and Material Conditions, 1879–1931* (Tucson: University of Arizona Press, 2003), 80.

Examining the Evidence

1. What major concerns do the women announce in this placard?

2. To what specific groups is the placard addressed? Why did the strikers single out these groups?

The Culture of Industry

> ↘ **FOCUS** How did writers and artists respond to the new industrial world?

Writers, artists, and ordinary people alike responded to the dramatic new sights and unexpected changes of industrialization. The railroad and expanded trade spread local customs, contributing to the development of national cultures. In

Japan, for example, sashimi and sushi, once known in only a few fishing towns, became popular dishes across the nation. Technological improvements helped knowledge flourish: gas lighting extended reading deep into the night, for example, and railroads exposed more travelers than ever to distant scenes. Increased productivity eventually led to more leisure time, and streams of workers entered cafés, dance halls, and parks to enjoy their new free time. Such changes in everyday life led to a torrent of cultural reflections on the dramatic new industrial world.

Industry and Thought

In some, industry inspired optimism. For such thinkers, the rational calculation and technological progress that had produced industry suggested that a perfect society could be created. A group of French and British thinkers, the "utopian socialists," spread this faith around the world. Their goal was to improve society as a whole, not just for the individual—hence the term **socialism**. They believed that rational planning would lead to social and political perfection—that is, to utopia—and to prove their point they often lived in communes where daily life could be as precisely organized as it was in the factory. The inefficient nuclear family became obsolete in their communes, where large numbers of people worked together to finish necessary tasks efficiently. Shunning monarchs and leisured aristocrats, **utopian socialism** valued technicians and engineers as future rulers of nations.

Two middle-class German theorists—the lawyer and economist Karl Marx (1818–1883) and the wealthy industrialist Friedrich Engels (1820–1895)—devised a completely different and globally influential plan for organizing society. Sharing the utopian socialists' appreciation of science, they saw the new industrial order as unjust and oppressive. In 1848 they published *The Communist Manifesto*, which became a rallying cry of modern socialism. Marx elaborated on what he called "scientific socialism" in his most important work, *Das Kapital* (*Capital*), published between 1867 and 1894.

Marx held that the fundamental organization of any society rested on the relationships developed around production. This idea, known as **materialism**, was that a society's structure was built on the class relationships involved in producing the goods that sustained life. These relationships were those between serf and medieval lord, slave and master, or worker and factory owner. Marx referred to these systems—feudalism, slavery, and **capitalism**, respectively—as modes of production. In the industrial era, people were in one of two classes: the workers, or **proletariat**, and the owners, or capitalists (also the **bourgeoisie**, in Marxist terms), who owned the means of production—the land, machines, factories, and other productive instruments. Rejecting the eighteenth-century liberal focus on individual rights, he held that the cause of the inequality between classes such as

socialism A social and political ideology dating from the early nineteenth century that stresses the need to maintain social harmony through communities based on cooperation rather than competition; in Marxist terms, a classless society of workers who collectively control the production of goods necessary for life.

utopian socialism A goal of certain French and British thinkers early in the nineteenth century, who envisioned the creation of a perfect society through cooperation and social planning.

materialism In Marxist terms, the idea that the organization of society derives from the organization of production.

capitalism An economic system in which the means of production—machines, factories, land, and other forms of wealth—are privately owned.

the proletariat and the capitalists was the owners' control of the means of production, which yielded profit. When capitalist control disappeared, as Marx was certain it would, a classless society of workers would arise.

Economic liberals such as Adam Smith thought the free market would ultimately produce a harmony of interests among people in all classes of society. In contrast, Marx believed that the workers' economic oppression by their bosses inevitably caused conflict. He predicted that workers would unite in revolt against their capitalist exploiters and bring about fundamental change worldwide. The proletariat would overthrow capitalism, and socialism would reign. The moment for revolt, Marx thought, was near. "The proletarians have nothing to lose but their chains.... WORKING MEN OF ALL COUNTRIES, UNITE!" So ends *The Communist Manifesto.*

Marx believed that a classless society would involve workers' control of production in large factories. In a socialist society, the end of private ownership of the means of production would in turn end the need for a state, whose only function, Marx claimed, was to protect wealthy people's property. Like many male intellectuals, Marx devoted little analysis to inequalities based on race and gender. He did conclude, however, that women's lives would automatically improve under socialism. The possibility of achieving Marxist socialism inspired workers around the world down to the present.

Industry and the Arts

The new industrial world also inspired artists. Some celebrated industry, welcoming the influences from far-off places. Japanese woodblocks showed trains racing through a countryside of cherry blossoms. Hiroshige's prints depicting roads teeming with working people inspired Western artists to turn from mythical topics and great historic scenes to the subject matter of everyday lives. Deeply influenced by the color, line, and delicacy of Japanese art as well as by its focus on ordinary life, French painters such as Claude Monet pioneered the artistic style known as "impressionism," so called for the artists' effort to capture a single moment by focusing on how the ever-changing light and color transformed everyday sights. Industry contributed to the new style as factories produced products that allowed Western painters to use a wider, more intense spectrum of colors.

Other Western artists interpreted the Industrial Revolution differently, focusing instead on the grim working conditions brought about by wrenching change. One was Germany's Käthe Kollwitz, whose woodcuts realistically depict starving artisans. British author Charles Dickens wrote of the dark side of industrialization in popular novels that reached even a Japanese audience. Among them was *Oliver Twist* (1837–1839), which many scholars speculate was based in part on the life of Robert Blincoe. *Uncle Tom's Cabin* (1852), U.S. writer Harriet Beecher Stowe's shocking tale of slave life in the American South, influenced some in the Russian nobility to lobby for freeing the serfs.

proletariat Under capitalism, those who work without owning the means of production.

bourgeoisie Originally a term meaning the urban middle class; Marx defined it as the owners of the means of production under capitalism.

Even musical forms showed the impact of the Industrial Revolution. Utopian socialists composed music celebrating the railroad and the sounds of industry. Concert halls, like factories, became bigger to accommodate the increasing urban population, and orchestras included more instruments to produce a massive sound. Military bands marched through the widening streets of capital cities. Their increasing precision and noise matched that of the new machines and the precise movements of the industrial workers tending them.

COUNTERPOINT: African Women and Slave Agriculture

FOCUS What contributions did African women agricultural workers make to industrial development?

The story of the Industrial Revolution often centers on individual inventors and the labor-saving machinery they pioneered. Entire groups, however, many of them anonymous and uncelebrated, piloted advances critical to industrialization. A good example comes from Africa, which many regarded as a continent full of unskilled people; this perspective justified both the enslavement of and discrimination against all people of color. Africans, however, were foremost among the collective innovators of their day.

Women and Farming in Africa

Many of these unnamed inventors were women, who have dominated African farming both as cultivators of their own land or as slaves. Women's agricultural labor supported African life. When they married, women received land to provide for themselves and their children. Free and slave women alike could themselves own slaves to increase their agricultural productivity. As farmworkers, women served as a counterpoint to independent and free male factory workers, peasants and large landowners alike. In Africa it was women, either as independent farmers or more usually as slave laborers, who introduced new varieties of seeds, new tools for farming, and more productive farming techniques. Today it is estimated that African women grow some 80 percent of all agricultural produce on the continent.

On the west coast of Africa, although men participated in some aspects of rice farming, rice cultivation was known as "women's sweat." Women developed complex systems for cultivating the important rice crop, especially a variety called "red" rice. To control water supplies, they installed canals, sluices, and embankments, depending on whether they were capturing water from rain, tides, or floods.

≡ **Nayemwezi Women Pounding Sorghum, 1864** As industrialization advanced around the world, women in Africa were central to its agricultural foundation, as this drawing shows. They planted, weeded, and harvested major crops such as sorghum, a grass whose kernels were pounded into flour and whose stalks were pressed to produce a sweet syrup. Sorghum is native to Africa, and there is evidence that slave women brought it, along with rice and other crops, to the Western Hemisphere.

They reaped bountiful harvests through this manipulation of the environment, experimenting with new seeds and plant varieties.[25]

Women Slaves in the North American South

Landowners in South Carolina and Georgia prized West African slave women, considering them "choice cargo" because of their knowledge of rice cultivation. In fact, it was slaves from West Africa who established the "red" rice variety as a preferred crop on American plantations and provided the initial technological systems for growing it. This rice was so important to the U.S. South's developing commercial economy that Thomas Jefferson, for one, sought more information about it. Its main advantage, he learned, was that if cultivated according to African techniques of water management, it could be grown outside of swamps. The more usual practice of cultivating rice in standing water "sweeps off numbers of the inhabitants with pestilential fevers,"[26] according to Jefferson, so a growing system that eliminated the threat of disease was advantageous.

The first African rice to be widely grown in North America was fragile, demanding special skills that planters such as Jefferson usually lacked. In contrast, West African women possessed an extensive knowledge of this and other forms of agriculture and passed this knowledge down through their families. Slavers added these women to their cargo along with unhusked rice and many other plants and seeds. When they arrived in the Western Hemisphere, the technological knowledge to grow them moved from Africans to Europeans, not the other way around. In this regard West African women farmers form a counterpoint to the celebrated inventors of machines. Although they have been overlooked in history books, they created wealth for their owners, most of whom in the early days of rice cultivation were adventurers with little knowledge of how to grow these crops. Their story of the introduction of rice to North America, the perfection of other seeds, and the complex technology of irrigation and processing that helped feed a growing global workforce—industrial and otherwise—has seemed less heroic than that of an individual who invented one labor-saving machine.

Conclusion

The Industrial Revolution changed not only the world economy but the lives and livelihoods of tens of millions of people, from workers and manufacturers to the politicians facing rapidly changing societies. By replacing simple machines operated by human energy with complex machines powered by steam engines, mechanization expanded productivity almost beyond measure. The results were both grim and liberating. Industrial laborers such as child mill worker Robert Blincoe suffered abuse, and the flow of cheap goods from industrial countries drove down prices and threw artisans around the world into poverty. Slavery not only flourished but made the advance of industry possible. Unsung slave women spread the cultivation of numerous plants, including rice, to help feed the growing population of workers worldwide. The new patterns of work in large factories transformed the rhythm of labor and the texture of urban life, and cities grew rapidly with the influx of both local and global migrants. Political ideas and the arts also changed with the rise of industry and the continuing expansion of global trade. Movements to end slavery and to create free workers succeeded in Europe and many parts of the Western Hemisphere.

Debate continues about whether industry was a force for good, but even opponents have appreciated that industry liberated people from the hardships of rural life and provided them a wider array of useful goods. The middle and working classes that developed with industrialization led different lives even within the same industrial cities, but they were often caught up in another global movement of the time—the development of the political form called the nation-state. As we will see in the next chapter, nation-state and empire were forms that accompanied the rise of industry and ushered in further complexity to the modern era.

✳ review

The major global development in this chapter: The Industrial Revolution and its impact on societies and cultures throughout the world.

Important Events	
c. 1750	Industrialization begins in Great Britain
1769	James Watt creates the modern steam engine
1780s–1790s	Interchangeability of parts developed in France
1803	Denmark becomes the first Western country to abolish the slave trade
1814	George Stephenson puts a steam engine on a carriage on rails, inventing the locomotive
1819	First Atlantic crossing by a steamship
1839–1842	Opium War between China and Britain
1840s–1864	Taiping Rebellion in China
1842	Treaty of Nanjing opens Chinese ports
1848	*Communist Manifesto* published
1853	U.S. ships enter Japanese ports
1865	U.S. Civil War ends, rapid U.S. industrialization begins
1868	Meiji Restoration launches Japanese industrialization
c. 1870–1900	Deep global recession with uneven recovery
1871	Germany gains resource-rich Alsace and Lorraine after defeating France
1890s	Argentina's leading textile manufacturer produces 1.6 million yards of cloth annually
1891–1904	Construction of trans-Siberian railroad

KEY TERMS

bourgeoisie (p. 868)
capitalism (p. 867)
cartel (p. 854)
Industrial Revolution (p. 841)

interchangeability
of parts (p. 845)
limited liability (p. 853)
materialism (p. 867)
outwork (p. 847)

proletariat (p. 868)
socialism (p. 867)
stock market (p. 854)
utopian socialism (p. 867)

CHAPTER OVERVIEW QUESTIONS

1. In what ways did the Industrial Revolution change people's work lives and ideas?
2. How did the Industrial Revolution benefit people, and what problems did it create?

3. How and where did industrial production develop, and how did it affect society and politics?

MAKING CONNECTIONS

1. How did the Scientific Revolution (see Chapter 19) and the Enlightenment (see Chapter 22) contribute to industrialization?
2. How did industrialization in the United States and in Japan differ, and why?

3. What was the role of slavery in industrial development?
4. In what ways was the Industrial Revolution a world event?

For further research on the topics covered in this chapter, see the Bibliography at the end of the book. For additional primary sources from this period, see *Sources for World in the Making*.

24

Nation-States and Their Empires 1830–1900

Modernizing Nations

FOCUS *How did some states transform themselves into modern nations?*

Building Empires

FOCUS *What motivated the imperialists, and how did they impose their control over other nations?*

Societies in an Age of Nations and Empires

FOCUS *How did nations and empires change lives and livelihoods around the world?*

COUNTERPOINT: Outsiders Inside the Nation-State

FOCUS *Which groups were excluded from full participation in the nation-state, and why?*

World in the Making The Meiji Restoration of 1868 was the foundation of Japanese nation-building and industrialization. Its Charter Oath, the founding document of Japan's new regime, is shown here being read in the presence of the emperor. The Charter Oath established the rule of law over "evil customs" of the past and opened the door to freedom in livelihoods. It also called on the Japanese to scour the world for new findings and advances, thus combining nation-building and economic development.

backstory

As we saw in Chapter 23, throughout the nineteenth century Europe and the United States industrialized rapidly, if unevenly, allowing the West to catch up economically with India and China. Industrialization offered a host of advantages to the West. Both Europe and the United States excelled in producing weaponry, which made them especially successful in opening trade and gaining diplomatic power. As the West's newly industrialized states extended their power around the world, industrialization also produced internal transformations. It gave rise to new social classes and new occupations, swelling the middle and working classes and giving both a stake in the growing prosperity of their nations.

The drive to increase national power was a prime motive for commercial and military expansion, an outgrowth of state efforts to gain control of resources, markets, and strategic locations around the world. As states jostled with one another for power, their rivalries were increasingly played out in a competition for possessions outside of their national boundaries.

In 1862 Matsuo Taseko, a prosperous Japanese peasant, hurried to the capital at Kyoto. Leaving her family behind and traveling alone, she had an unusual goal: to join with other conservative activists to restore the Japanese emperor, who for centuries had played second fiddle to the Tokugawa shogun, or first minister. "Despicable charlatans," she called the shogun's administration. Even worse to Taseko were the foreigners in the country's port cities, notably the Americans and British, who had demanded in the 1850s that Japan open its harbors to global trade. Taseko wrote this poem about them:

> The superficial
> foreign barbarians
> pile up mountains
> of silver,
> but even I, who am not
> a brave warrior
> from the land of the rising sun,
> I do not want their money,
> I would rather be poor.[1]

Beginning in 1862 members of Taseko's conservative group, aiming to free Japan from outside influences and to restore the emperor, waged a virtual civil war with reformers who wanted trade, the latest technology, and a modern nation-state. By 1868 Japan had restored the emperor to his central position in an act, para-doxically, of modern nation-building known as the Meiji Restoration—part of a global trend toward building strong, up-to-date states whose people felt bound together as citizens of a unified nation. New Latin American states also developed national allegiances, while in Europe the many individual German and Italian states unified into two distinct nations. The United States and Russia worked to fortify themselves by freeing millions of unfree laborers and by expanding their boundaries at the expense of neighboring peoples.

Historians sometimes treat the development of nation-states and of cohesive national identities among citizens as an inevitable process. However, it was not: millions of individuals in parts of eastern Europe, Africa, and Oceania, for example, maintained their local identities based in village life or ethnic ties. Once-powerful states such as the Ottoman Empire found it difficult to modernize the administra-tion of its vast holdings. China likewise failed to reform its governmental structures sufficiently to fight off inroads made by the European powers. Modern world-making was a complicated undertaking.

Other regions failed to change because modern nation-states were increasingly costly, due to growing bureaucracies, armies, and weaponry. In the nineteenth century, ambitious nations, including Matsuo Taseko's Japan, undertook a vigorous expansion of empire in the hope of boosting income to fund national power. Nation-states viewed the conquest of distant peoples as proof of their national superiority. National pride further united people within the metropole—that is, the homeland of an empire. As imperial rule of the globe increased, people in colonized countries had their independence denied. Those conquered were often terrorized and their resources stolen.

Britain, France, the Netherlands, Belgium, Germany, Russia, Japan, and the United States all shared an impulse to take over the wealth and, increasingly, the governments of other regions of the world. Historians use the term "new imperialism" to describe this obsession in the second half of the nineteenth century with global domination. Despite conflict and bloodshed, some in the colonies were inspired by the technological strength of nation-states and by theories of self-determination. The very existence of such ideals led many to fight for their freedom.

In the course of nation-building and the drive for empire, society and culture changed. Poets and artists reacted to the whirl of activity around them, sometimes deploring the changes and at other times seizing on ideas from other cultures to spark their creativity. Beyond what Matsuo Taseko could have imagined, tens of millions of people migrated to find opportunity, to escape colonial exploitation, or to serve as forced laborers and enslaved captives. As they took up livelihoods in faraway places, these migrants created new communities, such as the Chinese in Singapore and San Francisco and the Lebanese in Rio de Janeiro and Montreal. Oppression and opportunity coexisted, revealing the complexities of nation-building and imperial globalization.

OVERVIEW QUESTIONS

The major global development in this chapter: The rise of modern nation-states and their competition for empire.

As you read, consider:

1. Why did nation-states become so important to people in the nineteenth century?

2. What are the arguments for and against imperialism?

3. Which were the major imperialist powers, and what made them so capable of conquest?

4. Are there still outsiders inside nations?

Modernizing Nations

FOCUS How did some states transform themselves into modern nations?

Politicians at this time worked to unite diverse peoples within their borders and to develop more effective governments. Some created entirely new nation-states, as occurred in Italy and Germany. Even where industry was slower to thrive, nation-building occurred. People of the newly independent nations of Latin America began to develop a sense of themselves as citizens with common values. In Eurasia the Russian Empire instituted dramatic reforms in pursuit of a more effective and modern nation-state. This political and cultural form shaped the course of modern history, both for good and for ill.

"What Is a Nation?"

In an 1882 lecture, French writer Ernest Renan asked, "What is a nation?" The concept was much debated. Nations came to be seen as political units in which citizens feel an allegiance to one another and are active in the state that represents them. Thus *nation-state* and *nation* are often treated as synonyms. A **nation** differs from a kingdom—that is, the personal domain of a monarch, who sees people as subjects to be ruled, not as citizens demanding the rule of law and involvement in government. This active civic voice was essential to the rise of modern nations. Facing an enemy from without, people proudly protected the nation as patriotic soldiers rather than, as in a kingdom, military recruits forced to defend royal interests. Although they lacked political rights, women also began to consider themselves active contributors to national well-being, especially by rearing children to be virtuous citizens.

The nation-state bolstered its unity by coordinating economic development and eliminating tariffs among cities and localities. Importantly, it replaced disruptive regional armies with a single fighting force focused on advancing national power. Nation builders enlarged bureaucracies to oversee centralized institutions—constitutions, laws, and common military, education, and transportation systems. In this multifaceted undertaking, governments aimed to minimize competing allegiances, including local ones, and strengthen national loyalties.

nation
A sovereign political entity and defined territory of modern times representing a supposedly united people.

Latin American Nation-Building

After the regions of South and Central America gained independence from Spain and Portugal early in the nineteenth century, they did not generally develop efficient common institutions, but they did lay the groundwork for nation-states. Although some people of individual nations acquired a sense of themselves as citizens, Latin American nation-building was complex and often difficult (see Map 24.1).

Latin America, c. 1900

1821 Year independence gained

Civil war or rebellion

Colony

Boundaries, 1900

≡ **MAP 24.1   Latin America, c. 1900** The new nations of Latin America worked to create effective governments and institutions such as schools and draw citizens into the nation-building process. Like the new United States of America to the north, these nations often fought with their neighbors to expand boundaries and crushed native Americans to gain their lands.

For example, Brazil's dominant ruler for more than five decades was the emperor Pedro II (r. 1831–1889)—a committed nation builder. "I have no rights; all I have is a power resulting from birth and chance," he claimed. "It is my duty to use it for the welfare, the progress, and the liberty of my people."[2] Pedro surrounded himself with people of all races, ending the slave trade in 1850, partly in response to the growing voice of people of color expressed through their newspapers and clubs. Brazil ended slavery altogether in 1888 and produced one of the greatest Latin American writers, Joachim Machado de Assis (ma-KA-do day ah-SEES). Of African descent, Machado de Assis's masterful novels do not portray Pedro's rosy view. Instead, Machado satirically explored the worlds of the old moneyed classes, the new bureaucracies of the rising nation-state, and the outsider status of women—all shaped by the legacy of slavery.

The emancipation of Brazil's slaves enraged rural plantation and mine owners, who relied on slave labor for their profits and, billing themselves as "federalists," believed in regional autonomy. In 1889, these opponents overthrew Pedro's centralizing monarchy, returning power to their regional control and thus reversing the movement toward a strong, inclusive nation-state. As one newspaper complained of the takeover, "In Brazil there are no more citizens; we are all slaves!"[3] In fact, most Latin American nations were shaped by powerful landowners in the countryside, who controlled the production of commodities sold on the global market. Such men upheld the eighteenth-century liberal belief in minimal government and the building of individual wealth. Almost every Latin American state experienced this contest between centralization and **federalism**.

Many wealthy landowners were themselves strongmen with their own armies, but there were also independent military leaders, *caudillos*, men at the head of unofficial bands of warriors who controlled the countryside by force. Functioning as a law unto themselves, they gathered the support of peasants, workers, and the poor by offering protection. General Antonio Lopez de Santa Anna was the quintessential caudillo and a virtual dictator. In Mexico, the period from the 1830s to 1855 is called the "Age of Santa Anna" because his personal power actually stabilized the nation amidst political turmoil.

Despite regionalism, gradually governments built state institutions such as national armies and military schools to train nationally oriented officers and took control of infrastructure such as railroads and ports. As important, people themselves developed a sense of belonging that was crucial to nation-building. José Gregorio Paz Soldán, a judge in Peru, had first supported slavery in the new republic but soon became an ardent defender of liberty and equal treatment for all: "The Indians are no more savage or ferocious than other people who have been attracted to a social and civilized life."[4] Paz Soldán wanted solidarity among

federalism A form of government in which power and administration are located in regions such as provinces and states rather than in a centralized administration.

≡ **Brazilian Plantation Workers** Pedro II freed Brazil's slaves in 1888 in the belief that modern, unified nations needed to fully integrate all races into citizenship. Once regional leaders overthrew his monarchy, however, the weakened national authority could not protect newly freed workers such as these on a manioc plantation from exploitation by landowners.

citizens of all classes. The Peruvian constitution of 1828 stated, "All citizens may be admitted to public employment, without any difference except that of their talents and virtues."[5] The qualifications for citizenship were in theory the same for everyone, uniting people of different ethnicities and classes instead of dividing them as the Spanish monarchy had done by favoring the Spanish-born.

The Russian Empire's New Course

The Russian Empire modernized its institutions when wartime defeat dramatically revealed the need for change. In the 1800s, Russia continued its centuries-old expansionism across Asia. Tsar Nicholas I eyed the Ottoman Empire, which was fast becoming known as "the sick man of Europe" because of its administrative weakness. As Russia grew more aggressive, the Crimean War erupted in October 1853, beginning as a conflict between the Russian and Ottoman empires but soon expanding when Britain and France, enemies for more than a century, united in 1854 to declare war on Russia to defend the Ottoman Empire's sovereignty. To maintain power in the global economy, they needed secure access to the eastern Mediterranean.

The war coincided with the continuing spread of the Industrial Revolution, which introduced powerful new technologies into warfare: the railroad, breech-loading rifles, steam-powered ships, and the telegraph. Home audiences received news from the Crimean front rapidly. As a million men died, more than two-thirds from disease and starvation, wartime incompetence and poor sanitation showed that nations needed strong institutions. Citizens responded: London reformer Florence Nightingale organized battlefield nursing care for British troops, while Darya Mikhailova nursed Russian combatants. Along with Jamaican volunteer Mary Seacole, they pioneered nursing as a profession. Nightingale's postwar statistical studies showed that national effectiveness depended on organized health services for both the public and the military.

The war exposed Russia's weakness and transformed the global balance of power. With casualties mounting, Tsar Alexander II (r. 1855–1881) asked for peace. As a result of the peace treaty of 1856, Austria's and Russia's grip on European affairs weakened, making way for the rise of new powers. The defeat forced the authoritarian Russian state to embark on long-overdue reforms.

The public blamed Russia's loss on oppressed serf armies. In fact, the entire system of serf labor was seen as an intolerable liability for a country that clearly needed modernization to be an effective nation-state on the world stage. The Russian economy had stagnated compared with western Europe. Old-fashioned farming techniques led to worn-out soil and food shortages that in turn stoked serf rebellion.

Inspiration for reform also came from serf artists and writers—those among the serfs who were assigned artistic tasks such as piano tuning or fine cabinetry, some of whom became highly educated. One such lucky serf was Alexander Nikitenko (1804–1877). Enraged at his unfree condition, Alexander became known as one of the most learned young men in the land. In the late 1830s a powerful Russian prince obtained Nikitenko's freedom, allowing him to become a high government official—one advocating change (see Reading the Past: The Russian People Under Serfdom).

Faced with Russia's dire situation, Alexander II sponsored the Great Reforms, granting Russians new rights from above to fend off violence from below. The most dramatic was the emancipation of almost fifty million serfs beginning in 1861.

READING THE PAST

The Russian People Under Serfdom

Alexander Nikitenko gained his freedom from serfdom after proving himself a learned and conscientious teacher as well as an outstanding manager of households and general man of all work. Many serfs were accomplished; their achievements included painting and traveling in troupes of actors and singers, which brought Russians in contact with one another across vast spaces. Like Nikitenko, some of these serfs reached national eminence and came to be celebrated, but Nikitenko felt the degradation of serfdom long after he was free. These excerpts from his autobiography, first published in 1824, concern the early nineteenth century when he was between six and ten years old. They do not reflect the thinking of a child, however; Nikitenko observed serfdom for decades while honing this account of his life.

> The peasants suffered beneath the yoke of serfdom. If a master was wealthy and owned several thousand serfs, they suffered less oppression because most of them were tenant farmers. . . . On the other hand, small [landowners] literally sucked out the strength of unfortunates in their power. Neither time nor land was at their disposal. . . . In addition, sometimes there was inhuman treatment, and often cruelty was accompanied by debauchery. . . .

People could be bought and sold wholesale or in small numbers, by families, or singly like bulls and sheep. . . . Tsar Alexander I, during the humanitarian phase of his reign, talked about improving the lot of his serf-subjects, but attempts to limit the [landowners'] power vanished without trace. The nobility wanted to live in luxury befitting its station. . . .

[E]veryone bore the burdens generated by the People's War [Napoleon's 1812 invasion] without complaint. They supplied and equipped recruits at great personal expense. Yet I did not detect in their conversations a sign of deep interest in the events of the time. Evidently everyone was interested solely in their own affairs. The mention of Napoleon's name evoked awe rather than hate. The nonchalant attitude of our community toward the disaster hanging over Russia was startling. This may have been due in part to the distance of theater of war. . . .

But I think the main reason was apathy, characteristic of a people estranged from participation in society's affairs, as Russians were then. They were not accustomed to discussion [of] what went on around them and unconditionally obeyed the orders of the authorities.

Source: Alexander Nikitenko, *Up from Serfdom: My Childhood and Youth in Russia 1804–1824, trans.* Helen Saltz Jacobson (New Haven: Yale University Press, 2001), 54–56, 75.

Examining the Evidence

1. How does Nikitenko characterize Russian serfs?

2. How did serfdom affect the Russian people and state more generally?

3. What was the mood of the Russian people as a nation facing the Napoleonic invasion of 1812? How might the emancipation of the serfs in 1861 have changed the mood?

☰ **Russian Peasants at a Soup Kitchen** Even after emancipation from serfdom in 1861, Russian peasants were hard-pressed to earn a living. As a condition of emancipation, they were burdened with debt for farmland and could not migrate freely in search of greater opportunity. Only acts of charity, such as the soup kitchen distributing food shown here, relieved the misery of many.

Each liberated serf lived in a community called a *mir* (mihr), which received allocations of land from the state for which the new farmers had to reimburse the government. Male village elders distributed this land among its members and directed their economic activity. Thus, although the serfs were free, the requirements of communal landowning held back individuals with new ideas and those who wanted to find opportunity elsewhere. Nonetheless, former serf Alexander Nikitenko, like others, received this news "with an inexpressible feeling of joy."[6] As one writer said, the people, once treated like livestock, were "transfigured from head to foot. . . . The look, the walk, the speech, everything is changed."

    The state also reformed local administration, the judiciary, and the military in an effort to promote national allegiance. The changes diminished the personal prerogatives of the nobility, weakening its authority and sparking intergenerational rebellion. "An epidemic seemed to seize upon [noble] children . . . an epidemic of fleeing from the parental roof," one observer noted. Rejecting aristocratic values,

mir In Russia, the organization of land and former serfs following the emancipation of the serfs.

youthful rebels from the upper class identified with peasants and workers. Some turned to higher education to gain modern knowledge. Rebellious daughters of the nobility sported short hair, wore black, and abandoned their parents to study medicine and the sciences in European universities. Author Ivan Turgenev labeled radical youth *nihilists* (from the Latin for "nothing"), meaning they lacked belief in any values whatsoever. Youthful defiance soon fueled assassinations, including that of the reformer Alexander II in 1881. The next tsar and his inner circle held tightly to the reins of government, slowing the development of consensus politics and modern citizenship.

Risorgimento Italian for "rebirth," a nineteenth-century rallying cry for the unification of the Italian states.

A Unified Italy and a United Germany

With the European powers divided over the Crimean War of 1853 to 1856, politicians in the German and Italian states took the opportunity to unify and modernize their respective countries. Visionary leaders Camillo di Cavour and Otto von Bismarck took charge. Both depended on modern railroads, strong armies, and power diplomacy to transform disunited states into coherent nations.

The architect of the new Italy was Camillo di Cavour, prime minister of the kingdom of Piedmont-Sardinia in the economically modernizing north of Italy from 1852 until his death in 1861. A rebel in his youth, the young Cavour had conducted agricultural experiments on his aristocratic father's land, organized steamship companies, and inhaled the fresh air of modernization. Cavour promoted a healthy Piedmontese economy and a modern army to anchor Piedmont's drive to unite the Italian states.

To achieve this goal, however, Piedmont would have to confront Austria, which governed the northern provinces of Lombardy and Venetia. In 1859, with help from France, Piedmontese armies achieved rapid victories. In May 1860, an inspirational guerrilla fighter, Giuseppe Garibaldi, set sail from Genoa to liberate Sicily with a thousand red-shirted volunteers, half from the urban working class, "splendid in the dress and cap of the student, and in the more humble dress of the bricklayer, the carpenter, and the [black-smith]," as Garibaldi himself put it.[7]

Across the Sicilian countryside anticipation of ***Risorgimento***, the "rebirth" of a strong Italian state, grew. Farmers massacred oppressive landlords, leaving them to be "devoured by dogs . . . torn to pieces by their own brothers with a fury which would have horrified the hyenas."[8] The south secured, in 1861 the kingdom of Italy was proclaimed. Exhausted by overwork,

Unification of Italy, 1859–1870

≡ **Unification of Italy, 1859–1870**

Unification of Germany, 1866–1871

- Prussia before 1866
- Conquered by Prussia, 1866
- United with Prussia to form North German Confederation, 1867
- United with Prussia to form German Empire, 1871
- Ceded by France, 1871
- Boundary of German Empire, 1871

0   100 Miles

0   100 Kilometers

≡ **Unification of Germany, 1866–1871**

Cavour soon died. Despite huge difficulties such as poverty in the south, many "Italians" took pride in their new nation and came to see themselves as one people.

A momentous act of nation-building for both Europe and the world was the creation of a united Germany in 1871. Its architect was Otto von Bismarck from the prosperous kingdom of Prussia, who oversaw the merger of an array of cities and kingdoms under Prussian leadership within a single decade. Bismarck came from the landed nobility and high-ranking officialdom but spent his youth gambling and womanizing. His marriage to a pious Lutheran woman gave him new purpose: to establish Prussia as a dominant power.

In 1862, the king of Prussia appointed Bismarck as prime minister in hopes that he would build the army over the objections of liberals in parliament. Bismarck indeed managed to ram through programs to reform the military despite the opposition's belief in parliamentary control. His brand of nation-building was based on *realpolitik*—a political strategy of hardheaded realism, armed might, and rapid economic development. "Germany looks not to Prussia's liberalism, but to its power," he preached. "The great questions of the day will not be settled by speeches and majority decisions . . . but by iron and blood."[9] Next Bismarck undertook a series of victorious wars, against Denmark, Austria, and finally against France in 1870. These swift victories persuaded the individual German states to unify under Prussia's leadership. In January 1871, the king of Prussia was proclaimed the kaiser, or emperor, of a united Germany. The new constitution ensured the political dominance of the aristocracy and monarchy despite manhood suffrage. Germany's thriving industrial economy and efficient armies made it the foremost power on the European continent by the end of the nineteenth century.

Expansion and Consolidation of the United States

Two other newcomers, the United States and Japan, built national power in the nineteenth century and reformed their political structures to become more effective. The United States became a growing power in the nineteenth century and, like Italy and Germany, did so through warfare.

First, it fought Mexico and native American peoples in order to seize their resources and land. Between 1846 and 1848 the United States provoked and won a war with Mexico, and as a result almost doubled its territory, annexing Texas as well as large portions of California and the Southwest (see Map 24.2). Simultaneously,

realpolitik A practical, tough-minded approach to politics, wielded most famously by Otto von Bismarck in Germany.

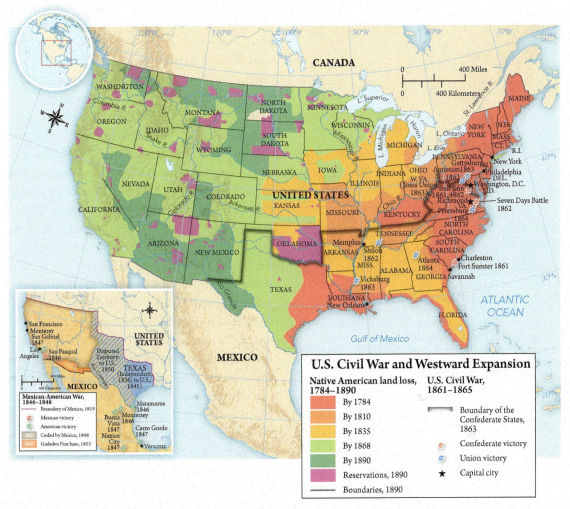

≡ **MAP 24.2   U.S. Civil War and Westward Expansion** U.S. nation-building advanced through the war with Mexico, the Civil War, and continuing battles to take the land of native Americans. Calls for unity during wartime and appeals asserting the superiority of white Americans welded the country together. They justified U.S. seizures of property as the right of advanced nations over backward tribes.

immigrants from around the world flocked to California where gold was discovered. Americans came to see this western expansion as part of the nation's **Manifest Destiny**—that is, the belief that whites had a God-given right to control the entire continent no matter how many native Americans were killed or displaced.

Second, the United States engaged in a devastating civil war over the plantation system based on slave labor. The main issue was whether new territories should be settled by free white farmers—a position held by the new Republican Party—or by

Manifest Destiny The nineteenth-century doctrine that the United States had the right and duty to expand throughout the North American continent.

≣ **English Porcelain Statue of Abraham Lincoln**
Although the British generally backed the Confederate
cause because they needed southern cotton for their
textile industry, the Staffordshire porcelain company
issued this statue on Abraham Lincoln's inauguration
in 1861. Portrayals of political heroes such as Lincoln
grew with the spread of the nation-state.

plantation owners bringing in their slaves. Following
Republican Abraham Lincoln's election to the presidency in 1860, most of the southern slaveholding
states seceded to form the Confederate States of
America. A bloody civil war, lasting from 1861 to
1865, began.

Lincoln did not initially aim to abolish slavery,
but in January 1863 his Emancipation Proclamation
came into force as a wartime measure officially freeing all slaves in the Confederate States, and turning
the war into a fight not only for union but for the end
of a plantation economy based on slave labor. "Believe
me," remarked one Pennsylvania industrialist, "I am
not eager for peace,"[10] as northern industrialization
flourished and overpowered the South. In April 1865
the prostrate Confederacy surrendered. For Lincoln,
the victory was short-lived. Within days a Confederate
sympathizer had assassinated the president.

After the war, abolitionists and freedmen's groups
helped achieve constitutional amendments ending slavery and granting the rights of citizenship and voting to
black males. By contrast, another nation-building effort
in the United States focused on crushing native American peoples and forcibly taking
their homelands for whites. To gain the land of the Cherokees, a group that had a constitution and practiced settled farming, in the 1820s the state of Georgia drove them
westward along the "Trail of Tears"—so named because of the number of deaths along
the way. Others displaced were Great Plains horse traders and herders of some forty
million buffalo. "There was always fat meat, glad singing, and much dancing in our
villages," one Crow woman remembered of her people's former prosperity.[11] As white
Americans murdered and spread disease, survivors were confined to reservations in
Oklahoma and other states, where they had no rights to participate in U.S. institutions (see again Map 24.2). As one Apache survivor described it, whites considered
reservations "a good place for the Apaches—a good place for them to die."[12] For white
Americans at the time, such conquest of "outsider" native Americans was cause for celebration, providing immigrants with livelihoods and the nation its unifying purpose.

Dramatic Change in Japan

As the activism of Matsuo Taseko shows, the arrival of U.S. ships with their unruly
white sailors and demanding agents in the 1850s threw Japan into turmoil. Some
among Japan's elites supported ending the Tokugawa shogun's control of foreign trade

and his monopoly on profits. Thus, in a dramatic realignment of power, Japanese of almost all political positions unified around the teenaged Meiji emperor (1852–1912), their "jewel." In 1868 the government announced the "Meiji Restoration"—*Meiji* means "enlightened rule"—as a combination of "Western science and Eastern values" offering both innovation and restoration. Japan's leaders were determined that the process of nation-building would serve Japan's interests, not the West's.

Amid revolutionary change, the Meiji government centralized power by forcing the daimyo (great lords) to surrender their control of the countryside. Tens of thousands of samurai were bought off with pensions and government bonds. Touring the world to view examples of modernizing reform, a prominent politician concluded that a centralized conscript army trained to cooperate in regiments using modern weaponry should replace the former samurai-based bands of individualistic would-be heroes. Japanese leaders limited the powers of elected representatives who might come from the general population however, instead creating a hereditary nobility, as in Europe. Despite centralization, Japan's government was not fully based on republican institutions or popular rule.

Disorder followed the Meiji remaking of society and the economy. The first to revolt were the displaced samurai, followed by farmers such as Matsuo Taseko, merchants, and countless others who had fought against the "barbarian" challenge posed by the West. They struggled for what were called "People's Rights" within the imperial system. The rural lower classes, squeezed by taxes and global competition, also rebelled. In Chichibu outside Tokyo, one resident expressed his despair: "The wind blows, / The rain falls, / Young men die. The groans of poverty / Flutter like flags in the wind."[13] In 1884, a force of eight thousand peasants in Chichibu aimed at "deposing evil rulers" by ousting corrupt officials. Government troops smashed the uprising, executing many participants. Meiji officials attributed the rising to criminals, but in fact, this revolt, like others occurring across Japan, showed that successful nation-building required attention to the needs of the Japanese population as a whole.

Building Empires

⬎ **FOCUS** What motivated the imperialists, and how did they impose their control over other nations?

The rise of modern nation-states went hand in hand with what historians call the **new imperialism**. Similar in its direct rule to the former Spanish Empire, the "new imperialism" did not target the Western Hemisphere, however, but rather made claims in Africa, Asia, and the Pacific. The British government, for example, assumed rulership of South Asian states, ending the East India Company's

new imperialism
The takeover in the second half of the nineteenth century of foreign lands by Western powers and Japan, which entailed political control as well as economic domination.

domination of the region. Other nations, including Japan and the United States, instituted direct rule of areas once linked to them by trade alone. Bureaucracies grew, migration accelerated, and the "tools of empire," including armies, became more powerful. The new imperialism was not, however, simply a story of violence inflicted by foreigners aiming for domination. Conquering nations provided social and cultural services such as schools to reflect the imperial power's values. In many instances local chieftains, merchants, and cultural leaders helped imperialists make their inroads.

Imperialism: What Is It?

Modern or "new" imperialism is associated with the intensified domination that modernizing states exercised worldwide in the second half of the nineteenth century. The term is all-encompassing, describing ambitions, conquests, ideologies, and power exercised over the trade, taxation, and governments of other states and their peoples—somewhat similar to the way in which the word **globalization** is used today to describe a variety of behaviors and processes that link the world's peoples. Modern imperialism was never a coherent system or a consistent set of practices except for its violence. Indeed, imperial rule was chaotic, rarely total, and constantly resisted.

Modern imperialism featured colonization—that is, the creation of settlements in foreign territories intended to dominate the land and its native peoples, take its wealth, and alleviate crowding in the mother country. Colonization shaped the Roman Empire and others, including the sixteenth-century Spanish and Portuguese Empires, and it remained a prominent part of the new imperialism. **Colonialism** is the term for the system that dominated people in these ways.

A second feature of imperialism was the range of motivations behind it. Some national leaders saw more extensive landholdings in and of themselves as a major ingredient of national strength; others saw the wealth that could be siphoned off to strengthen nations. Business leaders aimed to make money in underdeveloped areas by building harbors, railroads, and roads. **Business imperialism**, or "informal imperialism," based on foreign investment, commerce, and manufacturing, could also exist without political rule and the expense of standing armies or residential officials. Britain and later the United States exerted considerable power over Latin American states through investment in and control of key industries. Finally, for many, imperialism was an almost saintly undertaking. As one French economist put it in 1891, empire would bring civilization to "barbarous and savage tribes—knowing nothing of the arts and having so few habits of work and invention that they have no way of knowing how to get riches from the land."[14]

globalization A variety of behaviors and processes, such as trade, warfare, travel, and the spread of culture, that link the world's peoples.

colonialism The establishment of settler communities in areas ruled by foreign powers.

business imperialism The domination of foreign economies without military or political rule.

The Spanish and Portuguese Empires had based their superiority on their Catholic faith. In the second half of the nineteenth century, "scientific" theories of race reinforced imperialists' sense of cultural superiority. Charles Darwin, the English naturalist who developed the theory of evolution explicitly stated that nonwhites and women were less highly evolved than white men—ideas later used by "Social Darwinists" to justify European male domination. Scientific racism was not confined to Europeans: the Japanese considered themselves far in advance of foreigners such as the Koreans and local ethnic groups such as the Ainu. Cultural pride even prompted "civilizers" such as missionaries to support massacres of local people who resisted their rule.

Takeover in Asia

Great Britain, the era's mightiest colonial power, made a dramatic change of course by instituting governmental control of India. The Russians and British were also in constant competition to rule Central Asia, and the French and Dutch struggled with local peoples for empire in Southeast Asia. The contest in Central Asia has been called the "Great Game," but that hardly conveys the destruction inflicted—all in the name of advancing the nation by forging an empire (see Map 24.3).

By the nineteenth century and especially after the loss of Britain's thirteen North American colonies, the East India Company had become the major tax collector for rulers on the subcontinent, even de facto ruling some of these Indian states. In 1856, the Company took over the wealthy northern kingdom of Awadh, contrary to formal treaties with the king outlining his sovereignty. The takeover of Awadh fueled already rising anger over excessive taxation and the Company's increasingly high-handed ways.

In 1857, Indian troops serving the Company heard rumors that the new Enfield rifles they were to use had cartridges greased with cow and pig fat, forbidden to Hindus (for whom cows are sacred) and Muslims (for whom pigs are unclean). Believing this a plot to convert them to Christianity and spurred by the economic grievances of the peasant classes from which many sprang, the soldiers massacred their British officers. Then they conquered the Indian capital at Delhi, reinstating the emperor and declaring the independence of the Indian people.

Rebellions spread, justified, so the emperor explained, by "the tyranny and oppression of the infidel and treacherous English."[15] The Rani (Queen) Lakshmibai, widow of the ruler of the state of Jhansi in central India, for one, led a revolt when the East India Company tried to take over her lands. Indian recruits balked: "All black men are one," said a newly recruited soldier, who vowed he would not fight the rebels.[16] Eventually British-led forces from other regions crushed the Indian Uprising

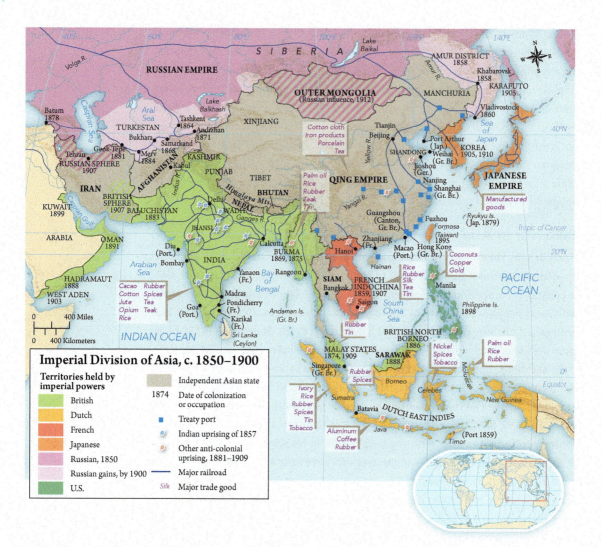

≡ **MAP 24.3 Imperial Division of Asia, c. 1850–1900** The Western powers and Japan expanded their influence in Asia by building railroads and using steamboats and, increasingly, destructive weaponry. They also made deals with local rulers and merchants who stood to profit by collaborating with imperialists in contrast to farmers and urban artisans whose livelihoods were often threatened.

of 1857, as this widespread revolt is now called. The British government substituted its control for that of the Company and in 1876 declared Queen Victoria the empress of India. The British constructed India as a single colony formed from kingdoms and small princely territories. Paradoxically, the "unification" of India helped lead wealthy and well-educated Indians in 1885 to create the Indian National Congress, an organization fostering nationalist sentiment, reform, and eventually independence.

Asia as a whole was a battlefield of competing interests and warring armies in a struggle for trade and empire. In Central Asia, Russian and British armies blasted former centers of Silk Road trade into ruins and slaughtered Afghan resisters during decades of destructive conflict for control. The British added to their holdings in Asia partly to block Russian and French expansion. Russia absorbed the small Muslim states of West and Central Asia, often encountering British competition but mostly fighting local peoples. It built the trans-Siberian railroad to help integrate Siberia—once considered a distant colony—into an expanding Russian Empire. Once completed, the line transported settlers and soldiers into the region (see again Map 24.3). Meanwhile the British military moved into Burma in 1869 and took the Malay peninsula in 1874. The environmental consequences were severe as the British built factories and leased forests in the north of Burma to private companies that stripped them bare, "denuding the country," as one official put it, "to its great and lasting loss."[17] Famine and drought followed this ecological nightmare, weakening the local population and resulting in the complete annexation of Burma in 1875.

In the 1860s the French established their own control in Cochin China (modern southern Vietnam). Missionaries, ambitious French naval officers, native officials looking for work, and even some local peoples making profits from European trade urged the French on. France then created the Union of Indochina from the ancient states of Cambodia, Tonkin, Annam, and Cochin China in 1887. Rubber plantations and other money-making projects followed. Modern agricultural projects increased the food supply. The French also improved sanitation and public health in Indochina, which proved a mixed blessing, as the changes led to population growth that strained resources. Cities such as Saigon gained tree-lined boulevards inspired by those in Paris and imported French theater and art. French culture was popular with colonial officials and upper-class Indochinese alike. Nonetheless, in the countryside ordinary people saw things differently. As one peasant protested to the governor-general in 1907, "The French are treating us like animals, looking at us like wood and stone."[18] Such treatment, along with exposure to Western ideas of "the rights of man," helped produce an Indochinese nationalist movement.

Europeans Scramble for Africa

Europeans also trained their sights on Africa in the second half of the nineteenth century, beginning with North Africa, and then moving to sub-Saharan Africa with its rich supplies of raw materials such as palm oil, cotton, diamonds, cacao, and rubber (see Map 24.4). Britain additionally hoped to keep the southern and eastern coasts of Africa secure for stopover ports on the route to Asia, especially India. North Africa's Mediterranean coast had strategic importance, as French emperor Napoleon III sponsored the building of the Suez Canal (1869) to shorten dramatically the route from Europe to Asia. Egyptian businessmen and government officials, borrowing at high rates of interest from European lenders,

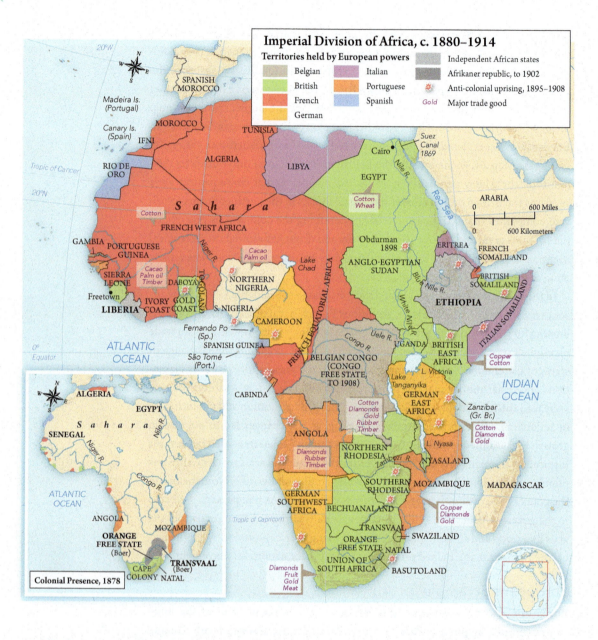

≡ **MAP 24.4   Imperial Division of Africa, c. 1880–1914** Though some Africans profited, most suffered from contacts with Europeans, which increased after the mid-nineteenth century, largely because the use of quinine cut down health risks for the invaders. Where environmental factors, especially famine and drought, failed to make Africans submit, the Europeans' outright brutality put down often stubborn resistance.

introduced technological improvements, including thousands of miles of railroad track, seen as essential to a modern future.

In 1882, the loans became the excuse for the British to invade, take over the government, and suppress Egyptian nationalists. Soon the capital of Cairo had the air of "an English town," as one Egyptian put it.[19] The English, in alliance with local entrepreneurs, shifted the Egyptian economy from a system based on multiple crops—a system that maintained the country's self-sufficiency—to one that emphasized a few highly marketable crops, notably cotton and wheat. As English and Egyptian elites grew rich, the bulk of the rural population, their livelihoods transformed, barely eked out an existence.

Meanwhile the French army occupied all of Algeria by 1870 and then neighboring Tunisia in 1881. As elsewhere, French rule in North Africa was aided by the attraction of local people to European trade and technology. Local leaders invested in infrastructure such as railroads and sent their children to European-style schools. They became "evolved"—as the French called those who adopted European ways. Other local people, however, attacked French soldiers and settlers. Many died from European-spread diseases. By 1872, the native population in Algeria had declined by more than 20 percent from five years earlier.

In the 1880s, European governments raced to the African interior, both playing to local elites' self-interest and using military force to overwhelm resistance. Eyeing "the magnificent cake of Africa," King Leopold II of Belgium (r. 1865–1909) inflicted unspeakable acts of cruelty on people in the Congo region of central Africa. German chancellor Otto von Bismarck established German control over Cameroon and a section of East Africa. Faced with stiff competition, the British spent millions attempting to take over the continent "from Cairo to Cape Town." The French cemented their hold on much of western Africa (see again Map 24.4), while the Ottomans hoped to compensate for its European losses with gains south and east of the Sahara and in southern Arabia.

Environmental disasters, regional tensions, and African rulers themselves scrambling for resources and territory helped the would-be conquerors. In 1882 the king of Daboya in northern Ghana explained his treaty with the British: "I want to keep off all my enemies and none to be able to stand before me."[20] The king expected guns and military backing from the British in his struggles with competing local rulers. Such struggles often aided the imperialists.

Competition escalated: farmers of European descent and immigrant prospectors battled the Xhosa (KOH-suh), Zulu, and other African peoples for the frontier regions of South Africa. British immigrants joined descendants of early Dutch settlers, called *Boers* (Dutch for "farmers"), in seizing land and mineral resources from natives. British businessman and politician Cecil Rhodes, sent to South Africa for his health at age seventeen, just as diamonds were being discovered, cornered the diamond market and claimed a huge amount of African territory with the help of official charters from the British government, all before he turned forty. His confidence in Britain and in himself was boundless: "I contend that we are the finest race in the world, and that the more of the world we inhabit the better it is."[21]

The scramble for Africa intensified tensions among the imperial powers, leading to the Berlin Conference in 1884. Statesmen from fourteen mostly European nations considered themselves fully entitled to the African continent. To resolve disputes, they decided that any nation that controlled a settlement along the African coast had the rights to the corresponding interior territory. The resulting dissection of the continent overrode the actual territorial borders of some 70 percent of Africa's ethnic groups. In theory the meeting was supposed to temper ambitions and reduce bloodshed in Africa, but European leaders remained committed to expanding their power.

Japan's Imperial Agenda

Japan escaped European domination by becoming an industrial nation with its own imperial agenda. The Japanese insisted on unity: "All classes high and low shall unite in vigorously promoting the economy and welfare of the nation," ran one government statement. The Meiji government entered the imperial fray by invading the Chinese island of Formosa (present-day Taiwan) in 1874. Japanese encroachments in Korea led to the 1894 Sino-Japanese War that left the once powerful Qing China humiliated and Japan the overlord of Taiwan and Korea. Tensions between Japan and Russia escalated with the extension of the trans-Siberian railroad through Manchuria and the arrival of millions of Russian settlers. Russia sponsored anti-Japanese groups in Korea, making the Korean peninsula appear, as one Japanese military leader put it, like "a dagger thrust at the heart of Japan."[22]

Technology, Environment, and the Imperial Advantage

Imperialists were helped by both technological development and a series of ecological disasters that weakened Asian and African societies. Powerful guns, railroads, steamships, and medicines accelerated conquest. As in China, gunboats forced African ethnic groups to give up their autonomy. Improvements to the breech-loading rifle and the development of the machine gun, or "repeater," after mid-century dramatically increased firepower. "The whites did not seize their enemy as we do by the body, but thundered from afar," claimed one resister at the 1898 Battle of Obdurman in Sudan, where the British mowed down some twenty-five thousand Africans with machine guns. "Death raged everywhere—like the death vomited forth from the tempest," as he put it.[23] Railroads sped troops and weapons to wherever there was resistance, cementing imperial domination.

The ecological balance of power changed too. Whereas once the tropical climate had given Africans an advantage, quinine extracted from cinchona bark from the Andes now protected Europeans from the deadly tropical disease malaria, which had once made Africa the "white man's grave." Disastrously for Africans and Asians, El Niño weather currents of the last quarter of the nineteenth century brought drought that resulted in deadly famine. Previous rulers had maintained water and food storage systems for such crises. Under the British, in contrast, one official noted that Mysore, India, contained "none but the dead and the dying."[24] Desperate for food, the population turned to theft, eating the dead, and, if they had the energy, rioting against big landowners and tax collectors. Lord Lytton, viceroy of India during the 1870s, refused to send food to the starving, calling people who wanted to restore the water storage infrastructure "irrigation quacks" and those proposing to give food to the starving "humanitarian hysterics." This environmental catastrophe allowed Europeans to increase their holdings. "Europeans," one African man observed, "track famine like a sky full of vultures."[25]

Mortality rates soared as smallpox, influenza, typhus, cholera, and other lethal diseases erupted in China, India, and other areas. Simultaneously the imperial powers introduced public health programs, mostly to protect their own soldiers and officials. These involved burning entire villages to the ground when contagious diseases struck a single household. Europeans also worked to increase hospital births in the colonies as a way to build the colonial workforce. Hospitalization ruined the livelihoods of midwives and other healers. Local people created their own stories in response to Western medicine. In African lore, the vampire, with its bloodsucking habit, reflected the natives' concern about colonial doctors who took blood. Modernizers in countries such as China, however, translated books on Western hygienic methods.

Societies in an Age of Nations and Empires

FOCUS How did nations and empires change lives and livelihoods around the world?

The consolidation of nation-states and the expansion of empires changed conditions of everyday life, both for good and for ill. Trade, migration, and warfare on a global scale brought benefits to some and disadvantaged many more. Migration burdened individuals and families while offering opportunities to others. Imperialists were able to dominate distant colonies only with the help of local people, many of whom gained new jobs governing on behalf of outsiders or fighting in their armies. Imported ways of thinking challenged traditions across societies. Empires could both undermine and fortify social unity, making this age one of contradictions.

Changing Conditions of Everyday Life

Citizens of nation-states paid heavy taxes to maintain empires, which usually cost the country as a whole more than it gained financially. Individuals, however, reaped huge profits, especially where colonies provided protected markets. Late in the century, for instance, French colonies bought 65 percent of France's exports of soap and 41 percent of its metallurgical exports. People in port cities around the world had steady jobs because of empires. Taxes to support imperial occupation, however, forced colonized men in particular to leave families to seek jobs in mines, on newly created plantations, or in the factories springing up around the world. While local peoples usually found empire oppressive, a few gained stupendous wealth.

Networks of guides and translators dealt with imperialists whose survival and livelihoods depended on local people. Nain Singh, principal of a school in the Himalayas and knowledgeable about a vast, uncharted region that included Tibet, could map terrain, take the temperature of water so as to chart altitudes, and speak many languages. He attached himself to caravans, posing as a Buddhist pilgrim or a merchant. In fact, Nain Singh was a skilled spy essential in Britain's drive to control Central Asia. Another local success, Chinese-born Khaw Soo Cheang, began his career as a fruit vendor in Thailand but ended as a magnate in the shipping and mining business and an official of the Thai government. He handed down his position to his five sons, who efficiently managed the southern states, collected taxes, and made improvements to roads, mines, and public buildings. The sons partnered with Europeans and Australians in their ventures, making the profitable area one where a Khaw "has his finger in every pie."[26] There were many ways to work with imperialists.

Under imperialism a system of indirect rule also emerged, one that used local officials, chiefs, and princes to enforce imperial laws and keep order. In India, for example, a few thousand British officials supervised close to half a million local civilian and military employees, who were paid far less than British employees would have been. As elsewhere, British civil servants attacked Indian cultural practices, such as female infanticide, child marriage, and *sati*, a widow's suicide on her husband's funeral pyre. Nonetheless, indirect rule invested local officials in the success of empire. Some in the upper classes of colonized countries were attracted to Japanese reforms or Western ideals—"the lofty tree of liberty," as one high Tunisian official praised them—and to notions of a technological society.[27]

The vast majority of colonized peoples, however, were exploited. For example, to prevent superior Indian textiles from competing with British cloth, the government worked to close Indian manufacturing centers and force artisans to become day laborers producing raw materials such as wheat and cotton. Once–self-sufficient farmers became landless workers wherever labor was needed, not only in their home region but around the world, as cash agriculture became an instrument of imperial rule. By confiscating land and demanding tax and other payments in cash, Europeans forced native peoples to work for them. As men left their families to work in mines, on urban docks, or on plantations, imperialists recruited local women into prostitution around these centralized workplaces. The agents of Leopold II of Belgium chopped off hands or simply shot Africans who did not provide their quota of rubber. "All of us wanted only one thing," reported a worker in a Belgian Congo mine, "to terminate our contract and return to our country—we were so frightened by the number of people who died each day."[28] Subsistence agriculture based on growing a variety of crops and raising animals declined around the world, and communities were undermined as men left their homes to earn cash.

Missionaries, rushing to newly secured areas of Africa and Asia, brought another kind of disorder. They thought of themselves as "God's soldiers," charged uniquely, as one put it, to keep local Asians from "going down, down into hell." In addition to their often unwanted presence and demands on native communities, missionaries fought among themselves, drawing locals into conflicts that sometimes brought on military intervention. Yet some women missionaries found their new settings liberating after the domestic confines of their homelands. For those whose new sense of empowerment made them feel entitled to change local people's lives, locals often set the price for attending church as lessons in languages and math.

Colonized people practiced everyday resistance such as slowdowns at work or petty theft. Indian merchants used traditional tactics to block tax increases: they closed up shop and left town. As imperial powers mapped the seas and controlled ports, local captains of small ships in the Arabian seas learned how to escape detection, smuggling in untaxed goods and even slave laborers. African merchants protested conditions around ports that favored white traders. In Freetown, Sierra Leone, local merchants found that the pathway to the customs house was constructed to block their goods while providing the European merchants direct access for their wares. Their protests ultimately forced European officials to modify the port. Although resistance sometimes led to compromise, more often violent repression followed. In early-twentieth-century German East Africa, local people refused to pay taxes, declaring, "We do not owe you anything. We have no debt to you."[29] In 1907, the Germans massacred these East Africans, seizing their food supplies and leaving survivors to die of starvation.

Migrants and Diasporas

The global expansion of industry and empire fostered mass migration in the second half of the nineteenth century (see Map 24.5). Migrants left rural areas for

MAP 24.5 **Global Migration, c. 1800–1910** People were on the move during these decades, concerned with finding livelihoods. Underemployed people from Asia and Africa migrated as indentured servants, which many saw as a new

Global Migration, c. 1800–1910

African
- Homeland
- Slave migration, c. 1800–1860
- Migration, c. 1840–1910

Chinese
- Homeland
- Migration, c. 1830–1914

Indian
- Homeland
- Migration, c. 1830–1914
- Destination of immigrants
- Boundaries, 1914

European Jewish
- Areas of settlement
- Migration, c. 1880–1914

Lebanese
- Homeland
- Migration, c. 1860–1914
- Other European migration, c. 1850–1914

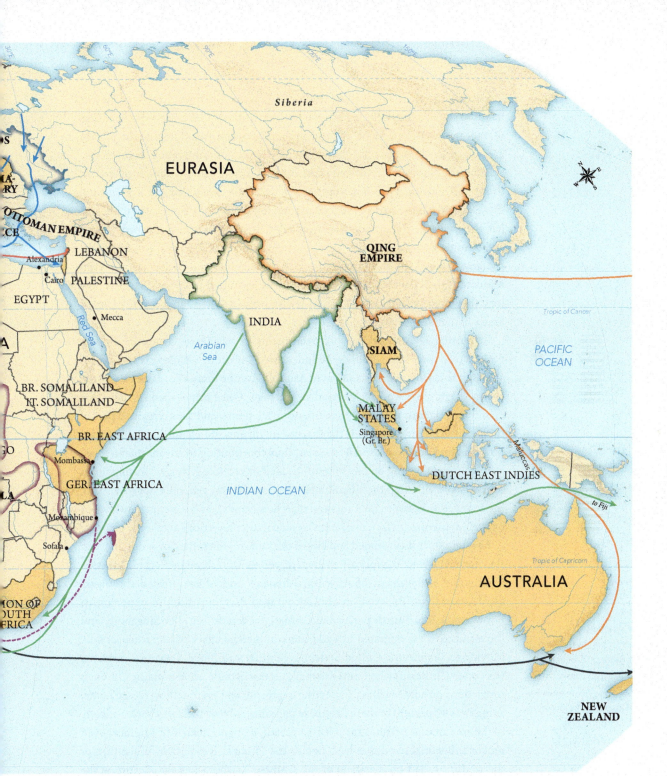

type of slavery. Europeans left rural areas as the global trade in grain drove down prices for produce; others hoped to escape religious and personal persecution.

industrializing cities, where they worked as masons, rickshaw drivers, or factory hands to supplement declining income from agriculture. In Africa, dense networks of trade took Africans, Arabs, and Indians hundreds and even thousands of miles in caravans packed with goods. In the colonies much regional migration was coercive.

In parts of Europe, China, and India the land simply could not produce enough to support rapidly expanding populations, especially when drought, agricultural diseases, and famine struck. Millions of rural Jews, especially from eastern Europe, left their villages for economic reasons, but Russian Jews also escaped vicious anti-Semitic **pogroms**. In the course of such state-approved riots, Russian mobs brutally attacked Jewish communities, destroyed homes and businesses, and even murdered Jews. "People who saw such things never smiled anymore, no matter how long they lived," recalled one Russian Jewish woman who migrated to the United States in the early 1890s.[30]

Recruiting agents working for governments or businesses determined destinations (see Lives and Livelihoods: Indentured Servitude). Railroads and steamships made journeys across and out of Asia and Europe more affordable and faster, even though most workers traveled in steerage. Once established in their new countries, migrants frequently sent money back home, and thus remained part of the family economy. The funds they earned might educate a younger brother or set up a daughter or son in a small business, thus contributing to advancement. Peasants welcomed having one less mouth to feed or receiving "magic" income from overseas kin, although the situation for the migrant was generally not rosy. Still, the connection between migrants and their homelands was not completely severed by their departure. In fact, migration created new connections across the globe.

As migrants from extended families or the same region settled near one another, they formed ethnic **diasporas,** clusters of people who shared an ethnic identity. Continuing enslavement of Africans, Russians, and others created the bleakest diasporas, but imperialism also encouraged diasporas born of opportunity. For example, the British persuaded Chinese traders to settle in Singapore, and thousands of them migrated to build this commercial city virtually from scratch. Moving to France, the United States, Argentina, and Brazil, Lebanese migrants were often Christians who wanted to make money in trade while avoiding Ottoman restrictions on non-Muslims. Expecting to prosper and eventually to return home, as many as 40 percent of these Lebanese migrants did find their way back—mostly to the area around Beirut—for at least a period, if not permanently. Migrants even proved influential in politics back home. The "Song of Revolution" of the turn of the century called on members of the Chinese diaspora to help overthrow the Manchu dynasty: "What use is the cumulation of silver cash? / Why not use it to

pogrom A systematic attack on Jews, as carried out, for example, in the late-nineteenth-century Russian Empire.

diaspora The dispersal of a population, often resulting in large settlements in different parts of the world.

eject the Manchus? / Ten thousand each from you isn't much / To buy cannons and guns and ship them inland."[31]

Migrating Cultures

Culture migrated with people. Bengali women moving to Calcutta to work as potters, basketmakers, dyers, and occasionally as factory workers, for example, celebrated their holidays in traditional ways, singing and dancing to stories of the gods and goddesses. Drug-smoking husbands and lovers who stole women's possessions were another favorite topic:

> My tears dry up in my eyes,
> I go around making merry. I'm writing in pain,
> Yet I act coy
> Swinging my hips.[32]

Such popular amusement outraged Calcutta's elites, who now preferred British middle-class norms for "civilized" female behavior. As a result, the number of women performers in Calcutta declined drastically, from over seventeen thousand in the 1870s to three thousand in 1890.

Elsewhere, local leaders were able to maintain cultural values and patterns of life. Japanese artists reinforced the nation-state by rejecting Chinese influences and creating an "authentic" Japanese style. In West Africa, the French allowed Islam to flourish while in return religious leaders preached accommodation to French rule. "God has given special victory, grace, and favor to the French," Sufi leader Malik Sy announced in the early twentieth century. "He has chosen them to protect our persons and property."[33] France financed pilgrimages to Mecca for Muslim leaders and local officials and supported the building of mosques and the observance of Islamic law.

Simultaneously, traditional patterns of thought and behavior loosened their hold on everyday life, especially in the world's teeming cities. Writers from many cultures read one another's works, and global celebrities such as Rabindranath Tagore emerged. Tagore, who won the Nobel Prize in Literature in 1913, was educated in Bengal and in London, but his grandfather's enormous wealth allowed him to travel the world

≡ **Indian Woman Dancing with Musicians** Indian women traditionally danced on many occasions in both public and private celebrations. Many in the growing Indian middle class came to see these dancers, whose entire bodies were in motion, as overly sexual and bordering on barbaric.

LIVES AND LIVELIHOODS

Indentured Servitude

After the decline of slavery in many countries during the first half of the nineteenth century, owners of plantations, mines, and refineries complained that they needed more workers. Agents searched colonized regions—especially those enduring famine and other economic distress—to find workers to transport to other parts of the world. By the system of indenture, workers were tricked, cajoled, or forced to sign contracts that obliged them to work for five to seven years in distant lands. Between 1830 and 1914, some 1.5 million Indians served as indentured laborers on European-owned plantations. Transported to Mauritania, British Guiana, Fiji, Trinidad, Guadeloupe, and Natal, to name a few destinations, their goal was to return home with some kind of savings.

"A new form of slavery," a British aristocratic opponent called the system of indentured servitude. Indentured laborers endured horrendous conditions cutting sugar cane, growing other cash crops, or working in mines. "I haven't had food for three days, my body is weak, my throat is parched," reported one worker in Fiji. Another worker in the Fiji

≡ **An African Indentured Servant** The end of slavery left global business people searching for cheap labor for plantations around the world. One solution was indenture, a system in which workers would serve an extended term of labor, usually in a far-off land. Here an indentured servant plants coconut trees on Fiji, one of the Solomon Islands.

cosmopolitanism The merging or acceptance of a variety of national and ethnic values and traditions.

at leisure while composing poems, songs, short stories, and essays. In his works, Tagore commented on the difficult lives of Bengali peasants while emphasizing Indian nationalism and education in Western knowledge. This ability to consider and often integrate different cultural traditions is called **cosmopolitanism**.

Art from distant cultures resonated in the imaginations of Western artists. The most striking changes came in the work of impressionist painters such as Claude cane fields said, "We were whipped for small mistakes. If you woke up late, i.e. later than three A.M., you got whipped." Others missed cultural life back home: "There are no temples, no festivals, no idols, . . . no schools for our children, who receive no education of any kind," an Indian indentured worker in Guadeloupe wrote in 1884. "It seems to us that animals are better treated than us in this colony."

Some African indentured laborers traveled back and forth between the Caribbean and the West African coast, sometimes serving as recruiters for the plantations. Many indentured laborers never returned to their homeland, however, constituting diasporas far from Africa and South Asia. They maintained many traditions: performing scenes from the *Ramayana*, for example, remains a joyous public celebration in Trinidad today. Indentured workers also transported African religions and rituals, which are still influential in binding descendants to the African continent.

Source: Quoted in Marina Carter and Khal Torabully, *Coolitude: An Anthology of the Indian Labour Diaspora* (London: Anthem Press, 2002), 90–91, 110.

Questions to Consider

1. How does the system of indentured servitude compare to slavery?
2. How did Africans and others help in the system of indentured labor, and why might they have cooperated?
3. What is the cultural legacy of indentured servitude?

Monet and Vincent Van Gogh who captured the color, line, and delicacy of Japanese art. Composers such as Claude Debussy largely abandoned centuries of Western musical patterns to create modern music based on sounds from around the world. In the same way, Western choreographers studied steps and movements from other cultures to develop modern dance. To get and stay in shape, men in Europe and the United States practiced martial arts, all of which came from Asia. African slaves

≡ **Vincent Van Gogh,** *Flowering Plum Tree* **(1887)**
Western artists' indebtedness to non-Western styles is epitomized in this painting by Dutch painter Vincent Van Gogh, who modeled this work on a print by Hiroshige (see page 852). The brief flowering of trees so dear to the Japanese represented the fleetingness of life, and impressionists built their entire style on capturing such rapid changes in light.

not only introduced new foods but reshaped American popular culture. They developed powerful musical forms such as blues and jazz from African traditions of the *griot* (or oral poet), while the sounds, rhythms, and tonalities of African music helped create square dancing, the Charleston, and other dances. Clothing traveled the world too. Chinese women had their portraits painted wearing perky Western straw hats adorned with feathers, while Western women dressed in kimonos and other slim clothing without massive petticoats or corsets.

Even as new global influences traveled the world, nation-building rested on loyalty to a single government. Official histories, monuments, and museums served as indications that the nation-state had deep roots, and government leaders became symbols of national unity. Monarchs' and presidents' portraits appeared on dishware and on household walls and adorned public spaces such as schools and office buildings. National flags were designed to serve a similar unifying purpose (see Seeing the Past: The Korean Flag). Royal births were widely reported in the press, and in Britain, for example, officials carefully staged royal marriages and funerals as public ceremonies. Nishimiya Hide, daughter of a samurai and lady-in-waiting to a member of the high Japanese nobility, found a way to use her experience after the samurai and grand nobility had lost their leading role. She supported herself in part under the Meiji Restoration by teaching ancient court ceremonies to members of the new elite. Reformers popularized and modified ideas from other parts of the world in the service of nation-building. Japanese author and educator Fukuzawa Yukichi came from an impoverished samurai family but quickly achieved fame and fortune through best-selling works that made people aware of current thinking in the West. Fukuzawa's theory differed from much of Western constitutional thought, however, when it maintained that once people had agreed to the formation of a state, they surrendered their right to criticize or protest, justifying both reform and an authoritarian, emperor-centered state.

Nationally minded reformers recognized public education as a crucial ingredient of national development. A Japanese law of 1872 mandated universal education so that in the modernized Meiji state there would be "no community with an

SEEING THE PAST

The Korean Flag

Flags existed in ancient times to distinguish regiments of an army, as was the case with Egyptian standards. Over the centuries, most flags continued to be standards for armies, but they also became important symbols of the nation. Designing a single flag around which citizens of an entire country could rally became a crucial part of the process of nation-building. Colors were carefully chosen to represent virtues such as courage and purity, and figures like lions, eagles, stars, and the sun were selected to portray a nation's strength and magnificence.

In the 1880s, as China, Russia, and Japan greedily eyed Korea for conquest, the kings of Korea adopted the more impressive title of emperor, and they also designed a flag. Its central figure represents the balance of yin and yang in the cosmos, while the four corners indicate the elements—fire, water, earth, and air—and the four seasons. After

The Korean Flag

Japan had defeated both China and (as we will see in the next chapter) Russia, it established a protectorate over Korea in 1905 and then annexed it in 1910, replacing the Korean flag with its own. On the defeat of Japan in World War II, the nineteenth-century flag became the standard of South Korea.

Examining the Evidence

1. What makes this flag or any flag distinctive to the nation?

2. Compare the Korean flag with the U.S. flag. What do the differences reveal about the political culture and national identity of each country?

illiterate family nor a family with an illiterate person."[34] Both citizen participation in the nation and imperial rule required a more literate population with a common culture and common skills and ideals—one that could prove cultural superiority. Reformers sought not only to imitate the Chinese tradition of an educated officialdom but also to expand education more generally as the foundation of strong nations. Emperor Pedro II of Brazil established a record number of schools as part of his commitment to nation-building. When he came to power in 1831, the capital of Rio de Janeiro had 16 primary schools; when he abdicated in 1889, the number had climbed to 118.

Reformers bucked tradition when they opened public schools for girls and young women. Across the globe these activists touted the education of women as key to modernization and to imperial rule, because ignorant or illiterate mothers would give children a poor start. The Russian Empire, comprising more than a hundred ethnicities, sought to reduce the threat of future rebellion by instructing the women of conquered peoples. It forced ethnic groups, from Poles to Afghans, to adopt the Russian language and culture and to worship in the Russian Orthodox church. When resistance to this "Russification" mounted, the government showed some leniency to encourage continued acceptance of the nation-state among conquered subjects.

COUNTERPOINT: Outsiders Inside the Nation-State

FOCUS Which groups were excluded from full participation in the nation-state, and why?

Who was a true Brazilian, Russian, Japanese, or other citizen? This central question emerged with the development of nation-states and rising global migration. All the while proclaiming the ideal of universal membership, legislators determined the exclusion of certain people from full citizenship. Sometimes these people— native Americans, for example—were those who had resisted nation-building, as the state took their land and devalued their beliefs. Other outsiders, notably women and freed slaves, often had helped in nation-building from the start but were excluded nonetheless. Nation-building created a body of insiders who assured themselves of their own belonging by discriminating against others, including imperial subjects, no matter how educated or wealthy.

Racial and Ethnic Difference

From Japan to South America, nation-building efforts had a devastating effect on indigenous peoples. Settlers in South America, Australia, New Zealand, and Siberia treated native peoples—who had lived in the territory for centuries and even for millennia—as remnants of barbarism. The *New York World* told its readers in 1874 that "the country never belonged to the Indians in any other sense than it belonged to the wolves and bears, which white settlers shoot without mercy."[35] Indigenous civilization was dismissed even though most settlements usually depended on receiving food, medicine, and knowledge from local peoples. In the United States they were excluded from voting and rights until 1924, and in Peru, native Americans paid an extra tax, which constituted almost half of Peru's national income. The Australian and Canadian governments took native children from their families, sending them to live in white homes or boarding schools to be "civilized." Russian officials simply moved settlers onto reindeer herders' lands in the name of strengthening the nation. As one U.S. newspaper argued, settlers "are the people who develop a country; who carry a civilization with them."[36]

Ethnic and racial thinking justified exploitation in the name of nation-building. Japanese nation builders taught that the Ainu peoples on the country's outer islands were dirty; their tattoos and physical features were judged as hideous. In the United States, Southerners withdrew the rights to citizenship given to black men in the Fourteenth Amendment to the Constitution. They passed "Jim Crow" laws segregating blacks from whites in public places and effectively disenfranchising them, while the Ku Klux Klan, a paramilitary group of white Southerners, terrorized, lynched, and mutilated black men. One woman's goal was to keep her daughter from the common livelihood for African American women of domestic service in a white family, "for [Southern men] consider the colored girl their special prey."[37] Many white Americans took the exclusion of blacks and native Americans from the rights of citizenship as the bedrock of national unity.

Women

Like Matsuo Taseko in Japan, women throughout the world joined the effort to create or preserve strong nation-states. "I am a U.S. soldier," wrote Clara Barton, nurse on a U.S. Civil War battlefield.[38] Women such as Barton were subject to the laws and taxes of the nation-state, but they too were denied rights of citizenship, including the rights to vote, to keep their own wages, and to participate in political life. In Japan and France, for example, the government criminalized women's attendance at political meetings, resulting in arrest and imprisonment. Nonetheless, the self-sacrifice of women to their nation or family was held up as a model for citizenship. Nations used mythical women as symbols on coins and other official artifacts even as state power denied women the rights of citizenship.

The Struggle for Citizens' Rights

Throughout the nineteenth century, reformers asserted the rights of native peoples, slaves and former slaves, and women in the face of the state's exclusionary power. Juan Manuel de Rosas, the powerful caudillo of Buenos Aires, Argentina,

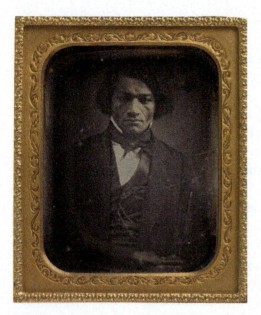

≡ **Frederick Douglass** Frederick Douglass was an escaped slave, journalist, and civil rights pioneer of the nineteenth century. His goal was freedom for slaves and civil rights for all, making him a hero to all outsiders down to the present day. As outsiders are integrated, histories cast them as heroes to portray the nation as inclusive.

pan-Africanism Originating in the late nineteenth century, an ideology that stresses the bonds of all people of African descent, both on the African continent and beyond.

Zionism A movement that began in the late nineteenth century among European Jews to form a Jewish state.

and its countryside, created unity by incorporating people of African and native American ancestry into his armies and promoting them to high ranks. In the United States, Frederick Douglass, an abolitionist before the Civil War, worked in its aftermath for the full inclusion of freed black men in the nation. Ida B. Wells, U.S. newspaper woman and daughter of a former slave, campaigned to end segregation of public facilities and to stop the lynching of black men. "I felt I owed it to myself and to my race to tell the whole truth now," Wells explained in her autobiography.[39] She received death threats and was forced to go into hiding.

Denied citizenship, minorities such as African Americans in the United States and former slaves in the Caribbean began to see the source of their common nationality not in the Western Hemisphere, to them a place of captivity, but in Africa. Thus **pan-Africanism**, an ideology stressing the common bonds of all people of African descent, took root. Similarly, Jews, who were excluded from civic equality in nations, aimed at building a nation in which they would have full rights. "Why should we be any less worthy than any other . . . people?" one Jewish leader asked. "What about our nation, our language, our land?"[40] By the late nineteenth century, a nationalist movement called **Zionism** advocated the migration of Jews to their ancestral homeland of Palestine and the creation there of a Jewish nation-state.

Because rising nation-states refused women a whole series of rights, activists began lobbying for women's full citizenship. As China moved toward a program of national strengthening, reformers denounced foot-binding and the lack of education for women. Activists often blamed men directly—"the basest of roughs," one German doctor called them—because it was their power that blocked women's inclusion.[41] In the United States the leading activists among a wide variety of mostly white women's organizations were Susan B. Anthony and Elizabeth Cady Stanton; black feminists included Sojourner Truth and Anna Maria Cooper, who worked for both racial and gender equality. In 1903 the most militant of suffrage movements arose in England; there Emmeline Pankhurst and her daughters founded the Women's Social and Political Union in the belief that women would accomplish nothing unless they threatened men's property. In 1907 WSPU members staged parades in English cities, and in 1909 they began a campaign of violence, blowing up railroad stations, slashing works of art, and chaining themselves to the gates of Parliament.

As nationalist movements arose in India, Egypt, the Middle East, and China, activist women focused on inclusion within an independent nation. Although these groups sometimes looked to Western **suffragists** for some of their ideas, European suffragists were themselves inspired by non-Western women's rights, including the right to own property. Latin American activists were also vocal, concerning themselves with education, the status of children, and the legal rights of women. Women from around the world met at international suffrage meetings. By 1904 feminist organizations from countries on almost all continents joined to form the International Woman Suffrage Alliance, showing that movements for women's inclusion in the nation took shape within a global context.

Conclusion

Regions across the globe witnessed dramatic change in the nineteenth century as leaders joined with ordinary people to create strong, centralized nation-states. Nations in Latin America felt the divisive forces of regionalism, while the United States experienced a devastating civil war over competing political and economic systems. In Russia, fear of revolution made the government change policies, liberating the serfs as a way to strengthen the state without enfranchising them. Fundamental flaws were woven into nation-building efforts, especially the creation of national unity by casting some people within national borders as unworthy of citizenship.

Beyond the nation-state lay populations targeted for colonization and unequal treatment, similar to the native peoples, people of color, and women within its borders. The nineteenth century is called an age of imperialism because of the growing contest among Western nation-states to dominate the world's peoples. New technology springing from industrialization helped people and ideas move more rapidly across the globe, while giving imperialists military and economic advantages. New forms of oppression such as indentured servitude developed; in colonies plantation agriculture increasingly replaced self-sufficient farming; and environmental catastrophes weakened societies and helped imperialism spread. Some colonized peoples prospered by participating in the system and simultaneously developed goals such as national independence, based on the Western values of rights and freedom that were denied them.

Imperial competition made the world more dangerous as distrust and insecurity among the powers intensified. When political ambitions clashed early in the twentieth century, catastrophic violence would follow.

suffragist An activist on behalf of the vote for women.

✳ review

The major global development in this chapter: The rise of modern nation-states and their competition for empire.

Important Events	
1833–1855	Mexican caudillo Santa Anna serves at intervals to lead the government
c. 1840–1910	Global migration because of indenture, imperial opportunity, and harsh environmental conditions
1846–1848	Mexican-American War
1853–1856	Crimean War
1857	Indian Uprising against the British
1859–1870	Unification of Italy
c. 1860–1900	Impressionism flourishes in the European arts, borrowing many non-Western techniques
1861	Emancipation of the serfs in Russia
1861–1865	U.S. Civil War
1863	Emancipation Proclamation in the United States
1866–1871	Unification of Germany
1868	Meiji Restoration of Japan
1869	Suez Canal completed
c. 1870–1900	European powers, Japan, and the United States extend formal and informal control over Asia, Africa, and parts of Latin America
1876	British Parliament declares Victoria empress of India
1880s	Popular uprisings in Japan
1881	Young rebels assassinate Alexander II of Russia
1884–1885	European nations carve up Africa at the Berlin Conference
1888	Emancipation of slaves in Brazil
1894–1895	Sino-Japanese War

KEY TERMS

business imperialism (p. 890)
colonialism (p. 890)
cosmopolitanism (p. 904)
diaspora (p. 902)
federalism (p. 880)
globalization (p. 890)

Manifest Destiny (p. 887)
mir (p. 884)
nation (p. 878)
new imperialism (p. 889)
pan-Africanism (p. 910)
pogrom (p. 902)

realpolitik (p. 886)
Risorgimento (p. 885)
suffragist (p. 911)
Zionism (p. 910)

CHAPTER OVERVIEW QUESTIONS

1. Why did nation-states become so important to people in the nineteenth century?
2. What are the arguments for and against imperialism?

3. Which were the major imperialist powers, and what made them so capable of conquest?
4. Are there still outsiders inside nations?

MAKING CONNECTIONS

1. How did the spread of industrialization (see Chapter 23) affect the rise of modern nation-states and the growth of empires?
2. What was the legacy of slavery in the new nations? How did it affect lives and livelihoods across the globe?

3. Recall the empires discussed in Part 3. What were the key differences between empires in the early modern period and empires in the nineteenth century?

For further research into the topics covered in this chapter, see the Bibliography at the end of the book. For additional primary sources from this period, see *Sources for World in the Making*.

Wars, Revolutions, and the Birth of Mass Society 1900–1929

≡ **World in the Making** Diego Rivera spent most of the Mexican Revolution in Europe, where he learned a range of classical Western styles of painting. The bloodshed of the revolution and World War I and the coming of communism to Russia inspired him to become a communist and to take up the cause of oppressed native American peasants and workers on his return to Mexico. This mural, *Blood of the Revolutionary Martyrs Fertilizing the Earth* (1927), reflects the traditional Mexican idea that martyrdom makes the earth fertile. "Rivera's art, reflecting his strong belief in the value of workers and signaling the brutality of the times, intersected with the politics and cultural aspirations of his day." The martyrs represented are peasant rebel leader Emiliano Zapata (right) and his follower Otilio Montano (left).

✴ # backstory

The competition among Western powers heated up in the second half of the nineteenth century, fueled by the drive for overseas expansion known as imperialism (see Chapter 24). European nations used the economic and military advantages that resulted from industrialization and nation-building to take direct and indirect control of territories in Asia, Africa, and Latin America. Resistance to both new and old empires and to political elites mounted during these years, even as imperialism multiplied the connections among the world's peoples and intensified the pace of cultural and economic exchange. Both competition for power and resistance to existing power structures contributed to the violence that marked the early twentieth century. The application of industrial technology to warfare made conflicts between and within states more destructive than ever.

The rebel leader Emiliano Zapata was a dandy, wearing blinding white shirts and fitted black pants adorned with silver. Before 1910 he had worked the land of his part-Indian family in central Mexico, where small farmers such as Zapata struggled—usually unsuccessfully—to block the takeover of their traditional lands by big hacienda (plantation) owners producing sugar and other commodities for the global market. A fighter against the takeover of local land, in 1910 he joined the revolution against the corrupt regime of Porfirio Díaz, a key ally of the big land-owners. Zapata's peasant army swept through central Mexico with the slogan "It is better to die on your feet than live on your knees." During the decade-long Mexican Revolution, peasants who had never seen Zapata boosted their spirits with cries of "Viva [Long Live] Zapata!"

By 1920, the Mexican Revolution had killed between one and two million people, some by rifles, machine guns, and bombs and others by disease, but it was just one of several lethal cataclysms in those years. At the turn of the twentieth century, China and Africa had been riddled with imperial violence, while Japan had defeated Russia in an astonishing war for territory in East Asia. Between 1900 and 1920, tens of millions fought and died around the world. After Mexico, revolution erupted in Qing China in 1911, and in 1912 and 1913 a host of Balkan peoples challenged the Ottoman and Austro-Hungarian Empires. Their struggle led to World War I, which lasted from 1914 to 1918, spawning the Russian Revolution. The legacy of these conflicts remade the world across the rest of the century.

These wars intersected with global trade and international politics. The Mexican Revolution was partly a struggle over U.S. control of the Mexican economy, and even the peasant leader Emiliano Zapata corresponded with foreign leaders. The fall of the Qing whetted the appetite of foreign powers for Chinese land and resources. World War I was a global war, fought not only on the European continent but in the Middle East, Africa, and the Pacific, often with the goal of imperial expansion. All wars brought the masses into global politics, but none of them settled problems as the combatants hoped. Instead, the Mexican Revolution destroyed the country's economy, while World War I produced turmoil, overturning the Russian, German, Ottoman, and Austro-Hungarian empires. Political uprisings continued into the 1920s, accompanying the rise of mass society.

Politics after the wars depended on mass culture and the postwar explosion of technology. Urban people from China to Argentina experienced the "Roaring Twenties," snapping up new consumer goods, drinking in the entertainment provided by films and radio, and relishing new personal freedoms. Modern communication technologies such as radio also spread political ideologies more widely than ever before. Some of these became the core of mass nationalist politics—some evil, like fascism, and some aimed at helping ordinary people, like the reform program of Emiliano Zapata.

OVERVIEW QUESTIONS

The major global development in this chapter: The wars and revolutions of the early twentieth century and their role in the creation of mass culture and society.

As you read, consider:

1. Why did the Mexican Revolution, the Chinese Revolution, World War I, and the Russian Revolution cause so much change far from the battlefield?

2. How did these wars help produce mass culture and society?

3. What role did technology play in these developments?

Imperial Contests at the Dawn of the Twentieth Century

> ⬇ **FOCUS** What were the main issues in the contests over empire, and what were the results of these contests?

Imperialism was increasingly chaotic and deadly at the start of the twentieth century. Large-scale rebellions by ordinary people fighting against imperial domination became more common; nationalist movements grew. Competition among the imperial powers themselves heated up as their ambitions swelled.

Clashes for Imperial Control

The British experienced an unexpected setback to their expansionist ambitions in 1896, when Cecil Rhodes, then prime minister of the Cape Colony at Africa's southern tip, directed a raid on Johannesburg to stir up trouble between the Boers, descendants of early Dutch settlers, and the more recent British immigrants in search of gold. Rhodes hoped the raid would justify a British takeover of the Boer-controlled territories. When the Boers unexpectedly won, the British waged the South African (or Boer) War against them. Journalists reported on appalling bloodshed, rampant disease, the unfit condition of the average British soldier, and the herding of the Boers into a shocking new institution—the concentration camp, where tens of thousands of women and children died. Britain finally defeated the Boers in 1902 and annexed the area, but the cost of war in money, loss of life, and public morale was enormous.

Soon after annexation, the government of South Africa passed a series of laws appropriating African-owned lands for whites and restricting their everyday lives, including their freedom of movement. It was the foundation for the policy of racial segregation and discrimination called apartheid. "We expected deliverance," one local chieftain commented bitterly on British policy, "whereas we have gone deeper into bond[age]."[1]

At about the time the British were fighting the South African War, Spain lost Cuba, Puerto Rico, and the Philippines to the United States, which defeated it in the Spanish-American War of 1898. The United States, a newcomer to imperialism overseas, annexed Hawaii in 1898 at the urgings of missionaries and businessmen, who had set up plantations on the islands. Before the Spanish-American War, both Cuba and the Philippines had vigorous independence movements backed by all classes of people. An inflammatory daily press goaded the U.S. government to help the independence movements. On victory, the United States annexed Puerto Rico and Guam and bought the Philippines from its former ruler. U.S. businesses virtually controlled an independent Cuba's sugar-exporting economy—an example of business imperialism. After that, the triumphant United States waged a bloody war against the independence-minded Filipinos. Several hundred thousand Filipinos died—a taste of more massive wars of empire to come.

Japan once more vigorously pursued empire, when, angered by Russian expansion in Manchuria, it attacked tsarist forces at Port Arthur in 1904 (see Map 25.1). Powerful machine guns mowed down combatants on both sides. To the astonishment of the world, the Japanese completely destroyed the Russian fleet in the 1905 Battle of Tsushima Strait. The victory was the first by a non-European nation over a European great power in the modern age. As one English general observed of the Russian defeat, "I have today seen the most stupendous spectacle it is possible for the mortal brain to conceive—Asia advancing, Europe falling back."[2] Bolstering its status and economy, Japan went on to annex Korea in 1910, while Russia itself erupted in the Revolution of 1905, forcing the tsar to institute a weak form of parliament, the Duma.

Growing Resistance to Foreign Domination

The Japanese victory over two important dynasties—the Qing in China and the Romanov in Russia—reverberated globally, with people under foreign domination believing that like Japan they too could conquer powerful forces. The Chinese

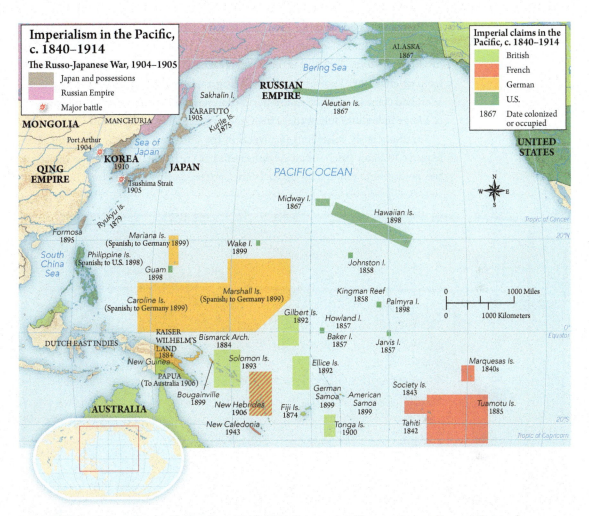

Imperialism in the Pacific, c. 1840–1914

The Russo-Japanese War, 1904–1905

- Japan and possessions
- Russian Empire
- ※ Major battle

Imperial claims in the Pacific, c. 1840–1914

- British
- French
- German
- U.S.

1867   Date colonized or occupied

MONGOLIA   MANCHURIA

Port Arthur 1904

QING EMPIRE

KOREA 1910

Sakhalin I.

KARAFUTO 1905

Kurile Is. 1875

Sea of Japan

Tsushima Strait 1905

JAPAN

RUSSIAN EMPIRE

Bering Sea

Aleutian Is. 1867

ALASKA 1867

UNITED STATES

PACIFIC OCEAN

Ryukyu Is. 1879

Formosa 1895

South China Sea

Philippine Is. (Spanish; to U.S. 1898)

Mariana Is. (Spanish; to Germany 1899)

Guam 1898

Wake I. 1899

Midway I. 1867

Hawaiian Is. 1898

Tropic of Cancer

20°N

Caroline Is. (Spanish; to Germany 1899)

Marshall Is. (Spanish; to Germany 1899)

Johnston I. 1858

Kingman Reef 1858

Palmyra I. 1898

0   1000 Miles

0   1000 Kilometers

DUTCH EAST INDIES

KAISER WILHELM'S LAND 1884

Bismarck Arch. 1884

New Guinea

PAPUA (To Australia 1906)

Bougainville 1899

AUSTRALIA

Solomon Is. 1893

New Hebrides 1906

New Caledonia 1943

Gilbert Is. 1892

Howland I. 1857

Baker I. 1857

Jarvis I. 1857

Ellice Is. 1892

Fiji Is. 1874

German Samoa 1899

American Samoa 1899

Tonga Is. 1900

Society Is. 1843

Tahiti 1842

Marquesas Is. 1840s

Tuamotu Is. 1885

0°
Equator

20°S

Tropic of Capricorn

≡ **MAP 25.1   Imperialism in the Pacific, c. 1840–1914** European and Japanese imperialists sent their traders, missionaries, military, and adventurers to China, Southeast Asia, and the Pacific Islands. They savagely put down the Boxer Rebellion, a Chinese uprising. The outbreak of the Sino-Japanese and Russo-Japanese Wars showed that imperial ambitions could lead to international warfare, with unpredictable results.

felt humiliated by the 1894–1895 defeat by Japan (discussed in Chapter 24): a range of reformers pressed for an efficient tax system, technology, and railroad networks. The Dowager Empress Cixi (che-shee) (1835–1908), who effectively ruled the empire, had would-be reformers rounded up and executed. In the face of new disasters, including famine, peasants organized to restore Chinese strength, though Cixi herself had earlier supported a variety of reforms. One organization, the Society of the Righteous and Harmonious Fists, or the Boxers, maintained that ritual boxing would ward off a variety of evils, including bullets. The Boxers appealed to the gods and spirits on behalf of China. Their European opponents did the same: "We know God could send relief thru rain if He thot [*sic*] best, " a woman missionary wrote.[3] By 1900 as the Boxers reached the height of their power, troops from seven imperial powers invaded, killing, raping, and looting to crush what the West had come to call "the yellow peril." Foreign military occupation and payment of a huge indemnity followed, as the Qing dynasty faced its downfall.

Simultaneously, rebellions in several of the Ottoman Empire's provinces challenged Ottoman rule. Sultan Abdul Hamid II (r. 1876–1909) tried to revitalize the multiethnic empire by using Islam and expanding its territory in order to

The Boxer Rebellion By 1900 imperial powers were exploiting China's resources in earnest and converting its population to Christianity. Simultaneously, famine was widespread, making Chinese rebels known as the Boxers determined to "Kill the Pig"—that is, foreign missionaries, diplomats, and merchants. Armies from the foreign powers suppressed the Boxers and further plundered the country's wealth.

counteract rising nationalism. Instead, dissident Turks, the dominant ethnic group in Asia Minor, embraced nationalism by focusing on the uniqueness of the Turkish culture, history, and language. Electrified by the Japanese victory over Russia, they sought to become "the Japan of the Middle East." In 1908, a group calling itself the Young Turks took control of the government in Istanbul, which had been weakened by nationalist agitation and by the empire's indebtedness to Western financiers and businessmen. Other dissident groups in the Middle East and the Balkans arose, including pan-Islamists and feminist nationalists who urged women across the empire to become modern activists. Once in control of the Ottoman government, the Young Turks brutally opposed movements in Egypt, Syria, and the Balkans modeled after their own.

Resistance to empire continued to grow everywhere in the wake of the Japanese victory. In India, fervently anti-British Hindu leader B. G. Tilak preached noncooperation, while the young took to assassinating officials. "We shall not give them assistance to collect revenue and keep peace," he maintained.[4] "We shall not assist them in fighting . . . with Indian blood and money." His forceful nationalism broke with the gradual change urged by the Indian National Congress. To repress Tilak, the British sponsored the Muslim League, a rival nationalist group, to divide Muslim nationalists from Hindus.

Inhabitants of the colonies—rulers and ruled alike—were often on edge amidst resistance and crackdowns. In German East Africa, colonial forces in 1905 used a scorched-earth policy to kill more than one hundred thousand Africans. Having set up police surveillance in colonies around the world, the French closed the University of Hanoi and executed Indochinese intellectuals to maintain their grip on Indochina. A French general there summed up the fears of many colonial rulers in the new century: "The gravest fact of our actual political situation in Indochina is not the recent trouble in Tonkin [or] the plots undertaken against us but in the muted but growing hatred that our subjects show toward us."

From Revolutions and Local Wars to World War

⬎ **FOCUS** What factors contributed to the wars of the early twentieth century?

The Mexican Revolution, the Chinese Revolution, the Balkan Wars, and ongoing colonial violence opened one of the bloodiest decades in human history. The reasons for the violence were many and complex, and the conflicts did not always produce the outcomes that had inspired individuals and nations to take up arms.

Guomindang The Chinese nationalist party founded by Sun Yatsen that overthrew the Qing dynasty and fought to rule mainland China from 1911 to 1949.

Revolutionaries and Warriors: Mexico, China, and the Balkans

The tensions created by imperialism and modern state-building exploded by 1910. In Mexico, liberal reformers headed by the wealthy landowner Francisco Madero began a drive to force the corrupt dictator Porfirio Diaz from office. Diaz saw himself as a modernizer, but only a handful of wealthy families and foreign investors reaped the riches of Mexico's development. By concentrating agricultural lands in the hands of a few, including U.S. mining and cattle-raising firms, Diaz's policies impoverished village people. By 1900, just 1 percent of the population held 85 percent of the land, much of it seized by the government for the wealthy.

In comparison to the liberal reformers' quest for a more open political system and the rule of law, peasants aimed for economic justice and survival, forming armies to fight for land reform. Zapata described their situation and their goals: "Considering that for the great majority, villages and citizens of Mexico possess not even the land that they work . . . the following is decreed: one-third of all monopolies will be expropriated . . . and distributed to those villages and citizens."[5]

In the north, landowner Pancho Villa headed another popular army that fought against U.S. citizens and others who were seizing local land and resources, further complicating the revolution.

Long after the ouster of Diaz in 1911 and amid assassinations of leaders, including Zapata, the Mexican government announced land reform in its Constitution of 1917. The hundreds of thousands of sacrificed lives, usually those of Indian or mixed blood like Zapata, inspired generations of Mexican writers and artists. Artist Diego Rivera's huge heroic depictions of the Mexican Revolution were meant to inspire the masses to remain committed to social justice.

As we have seen, the combination of Japan's lightning defeat of China in the Sino-Japanese War and the Boxer Rebellion thoroughly discredited the Qing dynasty. In 1911 to 1912 a group of revolutionaries organized as the **Guomindang** (gwo-min-DAHNG), or Nationalist Party, overthrew the long-lived dynasty and declared China a republic. Influenced by Western ideas of evolution, the Guomindang likened the Manchus, who descended from northern nomads, to peoples of past times who "lived in dens and wore pelts."[6] Nationalist leader and medical doctor Sun Yatsen (soon yot-SEN), who had been educated outside of China, used a cluster of Western ideas in his slogan

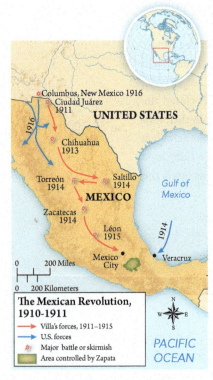

≡ **The Mexican Revolution, 1910–1911**

"nationalism, democracy, and socialism," albeit in the context of long-standing Chinese values. For example, whereas Marxist socialists called for an end to private property, Sun's socialism was based in such traditional charitable thinking as the view that all people should have enough food. Sun's Guomindang called for modernization and the end of foreign domination over China. He was not a capable administrator, however, and soon resigned as leader. When regional generals, using local armies, began to act as warlords, the country descended into chaos.

Adding to tensions, Balkan politicians aroused ethnic nationalism to challenge both Habsburg and Ottoman power. Nationalism had propelled Greece, Serbia, Bulgaria, Romania, and Montenegro to achieve autonomy, despite ethnically and religiously diverse populations. These small states sought strength as modern nations by taking Ottoman and Habsburg territory said to contain a majority of their own ethnic group—a complicated desire, given the centuries of intermingled ethnicities across the region. In the First Balkan War, in 1912, a united Serbia, Bulgaria, Greece, and Montenegro severed Macedonia and Albania from the Ottomans. The victors soon turned against one another and easily defeated Bulgaria in the Second Balkan War of 1913. After the fighting, Austria-Hungary enforced peace terms that further inflamed Serbs. Many Serbs dreamed of crushing Austria-Hungary with the help of their powerful Slavic ally Russia, a dream the Russian government did little to discourage as it too craved greater influence and even additional territory.

International tensions came to a head in June 1914 in the Habsburg-controlled Bosnian capital of Sarajevo when a Bosnian Serb, funded by the Serbian secret police, assassinated the heir to the Habsburg throne, Archduke Franz Ferdinand, and his wife Sophie, with the goal of freeing Bosnia from the Habsburgs and uniting it with Serbia. According to their revised alliance, Germany promised Austria-Hungary full support not just for a defensive war but also if it launched an offensive war to defeat the Serbians once and for all. So the Habsburgs issued a stern ultimatum. In response to Serbia's refusal to meet one of these demands, Austria declared war on Serbia on July 28. Armed to the teeth for war, the major European powers were eager to resolve the international tensions that existed among them over global, national, and even domestic issues. They got more than anyone bargained for.

Fighting World War I

World War I erupted in August 1914 (see Map 25.2). On one side stood the Central Powers—Austria-Hungary and Germany. On the other side were the

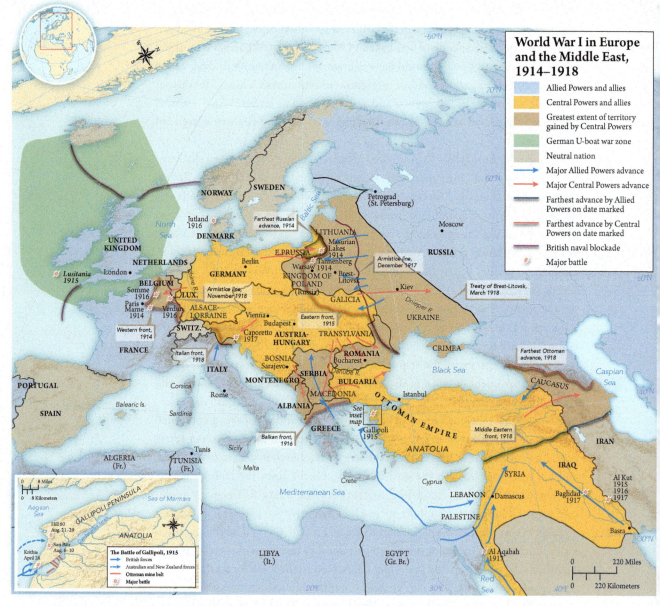

≡ **MAP 25.2   World War I in Europe and the Middle East, 1914–1918** Devastating weaponry transformed parts of Europe and the Middle East into wastelands during World War I. Farmlands were put out of commission for years; livestock near battlefields was decimated. On the western front the damage was mostly confined to northern France, but on the eastern front the armies' destructive power crossed some areas several times.

Allies—France, Great Britain, and Russia. In 1915, Italy, originally aligned with the Central Powers, went over to the Allies in hopes of making postwar gains. As the fighting spread to the combatants' overseas colonies, Japan, eager to extend its empire, soon joined the Allies, while in late October, amidst opposition, the

Ottoman Empire attacked its traditional enemy, Russia, and united with the Central Powers. In 1917, the United States entered the war as well.

The antagonists hungered for the same benefits that inspired imperialism. Germany hoped to acquire a far-flung empire by annexing Russian territory, parts of Belgium, France, and Luxembourg, and even Austria-Hungary. Austria-Hungary aimed to rebuild its power, which was under attack from the competing nationalist movements in the region. Russia wanted to reassert its great-power position as protector of the Slavs by adding all of Poland to the Russian Empire and by controlling other Slavic peoples. The French, too, craved territory, especially the return of Alsace and Lorraine, lost after the Franco-Prussian War of 1870 to 1871 (discussed in Chapter 24). The British sought to secure their world empire by defeating competitors. The secret Treaty of London (1915) promised Italy territory in Africa, Anatolia (modern Turkey), and the Balkans in return for joining the Allies.

In August 1914, armies had at their disposal machine guns and rifles, airplanes, battleships, submarines, and cars, railroads, and other motorized transport. Newer technologies such as chlorine gas, tanks, and bombs quickly developed. Nonetheless, officers on both sides held to a nineteenth-century strategy, the "cult of the offensive," in which, given the powerful technology on both sides, continuous spirited attacks and flashing sabers would be decisive. The colonies of the European powers were to provide massive assistance to wage such offensives. Some one million Africans, another two million Indians, and more than one million members of the British Commonwealth countries, notably Canada, Australia, and New Zealand, served on the battlefronts, while the imperial powers conscripted uncounted numbers of colonists as forced laborers. In the face of massive firepower, the outdated "cult of the offensive" would cost millions of these lives.

The first months of the war crushed hopes of quick victory. All the major armies mobilized rapidly. The Germans were guided by the Schlieffen Plan, which outlined a way to avoid a two-front war by concentrating on one foe at a time. It called for a rapid and concentrated blow to the west against France, defeating it in six weeks. Then German forces would be concentrated against Russia, which, the Germans believed, would mobilize slowly. The attack on France began in the summer of 1914 and proceeded through Belgium, where unexpected resistance slowed the German advance and allowed British and French troops to reach the northern front. In massive battles neither side could defeat the other, and casualties were in the millions. The expected offensive war of movement turned into a stationary, defensive stalemate along a line of nightmarish trenches that stretched from the North Sea through Belgium and northern France to Switzerland.

Meanwhile, on the eastern front, the Russian army, some twelve million strong, unexpectedly drove into German territory by mid-August. The Russian generals

≡ **The Dead of World War I** For most soldiers, the determination by heads of state to pursue the war at any cost meant ongoing suffering in the trenches, including hysteria, crippling wounds, or death. The bones of the unburied were collected from the battlefield as shown here in Verdun, for placement in ossuaries at the war's end.

believed that no matter how ill equipped their army was, no army could stand up to their numbers. Russian success was short-lived, and Germany's commanding generals demanded and received more troops for the eastern front. By year's end Germany was bogged down in the very two-front war its military planners had tried to avoid.

War at sea proved equally indecisive. The Germans responded to the Allied blockade of their ports with an intensive submarine, or U-boat ("underwater boat"), campaign against both Allied and neutral shipping. Despite U.S. deaths, President Woodrow Wilson maintained a policy of neutrality, and Germany, unwilling to provoke Wilson further, called off unrestricted submarine warfare— that is, attacks on neutral shipping. Throughout 1915 the British hoped to knock out the Ottomans and open ports to Russia by attacking at the Dardanelles Strait (see again Map 25.2). At Gallipoli, casualty rates for both sides of 50 to 60 percent only yielded stalemate. "A miserable time," one Irish soldier called Gallipoli, as his comrades from New Zealand, Australia, and elsewhere in the empire had their heads blown off and their limbs smashed to pulp. Horrific suffering in this single battle strengthened Australia's and New Zealand's will to break with Britain, which had led them into the tragedy.

Both sides refused a negotiated peace: "No peace before England is defeated and destroyed," Kaiser William II railed against his cousin, Britain's King George V. "Only amidst the ruins of London will I forgive Georgy."[7] In 1916, in an effort to break French morale, the Germans launched massive assaults on the fortress at Verdun, firing as many as a million shells in a single day during the attack. Combined French and German losses totaled close to a million men, whose anonymous bones today fill a vast shrine at the site.

Had the military leaders thoroughly dominated the scene, historians judge, all armies would have been demolished in nonstop offensives by the end of 1915. Yet ordinary soldiers in this war were not automatons, and in the face of what seemed to them suicidal orders, soldiers on both sides sometimes refused to engage in battle. Right up to the closing year of the war, soldiers fraternized with the "enemy," playing an occasional game of soccer and entering into silent agreements not to fight. A British veteran of the trenches explained to a new recruit that the Germans "don't want to fight any more than we do, so there's a kind of understanding between us. Don't fire at us and we'll not fire at you."[8] Male bonding aided survival as soldiers protected and came to love one another, sometimes even passionately.

Troops from Asian and African colonies often had different experiences, especially because colonial soldiers were frequently put in the front ranks where the risks were greatest. Many suffered from the rigors of a totally unfamiliar climate and strange food. Colonial troops' perspectives changed as they saw their "masters" completely "uncivilized." "I am greatly distressed in mind," one South Asian soldier wrote, echoing the general hopelessness on seeing comrades lose hands, feet, and entire limbs.[9] Colonizers and colonized could alike be reduced to hysteria through the sheer stress of battle; others became cynical. "It might be me tomorrow," a young British soldier wrote his mother in 1916. "Who cares?"

Citizens at War: The Home Front

World War I quickly became a "**total war**," one in which all resources of each nation were harnessed to the war effort, blurring lines between the home front and the battlefield. Civilians manufactured the machine guns, poisonous gases,

total war The vital involvement of civilians in the war industry, the blurring of home and battle fronts, and the use of industrial weaponry to destroy an enemy.

SEEING THE PAST

Wartime Propaganda

Propaganda agencies within governments on both sides in World War I touted the war as a patriotic mission to resist villainous enemies. They used both film and print to turn people who formerly saw themselves as neighbors into hate-filled enemies. British propagandists fabricated atrocities that the German "Huns" supposedly committed against Belgians, and German propaganda warned that French African troops would rape German women if Germany were defeated. Results were often questionable: a British film, *The Battle of the Somme* (1916), so obviously sanitized the war's horrors that soldiers in the audience roared with laughter, though civilians found it riveting.

Brightly colored propaganda posters, representing the best lithographic technology, were pasted to walls and placed in windows. Government experts hired the best graphic artists to execute their carefully chosen themes. In one of the images shown here, German propagandists picked up on the widespread

Lehtes Aufgebot der „Grande Armee".
Parole: Für die „Zivilisation" gegen die Barbarei!

The French Are Using Monkeys: A German Magazine Cover

bombs, airplanes, and tanks that were the backbone of modern warfare. Increased production of coffins, canes, wheelchairs, and artificial limbs was also a wartime necessity. In the cause of victory, civilians were required to work overtime and sacrifice. To supply the battlefront efficiently, governments took over the operation of the economy and suppressed dissent.

Initially, political parties in each combatant nation put aside differences. For decades socialist parties had preached that "the worker has no country" and that nationalism was mere ideology meant to keep workers obedient. In August 1914, however, most socialists backed the war, trading worker solidarity for national

(Walter Trier-Archiv, Konstanz)

use of African soldiers in the French army to make their point, depicting the enemy in this poster as monkeys. The "Fake Battalion—Senegal" mocks the effectiveness of the enemy. In contrast, an Australian artist drew this Allied poster representing the German enemy with a frightening face and its hands dripping blood.

Examining the Evidence

1. What accounts for these specific representations of the enemy?

2. What might the reaction have been to each representation, and how would these images have aroused commitment to the war?

3. Alongside this type of caricature was sentimental wartime propaganda depicting brave soldiers, faithful wives, and children in need of their hardy fathers' and other male protection. Why was there such variety in propaganda, and which type of image would you judge to be most effective?

unity in a time of crisis. Although many feminists were opposed to war, the British WSPU leader Emmeline Pankhurst was hardly alone in also becoming a militant nationalist.[10] "What is the use of fighting for a vote if we have not got a country to vote in?" she asked. Others hoped that the spirit of nationalism could end prejudices. "In the German fatherland there are no longer any Christians and Jews . . . , there are only Germans," one rabbi proudly announced. Governments mobilized the masses on the home front to endure long hours and food shortages by demonizing the enemy (see Seeing the Past: Wartime Propaganda). New laws made it a crime to criticize official policies.

As the war dragged on, some individuals and groups began to lobby for peace. In 1915, activists in the international women's movement met in The Hague to call for an end to war. "We can no longer endure . . . brute force as the only solution of international disputes," declared Dutch physician Aletta Jacobs.[11] Some socialists moved to neutral countries to work for a negotiated peace settlement.

The requirements of total war upset gender order. In the early days of fighting many women lost their jobs when nonmilitary establishments closed. New opportunities arose, however: as men left the workplace to join the fighting, women moved into a variety of high-paying jobs, including munitions production and services like streetcar conducting and ambulance driving. Workingmen often protested that women, in the words of one metalworker, were "sending men to the slaughter" and robbing them of their role as breadwinner. Many people, including some women, objected to women's loss of femininity, as workers cut their hair short and wore utilitarian slacks. Despite criticism, a "new woman" with a respectable job and new responsibilities for supporting her family was emerging from the war.

Rising social tensions revolved around issues of class as well as gender. Workers toiled longer hours eating less, while many in the upper classes bought abundant food and fashionable clothing. Governments allowed businesses to keep raising prices and thus earn high profits, resulting in a surging cost of living and social strife. Shortages of staples such as bread, sugar, and meat caused hardships. Starving Ottoman peasant women, their crops confiscated for the war effort, wrote hopelessly to the government in 1917, "Either deport us all to another place or cast us into the sea."[12] Civilians in such colonies as German East Africa suffered oppressive conditions, facing harsh forced labor along with skyrocketing taxes and prices. The prolonged conflict created grievances among people worldwide.

Revolution in Russia and the End of World War I

FOCUS Why did the Russian Revolution take place, and what changes did it produce in Russian politics and daily life?

By 1917 the situation was becoming desperate for everyone—politicians, the military, and civilians. In February of that year, the German government, responding to public anger over mounting casualties, resumed unrestricted submarine warfare. The move brought the United States into the war two months later, after German U-boats had sunk several American ships. In the spring of 1917, French soldiers mutinied against further offensives, while in Russia, wartime protest turned into outright revolution.

The Russian Revolution

Of all the warring nations, Russia sustained the greatest number of casualties—7.5 million by 1917. Unlike other heads of state, Tsar Nicholas II failed to unify his government or his people. Nicholas was capable of making patriotic gestures, such as changing the German-sounding name of St. Petersburg to Petrograd, but he stubbornly insisted on conducting the war himself instead of using experienced and knowledgeable officials: "Is this stupidity or treason?" one member of the Russian Duma asked. "Treason, treason," the deputies responded.[13] In March 1917, crowds of working women and civilians commemorating International Women's Day swarmed the streets of Petrograd and began looting shops for food; other workers joined them. Many in the army defected, angered by the massive casualties caused by their substandard weapons. Nicholas soon abdicated, bringing the three-hundred-year-old Romanov dynasty to an abrupt end.

Politicians from the old Duma formed a new ruling entity called the Provisional Government. Despite high hopes for a "pure, merry, and beautiful life," the abdication of the tsar unleashed popular forces that had been building. Spontaneously elected **soviets**—councils of workers and soldiers—campaigned to end favoritism toward the wealthy and urged concern for workers and the poor. The peasantry, another force competing for power, began to seize aristocratic estates. Meanwhile, the Provisional Government seemed unwilling to end the war and unable to improve living conditions.

In April 1917, Vladimir Ilyich Lenin, leader of a faction of the Russian Socialist Party, returned from exile in Switzerland, his safe rail transportation provided by the Germans, who hoped that Lenin might further weaken the Russian war effort. Son of a prominent provincial official, Lenin began his political activism while at university and then became an organizer of Marxist groups across Europe. Among his principles was the belief that workers needed to be led by an elite group of revolutionaries—not by the masses themselves. Those belonging to Lenin's faction were called **Bolsheviks**. Soon after returning, Lenin called on his countrymen to withdraw from World War 1, for the soviets to seize power on behalf of workers and poor peasants, and for all private land to be nationalized.

In November 1917, the Bolsheviks seized power from the Provisional Government in the name of the soviets. When in January 1918 elections for a constituent assembly failed to give the Bolsheviks a majority, the party simply took over the government by force. Following Marxist theory, the Bolsheviks abolished private property and nationalized factories in order to restore productivity. The new government asked Germany for peace and agreed to the Treaty of Brest-Litovsk (March 1918), which placed vast regions of the Russian Empire

soviet A council of workers and soldiers elected to represent the people in the Russian Revolutions of 1905 and 1917.

Bolshevik A faction of the Russian Socialist Party that advocated control of revolutionary activity by a disciplined group of the party elite instead of by the working class as a whole; renamed "Communist" by Lenin following the Russian Revolution.

under German occupation. To distinguish themselves from the socialists or Social Democrats who had voted for the disastrous war in 1914, the Bolsheviks formally adopted the name Communists. Lenin agreed to the huge loss of territory because he believed the rest of Europe would soon overthrow the capitalist order.

Opposition to Bolshevik policies swiftly formed and soon mushroomed into full-fledged civil war. The pro-Bolsheviks (or "Reds") faced an array of antirevolutionary forces (the "Whites"). Among the Whites, the tsarist military leadership, composed of many aristocratic landlords, was joined by non-Russian-nationality groups eager to regain independence. Russia's former allies, notably the United States, Britain, France, and Japan, landed troops in the country to defeat the Bolsheviks. The Whites failed, however, because its individual groups competed with one another. In contrast, the Bolsheviks had a more unified leadership, which, under commissar of war Leon Trotsky, built a highly disciplined army. The Cheka (secret police) set up detention camps for political opponents and often shot them without trial. The expansion of government undermined the Marxist belief that socialism would bring a "withering away" of the state.

The Bolsheviks organized revolutionary Marxism worldwide. In March 1919, they founded the **Comintern** (Communist International), a centrally run organization to achieve communism globally. By mid-1921, the Red Army had secured the Crimea, the Caucasus, and the Muslim borderlands in Central Asia, and in 1922 the Bolsheviks formally created the multiethnic Union of Soviet Socialist Republics (USSR). Despite disease, hunger, and rampant slaughter of enemies, people worldwide believed in the Soviet promise of a workers' utopia.

Ending the War: 1918

Although Russia withdrew from World War I in early 1918, the wider conflict continued. Relying on Arab, African, and Indian troops, the Allies took Baghdad as well as Palestine, Lebanon, and Syria from the Ottomans. Europeans conscripted more than a million Kenyans and Tanzanians to fight for control of East Africa. African civilians and soldiers died by the thousands, as resources were confiscated and villages burned by competing powers. The Japanese seized German holdings in China.

In the spring of 1918 the Central Powers made one final attempt to smash through the Allied lines, but Allied experimental use of tanks that could withstand machine-gun fire and the arrival of U.S. troops pushed back the Germans all along the western front. In an effort to shift the blame for defeat away from themselves, the German military leaders allowed a civilian government to ask for peace. After the war, the generals would falsely claim that this government had

Comintern An international organization of workers established by the Bolsheviks to spread communism worldwide.

dealt the military a "stab in the back" by surrendering when victory was still possible. As the Central Powers collapsed on November 11, 1918, the two sides signed an armistice.

In the course of four years, civilization had been sorely tested. Conservative figures put the battlefield toll at a minimum of ten million dead and thirty million wounded, incapacitated, or eventually to die of their wounds. In every European combatant country, industrial and agricultural production had plummeted, and much of the reduced output had been put to military use. From 1918 to 1919, the global population suffered an influenza epidemic that left as many as one hundred million more dead. "They carried the dead people on mule-drawn carts without even being in boxes," one fighter in Pancho Villa's army reported of the flu in Mexico. "Many poor people left their small children as orphans . . . without father, without mother, without anything."[14] The influenza pandemic only added to the tragic fact that total war had drained society of resources and population and had sown the seeds of future catastrophes.

Postwar Global Politics

↘ **FOCUS** What were the major outcomes of the peacemaking process and postwar conditions?

Across the globe, protest erupted after the war. The massive slaughter and use of forced labor damaged Western claims to be more advanced than other parts of the world, causing a surging resistance to colonialism even as the victorious Allies took steps to secure and expand their empires. Such was the highly charged backdrop for peacemaking.

The Paris Peace Conference, 1919–1920

The Paris Peace Conference opened in January 1919 with leaders of the United States, Great Britain, and France dominating the proceedings. Western leaders worried about civilian calls for revenge and communism spreading beyond the USSR's borders. France, for example, had lost almost an entire generation of young men, more than a million buildings, and thousands of miles of railroad lines and roads while the war was fought on French soil. The British slogan "Hang the Kaiser!" captured the public mood. U.S. president Woodrow Wilson's **Fourteen Points**, on which the truce had been based, were steeped in the language of freedom and called for an "open-minded" settlement of colonial issues and the self-determination of peoples—meaning the right of national groups to have

Fourteen Points
A proposal by U.S. president Woodrow Wilson for peace during World War I based on "settlement" rather than "victory" and on the self-determination of peoples.

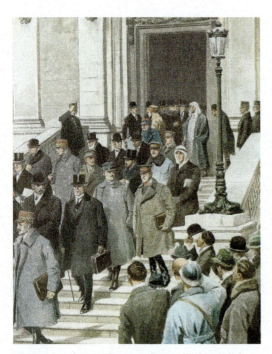

≡ **Paris Peace Conference, 1918** Allied heads of state and policy experts dominated the Paris Peace Conference of 1918. Also attending were leaders from the Middle East, who had rallied their own armed forces to fight for the Allies on the promise of postwar independence. The victors utterly disregarded those promises in the Peace of Paris settlement.

League of Nations
The international organization set up following World War I to maintain peace by arbitrating disputes and promoting collective security.

collective security The system of international diplomacy, especially involving the peaceful resolution of disputes, established by the League of Nations.

autonomy if they wanted it. Amid disagreements over punishing the Central Powers, representatives from Middle Eastern states, Japan, and other interested parties, having fought in the war, wanted a say in the peace.

After six months, the Allies produced the Peace of Paris (1919–1920), composed of individual treaties. The treaties separated Austria from Hungary, reduced Hungary by almost two-thirds of its inhabitants and three-quarters of its territory, and broke up the Ottoman Empire. The Habsburg Empire was replaced by a group of small, internally divided, and relatively weak states: Czechoslovakia, Poland, and the Kingdom of the Serbs, Croats, and Slovenes, soon renamed Yugoslavia. Austria and Hungary were both left reeling at their loss of territory and resources (see Map 25.3).

In the settlement with Germany (the Treaty of Versailles), France recovered Alsace and Lorraine, and Germany was ordered to pay crippling reparations for wartime damage and directed to give up its colonies, reduce its army, and deliver a large amount of free coal each year to Belgium and France. Average Germans saw the Treaty of Versailles as an unmerited humiliation: it branded their nation an outcast in the global community by blaming the war entirely on "the aggression of Germany and her allies."

Besides redrawing the map of Europe, the diplomats created the **League of Nations**, an organization whose members had a joint responsibility for maintaining peace through negotiation—a principle called **collective security**, which was to replace the divisive secrecy of prewar diplomacy. In Woodrow Wilson's vision, the league would guide the world toward disarmament and settle its members' disputes. However, the U.S. Senate both failed to ratify the peace settlement and refused to join the league. Germany and Russia initially were excluded from the league and were thus blocked from participating in international consensus-building. The absence of these three major powers weakened the league from the outset.

Instead of ending colonialism as promised to many non-Western combatants, the League of Nations organized the former territories of Germany and the Ottoman Empire into a system of mandates awarded to the victors, especially

The Peace of Paris in Central and Eastern Europe, 1920

— Boundaries of German, Russian, and Austro-Hungarian empires in 1914

▇ New and reconstituted nations

▇ Demilitarized or Allied occupation zone

-- Boundaries of 1920

≡ **MAP 25.3   The Peace of Paris in Central and Eastern Europe, 1920** Where mighty empires had once reigned over central and eastern Europe, new states appeared and new forms of government replaced dynastic rule. These small states were generally fragile due to their very novelty, postwar economic difficulties, and the need to modernize agriculture and to develop industrial capacity.

Britain and France who redrew borders in the Middle East (see Map 25.4). The league covenant justified the **mandate system** as providing governance by "advanced nations" over territories "not yet able to stand by themselves under the strenuous conditions of the modern world," leading some to see it as a "League of Empires."

Not surprisingly, the people of the new mandates were furious. Sharif Husayn ibn Ali had mobilized a substantial force to battle the Ottomans because of

mandate system A system of regional control over former Ottoman lands awarded by the League of Nations' charter to the victors in World War I.

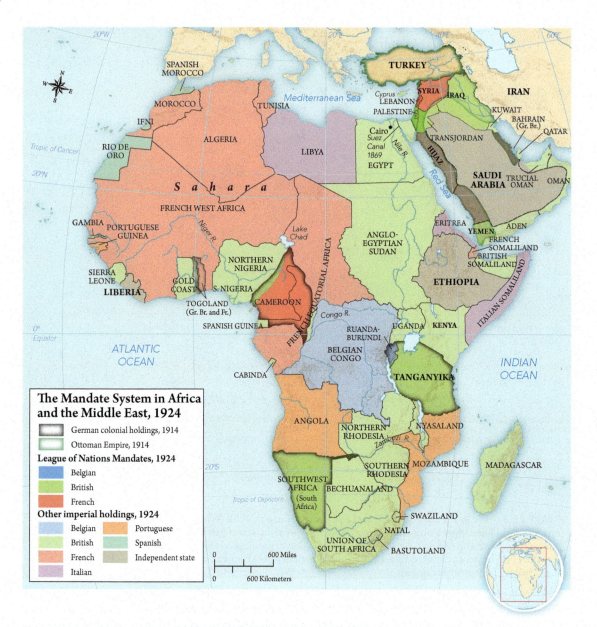

The Mandate System in Africa and the Middle East, 1924

| | German colonial holdings, 1914 |
| | Ottoman Empire, 1914 |

League of Nations Mandates, 1924

	Belgian
	British
	French

Other imperial holdings, 1924

	Belgian		Portuguese
	British		Spanish
	French		Independent state
	Italian		

≡ **MAP 25.4   The Mandate System in Africa and the Middle East, 1924**   Instead of granting Middle Eastern and African peoples the promised independence that had brought them into the war, the Allies scooped up former territories of the Germans and Ottomans and set boundaries that converted them into "mandates"—in effect, colonies. The growing importance of oil lay behind this seizure of control.

agreements with Britain for an independent Syria. His son Faisal was humiliated in Paris when it became clear that no such independence was forthcoming. On his return to the Middle East Faisal called on the crowds to "choose either to be slaves or masters of your own destiny."[15] Rebellions against France and Britain erupted in the Middle East, but they were put down most notably at the Battle of Maysalun in Syria. Outside of the Middle East, opposition movements such as pan-Africanism redoubled their efforts to build solidarity. "Never again will the darker people of the world occupy just the place they had before," the African American leader W. E. B. Du Bois predicted in 1918.[16] The postwar settlements, like the war itself, contributed to renewed activism among colonial peoples around the world.

Struggles for Reform and Independence

In the aftermath of war, many of the world's peoples took advantage of Western weakness to seek independence from outside domination. These struggles occurred in remnants of the Ottoman Empire, China, India, and Africa. In the face of such determination, imperial powers from Japan to Britain not only resisted loosening their domination, but continued to use violence to maintain and expand their empires.

The Allied invasion of the Ottoman Empire caused chaos and suffering from Anatolia through Syria, Lebanon, and Egypt. Allied blockades during the war produced widespread starvation, and Allied agents had provoked rebellion against the Ottoman grip to weaken the empire. An unacknowledged slaughter occurred during the war itself when the Ottoman leadership carried out the deportation of an estimated three hundred thousand to 1.5 million Armenians in the empire, claiming that they were plotting with the Russians. Armenians were rounded up and sent on marches into the desert to perish; their considerable property was stolen. The Ottoman position was that "the Armenians have only themselves to blame." They were, in the words of one official, "a menace to the Turkish race."[17]

As the Ottoman Empire was dismembered, Turkish military officers resisted the Allied occupation, which they viewed as a sign of the Allied desire to annex all Ottoman lands, including its center at Istanbul. Led by General Mustafa Kemal, the remnants of the Ottoman army traveled the countryside calling for a democratically elected national assembly and an end to British control of Istanbul: "All we want is to save our country from sharing the fate of India and Egypt."[18] He and his followers also pushed for the primacy of ethnic Turks, despite centuries-old intermixture of ethnic groups. As the Allies tried to partition Anatolia, Kemal, who later took the name Atatürk ("first among Turks"), countered with the founding an independent Turkish republic in 1923 (see Map 25.5).

As head of the new government, Kemal advocated Western modernity and a capitalist economy. "A nation must be strong in spirit, knowledge, science and morals," he announced.[19] In an effort to Westernize the new Turkish state, he mandated

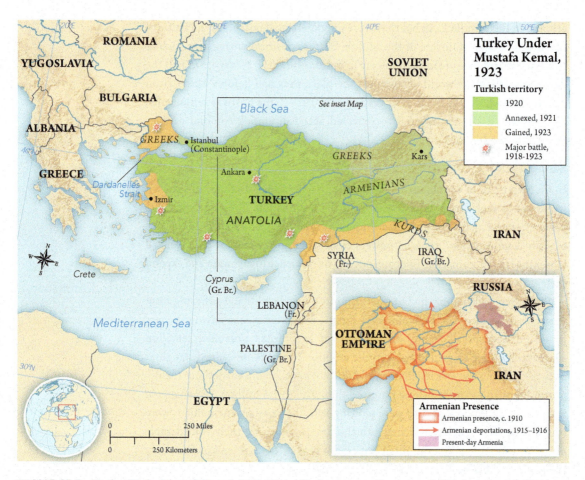

≡ **MAP 25.5   Turkey Under Mustafa Kemal, 1923** With Allied assistance, Greece invaded Turkey after World War I in an attempt to take it over. Armenia also attacked. Turkish nationalists commanded by Mustafa Kemal defeated both groups, despite a British drive to control Istanbul and the Dardanelles Strait.

Western dress for men and women, introduced the Latin alphabet, and abolished polygamy. Ordinary people reacted to their world being turned topsy-turvy: "It's a Christian hat," a barber warned a young soldier sporting a Western-style hat as part of his uniform. "If a Muslim puts such a shocking thing on his head the good God will surely punish him."[20] In 1936, women received the vote and became eligible to serve in the parliament.

China underwent similar turmoil as people from many walks of life protested Japan's 1915 takeover of Germany's sphere of influence in China, which included the birthplace of Confucius. The Allies' legal endorsement of that takeover, announced on May 4, 1919, galvanized student protest. Carrying signs that read

"China Belongs to the Chinese," they were joined by dockworkers, business people, and other citizens. The May Fourth Movement also targeted Chinese traditions—from patriarchal control of women to educational "backwardness"—as responsible for China's treatment on the world stage. Like the leaders of the new Turkey and Meiji Japan, they had come to see selective Westernization as key to independence.

Many other Chinese, however, declared that Western leaders at the Paris conference were "still selfish and militaristic and that they were all great liars," as one student put it.[21]

Reform in Turkey, 1923 Like other countries seeking to "modernize," Turkey under Atatürk made the condition of women an important element of modernization. Atatürk decreed that women and men alike dress in Western clothes, receive a secular education, and adopt the Latin alphabet. There was much for the citizens of the new Turkey to learn and unlearn.

Some adopted an alternative—communism. Supported by funds from the USSR, organized strikes erupted, but so did tensions between Communists and the Guomindang, which had been taken over by the military leader Jiang Jieshi (Chiang Kai-Shek) after the death of Sun in 1925. First Jiang led his troops to put down warlords. As he took the cities of Nanjing and Shanghai, his followers murdered the Communists in hopes of stopping their influence too. Jiang then turned to mobilizing his countrymen for modernization.

Prewar attempts at liberation continued elsewhere. In Ireland, pro-independence activists attacked government buildings in Dublin on Easter Monday 1916, in an effort finally to gain Irish

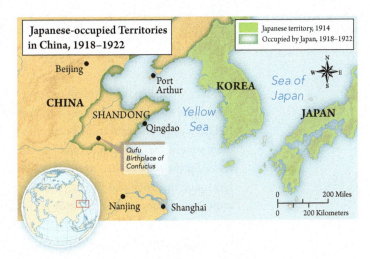

Japanese-Occupied Territories in China, 1918–1922

READING THE PAST

Léopold Sédar Senghor, "To the Senegalese Soldiers Who Died for France"

Among the colonial troops in World War I were the Senegalese Sharpshooters, who fought on the side of their French imperial masters. Though the Senegalese riflemen served on the front lines, they received little credit from the French and were even forced to march around rather than through, villages so that white citizens would not have to set eyes on black soldiers. They were immortalized in a poem by Léopold Sédar Senghor, who himself fought in the French colonial forces and who became the first president of an independent Senegal in 1960. Among the thousands of poems memorializing World War I, the one from which this excerpt was taken also served as Senegal's national anthem after liberation.

They put flowers on tombs and warm the Unknown Soldier.

But you, my dark brothers, no one calls your names.
. . .
Listen to me, Senegalese soldiers, in the solitude of the
      Black ground
And of death, in your deaf and blind solitude,
More than I in my dark skin in the depths of the
   Province,
Without even the warmth of your comrades lying close
      To you,
As in the trenches back then or the village palavers
      [conversations] long ago,
. . .
We bring you, listen to us, we who spelled your names

freedom from Britain. Ill-prepared, their Easter rebellion was easily defeated; many were executed. In January 1919, determined republican leaders proclaimed Ireland's independence from Britain. Instead of granting it, the British government sent in the "Black and Tans," a volunteer army of demobilized soldiers—so called for the color of their uniforms. Terror reigned as both the pro-independence forces and the Black and Tans took hostages, blew up buildings, and even shot into crowds at soccer matches. By 1921 public outrage forced the British to negotiate. The Irish Free State was declared a self-governing dominion, while Northern Ireland, a group of six northern counties containing many Protestants, became a self-governing British territory with representation in the British Parliament.

In the months of your deaths, we bring you,
In these fearful days without memory,
The friendship of your age-mates
Ah! If I could one day sing in a voice glowing
  like embers,
If I could praise the friendship of comrades as
  fervent
And delicate as entrails, as strong as tendons.

Listen to us, you Dead stretched out in water
  as far as
The northern and eastern fields.
Receive this red earth, under a summer sun this
  soil
Reddened with the blood of white hosts
Receive the salute of your black comrades,
Senegalese soldiers
WHO DIED FOR THE REPUBLIC

Source: Léopold Sédar Senghor, *The Collected Poetry,* trans. Melvin Dixon (Charlottesville: University Press of Virginia, 1991), 46–47.

Examining the Evidence

1. What emotions and values does Senghor express in this poem?

2. What views of World War I does the poem reveal?

3. Why do you think Senghor wrote this poem, and for whom?

4. Why would this poem about a specific group of people fighting on behalf of imperial powers become the national anthem of an independent country?

Partial independence and the rights of religious minorities remained contentious, producing violence for decades thereafter.

Colonial Protest and Imperial Expansion

Others from the colonies who had fought expected to gain the rights that European politicians had solemnly promised. Instead, they met worsening conditions at home. "Is our reward to have our tax raised . . . and for our ownership of land to be called into question?" one group of East Africans asked in 1921 (see Reading the Past: Léopold Sédar Senghor, "To the Senegalese Soldiers Who Died for France").[22] Fearful of losing India, British forces shot into crowds of protesters at

≡ **Ireland, 1921**

Amritsar in 1919 and put down revolts in Egypt and Iran in the early 1920s. The Dutch jailed political leaders in Indonesia; the French punished Indochinese nationalists; and in 1929 the British crushed Ibo women's tax protest as colonial rule became ever more brutal.

Maintaining empires was crucial to covering debts incurred during World War I, so amid protest imperialism reached its high tide in the 1920s and 1930s. Britain and France, enjoying control of Germany's African colonies and former Ottoman lands in the Middle East, were at the height of their global power. A new generation of adventurers headed for Middle Eastern and Indonesian oil fields, as the importance of oil increased along with the number of automobiles, airplanes, trucks, ships, and oil-heated homes. Investors from the United States and elsewhere grabbed land in the Caribbean and across Latin America, cornering markets in sugar, cocoa, and tropical fruit. Competition for territory and business thrived.

The balance of power among the imperial nations was shifting, however. The most important change was Japan's widening race for markets, resources, and influence. During the war, Japanese output of industrial goods such as ships and metal grew some 40 percent as the Allies outsourced their wartime needs for such products. Officials touted Japan's economic success as key to an Asia free from Westerners. Ardently nationalist, the Japanese government was not yet strong enough to challenge Western powers militarily. Thus, although outraged at Wilson's abrupt rejection (with British backing) of a nondiscrimination clause in the charter of the League of Nations, Japan cooperated in the Anglo-American-dominated peace, even agreeing both to restore Chinese possessions and to keep a ratio of English, American, and Japanese shipbuilding at 5:5:3 respectively. "Rolls Royce, Rolls Royce, Ford," a Japanese official commented bitterly.[23] This bitterness ultimately festered into war.

An Age of the Masses

⇘ **FOCUS** How did the rise of mass society affect politics, culture, and everyday life around the world?

With the collapse of autocratic governments from China to Germany, the sense of democratic potential based on mass participation grew. The condition of women came to symbolize the strength of the masses, which was reflected in the extension of the vote to many Western women during the 1920s. Modernizing the economy—a goal of many countries after the war—meant developing mass consumerism, while modern technology provided mass entertainment and news across the globe. By the end of the decade, a handful of political leaders were adopting new media to mobilize their citizenry.

Mass Society

The development of mass society was a global phenomenon, fueled by the growing connections among and within economies. Urbanization surged in Asia, Latin America, Africa, and the United States with the continued migration of rural people to cities. Global population, aided by the spread of medicine and improved sanitation, also soared. Tokyo had some 3.5 million inhabitants in 1920, New York 5.5 million, and Shanghai over 2 million. Calcutta's population quadrupled to 1.8 million from the late nineteenth century to 1920. City life was fast paced, brimming with trams, buses, and automobiles; in China rickshaws pulled by fast young men replaced the leisurely sedan chair. Tall buildings lifted skylines in cities throughout the world. New urban cultural livelihoods arose, such as performing jazz and managing nightclubs. Outside city centers, wealthy suburbs and exclusive beachside retreats flourished, such as that near the city of Bombay, India, started by the Tata family of industrialists (whom we met in Chapter 23).

Wartime innovations spurred new industries and created new jobs making cars, electrical products, and synthetic goods for peacetime use. The prewar pattern of mergers and cartels now gave rise to multinational food-processing firms such as Nestlé in Switzerland and global petroleum enterprises such as Royal Dutch Shell. Owners of these large manufacturing conglomerates wielded more financial and political power than entire small countries. Businessmen from around the world made pilgrimages to Henry Ford's trendsetting Detroit assembly line, which by 1929 produced a Ford automobile every ten seconds. The new livelihood of scientific manager also played a part, as efficiency experts developed methods to streamline workers' tasks for maximum productivity. Workers found these methods inhumane, with restrictions on time and motion so severe that often employees were allowed to use the bathroom only on a fixed schedule.

As industry spread, the number of people in unions increased around the world, with both skilled and unskilled workers organizing to advance their collective interests. Sometimes the reasons for joining were basic: local workers on the French railroads in West Africa complained of "unsanitary food seasoned with dried fish and full of worms" and began unionizing.[24] White-collar service and government workers also had large, effective unions. Male-dominated unions usually agreed with employers that women should receive lower wages, saving high-paying jobs for men.

Because they could mobilize masses of people, unions played a key role in politics, as when unionized workers in China struck against Britain's control of Hong Kong. "Down with imperialism!" was one of their cries, and they forced merchants to show that their goods did not originate in Britain.[25] India's ongoing industrialization during the war provided jobs, but in the postwar period some 125,000 Bombay textile workers were among those who struck for better pay. Labor flexed its muscle elsewhere: union members blocked coups against Germany's new democratic government, the Weimar Republic, and organized a general strike in Great Britain in the 1920s.

Modernization and rising global productivity affected traditional social divisions. Advances in industrialization boosted the size of the modern middle class by expanding the need for managers and professionals and for skilled workers in new jobs. Often these opportunities reduced the influence of traditional elites and in colonized areas such as India complicated long-standing caste and religious categories. In this atmosphere, reformers such as those in China's May Fourth Movement pointed to the irrationality of traditional patterns of deference within families.

Class and racial prescriptions were also breaking down as a result of the war: men of all classes and ethnicities had served in trenches together and were even buried in common graves. The war also caused daughters around the world to support themselves in jobs, and their mothers to take up their own housework because former servants could earn more money in factories. A middle-class "look" became common around the world, promoted by global advertising that appealed to consumers with vivid images of sleek, modern styles.

One emblem of postwar modernity in most parts of the world was the "new woman" or the "modern girl." In the 1920s many women cut their hair, abandoned traditional clothes such as kimonos, smoked, had money of their own from working in the service sector, and went out unchaperoned. Zhu Su'e, born in 1901 to a banking family in Changzhou, China, unbound her feet as a teenager and then left home in 1921 to study in Shanghai. She graduated from law school, married for love instead of having a traditional arranged marriage, and continued her career: "I understood that you must be able to earn money in order to be independent."[26] Some attempts to impose "modern" standards were

Miss Brazil in Texas, 1929 Healthful sports and a growing consumerism signaled postwar revival. In this photograph, Miss Brazil—an example of the new woman with her trim clothing and a cosmetically enhanced face—has traveled to the United States to participate in a beauty contest. International beauty contests displayed global styles in self-presentation for others to emulate.

rejected. When activists in the USSR urged Muslim women to remove their veils and "update" their way of life, fervent Muslims often attacked both the activists and any women who followed their advice.

Culture for the Masses

Wartime propaganda had aimed to unite classes, races, and countries against a common enemy. In the 1920s, phonographs, the radio, and film continued the development of mass or standardized culture. Mass media had the potential to create an informed citizenry, enhance democracy, and promote liberation in the colonies. Paradoxically, it also provided tools for would-be dictators aiming to mobilize the masses.

By the 1920s, film flourished around the world, with Shanghai and Hong Kong joining the United States, Europe, and South Asia as important centers of production and distribution (see Lives and Livelihoods: The Film Industry). In India, where movie theaters had sprung up at the start of the century, movies retelling the *Mahabharata* and history films on the story of the Taj Mahal developed Indians' sense of a common heritage. Bolshevik leaders underwrote the innovative work of director Sergei Eisenstein, whose films *Potemkin* (1925) and *Ten Days That Shook the World* (1927–1928) spread a Bolshevik view of history across international audiences. Films also helped standardize behavior. Popular comedies of the 1920s and 1930s such as the Shanghai hits *Three Modern Women* (1933) and *New Woman* (1934) showed women viewers the ways of flappers.

Cinematic portrayals also played to postwar fantasies and fears, as threats to class and caste systems shaped movie plots from India to the United States. Impersonators, "gold diggers," con artists, and gangsters abounded. English actor Charlie Chaplin in *Little Tramp* (1914–1915) won international popularity as the defeated hero, the anonymous modern man, trying to keep his dignity in a mechanical world. Sporting events such as cricket, boxing, and martial arts were shown as newsreels before featured movies. As popular films and books crossed national boundaries, global culture flourished.

Radio developed from the Italian inventor Guglielmo Marconi's wireless technology was first heard by mass audiences in public halls and featured orchestras and audience discussion. The radio quickly became a relatively inexpensive consumer item in private homes. Specialized programming for men (such as sports reporting) and for women (such as advice on home management) soon followed. By the 1930s, politicians, including anti-colonial ones, used radio to reach the masses.

The print media—newspapers and magazines—grew in popularity too, and their advertising encouraged new personal habits, presenting mass-produced razors and deodorants as essential to modern hygiene. Politicians joined in as modernizers:

LIVES AND LIVELIHOODS

The Film Industry

The development of the film industry worldwide from the late nineteenth century on led to dozens of new livelihoods. Although early films often were the work of a single author-director-cameraman, by the 1920s filmmaking involved many more jobs. Among the most notable new livelihoods were those of screenwriter, cameraman, art editor, and film financier, along with less-renowned jobs for stuntmen, animal trainers, baby actors, and, in the United States especially, film censors. The Chinese focus on martial arts in film increased the number of jobs for these experts. Before the "talkies," films with sound, were invented in the 1930s, silent movies featured pianists who provided mood-setting music and soloists who entertained during intermission. In Japan the *benshi* explained throughout the film the action on the screen, sometimes even singing and dancing.

From Southeast Asia to Central America, lavish cinema houses attracted hundreds of millions of weekly viewers, the majority of them women. The importance of the theater for film promoted architects, construction workers, and even the elegant usher, who frequently accompanied viewers to their seats in exchange for a tip. With India producing some fifteen hundred films of its own between 1912 and 1927, film viewing alone provided a rich array of jobs.

In the 1920s the "star" system turned performers into national, even global, celebrities. In Japan's thriving film industry, most stars were men, who played both male and female roles as they had done in kabuki and Noh theater. By contrast, in China, the highest-paid star was the actress Butterfly Hu, who starred in the first "talkie," *Sing Song Red Peony*, in 1930. Butterfly Hu also filled the pages of the print media as she became a style setter in terms of fashion and grooming. Hu, like other stars, was promoted by professional publicists and hired agents and managers, still other new livelihoods. Media entrepreneurs earned a handsome living founding magazines and engaging Hu and others to sell products. New lines of work arose to provide gossip about film celebrities, biographies of directors, and reviews of films. Film celebrity spawned hundreds of new livelihoods across mass culture.

Questions to Consider

1. What skills did those working in the film industry need, and to what extent were they new?

2. What accounts for the popularity of cinema in these decades?

3. In what ways was film important to global culture and the world economy?

≡ **Butterfly Hu and Chinese Cinema** By the 1920s films were distributed worldwide. *Twin Sisters* (1933), a product of Shanghai's bustling film industry, focused on the plight of twin sisters with utterly different personalities—both played by the Chinese star Butterfly Hu. The ease with which culture crossed borders made the movie a hit in China, Southeast Asia, Japan, and western Europe.

For Further Information:

Dixon, Wheeler Winston, and Gwendolyn Audrey Foster. *A Short History of Film*, 2nd ed. 2013.

Grieveson, Lee, and Peter Krämer, eds. *The Silent Cinema Reader.* 2004.

Wada-Marciano, Mitsuyo. *Nippon Modern: Japanese Cinema of the 1920s and 1930s.* 2008.

Zhang, Yingjin. *Cinema and Urban Culture in Shanghai, 1922–1943.* 1999.

Jiang Jieshi and Bolshevik leaders alike promoted toothpaste and toothbrushing as part of nation-building. "New woman" Rilda Marta of South Africa traveled to the United States to learn about African American cosmetics and on her return advocated the subtle use of lipstick and rouge: "The key to Happiness and Success is a good appearance," she proclaimed. "You are often judged by how you look."[27] Women from Tokyo to Buenos Aires bought mass-marketed cosmetics to achieve the appearance of film celebrities.

Mobilizing the Masses

The 1920s also saw politicians mobilizing the masses for their political causes. The Bolsheviks began massive propaganda efforts to bring news of communism to villages and cities, to peasants and workers, and to Muslims, Christians, and Jews alike. People around the world came to believe that the USSR was an ideal state, despite brutality and actual starvation, and even visited to join the experiment in communism. In the colonies and mandates, leaders like Mohandas Gandhi in India and groups such as the Muslim Brotherhood in Egypt mobilized the masses around spiritual teachings. In Italy, Benito Mussolini consolidated his coup with mass propaganda fueling postwar resentments.

From the beginning of the twentieth century, Indian leaders urged boycotts of British products. Indian activist Mohandas Gandhi (1869–1948) transformed this cause into a nonviolent mass movement that appealed to millions. Born of middle-class parents in a village on the west coast of India, Gandhi studied law in England and then began his practice in the Indian community in South Africa. The racism there made him determined to liberate the Indian masses from British imperialism. Returning to India permanently in 1915, he began a full-time drive for Hind Swaraj (HIHND swah-RAJ), or Indian Home Rule. Using the media and speeches, he challenged the view that Britain was "civilized" and thus worthy of respect. Rather, South Asia had an age-old tradition of civilization, he pointed out, while Britain and other Western countries, above all the United States, valued only one thing: material wealth. As Gandhi wrote early in his career, "Money is their God."[28] By contrast, Gandhi—dressed in a simple loincloth and shawl made from cloth he had woven himself—envisioned a nonviolent return to an India of small self-sufficient communities. In rejecting the West, Gandhi's movement resembled another potent force for the empowerment of ordinary people—the Muslim Brotherhood, founded in Egypt in 1928. This organization called for a return to Islam along with a rejection of the secular, "modern" mindset. "Islam is the solution" was the Brotherhood's watchword as it attacked British influence in the country, practiced abundant charity, and grew in mass appeal.

In contrast, communism promised a modern, technological culture. The reality was that workers' living conditions declined while Communist Party supervisors enjoyed a privileged life. In the early 1920s, workers, sailors, and peasant bands alike revolted against harsh Bolshevik policies toward ordinary people. The government ordered many of the rebels shot, but as production dropped to 13 percent of its prewar output, Lenin changed course. His **New Economic Policy** compromised with capitalism by allowing peasants to sell their grain freely and entrepreneurs to engage in trade and keep the profits.

Bolsheviks strove to make communism a cultural reality in the masses' daily lives through educational classes, especially those featuring reading. As commissar for public welfare, Aleksandra Kollontai promoted birth-control education and the establishment of day care centers. To advance literacy, she wrote simply worded novels about love and work in the new socialist state. Many found success: as one worker on a veterinary farm wrote, "I have discovered a new world for me in Marxism. I read with deep interest."[29]

Authoritarian rule came as well to Italy, though of a different nature from communism. Benito Mussolini (1883–1945) attained power as a mass hero. Blaming parliaments for economic ills, many Italians were enthusiastic when Mussolini built a personal army of veterans and the unemployed called the "Black Shirts" and used it to overturn parliamentary government. In 1922, his supporters, known as Fascists, started a march on Rome, leading to Mussolini's appointment as prime minister. Under Mussolini, criticism of the state became a criminal offense and violence, including murder of opponents and striking workers, a political tool. Yet the sight of hundreds of Black Shirts marching through the streets signaled the return of well-being to many Italians.

Besides violence, Mussolini used mass propaganda and the media to promote traditional values and prejudices, though **fascism**, unlike communism, was never a coherent doctrine. Only state supremacy mattered. Peasant men huddled around radios to hear him call for enhanced farm productivity on behalf of the state. Peasant women worshipped him for appearing to value motherhood as a patriotic calling. In the cities, the government built modern buildings and broad avenues for Fascist parades. Despite these signs of modernity, Mussolini introduced a "corporate" state that denied individual rights and outlawed independent labor unions, replacing them with state-controlled employer and worker groups, or "corporations." Mussolini cut women's wages and banned women from the professions, allowing them only to hold menial and low-paying jobs. His popularity soared among war-torn men, as he became a model for other militaristic leaders.

New Economic Policy Lenin's compromise with capitalism that allowed peasants to sell their grain on the market and entrepreneurs to engage in trade and keep the profits.

fascism A political movement originating in postwar Italy under Mussolini that stressed the primacy of the state over the individual and the importance of violence and warfare in making nations strong.

COUNTERPOINT: A Golden Age for Argentineans

> ↘ **FOCUS** In what ways did Argentina's history differ from that of countries caught up in World War I?

World War I allowed some societies outside of Europe to flourish. Both Japan and Australia increased their trade during the war. Indian entrepreneurs, aided by nationalist boycotts of British goods, continued to build metallurgical and other factories, replacing those of the warring European powers. In the Western Hemisphere, as many nations chose the road to war, Argentineans experienced a "golden age" in stark contrast to the suffering elsewhere.

A Flourishing Economy and Society

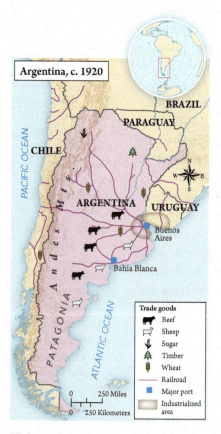

≡ **Argentina, c. 1920**

Starting in the 1880s, immigrants flooded to Argentina. Between 1900 and the outbreak of World War I in 1914, hundreds of thousands of newcomers moved to the bustling commercial city of Buenos Aires and the surrounding area. There traders imported European goods and ranchers supplied world markets with leather, meat, and agricultural products. Industry also thrived in Argentina, benefiting many in the laboring classes.

World War I broke Argentina's dependence on Britain's economy and turned its productivity inward, so that after the war the economy continued to grow. Landed elites controlled Argentina's politics for most of this time, though strikers and anarchists made vocal demands for change. Reform came in 1912 with universal and obligatory voting by secret ballot for all men. This led to the election in 1916 of Radical Civil Union leader Hipólito Yrigoyen, a candidate whose popularity with workers and the middle classes made for relatively stable politics. Instead of experiencing the surge of extremism elsewhere, the Argentinean political scene remained relatively moderate.

There was one glaring exception. After a general strike in December 1918, middle and upper classes, many of European heritage, began looking for scapegoats, encouraging vigilante groups to turn on Jews. From January 10 to 14, 1919, these groups attacked Jewish property and arrested Jews—the "tragic week" that would repeat itself in the 1960s and 1970s in Argentina.

Golden-Age Culture

Argentina's overall climate of growth, prosperity, and immigration sparked an outburst of cultural creativity. A vibrant working-class culture brought the world the tango, an erotic modern dance improvised from African, Spanish, and local music. Danced either by a man and woman or by two men together, the tango spread worldwide.

A participant in the 1920s cultural life of Buenos Aires was poet, essayist, and short story writer Jorge Luis Borges, one of the leading authors of the twentieth century. Moving beyond literary fashions, Borges was fascinated with the mysteries of learning, remembering, and forgetting. "Seek for the pleasure of seeking, not of finding," Borges counseled, and his whole life seemed more concerned with questions than with answers. As he wrote,

> I think about things that might have been and never
> were . . .
> The vast empire the Vikings declined to found.
> The globe without the wheel, or without the rose.[30]

Borges's imagination laid the groundwork for "magical realism," the late-twentieth-century movement in Latin American fiction. Even as much of Latin America, including Argentina, came to feel economic stresses as the century advanced, its Golden-Age culture has endured.

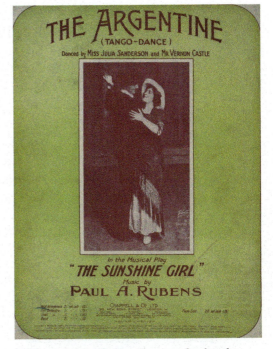

The Argentine Tango The tango developed in the cafés frequented by the sailors, dockworkers, and sex workers at the turn of the twentieth century. Born in "low-life" society, this creation of Argentina's Golden Age traveled to Europe, where it became a newly respectable if somewhat daring dance. Popular culture followed complicated routes in its global development.

Conclusion

Competition among nations and the clash of classes led to the loss of tens of millions of lives between 1900 and 1920. Major dynasties collapsed and governments fell while millions suffered starvation, disease, and permanent disability. Internationally, the Peace of Paris that settled World War I rearranged the map of Europe and the world beyond, dismantling the Habsburg and Ottoman Empires into new, intentionally small, and contested states—a settlement that failed to guarantee a peaceful future. The League of Nations allowed some Ottoman lands to be recolonized. Efforts increased for collective security such as that provided in the League of Nations. Some political leaders, such as Mustafa Kemal in Turkey, were inspired by Western ideals and models; others, such as Mohandas Gandhi in India, rejected them. The United States gained power even as it announced a policy of isolationism.

Alongside its mass armies, world war furthered the development of mass society and culture. It leveled social classes on the battlefield and standardized beliefs and behaviors through wartime propaganda and postwar popular culture. Wartime technology churned out postwar consumer goods while fostering innovations such as air transport, cinema, and radio programming for the masses. As in wartime, mass culture was a key ingredient in politicians' efforts to recruit supporters in the 1920s. The global economic collapse of 1929 would lead to further mobilization of the masses, this time to support dictators and even genocide.

✳ review

The major global development in this chapter: The wars and revolutions of the early twentieth century and their role in the creation of mass culture and society.

Important Events	
1910	Mexican Revolution begins
1911–1912	Revolutionaries overthrow Qing dynasty in China
1912	First Balkan War
1913	Second Balkan War
1914	World War I begins
1917	Russian Revolution begins; United States enters World War I; Lenin returns to Russia
1918	Bolsheviks take full control of Russian government; Treaty of Brest-Litovsk; armistice ends World War I
1919	Germany forms Weimar Republic; May Fourth Movement in China
1919–1920	Treaties comprising Peace of Paris signed, including the Treaty of Versailles with Germany
1920s	Mohandas Gandhi's nonviolent movement for India independence attracts millions; mass culture flourishes in film and publishing industries; growth of radio transmissions; technology increases global productivity
1921	Lenin introduces New Economic Policy in Russia
1922	Civil war ends in Russia; Mussolini comes to power in Italy
1923	Founding of the independent republic of Turkey under Mustafa Kemal; formation of Union of Soviet Socialist Republics

KEY TERMS

Bolshevik (p. 931)
collective security (p. 934)
Comintern (p. 932)
fascism (p. 949)

Fourteen Points (p. 933)
Guomindang (p. 922)
League of Nations (p. 934)
mandate system (p. 935)

New Economic Policy (p. 949)
soviet (p. 931)
total war (p. 927)

CHAPTER OVERVIEW QUESTIONS

1. Why did the Mexican Revolution, the Chinese Revolution, World War I, and the Russian Revolution cause so much change far from the battlefield?

2. How did these wars help produce mass culture and society?

3. What role did technology play in these developments?

MAKING CONNECTIONS

1. In what ways did conditions at the end of World War I differ from those expected at the outbreak of the war?

2. Consider the empires discussed in Chapter 24. How did they change in the 1920s, and why?

3. How did World War I affect work and livelihoods?

4. How did the mass political movements that emerged during and after the war differ from one another?

For further research into the topics covered in this chapter, see the Bibliography at the end of the book. For additional primary sources from this period, see *Sources for World in the Making*.

Global Catastrophe: The Great Depression and World War II 1929–1945

≡ **World in the Making** This photograph of a Nazi rally held in 1938 in Nuremberg reveals how young people, among others, admired Hitler and endorsed all that he stood for: quick fixes to a depressed economy and the promise of renewed global power. His rhetoric of hatred rallied Germans across the social order to envision a better future once their nation had been purified of enemies such as Jews, who were actually their neighbors and fellow Germans. Popular support for Hitler's violent bigotry has made historians aware that the history of Nazism is not just the story of one charismatic leader, but also of the masses whose devotion was the source of his power.

✳ backstory

As we saw in Chapter 25, in 1918 World War I ended, and with it fell four empires: the Ottoman, Russian, Austro-Hungarian, and German. The victorious Western powers took the colonies and other lands of the defeated German and Ottoman Empires, expanding the "new imperialism" (see Chapter 24). Significant changes in the nature of government and in the relationship between governments and their peoples accompanied the new geopolitical order. In countries around the world, governments grew larger and more powerful, taking advantage of the new mass media to promote a uniform culture that stressed the central importance of patriotism and national identity. In the political and economic turmoil that followed the war, the same mass media contributed to the rise of stridently nationalist dictators. When a worldwide depression struck in the late 1920s, these dictators, intent on expanding their nation's boundaries and empires, posed a grave threat to world peace.

Eva Kantorowsky worked as a secretary and teacher of English in Shanghai during World War II. A cosmopolitan city, Shanghai attracted refugees from war-torn Europe from the 1930s on, especially those fleeing Adolf Hitler's brutal Nazi regime in Germany. Eva Kantorowsky was one of these, helped by her uncle's successful acquisition of three exit visas so that she, her mother, and her father—a rabbi in Berlin—could make their way across two continents to China in 1940. They left only after Eva's father had been repeatedly beaten by the Nazis. Eva's uncle, however, had neglected to get an exit visa for her brother Hans, who the uncle mistakenly thought had already left the country. After World War II ended in 1945, Eva's family received the crushing news that Hans had died in Auschwitz, murdered along with millions of fellow Jews as well as Slavs, Roma ("gypsies"), and other persecuted groups, in the Nazi genocide.

Eva Kantorowsky escaped this genocide—the Holocaust—and survived the most destructive war in world history. World War II, with an estimated death toll of some one hundred million people, capped off a decade of suffering that began with the Great Depression of the 1930s, a global economic catastrophe that was sparked by the crash of the U.S. stock market in 1929. The crash opened a tragic era in history when people around the world were connected by their shared experience of economic hardship, war, and genocide. The Great Depression intensified discontent across the globe. In Japan, China, Italy, Germany, and across Latin America, strongmen took power and militarized the masses, promising an end their troubles. Adolf Hitler roused Germans to pursue national greatness by scorning democracy and scapegoating "inferior" and "menacing" Jews such as the Kantorowsky family. Joseph Stalin believed that the Soviet Union's rapid industrialization was worth the lives of the millions of citizens who died remaking their nation in the 1930s. For militaristic authoritarian regimes, human rights and democratic institutions were obstacles to national greatness.

Elected leaders in established democracies were often baffled by the Depression and the militarism it spawned. The League of Nations, formed after World War I to preserve world peace, ignored Japan's aggression in China, Italy's in Ethiopia, and Germany's in Europe. Aggression followed aggression until Hitler's invasion of Poland in 1939 and Japan's bombing of Pearl Harbor in 1941 finally pushed the democracies to declare war. By the end of 1941, Great Britain, France, the Soviet Union, and the United States were locked in combat with Germany, Italy, and Japan. The coalition to stop Germany and its partners was an uneasy one, however, and by the end of the war the world's new superpowers, the United States and the Soviet Union, regarded each other with deep, ideological distrust. As hot war

turned to cold war after 1945, tens of millions more became homeless refugees, among them Eva Kantorowsky. In this horrific war, however, global migration had helped her survive. The dense network of economic and political connections that had made the Great Depression a global event and drawn the world into war also provided routes for some individuals to escape persecution and suffering.

OVERVIEW QUESTIONS

The major global development in this chapter: The causes and outcomes of the Great Depression and World War II.

As you read, consider:

1. How did ordinary people react to the Great Depression, and how did their reactions differ from country to country?

2. Why were dictators and antidemocratic leaders able to come to power in the 1930s, and how did all countries—autocratic and democratic alike—mobilize the masses?

3. How are the Great Depression and World War II related historical events?

1929: The Great Depression Begins

FOCUS What was the global impact of both the Great Depression and the attempts to overcome it?

A rapid decline in agricultural prices in the 1920s followed by the U.S. stock market crash of 1929 threw tens of millions out of work and wrecked the prospects of rural people worldwide. People everywhere, from farmers to industrial workers, saw their livelihoods destroyed. Despair turned to outrage, as many rose up in rebellion, embracing militaristic solutions to their nation's problems.

Economic Disaster Strikes

In the 1920s, U.S. corporations and banks—as well as millions of individual Americans—invested in the stock market, which seemed to churn out endless profits. Confident that stock prices would continue to rise, they used easy credit to invest in companies based on electric, automotive, and other new technologies. At the end of the decade, the Federal Reserve Bank—the nation's central bank, which controlled financial policy—tightened the availability of credit in an attempt to stabilize the market. To meet the new restrictions, brokers demanded that their clients immediately pay back the money they had borrowed to buy stock. As investors sold their stocks to raise cash and repay their loans, the wave of selling caused prices on the stock market to collapse. Individuals lost their money, and a breakdown of the economy as a whole followed.

The stock market crash helped spark the global economic collapse known as the **Great Depression** because the United States had financed postwar economic growth by lending money for business development around the world. Suddenly strapped themselves, U.S. financiers cut back drastically on loans and called in debts, weakening banks and industry at home and abroad. Creditors to newly created industries in India, for example, demanded repayment of loans and refused to finance further expansion. In Europe, the lack of credit and the decline in consumer buying caused businesses to close, workers to be laid off, and the European economy to slump. By 1933, almost six million German workers, or about one-third of the workforce, were unemployed. The economic collapse was uneven, however: a few Latin American countries expanded domestic consumption enough partially to offset lost sales abroad.

For farmers, times had already been tough for years. In the 1920s, technological innovation and other factors combined to produce record crops and, consequently, falling farm prices. Canada, Australia, Argentina, and the United States had increased their production of wheat while World War I was raging in Europe but did not cut back when Europe became productive again. In the mid-1920s the price of wheat collapsed. Prices for other consumables, such as coffee and sugar, also tumbled, creating dire consequences in Africa, Asia, and some Latin American countries. Large-scale farmers bought up the land of debt-ridden small producers; with farmers receiving 50 percent less for their crops by 1931 than they had a few years earlier, rural consumption of manufactured goods dropped too. Problems in agriculture were directly connected to the industrial decline.

Government responses to the crisis, which followed accepted economic theory at the time, aggravated the situation. Great Britain went off the gold standard, which depreciated its currency and increased the cost of living. Other countries blocked imports with high tariffs in hopes of sparking purchases of domestically produced goods. Measures such as cutting budgets led to reduced purchasing power and thus more business failures and higher unemployment. Governments in Latin America and eastern Europe often ignored the farmers' plight as they poured available funds into industrialization, increasing tensions in rural society.

Great Depression The economic crisis of the 1930s that began in agricultural regions through a severe drop in commodity prices in the 1920s and then, with the U.S. stock market crash of 1929, spread to industrial countries.

One solution for the imperial powers was to increase economic exploitation in the colonies, whose surging population made them more attractive as markets and sources of tax revenue. Now the imperial powers demanded that colonial subjects pay higher taxes, no matter how desperate the local peoples' plight, to compensate for falling revenues back home. In the Belgian Congo, local farmers paid a per-person tax—called a poll or head tax—equivalent to one-sixth of their crops in the 1920s and one-fourth in the 1930s. Britain forced colonies such as India to pay taxes and other charges in gold. India's farmers stripped the subcontinent of every scrap of the precious metal, including women's jewelry, to meet Britain's increased demands.

Social Effects of the Great Depression

The Great Depression's social effects were complex and not entirely negative. Despite the economic crisis, modernization proceeded, whether in the form of building new roads in Africa or bringing electricity to the Soviet Union. Wealthy individual Chinese living abroad poured money into modernizing their homeland, investing in profitable development projects. In Northern Nigeria, as the price of imported fabrics rose, women revived textile weaving and thus were able to help unemployed family members. Bordering English slums, one British observer in the mid-1930s noticed, were "filling stations and factories that look like exhibition buildings, giant cinemas and dance halls and cafés, bungalows with tiny garages, cocktail bars, Woolworth's [and] swimming pools."[1] Municipal and national governments modernized sanitation; and running water, electricity, and sewage pipes were installed in many homes throughout the world for the first time.

Many in the upper classes prospered during the Great Depression. In Kenya, southern Indochina, and elsewhere, large landowners evicted tenants who were unable to pay their rents and replaced them with cheaper day laborers. Moneylenders in India and Burma loaned peasants money to pay their rising taxes—due before the harvest. When agricultural prices fell, moneylenders and large landowners alike took over the indebted peasants' lands. Although the loss of foreign markets such as Britain hurt many international traders, merchants engaged in domestic trade managed to survive. Colombia, Brazil, Chile, Mexico, and Argentina actually showed either rising production or increased exports by 1932–1933. Throughout the Great Depression arms manufacturers made huge profits as nations such as Germany militarized. The majority of Europeans and Americans actually had jobs throughout the 1930s, allowing them to benefit from the decline in consumer prices.

Even employed people, however, were aware of the millions of others struggling for a bare existence. In Cuba, where sugar prices collapsed, workers who did not lose their jobs were no longer paid, but simply fed a meal of "black or *caritas* beans, with their accompanying scum of weevils and worms . . . garbage that had no market," as one sugar worker described the food.[2] Because of the slump in agricultural prices, Japanese farmers were often reduced to eating tree bark, grass, and acorns and even gave up working: "Better to remain idle and eat less than work hard and eat more than can be earned," was the motto of some.[3] In a 1932 school assignment, a German youth wrote, "My father has been out of work for two-and-a-half years. He thinks that I'll never find a job." A storm cloud of fear and resentment settled over many parts of the globe.

Economic catastrophe strained social stability and upset gender relations. The collapse of prices made some Japanese peasants so desperate that they sold their daughters into prostitution. African men migrated hundreds of miles from their families in search of better jobs, weakening family ties. In urban areas of Europe and the United States unemployed men stayed home all day, increasing the tension in small, overcrowded apartments. Some took over housekeeping chores, but others found this "women's work" emasculating. Women around the world could often find low-paying jobs doing laundry or brewing and marketing beer from their homes. As many women became breadwinners, albeit for low wages, men could be seen standing on street corners begging—a reversal of gender expectations that fueled discontent. Rural men also faced the erosion of patriarchal authority, as some lost their land entirely. Family-planning centers opened to help working people reduce family size in hard times. The Great Depression disrupted the most fundamental human connections—the relationships among family members.

Protesting Poverty

The Great Depression produced rising protest. Often led by activists trained in the USSR, Communist parties flourished in the Chinese countryside, Indochina, the United States, Latin America, and across Europe, because they promised to end joblessness and exploitation. Mexican artist Diego Rivera captured the experiences of ordinary working people and the appeal of communism in huge murals he painted for public buildings. These massive paintings featured workers in factories and on farms, with portraits of communist heroes like Marx and Lenin intermingled with those of ordinary laborers. Union members worldwide took to the streets to demand relief. In 1935, women textile workers in Medellín, Colombia, rose in angry protest about low wages and the insulting behavior of bosses. "Look, they'd go after the companies or whatever it was with rocks," said one woman of the strikers. "It was rough, it was bitter," she added.[4] "Revolutions grow out of the depths of hunger," warned William Green, head of the American Federation of Labor, in 1931.[5] For their part, governments and even factory owners responded with guns:

police in Kobe, Japan, fought dockworkers, and government troops joined in crushing the demonstrators. U.S. automobile magnate Henry Ford turned his private police force on unemployed workers, killing four of them and wounding far more. During the Great Depression, the masses defended their lives as well as their livelihoods.

Economic distress added to smoldering grievances in the colonies. As prices on commodities such as coffee, tin, and copper sank, colonial farmers withheld their produce from imperial wholesalers. Farmers in Ghana, for example, refused to sell cocoa in the 1930s. Discontent ran deep across the Middle East and Asia as well, fueled by the injustices of the World War I peace settlement, increasing colonial taxa-

≡ **Diego Rivera, *Man at the Crossroads* (1934)** Mexican artist Diego Rivera had no love for the Soviet Union, yet he considered communism the only remedy for the oppressed worldwide during the Great Depression. In this mural, painted for Rockefeller Center in New York City but then torn down because of its image of Lenin, workers from many ethnicities flock to the red flag and the Communist leadership.

tion, and hard economic times. General strikes rocked Palestine and India in 1936 and 1937, respectively. Their resolve fortified by bitter experiences, by the example of Japan's rising power, and by their own industrial development, colonial peoples roused themselves in an effort to overturn the imperial order.

Western-educated native leaders such as Ho Chi Minh, founder of the Indochinese Communist Party, led popular movements to contest their people's subjection. In 1930 the French government brutally crushed the peasant uprising Ho led. During the 1930s millions more working people came to follow Mohandas Gandhi, the charismatic leader of the Indian independence movement. The British jailed Gandhi repeatedly, stirred up Hindu-Muslim antagonism, and massacred protesters. European officials were quick to use their military might to put down colonial uprisings, but they were slow to recognize a much greater threat to their well-being: the spread of totalitarianism

Militarizing the Masses in the 1930s

> ⬦ **FOCUS** How did dictatorships and democracies attempt to mobilize the masses?

totalitarianism A single-party form of government emerging after World War I in which the ruling political party seeks to control all parts of the social, cultural, economic, and political lives of the population, typically making use of mass communication and violence to instill its ideology and maintain power.

five-year plan One of the centralized programs for economic development instituted by Joseph Stalin in the USSR and copied by Adolf Hitler in Germany; these plans set production priorities and targets for individual industries and agriculture.

central economic planning A policy of government direction of the economy, established during World War I and increasingly used in peacetime.

Representative government collapsed in many countries under the sheer weight of social and economic crisis. Japanese military men promoted overseas conquest as a solution to the Depression, and even poor peasants donated funds to Japan's military cause. After 1929, Italy's Benito Mussolini, the Soviet Union's Joseph Stalin, and Germany's Adolf Hitler gained vast support by mobilizing the masses in ways that had previously been attempted only in times of war. This common commitment to militarism alongside the use of political violence has led historians to apply the term **totalitarianism** to the Fascist, Communist, and Nazi regimes of the 1930s. The term refers to highly centralized systems of government that attempt to control society and ensure obedience through a single party and police terror. Many citizens admired Mussolini, Stalin, and Hitler for the discipline they brought to social and economic life, and overlooked the brutal side of totalitarian government. Unity and soldier-like obedience—not individual rights and open debate—were seen as keys to recovery.

To mobilize the masses, politicians also appealed to racism. "Superior" peoples were selfishly failing to breed, Hitler charged, while the numbers of "inferior" peoples were growing. Targeting an enemy—whether fellow citizens of different faiths, colors, or ethnicities, or an entire country—enabled popular leaders to mobilize the masses to fight this internal or external enemy instead of building national unity around democratically solving problems.

The Rise of Stalinism

Joseph Stalin, who succeeded Lenin in 1929, led the astonishing transformation of the USSR in the 1930s from a predominantly agricultural society into a formidable industrial power. In 1929 Stalin ended Lenin's New Economic Policy (see Chapter 25) and replaced it with the first of several **five-year plans** intended to mobilize Soviet citizens to industrialize the nation.

Stalin outlined a program for massive increases in the output of coal, iron ore, steel, and industrial goods over successive five-year periods. Without an end to economic backwardness, Stalin warned in a 1931 speech, the advanced countries will "crush us."[6] He thus established **central economic planning**, a policy of government direction of the economy, as used in World War I. Between 1929 and 1940, the number of Soviet workers in industry, construction, and transport grew from 4.6 million to 12.6 million, and production soared. Stalin's first five-year plan helped make the USSR a leading industrial nation, and one that was ultimately able to withstand the test of total war.

Central planning created a new elite class of bureaucrats and industrial officials, who forced workers to leave the countryside for jobs in state-run factories. While Communist officials enjoyed benefits such as country homes and luxurious vacations, untrained workers from the countryside were herded into barrack-like dwellings or tents and endured dangerous factory conditions. Still, many believed in communism and took pride in learning new skills: "We mastered this profession—completely new to us—with great pleasure," a female lathe operator recalled.[7] They tolerated intense suffering because, as one worker put it, "Man himself is being rebuilt."[8] Nonetheless, new workers often lacked the technical education necessary to achieve the goals of the five-year plan, and official lying about productivity became a regular practice.

Brutality reigned, especially on the land. Faced with peasants' refusal to turn over their grain to the government, Stalin called for the "liquidation of the kulaks" (koo-LAHKS). The word *kulak*, which literally means "fist," was first insultingly applied to a prosperous peasant, then to any independent farmer. One Russian remembered believing kulaks were "bloodsuckers, cattle, swine" and "enemies of the state." Party workers robbed farmers, left them to starve, or even murdered them outright. Confiscated kulak land became the new collective farms, where the remaining peasants were forced to share facilities and modern machinery. Traditional peasant life was brought to a violent end.

The Communist experiment with collective farming resulted in mass starvation, as Soviet grain harvests declined from eighty-three million tons in 1930 to sixty-seven million in 1934. Stalin blamed the crisis on enemies of communism and instituted **purges**—state-approved violence that included widespread arrests, imprisonments in labor camps, and executions. Beginning in 1936, a series of "show trials" based on trumped-up charges resulted in the execution of early Bolshevik leaders and thousands of military officers for conspiring against the USSR. Simultaneously, the government expanded the system of lethal prison camps—called the *Gulag*, an acronym for the department that ran the camps—where prisoners did every kind of work, from digging canals to building apartment complexes in Moscow. With untold millions dying from the harsh conditions and famines, the USSR ended the reproductive freedom of the early revolutionary years, restricting access to birth-control information and abortion and criminalizing homosexuality. The casualties of the Soviet system far exceeded those in Nazi Germany in the 1930s.

Stalin used artists and writers—"engineers of the soul," he called them—to help mobilize the masses. In return for housing, office space, and secretarial help, the

purge In the USSR in the 1930s, one of a series of attacks on citizens accused of being enemies of the state.

≡ **Socialist Realist Art** The early days of the
Bolshevik Revolution witnessed experimentation
in social and sexual relationships and in the arts.
Under Stalin, the government sponsored the official
artistic style called "socialist realism"; it featured
smiling workers who radiated supreme happiness.
Often taken as hypocritical, socialist realist art
depicted the perfect socialist society of the future.

"comrade artist" followed the official style of "socialist
realism," which depicted workers as full of rosy emotions. Some artists, such as the poet Anna Akhmatova
(ahk-MAH-toh-vah), protested the harsh Soviet reality. "Stars of death stood over us/ as innocent Russia
squirmed, / Under the blood-spattered boots and tyres/
of the black marias," wrote Akhmatova of the 1930s,
as she stood in line outside a Soviet prison, where her
son was being held.[9] Once a prosperous and celebrated
writer, Akhmatova was reduced to living off the generosity of her friends because of her resistance.

Despite such examples, Stalin militarized the masses
in his warlike campaign to industrialize in the 1930s, becoming to them, as one worker put it, "a god on earth."[10]
As women's literacy grew and health care improved, admirers from around the world headed to the USSR to
see the "workers' paradise" for themselves.

Japanese Expansionism

The Great Depression struck Japan's economy as it
was recovering from a catastrophic earthquake that
had killed more than 140,000 people and laid waste to
both the capital of Tokyo and the bustling port city of
Yokohama. The earthquake sparked murders—led by the military—of Korean
and Chinese workers in the area who were seen somehow as being responsible for
the devastation. In 1925, men over the age of twenty-five had gained the vote and
the young Hirohito (heer-oh-HEE-toh) had become emperor, but the economic
downturn and social unrest made Japan unstable.

An ambitious military, impatient with democratic institutions, sought control of
the government, as did politicians favoring improved representative institutions.
A modernizing economy and growing world trade had unleashed social change,
and reformers challenged traditional values such as women's obedience. Author
Junichiro Tanizaki captured the clash of old and new worldviews in novels such as
Naomi (1924–1925), in which an engineer is totally obsessed with an independent
"new woman," and *The Makioka Sisters* (1943–1948), some of whose characters
struggle to protect tradition amid relentless change.

Gaining control, military leaders offered their own solution to the depressed
conditions: conquer nearby regions to provide new farmlands and create markets.

Japanese peasants would revive their livelihoods by settling areas such as Manchuria, while business people would benefit from consumers, workers, and raw materials in annexed lands. Viewing China and the Western powers as obstacles to prosperity, Japan's military leaders promoted the idea that the military was an "emperor's army" not subject to civilian control, and that it would bring about a new world order. By the 1930s, Emperor Hirohito and his advisers had built public support for renewed military vigor as key to Japan's claims to racial superiority and its entitlement to the lands of "inferiors"—such as the Chinese.

The Japanese army took the lead in making these claims a reality: in September 1931 it blew up a Japanese-owned train in the Chinese province of Manchuria and made the incident look like an attack on Japan by placing corpses dressed in official Chinese uniforms alongside the tracks. The military then used the explosion as an excuse to invade the territory, set up a puppet government, and push farther into China (see Map 26.1). China appealed to the League of Nations in protest, but the league imposed no economic sanctions against Japan. The Japanese army dealt with democratic opponents by assassinating them.

The Chinese did not sit idly by in the face of Japan's invasion. In 1934 Jiang Jieshi (Chiang Kai-shek) introduced the "New Life" Movement, whose aim was "to militarize the life of the people" and to make them "willing to sacrifice for the nation at all times."[11] The New Life Movement was inspired by European fascist militarism; it also promoted discipline in everyday life through cleanliness and exercise. Some nationalist reformers saw the position of women as key to modernizing and strengthening China. Traditions such as foot-binding were attacked as old-fashioned, and by the mid-1930s there were some six thousand institutions of higher education for

≡ **Jiang Jieshi and Mai-ling Soong** Jiang Jieshi, heading the Nationalist government in China, promoted regular exercise and hygiene as part of his modernization efforts. At the time of this 1927 photograph, Mai-ling Soong, from one of China's wealthiest families, was Jiang's fiancée. She represented the "new woman" with her U.S. college education, unbound feet, and Western clothing.

≡ **MAP 26.1** **Japanese Expansion, 1931–1942** Japan's rise as a modern industrial power began in the nineteenth century with the Meiji Restoration. Like most powers and would-be powers, its leaders believed that the nation should dominate others to create its own empire. Expansion into much of Asia in the 1930s aimed to bring the island nation much-needed new resources.

women in China. To Jiang, national unity demanded mobilization against the Chinese Communist Party—not the Japanese. Ultimately, however, Jiang joined the Communists in fighting the Japanese instead of fighting one another.

Japanese army leaders, countering the Chinese, mobilized their own people, using the mass media to create a "people's patriotism." In 1933, the film *Japan in the National Emergency* depicted the utopian mission of Japan "to create an ideal land in East Asia" where under Japanese leadership the races would harmoniously join together. Decadent Western culture—notably its racism, the film noted—showed that Japan as a whole needed to turn away from the West, renounce individual rights, and promote the "sacred spirit" of the nation.[12] Labor unions supported militarization, pressing impoverished workers to contribute funds for the military. By 1937, Japan's government was spending 47 percent of its budget on weaponry.

Hitler's Rise to Power

Mass politics reached terrifying proportions in Germany when Adolf Hitler finally achieved his goal of overthrowing German democracy. In his book *Mein Kampf* (*My Struggle*, 1925), he laid out his vision of "scientific" anti-Semitism and the rebirth of the German "race," a vision he attempted to implement through his leadership of the Nazi Party (National Socialist German Workers' Party). When the Great Depression struck Germany, the Nazis began to outstrip their rivals in elections, thanks in part to backing in the press.

Foremost among the Nazis' supporters were idealistic youth, who believed that Germany could recapture its former glory under Hitler, and also white-collar workers and the lower middle class, whose savings the postwar inflation had destroyed. By targeting all their parliamentary opponents as a single, monolithic group of "Bolshevik" enemies, the Nazis won wide approval. Many thought it was time to replace democratic government with a bold new leader who would take on these enemies.

Hitler devised modern propaganda techniques to build his appeal. Thousands of recordings of Hitler's speeches and other Nazi souvenir items circulated among the public, and Nazi rallies were masterpieces of mass spectacle. Hitler, however, viewed ordinary people with contempt: "The receptivity of the great masses is very limited, their intelligence is small. In consequence of these facts, all effective propaganda must be limited to a very few points and must harp on those in slogans."[13] Military, industrial, and political elites, fearing the Communists for their opposition to private property, saw to it that Hitler legally became chancellor in 1933. Millions celebrated. "My father went down to the cellar and brought up our best bottles of wine. . . . And my mother wept for joy," one German recalled.

Hitler closed down representative government. Nazis suspended civil rights, imposed censorship of the press, and prohibited meetings of the political parties. Hitler made his aims clear: "I have set myself one task, namely to sweep those parties out of Germany." Storm troopers—the private Nazi army that existed in addition to Germany's regular forces—harassed democratic politicians into allowing passage of the Enabling Act, which suspended the constitution for four years and allowed Nazi laws to take effect without parliamentary approval. The elite SS (*Schutzstaffel*), yet another military organization, along with the Gestapo, or political police, enforced obedience to Nazism. These organizations arrested Communists, Jews, homosexuals, and activists and either executed them or imprisoned them in concentration camps, the first of which opened at Dachau near Munich in March 1933.

To improve economic conditions, the government pursued pump priming—that is, stimulating the economy by investing in public works projects such as constructing tanks, airplanes, and highways. Unemployment declined from a peak of almost 6 million in 1932 to 1.6 million by 1936. The Nazi Party closed down labor unions, and government managers classified jobs and set pay levels, rating women's jobs lower than men's. People believed that Hitler was working an economic miracle.

The Nazi government aimed to control everyday life, including gender roles. A law encouraged Aryans (those people legally defined as racially German) to have children by providing loans to Aryan newlyweds, but only if the wife left the workforce. Nazi marriage programs enforced both racial and gender ideology; women were supposed to be subordinate so men would feel tough and industrious despite military defeat and economic depression. A woman "joyfully sacrifices and fulfills her fate," one Nazi leader explained.[14] Censorship flourished. Radio broadcasts were clogged with propaganda; book-burnings destroyed works by Jews, socialists, homosexuals, and modernist writers. Hitler claimed to be rebuilding the united community destroyed by modernity, but for millions of Germans Nazi surveillance brought anything but harmony and well-being.

The Nazis defined Jews as an inferior "race" dangerous to the superior Aryan "race" and responsible for both Germany's defeat in World War I and the Great Depression. Jews were "vermin," "parasites," and "Bolsheviks" to be eliminated. In 1935, the Nuremberg Laws deprived Jews of citizenship and prohibited marriage between Jews and other Germans. Whereas women defined as Aryan had increasing difficulty obtaining abortions or birth-control information, these were readily available to Jews and other outcast groups. Doctors in the late 1930s helped organize the T4 project, which used carbon monoxide poisoning and other means to kill two hundred thousand "inferior" people—especially the disabled.

Jews were forced into slave labor, evicted from their apartments, and prevented from buying most clothing and food. In 1938, a Jewish teenager, reacting to the harassment of his parents, killed a German official. In retaliation, Nazis attacked synagogues, smashed windows of Jewish-owned stores, and threw more than twenty thousand Jews—including Eva Kantorowski's brother—into prisons and work camps. The night of November 9–10 became known as *Kristallnacht* (kris-TAHL-nahkt), or the Night of Broken Glass. To escape, by 1939 more than half of Germany's five hundred thousand Jews had emigrated. Hitler used the totalitarian tactic of mobilizing the masses by targeting an enemy—in this instance and in many others, the Jews. Their persecution brought Germans new financial resources as they simply stole Jewish property and took Jewish jobs.

Democracies Mobilize

Facing economic depression and totalitarian aggression, democracies rallied in support of individuals' rights and citizens' well-being, though they usually limited their efforts to whites. To many, however, representative government appeared feeble compared with totalitarian leaders' military style of mobilizing the masses. As the Depression wore on, some governments—notably the United States and Sweden—undertook bold social and economic experiments while still emphasizing democratic values.

Initially, U.S. lawmakers opposed giving direct aid to the unemployed and even used military force to put down a demonstration by jobless veterans. Government policy changed, however, after Franklin Delano Roosevelt was elected president in 1932. Roosevelt pushed through a torrent of legislation: relief for businesses, price supports for struggling farmers, and public works programs for the unemployed. The Social Security Act of 1935 set up a fund to which employers and employees contributed to provide retirement and other benefits for citizens. Like other politicians of the 1930s and thereafter, Roosevelt used the new mass media expertly, especially in his radio series of "fireside chats" to the American people. In sharp contrast to Mussolini and Hitler, Roosevelt—with the able assistance of his wife Eleanor—aimed to build faith in democracy: "We Americans of today . . . are characters in the living book of democracy," he declared in 1939.[15] The president's bold programs and successful use of the media mobilized citizens, even those facing racial discrimination, to believe in a democratic future.

Sweden's response to the crisis of the 1930s focused on instituting social welfare programs and central planning of the economy. Pump-priming projects increased Swedish productivity by 20 percent between 1929 and 1935, a period when other democracies were floundering. Government programs also addressed the population problem, but without coercion. One architect of the program to boost childbirth was activist Alva Myrdal (MEER-dahl), a young sociologist and member of parliament. Myrdal's mother had so opposed modern education that she forbade library books in the house, claiming that they promoted diseases. Myrdal made it to university, but then turned to activism, promoting causes such as "voluntary parenthood" and improved work opportunities for women—even married ones. Following Myrdal's lead, the Swedish government introduced pre-natal care, free childbirth in a hospital, and subsidized housing for large families. Because all families—rural and urban, poor or prosperous—received these benefits, there was widespread support for this developing, democratic welfare state. Alva Myrdal went on to become a tireless worker for the United Nations and world peace and a Nobel Prize recipient.

Facing the economic and political turmoil of the 1930s, France narrowly avoided a fascist takeover. Politicians with opposing views frequently came to blows in the Chamber of Deputies, and right-wing paramilitary groups took to the streets, demonstrating against representative government. Shocked French liberals, socialists, and Communists formed an antifascist coalition known as the Popular Front. This alliance was made possible when Stalin allowed Communist parties to join in the protection of democracy rather than work to destroy it. For just over a year in 1936–1937 and again very briefly in 1938, the French Popular Front, headed by socialist leader Léon Blum, led the government. Like American and Swedish reformers, the Popular Front enacted welfare benefits and mandatory two-week paid vacations for workers. Bankers and industrialists greeted Blum's programs by sending their savings out of the country, leaving France financially strapped. "Better Hitler than Blum" was the slogan of the upper classes, and the Popular Front fell, evidence of the difficulties of defending democracy during economic crises and growing militarism.

Democratic cultural life also fought the lure of fascism. During its brief existence, the Popular Front encouraged citizens to celebrate democratic holidays such as Bastille Day with new enthusiasm. Artists produced work that applauded ordinary people and captured their everyday struggles. In Charlie Chaplin's film *Modern Times* (1936), his famous character, the Little Tramp, was a worker in a modern factory molded by his monotonous job to believe that even his co-workers' bodies needed mechanical adjustment. Viewers laughed with him instead of growing resentful. Heroines in immensely popular musical comedies behaved bravely, pulling their men out of despair and thus away from fascist temptation. In the film *Keep Smiling* (1938), for example, British comedienne Gracie Fields portrayed a spunky working-class woman who remained cheerful despite hard times.

Novelists affirmed human rights and the dignity of the poor in the face of dictatorial power and bombast. In a series of novels based on the biblical figure Joseph, German writer and Nobel Prize winner Thomas Mann conveyed the conflict between humane values and barbarism. The fourth volume, *Joseph the Provider* (1944), praised Joseph's welfare state, in which the granaries are full and the rich pay taxes so the poor might live decent lives. Chinese author Pa Chin used his widely influential novel *Family* (1931) to criticize the dictatorial powers of traditional patriarchy, which destroyed humane values and loving relationships. In one of her last works, *Three Guineas* (1938), English writer Virginia Woolf directly attacked militarism, poverty, and the oppression of women, showing that these were interconnected parts of the single, dangerous worldview of the 1930s.

Global War 1937–1945

⬇ **FOCUS** How did World War II progress on the battlefield and the home front?

The Depression intensified competition among nations for access to land, markets, and resources. Mobilizing the masses around national and military might, Hitler, Mussolini, and Japan's military leaders marched the world toward another catastrophic war. Democratic statesmen hoped that sanctions imposed by the League of Nations would stop new aggression, but military assaults escalated with Japan's invasion of China and the outbreak of war there in 1937. An era of destruction that opened at war's end left some one hundred million of the world's peoples dead and tens of millions more starving and homeless.

Europe's Road to War

The surge in global imperialism that occurred during the 1930s has shaped international politics to the present day. Hitler's harsh anti-Semitic policies drove European Jews to migrate to Palestine, bringing clashes between Palestinians and Jewish newcomers. Western imperialist powers, including Britain, France, the United States, and the Netherlands, increased their exploitation of resource-rich regions outside their borders amid mounting local resentment. The authoritarian regimes in Germany, Italy, and Japan unleashed bolder aggression in the name of their own people's superior rights to empire.

Like Japanese leaders, Hitler and Mussolini presented their countries as "have-nots" and demanded more resources and land. Hitler aimed for further *Lebensraum*

Italian Invasion of Ethiopia, 1935–1936

(LAY-buns-rowm), or living space, in which supposedly superior "Aryans" could thrive. This space would be taken from the "inferior" Slavic peoples, who would be moved to distant Siberia or enslaved. In 1935 Hitler rejected the Treaty of Versailles's limitations on German military strength and openly began rearming. In the same year, Mussolini invaded Ethiopia, one of the few African states not overwhelmed by European imperialism. "The Roman legionnaires are again on the march," one Italian soldier exulted at this colonial adventure.[16] Despite the resistance of the poorly equipped Ethiopians, their capital, Addis Ababa, fell in the spring of 1936. The League of Nations voted to impose sanctions against Italy, but it showed a lack of will to fight aggression.

Nazi territorial expansion began in 1938, when Hitler's troops entered Austria (see Map 26.2). The enthusiasm of Nazi sympathizers there made Germany's subsequent annexation appear to demonstrate Wilsonian "self-determination." Nazis generated support in Austria by building factories to solve the unemployment problem and by reawakening Austrians' sense that they belonged once more to a mighty empire. Hitler turned next to Czechoslovakia and its rich resources. Hitler gambled that the other Western powers would not interfere with any takeover if he could convince them that this was his last territorial claim. In the fall of 1938, British Prime Minister Neville Chamberlain, French Premier Édouard Daladier, and Mussolini met with Hitler in Munich, Germany, and, despite strong Czech opposition, agreed to allow Germany's claim to the Sudetenland (sue-DAY-ten-lahnd)—the German-populated border region of Czechoslovakia. Their strategy was to make concessions for grievances (in this case, injustices to Germany in the Peace of Paris), a policy called **appeasement**. Chamberlain announced that he had secured "peace in our time" for a continent fearing another devastating war. Appeasement proved a failure: in March 1939, Hitler invaded the rest of Czechoslovakia.

The Early Years of the War, 1937–1943

Amid this expansion, World War II had actually begun in East Asia. In 1937, the Japanese military, after skirmishes around Beijing, attacked Shanghai, justifying its offensive as liberating the region from Western imperialism (see again Map 26.1, page 966). The Japanese army next took the Chinese capital of Nanjing, massacring hundreds of thousands of Chinese in the "Rape of Nanjing," an atrocity so named because of the special brutality toward girls and women before they were

appeasement The strategy of preventing a war by making concessions to aggressors.

Nazi Expansion, 1933–1939

——	International boundaries, 1936
▢	Germany, 1933
▢	Remilitarized, 1936
▢	Annexed, 1938
▢	Satellite state, March 1939
▢	Conquered by Germany, September 1939
▢	Annexed by Soviet Union, September, 1939

≡ **MAP 26.2   Nazi Expansion, 1933–1939** Germany's conquests in the 1930s resulted from greed and the conviction that its superior people deserved the wealth of others. Throughout the decade, the Nazis advanced across central and eastern Europe to seize the property of Jews and Slavs along with the gold and other wealth of conquered nations.

killed. In 1938, the Japanese government described its expansionism as the foundation for a "New Order" in Asia, the **Greater East Asia Co-Prosperity Sphere** that would free Asians and indeed the world from the oppressive white race. In reality, however, the Japanese made enormous demands on Asians for resources while treating them with brutality (see Reading the Past: "Comfort Women" in World War II).

Greater East Asia Co-Prosperity Sphere A region of Asian states to be dominated by Japan and, in theory, to benefit from Japan's superior civilization.

READING THE PAST

"Comfort Women" in World War II

Oh Omok was sixteen when she left home in Chongup, Korea, in 1937 to take up a new livelihood: that, she was told, of a factory worker in Japan. Instead, like thousands of other young Korean women, she ended up in a military brothel. This is a small part of her story, among the mildest of those gathered in the 1990s from former "comfort women" and meticulously documented by researchers.

> At first I delivered food for the soldiers and had to serve the rank and file, to have sex with them. . . . On receiving orders we were called to the appropriate unit and served five or six men a day. At times we would serve up to ten. We served the soldiers in very small rooms with floors covered with Japanese-style mats, tatami. . . . When the soldiers were away on an expedition it was nice and quiet, but once they returned we had to serve many of them. Then they would come to our rooms in a continuous stream. I wept a lot in the early days. Some soldiers tried to comfort me saying "kawaisoni" or "naitara ikanyo," which meant something like "you poor thing" and "don't cry." Some of the soldiers would hit me because I didn't understand their language. If we displeased them in the slightest way they shouted at us and beat us: "bakayaro" or "kisamayaro," "you idiot" and "you bastard." I realized that I must do whatever they wanted of me if I wished to survive.
>
> The soldiers used condoms. We had to have a medical examination for venereal infections once a week. Those infected took medicine and were injected with "No. 606" [a medicine regularly injected into the forced sex workers, often with bad side effects]. Sometime later, I became quite close to a Lieutenant Morimoto, who arranged for Okhui [a friend of Oh Omok] and me to receive only high-ranking officers. Once we began to exclusively serve lieutenants and second lieutenants, our lives became much easier.

Source: Keith Howard, ed., *True Stories of the Korean Comfort Women: Testimonies Compiled by the Korean Council for Women Drafted for Military Sexual Slavery by Japan and the Research Association on the Women Drafted for Military Sexual Slavery by Japan,* trans. Young Joo Lee (London: Cassell, 1995), 66–67.

Examining the Evidence

1. How would you describe Oh Omok's attitude toward her situation?

2. How might her experience as a "comfort woman" shape her ideas about gender and class relations?

As the Japanese fought to conquer China, Hitler launched an all-out attack on Poland on September 1, 1939. The way was prepared a week earlier on August 23, 1939, when Germany and the USSR signed a nonaggression agreement—the Nazi-Soviet Pact—providing that if one country became embroiled in war, the other country would remain neutral. Feeling confident, German forces let loose an overpowering *Blitzkrieg* ("lightning war"), a concentrated onslaught of airplanes, tanks, and motorized infantry, to stun the ill-equipped Polish defenders. Allowing the army to conserve supplies, the Blitzkrieg assured Germans at home that the human costs of conquest would be low. On September 17, 1939, the Soviets invaded Poland from the east, and the victors then divided the country according to secret provisions in the Nazi-Soviet Pact (see again Map 26.2). Within Germany, Hitler called for defense of the fatherland against the "warlike menace" of world Jewry.

In April 1940, the Blitzkrieg crushed Denmark and Norway; Belgium, the Netherlands, and France fell in May and June. Stalin meanwhile annexed the Baltic states of Estonia, Latvia, and Lithuania (see Map 26.3). As Winston Churchill, an early advocate of resistance, took over as prime minister, Hitler ordered the bombardment of Britain. Churchill, another savvy orator, rallied the British people by radio to protect the ideals of liberty with their "blood, toil, tears, and sweat." In the Battle of Britain, or the Blitz as the British called it, the German air force bombed homes, public buildings, harbors, weapons depots, and factories. Britain poured resources into anti-aircraft weapons, its highly successful code-detecting group called Ultra, and further development of radar. By year's end, the British airplane industry was outproducing the Germans by 50 percent.

By the fall of 1940, German air losses had driven Hitler to abandon his planned conquest of Britain. Forcing Hungary, Romania, and Bulgaria to become its allies, Germany gained access to more food and oil. In violation of the Nazi-Soviet Pact, Hitler launched an all-out campaign in June 1941 against what he called the "center of judeobolshevism"—the Soviet Union. Deployed along a two-thousand-mile front, 3 million German and allied troops quickly penetrated Soviet lines and killed, captured, or wounded more than half of the 4.5 million Soviet soldiers defending the borders. The Soviet people fought back. Because Hitler feared that equipping his army for Russian conditions would suggest to civilians that a long war lay in store, the Nazi soldiers were unprepared for the onset of winter.

Meanwhile, as Japan swiftly captured Western colonies in Asia, the United States stopped supplying Japan with essential industrial goods. In December 1941, Japanese planes bombed American bases at Pearl Harbor in Hawaii and then destroyed a fleet of airplanes in the Philippines. President Roosevelt summoned the Congress to declare war on Japan. By spring 1942, the Japanese had conquered

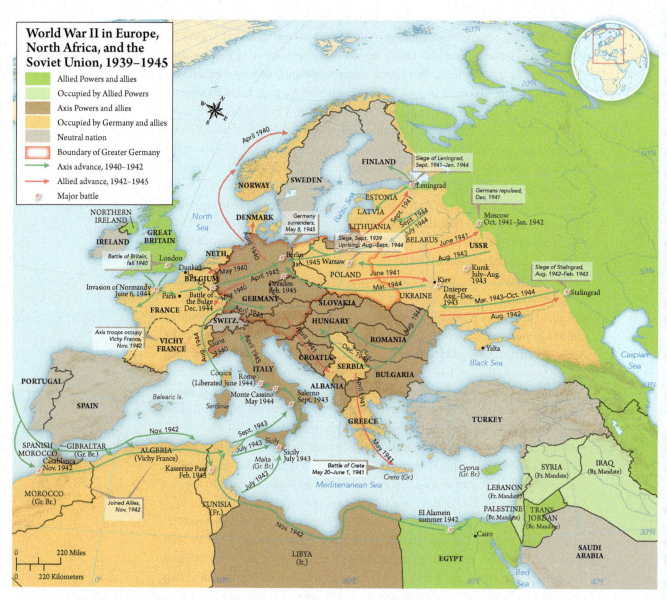

World War II in Europe, North Africa, and the Soviet Union, 1939–1945

Allied Powers and allies
Occupied by Allied Powers
Axis Powers and allies
Occupied by Germany and allies
Neutral nation
Boundary of Greater Germany
Axis advance, 1940–1942
Allied advance, 1942–1945
Major battle

≡ **MAP 26.3   World War II in Europe, North Africa, and the Soviet Union, 1939–1945**   Across Europe increasingly powerful bombers, tanks, and artillery were unleashed on soldiers and civilians alike. After its initial success early in 1940, Germany pursued war against the USSR despite failing to conquer Britain. By May 1945, much of the European continent and parts of the Middle East and North Africa had been reduced to rubble.

Guam, the Philippines, Malaya, Burma, Indonesia, Singapore, and much of the southwestern Pacific (see Map 26.4). As had happened with Germany's expansionist drive, the victories strengthened the appeal of the Japanese military's ideology. "The era of democracy is finished," the foreign minister announced confidently.[17] Japanese officials portrayed Emperor Hirohito as the monarch who would liberate Asians everywhere.

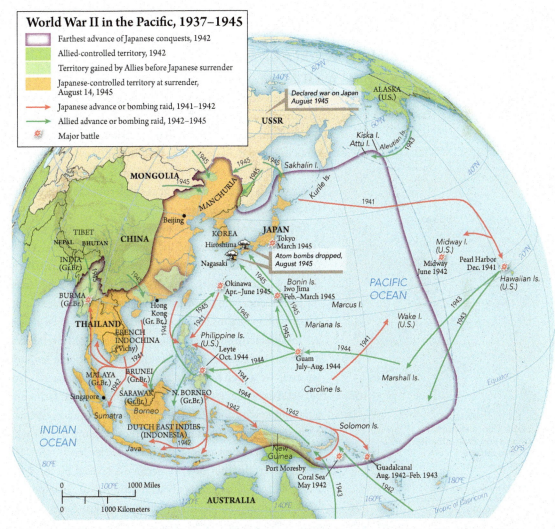

World War II in the Pacific, 1937–1945

- Farthest advance of Japanese conquests, 1942
- Allied-controlled territory, 1942
- Territory gained by Allies before Japanese surrender
- Japanese-controlled territory at surrender, August 14, 1945
- → Japanese advance or bombing raid, 1941–1942
- → Allied advance or bombing raid, 1942–1945
- ✳ Major battle

≡ **MAP 26.4   World War II in the Pacific, 1937–1945** The "Europe first" strategy of the Allies permitted Japan a comparatively free hand in the Pacific except for steady Chinese resistance. Japan's victories were short-lived, though the conquered peoples of the Pacific suffered mightily under Japanese rule, performing forced labor, serving as sex slaves, and bearing the brunt of the war's horrendous end.

Allies The alliance of Great Britain, France, the Soviet Union, and the United States and their coalition partners in World War II.

Axis The alliance of Italy, Germany, and Japan and their client states in World War II.

Germany and Italy quickly joined Japan and declared war on the United States—an appropriate enemy, Hitler proclaimed, as it was "half Judaized and the other half Negrified." The United States and the Soviet Union mistrusted each other, yet the Soviet Union joined with Great Britain, the Free French (an exile government based in London), and the United States to form the "Grand Alliance." Twenty other countries joined this coalition—known collectively as the **Allies**—who fought the **Axis** powers of Germany, Italy, and Japan. In the long run the Allies held advantages in terms of manpower and access to resources, but both sides faced the bloodiest fight in world history (see Lives and Livelihoods: Soldiers and Soldiering).

War and the World's Civilians

Victory in World War II depended on industrial production geared toward total war and mass killings. From the Rape of Nanjing to the horrors of the Holocaust, far more civilians than soldiers died in World War II. The Axis and the Allies alike bombed cities to destroy civilians' will to resist—a tactic that often inspired defiance rather than surrender, as in the Battle of Britain. Mass slaughter had a rationale behind it: in a total war, workers were as important as soldiers because they manufactured the tools of war.

The new "master races" believed it was their mission to rid the world of subhumans and then repopulate it themselves. As the German army swept through eastern Europe, it slaughtered Jews, Communists, Slavs, and others whom Nazi deemed "racial inferiors" and enemies. The number of deliberately murdered civilian victims in China alone is estimated to be at least 2.5 million, with some 14 million Chinese deaths overall and millions more murdered elsewhere in the region. Some 3 million Japanese were then relocated as "civilizers" in conquered areas of East Asia, while "racially pure" Germans took over farms and homes in Poland and elsewhere. To lessen resistance, German occupiers tested the reading skills of those captured; those who could read were shot as potential resistance leaders.

The extermination of Jews became a special focus of the Nazis. Forced into urban ghettos, stripped of their possessions, and living on minimal rations, countless eastern European Jews died of starvation and disease—the Nazis' initial plan for reducing the Jewish population. Soon the Nazis put into operation the "Final Solution," the organized rounding up

Major Concentration Camps and Extermination Sites in Europe

- Axis Powers and allies
- Occupied by Germany and allies
- ■ Extermination camp
- ● Other major concentration camp
- ◆ Site of mass killing
- ✶ Major ghetto

≡ **Major Concentration Camps and Extermination Sites in Europe**

≡ **The Warsaw Ghetto, 1943** From the 1930s on, the Nazis drove Jews into ghettos, confiscated their property, and deprived them of food and fuel. Despite being cut off, residents learned of the Holocaust, and in 1943 the people of the Warsaw ghetto staged an uprising. Those shown here were taken prisoner, and the uprising was brutally put down.

of Europe's Jews for transport to death camps. Some camps, like Auschwitz-Birkenau in Poland, served as both death and labor camps. Captives, among them Hans Kantorowsky, were herded into gas chambers where they were killed by lethal gas; their corpses were then burned in specially designed crematoria. As of 1943, Auschwitz had the capacity to burn 1.7 million bodies per year.

Soldiers, ordinary civilians, police, scientists, and doctors—all participated in the **Holocaust**. For all their public anti-Semitism, the Nazis took pains to hide the true purpose of the camps. Those not chosen for immediate murder in the camps had their heads shaved, were disinfected, and then given tattered prison garments. So began life in "a living hell," as one survivor wrote of the starvation, overwork, and disease. In the name of advancing "racial science," doctors in German concentration camps performed cruel experiments and operations with no anesthesia on pregnant women, twins, and other innocent people. Yet prisoners developed strategies for survival, forging friendships that sustained them. Thanks to the food and favors he received from fellow prisoners, wrote Auschwitz survivor Primo Levi, "I managed not to forget that I myself was a man."[18] In the end, six million Jews, the vast majority from eastern Europe, along with millions of Roma, homosexuals, Slavs, and others, were murdered in the Nazis' genocidal fury.

Holocaust The genocidal murder of some six million Jews by the Germans during World War II in an attempt to exterminate European Jewry.

LIVES AND LIVELIHOODS

Soldiers and Soldiering

Between 1930 and 1945 tens of millions of men and women worldwide became soldiers, joining both regular armies and paramilitary groups such as those run by the Chinese Communist Party and the German National Socialist (Nazi) Party. In 1927, for example, Mao Zedong, a young leader among Chinese Communists, helped decide that the groups should become a "Red Army" rather than organize into a traditional army. This paramilitary group marched northward through rural regions of China, adding recruits and ministering to the needs of peasants even as it indoctrinated them and took their resources. The German Nazi and Italian fascist paramilitary groups inflicted violence on strikers, on Communists, and, in the case of the Nazis, on Jews. During tough economic times, when jobs in the civilian workforce were lacking, men found a livelihood in paramilitary armies.

Thus, active soldiering and warfare marked the decades before World War II. Indeed, many people wondered if war ever really ended. In the deadly Chaco War (1932–1935) between Bolivia and Paraguay to increase territory, especially where oil exploration was taking place, conscripts included teenage boys. One Bolivian survivor, drafted at age fifteen, recalled, "[Our commanders] didn't lead us. . . . They sent all the soldiers to the front, and they stayed behind. They didn't give us a single thing to eat nor a single thing to drink. . . . For this simple reason [soldiers] collapsed . . . they died."[1]

The highest ranks of the military were generally staffed by social elites and treated well. In China, Jiang Jieshi, from a relatively prosperous family, attended Baoding Military Academy. He then trained in Japan, where high levels of literacy and knowledge of the classics were central, so officers usually came from homes that were cultured. In the United States, movie stars and children from the highest ranks of society, including the sons and daughters of senators and millionaires, volunteered for World War II and were often placed in less dangerous regions. Ordinary members of the infantry, however, were on the front lines, where the most common activity was digging, especially the foxholes in which they lived and protected themselves.

For many, political belief was a major factor in warfare. "The only thing that keeps me always on my feet and always ready: faith in God and the Duce [Mussolini]," one Italian soldier wrote from the front. From their training, Japanese soldiers came to believe "we are all samurai now," and an Australian soldier observed that whatever the character of the individual Japanese soldier, "good or bad, kind or sadistic, they had one supreme virtue . . . a courage that I believe to be unequalled in our time."[2]

There were failures in instilling belief, however. After their increasing exploitation during the Depression, Africans often hid from recruiters and village chiefs in charge of wartime forced labor. In Southern Rhodesia, they used colonial ideology to justify their draft dodging. "We are women. The

≡ **African American Sailors in World War II** Even as African American soldiers faced discrimination in the U.S. military, many saw the war as a campaign to promote universal rights and to defeat the forces of racism and ethnic supremacy. Having participated in defeating violent bigotry abroad, they often joined the postwar civil rights campaign to defeat violent bigotry at home.

White people are our menfolk to whom we look for guidance and protection. We have never had the courage or the ability to fight in war."[3]

War was a grim experience for most—they might face starvation in prison camps, epidemic disease, horrific wounds, wrenching physical and mental torture, suicide, cannibalism, and death. Yet soldiers' lives also had a bright side based on the loyal comradeship that developed during combat. Many professed to fight not for a cause but for the well-being of those fighting alongside them, and others found love and support on ships, in hospitals, and on the battlefield. Some believed that the military offered opportunity, among them African Americans; Soviet women in massive numbers volunteered to fight. Soldiers might gain new technological skills and even find wholly new livelihoods to pursue in the future.

Questions to Consider

1. What specific advantages did soldiers from many walks of life see in joining the military?
2. How would you describe soldiers' lives from 1930 to 1945, and how did they vary?
3. What were the class dimensions of the military?

For Further Information:

Johnson, David. *World War II and the Scramble for Labour in Colonial Zimbabwe, 1939–1948*. 2000.
Keegan, John. *Soldiers: A History of Men in Battle*. 1986.
Krylova, Anna. *Soviet Women in Combat*. 2011.
Montgomerie, Deborah. *Love in a Time of War: Letter-Writing in the Second World War*. 2005.

1. Christobal Arancibia, quoted in "Cristobal Arancibia: The Life of a Bolivian Peasant During the Chaco War, 1932–1935," ed. W. H. Beezley and J. Ewell, *Human Tradition in Latin America: The Twentieth Century* (Wilmington, DE: Scholarly Resources, 1987), 97.
2. Quoted in John Keegan, *Soldiers: A History of Men in Battle* (New York: Viking Penguin, 1986), 51.
3. Quoted in David Johnson, *World War II and the Scramble for Labour in Colonial Zimbabwe, 1939–1948* (Harare: University of Zimbabwe Press, 2000), 18.

The Axis countries remained at a disadvantage throughout the war despite their early conquests. Although the war accelerated economic production some 300 percent between 1940 and 1944 in all belligerent countries, the Allies produced more than three times as much as the Axis in 1943 alone. Even while some of its lands were occupied and its cities besieged, the Soviet Union increased its production of weapons. Both Japan and Germany made the most of their lower capacity, with such tactics as Japan's suicide, or *kamikaze,* attacks in the last months of the war. Whereas Hitler had come to power promising to end economic suffering, Japanese propaganda persuaded civilians to endure extreme scarcity for the sake of the nation. The use of millions of forced laborers and resources from occupied areas reduced Axis deprivation.

Allied governments were successful in generating civilian participation, especially among women. Soviet women constituted more than half the workforce by war's end and, as the Germans invaded, helped move entire factories eastward. They dug massive antitank trenches around threatened cities, and eight hundred thousand volunteered for the military, even serving as pilots. German and Italian officials began to realize too late that women were desperately needed in offices and factories. Japanese women rushed to help, but changing the propaganda did not convince enough German women to join the low-paid female workforce.

Even more than in World War I, propaganda saturated society in movie theaters and on the radio. People were glued to their radios for war news, but much of it was tightly controlled. Japan, like Germany, generally withheld news of defeats and large numbers of casualties to maintain civilian support. The antireligious Soviet government found that radio programming from the Russian Orthodox clergy boosted patriotism, as did films such as "Two Soldiers" (1943) with its tear-jerking hit song "Dark Night." Filmmakers were subject to censorship unless their films conveyed the "right" message, including racial thinking. The German government continued to advertise ugly caricatures of Jews, Slavs, and Roma; Allied propaganda depicted Germans as gorillas and "Japs" as uncivilized, insect-like fanatics.

Such characterizations eased the way for the U.S. government to force citizens of Japanese origin into its own concentration camps. Fred Korematsu, born in Oakland, California in 1919, was one U.S. citizen of Japanese descent who refused to leave his home on the grounds that only a handful of Americans of Italian and German descent were similarly interned. Korematsu was arrested and ultimately sent to a camp surrounded by barbed wire, machine guns, and watchtowers. Like that of many interned Japanese Americans, his family's property was taken and sold and he was left to find odd jobs, but he continued to fight, becoming a pioneer for civil rights.

As before, colonized peoples were conscripted into armies and forced labor. Some two million Indian men served the Allied cause, as did several hundred thousand Africans, even as governments stripped their families of resources. To prevent Japanese access to Indian resources, the British withdrew all shipping from Bengali ports, leaving the region with no food deliveries. "When I was nine years old we had the Bengal famine," one distinguished Indian remembered. "The victims suddenly emerged in millions—it seemed from absolutely nowhere, dying in incredible numbers."[19] Some three to seven million Bengali civilians died of starvation—a British-inflicted Holocaust because Churchill refused relief offered by Canada, Australia, and other countries. Soviet civilians were also at risk; during the siege of Leningrad (1941–1944) alone, one million residents starved to death.

Collaboration with Axis conquerors was common among colonial people who had suffered the racist oppression of the Western powers. As the Japanese swept through the Pacific and parts of East Asia, they conscripted local men into their army; many volunteered willingly. Subhas Bose, educated in England and accepted into the Indian Civil Service, became prominent in the Indian Congress Party, spending time in British prisons for his activities. When World War II broke out and the British refused to grant India home rule, he went over to the Axis side and recruited an all-Indian army to fight the British in South Asia. "Gandhi wants to change human beings, and all I want to do is free India," Bose maintained, as he fought on Japan's side.[20] Throughout the Axis-occupied areas, collaborationist leaders such as Wang Jingwei in China, Philippe Pétain in France, and Vidkun Quisling in Norway provided support for the Axis cause. An ordinary person could benefit from working for the occupiers.

Resistance to the Axis also began early in the war. Escaping France in 1940, General Charles de Gaulle from his haven in London directed the Free French government, resisters on the continent, and Free French military—a mixed organization of troops of colonized Asians and Africans and soldiers and volunteers from France and other occupied countries. Other resisters, called partisans, planned assassinations of collaborators

≡ **Forced Labor in Vietnam** Japan promised colonized peoples that Japanese rule would bring liberation to those dominated by the Western powers. In reality, Korean and other women served as sex slaves to members of the Japanese military, and other civilians provided forced labor, such as these Vietnamese women digging a trench to defend the military against tanks and other enemy vehicles.

and enemy officers and bombed bridges and rail lines. Although the Catholic Church officially supported Mussolini, Catholic and Protestant clergy and their parishioners set up resistance networks, often hiding Jews and political suspects. Ordinary people also fought back through everyday activities. Homemakers circulated newsletters urging demonstrations at Nazi prisons and in marketplaces where food was rationed. Jews rose up against their Nazi captors in Warsaw in 1943 but were mercilessly butchered; even then resistance in Poland remained strong. Resisters played on stereotypes: women often carried weapons to assassination sites and seduced and murdered enemy officers. "Naturally the Germans didn't think that a woman could have carried a bomb," explained one female Italian resister, "so this became the woman's task."[21]

From Allied Victory to the Cold War 1943–1945

FOCUS How did the Allied victory unfold, and what were the causes of that victory?

Allied victory began to look certain in 1943, even though tough fighting still lay ahead. In a series of meetings, Churchill, Stalin, and Roosevelt—nicknamed the Big Three—planned the peace they expected to achieve, including the creation of a new organization called the United Nations to prevent another world war. On the eve of victory, however, distrust among the Allies was about to provoke yet another struggle for supremacy—the Cold War between the United States and the Soviet Union.

The Axis Defeated

The Battle of Stalingrad in 1942–1943 marked a turning point in the war in Europe. In August 1942 the German army began a siege of this city, whose capture would give Germany access to Soviet oil. The fighting dragged on longer than the Germans expected, and when winter arrived, the German army was ill-equipped. In February 1943, the Soviet army captured the ninety thousand Germans who survived the freezing cold and near-constant combat. Meanwhile, the British army in North Africa faced off against German troops led by General Erwin Rommel. Skilled in the new mobile warfare, Rommel let his tanks move hundreds of miles from supply lines. He could not, however, overcome Allied access to secret German communication codes, which ultimately helped the Allies capture Morocco and Algeria in the fall of 1942. After driving Rommel out of Africa, the Allies landed in Sicily in July 1943, winning back the Italian peninsula only in April 1945. Almost simultaneously, partisans shot Mussolini and his mistress and hung their dead bodies for public display.

After Stalingrad the Soviet drive westward unfolded, with the Soviets still bearing the brunt of the Nazi war machine. British and U.S. warplanes bombed German cities, and on June 6, 1944, known as D-Day, combined Allied forces attacked the heavily fortified Normandy coast and then fought their way through the German-held territory of western France. Meanwhile the Soviets took Poland, Bulgaria, Romania, and finally Hungary during the winter of 1944–1945. Facing defeat, Hitler refused to spare the German people by surrendering. Instead, he committed suicide with his wife, Eva Braun, as the Soviet army took Berlin in April. Germany finally surrendered on May 8, 1945.

The Allies had followed a "Europe first" strategy for conducting the war. In the meantime, the Chinese had fought Japan virtually alone since 1937. In 1942, Allied forces destroyed part of Japan's formidable navy in battles at Midway Island and Guadalcanal. Japan lacked the capacity to recoup losses of ships and men, while the Allies had not only their own productive power but access to materiel manufactured around the world. The Allies stormed one Pacific island after another, gaining more bases from which to cut off Japanese supply lines and launch bombers toward Japan. In response to the kamikaze resistance of soldiers and civilians alike, the Allies stepped up their bombing of major cities, killing some 120,000 civilians in its spring 1945 firebombing of Tokyo.

Meanwhile an international team of more than one hundred thousand scientists, technicians, and other staff had secretly developed the atomic bomb. The Japanese practice of fighting to the last man rather than surrendering persuaded Allied military leaders that the defeat of Japan might cost the lives of an additional hundreds of thousands of Allied soldiers (and even more Japanese). On August 6, 1945, the U.S. government unleashed the new atomic weapon on Hiroshima and on August 9 a second bomb on Nagasaki. The two bombings killed 140,000 people instantly; tens of thousands died later from burns, radiation poisoning, and other wounds. Hardliners in the Japanese military wanted to continue the war, but on August 15, 1945, Japan surrendered.

Postwar Plans and Uncertainties

Conditions for lasting peace were poor at best. Japan, Europe, and large parts of East Asia and the Pacific lay in ruins. Governments and social order in many parts of the world were fragile if not totally broken. An estimated hundred million people had died in the war, and perhaps an equal number were homeless refugees. Colonial peoples were in full rebellion or close to it: for a second time in three decades, they had seen their imperial masters killing one another with the very technology that supposedly made Western civilization superior (see Seeing the Past: Technological Warfare: Civilization or Barbarism?). It was only a matter of time before colonized peoples would mount battles for their independence.

Amid chaos, a wartime agreement led to the founding of the **United Nations** (UN)—a name first applied to the alliance of twenty-six countries formed in 1942, to fight the Axis. With the collapse of the League of Nations after the outbreak of war, the formation of the United Nations had a new urgency and the term a new meaning. In 1944, even as the war proceeded, delegates from the United States, Britain, the USSR, and China met in Washington, DC, to draw up plans for the UN. As a result of this wartime conference, in June 1945, before the war was over, representatives from fifty countries signed the UN charter, setting the conditions for peaceful international cooperation. It remained to be seen whether this new organization would be successful at maintaining world peace.

The outlook was grim: a new struggle called the Cold War was taking root between the world's two military powers—the United States and the Soviet Union. At war's end, Stalin saw the world as hostile to his nation; the United States, for example, abruptly cut off many aid programs to the starving Soviet Union. Thus he believed that Soviet security depended on a permanent "buffer zone" of European states loyal to the USSR as a safeguard against a revived Germany in particular and the anti-Soviet Western states more generally. Across the Atlantic, President Harry S. Truman, who had succeeded Roosevelt after his death in April 1945, foresaw Communist expansion into the areas of eastern Europe the Allies had liberated. By 1946, U.S. officials were describing Stalin as a "neurotic" Asian ruler prepared to achieve world domination. For his part, Stalin claimed that "it was the Soviet army that won" World War II and warned Anglo-American forces not to continue moving eastward. In a March 1946 speech, former British Prime Minister Churchill warned that an "iron curtain" had fallen across Europe, dividing the world into two hostile camps.

As the Cold War came to inflame global politics, it affected the world's peoples. Eva Kantorowsky was again ensnared in global developments as she and her family tried to immigrate to the United States. Many Americans, even though they had opposed Hitler, remained anti-Semitic, and the U.S. Congress blocked the immigration of Jewish refugees. Jews were Communists, members of Congress claimed, echoing Nazi ideology as they played the Cold War card. Eva eventually arrived in the United States despite the growing intensity of the Cold War.

United Nations The international organization of nations established at the end of World War II to replace the League of Nations and to promote diplomacy and the peaceful settlement of disputes for countries worldwide.

SEEING THE PAST

Technological Warfare: Civilization or Barbarism?

Hiroshima, September 2, 1945

This photograph of Hiroshima, Japan, shows the near-total destruction that resulted from the dropping of the first atomic bomb on August 6, 1945. The atomic bomb was the work of the world's top scientists during World War II, and its development resulted from the theories of brilliant people like Albert Einstein. So too, other increasingly sophisticated weaponry and methods for mass killing paralleled great advances in a number of scientific fields. For some two centuries, the West characterized its scientific achievements as the hallmark of advanced civilization and viewed as backward those countries without them. It continued to make such claims as increasingly powerful nuclear weapons were tested in the Pacific and on the Asian continent, resulting in the annihilation of entire islands and the destruction of the environment. The visual and other evidence from Hiroshima can lead us to reflect to what degree the ability to destroy more lives than ever before and with less effort is a mark of high civilization or of barbarism.

Examining the Evidence

1. How is a moral argument for the atomic bomb possible?

2. How would you situate the atomic bomb and its use during World War II in the scientific and intellectual history of the West?

COUNTERPOINT: Nonviolence and Pacifism in an Age of War

FOCUS In what ways did peace movements serve as a counter-trend to events in the period from 1929 to 1945?

While leading nations saw military capacity as the measure of national greatness, some activists and ordinary people realized that nonviolent tactics could be powerful tools to undermine both colonialism and the doctrine of total war. Traditional modes of resistance shaped some efforts, while religious precepts underlay others.

Traditional Tactics: The Example of Nigerian Women

Some used traditional modes of resistance. In 1929, women in British-controlled Nigeria rebelled at a new tax the government tried to impose on them to solve its economic problems. They painted their bodies and sang and danced in the nude outside the homes of local tax collectors, who attacked and even burned some of the women's houses. Their method was called "sitting on a man," because it was generally used against rulings by men that the women considered unjust. British officials justified shooting the women, killing fifty-three of them, by calling the women's behavior irrational and dangerous. Up into the 1980s, women in Nigeria used traditional nonviolent tactics, including removing all their clothing, to protest low prices for their palm products and the exploitative practices of corporations in their region.

Gandhi and Civil Disobedience

Other pacifist traditions were mobilized during the 1920s and 1930s. Jainism, an ancient South Asian religion, held to the belief in *ahimsa*—the idea of doing no harm—and led many to become pacifists. Growing up amid Jains, Mohandas Gandhi led his followers in 1930 on a twenty-three-day "Salt March" to break the law giving the British a monopoly on salt—a necessity of life that exists freely in nature. Professing to model his activism on the teachings of Jesus, Buddha, and other spiritual leaders, Gandhi differentiated his nonviolent protest from militaristic, genocidal Western behavior. He called his strategy *Satyagraha* (SAH-ty-ah-GRAH-hah)—truth and firmness—and rejected the view that his tactics were "passive." Rather, such acts as taking salt and then being beaten or arrested (as Gandhi was) demanded incredible discipline to remain opposed but at the same time nonviolent.

Pacifism, including the tactics of Gandhi, unfolded with real conviction during the pre–World War I arms race and with even greater fervor in the aftermath of World War I. Feminists played key roles in the development of the Women's International League for Peace and Freedom after that war, and religious groups in many parts of the world contested what they saw as a new militarism developing in the interwar years. Many of these groups remained firmly pacifistic even with the rise of fascism, and were ridiculed either as deluded or as traitors. After World War II, civil rights activists in the United States embraced nonviolence and **civil disobedience**. In the 1950s and early 1960s they "sat in" to desegregate lunch counters, buses, and public facilities that were closed to them, even as officials whipped, hosed, and murdered them. Many still see committed pacifists as deluded thinkers or as traitors to the nation-state, but for some causes pacifists have been effective.

≡ **Mohandas Gandhi and Nonviolence** Indian leader Mohandas (also called Mahatma, "great souled one") Gandhi led a mass movement, whose message differed entirely from those of Mussolini and Hitler. Gandhi was neither bombastic nor wedded to material and militaristic display. Instead he denounced the violence and materialism of the West, preferring Satyagraha—"soulforce"—to physical conflict, and spinning by hand to parading tanks.

Conclusion

The Great Depression, which destroyed the lives and livelihoods of millions of people throughout the world, created conditions in which totalitarian rulers thrived by promising to restore national greatness and wealth. Mobilized by the mass media, many people turned from representative institutions to militaristic leaders who guaranteed a gleaming future. Authoritarian leaders used violence to gain support, even as others, including nonviolent resisters in the colonies and those with memories of World War I, took up pacifism or civil disobedience to achieve their objectives.

Leaders of the Western democracies, hoping to avoid another war, permitted Hitler and Mussolini to menace Europe throughout the 1930s. In Asia, the Japanese military convinced citizens to seek an extensive empire and an end to white domination. The uneasy coalition that formed to stop Germany, Italy, and Japan included the Allied powers of France, Britain, the Soviet Union, China, and the United States. At the war's end, Europe's population was reduced, its colonies on the verge of independence, its

civil disobedience A political strategy of deliberately but peacefully breaking the law to protest oppression and obtain political change.

peoples starving and homeless. Occupied by the victorious U.S. Army, Japan was similarly devastated, as were large swaths of North Africa, Asia, and the Pacific Islands. People who had been dislocated by the war—such as Eva Kantorowsky and her family—were dislocated once again. With Europe's global dominance ended, the Soviet Union and the United States reigned as the world's superpowers, with the newly formed United Nations established to achieve global governance.

In the decades following World War II, the United States and the Soviet Union competed for power and influence in every corner of the globe, seeing each local and regional development through the prism of the Cold War ideological split. Amid this growing divide, the experience of global war also convinced millions of people that colonialism should not survive.

✳ review

The major global development in this chapter: The causes and outcomes of the Great Depression and World War II.

Important Events	
1920s	Collapse of commodity prices around the world
1929	Crash of the U.S. stock market; global depression begins; Stalin's "liquidation of the kulaks"
1930	Gandhi's Salt March
1930s	Sweden begins setting up welfare state
1931	Japan invades Manchuria
1933	Hitler comes to power in Germany and ends representative government
1935	Nuremberg Laws enacted against the Jews in Germany; Italy invades Ethiopia
1936	Purges and show trials begin in USSR
1937	Japan attacks China; World War II begins in Asia
1939	Germany invades Poland; World War II begins in Europe
1941	Germany invades USSR; Japan attacks Pearl Harbor; United States enters the war
1941–1945	Holocaust
1943	USSR defeats Germany at Stalingrad
1945	Fall of Berlin and surrender of Germany; UN charter signed; United States drops atomic bombs; Japan surrenders

KEY TERMS

Allies (p. 978)
appeasement (p. 972)
Axis (p. 978)
central economic planning (p. 962)
civil disobedience (p. 989)

five-year plan (p. 962)
Great Depression (p. 958)
Greater East Asia Co-Prosperity
Sphere (p. 973)
Holocaust (p. 979)

purge (p. 963)
totalitarianism (p. 962)
United Nations (p. 986)

CHAPTER OVERVIEW QUESTIONS

1. How did ordinary people react to the Great Depression, and how did their reactions differ from country to country?
2. Why were dictators and antidemocratic leaders able to come to power in the 1930s, and how did all countries—autocratic and democratic alike—mobilize the masses?
3. How are the Great Depression and World War II related historical events?

MAKING CONNECTIONS

1. What are the main differences between World War I (see Chapter 25) and World War II?
2. In what specific ways did World Wars I and II affect the African and Asian colonies of the imperial powers?
3. How do the strengths and weaknesses of the Allies and the Axis compare?
4. How would you describe the importance of World War II not only to the unfolding of history but also to present-day concerns?

For further research into the topics covered in this chapter, see the Bibliography at the end of the book. For additional primary sources from this period, see *Sources for World in the Making*.

27

The Emergence of New Nations in a Cold War World 1945–1970

backstory

As we saw in Chapter 26, imperial rivalries played a key role in the outbreak of World War II, the most destructive conflict in human history. By the time the war was over, as many as one hundred million people had died, countries around the world lay in ruin, and the imperial system that had helped produce the war was in disarray. The chaos and confusion of the postwar world gave rise to a new set of global political trends. The formation of organizations such as the United Nations reflected new levels of cooperation among nations. At the same time, rising nationalism among colonized peoples sparked the process of decolonization. Finally, the Cold War between the United States and the Soviet Union shaped politics around the world and posed an unprecedented threat to world peace.

≡ **World in the Making** After World War II, colonized peoples created independent nations, sometimes wrenching freedom through armed struggle and bloodshed. Ghanaians celebrated their achievement of nationhood in 1957 with festive ceremonies, including lavish dress such as that worn by this young girl. She adorns her body with a headdress and a salute to independence on her skin along with white ceremonial body markings. Others wore clothing printed with images of new political leaders—a clear sign of this next stage of world-making.

During the early 1950s, on the first Thursday of the month, life in Cairo and other cities of the Arab world came to a standstill. Patrons of cafés huddled around the radio, and shoppers dashed home to catch the broadcast. All were eager to hear featured singer Umm Kulthum, whose repertoire included traditional desert songs, religious verses, and romantic ballads. Born at the beginning of the twentieth century, she first sang disguised as a boy because girls were not supposed to perform in public. By the 1950s she had become "the voice of Egypt" for the newly independent republic. Her singing, one fan said, "shows our ordinary life." Even Egypt's leader Gamal Abdel Nasser broadcast his speeches just before Umm Kulthum's program to link himself to her appeal. Traveling widely, she used her vocal talent to encourage Arab-speaking peoples to celebrate their own culture as another sign of independence.

The creation of a fully independent Egyptian republic was just one of many acts of liberation in the postwar world. From the Middle East through Africa and Asia, independence movements of workers, veterans, and other activists toppled colonial governments. **Decolonization** was followed by the difficult process of nation-building. While creating government structures, newly independent states had to rebuild roads destroyed in the war, create systems for educating citizens, and foster solidarity among them. Like Kulthum, patriots throughout the new nations devoted their livelihoods and talents to this cause.

Postcolonial nation-building occurred amidst the collapse of the old European-dominated international order and its replacement by intense rivalry between the United States and the Soviet Union. The nuclear arsenals of these two "superpowers" grew massively in the 1950s, but they were enemies who did not fight outright on their own soil—thus the term **Cold War**. Instead, they confronted each other in the developing world. When the United States discovered Soviet missile sites on the island of Cuba in 1962, the world stood on the brink of nuclear disaster.

Decolonization The process of freeing regions from imperial control and creating independent nations.

Cold War The rivalry between the Soviet Union and the United States that followed World War II and shaped world politics between 1945 and 1989.

Yet optimism surged after World War II. The birth of new nations and the defeat of authoritarian militarism inspired hope that life would become fairer as people everywhere gained freedom. Revolutionary-minded thinkers poured out new political theories, while novelists explored the often-harsh realities of independence. Vast nation-building projects for citizens' well-being took shape; the welfare state expanded; and by the 1960s economic rebirth had made many regions prosperous. People caught up in events precipitated by Cold War rivalries, however, faced a grim, often violent, reality. In the 1950s and 1960s, while Kulthum gave Arabs hope, youthful followers of China's Mao Zedong banded together to bring about a deadly "cultural revolution" that would shake society. Across the globe, other youth rose up in the 1960s, envisioning an end to war and injustice. The search for freedom differed—sometimes drastically—from place to place in this age of Cold War extremes.

OVERVIEW QUESTIONS

The major global development in this chapter: The political transformations of the postwar world and their social and cultural consequences.

As you read, consider:

1. How did the Cold War affect the superpowers and the world beyond them?

2. How did the Cold War shape everyday lives and goals?

3. Why did colonial nationalism revive in the postwar world, and how did decolonization affect society and culture?

4. Why did the model of a welfare state emerge after World War II, and how did this development affect ordinary people?

World Politics and the Cold War

⬇ **FOCUS** Why was the Cold War waged, and how did it reshape world politics?

In 1945, Europe's world leadership ended and the reign of the United States and the Soviet Union as the world's new superpowers began. The United States, its territory virtually untouched in the war, was now an economic giant, and the Soviet Union, despite suffering immense destruction, had developed enormous military might. By the late 1940s, the USSR had imposed Communist rule throughout most of eastern Europe, while the United States poured vast amounts of money and military equipment across the globe to win allegiance. Unwilling to confront each other head-on, they fought **proxy wars** in smaller, contained areas such as Korea and Vietnam, while amassing stockpiles of nuclear weapons that could annihilate the world.

proxy war During the Cold War, a conflict in another part of the world backed by the USSR or the United States as part of their rivalry.

The New Superpowers

The situation of the two superpowers in 1945 differed dramatically. The United States, the world's richest nation, had increased industrial output 15 percent annually between 1940 and 1944, a rate of growth reflected in workers' wages. Casting aside its post–World War I policy of nonintervention, the United States embraced its position as global leader. Americans had tracked the progress of World War II; hundreds of thousands of U.S. soldiers and relief workers gained direct experience of Europe, Africa, and Asia. Despite Cold War fears, most Americans were optimistic about their futures.

The Soviets emerged from the war with a well-justified sense of accomplishment. Withstanding the deaths of tens of millions, they had successfully resisted the most massive onslaught ever launched against a modern nation. Thus, Soviet citizens believed that everyday conditions would improve. "Life will become pleasant," one writer prophesied at war's end. "There will be much coming and going, and a lot of contacts with the West."[1] Stalin, however, moved ruthlessly to reassert control. In 1946, his new five-year plan increased production goals and mandated more stringent collectivization of agriculture. To raise the low wartime birthrate he introduced an intense propaganda campaign emphasizing that women should hold down jobs and also fulfill their "true nature" by producing many children.

The Cold War Unfolds 1945–1962

The Cold War afflicted the world for more than four decades, with lasting effects. Its origins remain a matter of debate. Some historians point to consistent U.S., British, and French hostility that began with the Bolshevik Revolution in 1917. Others stress Stalin's policies, notably the Nazi-Soviet alliance in 1939 and his quick claims on the Baltic states and Polish territory when World War II broke out. During that war, suspicions among the Allies ran deep. Stalin felt that Churchill and Roosevelt were deliberately letting the USSR bear the brunt of Hitler's onslaught on Europe. Some believed that dropping the atomic bomb on Japan was a heartless U.S. ploy to frighten the Soviets from seizing more land. Early on, the U.S. State Department described Stalin as continuing the centuries-old Russian thirst for "world domination." In August 1949, the USSR tested its own atom bomb; thereafter the superpowers built and stockpiled ever more sophisticated nuclear weapons, including hydrogen and neutron bombs. The Cold War now threatened global annihilation.

The United States acknowledged Soviet influence in areas the USSR occupied but feared the spread of communism around the world. The difficulties of postwar life in western and southern Europe made Communist ideas and programs promising better conditions attractive, and Communist leadership in the resistance movements of World War II gave the party a powerful appeal. When in 1947 Communist insurgents threatened the British-installed Greek monarchy,

U.S. president Harry S. Truman announced what quickly became known as the Truman Doctrine, the countering of possible Communist rule with economic and military aid. Truman promoted a large aid program as necessary to prevent global Soviet conquest, warning that "the seeds of totalitarian regimes are nurtured by misery and want."[2] The Truman Doctrine thus began the U.S. Cold War policy of **containment**—the attempt to keep communism from spreading.

The European Recovery Program, or Marshall Plan, providing massive U.S. economic support to Europe, followed. Secretary of State George C. Marshall claimed that the plan was directed not "against any country or doctrine but against hunger, poverty, desperation, and chaos." Stalin, however, saw it as a U.S. political ploy to bolster American influence in Europe. By the early 1950s, the United States had sent western Europe more than $12 billion in food, equipment, and services and then sent the same amount to Japan alone with the same goal.

Countering, the USSR turned its military occupation of eastern Europe into a buffer zone of satellite states directed by "people's governments." In such Soviet-allied states as Poland,

American Aid to Tokyo's Orphans In addition to postwar homelessness, disease, and starvation, Japan's citizens lost family members in the atomic bombings and firebombings. As part of the Cold War effort to win allies, the United States hurried to make things better for those most in need—including defeated enemies Japan and Germany—by giving them aid.

Czechoslovakia, and Hungary, Stalin enforced collectivized agriculture, centralized industrialization, and the nationalization of private property. Enforced collectivization of farming was a brutal process for many, but others felt differently. "Before [communism] we peasants were dirty and poor, we worked like dogs. . . . Was that a good life? No sir, it wasn't. . . . I was a miserable sharecropper and my son is an engineer," said one Romanian.[3] Thus modernization of production in the Soviet bloc opened technical and bureaucratic careers. People's livelihoods changed dramatically, as they moved to cities to receive better education, health care, and jobs. The price was political repression and immersion in Russian rather than their own national cultures.

Cold War competition also led to the division of Germany. Allied agreements at Yalta in 1945 provided for the division of Germany and its capital city, Berlin,

containment The U.S. policy developed during the Cold War to prevent the spread of communism.

≡ **MAP 27.1   Divided Germany**   Temporarily divided among the Allied powers, postwar Germany was caught in the tentacles of Cold War politics. By 1949, the former industrial center of Europe had been divided into two nations, commonly called East and West Germany. Deep in the Soviet-dominated eastern sector was the once-vibrant city of Berlin, itself divided east and west.

into four zones, individually occupied either by the United States, the Soviet Union, Britain, or France (see Map 27.1). On June 24, 1948, Soviet troops blockaded the American, British, and French zones of Berlin, located more than one hundred miles deep in the Soviet zone. Instead of handing over Berlin, the United States flew in millions of tons of provisions to the city in the Berlin Airlift, or as U.S. pilots called it, "Operation Vittles." The blockade was lifted in May 1949, with West Berlin remaining a symbol of freedom to many. France, Britain, and the United States then merged their zones into a West German state that would serve as a buffer against the Soviets, who in turn created an East German state to counter West Germany. In 1961, the East German government began construction of the Berlin Wall to block the route by which some 3 million East Germans had escaped to the freer, more prosperous West.

The People's Republic of China 1949

Amid superpower struggles in Europe, Chinese Communist forces triumphed over the Nationalists in 1949. Before, during, and after World War II, the Nationalist armies led by Jiang Jieshi (Chiang Kai-shek) had fought to defeat Japan but also to eliminate rival Communist forces. The Allies aided Jiang and urged these two Chinese factions to concentrate on defeating Japan during World War II. Once the war was over, however, in 1949, Mao Zedong's (MOW zuh-DOONG) army of Communists defeated the Nationalists.

From a prosperous peasant family, Mao had little in common with the farmers whom he targeted for support. He never worked as an agricultural laborer but rather spent his entire life as a politician. Initially he gravitated toward communism with USSR financial support, but in power, Mao's new People's Republic of China focused on the welfare of the peasantry rather than the industrial proletariat. Mao's government instituted social reforms such as civil equality for women and at the same time copied Soviet collectivization, rapid industrialization, and brutal repression of the privileged classes. Jiang's Nationalist forces escaped to the island of Taiwan; from there, with Jiang supported by the United States, Cold War fires spread to East Asia.

Proxy Wars and Cold War Alliances

The superpowers now pulled much of the globe into the Cold War. Africa and Latin America felt the Cold War's impact as opposing guerrilla fighters, spies, and propagandists blanketed their regions. The Cold War even reached into space: in 1957, the Soviets successfully launched the first artificial earth satellite, *Sputnik*, and in 1961 they put the first cosmonaut, Yuri Gagarin, in orbit around the earth. The Soviets' edge in space technology shocked the Western bloc amid massive weapons buildup (see Lives and Livelihoods: Cosmonauts and Astronauts).

The two superpowers faced off indirectly in Korea, which after World War II had been divided into two nations, North and South Korea. After border skirmishes by both sides, in 1950 the North Koreans, supported by the Soviet Union, invaded the U.S.-backed South. The United States maneuvered the UN Security Council into approving a "police action" against the North, and UN forces quickly drove well into North Korean territory. The war continued for two and a half years, killing three million civilians alone and ending in stalemate. The settlement in 1953 changed nothing, with Korea divided as before.

U.S. military spending soared from $10.9 billion in 1948 to almost $60 billion in 1953 to "contain" communist expansion, as U.S. President Dwight Eisenhower likened Asian countries to a row of dominoes: "You knock over the first one and what will happen is that it will go over [to communism] very quickly,"[4] contaminating the entire world. The USSR and the United States formed competing military alliances that split most of the world into two opposing camps. In 1949 the United States, Canada, and their European allies formed the **North Atlantic Treaty Organization** (NATO). In 1955, after the United States forced France and Britain to invite West Germany to join NATO, the Soviet Union established

North Atlantic Treaty Organization
A Cold War alliance formed in 1949 among the United States, its western European allies, and Canada.

LIVES AND LIVELIHOODS

Cosmonauts and Astronauts

≡ **Soviet Leaders Honor Yuri Gagarin and Valentina Tereshkova** The Soviets made these two cosmonauts special heroes: Gagarin (second from the left) because he was the first man in space, and Tereshkova because she represented the equality for women said to exist only in the Soviet bloc. Today, mementos of these heroes on T-shirts and caps across the former Soviet Union are reminders of the Cold War.

The space race gave rise to many new livelihoods, but none more celebrated than that of USSR cosmonauts and U.S. astronauts. The parents of cosmonaut Yuri Gagarin, the first person in space, worked on a Communist collective farm, and Gagarin himself labored in a foundry before the Soviet government selected him for technical education and eventual training as a pilot. Standing five feet, two inches helped him fit into the small cockpit of the first manned spacecraft—*Vostok I.*

After the successful 1957 launch of *Sputnik*, the Soviets' shocking lead in space motivated the creation in 1958 of the U.S. National Aeronautics and Space Administration (NASA). Like Gagarin, U.S. astronauts became heroes to many: astronaut John Glenn, for example, later served as a U.S. senator. Yet civil rights activists protested the expenditure of funds to get men on the moon where no one lived instead of alleviating the poverty of those on Earth. A rapper composed "Whitey on the Moon" pointing to the rats and broken toilets in ordinary lives while billions from people's taxes funded Whitey's space jaunts.

Despite the dominance of the superpowers in space, some thirty-five countries contributed their citizens to the world's various space programs, recognizing that capabilities in space were needed to participate in satellite technology and advanced military capability. Trained space travelers are generally drawn from the ranks of jet pilots (like Gagarin) and space engineers, with mathematicians and scientists added to oversee experiments. However, to fend off criticism and give these costly programs more widespread appeal, people of diverse ethnicities and women have joined the ranks.

Space travel is one of the more dangerous livelihoods created since the end of World War II. Not only have dozens of trained astronauts and cosmonauts died, but so have ground workers supporting space programs. In 2003, twenty-one workers and scientists died in a rocket explosion at Brazil's space site, and the following year six people in India's space program were killed when a rocket motor burst into flames. Yuri Gagarin himself died in 1968 during a jet training flight.

Questions to Consider

1. What roles did astronauts and cosmonauts play in the Cold War?

2. Why did so many countries besides the superpowers begin their own space programs?

3. What livelihoods do you find comparable to those of astronaut and cosmonaut?

For Further Reading:

Brzezinski, Matthew. *Red Moon Rising: Sputnik and the Hidden Rivalries That Ignited the Space Age.* New York: Times Books, 2007.

De Groot, Gerard. *Dark Side of the Moon: The Magnificent Madness of the American Lunar Quest.* New York: New York University Press, 2006.

Maher, Neil M. *Apollo in the Age of Aquarius.* Cambridge, MA: Harvard University Press, 2017.

Wolfe, Tom. *The Right Stuff.* New York: Farrar, Straus, and Giroux, 1979.

Warsaw Pact A Cold War alliance formed in 1955 among the Soviet Union and its eastern European satellite states.

Organization of American States An alliance formed in 1948 among nations in the Western Hemisphere.

its own military organization, commonly called the **Warsaw Pact**, which included Albania, Bulgaria, Czechoslovakia, East Germany, Hungary, Poland, and Romania. These two massive regional alliances replaced the individual might of the European powers (see Map 27.2).

Distant from Europe, twenty-one nations from the Western Hemisphere formed the **Organization of American States** (OAS) in 1948. As in Europe, the United States gave individual countries of the OAS economic as well as military aid. This aid guaranteed Latin American military regimes' increased power over civilians, wounding democratic politics. The **Southeast Asia Treaty Organization** (SEATO), established in 1954 as a counterpart to NATO, included Pakistan,

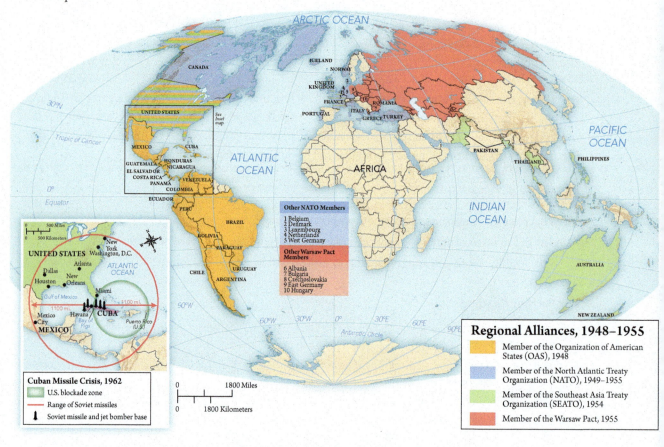

MAP 27.2 Regional Alliances, 1948–1955 During the Cold War, the United States and the Soviet Union divided the world into regional alliances, which were pitted against one another like the two superpowers themselves. Individual states in these alliances rearmed, even building their own nuclear capacity. Military budgets soared, as the USSR and the United States took the Cold War into space.

Thailand, the Philippines, Britain, Australia, New Zealand, France, and the United States. The United States thus pulled as much of the world as possible into its orbit.

One Latin American nation stood apart. In 1959 a revolution in Cuba brought to power the young Fidel Castro. Born in 1926 to the owner of a large plantation and his housekeeper, Castro as a child played with others far less privileged than he. Soon, however, the boy was separated from his poorer friends and given an elite education. At the university, Castro was a political leader, eventually becoming a major opposition figure in Cuban politics. In 1959 Castro's forces overthrew the island's corrupt regime, which was controlled mostly by U.S. sugar interests and the mob. After being rebuffed by the United States, Castro, initially opposed to communism, turned to the Soviet Union for aid to rebuild his country.

Cuba's connection to the Soviet Union alarmed American decision makers, including John F. Kennedy, who became U.S. president in 1961. Almost immediately Kennedy authorized an invasion of Cuba at the Bay of Pigs to overthrow Castro. The CIA had similarly overthrown a populist nationalist regime in Iran to install the Shah, and in Guatemala imposed a president friendly to U.S. interests. The Bay of Pigs invasion, however, failed miserably and humiliated the United States, as Castro's tiny air force sank U.S. ships and captured more than a thousand invaders.

Another incident involving Cuba brought the world even closer to nuclear war. In October 1962, the CIA reported the installation of launching pads for Soviet nuclear missiles in Cuba (see again Map 27.2). In response, Kennedy called for a blockade of Soviet ships headed for Cuba and threatened nuclear war if the installations were not removed. As the superpowers hovered on the brink of nuclear disaster, a high Soviet official told his wife to leave Moscow immediately; men in Kennedy's cabinet reported looking at the sunset, believing it to be the last they would see. Then, between October 25 and 27, Nikita Khrushchev, Stalin's successor, and Kennedy negotiated an end to the crisis, clearly fearing the nuclear future.

Southeast Asia Treaty Organization
A Cold War coalition of U.S. Asian allies formed in 1954.

Decolonization and the Birth of Nations

⭘ **FOCUS** How did colonized peoples achieve their independence from the imperialist powers after World War II?

For decades, colonized peoples had aimed for relief from imperial rule, the more so after World War II when they had witnessed the full barbarism of imperial warfare— and also the West's weaknesses. "We felt that the British were not supermen as we used to think," one Singapore worker put it. Another was enraged at seeing "the same old arrogance that you saw before the war."[5] Excluded from victory parades so the Allies could maintain the illusion of white supremacy, colonized veterans were determined to be free. People from many walks of life, often led by individuals experienced in warfare and steeped in nationalism, fought for liberation after 1945.

The path to independence was paved with difficulties. In Africa, a continent whose peoples spoke several thousand languages, the European conquerors' creation of administrative units such as "Nigeria" and "Rhodesia" had undermined ethnic ties and local cultures. In the Middle East and North Africa, pan-Arab and pan-Islamic movements might seem to have been unifying forces. Yet many Muslims were not Arab, and not all Arabs were Muslim: Islam itself encompassed many beliefs and sects. In India, anti-colonialist Hindus, Sikhs, and Muslims battled one another as well as the British. Despite these complications, in the decades after World War II colonized peoples succeeded in creating independent nations, often to become entangled in Cold War machinations.

The End of Empire in Asia

At the end of World War II, Asians mobilized against the inflation, unemployment, and other harsh conditions the war had imposed on them. Britain had promised in the 1930s to grant India its independence, but postponed the plan when war broke out. Two million Indian veterans of the war joined forces with powerful Indian Congress politicians, many of whom had helped finance the British war effort, making India one of Britain's major creditors. Bankrupt from the war, Britain in 1947 finally parted with India. As some half a billion Asians gained their independence, Britain's sole notable remaining colony was Hong Kong.

Independent countries emerged along the lines of religious rivalries that Britain had fomented under colonialism. In 1947, political leaders agreed to partition British India into an independent India for Hindus and the new state of Pakistan for Muslims; both were artificial divisions, because there were people from many religions living together across the subcontinent. The new state of India, in fact, had the second largest Muslim population in the world after Indonesia. Ordinary people had violent reactions as **Partition** unfolded, even setting up paramilitary groups (see Map 27.3). A powerful religious minority—the Sikhs—bitterly resented receiving nothing. Hundreds of thousands were massacred in the great shift of religious populations between India and Pakistan—"appalling sights," a journalist reported, as trains reached their destination filled with nothing but corpses.[6] Indian and Pakistani soldiers began fighting for control of Kashmir along the border between the two countries. In the midst of tragic bloodshed and nation-building, in 1948 a radical Hindu assassinated Gandhi, who had championed religious reconciliation and a secular Indian democracy.

Partition The division of the Indian subcontinent into different states in 1947 and the violence accompanying it.

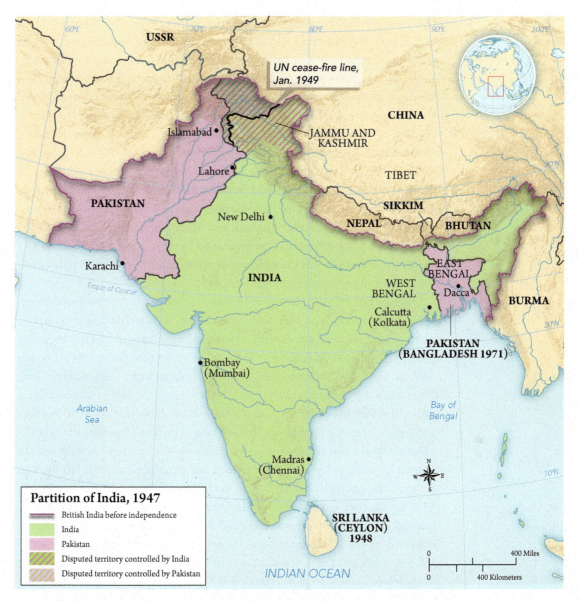

UN cease-fire line,
Jan. 1949

Partition of India, 1947

	British India before independence
	India
	Pakistan
	Disputed territory controlled by India
	Disputed territory controlled by Pakistan

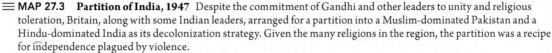

≡ **MAP 27.3   Partition of India, 1947**   Despite the commitment of Gandhi and other leaders to unity and religious toleration, Britain, along with some Indian leaders, arranged for a partition into a Muslim-dominated Pakistan and a Hindu-dominated India as its decolonization strategy. Given the many religions in the region, the partition was a recipe for independence plagued by violence.

In Indonesia in the closing days of World War II, the Japanese, eager to foil the Dutch, allowed Western-educated Achmed Sukarno and his followers to declare Indonesia an independent state. Sukarno's nationalist vision brought all the islands of the archipelago into a unified nation. His task was complicated by three factors.

First, Indonesia had a tradition of local princely rule, even under Dutch control. Second, from the beginning of the twentieth century Indonesians had built an array of competing organizations, including Islamic ones, that pushed for freedom. Third, Allied military forces had helped the Dutch to reclaim their empire, even enlisting the help of remaining Japanese troops to crush pro-independence fighters.

These fighters engaged in relentless **guerrilla warfare**. In 1949 the Dutch conceded Indonesian independence, and in 1957 Sukarno, as head of the new state, legislated that all Dutch leave the country. Sukarno's policies entailed economic modernization and a cultural unity based on the belief in one God, whether Islamic, Christian, or other. The new Ministry of Religion fostered unity through Islamic institutions, such as the building of mosques and establishment of Islamic welfare programs, but ethnic, religious, and economic interests diverged in the archipelago, leading to constant governmental struggle against dissenters. For a time, Sukarno himself was the mainstay of unity, becoming a charismatic champion of newly independent countries (see Map 27.4).

In Indochina nationalists struggled to prevent the postwar revival of French imperialism. From the 1930s on, their leader, Ho Chi Minh (hoe chee min), built a powerful organization, the Communist Viet Minh, to fight colonial rule. He began his career, however, by working aboard a French ocean liner, then taking jobs in London and Paris during World War I, experiences that brought him in direct contact with white racism. Ho became interested in Marxism, which led him to Moscow. Once head of the Viet Minh, he advocated land redistribution, especially in southern Indochina where some six thousand owners held more than 60 percent of the land.

During World War II, Ho worked to overthrow the Japanese; at war's end, he declared Vietnam independent. The French reasserted their control, but the Viet Minh peasant guerrillas defeated them in the bloody battle of Dien Bien Phu in 1954. The Geneva Conference held later that year carved out an independent Laos and divided Vietnam into North and South, each free from French control. Supported by the USSR and China, Ho established a Communist government in North Vietnam, and a non-Communist government was installed in South Vietnam (see again Map 27.4). The United States supported South Vietnam, and cancelled its elections in 1956 to prevent a Communist victory.

The Struggle for Independence in the Middle East

guerrilla warfare
Unconventional combat, often undertaken by those who are not members of official armies.

By war's end in 1945, much of the world had become almost fully dependent on the Middle East's rich petroleum resources to fuel cars and airplanes, heat homes, and create products such as plastics. "The oil in this region is the greatest single prize in all history," as one geologist put it.[7] Empowered, the Middle Eastern nations that emerged from imperial domination maneuvered between the Cold War rivals.

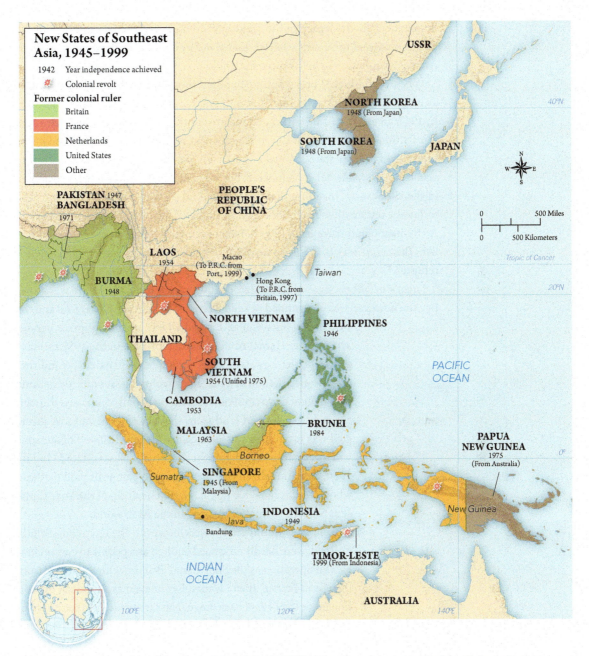

New States of Southeast Asia, 1945–1999

1942 — Year independence achieved

✳ — Colonial revolt

Former colonial ruler

- Britain
- France
- Netherlands
- United States
- Other

PAKISTAN 1947
BANGLADESH 1971

USSR

NORTH KOREA
1948 (From Japan)

SOUTH KOREA
1948 (From Japan)

JAPAN

PEOPLE'S
REPUBLIC
OF CHINA

LAOS
1954

Macao
(To P.R.C. from
Port., 1999)

Hong Kong
(To P.R.C. from
Britain, 1997)

Taiwan

BURMA
1948

NORTH VIETNAM

THAILAND

PHILIPPINES
1946

SOUTH
VIETNAM
1954 (Unified 1975)

PACIFIC
OCEAN

CAMBODIA
1953

MALAYSIA
1963

BRUNEI
1984

PAPUA
NEW GUINEA
1975
(From Australia)

Borneo

SINGAPORE
1945 (From
Malaysia)

Sumatra

New Guinea

INDONESIA
1949

Java

Bandung

INDIAN
OCEAN

TIMOR-LESTE
1999 (From Indonesia)

AUSTRALIA

500 Miles

500 Kilometers

Tropic of Cancer

40°N

20°N

0°

100°E

120°E

140°E

≡ **MAP 27.4 New States of Southeast Asia, 1945–1999** The French were determined to keep their empire in Southeast Asia, but their forces were defeated by the Vietnamese in 1954. As the Bandung Conference proceeded in Indonesia, the emerging nations of Southeast Asia became pivotal to the Cold War: the long and lethal proxy war continued in Vietnam, and genocide erupted in neighboring Cambodia.

Simultaneously the legacy of the Holocaust complicated the commitment of the Western powers to secure a Jewish homeland in the Middle East, which stirred Arab determination to hold onto their lands.

When World War II broke out, six hundred thousand Jewish settlers and twice as many Arabs lived, amid intermittent conflict, in British-controlled Palestine. In 1947, an exhausted Britain ceded the area to the United Nations, which voted to partition Palestine into an Arab region and a Jewish one. In May 1948 Israelis proclaimed the new state of Israel. "The dream had come true," Golda Meir, future prime minister of Israel, remembered, but "too late to save those who had perished in the Holocaust."[8] Arguing that the UN had no right to award Palestinian land to Jewish settlers, five neighboring Arab states attacked Israel and were beaten. A UN-negotiated truce in 1949 gave Israel even more territory than granted earlier. The result was that some two-thirds of Palestinian Arabs became stateless refugees.

Israel's neighbor, Egypt, demanded complete independence at the war's end. Britain, however, was determined to keep its control of Middle Eastern oil and the British-run Suez Canal. Backed widely by the Egyptian people, army officer Gamal Abdel Nasser took part in the 1952 military ouster of the Egyptian king, a puppet of Britain's behind-the-scenes rule. The son of a postal inspector, Nasser quickly became president of Egypt in 1956, working on behalf of peasants through the redistribution of land from the wealthiest estates. A prime goal was reclaiming the Suez Canal, "where 120,000 of our sons had lost their lives in digging it [by force]," Nasser stated.[9] In July 1956, he nationalized the Suez Canal to gain tolls paid by those who used the canal for Egypt. Nationalization of the Suez Canal sent Nasser's reputation soaring in the Arab world.

It enraged the imperial powers, however. The Egyptians, Britain claimed, were hardly advanced enough as a people to run as complex an operation as the Suez Canal. Britain, with assistance from Israel and France, then invaded Egypt even as American opposition made the British back down. Nasser's triumph inspired confidence that the Middle East could confront the West and win.

New Nations in Africa

Displaced from their traditional agricultural livelihoods during the war, many Africans flocked to cities such as Lagos and Nairobi, where they lived in shantytowns and survived by scavenging and doing menial labor for whites. After the war, struggling urban

≡ **The Arab-Israeli War of 1948–1949**

(map labels)

LEBANON

Mediterranean Sea

SYRIA

ISRAEL

Jerusalem

Dead Sea

EGYPT

JORDAN

0   100 Miles
0   100 Kilometers

The Arab-Israeli War of 1948–1949
UN partition of Palestine, 1947
■ Proposed Jewish state
■ Proposed Arab state
— Boundary of Israel after UN truce, 1949

SAUDI ARABIA

workers formed the core of the nationalist movement. High taxes imposed by white settlers further spurred the decolonization movement. Leaders who had studied abroad were determined to have their freedom.

In sub-Saharan Africa, increasingly discontented peoples challenged the European imperialists. In the British-controlled Gold Coast of West Africa, Kwame Nkrumah (KWAH-may ehn-KROO-mah), formerly a poor schoolteacher, led the region's diverse inhabitants in Gandhi-style civil disobedience. A student in the United States in 1936, Nkrumah had been radicalized by Italy's invasion and defeat of Ethiopia. After the war, he joined fellow West Africans in London in planning African liberation. Nkrumah returned to the Gold Coast, leading protests against British rule that resulted in the independence of Ghana in 1957 (see Seeing the Past: African Liberation on Cloth).

Nkrumah lobbied for the unity of all African states: "How except by our united efforts will the richest and still enslaved part of our continent be freed from colonial occupation . . . ?" he asked in 1963.[10] Still, individual nation-building remained the order of the day. In the most populous African colony, Nigeria, workers and veterans struck for higher wages, better working conditions, and greater respect. During a miners' strike in 1949, the British police commissioner ordered his troops to shoot because, he said, the miners were "dancing around and around" and chanting "We are all one."[11] Nigeria gained its freedom in 1960 and developed a federal-style government. In African states where the population was mostly black, independence came less violently than in more mixed-race territory (see Map 27.5).

European settlers along Africa's eastern coast and in the southern and central areas of the continent violently resisted independence movements. In British East Africa, white settlers protected their privilege by driving blacks off the land and into cities. Some of these displaced persons, including returning veterans, began forming secret political groups to oppose British rule and recover land from the whites. The rebels, who were mostly from the Kikuyu (kih-KOO-you) ethnic group and included women who served as provisioners, messengers, and weapons stealers, called themselves the Land and Freedom Army. Whites referred to them as "Mau Mau." The British rounded up Kikuyus by the hundreds of thousands, placed them in secret concentration camps, and slaughtered an estimated 150,000 to 320,000. Nonetheless, the Land and Freedom Army helped gain Kenya's independence in 1963.

As the wave of liberation spread, colonial leaders in North and West Africa, where European settlers and military forces were few, convinced France to leave peaceably. Declared an integral part of France, Algeria was another story altogether. In 1954 the Front for National Liberation (FLN) rose up, broadcasting by

SEEING THE PAST

African Liberation on Cloth

Many African societies used commemorative textiles such as this example from Nigeria to mark special occasions. Nations gaining their independence from the European powers issued such textiles in the 1960s and 1970s as they threw off imperial rule. This cloth clearly proclaims "Independence," but others presented the portraits of liberation heroes as they announced their freedom to the world. The textiles, sometimes fashioned by women artisans, were immensely popular, hanging in homes and public buildings or serving as clothing. Paradoxically, the independence textiles symbolized unity in the face of divisions among regions and ethnic groups within a country that had been artificially created by imperialist designs.

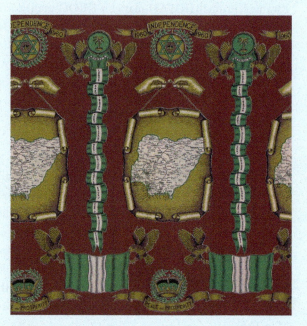

Nigerian Commemorative Textile

Examining the Evidence

1. What was the purpose of these commemorative textiles?

2. What accounts for their popularity, given the many divisions among the peoples of new nations?

3. Why would some commemorative textiles feature brutal dictators?

radio the FLN's goal: the "restoration of the Algerian state, sovereign, democratic, and social, within the framework of the principles of Islam."[12] The French sent in more than four hundred thousand troops to protect over one million European settlers by crushing the uprising.

Neither side fought according to the rules of warfare. The French tortured native people, mutilating and beheading them. The FLN fought a guerrilla war, fading

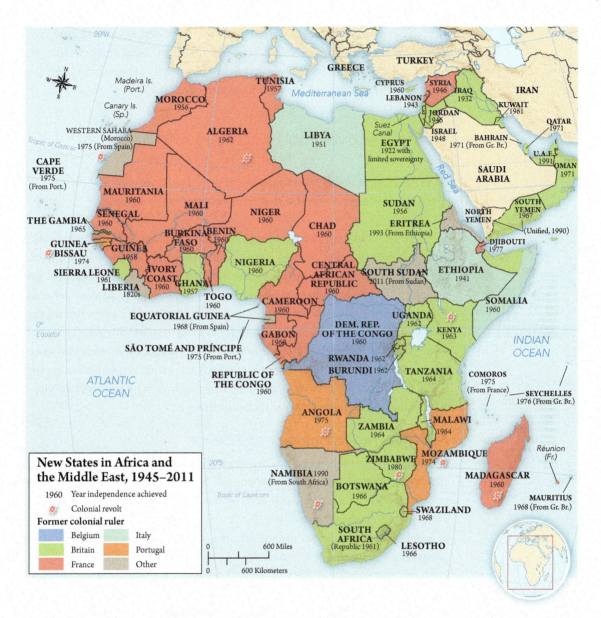

New States in Africa and the Middle East, 1945–2011

1960   Year independence achieved

✹   Colonial revolt

Former colonial ruler

Belgium		Italy	
Britain		Portugal	
France		Other	

≡ **MAP 27.5   New States in Africa and the Middle East, 1945–2011**   The British, French, and Belgians fought brutal wars in Kenya, Algeria, and Congo, where they killed tens of thousands of local people. Other African countries became independent relatively peacefully, while in contrast, the superpowers and other nations competed fiercely for Middle Eastern oil and control of the region's other assets, such as the Suez Canal.

into the mountains and countryside, while Algerian women, defying gender stereotypes, planted bombs in European cafés and carried weapons to assassination sites. Outgunned, Algerian nationalists used modern public relations methods to turn the United States and other influential nations against the French, convincing them that France stood in the way of Algerian economic development and the fight against communism. In 1962 French president Charles de Gaulle negotiated independence for Algeria, which, like other newly independent states, now faced the challenge of establishing an effective, unified nation.

World Recovery in the 1950s and 1960s

FOCUS What were the major elements of recovery in different parts of the world in the decades following World War II?

The Cold War and struggles against colonialism took place alongside remarkable economic growth. Some parts of the world had prospered during the war. Latin America, for example, benefited from the wartime demand for raw materials and manufactured goods. Cuba's exports of sugar grew almost 300 percent between 1938 and the end of the war. Other peoples, within a few decades after suffering the devastation of total war, came to live longer lives and to enjoy a higher standard of living than ever before. In Europe this newfound prosperity was celebrated as an "economic miracle." As some governments took increasing responsibility for the health and well-being of citizens, the menacing Cold War also saw rapid development of the welfare state and scientific breakthroughs.

Advances in Technology and Science

Revolutionary developments in technology and science reshaped global society after World War II and contributed to well-being, if unevenly. Wartime technology adapted for civilian use—such as the massive development of nuclear power—continued to improve daily life. The spread of technology allowed billions of people access to radio and television news, to new forms of contraceptives to control reproduction, and to the advantages of computers. Satellites orbiting the earth reported weather conditions, relayed telephone signals, and collected military intelligence. While the "information revolution" changed politics, it also made everyday life more agreeable. In the last third of the century, television, computers, and telecommunications linked once-remote towns to urban capitals on the other side of the globe, acting as a crossroads for ideas and beliefs.

Americans embraced television in the 1950s; following the postwar recovery, television became a major entertainment and communications medium in countries around the world. As with radio, many governments funded television broadcasting with tax dollars and initially controlled TV programming to avoid what they perceived as the substandard fare offered by American commercial TV.

The Indian official in charge of early television programming forbade pop music, for example, and some European countries initially broadcast mostly classical drama and news. States thus began to organize their citizens' leisure time and their daily lives.

Communications satellites in the 1960s challenged state-sponsored television by transmitting to a worldwide audience. What statesmen and intellectuals considered the junk programming of the United States—soap operas, game shows, sitcoms—arrived dubbed in the native language. More interesting to Brazilians, however, were their own soap operas and those imported from Mexico. Amid censorship of news under the Brazilian dictatorship, soap operas seemed to show real life, and Mexican programming added to their pool of information. Educational programming united the far-flung population of the USSR with shows featuring Soviet specialties such as ballet. By late in the century, houses in remote African oases sported satellite dishes to become globally connected. Heads of state such as Fidel Castro, however, used television to maintain national leadership by addressing Cuban citizens. Thus the medium of television operated nationally and globally.

Similarly, the computer reshaped work in science, defense, and industry and eventually came to affect everyday life. As large as a gymnasium in the 1940s, computing machines shrank, becoming far less expensive and fantastically more powerful, thanks to the development of sophisticated digital electronic circuitry implanted on tiny silicon chips. The pace and patterns of work changed, by speeding up tasks and making them easier. Many livelihoods became obsolete. In garment making, for example, experienced workers no longer painstakingly figured out how to arrange patterns on cloth for maximum economy. Instead, a computer gave instructions for the best positioning of pattern pieces. In 1981 the French phone company launched a public Internet server, the Minitel—a forerunner of the World Wide Web—through which French users made dinner reservations, performed stock transactions, and gained information. Whereas in the Industrial Revolution, machine capabilities had replaced physical power, in the information revolution computer technology augmented brainpower. Computers, in the words of one scientist, provided "boundless opportunities . . . to resolve the puzzles of cosmology, of life, and of the society of man."[13] Others maintained that computers programmed people, reducing human capacity for inventiveness and problem solving.

The Space Age

After the Soviet launch of the satellite *Sputnik* in 1957, the space race took off as part of the technology revolution. The competition produced increasingly complex space flights that tested humans' ability to survive space exploration and its

☰ **Computer Programmers in the 1940s** Many women, such as these U.S. workers, were among the first programmers of early computers, perhaps because the process resembled large telephone operations. Technological advances brought increasing miniaturization of ever more powerful computers—a true knowledge revolution that shaped the development of postindustrial society and globalization.

effects. Astronauts walked in space, endured weeks (and later, years) in orbit, docked with other craft, fixed satellites, and carried out experiments for the military and private industry. Meanwhile, a series of unmanned rockets filled the earth's gravitational sphere with weather, television, intelligence, and other communications satellites. In July 1969, U.S. astronauts Neil Armstrong and Edwin "Buzz" Aldrin walked on the moon's surface—a climactic moment in the space race.

Alongside Cold War rivalry, the space age offered the possibility of global political cooperation and communication. The exploration of space came to involve the participation of many countries. In 1965, an international consortium headed by the United States launched the first commercial communications satellite, *Intelsat I*, and by 1969, with the launch of *Intelsat III* covering the Indian Ocean region, the entire world was linked via satellite. Although some 50 percent of satellites were for military and espionage purposes, the rest promoted international communication and were sustained by transnational cooperation: by the 1970s some 150 countries collaborated to maintain the global satellite system. Satellite transmission eventually allowed billions of people worldwide to watch feats of space exploration, not to mention World Cup soccer games and twenty-four-hour news broadcasts.

Experiments in space brought advances in pure science. Unmanned spacecraft provided data on cosmic radiation, magnetic fields, and infrared sources. Utilizing a range of technology, including the radio telescope—which depicted space by receiving, measuring, and calculating nonvisible rays—these findings reinforced the so-called big bang theory of the origins of the universe and brought other new information, such as data on the composition of other planets, to scientists around the world. Long before politicians resolved Cold War differences, scientists were sharing their knowledge of the universe.

A New Scientific Revolution

Sophisticated technologies extended to the life sciences, bringing dramatic health benefits and ultimately changing reproduction itself. In 1952, English molecular biologist Francis Crick and American biologist James Watson discovered the configuration of DNA, the material in a cell's chromosomes that carries hereditary information. Crick and Watson showed how the double helix of the DNA molecule splits in cellular reproduction to form the basis of each new cell, providing the chemical pattern for an individual organism's life. Growing understanding of nucleic acids and proteins advanced knowledge of viruses and bacteria. Effective worldwide campaigns—again, bridging the Cold War divide—against polio, tetanus, syphilis, tuberculosis, and such dangerous childhood diseases as mumps and measles followed, thus boosting population. Understanding how DNA works also allowed scientists both to alter the makeup of plants and to bypass natural animal reproduction in a process called cloning—obtaining the cells of an organism and dividing or reproducing them (in an exact copy) in a laboratory.

Science and technology influenced the most intimate areas of human relations—sexuality and procreation. In postwar urban societies the growing availability of reliable birth-control devices permitted young people to begin sexual relations earlier, with less risk of pregnancy. These trends accelerated in the 1960s when the birth-control pill, developed in a Mexican research institute and later mass-produced in the United States and tested on women in Puerto Rico and other developing areas, came on the Western market and then spread around the world.

Childbirth and conception itself became the work of doctors operating in hospitals and laboratories. In 1978, the first "test-tube baby," Louise Brown, was born to an English couple. She had been conceived when her mother's eggs were fertilized with her father's sperm in a laboratory dish and then implanted in her mother's uterus—a complex process called *in vitro fertilization*.

Science also helped boost grain harvests around the world. In Mexico City in the 1940s, a team of scientists led by Norman Borlaug experimented with blending Japanese strains of wheat with Mexican ones, devising hardier seeds that raised yields by some 70 percent. Borlaug became part of "an army of hunger fighters," as he called those who next worked to devise rice that would thrive in India, the Philippines, and other countries.[14] Large landowners who could afford the irrigation, fertilizers, and the new seeds themselves profited, while high costs caused many small farmers to fail. Still, the **Green Revolution** helped countries such as India, where rural poverty fell from close to 50 percent of the population in the 1960s to 30 percent in the 1990s.

Green Revolution
The application of DNA and other scientific knowledge to the production of seeds and fertilizers to raise agricultural productivity in developing parts of the world.

Expanding Economic Prosperity

In the immediate aftermath of World War II, governments rebuilt infrastructure—transportation, communications, and industrial capacity. Food and consumer goods became more plentiful, and demand for them increased. The growth in production alleviated unemployment among those whose livelihoods the war had destroyed. Oil-rich countries imported people from many parts of Asia and Africa to perform menial labor: women from the Philippines, Indonesia, and the Caribbean were among those who migrated as nurses, nannies, and household help. Northern Europe, short of labor, arranged for "guest" workers to arrive from Sicily, Turkey, and North and sub-Saharan Africa to help rebuild cities. The outbreak of war in Korea in 1950 encouraged manufacturing in Japan and elsewhere. Korea itself, however, was devastated. The Cold War thus spurred economic advance in some parts of the world while others experienced political convulsions including those of proxy wars and nation-building.

In Europe international cooperation and economic growth led to the creation in 1957 of the **European Economic Community** (EEC), known popularly as the Common Market, the foundation of the European Union of the 1990s. Belgium, the Netherlands, Luxembourg, France, West Germany, and Italy established the EEC, which reduced tariffs among the six partners and worked to develop common trade policies. According to its founders, the EEC aimed to "prevent the race of nationalism, which is the true curse of the modern world."[15] Increased cooperation produced great economic rewards for the six members: the Italian economy, which had lagged behind that of France and Germany, boomed, and as additional countries joined from the 1970s on, many of them flourished.

Even as new nations came into being, the trend in postwar and postcolonial government was to intervene in people's everyday lives to improve social conditions and thus to prevent the political extremism and discontent of the 1930s. This policy became known as the **welfare state**, a term suggesting that, in addition to building their military power, states would guarantee a minimum level of well-being for their citizens. Postwar governments devised forms of financial assistance—including family allowances, healthcare and medical benefits, and programs for pregnant women—to promote overall welfare. The combination of better material conditions and state provision of health care dramatically extended life expectancy.

State initiatives in other areas also helped raise the standard of living. Government-built atomic power plants brought electrification to many more rural areas. States sponsored construction to alleviate housing shortages resulting from three decades of economic depression and war. Such efforts often drained the economies of newly independent countries. Moreover, housing shortages persisted, and

European Economic Community A consortium of European countries established in 1957 to promote free trade and economic cooperation among its members.

welfare state The postwar system of government-sponsored programs designed to provide citizens with basic standards of health care, housing, and income.

growing cities like Rio de Janeiro were surrounded by shantytowns. Still, many of the world's cities were refurbished or gained a modern look.

Citizen welfare became the backbone of politics in many regions. In Argentina, for example, army colonel Juan Perón became president in 1946 on a platform of worker well-being and an end to British and U.S. financial domination. Hundreds of thousands of workers backed Perón's array of economic benefits for "the shirt-less ones" and his dramatic use of surplus government funds to free Argentina from Western business imperialism. While Perón added to workers' wallets, his wife Eva, who was from the lower class, won their hearts. During the Depression, at the age of fifteen, she had migrated from the countryside to Buenos Aires, quickly succeeding in radio and film. As Perón's wife, "Evita" joined him in providing the poor with housing and other benefits, which she virtually extorted from businesses. In exchange, the masses, if not the upper classes, loyally supported the Peróns. After Eva Perón's death from cancer at the age of thirty-two, in 1955, the military drove Perón out, reducing both the welfare state and anti-Western rhetoric.

≡ **Rio de Janeiro** In 1946 Brazil threw off its dictatorship and became a democracy. Central to modernizing the nation was the construction of the Maracanã in Rio de Janeiro, the largest soccer stadium in the world at the time. Other modern urban construction followed, but as migrants arrived from rural areas many lived in shantytowns on Rio's outskirts, shown in the lower left of this photograph.

Building and Rebuilding Communism

Two countries in particular bore the brunt of World War II in terms of population loss and outright destruction. The Soviet Union lost between forty-two and forty-seven million people, new estimates suggest, while the Japanese invasion and more than a decade of civil war killed some thirty million people in China. Both Stalin and Mao Zedong were committed to rebuilding their countries, and both revived the crushing methods that had served before to modernize and industrialize traditional peasant economies.

Stalin's death in 1953 created an opening for a less repressive society in the USSR. Political prisoners in the labor camps pressed for reform, leading to the release of millions. Growing protests over shortages of food and other items led the government to increase production of consumer goods. Nikita Khrushchev, an illiterate coal miner before the Bolshevik Revolution, outmaneuvered other rivals to become in 1955 the undisputed leader of the Soviet Union, but he did so without the usual executions. At a party congress in 1956, Khrushchev attacked the "cult of personality" Stalin had built about himself and announced that Stalinism did not equal socialism. The so-called Secret Speech—it was not published in the USSR but became widely known—sent tremors through hard-line Communist parties around the world.

In 1956, discontented Polish railroad workers successfully struck for better wages. Inspired by the Polish example, Hungarians rebelled later that year, eventually targeting the entire communist system. Tens of thousands of protesters filled the streets of Budapest, urged on by the U.S. bloc. Soviet troops moved in, killing tens of thousands and causing hundreds of thousands more to flee to the West. The U.S. refusal to act showed that, despite its rhetoric of "freedom," it would not risk World War III by military intervention in the Soviet bloc.

In the People's Republic of China, Mao Zedong faced the problem of rebuilding a war-torn peasant society. Like Stalin, Mao saw modernization as the answer. In 1959, he initiated the **Great Leap Forward**, an economic plan to increase industrial production. The plan ordered country people to stop tending their farms and instead produce steel from their shovels, pots, and pans in their own small backyard furnaces (see Reading the Past: The Great Leap Forward in China). This plan of industrial production proved to be a disaster, as much of the do-it-yourself iron and steel was worthless. Meanwhile, the halting of agriculture resulted in massive famine. An estimated thirty million people died, and millions more went hungry. "A revolution is not a dinner party," Mao remarked with grim irony, as his government touted the virtues of being thin.[16]

Great Leap Forward The Chinese Communist program of the mid-1950s designed to push the country ahead of all others in industrial and other production.

READING THE PAST

The Great Leap Forward in China

In 1949, life in China changed for most people because of the Communist Revolution that brought Mao Zedong to power. Kang Zhengguo was a student in the 1950s as the full weight of change began. His grandfather owned land and was a Buddhist leader; his father was a highly trained engineer. In this early passage from Zhengguo's memoir, he describes one of Mao's earliest programs, "The Great Leap Forward," when China was supposed to industrialize rapidly as the Soviets had done. Later parts of his memoir present bloody and terrifying incidents, including those that he himself endured.

> In 1958, the year of the Great Leap Forward, the nation became caught up in a frenzy of smelting "back-yard steel." It was our "glorious mission" to donate scrap iron to this cause, so our school playground, like most other work units, was heaped with it, along with piles of burned charcoal. Some enthusiasts had tossed in their pots and pans or drawer handles for good measure, even if they were made of copper or tin. The student cafeteria had been temporarily converted into a foundry, equipped with a mighty blower that shook the classrooms with its roar and filled the air with a sooty purplish haze. Nobody seemed to have time for mundane pursuits like eating and sleeping. The upperclassmen manned the furnaces around the clock with holiday spirit, belting out all of their new songs and charring for the molten "steel" as it poured out of the furnaces. Once it congealed into hard black slag, we deemed it a success and swathed it in bright red silk. Then, banging on drums and gongs and carrying big red paper placards that read "SURPASS ENGLAND AND CATCH UP TO AMERICA," we marched it triumphantly over to the district party committee.
>
> Classes were canceled more often than not, and even we younger students had to help out at the foundry.

Source: Kang Zhengguo, *Confessions: An Innocent Life in Communist China*, trans. Susan Wilf (New York: W. W. Norton, 2007), 14–15.

Examining the Evidence

1. What impression does this passage give you of the Great Leap Forward?

2. What is the place of politics in education, as suggested by this excerpt?

3. How would you describe the industrialization taking place during the Great Leap Forward?

4. How would you describe the student life?

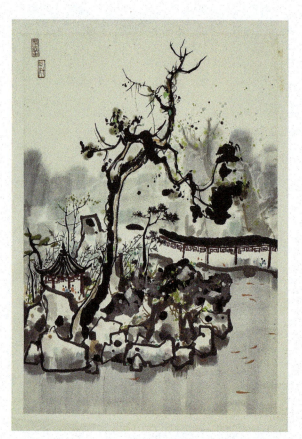

≣ **Wu Guanzhong, *Gardens of Suzhou*** Wu Guanzhong's studies in Europe influenced his art after his return to China to teach in Beijing in the 1950s. Forbidden to paint during the Cultural Revolution of the 1960s, Wu returned to his hybrid style, which mixed abstract representations from the West with Chinese styles that he modernized in his work. (Photograph courtesy of Sotheby's Picture Library)

In the early 1960s, Mao's slipping popularity led to the brutal **Cultural Revolution**. To break opposition to the Great Leap Forward, Mao turned to China's youth to reinvigorate the revolution. Brought up to revere Mao, young people responded to his call to rid society of the "four olds"—old customs, old habits, old culture, and old ideas. In Mao's name they destroyed artistic treasures and crushed individual lives. Any kind of skilled person was branded un-Communist and thus criminal.

One such target of the Cultural Revolution was painter Wu Guanzhong. Wu went to Paris in 1947 on a government scholarship to learn the techniques of Western masters, but after three years Mao's administration summoned him back to teach in Beijing. By the mid-1950s, the Chinese leadership had come to see Wu's work, which mixed Chinese and Western styles, as a "poisonous weed." Wu was sent to the countryside, where he was forbidden to paint or to talk to his wife, who accompanied him. After Mao's death in 1976, the brutality of the Cultural Revolution eased. Wu Guanzhong's reputation as one of the world's outstanding artists was restored, and the skills of the Chinese people in the arts and industry were once again valued.

Cultural Revolution
The Chinese Communist program of the 1960s and early 1970s carried out by Mao Zedong's youthful followers to remake Chinese thought, behavior, and everyday life.

Cultural Dynamism amid Cold War

⬎ **FOCUS** How did the experience of world war, decolonization, and Cold War affect cultural life and thought?

As the Cold War unfolded, people around the world vigorously discussed the devastating World War II experience, the effects of colonialism, the rationale for decolonization, and the dangers of the Cold War itself. Writers tried to understand the meaning of war and genocide. Literature exploring concepts of freedom and liberation poured out of Africa, Latin America, and Asia and reached the West, where oppressed minorities were likewise demanding better treatment. Students and women also took up the cause. Thus, the postwar period was one of intense cultural ferment.

Confronting the Heritage of World War

In 1944, during the last months of the war, University of Tokyo professor Tanabe Hajime began a soul-searching book, turning to Buddhism for enlightenment. In *Philosophy as Matonetics* (an act of repentant confession), Tanabe urged the Japanese to enter higher realms of wisdom as they faced defeat. His program for a return to Buddhist values allowed the Japanese to see in their defeat a lofty purpose, elevating them above the brute power politics of the Western victors. Such programs for exalting the wartime losers took place alongside intense indoctrination in democratic values and the dramatic trials of Axis leaders conducted at Nuremberg, Germany, in 1945 and in Tokyo, Japan, in 1946. As defendants received long imprisonment or death sentences, the trials introduced the concept of "crimes against humanity" and an international order based on human rights.

Nonetheless, civilians in the defeated Axis nations struggled to survive, causing many Japanese and Germans to believe that they were the main victims of the war. The Cold War helped reinforce that view when American officials began to rely on the intelligence reports of high-ranking Japanese militarists and Nazis, casting war crimes as trivial when compared to the Soviet menace.

Memoirs of the death camps and tales of the resistance told a starkly different story. Anne Frank's *Diary of a Young Girl* (1947) was the poignant record of a German Jewish teenager hidden with her family for two years in the back of an Amsterdam warehouse before they were discovered and sent to concentration camps, where all died except Anne's father. Confronted with the small miseries of daily life and the grand evils of Nazism, Frank wrote that she never stopped believing that "people are really good at heart."[17] After years of censorship, Japanese publishers slaked the thirst of readers with collections of letters from soldiers that quickly became best-sellers. Into the twenty-first century, filmmakers around the world depicted the memories and nightmares of World War II.

By the 1950s, **existentialism**—a philosophy that explored the meaning of human existence in a world where evil flourished—had become globally popular. The principal theorists of existentialism, Frenchmen Jean-Paul Sartre and Albert Camus, asked what "being" meant, given what they saw as the absence of God and the breakdown of morality under Nazism. "Being," or existing, to them, was not birth into the natural world. Instead, through action and choice, including political

existentialism A philosophy prominent after World War II, developed primarily by French thinkers, that stresses the importance of active engagement with the world in the creation of an authentic existence.

resistance, the individual created an "authentic" or meaningful existence. In 1949, Simone de Beauvoir, Sartre's lifetime companion, published *The Second Sex*, the twentieth century's most influential work on women. According to Beauvoir, most women failed to lead authentic lives, instead devoting themselves to reproduction and motherhood because it was society's expectation. Failing to become a self or subject through considered action, they had become its opposite—an object, or "Other," who followed norms set by men. Translated into many languages, Beauvoir's book urged women to create their own freedom.

Cold War Culture

In the effort to win the Cold War, both sides poured vast sums of money into high and popular culture. The United States secretly channeled government money to promote specific artists and favorable journalism around the world. In the USSR, official writers churned out spy stories, while espionage novels also topped best-seller lists in the West. *Casino Royale* (1953), by the British author Ian Fleming, introduced James Bond, British intelligence agent 007, whose wits and physical prowess Communist and other political villains tested. Soviet pilots would not take off for flights when the work of Yulian Simyonov, the Russian counterpart of Ian Fleming, was playing on radio or television.

In postwar Europe and the United States, everyday life also revolved around the growing availability of material goods and household conveniences. The advertising business boomed, enticing war-deprived adults and rollicking youth alike. America came to stand for freedom and plenty versus the scarcity in the Communist world. Women's magazines in the West publicized a sexy "new look," while Communists displayed women's utilitarian, but tasteful garb. European Communists wanted to ban American products such as Coca-Cola, while the Soviets also emphasized a warm, private life without so wide an array of consumer goods.

Radio was key to spreading Cold War culture and values; both the United States and the USSR used the medium to broadcast news and propaganda. During the late 1940s and early 1950s, the Voice of America, broadcasting in thirty-eight languages from one hundred transmitters, provided an alternative source of news for people around the world. The Soviet counterpart broadcast in Russian around the clock, stressing its Communist culture while also jamming U.S. programming. Both sides used the media to whip up fear of enemies within. People heard reports of nuclear buildups; in school, children rehearsed what to do in case of nuclear war; and some families built bomb shelters in their backyards. Art became part of the Cold War, along with consumer goods and books. The USSR promoted an official Communist culture based on the socialist realist style highlighting the heroism of the working classes. Dissenters in the USSR were both feared and bullied. For example, Khrushchev forced Boris Pasternak to refuse the 1958 Nobel Prize in Literature because Pasternak's novel *Doctor Zhivago* (1957) cast doubt on the glory of the Bolshevik Revolution and affirmed the value of the individual. The government sponsored classical training in ballet and music and harassed innovators in the arts. When a show of Western abstract art opened in the Soviet Union, Khrushchev yelled that it was "dog shit."

Liberation Culture

In decolonizing areas, thinkers mapped out new visions of how to construct the future. In the 1950s and 1960s Frantz Fanon, a black psychiatrist from the French Caribbean colony of Martinique, wrote that the mind of the colonized person had been traumatized by the brutal imposition of an alien culture. Ruled by guns, the colonized person knew only violence and would thus naturally decolonize by means of violence. Translated into many languages, Fanon's *Black Skin, White Masks* (1952) and *The Wretched of the Earth* (1961) discussed how to "decolonize" one's mind. Nigerian novelist Chinua Achebe's trilogy about generations of a Nigerian family (1958–1964) boldly detailed Africans' painful choices as British colonialism entered people's lives, tempting and even absorbing them. South African writer Bessie Head, the daughter of a white mother and an African father, showed characters dancing on the edge of madness because of their complicated identities springing from colonialism, clashing ethnicities, and education. A teacher in Head's novel *Maru* (1971) has an English education but is despised by other Africans because she belongs to the darkest-skinned "Bushmen." As with colonialism itself, independence was confusing, with the relationship between tradition and freedom to be puzzled out.

Ideas about liberation circled the world. Mao Zedong's "Little Red Book" contained brief maxims intended to guide hundreds of millions of postcolonial citizens. Fanon's ideas also circulated among Africans, North Americans, and Latin Americans. They intersected with those of Jamaica-born Marcus Garvey, who in the interwar years had promoted a "back to Africa" movement as the way for African Americans to escape U.S. racial discrimination. In the 1960s physician and upper-class guerrilla warrior Che Guevara, though a Marxist, advocated against the centralized and dictatorial Marxism of the USSR and China. He popularized a compassionate Marxism based on appreciation of the oppressed, not domination of them.

Liberation movements throughout the world included African Americans' agitation for civil rights in the 1950s. African American troops had fought to defeat Nazi genocide and the cause of white racial supremacy; now their goal was to overcome white racial superiority at home in the United States. In 1954, the U.S.

Supreme Court declared segregated education unconstitutional in *Brown v. Board of Education* as talented individuals emerged to lead the civil rights movement. Martin Luther King Jr., a minister from Georgia, galvanized African Americans to Gandhian nonviolence despite murderous white retaliation. By the 1960s, other activists came to follow thinkers such as Fanon, proclaiming "black power" to achieve rights through violence if necessary. Racism belied American claims to moral superiority in the Cold War, while civil rights leaders publicized the massive cost of the space program despite minority poverty. Criticism at home and abroad prompted President John F. Kennedy to introduce civil rights legislation forbidding segregation or discrimination based on "race, color, national origin, religion, and sex."

≡ **Mexico City Protest, 1968** In Mexico City, which in the spring of 1968 was about to host the summer Olympics, university students protested police violence and government repression after the slaying of several high school students. They, too, were mowed down by the police. Notice in this photograph an element of student protest common across the world: a banner featuring the revolutionary Che Guevara.

Despite civil rights legislation, change came too slowly for some minority activists. Among those were César Chavez and Dolores Huerta, who in the 1960s led oppressed Mexican American migrant workers in the California grape agribusiness to nonviolent resistance in their struggle for their right to collective bargaining and for an end to discrimination. Chavez knew their plight firsthand—he had lived in miserable conditions as a son of migrant workers. A teacher had put a sign around his neck: "I am a clown. I speak Spanish." Huerta—a "firebrand," she was called—had attended community college but faced racial discrimination despite her education. Both Chicano and African American activists identified more with decolonizing people than with other Americans; like them, they needed to protect themselves against antagonistic whites.

Young people, critical of racism, militarism, the war in Vietnam, and the environmentally harmful effects of technology, closed down classes in campuses around the world. In western Europe, students went on strike, invading administration offices to protest their inferior education and status. They called themselves a proletariat—an exploited working class in the new high-tech, service society—and, rejecting the Soviets, considered themselves part of a New Left. With their long hair, communal living, and scorn for sexual chastity, students proclaimed their rejection of middle-class values.

Women around the world also turned to activism, calling for equal rights and an end to gender discrimination.

Middle-class women eagerly responded to the international best-seller *The Feminine Mystique* (1963) by American journalist Betty Friedan. Pointing to the stagnating talents of many housewives, Friedan helped organize the National Organization for Women in 1966 to lobby for equal pay and legal reforms. Women worldwide demonstrated on behalf of such issues as abortion rights and were soon joined by gays demanding the decriminalization of their sexuality. African American women pointed to the "double jeopardy" of being "black and female." Many realized that men in protest organizations devalued women just as the society at large did. As African American activist Angela Davis complained, women aiming for equality supposedly "wanted to rob [male protesters] of their manhood."[18] Some concrete changes resulted. After the war, women in Chile and other Latin American countries lobbied successfully for the vote, while in India women persuaded the government to take action to improve job prospects and remedy a range of abuses. In Catholic Italy, feminists won the rights to divorce, to gain access to birth-control information, and to obtain legal abortions. The demand for protection from rape, incest, and battering became the focus of thousands of women's groups, as they combated a long-held social value—the inferiority of women.

Protests erupted in the Soviet bloc too, with students at a Czech May Day rally in 1967 publicly chanting, "The only good communist is a dead one." In 1967 the Czechoslovak Communist Party took up reform when Alexander Dubček (DOOB-chehk), head of the Slovak branch of the party, called for more openness, gaining support from party officials, technocrats, and intellectuals. With censorship ending and political groups allowed to form, the Prague Spring had begun—"an orgy of free expression," one Czech journalist called the almost nonstop political debate that followed.[19] Then in August 1968, Soviet tanks rolled into Prague in a massive show of antirevolutionary force. Citizens turned to sabotage and self-immolation to defend their new rights. Still, the Cold War continued.

COUNTERPOINT: The Bandung Conference, 1955

↘ **FOCUS** How did the Bandung Conference and its aims represent an alternative to the Cold War division of the globe?

In April 1955, Achmed Sukarno, who led the struggle for Indonesian independence from the Dutch, hosted a conference of emerging nations in Bandung, Indonesia. The Bandung Conference was meant to ensure the independence of the

The Bandung Conference In 1955, leaders participating in the Bandung Conference shared the goal of building unity among emerging nations while they began a policy of "nonalignment" in the Cold War. This policy was hard for many to maintain because the need for support was so great in regions devastated by imperial pillaging and total war.

new Asian and African nations despite the temptations of aid from the superpowers. The conference was thus a counterpoint to the superpowers' Cold War hold on international politics.

Representatives from twenty-nine countries, most of them newly independent, attended. They constituted a who's who of anti-colonialism: Kwame Nkrumah of Ghana, Gamal Abdel Nasser of Egypt, Zhou Enlai of China, and Ho Chi Minh of Vietnam alongside Sukarno and Jawaharlal Nehru, prime minister of India. Activists throughout the world were inspired by their independent, even defiant, stand. Attendee African American author Richard Wright was riveted by the meaning of such an assembly: "The despised, the insulted, the hurt, the dispossessed—in short, the underdogs of the human race were meeting. . . . Who had thought of organizing such a meeting? And what had these nations in common? Nothing, it seemed to me. . . . This meeting of the rejected was in itself a kind of judgment upon the Western world!"[20] Leaders at the meeting represented more than half the world's population.

Shared Goals

Participants discussed economic development outside the structures of colonialism and the achievement of political well-being without following the dictates of either the Soviet Union or the United States. Nehru argued strongly for nonalignment, maintaining that nations affiliating with one side or the other would lose their identity. Moreover, Nehru claimed, the superpowers had come to equate a nation's worth with its military power. To his mind this was evidence that "greatness sometimes brings quite false values, false standards."[21] In India, Nehru tried to follow a middle course between the superpowers in his policies.

Nehru admired the goals of the UN, including the charter outlining a collective global authority that would adjudicate conflicts and provide military protection to any member threatened by aggression. Meetings of both the UN and, as in Bandung, emerging nations began shifting global issues away from superpower priorities. Human rights, humane treatment, and economic inequities nudged their way into public consciousness despite serious issues dividing conference participants.

Divisive Issues

Among these was the legacy of mistrust between India and Pakistan over their rival claims to the state of Kashmir. The leaders at Bandung argued both in favor of nationalism and in support of movements that transcended nationalism, such as pan-Islam and pan-Africanism. The Bandung Conference also foresaw an evolving recognition of a North-South divide. Those living in the northern half of the globe were wealthy compared with those in the south, impoverished because imperialism's legacy had relegated them to low-paid production of commodities. Overall, however, the Bandung Conference strengthened the new nations' commitment to independence in the face of the superpowers' overwhelming might.

Conclusion

The Cold War began the atomic age and transformed international power politics. The two new superpowers, the Soviet Union and the United States, each built massive atomic arsenals, replacing the former European leadership and menacing the entire world. The Cold War saturated everyday life, producing an atmosphere of division. Within this rivalry an astonishing worldwide recovery occurred based on a burgeoning welfare state and wartime technology converted to peacetime purposes.

Postwar activism of many types—like that of Umm Kulthum—loosened the grip of the colonial powers. From India to Ghana, colonial peoples won their independence. Many, as in the case of Algeria and Kenya, had to take up arms against the brutality of the imperialists to become free. Nation-building in newly independent states, however, turned out to be slow and halting.

As the world grew overall in prosperity, its cultural life focused on eradicating wartime evil and developing theories to explain the struggles of decolonized peoples for full independence. Thinkers questioned Cold War threats of nuclear annihilation while leaders of newly independent nations, through such activities as the Bandung Conference, favored nonalignment with either superpower. This and other activism matured amidst another burst of technological creativity and efforts to improve the world—including putting an end to the Cold War.

✱ review

The major global development in this chapter: The political transformations of the postwar world and their social and cultural consequences.

	Important Events
1945	World War II ends
1947	India and Pakistan win independence
1948	Israel gains independence
1948–1949	Arab-Israeli War
1949	Communists take control of China; Western powers form NATO; USSR detonates atomic bomb; Indonesia gains independence
1950–1953	Korean War
1952	Egypt achieves full independence under Nasser
1953	Death of Stalin
1954	Vietnamese defeat French army at Dien Bien Phu
1956	Khrushchev denounces Stalin; Suez crisis; revolution in Hungary
1957	USSR launches *Sputnik*
1958	Khrushchev forces Boris Pasternak to refuse Nobel Prize in Literature
1961	Construction of the Berlin Wall
1962	Algeria wins independence; Cuban Missile Crisis
c. 1966–1976	Mao Zedong's "Cultural Revolution"

KEY TERMS

Cold War (p. 994)
containment (p. 997)
Cultural Revolution (p. 1020)
decolonization (p. 994)
European Economic
Community (p. 1016)
existentialism (p. 1021)

Great Leap Forward (p. 1018)
Green Revolution (p. 1015)
guerrilla warfare (p. 1006)
North Atlantic Treaty
Organization (p. 999)
Organization of American
States (p. 1002)

Partition (p. 1004)
proxy war (p. 995)
Southeast Asia Treaty
Organization (p. 1003)
Warsaw Pact (p. 1002)
welfare state (p. 1016)

CHAPTER OVERVIEW QUESTIONS

1. How did the Cold War affect the superpowers and the world beyond them?
2. How did the Cold War shape everyday lives and goals?

3. Why did colonial nationalism revive in the postwar world, and how did decolonization affect society and culture?
4. Why did the prewar model of a welfare state spread after World War II, and how did this development affect ordinary people?

MAKING CONNECTIONS

1. Recall Chapters 25 and 26. Why did economic well-being seem so much stronger for three decades after World War II than it had been after World War I?
2. Why did proxy wars play such a constant role in the Cold War? Some historians see these wars as part of a new imperialism. Do you agree?

3. What was the role of culture in shaping the Cold War?
4. What remnants of decolonization and the Cold War still affect life today?

For further research into the topics covered in this chapter, see the Bibliography at the end of the book. For additional primary sources from this period, see *Sources for World in the Making*.

A New Global Age 1989 to the Present

≡ **World in the Making** The Burj Khalifa makes a statement about its home—Dubai, the United Arab Emirates—as a global crossroads. Its name signals regional pride while the tower itself is a hotel that welcomes visitors from around the world. With vast international experience, Tom Wright from England and Kunan Chew from Singapore designed the exterior and the interior, respectively. Like the designers and visitors, many of the men and women who built the tower came from beyond Dubai's borders to keep the world evolving.

backstory

As we saw in Chapter 27, a burst of technological innovation from the 1960s on changed the way many people lived and worked. In much of the West, the service sector surpassed industry and manufacturing as the most important components of the economy, with knowledge-based jobs leading the way. At the same time, industrial jobs were shipped overseas, and countries such as China and Japan joined the United States and Germany as centers of global manufacturing. As the economic balance of power began to shift, the United States and the Soviet Union found it more and more difficult to shape and control events around the world. In 1989, internal tensions led to the collapse of the Soviet Union, bringing the Cold War to a close and opening the way for still more dramatic change in the global landscape.

On February 11, 1990, South Africans celebrated the news that Nelson Mandela, deputy head of the African National Congress (ANC), had been freed after three decades in prison. Later that day Mandela stood before some fifty thousand cheering supporters in Cape Town, announcing his determination to end apartheid, the brutal South African system of racial discrimination. "Our path to freedom is irreversible," he stated. "Now is the time to intensify the struggle on all fronts." These were brave words in a society where the minority white population had not hesitated to murder anyone who criticized their racist rule. Black youth in crowded ghettos had taken up arms, protesting repression. By 1994 it was clear that white rule would not hold, and in April of that year nearly 90 percent of South Africans went to the polls, many of them standing for hours in mile-long lines to vote in a free and fair election. One voter summed up his feelings at participating in democracy: "Now I am a human being." The ANC won 62 percent of the vote, as Nelson Mandela became president of South Africa.

Nelson Mandela's release from prison was noted by people around the world. Powerful multinational companies had come to insist on racial equality in hiring at their South African plants, but as the apartheid government continued to torture and kill blacks, Coca-Cola, IBM, and others closed down their factories. The U.S. Congress legislated a boycott of South African products. Other countries took similar measures. The South African economy crashed, giving its leaders a harsh lesson. As satellite television and human rights groups made the brutality of apartheid a concern of people everywhere, Nelson Mandela's release from prison and his election as president of South Africa symbolized a new global stage in human history.

Almost simultaneously, the Cold War ended, accelerating the ongoing process of **globalization**. The abrupt collapse of the Soviet empire between 1989 and 1992 meant that people around the world could envision working and living together as global citizens instead of as dangerous adversaries or as pawns in international politics. Global organizations, regional trade alliances, and international businesses multiplied, while films, books, and other expressions of local culture traveled the world. Migration increased, with many migrants moving to find opportunity or to escape new dangers in Africa, the former Soviet Union, the Middle East, and elsewhere. While improvements in medicine benefited many, globalization also spread infectious diseases worldwide. Interconnectedness, people realized, increased the potential for worldwide economic, environmental, and cultural disasters.

globalization The economic, cultural, political, and social interactions and integration of the world's peoples.

The process of globalization helped advance many national economies, while producing a backlash from those determined to preserve their traditional values, livelihoods, and distinctive identities. In some cases, resistance to globalization included terrorist attacks and surges in populist movements against those seen as responsible for the erosion of their way of life. The Cold War threat of nuclear devastation gave way to a world seemingly in disarray.

As historians, the authors of this book have no firm idea of how recent events will appear a century from now, but in this chapter we consider both the very near past and trends that have in fact evolved over decades and even centuries. In choosing events to recount in this analysis we have used generally accepted criteria for spotting historical significance. We hope—and you can be the judge several decades from now—that this account of our own global age stands the test of time and of history.

OVERVIEW QUESTIONS

The major global development in this chapter: The causes and consequences of intensified globalization.

As you read, consider:

1. What were the elements of globalization in the early twenty-first century?

2. How did globalization affect lives and livelihoods throughout the world?

3. How did globalization affect local cultures?

4. What people do you know whose roots and livelihoods are global?

Ending the Cold War Order

↘ **FOCUS** Why did the Cold War order come to an end?

During the 1970s the superpowers faced internal corruption, competition from oil-producing states and rising Asian economies, and the increasing costs of attempting to control the world beyond their borders. Oil-producing countries brought postindustrial prosperity in the West to a crashing halt. Reformers Mikhail Gorbachev in the USSR and Margaret Thatcher in Great Britain began implementing strikingly new policies in the 1980s to revive their economies. In the Soviet bloc, efforts to restore prosperity ended in failure, and in 1989, the Soviet Empire collapsed. The Cold War came to an abrupt end as the USSR itself dissolved, finally disappearing on December 31, 1991.

A Change of Course in the West

What was the backstory to such dramatic change? One major event was sparked by the draining proxy war in Vietnam. In 1972 U.S. president Richard Nixon took advantage of growing tensions between the two communist giants, China and the USSR, to open relations with China through a formal visit—a high-profile diplomatic victory to counter increasing antiwar protest at home. Within China, the meeting—supported by pragmatist Chinese officials interested in technology and economic growth—helped stop the brutality of Mao's Cultural Revolution. U.S.-Soviet relations advanced as well. Fearful of the Chinese diplomatic advantage, the Soviets joined the United States later that year to sign the first Strategic Arms Limitation Treaty (SALT I), which capped the number of antimissile defenses for each country. In 1975, in the Helsinki Accords, the Western bloc officially acknowledged Soviet territorial gains in World War II in exchange for the Soviets' guarantee of basic human rights.

Meanwhile, tension between Israel and the Arab world dealt Western dominance a major blow. On June 5, 1967, Israeli forces seized Gaza and the Sinai peninsula from Egypt, the Golan Heights from Syria, and the West Bank from Jordan in a stunning victory that came to be known as the Six-Day War (see Map 28.1). Retaliating, in 1973, Egypt and Syria attacked Israel on Yom Kippur. Israel, with assistance from the United States, stopped the assault. Reprisal for U.S. support of Israel followed when the Arab member nations of **OPEC** (Organization of Petroleum Exporting Countries) quadrupled the price of its oil and imposed an embargo of its oil to the United States.

For the first time since imperialism's heyday, the producers of raw materials—not the industrial powers—controlled the flow of commodities and set prices. The oil embargo and price hike caused a significant rise in unemployment in Europe and the United States, and by the mid-1970s inflation soared, discouraging both industrial investment and consumer buying globally—conditions dubbed **stagflation.** Western Europe and Japan cut back on their oil dependence through conservation, but more was clearly needed.

Stagflation forced drastic measures in noncommunist governments in the West. More than anyone, Margaret Thatcher, leader of Britain's Conservative Party and prime minister from 1979 to 1990, reshaped the West's approach and policies in meeting the crisis. She called herself "a nineteenth-century liberal" in reference to the private enterprise she favored; she also rejected the politics of democratic consensus building, calling unions, immigrants, and welfare recipients the enemies of British well-being. Conservatives aimed to end policies based on economic democracy.

OPEC A consortium of oil-producing countries in the Middle East established to control the production and distribution of oil.

stagflation A surge in prices and interest rates combined with high unemployment and a slowdown in economic growth.

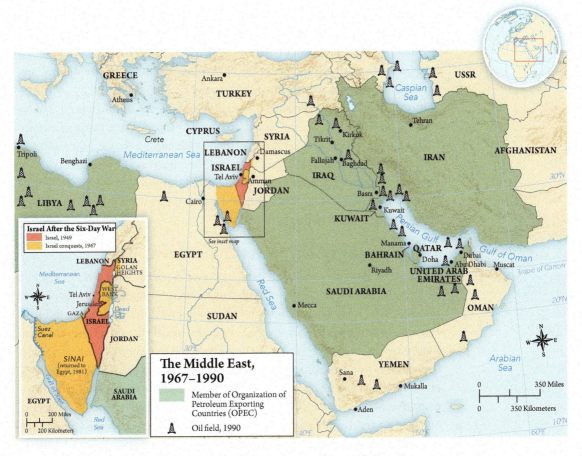

The Middle East, 1967–1990

Israel After the Six-Day War
- Israel, 1949
- Israel conquests, 1967

Member of Organization of
Petroleum Exporting
Countries (OPEC)

Oil field, 1990

≡ **MAP 28.1   The Middle East, 1967–1990** Middle Eastern wealth in oil bolstered
dictators in the region and gave jobs in its oil fields and cities to workers from around the
world. Inequality was great because of the oligarchic control of resources, which created
social and political tensions. The most persistent and violent occurred between Israelis and
Arabs, especially Palestinians.

The policies of Thatcherism followed monetarist, or supply-side, economic theories, which state that inflation results when government pumps money into the
economy at a pace higher than a nation's economic growth rate. Supply-siders thus
advocate tight control of the money supply to keep prices from rising rapidly. They
maintain that the economy as a whole flourishes when businesses grow and prosperity "trickles down" throughout the society. To implement such theories, the
British government cut income taxes on the wealthy to encourage their investment
in industry and the economy more generally. It then increased sales taxes on everyday purchases to compensate for the lost revenue. The result was fairly successful,

but economic growth came at the price of cuts to education and health programs and an increased burden on working people, who bore the brunt of the sales tax and lost jobs when businesses downsized their workforces through technological innovation. The package of economic policies came to be known as **neoliberalism**, and from then on it shaped practices worldwide.

In the United States, President Ronald Reagan followed Thatcher's lead by blaming both "welfare queens" and spendthrift liberals for stagflation and by introducing "Reaganomics," a program of income tax cuts for the wealthy combined with massive reductions in federal spending for infrastructure and education. In foreign policy, Reagan increased military expenditures to fight the USSR, or "evil empire." The combination of tax cuts and military expansion pushed the federal budget deficit to $200 billion by 1986.

The Collapse of Communism in the Soviet Bloc

Facing more difficult challenges than the West, Soviet leaders after Stalin had periodically taken small, half-hearted steps toward reform. In 1985 a new Soviet leader, Mikhail Gorbachev, introduced much more thorough-going reforms and unexpectedly opened an era of change. The son of peasants, Gorbachev had watched for years a lower standard of living unfold. After working a full day, Soviet homemakers stood in long lines to obtain basic commodities. Alcoholism reached crisis levels, diminishing productivity and damaging the nation's morale. The mismanagement of the state-directed economy was so great that 20 to 30 percent of homegrown grain rotted before it could be harvested or shipped to market. A privileged party bureaucracy stifled effective use of technology, while Soviet military spending of 15 to 20 percent of the gross national product (more than double the U.S. proportion) further reduced living standards. A new generation was cynical: "They believe in nothing," a mother said of Soviet youth in 1984.

Gorbachev quickly proposed several new programs to help move forward. A crucial economic reform, *perestroika* ("restructuring"), aimed to reinvigorate the Soviet economy by encouraging more up-to-date technology and introducing such market features as prices and profits. The policy of *glasnost* (translated as "openness") called for disseminating "wide, prompt, and frank information" and for allowing Soviet citizens freer speech. Television reporting opened up, and newspapers, instead of publishing made-up letters praising the Soviet state, printed real ones complaining of shortages and abuse. One outraged "mother of two" protested that the cost-cutting policy of reusing syringes in hospitals was a source of AIDS. "Why should little kids have to pay for the criminal actions of our Ministry of Health?" she asked. "We saw television programs about U.S. racism,"

neoliberalism A theory first promoted by British prime minister Margaret Thatcher, calling for a return to nineteenth-century liberal principles, including welfare-state program reductions and tax cuts for the wealthy to promote economic growth.

one young man reported, "but blacks there had cars, housing, and other goods that we didn't."[1] Gorbachev cut missile production, defusing the Cold War, and in early 1989 withdrew Soviet forces from the disastrous war in Afghanistan.

Dissent had long rippled across the Soviet bloc. In the summer of 1980, Poles reacted to rising food prices by striking and forming an independent labor movement called Solidarity under the leadership of electrician Lech Walesa and crane operator Anna Walentynowicz. Waving Polish flags and parading giant portraits of the Virgin Mary and Pope John Paul II—a Polish native—Solidarity workers occupied factories in protest against the deteriorating conditions of everyday life, which Communist administrations had promised to bolster. The scarcity of food likewise drove tens of thousands of women, who were simultaneously workers and homemakers, into the streets crying, "We're hungry!" In the winter of 1981 Solidarity was outlawed. Yet workers kept meeting and a new culture emerged, publicizing Polish poetry and honest history about the Polish past. The stage was set for communism's downfall.

Communist power in Europe further disintegrated during Gorbachev's visit to China's capital, Beijing, in the spring of 1989. There, hundreds of thousands of students massed in the city's Tiananmen Square to demand democracy and greet Gorbachev as democracy's hero. Workers joined the prodemocracy students: "They say and they do what I have only dared to think," one man commented.[2] As the international press broadcast the events, government forces crushed the swelling movement, killing and executing untold numbers.

The televised protests in Tiananmen Square offered inspiration to opponents of communism in Europe. In June 1989, free parliamentary elections in Poland saw Solidarity candidates overwhelmingly defeat the Communists, and in early 1990, Walesa became president. In Hungary, where citizens had boycotted communist holidays and lobbied against ecologically unsound projects such as the construction of new dams, popular demand led to the dismissal of the Communist Party. Meanwhile, Gorbachev reversed Soviet policy by refusing to interfere in the politics of satellite nations. East Germans had likewise long protested communism, holding peace vigils throughout the 1980s, while satellite news brought them open public debate from West Germany. In the summer of 1989, crowds of East Germans amassed at the borders of the crumbling Soviet bloc. On November 9, East Berliners crossed the Berlin Wall unopposed. Soon thereafter, citizens—East and West—assaulted the wall with sledgehammers and then celebrated the reunification of the two Germanys in 1990.

The fall of communism in Czechoslovakia and Romania formed two extremes. In November 1989 Alexander Dubček, leader of the Prague Spring of 1968, addressed the crowds in Prague's Wenceslas Square after police had beaten student protestors. Almost immediately, the Communist leadership resigned, in a bloodless or "velvet" revolution. By contrast, workers and much of the army rose up and crushed the forces of Romanian dictator Nicolae Ceaușescu (nee-koh-LIE chow-SHES-koo). On Christmas Day 1989, viewers watched on television as the dictator and his wife were executed. Next, Yugoslavia's ethnically diverse population broke up into multiple states (see Map 28.2). When Serbian president Slobodan Milosevic attempted in 1991 to seize territory and create a "greater Serbia," a tragic civil war broke out. Throughout the 1990s, the peoples of the former Yugoslavia fought one another, murdering neighbors.

Meanwhile, the Soviet Union itself collapsed amidst unemployment and escalating scarcity. In 1991, a group of eight antireform top officials, including the powerful head of the Soviet secret police (the KGB), attempted a coup, holding

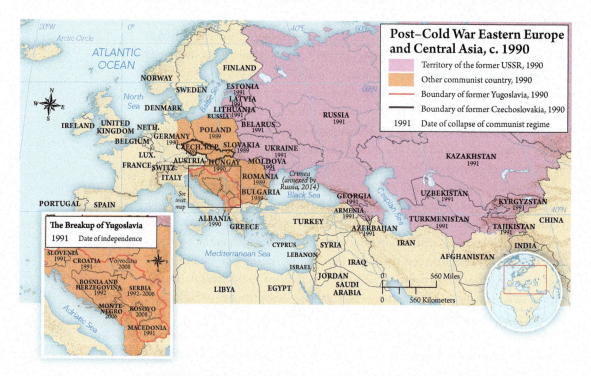

≡ **MAP 28.2 Post–Cold War Eastern Europe and Central Asia, c. 1990** The collapse of the Soviet Union brought social, economic, and political change to the region. Former nations fragmented as regions became independent states; many jobs disappeared; and the postcommunist social order appeared unpredictable. The new Russian nation, however, remained influential as it began drawing on and marketing its natural resources more effectively.

Gorbachev under house arrest. Hundreds of thousands of residents of Moscow and Leningrad filled the streets, and units of the army defected to protect reformers in the Russian Parliament. As the coup failed, the Soviet Union disintegrated and officially dissolved on December 31, 1991.

Regions and Nations in a Globalizing World

⬆ **FOCUS** How has globalization affected the distribution of power and wealth throughout the world in the early twenty-first century?

The end of the Cold War brought many advantages in terms of free speech, human rights, and economic opportunity, and some nations began to flourish as never before, often thanks to adopting new technology. Yet the aftermath was not all positive—the weapons and financial aid given by the superpowers promoted dictatorships and civil wars. Vast differences appeared between regions emerging from colonialism and those that already enjoyed freedom.

North Versus South

During the 1980s and 1990s, world leaders tried to address the growing economic schism between the earth's northern and southern regions. Other than Australians and New Zealanders, southern peoples (those from Africa, South Asia, Southeast Asia, and Latin America) generally had lower standards of living than northerners. Long ruled as colonies or exploited economically by northerners, citizens in the southern regions could not yet count on their governments to provide sufficient welfare services or education. International organizations such as the World Bank and the International Monetary Fund provided loans for economic development, but tied neoliberal conditions, such as cutting government spending for health and education, to such funding. Disease soared and the pace of literacy and capacity-building slowed.

Although the Southern Hemisphere had highly productive agriculture and abundant natural resources, the United States and the European Union—despite their advocacy of free trade—imposed tariffs on imported agricultural products while subsidizing their own farmers so that they could better compete on the world market. These policies raised prices of imported products and lowered them for domestic ones. As Amadou Toumani Touré, president of Mali, complained, "The North cannot massively subsidize its farm exports and at the same time try and give lessons in competitiveness to the South."[3] Tariffs and financial aid to wealthy farmers in the north diverted an estimated $100 billion worth of business away from poorer nations. "We cannot compete against this monster, the United States," one Mexican farmer claimed in 2008. "It's not worth the trouble to plant."[4]

Southern regions also experienced internal barriers to peaceful development. Latin American nations grappled with crushing government corruption, multibillion-dollar debt owed to international banks, widespread crime, and grinding poverty. Nonetheless, some countries—Mexico and Brazil, for example—strengthened their economies by marketing their oil and other natural resources effectively on the global market.

In some southern nations a toxic mixture of military rule, ideological factionalism, and ethnic antagonism resulted in conflict and even genocide from the 1990s on. In 2017 the Buddhist military killed thousands of predominantly Muslim Rohingya in Myanmar and drove hundreds of others from the nation into homeless exile. Earlier, millions had perished in Rwanda, Burundi, and Sudan; others were left starving and homeless while leaders used foreign aid and drained national resources to build up their militaries and enrich themselves. Common to Africa and some other embattled regions was the recruitment of children into armies, further militarizing affected societies.

Advancing Nations in the Global Age

Despite the challenges, the developing world was also the site of dramatic successes. After decades of strife and Cold War pressures, the diverse peoples of India, Brazil, and South Africa rebuilt prosperity by taking advantage of global technology and markets. They also helped democracy materialize in Brazil and South Africa and mature in India. Politicians in many places worked to accommodate opposition parties instead of stifling their critics, and they pulled citizens into a common national cause.

By the twenty-first century, democratic India had become increasingly successful economically, possessing robust worldwide industrial and service sectors. Its path to prosperity was hardly smooth, however. India's leaders from the Congress Party had to overcome ethnic, religious, class, and caste conflict: Jawaharlal Nehru's daughter and grandson, who followed him as prime ministers, were assassinated by offended members of religious and ethnic minorities. Nonetheless, India remained the world's largest democracy.

Two different prime ministers in the twenty-first century, Sikh economist Manmohan Singh, known as "the cleanest politician in India,"[5] and Hindu politician Narendra Modi, advanced technological and infrastructure development. Even as its economy soared, India continued to face problems that were part of the legacy of colonialism: lack of education for all, the poverty of several hundred million citizens, and persistent ethnic and religious terrorism. Amid both turmoil and prosperity, India's cities grew and its middle class expanded, in large part thanks to its technological expertise and the global economic activities of its innovative business people.

≡ **Globalized Agriculture in India** This up-to-date Indian farmer harvests a bumper crop of wheat using machinery from the U.S.-based John Deere corporation. Not only did this harvester have parts made in other countries, but the seeds he used were probably developed in Mexico-based scientific laboratories to suit varying climate and soil composition. The result was the "Green Revolution" that began in the 1960s.

Like other Latin Americans in the 1960s and 1970s, Brazilians had endured military dictatorship, soaring inflation, rising poverty, and grossly inadequate systems of education and social services. In 1985 Brazilian voters, tired of government brutality and human rights abuses, ousted the military dictatorship and installed an elected government. Civilian rule brought with it an emphasis on human rights and, despite the persistence of crime and poverty, economic expansion over 5 percent in the early twenty-first century.

In the slums or *favelas* of the country's major cities, Rio de Janeiro and São Paulo, poverty-stricken residents organized, teaching one another to read and holding self-education meetings. "I go to meetings every week now," one woman reported of her activism. "I think we women should participate in political parties."[6] In 2002, Luiz Inácio Lula da Silva, a metalworker and union leader, was elected president—an incredible journey for a poor child who only learned to read when he was ten. He increased taxation on the wealthy to pay for improvements and negotiated over the state of the rainforests, where developers sought to dispossess local peoples of their land. A settlement unfolded, but it turned out that Lula da Silva, his two successors in office, and an array of elected officials and big businessmen had engaged in massive corruption. Overall well-being sank, fueled by the economic crisis of 2008 (discussed later in this chapter). A decade later a shaky comeback was underway.

As president of South Africa, Nelson Mandela faced pressing issues similar to those in other rising nations. Foremost among them were calming ethnic tensions and unifying the nation around consensus-building rather than violence—the main political strategy of the previous **apartheid** government. It had included taking homes and land from blacks and herding them into small "townships." "We want equal education, not slave education,"[7] youth had chanted at Soweto in 1976 while troops mowed them down. After Mandela took control, the African National Congress set up in 1995 a Truth and Reconciliation Commission to adjudicate past violence. The commission allowed those whom the apartheid government had persecuted to talk about their experiences in public; then it allowed those who had participated in the persecutions to confess their deeds and request amnesty. Reconciliation, it was recognized, fostered democracy; divisiveness fathered dictatorship (see Reading the Past: Testimony to South Africa's Truth and Reconciliation Commission).

Mandela's presidency reopened world markets to South African products, increased the flow of technology to the country, and created policies based on fairness to all social groups. For example, South African women, having played a leadership role in opposing apartheid, received a quota of seats in the new government. Health care was declared a constitutional right of all citizens. The government also negotiated land reform, resolving the claims of dispossessed whites and blacks alike. Still, South African blacks remained an underclass, and migrants from neighboring Zimbabwe, Mozambique, and other hard-pressed African regions competed with them for jobs. At the same time, the rapid spread of HIV/AIDS engulfed the nation in a horrific health crisis, magnified by the arrival of tens of thousands of other afflicted Africans to receive treatment. Twenty-four percent of all inhabitants of South Africa were HIV-positive in 2007. After Mandela's death in 2013, the rising political corruption of his successors weakened South Africa's hard-won democracy. In 2018, hoping to restore South Africa's reputation and momentum, reformers pushed one of these successors, Jacob Zuma, from the presidency.

apartheid The South African system of laws and behaviors that enforced segregation of the black from the white population, with the intention of creating a society dominated by whites; apartheid laws were repealed in 1991.

The Pacific Century?

From Japan to Singapore, people of the Pacific region produced explosive economic growth. In 1959 Japan's Ministry of Trade and Industry had announced a goal of "income doubling" within ten years, ultimately because of U.S. purchases across the region. By 1982, Asian Pacific nations accounted for 16.4 percent of global production, while China's abandonment of Mao's disastrous economic experiments yielded economic growth rates of 14 percent by 2007. Japan became the world's

READING THE PAST

Testimony to South Africa's Truth and Reconciliation Commission

In 1995 the South African government established the Truth and Reconciliation Commission to hear testimony from accusers and perpetrators alike about violence and human rights abuses during the apartheid regime. Usually the commission imposed fines, but in the aftermath of the hearings victims were often angrier than before. They saw the punishment as inadequate and complained that the fines were ridiculously low or never paid. Despite the drawbacks and objections, many around the world hailed the Truth and Reconciliation model as one with great potential.

Accounts by perpetrators of the violence make for especially horrific reading. In this excerpt, researchers followed up with one member of government security forces to hear in more depth how he pursued his grim job in the 1970s and 1980s, getting paid by the head for black resisters captured and for black resisters killed.

> We would volunteer for a three-month stint on the border for the Security Branch up there. . . . It sounded like a bit of an adventure and [a] nice getting away kind of ploy, because my girlfriend and

I were having hassles, probably because we were staying at my parents' place. I'd always been interested in doing something unconventional anyway, and I thought, well, this is it. This is my chance. . . .

The amount of adrenaline that we were producing on a daily level, constantly aware that we could die or be wounded at any moment. . . . Having that adrenaline pumping, we became adrenaline junkies. . . . It became like a drug to me, to go out there and follow up on those tracks. . . . [It is] almost a sexual kind of stimulation. Not physical sexual, but mental sexual. . . .

[On one particular captive] I knew that he was a veteran and that he would have been an excellent source of info. Sean, the Army medic, started patching him up while I was busy interrogating him. . . . Even at that stage he was denying everything and I just started to go into this uncontrollable [expletive deleted] rage and I remember thinking, "How dare you?" And then—this is what I was told afterwards—I started ripping. I ripped all the bandages, the drip that Sean had put into this guy . . . pulled out my 9 mm, put the barrel between his eyes and . . . I executed him.

Source: Don Foster et al., *The Theatre of Violence: Narratives of Protagonists in the South African Conflict* (Oxford, UK: James Currey, 2005), 130, 137, 140.

Examining the Evidence

1. What values appear to have motivated this member of the security forces as he pursued his livelihood?

2. Do you detect a change over time in his conduct, and if so, how do you explain it?

3. Why do you think the Truth and Reconciliation Commission came to be viewed as a powerful model in nation-building?

second largest economy in 1978 after the number one–ranked United States. It led the world in developing high-tech industry. In 2012, Japan had more than 300,000 industrial robots in operation while the United States had 163,000 and Germany 161,000. Meanwhile South Korea, Taiwan, Singapore, and Hong Kong came to be called "Pacific tigers" for the ferocity of their growth in the 1980s and 1990s.

In 2010 China took Japan's place as the world's second largest economy. Of all the developing nations, China's was the most striking success story. After Mao Ze-dong's death in 1976, Deng Xiaoping led China to become an economic titan, at once producing an array of inexpensive products for the global marketplace and providing its citizens with jobs that raised their standard of living. As people from the countryside flocked to cities to find jobs, skyscrapers replaced one- and two-story buildings: "Buildings are being knocked down at such a rate that one doesn't even have time to film them anymore," said one Beijing resident.[8] Throughout, the Communist Party kept its grip on government, clamping down hard on free speech, even on the Internet. China found business partners around the world, making deals for raw materials and used factories, which it dismantled piece by piece and then reconstructed in new Chinese industrial parks. By 2017 it owned 1.1 trillion dollars in U.S. government bonds. To some, the flow of wealth and productive energy appeared to have shifted away from the Atlantic and toward the Pacific, especially as the United States appeared to decline in global leadership.

Global Livelihoods and Institutions

> ↘ **FOCUS** How has globalization reshaped the global workforce and traditional political institutions?

The same forces that created a global market for products and services created a global market for labor: factories moved to wherever labor was cheapest. Workers around the world faced greater competition for employment, as many well-paid jobs increasingly disappeared in the twenty-first century. At the same time, better transportation and communication led people to travel thousands of miles to find jobs. Indonesian village women, for instance, left their families to work as domestic servants in the Middle East, and Filipino nurses went to Japan and elsewhere as healthcare providers in better-paying environments. Migration, innovations in communication technology, and the globalization of business combined to create global cities. Finally, global financial, political, and activist institutions such as the World Trade Organization, the United Nations, and Doctors Without Borders operated beyond any single nation-state, making a global order based on relationships among individual states seem obsolete.

Global Networks and Changing Jobs

The Internet in particular advanced globalization, bringing new jobs to previously impoverished countries. One of the first to recognize the possibilities of computing and call desk services was Ireland, which attracted global business by stressing computer literacy. From the 1990s on, as the people of this traditionally poor country began to prosper while

☰ Doctors Without Borders This doctor from the global NGO Doctors Without Borders distributes plastic sheeting to construct refugee shelters during the 1994 civil war and genocide in Rwanda. In an age of ethnic conflict and civil war, refugees were an all-too-common type of global citizen, one lacking the most basic of human rights—adequate health care.

working for clients throughout the world, the trend reached other nations: Moroccans could do help-desk work for French or Spanish speakers, and Filipinos could repair computers across the globe. Three percent of Indian domestic product came from the outsourcing work it did in payroll and other services, but jobs flowed in multiple directions: in 2017 a major Indian company, Infosys, planned to send some ten thousand jobs to America. Local knowledge was becoming important to many employers' success abroad.

Those who worked in outsourced jobs were more likely to participate in the global consumer economy. Thus, consumption soared in India, China, Brazil, and other emerging markets. A twenty-one-year-old Indian woman, working for a service provider in Bangalore under the English name "Sharon," was able to buy a cellphone from the Finnish company Nokia with her salary. "As a teenager I wished for so many things," she said. "Now I'm my own Santa Claus."[9] North Africans, Indians, and eastern Europeans had access to automobiles and iPhones; these would have been beyond their means before the 1990s. Critics called the phenomenon "Consumania."[10]

Consumerism developed unevenly, however: many in southern nations lacked the means for even basic purchases. Competition among lower-level workers for good jobs across the globe led to low wages everywhere. "How can I prepare my children for a knowledge-based society when I can't even put food on the table," one French mother objected.[11] Those with advanced managerial, technological, and other skills derived from university education fared better, showing the increasing importance of education to prosperity.

Neoliberalism added to worker impoverishment. An important tenet of neoliberalism was that profit and investment increase through downsizing—that is, reducing the number of jobs and enhancing the productivity of any remaining individual workers. Although Europeans still believed government should provide social services and education for all, the tightening of budgetary rules in the European Union meant that these services had to constitute a smaller part of the budget. The Swedish government drastically cut pensions, leading one union member to complain: "It means that we have to work our entire life."[12] Because employers (like workers) paid taxes for social service programs, reductions in benefits meant smaller employer contributions, which employers obviously favored to boost profits. Still, some nations believed in promoting the public good: these governments continued to run high-quality education, health, and transportation systems and to provide well-maintained roads, for example.

Beyond the Nation-State

Supranational organizations fostered globalization by creating worldwide networks to provide information and aid and set global standards for interactions such as trade. In the 1990s and thereafter Europeans expanded the range of their common governmental institutions, while countries of the "southern cone" of South America joined the effort to achieve even greater economic and social progress through cooperation.

The International Monetary Fund (IMF) and the World Bank grew in power by raising money from individual governments and then using it to assist developing countries in modernizing projects and in repayment of debts. The condition for such aid, however, was restructuring of the economy according to neoliberal principles. Other supranational organizations not connected to governments and hence called **nongovernmental organizations** (NGOs) were charitable or policy-oriented foundations. Those NGOs possessing great wealth often shaped national policies. Some NGOs, such as the France-based Doctors Without Borders, used contributions to provide medical aid in such places as the former Yugoslavia or Afghanistan, where people at war lacked any medical help except what outsiders could provide.

Globalization also entailed the rise of global activism, even against globalization itself. Political leaders flocked to an "alternative" conference at Porto Alegre, Brazil,

nongovernmental organization A group devoted to activism outside the normal channels of government, such as Doctors Without Borders.

in 2002 to protect people from the worst of globalization's effects, even as they attended the more traditionally global Davos forum held annually in Switzerland for the world's leading officials and executives.[13] Women activists also held global meetings, such as the UN Fourth World Conference on Women held in Beijing, China, in 1995 to negotiate a common platform for political action. The event was eye-opening for many participants, especially those from industrialized countries who had thought themselves more advanced than women from Africa and South America. The reverse proved to be true. In the end, their joint Declaration aimed "to advance the goals of equality, development, and peace for all women everywhere in the interest of all humanity."[14] In the twenty-first century, while women became heads of state in Germany, Liberia, Chile, Great Britain, Brazil, and some twenty other nations, they also held high positions in global organizations such as the United Nations and the IMF.

In 1992, the twelve countries of the European Economic Community (or Common Market) ended national distinctions in the spheres of business activity, border controls, and transportation, with citizens of member countries carrying a common burgundy-colored passport. In 1994 by the terms of the Maastricht Treaty, the European Economic Community became the **European Union** (EU), and in 1999 a common currency, the European Currency Unit—the ECU, or euro—was established. The EU parliament convened regularly in Strasbourg, France, while its central bank gained more control over region-wide economic policy. Beginning in 2004 the EU admitted fifteen new members, mostly from central and eastern Europe with other candidates including Turkey waiting for acceptance (see Map 28.3).

The success of the EU prompted the creation of other cooperative zones that imitated the early Common Market. In 1967 five countries—Indonesia, Malaysia, the Philippines, Singapore, and Thailand—formed the **Association of Southeast Asian Nations** (ASEAN), later expanded to include Brunei Darussalam (1984), Vietnam (1995), Laos and Myanmar (1997), and Cambodia (1999). ASEAN members engaged in a range of cooperative ventures, focused especially on rapid economic cooperation and expansion. The **North American Free Trade Agreement** (NAFTA), implemented in 1994, eliminated nearly all tariffs on goods traded between Canada, the United States, and Mexico. **Mercosur**, formed in 1991, established a free trade zone among South America's "southern cone" countries: Argentina, Brazil, Uruguay, and Paraguay, all of which were full members, and Chile and Bolivia as associates. These transnational organizations hardly matched the integration of the EU, and NAFTA explicitly rejected the kind of borderless opportunities for workers that the EU allowed. Workers in the United States watched

European Union An expanded version of the European Economic Community, established in 1994 to increase political and economic cooperation among European nations.

Association of Southeast Asian Nations A transnational organization formed in 1967 to facilitate economic cooperation among Southeast Asian countries.

North American Free Trade Agreement An agreement among Canada, Mexico, and the United States established in 1994 that eliminated most tariffs on goods traded among the signatories.

Mercosur The establishment in 1991 of a free trade zone among nations of South America's "southern cone."

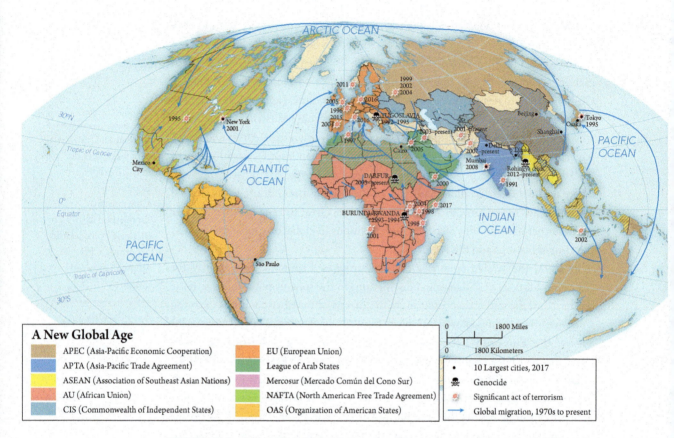

≡ **MAP 28.3** **A New Global Age** By the start of the twenty-first century, the world's peoples were bound together more significantly than ever. Migration brought unprecedented ethnic and cultural diversity to entire regions, while large regional alliances fostered unity—at least superficially. No less real in their impact were the mixing of cultures and the shared experience of terrorism and disease.

in dismay as jobs moved to fuel Mexico's industrial zones on its U.S. border, but it turned out that five to six million jobs in the United States stemmed from NAFTA agreements.

A cluster of cities were also global powerhouses, competitive with some nations. Old urban areas, including Hong Kong, Paris, Tokyo, London, and New York, used innovations in transportation and communication to become magnets for economic activity and for migrants from all over the world. Within these cities, high-level decision makers interacted with one another to set global economic policy and to transact business worldwide. Their high pay drove up living costs and sent middle managers and engineers to live in lower-priced suburbs with good schools and other amenities for these well-educated white-collar workers. Living in often squalid conditions in the run-down neighborhoods of global cities were the maintenance, domestic, and other workers—sometimes called "lumpentrash"—who needed to be at the beck and call of global enterprise. Suburbanization and ghettoization flourished simultaneously, testifying to globalization's uneven economic and social effects.

Huge numbers of willing migrants flocked to leading global cities. In 2015, for example, more than a hundred thousand Japanese lived in England staffing Japan's global enterprises located there. These migrants did not aim to become citizens, nor did they make any financial claim on the adopted country. Global cities were sometimes criticized for producing a "de-territorialization of identities"—meaning that residents of these areas lacked both a national and a local sense of themselves, so much so that they were at home anywhere in the world (see Seeing the Past: The Globalization of Urban Space).

Global Culture

A crucial ingredient of globalization was the deepening relationship among cultures through shared books, films, and music from different traditions. Latin American authors, prominent among them Colombian-born Nobel Prize winner Gabriel Garcia Marquez, developed a style known as magical realism, which melded everyday events with elements of Latin American history, myth, magic, and religion. His lush fantasies, including *One Hundred Years of Solitude* (1967), represented the Latin American creative "boom" to millions of readers worldwide and gave eager authors a style to emulate into the twenty-first century.

Authors charted the horrors of twentieth- and twenty-first century history—among these Stalinism, colonialism, and U.S. domination. Svetlana Alexievich was a Russian journalist and writer who devoted her career to investigating women's testimonies of World War II and the sweep of Russian history under Stalin, Gorbachev, and Putin—among others. For taking on these subjects, she passed long stretches of her life in exile, though eventually winning the Nobel Prize in Literature. The Nigerian-born writer Chimamanda Adichie depicted the complexities of living in West Africa after colonialism had spawned authoritarian governments. Her *Purple Hibiscus* (2003) featured the complicated hope that educated Africans living in dictatorships found in thinking about exile to the United States. Similarly writing across cultures, Indian-born Amitav Ghosh presented in works like *The Glass Palace* (2000) and *Ibis Trilogy* (2008–2015) a global cast of characters intersecting for both good and ill in the context of global capitalism, poverty, drugs, and imperial domination.

SEEING THE PAST

The Globalization of Urban Space

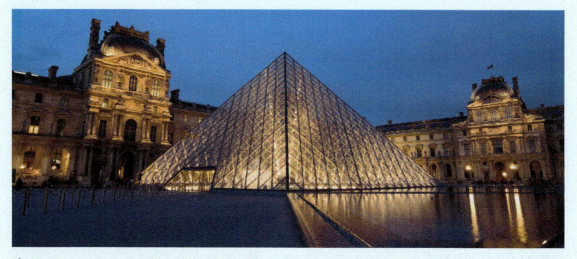

The New Louvre, Paris, France

One everyday sign of globalization is the homogenization of urban architecture. Travelers to urban capitals may see carefully preserved and distinctive buildings from centuries past that differ from one continent to another. Alongside these ancient buildings are recent ones, similar in style whether they are in Dubai, Malaysia, Japan, Brazil, or the United States. The similarity arises not only from the globalization of style but from the globalization of architects themselves, who bid on and construct buildings far beyond their home countries, often in collaboration with architects from other parts of the world.

The Louvre was once a royal palace. It evolved from a twelfth-century fortified residence of kings to a museum not only for the French but for millions of international tourists. In the 1980s the French government undertook a major renovation of the central entrance to the Louvre, which was no longer adequate to deal with the throngs of tourists. The Japanese architect I. M. Pei, who designed buildings around the world, produced this entryway through a glass pyramid.

Examining the Evidence

1. Why might so ancient a structure as a pyramid have been chosen to be placed in front of the Louvre?

2. Why might glass have been used instead of the stone from which the Egyptian pyramids were constructed?

3. What message does this update of the entrance to the Louvre convey?

Popular music also thrived in the global market-place, mixing styles from all over the world. Hip-hop, rap, and salsa music, for example, combined African, Latin American, and African American traditions into new musical genres. African hip-hop artists claimed hip-hop and rap as part of an African heritage based on the poet singers, or griots, who for centuries had lyrically recited history and legends. In 1988 the South African group Black Noise, active in the anti-apartheid movement, produced the region's modern version of rap. Salsa music likewise circled the world, flourishing not just in Latin America and the Caribbean but also in the United States as more Hispanics migrated there. African influences shaped salsa, too, via the slave heritage of the Western Hemisphere. Raï, the popular music of North African cities, echoed in the Algerian suburbs of Paris, and performances by raï stars attracted tens of thousands of fans. Dangdut, a form of popular music in Indonesia, used tunes from Bollywood film while its lyrics expressed Islamic values—the combination appealing to diasporas in the world's largest Islamic state. "Chutney" generally described the fusion music of the Caribbean, but particularly the influence of the many South Asian indentured workers who settled there in the nineteenth and early twentieth centuries.

Religion also operated globally but few practices of any single religion were uniform from culture to culture. While all Muslims practiced the Five Pillars of their faith, including charitable giving, they embraced a wide variety of interpretations of Islam (see Lives and Livelihoods: Readers of the Qur'an). In the 1990s, Turkish youth, raised with the nation's republican and secular beliefs, began to follow "green" pop stars and to read "green" romances—green being the color of paradise in the Muslim faith. While enjoying gossip, jokes, and the company of their best friends, young women decided to wear headscarves and follow the call to prayer, explaining, "We pray like you have fun."[15]

≡ **Global Pop Culture** Inul Daratista, a sensation in Indonesia and beyond for her singing and dancing performances, blends Indian, Middle Eastern, Malay, and Portuguese styles. Inul's body moves sensuously and rapidly, and Muslim clergy object to her lack of modesty. Although Inul Daratista's "dangdut" music originates in local folk performances, she has made it a global phenomenon.

LIVES AND LIVELIHOODS

Readers of the Qur'an

Among the most popular stars in the global media are those who chant the Qur'an in recordings available on cassettes, CDs, radio, and cellphones. Specially trained and tested Qur'an reciters—literally thousands of them—make their recordings in dozens of cities in the Islamic world (ummah), but only after being certified by official examining boards. Readers must know the Qur'an to perfection, because errors such as stopping in the middle of a word would mar the holy words of Allah as handed down through the Prophet Muhammad. Cassettes allow the Qur'an to inspire Muslims at home or work. For example, a carpenter in Cairo keeps his tape playing during the day: "I have two ears," the carpenter reports, "one for work, and one for listening to the Qur'an."

Readers of the Qur'an in Kazan, Russia Despite the Soviet Union's official policy of atheism, Kazan has remained a center of Islamic culture and practice. It is the site of magnificent mosques and hosts expert readings of the Qur'an. In this 2008 photograph of a Qur'an reading contest, a young expert reciter vies with others from across Russia for the best and truest performance.

Although most reciters of the Qur'an are men, one of the best known is Maria Ulfah, a reciter from Indonesia. Taught as a child that men and women are equal, she has traveled to many parts of the world

The Promises and Perils of Globalization

> **FOCUS** What major benefits and dangers has globalization brought to the world's peoples?

Despite growing prosperity, the global age has been called "a world in disarray." First, the health of the world's peoples and their environments came under a multipronged attack from industrial disasters, acid rain, epidemics, and global warming.

to read. Like Ulfah, well-loved readers of the Qur'an become celebrities. In Egypt Sheik Mohammed Gebriel is the most appreciated; listeners immediately recognize his voice. He is known to bring in crowds of over half a million when reading in public. "When I hear Sheik Gebriel, I feel that the angels are reading with him," a retired army officer said.

Despite the standardization involved in certification, the reading of the Qur'an and the issuing of calls to prayer five times a day have their variations according to region and language. Muslims in Kenya, for example, prefer the sounds of the call to prayer by their country's readers to those recorded in Egypt. Recordings by the thousands of reciters show, in fact, differences and nuances by region, again proving that even in the face of standardization and globalization, local identities remain important to carrying out one's daily life. "You can get bored by a song in a few days," a record store owner said, "but no one gets bored listening to the Qur'an."

Source: Douglas Jehl, "Above the City's Din, Always the Voice of Allah," *New York Times International,* March 6, 1996.

Questions to Consider

1. In the case of the Qur'an in people's lives, what has been the effect of modern communications technology?
2. How would you describe the role of the reciter of the Qur'an in modern society? Is he or she a religious leader, service worker, or media personality?
3. Over time, what has been the effect of books, television, CDs, and other media on religion generally?

For Further Information:

Jehl, Douglas. "Above the City's Din, Always the Voice of Allah." *New York Times International*, March 6, 1996.

Quran Explorer (recordings of recitations of the Qur'an in several languages, including Arabic, Urdu, and English). http://www.quranexplorer.com/.

Quran Reciters (including images of especially important reciters of the past). http://www.quranreciters.com/wp/.

Second, a surging population, especially in southern regions, increased demands on resources and often fed strife. Migration from imperiled areas surged dramatically, and transnational religious and ethnic movements also competed, sometimes through the use of terrorism. Finally, a devastating economic crisis that broke out in 2008 ricocheted into geopolitics, leading to the rise of nationalist authoritarianism in some nations and to reassertions of democracy and global cooperation in others.

Environmental Challenges

In the early twenty-first century, people continued to worry about the impact of technological development on the environment. In 1984 poisonous gas leaking from a Union Carbide plant in Bhopal, India, had killed an estimated ten to fifteen thousand people, harmed tens of thousands permanently, and left the region completely contaminated by chemicals. In 1986 an explosion at the Chernobyl nuclear power plant in present-day Ukraine killed thirty people instantly and left many more to die from radiation. Clearing the world's rainforests depleted the global oxygen supply and threatened the biological diversity of the entire planet (see Map 28.4).

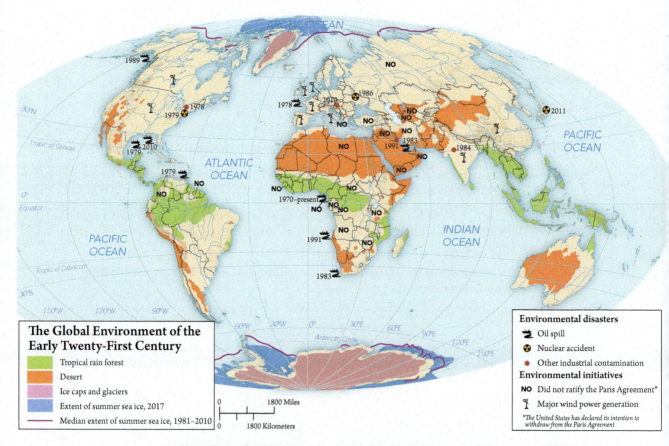

The Global Environment of the Early Twenty-First Century

- Tropical rain forest
- Desert
- Ice caps and glaciers
- Extent of summer sea ice, 2017
- Median extent of summer sea ice, 1981–2010

0 — 1800 Miles
0 — 1800 Kilometers

Environmental disasters
- Oil spill
- Nuclear accident
- Other industrial contamination

Environmental initiatives
- **NO** Did not ratify the Paris Agreement*
- Major wind power generation

*The United States has declared its intention to withdraw from the Paris Agreement

≡ **MAP 28.4 The Global Environment of the Early Twenty-First Century** As industry advanced and population grew, the earth itself came under assault. Degradation of the environment—including desertification (the transformation of formerly agrarian land into desert), depletion of rainforests, climate extremes, industrial catastrophes, and other changes caused by humans—threatened the sustainability of life.

By the late 1980s, scientists determined that the use of chlorofluorocarbons (CFCs), chemicals found in aerosol and refrigeration products, had blown a hole in the earth's ozone layer, the part of the blanket of atmospheric gases that prevents harmful ultraviolet rays from reaching the planet. The buildup of CFCs, carbon dioxide produced by the burning of fossil fuels, and other atmospheric pollutants produced a "greenhouse effect" that resulted in **global warming**. By 2017, global warming had produced weather extremes such as more frequent and stronger hurricanes and droughts and the breakup of the Arctic ice pack as measurable through space technology.

global warming An increase in the temperature of the earth's lower atmosphere, resulting in dramatic weather cycles and melting of glaciers.

Activism over decades against unbridled industrial growth led in 1979 to the founding of the Green Party in West Germany, followed by Green Party development worldwide. Nation-building, however, led politicians to push big and questionable projects such as dams. Egypt's Aswan Dam, built in the 1960s, and China's Three Gorges Dam, constructed between 1994 and 2015, destroyed miles of villages and farmland and cost thousands of lives even as it produced massive hydroelectric power. Chinese Nobel Laureate Gao Xingjian explored questions of

The Arctic Ice Pack Arctic sea ice was more than 25 percent smaller in 2011 than its average extent during the period 1979–2000. Whereas the Arctic ice pack once virtually closed shipping, by the early twenty-first century some ships could navigate the waters around it for an extended period. Scientists saw coastal cities around the world and marine life threatened.

ecological disaster, as he described peasant reactions to the destruction and invoked the responsibilities of the human community for the earth's well-being in his novel *Soul Mountain* (2000). Gao was denounced by modernizers around the world and punished more than once in China, leading to his self-imposed exile, during which he gathered stories for his novel.

People attacked environmental problems on both the local and global levels. Beginning in 1977, Wangari Maathai (wan-GAH-ree mah-DHEYE) enlisted women to plant trees to create green belts around Kenya's capital city of Nairobi. Born in Kenya, Maathai had studied botany in the United States and veterinary medicine in Africa. Local deforestation led her to create a citizens' movement. "It's important for people to see that they are part of the environment and that they take responsibility for it,"[16] she explained. Powerful politicians and business people had her beaten up and run out of the country. In 2004 Maathai won the Nobel Peace Prize for her efforts to improve the environment and livelihoods of Africans.

Frankfurt, Germany, and other European cities developed car-free zones. The Smart, a very small car using reduced amounts of fuel, became a popular way for Europeans to cut their use of fossil fuels. Cities also developed bicycle lanes on major streets. Germany, Spain, the United States, Denmark, and China had some 80 percent of the world's wind installations to generate electricity in 2005. In 2016 the Paris Climate Agreement went into effect and by 2017 had 195 signatories, with the United States, the second worst global polluter after China, withdrawing from the plan to reduce dangers to the environment.

Population Pressures and Public Health

Nations with less-developed economies struggled with rapidly rising population as life expectancy globally rose by an average of sixteen years between 1950 and 1980. Censuses in 2015 showed eastern Europe and Japan actually experiencing negative growth (that is, more deaths than births); less industrially developed countries accounted for 98 percent of worldwide population growth, thanks to medicine increasing the life span of people there. By 2015, the earth's population had reached 7.3 billion and by 2050 was projected to reach 9.8 billion.

Non-Western governments were alarmed at their nation's rising population and took action. In 1979 Deng introduced the one-child policy for urban Chinese families, which was not lifted until 2015. By the 1990s, the Iranian government was urging families to space their children: the birth rate fell from 6.5 live births per Iranian woman in the 1970s to below 2 in 2010. For a time in the 1970s, the Indian government used a policy of forced sterilization. Mullahs in Afghanistan also studied population: "If you have too many children and you can't control them," one reported after a class on birth control, "that's bad for Islam."[17]

Vaccines and drugs for diseases such as malaria and smallpox helped improve health in developing nations. However, half of all Africans lacked access to basic public health facilities such as safe drinking water. In the early 1980s, medical expertise was further challenged by a global epidemic disease: acquired immunodeficiency syndrome (AIDS), caused by human immunodeficiency virus (HIV). The government of Vietnam launched a dramatic poster campaign: "Do not use or accept harmful cultural products. Do not become addicted to smoking or injecting drugs." [18] In fact, the major culprits for the spread of AIDS in Vietnam were privileged and sexually adventurous public officials. By 2010, no cure had yet been discovered, though scientists developed strong drugs that alleviated the symptoms. Activists protested that these costly drugs existed but only white victims were being saved. Alongside AIDS, the deadly Ebola virus, bird flu, swine flu, and dozens of other viruses harbored the potential for global pandemics. Interconnectedness via diseases and scientific advances gained from combating them showed both the perils and promises of globalization.

Worldwide Migration

The twenty-first century witnessed accelerating migration worldwide, building on the migration that followed decolonization and often adding to the diversity of many regions of the world (see again Map 28.3). An estimated 190 million rural Chinese traveled to China's industrial cities to find work in 2004, while millions more went to Malaysia, Indonesia, and other regions in Southeast Asia to get jobs. Sometimes danger prompted migration. Africans fled civil wars in Rwanda, Congo, and Sudan, often heading for Europe, Canada, and the United States, or to nearby South Africa. Civil wars and ethnic oppression drove civilians from states of the former Soviet Union and its satellites to Germany, Scandinavia, Austria, France, and England. Jordan and other countries of the Middle East and Europe were home to Palestinians, Iraqis, and Syrians—all driven from their homelands by violence. A particularly abhorrent form of coerced migration was the increasing trafficking in children and women for sexual and other kinds of forced labor.

The conditions of migration varied depending on one's class, gender, and regional origin. Among the most fortunate migrants were professionals in science and technology. Less fortunate were women from the Philippines, Indonesia, and other southern regions who migrated to perform domestic service. They frequently suffered rape by their employers, oppressive working conditions, and confiscation of their wages. Men and women alike traveled into the European Union or the United States packed into airless storage containers in trucks or on unsafe boats to find opportunity or to escape political turmoil. By 2015, millions of distressed migrants from violent regions were receiving a hostile, even brutal reception. Ironically, given the country's history of innovation by immigrants, U.S. politics increasingly centered on the presence of "illegal aliens." Malaysian politicians blamed the Chinese in their midst for problems of modernization, whereas Indonesians rampaged against both Chinese and Christians. Authoritarian politicians and would-be dictators worldwide won support by promising to fix the immigrant "problem."

Migration stories, many of them best-sellers, related would-be migrants' dreams of magnetic other worlds, conjured up amid oppressive conditions. Expatriate Russian author Andrei Makine, who immigrated to France, produced lyrical accounts of Siberian people's powerful imaginings of a better world in *Once Upon the River Love* (1998). *Reading Lolita in Tehran* (2003), a memoir by Iranian author Azar Nafisi, an immigrant to the United States, and *Balzac and the Little Chinese Seamstress* (2003) by Dai Sijie, a Chinese refugee in Europe, detail the powerful influence of Western literature under conditions of oppression. Nafisi, who left her post at a Tehran university during the Iranian theocracy, writes of bringing a group of young women to her home to read forbidden books. The two young men in Sijie's novel are banished to the countryside during China's Cultural Revolution and discover there a supply of nineteenth-century Western classics.

Terrorism Confronts the World

Even as literature portrayed diverse global relationships, the world's people also experienced interconnectedness as terrifying. In the 1970s, European terrorist bands, such as Italy's Red Brigades, responded to post-1968 politics with kidnappings, bank robberies, bombings, and assassinations. In 1972, Palestinian terrorists kidnapped and murdered eleven Israeli athletes at the Olympic Games in Munich. After Bloody Sunday (January 30, 1972) in Northern Ireland, when British troops fired on unarmed civil rights demonstrators, a cycle of violence ensued that left thousands dead. Prime Minister Indira Gandhi was assassinated by her Sikh security guards in 1984 after the Indian government attacked a Sikh temple; Tamil separatists from Sri Lanka assassinated Indira Gandhi's son Rajiv for his lack of support in 1991; antigovernment U.S. terrorists blew up a federal building in Oklahoma City in 1995; in the same year Japanese religious radicals released deadly poisonous gas in the Tokyo subway system to promote their beliefs; in 2011 a Norwegian fundamentalist Christian and anti-Muslim extremist massacred close to eighty young political activists and wounded hundreds more; terrorists from the Middle East and North Africa planted bombs in many European cities, blew up European airplanes, and bombed the Paris subway system—among other acts from the 1980s into the twenty-first century. Some attacks were said to be punishment for the West's support for both Israel and repressive regimes in the Middle East.

On September 11, 2001, Middle Eastern militants hijacked four planes in the United States and flew two of them into the World Trade Center in

New York and one into the Pentagon in Virginia. The fourth plane crashed in Pennsylvania. The hijackers, most of whom were from Saudi Arabia, were inspired by Osama bin Laden, the charismatic founder of the al-Qaeda transnational terrorist organization, who was supported by the United States during the Cold War but now wanted U.S. military forces removed from Saudi Arabia. The loss of some three thousand lives led the United States to declare a "war on terrorism."

Global cooperation followed the September 11 attacks and the continuing lethal bombings around the world, from Bali to Britain (see again Map 28.3). European countries rounded up terrorists and conducted the first successful trials of them in the spring of 2003. Ultimately, Western cooperation fragmented when the United States invaded Iraq in March 2003, claiming falsely that Iraq's Saddam Hussein had weapons of mass destruction (see Map 28.5). In 2011 American forces scored a symbolic victory in the "war on terror" through the capture and execution of Osama bin Laden. As the invasion of Iraq fragmented civic unity, a new transnational terrorist group—the Islamic State (or ISIS or ISIL)—became operational and thrived in the country. Alongside the many promises of globalization was the incredible toll in lives taken by terrorism and the worldwide xenophobia—or hatred of foreigners—that followed.

Even as terrorism continued, a new manifestation of antigovernment sentiment appeared that brought hope across the Middle East. In late 2010 and 2011, an "Arab Spring" began in a series of popular uprisings, some of which forced dictators in North Africa and the Middle East to step down or to reform government. Uprisings in Tunisia, Egypt, and Libya succeeded, even in the face of brutal repression. In Egypt, long-time dictator Hosni Mubarak surrendered power and was tried for the murder of many protesters. Hard on the heels of the Egyptian success, protest mounted against dictators in Libya and Syria, with NATO planes helping the Libyan rebels defeat Muammar Qaddafi.

In the place of these dictators, tribal organizations—long an alternative political form to the nation-state— sometimes came to control decision making, and in Syria rebel forces confronted the dictator Bashar al' Asad in what became a deadly civil war.

≣ **Arab Spring, 2010–2011**

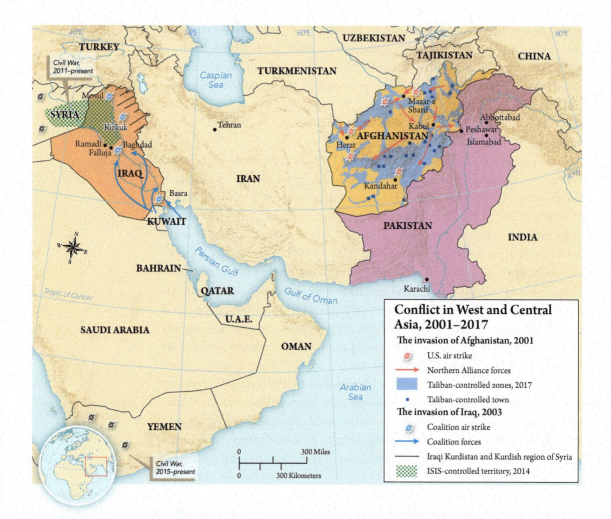

≡ **MAP 28.5   Wars in Afghanistan and Iraq, 2001–2011** After the terrorist attack on September 11, 2001, the U.S. government, with the help of Western and Afghani allies, launched an attack on the Taliban—a group in control of Afghanistan and a supporter of al-Qaeda. In 2003, the United States and its allies invaded Iraq on the grounds that it had weapons of mass destruction—which was not true.

Still, the sophisticated means by which protesters had mobilized, including the use of e-mail and social networking to create meeting points and devise strategies, seemed hopeful. The promise of the Arab Spring was not just in its accomplishments but in the "virtual" societies young and older citizens had constructed through technology. Yet these same techniques benefited the highly violent Islamic State, which only added to death and destruction in the Middle East. Youth worldwide, often facing unemployment due to globalization and restructuring, served as the shock troops first of al-Qaeda and then of ISIS in escalating global terrorism in the second decade of the twenty-first century.

Global Economic Crisis and the Rise of Authoritarian Politicians

As the twenty-first century opened, the global economy suffered a series of shocks including terrorism and civil war. In 1997 many East Asian economies faced collapse after a period of rapid growth but also rapid indebtedness. As "hot money" in the form of investment loans flowed into these so-called Pacific Tigers, the decline in value of their currencies made it difficult to repay. The International Monetary Fund helped bail them out but the region's economies faltered badly. Their fragile recovery was followed by the bursting in 2008 of a real estate bubble in the United States. Housing prices had escalated because of mortgage financing available on easy or even dishonest terms. Then, financiers distributed this often fraudulent debt around the world to those who hoped to make handsome profits because adjustable mortgage rates were set to rise dramatically. When people became unable to repay their mortgage and credit card debt, credit became unavailable both to ordinary people and to banks and industry. A credit collapse followed, just as it had in the stock market collapse of 1929. Governments around the world tried to save banks and industries with the infusion of billions of dollars. Unemployment rose as businesses and consumers alike stopped purchasing goods. In 2011 some European governments faced possible bankruptcy, especially as the price of commodities plunged. The globalization of economic crises haunted the world's population even as recovery was at hand by 2017.

As in the past, hard times encouraged the rise of authoritarian figures with quick and easy solutions. In Europe, which faced the influx of millions of refugees from Iraq, Syria, and other threatened regions, this issue when combined with economic difficulties benefited strongmen. Pounding the idea that migration and globalization—not technological innovation and dishonest businesses—caused the crash, politicians employed the techniques of divisiveness and social pessimism that had been the stock in trade of twentieth-century dictators. Whereas enemies then had been Jews, gays, and Roma, people now were set against migrants within their borders or competitors on the global stage. Hungary, Poland, Russia, Czechoslovakia, Italy, and the United States saw the appeal to hatred for migrating peoples weaken the politics of consensus building and freedom of speech. Ironically, globalization helped these antiglobalization politicians, as social network meddling by Russia sowed the divisiveness that authoritarian politicians claimed to be the result of democratic politics. Almost uniformly, the disappearance of jobs due to technological innovation was cast as due instead to evil foreigners and nations. People in Europe and the United States turned

≡ **Women's March Inside Karura forest in Kenya's capital Nairobi** Women across the globe had been organizing mass meetings and protests locally, nationally, and internationally for more than a century. On January 21, 2017, demonstrations occurred worldwide to mark women's disagreement with what they believed were President Donald Trump's beliefs, agenda, and behavior, in particular toward women. Kenya's women came out in force to show solidarity.

against multilateral, global alliances such as the European Union, NAFTA, and the Trans-Pacific Partnership—and in some cases even against their fellow citizens.

COUNTERPOINT: Defending Local Identity in a Globalizing World

⬂ **FOCUS** How have peoples worked to maintain distinctive local identities in today's global age?

Amid globalization, individuals sought to reclaim local, personal, and even national identities. The advance of globalization produced both a sense of loss and a feeling that something other than global forces and even nation-states was needed to provide values and well-being. People sought various ways to proclaim their personal identities: through local religious customs, or by reviving age-old traditions of dress, food, and celebration, or by showing loyalty to local sports teams (despite the fact that most teams were allied with global business, including television networks and marketers of consumer goods). In some countries such as the United States, Hungary, and Poland, populist politicians promised a return to past prosperity and so-called racial order.

Ethnic Strife and Political Splintering

One counter to globalization aimed at creating and empowering smaller political units. Such groups as the Tamils in Sri Lanka and Sikhs in India struggled unsuccessfully for autonomy for their people from the homogenizing nation-state. The wealthy Catalonian region of Spain also sought to become an independent nation. By 2010 there were more nations than there were at the end of World War II in 1945 because people divided some countries according to ethnicity. Since 1990, some twenty-nine new nations have been born, including South Sudan in 2011. The post-Communist emergence of Kazakhstan, Uzbekistan, Serbia, and other eastern European states often involved bitter civil wars among ethnic groups and the forcible ejection or genocide of minority groups.

Many a politician found the cause of secession a route to public office; for example, a number of those working to separate Scotland from Great Britain and Great Britain itself from the European Union. The latter movement, dubbed Brexit, was a successful campaign to restore the "greatness" of the nation in the face of absorption in a transnational cooperative—the EU. The Russian use of social media to sow division in other nations aimed to make Russia appear larger on the global stage as the European Union fragmented and as individual societies became dysfunctional.

Movements to Protect Tradition

The desire to maintain a local identity also encompassed movements to preserve local customs and practices, including some of the world's thousands of languages, which were under threat of being swallowed up by Chinese, Hindi, Spanish, and English. In January 2005 Guatemalan forces killed a Maya-Kakchiquel man who sought to block a global mining firm's inroads into his community. At issue in hundreds of other similar protests was the preservation of local customs, livelihoods, and traditional rights. In late 1993 a group of activists in the Chiapas state of Mexico declared themselves a local liberation army devoted to stanching the "bleeding" of their locality by stopping the flow of oil, coffee, bananas, and other

Nambikwara family, late 1930s

Nambikwara boys today

≡ **The Nambikwara of Brazil** The Nambikwara, described in the preface to this book, have themselves struggled to preserve their way of life from those bringing in modern technology, farming, logging, scholarly, and missionary activity. Although preserving their way of life and "untouched" by modernity, in fact the Nambikwara are constantly being photographed, studied, and "reorganized" by these outside forces. Some subgroups of the Nambikwara have become extinct, especially because of imported diseases. But these healthy youngsters are carrying on the Nambikwara contribution to world-making.

resources out of the area and onto the world market, leaving the local people destitute. These activists, known as the Zapatistas (recalling the name of the hero of the 1910 revolution), also decried the ridicule heaped on their way of life by globalizers.

In seeking to preserve their local Mayan identity, the activists were similar to the pilgrims in Vietnam who brought fruit to special shrines around Hanoi to be blessed by local gods. The rap group Xplastaz in Tanzania promoted the wearing of traditional garb to fight the globalization of clothing that threatened to erase their local culture. South American indigenous women also organized in 2009 to preserve their traditional values: "As we women are part of nature and the universe, we are called to care for and defend our mother earth. From her, comes the ancient history and culture that makes us what we are."[19] The Nambikwara of Brazil, with whom this book began, although losing their variety of inherited languages and many of their diverse peoples, continue to pursue their centuries-old way of life, even though surrounded by "modernizing" forces. Finally, rural people, left behind by globalization's steamroller, joined anti-urban populist political movements that promised to restore the well-paying local jobs lost to the global market—yet another facet of making the world.

Conclusion

"Sometimes I tell myself, I may only be planting a tree here, but just imagine what's happening if there are billions of people out there doing something. Just imagine the power of what we can do."[20] Wangari Maathai's motivation reflected a belief that billions of citizens, acting locally as individuals, could effect change on a global scale as part of a worldwide effort. Innovations in communications, transportation, and the development of strong transnational organizations have accelerated the pace of globalization in the past four decades. Globalization is evident everywhere: in the worldwide spread of disease, worldwide migration, and the worldwide consequences of industrialization. It is seen in the spread of campaigns like Nelson Mandela's on behalf of human rights and in dastardly acts of global terrorism.

As the world's peoples come to work on common projects and share elements of one another's cultures, their mental outlook has become more global, more cosmopolitan. The Chinese painter Wu Guanzhong, even after years of repression for his cosmopolitan style, combined elements from around the world in his work. "In my art," Wu said, "I really belonged to a hybridized breed."[21] Many rightly protest that much of value can be lost at the hands of global forces or in authoritarian populism at work in the world today; others foresee some great irreconcilable clash among civilizations. The question remains whether, given human interaction in a globalizing world, we are not all hybrids—that is, mixtures of one another's thoughts, traditions, cultures, and livelihoods as we engage in making and remaking the world. Isn't this mixture of the world's peoples what has given texture to the recent history of the world?

✳ review

The major global development in this chapter: The causes and consequences of intensified globalization.

Important Events	
1986	Nuclear accident at Chernobyl power plant in Soviet Union
1989	Eastern European states liberate themselves from USSR domination pro-democracy protests in Beijing's Tiananmen Square
1990s	New Eurasian nations emerge in wake of USSR collapse
1991	USSR dissolves December 31. Mercosur establishes a free-trade zone among southern South American nations
1994	Nelson Mandela elected president of South Africa; European Union officially formed; North American Free Trade Agreement implemented
1995	United Nations Fourth World Conference on Women held in Beijing
1999	European Union adopts the euro as its new currency
2001	Terrorists attack United States; United States declares "war on terrorism"
2002	Luiz Inácio Lula da Silva elected Brazilian president
2003	United States invades Iraq
2004	Manmohan Singh becomes prime minister of India
2007–2008	Global economic crisis begins to unfold
2016	Paris Climate Agreement goes into effect

KEY TERMS

apartheid (p. 1042)
Association of Southeast Asian Nations (p. 1047)
European Union (p. 1047)
global warming (p. 1055)

globalization (p. 1032)
Mercosur (p. 1047)
neoliberalism (p. 1036)
nongovernmental organization (p. 1046)

North American Free Trade Agreement (p. 1047)
OPEC (p. 1034)
stagflation (p. 1034)

CHAPTER OVERVIEW QUESTIONS

1. What were the elements of globalization at the beginning of the twenty-first century?
2. How did globalization affect lives and livelihoods throughout the world?
3. How did globalization affect local cultures?
4. What people do you know whose roots and livelihoods are global?

MAKING CONNECTIONS

1. What have been the most important features of globalization—good and bad—in the past thirty years, and why are they so significant?
2. Consider Chapter 23. How have livelihoods changed since the era of industrialization, and what factors have caused these changes?
3. Do you consider local or global issues more important to people's lives? Explain your choice.
4. How do you describe your identity—as global, national, local, familial, religious—and why?

For further research into the topics covered in this chapter, see the Bibliography at the end of the book. For additional primary sources from this period, see *Sources for World in the Making*.

Notes

Chapter 1

1. Charles Darwin, *On the Origin of Species*, ed. Joseph Carroll (Peterborough, Ontario, Canada: Broadview, 2003), 432.

2. J. C. Beaglehole, ed., *The Voyage of the Endeavour 1768–1771: The Journals of Captain James Cook on His Voyages of Discovery [Series]* (Cambridge: Cambridge University Press, 1955), 1:399.

Chapter 2

1. H. L. J. Vanstiphout, ed., *Epics of Sumerian Kings: The Matter of Aratta* (Atlanta, GA: Society of Biblical Literature, 2004), 85.

2. Martha T. Roth, *Law Collections from Mesopotamia and Asia Minor* (Atlanta, GA: Society of Biblical Literature, 1997), 121.

3. J. A. Black, et al., *The Literature of Ancient Sumer* (Oxford: Oxford University Press, 2004), 319.

4. Translated from E. Edel, *Die ägyptisch-hethitische Korrespondenz aus Boghazkoy* (Opladen, Germany: Westdeutscher Verlag, 1994), 40–41.

Chapter 3

1. Burton Watson, trans., *Records of the Grand Historian by Sima Qian: Han Dynasty II* (New York: Columbia University Press, 1993), 129.

2. *The Laws of Manu*, trans. Georg Bühler (New York: Dover, 1969), 327–328.

3. Wendy Doniger O'Flaherty, *The Rig Veda: An Anthology* (New York: Penguin Books, 1981), 10.90, 30–31.

4. Burton Watson, trans., in Wm. Theodore de Bary and Irene Bloom, eds., *Sources of Chinese Tradition*, 2nd ed. (New York: Columbia University Press, 1999), 1:38.

Chapter 4

1. Translated from Florence Malbran-Labat, *La version akkadienne de l'inscription trilingue de Darius à Behistun* (Rome: GEI, 1994), 93–103.

2. Yasna 30:3. In S. Insler, *The Gathas of Zarathustra* (Leiden: Brill, 1975), 33.

Chapter 5

1. Susan Sherwin-White and Amélie Kuhrt, *From Samarkhand to Sardis: A New Approach to the Seleucid Empire* (Berkeley: University of California Press, 1993), 179.

2. Ainslie T. Embree, ed., *Sources of Indian Tradition*, 2nd ed. (New York: Columbia University Press, 1988), 1:282.

3. *Sources of Indian Tradition*, 1:148.

4. Leonard Nathan, *The Transport of Love* (Berkeley: University of California Press, 1976), 83.

5. Confucius, *Analects* 15, 17, *Chinese Civilization: A Sourcebook*, 2nd ed., trans. Patricia Buckley Ebrey (New York: Free Press, 1993), 18.

6. *Sophocles I*, trans. Elizabeth Wyckoff (Chicago: University of Chicago Press, 1954), 174.

7. Tacitus, *Annals*, Book 14, Ch. 35. Quoted from http://www.athenapub.com/tacitus1.htm.

Chapter 6

1. H. Mattingly, trans., *Tacitus on Britain and Germany* (Harmondsworth, Middlesex, UK: Penguin Books, 1978), 72.

2. Horace, *Epistles* 2.1, lines 156–157.

3. Herbert Musurillo, ed. and trans., *The Acts of the Christian Martyrs* (Oxford, UK: Clarendon Press, 1972), 119.

4. Ammianus Marcellinus, 24.6.7, quoted. in M. Brosius, *The Persians* (London: Routledge, 2006), 187.

5. Josef Wiesehöfer, *Ancient Persia from 550 B.C. to 650 A.D.* (London: Tauris, 1996), 199.

Chapter 7

1. *The Endeavour Journal of Joseph Banks, 1768–1771*, ed. J. C. Beaglehole (Sydney, Australia: Halstead Press, 1962), 1:368. Spellings retained from the original source.
2. *The Endeavour Journal of Joseph Banks, 1768–1771*, ed. J. C. Beaglehole (Sydney, Australia: Halstead Press, 1962), 2:37. Spellings retained from the original source.
3. Martin West, trans., "A New Sappho Poem," *The Times Literary Supplement*, June 24, 2005.

Chapter 8

1. Jo Ann McNamara and John E. Halborg, eds. and trans., *Sainted Women of the Dark Ages* (Durham, NC: Duke University Press, 1992), 65, 72, 75.
2. Procopius, *The Secret History*, trans. G. A. Williamson (London: Penguin, 1966), 106.
3. Alcuin, "Letter 8" (to Charlemagne), in Stephen Allott, *Alcuin of York, c. A.D. 732 to 804: His Life and Letters* (York, UK: Sessions, 1974), 11.
4. Gregory, *Pastoral Care*, 1.1, trans. Henry Davis, in *Ancient Christian Writers* (New York: Newman Press, 1950), 11:21.
5. S. H. Cross and O. P. Sherbovitz-Wetzor, *The Russian Primary Chronicle, Laurentian Text* (Cambridge, MA: Medieval Academy of America, 1953), 53, referring to the Poliane people inhabiting modern-day Ukraine.
6. Procopius, *History of the Wars*, trans. H. B. Dewing (Cambridge, MA: Harvard University Press, 1924), 7:14, 22–30.
7. Quoted in Gaston Wiet, *Baghdad: Metropolis of the Abbasid Caliphate* (Norman: University of Oklahoma Press, 1971), 11.
8. Sufyan al-Thawri, quoted in Francis Robinson, ed., *The Cambridge Illustrated History of the Islamic World* (Cambridge: Cambridge University Press, 1996), 22.
9. Charles Plummer, ed., *Two of the Saxon Chronicles* (Oxford, UK: Clarendon Press, 1892), 57.
10. *Beowulf*, lines 4–11, from *Beowulf: A Verse Translation*, trans. Michael Alexander (London: Penguin, 1973), 3.

Chapter 9

1. Translated from Xuanzang, *Record of the Western Regions*.
2. Translated from *The Chronicles of Japan*, Chapter 19.
3. Translated from Xuanzang, *Western Regions*, Book 2.
4. Ibid., Book 7.
5. Translated in Munshi Debiprasad, "Ghatayala Inscription of the Pratihara Kakkuka of [Vikrama-] Samvat 918," *Journal of the Royal Asiatic Society* (1895): 519–520.
6. Cosmas Indicopleustes, *Christian Topography* (c. 547–550) (London: Hakluyt Society, 1897), Book II, 47.

Chapter 11

1. Quotations from S. D. Goitein, "Portrait of a Medieval India Trader: Three Letters from the Cairo Geniza," *Bulletin of the School of Oriental and African Studies*, 50, no. 3 (1987): 461; S. D. Goitein, *A Mediterranean Society: The Jewish Communities of the World as Portrayed in the Documents of the Cairo Geniza* (Berkeley: University of California Press, 1978–88), 3:194; 5:221.
2. Kekaumenos, *Strategikon*, quoted in Angeliki E. Laiou, "Economic Thought and Ideology," in Angeliki E. Laiou, ed., *The Economic History of Byzantium from the Seventh Through the Fifteenth Century* (Washington, DC: Dumbarton Oaks Research Library and Collection, 2002), 3:1127.
3. Ibn Hazm, *The Ring of the Dove: A Treatise on the Art and Practice of Arab Love* (London: Luzac, 1953), 74.
4. Al-Muqaddasi, *The Best Divisions for Knowledge of the Regions*, trans. Basil Anthony Collins (Reading, UK: Garnet, 1994), 181.
5. Quoted in Goitein, *A Mediterranean Society*, 1:200.
6. Translation adapted from Yuan Ts'ai, *Family Instructions for the Yuan Clan*, quoted in Patricia Buckley Ebrey, *Family and Property in Sung China: Yuan Ts'ai's Precepts for Social Life* (Princeton, NJ: Princeton University Press, 1984), 267.
7. Ibn Hawqal, *The Picture of the Earth*, translated in N. Levtzion and J. F. P. Hopkins, eds., *Corpus of Early Arabic Sources for West African History* (Cambridge: Cambridge University Press, 1981), 49.
8. Al-Bakri, *Kitab al masalik wa-'l-mamalik*, translated in Levtzion and Hopkins, eds., *Corpus of Early Arabic Sources*, 79.
9. Al-Umari, "The Kingdom of Mali and What Appertains to It" (1338), cited in Levtzion and Hopkins, eds., *Corpus of Early Arabic Sources*, 270–271.

Chapter 12

1. Lady Murasaki, *The Tale of Genji*, quoted in Ivan Morris, *The World of the Shining Prince: Court Life in Ancient Japan* (New York: Knopf, 1964), 308–309.
2. *The Letters of Abelard and Heloise*, trans. Betty Radice (Harmondsworth, UK: Penguin, 1974), 58.
3. *The Anglo-Saxon Chronicle*, trans. G. N. Garmonsway (London: J. M. Dent, 1954), 216.
4. Farid al-Din Attar, *Tadhkirat al-Awliya*, quoted in Margaret Smith, *Rabi'a the Mystic and Her Fellow Saints in Islam* (Cambridge: Cambridge University Press, 1928), 3–4.
5. W. Montgomery Watt, *The Faith and Practice of al-Ghazali* (London: George Allen & Unwin, 1967), 57.
6. Ali Hujwiri, *The Kashf al-Mahjūb: The Oldest Persian Treatise on Sufism*, trans. Reynold A. Nicholson (rpt. ed.; London: Luzac, 1976), 213.
7. Quoted in Ichisada Miyazaki, *China's Examination Hell: The Civil Service Examinations of Imperial China* (New Haven, CT: Yale University Press, 1981), 17.

Chapter 13

1. *The Deeds of the Franks and the Other Pilgrims to Jerusalem*, cited in James Harvey Robinson, ed., *Readings in European History* (Boston: Ginn, 1904), 1:312.
2. Ibn Jubayr, "Relation de voyages," *Voyageurs arabes: Ibn Fadlan, Ibn Jubayr, Ibn Battuta et un auteur anonyme*, trans. Paul Charles-Dominique (Paris: Éditions Gallimard, 1995), 310.
3. Bernard of Clairvaux, *Letters*, trans. Bruno Scott James (London: Burns, Oates, 1953), 467.
4. Cited in Bartlett, *The Making of Europe*, 132.
5. Nicole Oresme, "Le Livre de Politiques d'Aristotle," *Transactions of the American Philosophical Society*, new series, vol. 60, part 6 (1970), 292.
6. *Marco Polo: The Description of the World*, eds. A. C. Moule and Paul Pelliot (London: George Routledge & Sons, 1938), 1:192.
7. *Rashiduddin Fazullah's* Jami'u't-tawarikh (Compendium of Chronicles): *A History of the Mongols*, trans. W. M. Thackston (Cambridge, MA: Harvard University, Department of Near Eastern Languages and Civilizations, 1998), Part I, 6.

Chapter 14

1. Giovanni Boccaccio, *The Decameron* (New York: Modern Library, 1931), 8–9.
2. Quoted in Adel Allouche, *Mamluk Economics: A Study and Translation of Al-Maqrizi's* Ighathah (Salt Lake City: University of Utah Press, 1994), 75–76 (translation slightly modified).
3. Quoted in Michael W. Dols, "Ibn al-Wardi's *Risalah al-naba' 'an al'waba'*: A Translation of a Major Source for the History of the Black Death in the Middle East," in *Near Eastern Numismatics, Iconography, Epigraphy and History: Studies in Honor of George C. Miles*, ed. Dickran K. Kouymjian (Beirut, Lebanon: American University of Beirut, 1974), 454.
4. *Anonimalle Chronicle*, in *The Peasants' Revolt of 1381*, ed. R. B. Dobson (London: Macmillan, 1970), 164–165.
5. Ibn Battuta, "The Sultan of Mali," in *Corpus of Early Arabic Sources for West African History*, trans. J. F. P. Hopkins, ed. N. Levtzion and J. F. P. Hopkins (Cambridge: Cambridge University Press, 1981), 296.
6. Leo Africanus, *History and Description of Africa*, trans. John Poy (London: Hakluyt Society, 1896), 3:825.
7. Shihab al-Din Ahmad ibn Majid, "Al'Mal'aqiya," in *A Study of the Arabic Texts Containing Material of South-East Asia*, ed. and trans. G. R. Tibbetts (Leiden, Netherlands: Brill, 1979), 206.
8. Simone Sigoli, "Pilgrimage of Simone Sigoli to the Holy Land," in *Visit to the Holy Places of Egypt, Sinai, Palestine and Syria in 1384 by Frescobaldi, Gucci, and Sigoli*, trans. Theophilus Bellorini and Eugene Hoade (Jerusalem: Franciscan Press, 1948), 182.
9. Quoted in Lisa Jardine, *Worldly Goods: A New History of the Renaissance* (New York: Doubleday, 1996), 126.
10. Declaration of Oshima and Okitsushima shrine association, dated 1298, quoted in Pierre François Souyri, *The World Turned Upside Down: Medieval Japanese Society* (New York: Columbia University Press, 2001), 136.

Chapter 15

1. For the archaeologist's own account of these discoveries, see Johan Reinhard, *The Ice Maiden: Inca Mummies, Mountain Gods, and Sacred Sites in the Andes* (Washington, DC: National Geographic, 2005).
2. Miguel León-Portilla, *Pre-Columbian Literatures of Mexico* (Norman: University of Oklahoma Press, 1969), 87.
3. Juan de Betanzos, *Narrative of the Incas*, c. 1557, trans. Roland Hamilton and Dana Buchanan (Austin: University of Texas Press, 1996), 92.

Chapter 16

1. Christopher Columbus, *The Four Voyages*, trans. J. M. Cohen (New York: Penguin, 1969), 300.
2. Gomes Eannes de Azurara, quoted in John H. Parry and Robert G. Keith, *New Iberian World: A Documentary History of the Discovery of Latin America to the Seventeenth Century* (New York: Times Books, 1984), 1:256.
3. Alfred Crosby, *The Columbian Exchange: Biological and Cultural Consequences of 1492*, 2nd ed. (Westport, CT: Praeger, 2003).
4. Quoted in Ross Hassig, *Aztec Warfare: Imperial Expansion and Political Control* (Norman: University of Oklahoma Press, 1992), 124.

Chapter 17

1. The story of Domingo Angola is reconstructed from notary documents found in the Ecuadorian National Archive in Quito (Archivo Nacional del Ecuador, Protocolos notariales 1:19 FGD, 1-x-1601, ff. 647–746, and 1:6 DLM, 5-x-1595, f. 287v) and various studies of the early slave trade, especially Linda Heywood and John Thornton, *Central Africans, Atlantic Creoles, and the Foundation of the Americas, 1585–1660* (New York: Cambridge University Press, 2007). On the Jesuits in Luanda and their involvement in the slave trade at this time, see Dauril Alden, *The Making of an Enterprise: The Society of Jesus in Portugal, Its Empire, and Beyond, 1540–1750* (Stanford, CA: Stanford University Press, 1996), 544–546.
2. Joseph Miller, *Way of Death: Merchant Capitalism and the Angolan Slave Trade, 1730–1830* (Madison: University of Wisconsin Press, 1988), 4–5.
3. George E. Brooks, *Landlords and Strangers: Ecology, Society, and Trade in Western Africa, 1000–1630* (Boulder, CO: Westview Press, 1994).
4. This and other letters are published in António Brásio, ed., *Monumenta Missionaria Africana*, vol. 1, *África Ocidental (1471–1531)* (Lisbon: Agência Geral do Ultramar, 1952), 470–471. (Special thanks to José Curto of York University, Canada, for pointing out this reference.)
5. Olaudah Equiano, *The Interesting Narrative of the Life of Olaudah Equiano, Written by Himself*, 2nd ed., introduction by Robert J. Allison (Boston: Bedford/St. Martin's, 2007).

Chapter 18

1. Marshall Hodgson, *The Venture of Islam* (Chicago: University of Chicago Press, 1974), 2:34.
2. Robert Sewell, *A Forgotten Empire (Vijayanagar): A Contribution to the History of India* (London: Sonnenschein, 1900), 245.
3. Thackston Wheeler, ed. and trans., *The Baburnama: Memoirs of Babur, Prince and Emperor* (Washington, DC: Smithsonian Institution, 1996), 326, 384.
4. Vasco da Gama, *The Diary of His Travels Through African Waters, 1497–1499*, ed. and trans. Eric Axelson (Somerset, UK: Stephan Phillips, 1998), 45.

Chapter 19

1. Mustafa Celalzade, *Selim-name* [In praise of Selim] (eds. Ahmet Uğur, Mustafa Huhadar), Ankara 1990; as it appears in Halil Berktay and Bogdan Murgescu, *The Ottoman Empire* (Thessaloniki: CDRSEE, 2005), 53.
2. Habsburg ambassador Ghiselin de Busbecq, quoted in Gérard Chaliand, ed., *The Art of War in World History* from Antiquity to the Nuclear Age (Berkeley: University of California Press, 1994), 457.
3. Catherine Pagani, *Eastern Magnificence & European Ingenuity: Clocks of Late Imperial China* (Ann Arbor: University of Michigan Press, 2001), 18.

Chapter 20

1. Bashō, "The Records of a Weather-Exposed Skeleton" (c. 1685), ed. and trans. Nobuyuki Yuasa, *The Narrow Road to the Deep North and Other Sketches* (London: Penguin, 1966).

Chapter 21

1. Sor Juana Inés de la Cruz, quoted in Irving Leonard, *Baroque Times in Old Mexico: Seventeenth-Century Persons, Places, and Practices* (Ann Arbor: University of Michigan Press, 1959), 189.
2. Saramakan elder Lántifáya, quoted in Richard Price, *First-Time: The Historical Vision of an Afro-American People* (Baltimore, MD: Johns Hopkins University Press, 1983), 71.

Chapter 22

1. Luis Peru de Lacroix, *Diario de Bucuramanga* (Caracas: Comité ejecutivo del Bicentenario de Simón Bolívar, 1982), 67, quoted in Charles Minguet, ed., *Simon Bolivar: Unité impossible* (Paris: La Découverte, 1983), 13.
2. Voltaire, *Essai sur les moeurs*, 3:179.
3. Quoted in Hilda L. Smith and Berenice A. Carroll, eds., *Women's Political and Social Thought* (Bloomington: Indiana University Press, 2000), 133.
4. "Political Testament," in George I. Mosse et al., eds., *Europe in Review* (Chicago: Rand McNally, 1957), 111–112.
5. Quoted in Richard Wortman, *Scenarios of Power: Myth and Ceremony in Russian Monarchy, Volume 1: From Peter the Great to the Death of Nicholas I* (Princeton, NJ: Princeton University Press, 1995), 130.
6. *Seminario Económico de México*, 1811, quoted in Silvia Marina Arrom, *The Women of Mexico City, 1790–1857* (Palo Alto, CA: Stanford University Press, 1985), 18.
7. Edward Long, quoted in Barbara Bush, *Slave Women in the Caribbean, 1650–1838* (London: Heinemann, 1990), 15, 51.
8. Quoted in Paul Dukes, ed. and trans., *Russia Under Catherine the Great: Select Documents on Government and Society* (Newtonville, MA: Oriental Research Partners, 1978), 112, 115.
9. Alexander Hamilton, *Federalist Papers*, Number 15.
10. Letter to John Jay, March 14, 1779, http://www.c250.columbia.edu/c250_celebrates/remarkable_columbians/alexander_hamilton.html.
11. Quoted in Ron Chernow, *Alexander Hamilton* (New York: Penguin, 2004), 316.
12. Quoted in Lynn Hunt, *The French Revolution and Human Rights: A Brief Documentary History* (Boston: Bedford/St. Martins, 1996), 65.
13. Quoted in Annie Jourdan, *Napoléon: Héros, Imperator, Mécène* (Paris: Aubier, 1998), 34.
14. Quoted in Albert Hourani, *Arabic Thought in the Liberal Age, 1798–1939* (London: Oxford University Press, 1962); "Address to the National Assembly, to Our Lords the Representatives of the Nation," quoted in Laurent Dubois and John D. Garrigus, eds., *Slave Revolution in the Caribbean, 1789–1804: A Brief History with Documents* (Boston: Bedford/St. Martins, 2005), 69.
15. Quoted Dubois and Garrigus, *Slave Revolution*, 77.
16. "Notes [from Napoleon Bonaparte] to Serve as Instructions to Give to the Captain General Leclerc," quoted in Dubois and Garrigus, *Slave Revolution*, 176.
17. "Proclamation of 1809," quoted in Peter Bakewell, *A History of Latin America: Empires and Sequels, 1450–1930* (Oxford, UK: Blackwell, 1997), 362.
18. Juan Ruiz de Apodaca, quoted in Richard Boyer and Geoffrey Spurling, eds., *Colonial Lives: Documents on Latin American History, 1550–1850* (New York: Oxford University Press, 2000), 305.
19. Quoted in George Reid Andrews, *Afro-Latin America, 1800–2000* (New York: Oxford University Press, 2004), 57.
20. Quoted in John Lynch, "The Origins of Spanish American Independence," in *The Cambridge History of Latin America* (Cambridge: Cambridge University Press, 1985), 3:32.
21. Quoted in Martyn Lyons, *Napoleon Bonaparte and the Legacy of the French Revolution* (London: Macmillan, 1994), 232.
22. Quoted in Lyons, *Napoleon Bonaparte*, v.
23. William Briggs, quoted in Phyllis Mack, *Heart Religion in the British Enlightenment: Gender and Emotion in Early Methodism* (New York: Cambridge University Press, 2008), 2.
24. John Esposito, *Islam: The Straight Path* (New York: Oxford University Press, 1991).
25. "Letter from Jamaica," 1815, http://faculty.smu.edu/bakewell/bakewell/texts/jamaica-letter.html.

Chapter 23

1. James R. Simmons Jr., ed., *Factory Lives: Four Nineteenth-Century Working-Class Autobiographies* (Peterborough, Ontario: Broadview, 2007), 110.
2. Ibid., 123.
3. Quoted in Brian Dolan, *Wedgwood: The First Tycoon* (New York: Viking, 2004), 54.
4. Quoted in Sally and David Dugan, *The Day the World Took Off: The Roots of the Industrial Revolution* (London: Macmillan, 2000), 54.
5. Quoted in Ken Alder, *Engineering the Revolution: Arms and Enlightenment in France, 1763–1815* (Princeton, NJ: Princeton University Press, 1997), 223.
6. Quoted in Tessa Morris-Suzuki, *The Technological Transformation of Japan from the Seventeenth to the Twenty-First Century* (Cambridge, UK: Cambridge University Press, 1994), 65.
7. Quoted in ibid., 73.
8. Quoted in T. R. Havens, "Early Modern Farm Ideology and Japanese Agriculture," in *Meiji Japan: Political, Economic and Social History*, ed. Peter Kornicki (Routledge: New York, 1998), 1:235.
9. Quoted in Edward Beatty, *Institutions and Investment: The Political Basis of Industrialization in Mexico Before 1911* (Stanford, CA: Stanford University Press, 2001), 59.

10. Thomas Munro, quoted in Romash Chunder Dutt, *The Economic History of India* (Delhi: Low Price, 1990 [orig. pub. 1902–1904]), 185–186.

11. "The Land System of the Heavenly Dynasty" (1853), quoted in *China: Readings in the History of China from the Opium War to the Present*, ed. J. Mason Gentzler (New York: Praeger, 1977), 56.

12. Quoted in Michael E. Meeker, *A Nation of Empire: The Ottoman Legacy of Turkish Modernity* (Berkeley: University of California Press, 2002), 103.

13. Afaf Lutfi Al-Sayyid Marsot, *Egypt in the Reign of Muhammad Ali* (Cambridge: Cambridge University Press, 1984), 169–171.

14. Quoted in Carolyn Brown, *"We Were All Slaves": African Miners, Culture, and Resistance at the Enugu Government Colliery* (Portsmouth, NH: Heinemann, 2003), 36.

15. Mr. Laird, quoted in Joseph Inicori, *Africans and the Industrial Revolution in England: A Study in International Trade and Economic Development* (New York: Cambridge University Press, 2002), 394.

16. Debendranath Tagore, quoted in Blair B. Kling, *Partner in Empire: Dwarkanath Tagore and the Age of Enterprise in Eastern India* (Berkeley: University of California Press, 1976), 184.

17. Quoted on the Tata Group website, http://www.tata.com/0_about_us/history/pioneers/quotable.htm.

18. Quoted in Susie Tharu and K. Lalita, eds., *Women Writing in India: 600 B.C. to the Early Twentieth Century* (London: Pandora, 1991), 1:214.

19. Quoted in Caroline Arscott, "'Without Distinction of Party': The Polytechnic Exhibitions in Leeds, 1839–1945," in *The Culture of Capital: Art, Power, and the Nineteenth-Century Middle Class*, ed. Janet Wolff and John Seed (Manchester, UK: Manchester University Press, 1988), 145.

20. Quoted in Susie Porter, *Working Women in Mexico City: Public Discourse and Material Conditions, 1879–1931* (Tucson: University of Arizona Press, 2003), 3–4.

21. Quoted in E. Patricia Tsurumi, *Factory Girls: Women in the Thread Mills of Meiji Japan* (Princeton, NJ: Princeton University Press, 1990), 139.

22. Quoted in Ivy Pinchbeck, *Women Workers and the Industrial Revolution, 1750–1850* (London: Virago, 1981 [orig. pub. 1930]), 195.

23. Quoted in Eric Hobsbawm and George Rudé, *Captain Swing: A Social History of the Great English Agricultural Uprising of 1830* (New York: Norton, 1968), 208.

24. Quoted in Victoria E. Bonnell, *The Russian Worker: Life and Labor Under the Tsarist Regime* (Berkeley: University of California Press, 1983), 197.

25. Judith A. Carney, *Black Rice: The African Origins of Rice Cultivation in the Americas* (Cambridge, MA: Harvard University Press, 2001), 31.

26. Ibid., 147.

Chapter 24

1. Anne Walthall, *The Weak Body of a Useless Woman: Matsuo Taseko and the Meiji Restoration* (Chicago: University of Chicago Press, 1998), 98, 107.

2. Quoted in John Armstrong Crow, *The Epic of Latin America*, 4th ed. (Berkeley: University of California Press, 1992), 542.

3. Quoted in George Reid Andrews, *Afro-Latin America, 1800–2000* (New York: Oxford University Press, 2004), 113.

4. Quoted in Sarah C. Chambers, *From Subjects to Citizens: Honor, Gender, and Politics in Arequipa, Peru, 1780–1854* (University Park: Pennsylvania State University Press, 1999), 234–235.

5. Quoted in ibid., 184.

6. "Alexander Nikitenko Responds to the Emancipation of the Serfs, 1861," http://artsci.shu.edu/reesp/documents/nikitenko.htm.

7. Quoted in Jasper Ridley, *Garibaldi* (London: St. Martins, 2001), 443.

8. Ibid., 448.

9. German Historical Institute, http://ghdi.ghi-dc.org/sub_document.cfm?document_id=250.

10. Quoted in James L. Roark et al., *The American Promise: A History of the United States*, 4th ed. (Boston: Bedford/St. Martins, 2009), 537.

11. Quoted in Frank Linderman, *Pretty-Shield: Medicine Woman of the Crows* (Lincoln: University of Nebraska Press, 1972), 83.

12. Daklugie quoted in Colin G. Calloway, *First Peoples: A Documentary Survey of American Indian History*, 3rd ed. (Boston: Bedford/St. Martins, 2008), 312.

13. Quoted in Mikiso Hane, *Peasants, Rebels, and Outcastes: The Underside of Modern Japan* (New York: Pantheon, 1982), 24.

14. Paul Leroy-Beaulieu, quoted in *Histoire de la colonisation française* (Paris: Fayard, 1991), 2:149.

15. Rachel Fell McDermott et al., eds., *Sources of Indian Traditions: Modern India, Pakistan, and Bangladesh* (New York: Columbia University Press, 2014), 99.

16. Quoted in Rudrangshu Mukherjee, "The Sepoy Mutinies Revisited," in *War and Society in Colonial India, 1807–1945*, ed. Kaushik Roy (Delhi: Oxford University Press, 2006), 121.

17. Quoted in Charles Lee Keeton, *King Thebaw and the Ecological Rape of Burma: The Political and Commercial Struggle Between British India and French Indo-China in Burma, 1878–1886* (Delhi, India: Manohar Book Service, 1974), 202.

18. Phan Chau Trinh, in Truong Buu Lam, *Colonialism Experienced: Vietnamese Writing on Colonialism, 1900–1931* (Ann Arbor: University of Michigan Press, 2000), 130.

19. William Morton Fullerton, *In Cairo*, quoted in Max Rodenbeck, *Cairo: The City Victorious* (New York: Knopf, 1999), 136.

20. Letter from the king of Daboya to governor of the Gold Coast, July 8, 1892, quoted in A. Adu Boahen, *African Perspectives on Colonialism* (Baltimore, MD: Johns Hopkins University Press, 1987), 37.

21. Cecil Rhodes, "Confession of Faith" (1877), in John E. Flint, *Cecil Rhodes* (Boston: Little Brown, 1974), 248–250.

22. Ramon Hawley Myers and Mark R. Peattie, eds., *The Japanese Imperial Colonial Empire, 1895–1945* (Princeton, NJ: Princeton University Press, 1984), 15.

23. Quoted in Mike Davis, *Late Victorian Holocausts: El Niño Famines and the Making of the Third World* (London: Verso, 2001), 46.

24. Jack Kelly, *Gunpowder: Alchemy, Bombards, and Pyrotechnics: The History of the Explosive That Changed the World* (New York: Basic Books, 2004), 233.

25. Davis, *Late Victorian Holocausts*, 139.

26. Quoted in Jennifer W. Cushman, *Family and State: The Formation of a Sino-Thai Tin-Mining Dynasty, 1797–1832* (Singapore: Oxford University Press, 1991), 62.

27. Khayr al-Din al-Tunisi, "The Surest Path to Knowledge Concerning the Condition of Countries," quoted in *Colonial Rule in Africa: Readings from Primary Sources*, ed. Bruce Fetter (Madison: University of Wisconsin Press, 1979), 57.

28. Quoted in Bruce Fetter, ed., *Colonial Rule in Africa*, 117.

29. Quoted in Robert O. Collins, ed., *Eastern African History*, vol. 2, *African History: Text and Readings* (New York: Markus Wiener, 1990), 124.

30. Mary Antin, *The Promised Land* (Boston: Houghton Mifflin, 1912), 8.

31. "Song of Revolution," in Gungwu Wang, *Community and Nation: China, Southeast Asia and Australia* (St. Leonards, Australia: Allen and Unwin, 1992), 10.

32. Quoted in Sumanta Banerjee, "Women's Popular Culture in Nineteenth Century Bengal," in *Recasting Women: Essays in Indian Colonial History*, ed. Kumkum Sangari and Sudesh Vaid (New Brunswick, NJ: Rutgers University Press, 1990), 142.

33. Quoted in David Robinson, *Muslim Societies and French Colonial Authorities in Senegal and Mauritania, 1880–1920* (Athens: Ohio University Press, 2000), 204.

34. Quoted in Irokawa Daikichi, *The Culture of the Meiji Period*, ed. and trans. Marius B. Jansen (Princeton, NJ: Princeton University Press, 1985), 56.

35. Quoted in Richard Slotkin, *The Fatal Environment: The Myth of the Frontier in an Age of Industrialization* (Norman: University of Oklahoma Press, 1985), 339.

36. Ibid., 347.

37. "The Race Problem: An Autobiography: A Southern Colored Woman," *Independent*, 56 (1904): 586–589.

38. Quoted in Stephen Oates, *A Woman of Valor: Clara Barton and the Civil War* (New York: Free Press, 1994), 157–158.

39. Ida B. Wells, *Crusade for Justice: The Autobiography of Ida B. Wells*, ed. Alfreda M. Duster (Chicago: University of Chicago Press, 1970), 49.

40. Eliezer Perlman (Ben Yehuda), quoted in Howard M. Sachar, *A History of the Jews in the Modern World* (New York: Random House, 2006), ebook, np.

41. Grete Meisel-Hess, *The Sexual Crisis*, trans. Eden and Cedar Paul (New York: Critic and Guide, 1917), 6.

Chapter 25

1. Chief Segale, quoted in Peter Warwick, *Black People and the South African War, 1899–1902* (Cambridge: Cambridge University Press, 1983), 177.

2. General Sir Ian Hamilton, *A Staff-Officer's Scrap-Book During the Russo-Japanese War* (New York: Longman's Green, 1907), 2:64.

3. Quoted in Paul A. Cohen, *History in Three Keys: The Boxers as Event, Experience, and Myth* (New York: Columbia University Press, 1997), 80.

4. Bal Gangadhar Tilak, "Address to the Indian National Congress, 1907," *https://sourcebooks.fordham.edu/mod/1907tilak.asp*.

5. Emiliano Zapata, "Plan de Ayala," quoted in Manuel Plana, *Pancho Villa et la Révolution Mexicaine*, trans. Bruno Gaudenzi (Florence, Italy: Castermann, 1993), 28.

6. Wang Jingwei, quoted in Prasenjit Duara, *Rescuing History from the Nation: Questioning Narratives of Modern China* (Chicago: University of Chicago Press, 1995), 141.

7. Quoted in Isabel V. Hull, *The Entourage of Wilhelm II, 1888–1918* (New York: Cambridge University Press, 1982), 266.

8. Quoted in Michael S. Neiberg, *The World War I Reader* (New York: New York University Press), 212.

9. Anonymous letter, February 17, 1915, in David Omissi, ed., *Indian Voices of the Great War: Soldiers' Letters, 1914–1918* (London: Macmillan, 1919), 38.

10. Philip Sauvain, *Key Themes of the Twentieth Century* (Cheltenham, UK: Stanley Thornes, 1996), 32.

11. "This Day in History," https://www.history.com/this-day-in-history/international-congress-of-women-opens-at-the-hague.

12. Yigit Akin, "War, Women, and the State: The Politics of Sacrifice in the Ottoman Empire During the First World War," *Journal of Women's History*, 26, no. 3 (Fall 2014): 13.

13. Laura Engelstein, *Russia in Flames: War, Revolution, Civil War, 1914–1921* (New York: Oxford University Press, 2017), 96.

14. Quoted in Oscar J. Martinez, *Fragments of the Mexican Revolution: Personal Accounts from the Border* (Albuquerque: University of New Mexico Press, 1983), 52.

15. Quoted in Margaret Macmillan, *Paris 1919: Six Months That Changed the World* (New York: Random House, 2001), 403.

16. "The Black Soldier," *Crisis*, 16, no. 2 (June 1918): 60.

17. Quoted in Merrill Peterson, *"Starving Armenians": America and the Armenian Genocide, 1915–1930* (Charlottesville: University of Virginia Press, 2004), 48.

18. Quoted in Andrew Mango, *Atatürk: The Biography of the Founder of Modern Turkey* (Woodstock, NY: Overlook, 1999), 278.

19. Quoted in Mango, *Atatürk*, 219.

20. Irfan Organ, *Portrait of a Turkish Family* (London: Eland, 1993), 223.

21. Quoted in Macmillan, *Paris 1919*, 340.

22. Quoted in Geoffrey Hodges, "Military Labour in East Africa," in *Africa and the First World War*, ed. Melvin Eugene Page (New York: St. Martin's Press, 1987), 146.

23. Quoted in Sally Marks, *The Ebbing of European Ascendancy: An International History of the World, 1914–1945* (London: Arnold, 2002), 219.

24. Quoted in Babacar Fall, *Le travail forcé en Afrique occidentale française (1900–1946)* (Paris: Karthala, 1993), 181.

25. Quoted in Michael Tsin, *Nation, Governance, and Modernity in China: Canton, 1900–1927* (Palo Alto, CA: Stanford University Press, 1999), 151.

26. Quoted in Wang Zheng, *Women in the Chinese Enlightenment: Oral and Textual Histories* (Berkeley: University of California Press, 1999), 196.

27. Quoted in Lynn Thomas, "The Modern Girl and Racial Respectability in South Africa," *Journal of African History*, 47, no. 3 (2006): 487.

28. Mohandas Gandhi, "Hind Swaraj," in *The Collected Works of Mahatma Gandhi* (Ahmedabad: Navjivan Trust, Government of India, Publications Division, 1963), 23.

29. Quoted in Jochen Hellbeck, *Revolution on My Mind: Writing a Diary Under Stalin* (Cambridge, MA: Harvard University Press, 2006), 146.

30. Jorge Luis Borges, "Things That Might Have Been," in *Selected Poems*, ed. Alexander Coleman (New York: Viking, 1999), 405.

Chapter 26

1. J. B. Priestley, *English Journey; being a rambling but truthful account of what one man saw and heard and felt and thought during a journey through England during the autumn of the year 1933* (London: Harper & Brothers, 1934), 319.

2. Ana Núñez Machin, quoted in Angel Santana Suárez, "Angel Santana Suárez: Cuban Sugar Worker," in *The Human Tradition in Latin America: The Twentieth Century*, ed. William H. Beezley and Judith Ewell (Wilmington, DE: Scholarly Resources, 1987), 85, 86.

3. Quoted in Piers Brendon, *The Dark Valley: A Panorama of the 1930s* (London: Jonathan Cape, 2000), 175.

4. Quoted in Ann Farnsworth-Alvear, *Dulcinea in the Factory: Myths, Morals, Men, and Women in Colombia's Industrial Experiment, 1905–1960* (Durham, NC: Duke University Press, 2000), 124, 125.

5. Quoted in James L. Roark et al., *The American Promise: A History of the United States*, 4th ed. (Boston: Bedford/St. Martins, 2009), 856.

6. Quoted in John Eric Marot, *The October Revolution in Prospect and Retrospect: Interventions in Russian and Soviet History* (Leiden: Brill, 2012), 54.

7. Barbara Evans Clements et al., *Russia's Women: Accommodation, Resistance, Transformation* (Berkeley: University of California Press, 1991), 270.

8. Quoted in Eric Weitz, *A Century of Genocide: Utopias of Race and Nation* (Princeton, NJ: Princeton University Press, 2015), 58.

9. "Requiem," https://the-eye.eu/public/Books/Poetry/Anna%20Akhmatova%20-%20Poems.pdf.

10. Edvard Radzinsky, *Stalin: The First In-Depth Biography Based on Explosive New Documents from Russia's Secret Archives*, trans. H. T. Willetts (New York: Doubleday, 1996), 363.

11. Jiang Jieshi, quoted in Patricia Buckley Ebrey, *Cambridge Illustrated History of China* (Cambridge: Cambridge University Press, 1996), 277.

12. Herbert Bix, *Hirohito and the Making of Modern Japan* (New York: HarperCollins, 2000), 274–276.

13. Adolf Hitler, *My Struggle* (London: Hurst and Black-ett, 1939 [1926]) vol. 1, chapter 6, Project Gutenberg, http://gutenberg.net.au/ebooks02/0200601.txt.

14. Claudia Koonz, *Mothers in the Fatherland: Women, the Family and Nazi Politics* (London: Routledge, 2013 [1987]), 157.

15. Edward Keynes and David W. Adamany, eds., *Borzoi Reader in American Politics* (New York: Knopf, 1971), 111.

16. Quoted in David Clay Large, *Between Two Fires: Europe's Path in the 1930s* (New York: Norton, 1991), 162.

17. Matsuoka Yosuke, quoted in Bix, *Hirohito*, 374.

18. Primo Levi, *Survival in Auschwitz* and *The Reawakening*, Stuart Woolf trans. (New York: Summit, 1985), 122.

19. Amartya Sen in Arjo Klamer, "Interview with Amartya Sen," *Journal of Economic Perspectives*, 3, no. 1 (Winter 1989): 136.

20. Quoted in John Lancaster, "An Indian Revolutionary Gains Favor Posthumously," *Washington Post*, May 23, 2005.

21. Carla Capponi, interviewed in Shelley Saywell, *Women in War: From World War II to El Salvador* (New York: Penguin, 1986), 82.

Chapter 27

1. Timothy Dunmore, *Soviet Politics, 1945–1953* (London: Macmillan, 1984), 129.

2. Harry S. Truman, "Truman Doctrine Speech," March 12, 1947.

3. Katherine Verdery, *Transylvanian Villagers: Three Centuries of Political, Economic, and Ethnic Change* (Berkeley: University of California Press, 1983), 33–34.

4. Dwight D. Eisenhower, press conference, April 7, 1954.

5. Quoted in Ronald J. Spector, *In the Ruins of Empire: The Japanese Surrender and the Battle for Postwar Asia* (New York: Random House, 2007), 78.

6. Quoted in Alex von Tunzelmann, *Indian Summer: The Secret History of the End of an Empire* (New York: Henry Holt, 2007), 225.

7. Everette Lee DeGoyler, quoted in Daniel Yergin, *The Prize: The Epic Quest for Oil, Money, and Power* (New York: Simon & Schuster, 1991), 393.

8. Golda Meir, *My Life* (New York: Putnam, 1975).

9. Gamal Abdel Nasser, "Nationalization Speech, 1956," in Carol A. Fisher and Fred Krinsky, eds., *Middle East in Crisis: A Historical and Documentary Review* (Syracuse, NY: Syracuse University Press, 1959), 136ff.

10. "Africa Must Unite" (1963), quoted in Michael Hunt, *The World Transformed, 1945 to the Present* (Boston: Bedford/St. Martin's, 2004), 144.

11. Superintendent of Police Philip, quoted in Carolyn A. Brown, *"We Were All Slaves": African Miners, Culture, and Resistance at the Enugu Government Colliery* (Portsmouth, NH: Heinemann, 2003), 310.

12. "Proclamation of the Algerian National Liberation Front (FLN), November 1, 1954," Cornell Middle East Library, https://middleeast.library.cornell.edu/content/proclamation-algerian-national-liberation-front-fln-november-1-1954.

13. W. O. Baker, "Computers as Information-Processing Machines in Modern Science," *Daedalus*, 99, no. 4 (Fall 1970): 1120.

14. Norman Borlaug, "Nobel Prize Acceptance Speech," 1970, http://www.nobel.se.

15. Jean Monnet, quoted in Ghita Ionescu, ed., *The New Politics of European Integration* (London: Palgrave Macmillan, 1972), 38.

16. "Mao Zedong on War and Revolution," Asia for Educators, http://afe.easia.columbia.edu/special/china_1900_mao_war.htm.

17. Anne Frank, *Diary of a Young Girl*, trans. B. M. Mooyaart. Doubleday (New York: Simon & Schuster, 1953), 237.

18. Quoted in Paula Giddings, *Where and When I Enter: The Impact of Black Women on Race and Sex in America* (New York: William Morrow, 1984), 316.

19. David Caute, *Sixty-Eight* (London: Hamilton, 1988), 165.

20. Richard Wright, *The Color Curtain: A Report on the Bandung Conference* (Jackson, MS: Banner, 1995).

21. Jawaharlal Nehru, "Speech to Bandung Conference Political Committee, 1955," Fordham Modern History Sourcebook, https://sourcebooks.fordham.edu/halsall/mod/1955nehru-bandung2.html.

Chapter 28

1. *Small Fires: Letters from Soviet Citizens to Ogonyok Magazine, 1887–1990* (New York: Summit, 1990), 178; author interview with Russian citizen, July 1994.

2. Quoted in Orville Schell, "China's Spring," in *The China Reader: The Reform Era*, ed. Orville Schell and David Shambaugh (New York: Vintage, 1999), 194.

3. Quoted in *Guardian Weekly*, September 19–25, 2002.

4. Quoted in James C. McKinley Jr., "Mexican Farmers Protest End of Corn-Import Taxes," *New York Times*, February 1, 2008.

5. Soutik Biswas, "India's Architect of Reforms," *BBC News*, May 22, 2004.

6. Quoted in Yvonne Corcoran-Nantes, "Female Consciousness or Feminist Consciousness: Women's Consciousness-Raising in Community-Based Struggles in Brazil," in *Global Feminisms Since 1945*, ed. Bonnie G. Smith (London: Routledge, 2000), 89.

7. William H. Worger, *Africa and the West: A Documentary History: From Colonialism to Independence, 1875 to the Present* (New York: Oxford University Press, 2010), 204.

8. Quoted in Michael Dutton, et al., *Beijing Time* (Cambridge, MA: Harvard University Press, 2008), 10.

9. Saranya Sukumaran, quoted in Saritha Rai, "India Is Regaining Contracts with the U.S.," *New York Times*, December 25, 2002, W7.

10. Georges Quioc, "La 'consomania' de l'Europe de l'Est électrise les distributeurs de l'Ouest," *Le Figaro économie*, January 13, 2003.

11. Quoted in *Le Monde*, June 2, 2002.

12. Quoted in *Le Monde*, January 17, 2003.

13. Quoted in *Libération*, January 20 and 21, 2002.

14. "Fourth World Conference on Women Beijing Declaration, 1995," http://www.un.org/womenwatch/daw/beijing/platform/declar.htm.

15. Quoted in Ayse Saktanber, "'We Pray Like You Have Fun': New Islamic Youth in Turkey Between Intellectualism and Popular Culture," in *Fragments of Culture: The Everyday of Modern Turkey* (London: I. B. Tauber, 2006), 254.

16. Quoted in "Nobel Peace Prize for Woman of 30m Trees," *Guardian*, October 9, 2004.

17. Quoted in "At Birth Control Class, Mullahs Face New Reality," *International Herald Tribune*, November 12, 2009.

18. Lisa Drummond and Mandy Thomas, eds., *Consuming Urban Culture in Contemporary Vietnam* (London: Routledge, 2003), 115.

19. Excerpted from "Mandato de la Primera Cumbre Continental de Mujeres Indigenas de Abya-Yala," posted on Abya-Yala Net, http://www.abyayalanet.org/index.php, translated by Pamela Murray in Pamela Murray, ed., *Women and Gender in Modern Latin America: Historical Sources and Interpretations* (New York: Routledge, 2014), 328–330.

20. "Wangari Maathai, Nobel Laureate," Marion Institute, https://www.marioninstitute.org/wangari-maathai-nobel-laureate/.

21. Wu Guanzhong, "Preface by the Artist," in Anne Farrer, *Wu Guanzhong: A Twentieth-Century Chinese Painter* (London: British Museum, 1991), 9.

Bibliography (Resources for Research)

Chapter 1

The study of the earliest stages of world history relies to a great extent on archaeological sources, but because the evolution of natural species, including humans, is involved, the disciplines of anthropology, genetics, and linguistics also contribute. The literature is extensive, and ideas change rapidly due to new finds.

Bahn, Paul G. *The Cambridge Illustrated History of Prehistoric Art*. 1997.

Barker, Graeme. *The Agricultural Revolution in Prehistory: Why Did Foragers Become Farmers?* 2009.

Bellwood, Peter. *First Farmers: The Origins of Agricultural Societies*. 2005.

Fagan, Brian. *World Prehistory: A Brief Introduction*, 9th ed. 2016.

Human origins: http://humanorigins.si.edu/

"Lascaux: A Visit to the Cave." http://www.lascaux.culture.fr/#/en/00.xml

Palmer, Douglas, *Origins: Human Evolution Revealed*. 2010.

Scarre, Chris, ed. *The Human Past*, 3rd ed. 2013.

Simmons, Alan H. *The Neolithic Revolution in the Near East: Transforming the Human Landscape*. 2007.

Tattersall, Ian. *Masters of the Planet: The Search for Our Human Origins*. 2012.

Wenke, Robert J., and Deborah I. Olszewski. *Patterns in Prehistory: Humankind's First Three Million Years*, 5th ed. 2007.

Chapter 2

Early developments in Mesopotamia interest historians, archaeologists, and anthropologists because they present the first appearance in world history of many aspects of human culture, such as cities, states, empires, and laws.

Aruz, Joan, ed. *Beyond Babylon: Art, Trade, and Diplomacy in the Second Millennium B.C.* 2008.

Black, Jeremy, and Anthony Green. *Gods, Demons and Symbols of Ancient Mesopotamia*. 1992.

*George, Andrew. *The Epic of Gilgamesh*. 2000.

Pollock, Susan. *Ancient Mesopotamia: The Eden That Never Was*. 1999.

Postgate, J. N. *Early Mesopotamia: Society and Economy at the Dawn of History*. 1992.

*Roth, Martha T. *Law Collections from Mesopotamia and Asia Minor*, 2nd ed. 1997.

Uluburun shipwreck: http://ina.tamu.edu/vm.htm

Van De Mieroop, Marc. *The Ancient Mesopotamian City*. 1999.

Van De Mieroop, Marc. *The Eastern Mediterranean in the Age of Ramesses II*. 2007.

Van De Mieroop, Marc. *A History of the Ancient Near East ca. 3000–323 B.C.*, 3rd rev. ed. 2016.

Wenke, Robert J., and Deborah I. Olszewski. *Patterns in Prehistory: Humankind's First Three Million Years*, 5th ed. 2007.

*Primary source.

Chapter 3

Most histories of early South and East Asia treat the periods before the appearance of written sources. They tend to focus on urban cultures, but pastoral aspects also draw attention. Several websites provide access to translations of primary sources.

Avari, Burjor. *India, the Ancient Past: A History of the Indian Sub-Continent from c. 7000 BC to AD 1200*. 2007.

*East Asian sources: http://www.fordham.edu/halsall/eastasia/eastasiasbook.html

Ebrey, Patricia Buckley. *The Cambridge Illustrated History of China*, 2nd ed. 2010.

Family Tree of Indo-European Languages: http://www.danshort.com/ie/

Golden, Peter B. "Nomadism and Sedentary Societies in Eurasia." In *Agricultural and Pastoral Societies in Ancient and Classical History*, edited by M. Adas, 71–115. 2001.

Hansen, Valerie. *The Open Empire: A History of China to 1800*, 2nd ed. 2015.

Indus Civilization: http://www.harappa.com/har/har0.html

*Internet Indian History Sourcebook: http://www.fordham.edu/halsall/india/indiasbook.html

Mallory, J. P. *In Search of the Indo-Europeans*. 1991.

Thapar, Romila. *Early India from the Origins to A.D. 1300*. 2002.

Visual Sourcebook of Chinese Civilization. http://depts.washington.edu/chinaciv/index.htm

Wright, Rita P. *The Ancient Indus: Urbanism, Economy, and Society*. 2010.

*Primary source.

Chapter 4

In their general surveys of the culture, many of the plentiful books on ancient Egypt treat the New Kingdom's imperial period and the period when Nubians ruled Egypt. The empires of Assyria and ancient Persia are often discussed in general surveys of ancient Near Eastern history.

*Achaemenid Persia: http://www.achemenet.com/en/

Allen, Lindsay. *The Persian Empire: A History*. 2005.

Ancient Egypt: http://www.ancient-egypt.co.uk

British Museum on Mesopotamia: http://www.mesopotamia.co.uk

*Kuhrt, Amélie. *The Persian Empire: A Corpus of Sources from the Achaemenid Period*. 2007.

Morkot, Robert G. *The Black Pharaohs: Egypt's Nubian Rulers*. 2000.

Radner, Karen. *Ancient Assyria: A Very Short Introduction*. 2015.

Theban Mapping Project: http://www.thebanmappingproject.com

Van De Mieroop, Marc. *A History of Ancient Egypt*. 2010.

Waters, Matt. *Ancient Persia: A Concise History of the Achaemenid Empire, 550–330 BCE*. 2014.

Welsby, Derek A. *The Kingdom of Kush: The Napatan and Meroitic Empires*. 2002.

*Primary source.

Chapter 5

The ancient cultures of India, China, and Greece are discussed in numerous historical surveys and more specialized publications. Because Buddhism and Hinduism had a lasting influence, many books treat the early developments of these religions within a long-term context. Studies of the Atlantic peoples, who left no writings of their own, are archaeological in nature and include Celtic tales that were written down much later.

Avari, Burjor. *India, the Ancient Past: A History of the Indian Sub-Continent from c. 7000 B.C. to A.D. 1200*. 2007.

Cartledge, Paul. *Alexander the Great: The Hunt for a New Past*. 2004.

Cunliffe, Barry. *The Celts: A Very Short Introduction*. 2003.

Erskine, Andrew, ed. *A Companion to the Hellenistic World*. 2003.

*Freeman, Philip. *Celtic Mythology: Tales of Gods, Goddesses, and Heroes*. 2017.

Gascoine, Bamber. *A Brief History of the Dynasties of China*. 2003.

Hansen, Valerie. *The Open Empire: A History of China to 1800*, 2nd ed. 2015.

Ivanhoe, Philip J., and Bryan W. Van Norden, eds. *Readings in Classical Chinese Philosophy*, 2nd ed. 2005.

Keown, Damien. *Buddhism: A Very Short Introduction*. 1996.

Kinzl, Konrad H., ed. *A Companion to the Classical Greek World*. 2006.

Knott, Kim. *Hinduism: A Very Short Introduction*. 1998.

Puett, Michael, and Christine Gross-Loh. *The Path: What Chinese Philosophers Can Teach Us About the Good Life*. 2016.

Sources of Indian Tradition: http://www.columbia.edu/itc/mealac/pritchett/00sources/#one

*Primary source.

Chapter 6

Ancient Rome is the subject of a vast amount of research and writing and works continue to be published on every aspect of its history and culture. In contrast, publications on the empires of Persia that existed alongside the Roman were highly specialized until recently.

Beard, Mary. *SPQR: A History of Ancient Rome*. 2015.

Bowersock, G. W., Peter Brown, and Oleg Grabar, eds. *Late Antiquity: A Guide to the Postclassical World*. 1999.

Goodman, Martin. *The Roman World 44 BC–AD 180*, 2nd ed. 2013.

Green, Bernard. *Christianity in Ancient Rome: The First Three Centuries*. 2010.

Harries, J. D. *Imperial Rome AD 284–363: The New Empire*. 2012.

Harris, William V. *Roman Power: A Thousand Years of Empire*. 2016.

*Internet Ancient History Sourcebook: Rome: http://www.fordham.edu/halsall/ancient/asbook09.html

Lee, A. D. *From Rome to Byzantium AD 363 to 565: The Transformation of Ancient Rome*. 2013.

Matyszak, Philip. *Chronicle of the Roman Republic: The Rulers of Ancient Rome from Romulus to Augustus*. 2008.

Parker, Geoffrey, and Brenda Parker. *The Persians: Lost Civilizations*. 2017.

Parthian Empire: http://parthia.com/

*Perseus digital texts: http://www.perseus.tufts.edu

Scarre, Christopher. *Chronicle of the Roman Emperors: The Reign-by-Reign Record of the Rulers of Imperial Rome*. 2012.

Vermes, Geza. *Christian Beginnings: From Nazareth to Nicaea (AD 30–325)*. 2012.

Woolf, Greg, ed. *Cambridge Illustrated History of the Roman World*. 2003.

*Primary source.

Chapter 7

In the absence of written sources, historians draw deeply on works from the archaeological perspective. The varied cultures discussed in this chapter are spread all over the world and are unevenly studied. There are many more studies of those on the American continent, for example, than on those of the Pacific.

African Archaeology: http://www.african-archaeology.net/

African history: https://networks.h-net.org/h-africa

Ehret, Christopher. *The Civilizations of Africa: A History to 1800*. 2002.

Fagan, Brian. *Ancient North America*, 4th ed. 2005.

Kirch, Patrick V. *The Lapita Peoples*. 1997.

Kirch, Patrick V. *On the Road of the Winds: An Archaeological History of the Pacific Islands Before European Contact*. 2000.

Houston, Stephen D., ed. *The First Writing: Script Invention as History and Process*. 2004.

Milleker, Elizabeth J., ed. *The Year One: Art of the Ancient World East and West*, 2000.

Moche culture: http://www.huacas.com/

Scarre, Chris, ed. *The Human Past: World Prehistory and the Development of Human Societies*, 2005.

Stahl, Ann, ed. *African Archaeology: A Critical Introduction*. 2005.

Stone, Rebecca. *Art of the Andes: from Chávin to Inca*, 3rd ed. 2012.

Wenke, Robert J., and Deborah I. Olszewski. *Patterns in Prehistory: Humankind's First Three Million Years*, 5th ed. 2007.

Chapter 8

Both Christianity and Islam spread across vast regions of Eurasia and Africa during this era, yet these religious traditions also assumed a multitude of forms in different societies. Recent research emphasizes the enduring influence of Roman culture and institutions on both Latin and Byzantine Christianity, and the ways in which Muhammad's teachings and the Islamic movement were shaped by interactions among the complex mosaic of cultures in Arabia and surrounding regions.

Al-Azmeh, Aziz. *The Emergence of Islam in Late Antiquity: Allāh and His People*. 2014.

Barraclough, Eleanor Rosamund. *Beyond the Northlands: Viking Voyages and the Old Norse Sagas*. 2016.

Berkey, Jonathan. *The Formation of Islam: Religion and Society in the Near East, 600 to 1800*. 2003.

Bowerstock, G. W. *The Crucible of Islam*. 2017.

Brown, Peter. *The Rise of Western Christendom*, rev. ed. 2013.

Christiansen, Eric. *The Norsemen in the Viking Age*. 2006.

Donner, Fred. *Muhammad and the Believers: At the Origins of Islam*. 2010.

Gordon, Matthew S. *The Rise of Islam*. 2005.

Heather, Peter. *Empires and Barbarians: The Fall of Rome and the Birth of Europe*. 2010.

Herrin, Judith. *Byzantium: The Surprising Life of a Medieval Empire*. 2007.

Islamic Studies on the Internet: http://www.fordham.edu/halsall/islam/islamsbook.html

Kreuger, Derek, ed. *Byzantine Christianity*. 2006.

Lapidus, Ira M. *A History of Islamic Societies*, 3rd ed. 2014.

MacMullen, Ramsay. *Christianity and Paganism in the Fourth to the Eighth Centuries*. 1997.

McKitterick, Rosamond. *Charlemagne: The Formation of a European Identity*. 2008.

McNamara, Jo Ann, and John E. Halborg, eds. and trans. *Sainted Women of the Dark Ages*. 1992.

Winroth, Anders. *The Age of the Vikings*. 2014.

Worlds of Late Antiquity (post-Roman Mediterranean): http://www9.georgetown.edu/faculty/jod/wola.html

Chapter 9

The spread of religious ideas and practices, political ideologies and institutions, and written languages and literary traditions shaped the formation of common civilizations in East, South, and Southeast Asia during the first millennium C.E. Much scholarly attention has focused on the role of the overland Central Asian "Silk Road" in stimulating cultural and economic interaction across Asia, but maritime routes also fostered such exchanges and promoted regional integration.

A Visual Sourcebook of Chinese Civilization: http://depts.washington.edu/chinaciv/

Adshead, S. A. M. *T'ang China: The Rise of the East in World History*. 2004.

Ali, Daud. *Courtly Culture and Political Life in Early Medieval India*. 2004.

Bentley, Jerry H. *Old World Encounters: Cross-Cultural Contacts and Exchanges in Pre-Modern Times*. 1993.

Chattopadhyaya, Brajadulal. *The Making of Early Medieval India*. 1994.

Doniger, Wendy. *On Hinduism*. 2014.

Farris, William Wayne. *Sacred Texts and Buried Treasures: Issues in the Historical Archaeology of Ancient Japan*. 1998.

Hall, Kenneth R. *A History of Early Southeast Asia: Maritime Trade and Societal Development, 100–1500*. 2011.

Hansen, Valerie. *The Silk Road: A New History with Documents*. 2016.

Higham, Charles. *The Civilization of Angkor*. 2002.

Holcombe, Charles. *The Genesis of East Asia, 221 B.C.-A.D. 907*. 2001.

International Dunhuang Project: http://idp.bl.uk/

Liu, Xinru. *The Silk Road in World History*. 2010.

Lockard, Craig A. *Southeast Asia in World History*. 2009.

Pai, Hyung-Il. *Constructing "Korean" Origins: A Critical Review of Archaeology, Historiography, and Racial Myth in Korean State-Formation Theories*. 2000.

Skaff, Jonathan. *Sui-Tang China and Its Turko-Mongol Neighbors: Culture, Power and Connections, 580–800*. 2012.

Thapar, Romila. *Early India: From the Origins to A.D. 1300*. 2002.

de la Vaissière, Étienne. *Sogdian Traders: A History*. 2005.

Whitfield, Susan, and Ursula Sims-Williams, eds. *Silk Road: Trade, Travel, War, and Faith*. 2004.

Wolters, O. W. *History, Culture, and Region in Southeast Asian Perspectives*. 1999.

Chapter 10

Our knowledge of the history of all the societies in this chapter except the Maya depends on research in fields such as archaeology and linguistics rather than written sources. Comparative and interdisciplinary research has revealed common features in the formation of social identity and political power, the broad reach of the cultural heritage of Mesoamerica, and human responses to ecological crises and the collapse of social systems.

Cahokia Mounds historical site: https://cahokiamounds.org/

Coe, Michael D. *The Maya*, 9th ed. 2015.

Cowgill, George L. *Ancient Teotihuacan: Early Urbanism in Central Mexico*. 2015.

Diamond, Jared. *Collapse: How Societies Choose to Fail or Succeed*. 2004.

Drew, David. *The Lost Chronicles of the Maya Kings*. 1999.

Earle, Timothy. *How Chiefs Come to Power: The Political Economy in Prehistory*. 1997.

Fagan, Brian. *Chaco Canyon: Archaeologists Explore the Lives of an Ancient Society*. 2005.

Homman, Robert J. *The Ancient Hawaiian State: Origins of a Political Society*. 2013.

Howe, K. R., ed. *Vaka Moana, Voyages of the Ancestors: The Discovery and Settlement of the Pacific*. 2007.

Janusek, John Wayne. *Ancient Tiwanaku*. 2008.

Kirch, Patrick V. *On the Road of the Winds: An Archaeological History of the Pacific Islands Before European Contact*. 2000.

Kolata, Alan. *The Tiwanaku: Portrait of an Andean Civilization*. 1993.

Milner, George R. *The Moundbuilders: Ancient Peoples of Eastern North America*. 2005.

Pauketat, Timothy R. *Ancient Cahokia and the Mississippians*. 2004.

Quilter, Jeffrey, and Mary Miller, eds. *A Pre-Columbian World*. 2006.

Sahlins, Marshall. *Social Stratification in Polynesia*. 1958.

Sharer, Robert J. *Daily Life in Maya Civilization*, 2nd ed. 2009.

Spriggs, Matthew. *The Island Melanesians*. 1997.

Stanish, Charles. *Lake Titicaca: Legend, Myth, and Science*. 2011.

Chapter 11

The diffusion of crops, technological innovations, and new commercial institutions and practices gave impetus to major advances in agricultural productivity, industrial growth, and commercial exchange across Eurasia between 900 and 1300. Far-flung merchant networks not only fostered the spread of goods and ideas, but also gave birth to multicultural trading communities in the great port cities and major commercial centers.

Abu-Lughod, Janet. *Before European Hegemony: The World System, A.D. 1250–1350*. 1989.

Austen, Ralph A. *Trans-Saharan Africa in World History*. 2010.

Chaudhuri, K. N. *Asia Before Europe: Economy and Civilization of the Indian Ocean from the Rise of Islam to 1750*. 1990.

Duby, Georges. *The Early Growth of the European Economy: Warriors and Peasants from the Seventh to the Twelfth Century*. 1974.

Epstein, Steven A. *An Economic and Social History of Later Medieval Europe, 1000–1500*. 2009.

Favier, Jean. *Gold and Spices: The Rise of Commerce in the Middle Ages*. 1998.

Goldberg, Jessica L. *Trade and Institutions in the Medieval Mediterranean: The Geniza Merchants and their Business World*. 2012.

Herlihy, David. *Opera Muliebria: Women and Work in Medieval Europe*. 1990.

Kirch, Patrick V. *A Shark Going Inland Is My Chief: The Island Civilization of Ancient Hawai'i*. 2012.

Kirch, Patrick V., and Jean-Louis Rallu, eds. *The Growth and Collapse of Pacific Island Societies: Archaeological and Demographic Perspectives*. 2007.

Laiou, Angeliki E., and Cécile Morrison. *The Byzantine Economy*. 2007.

Medieval Europe: http://sourcebooks.fordham.edu/Halsall/sbook1j.asp

Sen, Tansen. *Buddhism, Diplomacy, and Trade: The Realignment of Sino-Indian Relations, 600–1400*. 2003.

Verhulst, Adriaan. *The Carolingian Economy*. 2002.

Von Glahn, Richard. *The Economic History of China from Antiquity to the Nineteenth Century*. 2016.

Watson, A. M. *Agricultural Innovation in the Early Islamic World: The Diffusion of Crops and Farming Techniques, 700–1100*. 1983.

Chapter 12

In contrast to the control that religious and legal institutions wielded over educational institutions and intellectual life in Islamic and Christian societies, in China the civil service examinations implanted secular Confucian ideas and values in the ruling elite. This era witnessed both the circulation of knowledge across cultural and religious boundaries—for example, the rediscovery of Greek philosophy and science in Latin Christendom via translations from Arabic—and increasing regional diversity in vernacular languages and literary cultures.

Asher, Catherine B., and Cynthia Talbot. *India Before Europe*. 2006.

Asia for Educators: 1000 to 1450, Intensified Hemispheric Interactions (see sections on Neo-Confucianism): http://afe.easia.columbia.edu/tps/1000ce.htm

Berkey, Jonathan. *The Transmission of Knowledge in Medieval Cairo: A Social History of Islamic Education*. 1992.

Bol, Peter K. *Neo-Confucianism in History*. 2008.

Clanchy, M. T. *Abelard: A Medieval Life*. 1997.

Cobban, A. B. *The Medieval Universities: Their Development and Organization*. 1975.

Coe, Michael D. *Breaking the Maya Code*, rev. ed. 1999.

Eaton, Richard M., ed. *India's Islamic Traditions, 711–1750*. 2003.

Ephrat, Daphna. *A Learned Society in a Period of Transition: The Sunni Ulama of Eleventh-Century Baghdad*. 1995.

Miyazaki, Ichisada. *China's Examination Hell: The Civil Service Examinations of Imperial China*. 1981.

Moore, R. I. *The First European Revolution, c. 970–1215*. 2000.

Morris, Ivan. *The World of the Shining Prince: Court Life in Ancient Japan*. 1964.

Orme, Nicholas. *Medieval Schools: From Roman Britain to Renaissance England*. 2006.

Pollock, Sheldon. *The Language of the Gods in the World of Men: Sanskrit, Culture, and Power in Premodern India*. 2006.

Ridgeon, Lloyd, ed. *The Cambridge Companion to Sufism*. 2015.

Schele, Linda, and Peter Mathews. *The Code of Kings: The Language of Seven Sacred Maya Temples and Tombs*. 1998.

Starr, S. Frederick. *Lost Enlightenment: Central Asia's Golden Age from the Arab Conquest to Tamerlane*. 2015.

Tedlock, Dennis. *2000 Years of Mayan Literature*. 2010.

Wink, André. *Al-Hind: The Making of the Indo-Islamic World*, 2nd ed. 1997.

Chapter 13

The era of the Crusades sharpened the boundaries between the Christian and Islamic worlds, launched Latin Christendom's expansion into eastern and northern Europe and Spain, and gave rise to more distinctive religious, political, and cultural identities among Christians and Muslims alike. Although the Mongol conquests unleashed widespread destruction, Mongol rule had a transformative influence on many societies, including Russia, Iran, and China, and sparked a cultural renaissance in Central Asia.

Barber, Malcolm. *The Crusader States*. 2012.

Barber, Malcolm. *The New Knighthood: A History of the Order of the Temple*. 1994.

Bartlett, Robert. *The Making of Europe: Conquest, Colonization, and Cultural Change, 950–1350*. 1993.

Biran, Michal. *Chinggis Khan*. 2007.

Bisson, Thomas N. *The Crisis of the Twelfth Century: Power, Lordship, and the Origins of European Government*. 2009.

Christiansen, Eric. *The Northern Crusades: The Baltic and the Catholic Frontier, 1100–1525*, 2nd ed. 1997.

Crusades: Introduction: http://www.theorb.net/encyclop/religion/crusades/crusade_intro.html

France, John. *The Crusades and the Expansion of Catholic Christendom, 1000–1714*. 2005.

Hillenbrand, Carole. *The Crusades: Islamic Perspectives*. 2000.

Kafadar, Cemal. *Between Two Worlds: The Construction of the Ottoman State*. 1995.

Lane, George. *Early Mongol Rule in Thirteenth-Century Iran: A Persian Renaissance*. 2003.

Larner, John. *Marco Polo and the Discovery of the World*. 1999.

May, Timothy. *The Mongol Conquests in World History*. 2012.

Military Orders: A Guide to On-line Resources: https://www.arlima.net/the-orb/encyclop/religion/monastic/milindex.html

Morgan, David. *Medieval Persia, 1040–1797*, 2nd ed. 2015.

Morgan, David. *The Mongols*, 2nd ed. 2007.

Nicholson, Helen. *Templars, Hospitallers and Teutonic Knights: Images of the Military Orders, 1128–1291*. 1993.

Ostrowski, Donald. *Muscovy and the Mongols: Cross-Cultural Influences on the Steppe Frontier, 1304–1589*. 1998.

Riley-Smith, Jonathan. *The Crusades: A History*, 3rd ed. 2014.

Tyerman, Christopher. *The Invention of the Crusades*. 1998.

Wickham, Chris. *Medieval Europe*. 2016.

Chapter 14

The Black Death pandemic that erupted in the mid-fourteenth century had devastating consequences in Europe and the Islamic world, bringing an abrupt halt to the rising prosperity of the previous centuries. Despite the fall of the Mongol-ruled Yuan Empire in China, maritime Asia was spared the ravages of the Black Death and continued to enjoy robust cultural and economic interchange. By 1400 economic recovery in Italy gave birth to a new age of intellectual and artistic vigor—the Renaissance—which was shaped by transformative changes in trade, industry, material culture, and lifestyles.

Aberth, John. *The Black Death, the Great Mortality of 1348–1350: A Brief History with Documents*, 2nd ed. 2016.

Adolphson, Mikael S. *The Gates of Power: Monks, Courtiers, and Warriors in Premodern Japan*. 2000.

Barker, Juliet R. V. *1381: The Year of the Peasants' Revolt*. 2014.

Borsch, Stuart J. *The Black Death in Egypt and England: A Comparative Study*. 2005.

Brook, Timothy. *The Confusions of Pleasure: Commerce and Culture in Ming China*. 1998.

Dreyer, Edward L. *Zheng He: China and the Oceans in the Early Ming Dynasty*. 2007.

Dunn, Ross E. *The Adventures of Ibn Battuta: A Muslim Traveler of the 14th Century*, rev. ed. 2005.

Finlay, Robert. *The Pilgrim Art: Cultures of Porcelain in World History*. 2010.

Goldthwaite, Richard A. *Wealth and the Demand for Art in Italy, 1300–1600*. 1993.

Green, Monica H., ed. *Pandemic Disease in the Medieval World: Rethinking the Black Death*. 2015.

Imber, Colin. *The Ottoman Empire, 1300–1650: The Structure of Power*, 2nd ed. 2009.

Jardine, Lisa. *Worldly Goods: A New History of the Renaissance*. 1996.

Manz, Beatrice Forbes. *The Rise and Rule of Tamerlane*. Rpt. 1999.

Medieval Japan Through Art: Samurai Life in Medieval Japan: http://www.colorado.edu/cas/tea/curriculum/imaging-japanese-history/medieval/index.html

Reid, Anthony. *Southeast Asia in the Age of Commerce, 1350–1750*. Vol. 1, *The Land Below the Winds*; Vol. 2, *Expansion and Crisis*. 1989, 1993.

Robinson, David. *Muslim Societies in African History*. 2004.

Souyri, Pierre-François. *The World Turned Upside Down: Medieval Japanese Society*. 2001.

Wakita, Haruko. *Women in Medieval Japan: Motherhood, Household Economy, and Sexuality*. 2006.

Chapter 15

The "pre-contact" cultures of the Americas are no longer considered "prehistoric." Scholars from many disciplines have combined resources and methods to explain the rise of empires such as those of the Incas and Aztecs as well as the far more common appearance of regional chiefdoms from Canada to Patagonia.

Boone, Elizabeth, and Gary Urton. *Their Way of Writing: Scripts, Signs, and Pictographies in Pre-Columbian America*. 2011.

Carrasco, David. *The Aztecs: A Very Short Introduction*. 2011.

Carrasco, David. *City of Sacrifice: The Aztec Empire and the Role of Violence in Civilization*. 1999.

Clendinnen, Inga. *Aztecs: An Interpretation*. 1994.

D'Altroy, Terrence. *The Incas*, 2nd ed. 2014.

Denevan, William. *The Native Population of the Americas in 1492*, 2nd. ed. 1992.

Richter, Daniel K. *Facing East from Indian Country: A Native History of Early America*. 2003.

Trigger, Bruce, ed. *The Cambridge History of the Native Peoples of the Americas*. 3 vols. 1999.

Trigger, Bruce. *The Children of Aataentsic: A History of the Huron People to 1660*, 2nd. ed. 1987.

Urton, Gary. *Inka History in Knots: Reading Khipus as Primary Sources*. 2017.

Von Hagen, Adriana, and Craig Morris. *The Cities of the Ancient Andes*. 1998.

Chapter 16

Europe's transatlantic expansion in the wake of Columbus's 1492 voyage was audacious and often violent, but scholars have re-examined evidence that points to a complex range of interactions with native peoples as well as enslaved and free Africans. Early American colonialism was no picnic, but even in resistance it was a shared and also global project.

Bakewell, Peter. *A History of Latin America to 1825*, 3rd ed. 2009.

Clendinnen, Inga. *Ambivalent Conquests: Maya and Spaniard in Yucatan, 1517–1570*, 2nd ed. 2003.

Crosby, Alfred. *The Columbian Exchange*, 2nd ed. 2003.

Dillehay, Tom. *Monuments, Empires, and Resistance: The Araucanian Polity and Ritual Narratives*. 2007.

Disney, Anthony. *A History of Portugal and the Portuguese Empire*. 2009.

Gómez, Pablo F. *The Experiential Caribbean: Creating Knowledge and Healing in the Early Modern Atlantic*. 2017.

Mangan, Jane E. *Trading Roles: Gender, Ethnicity, and the Urban Economy in Colonial Potosí*. 2005.

Melville, Elinor. *A Plague of Sheep: Environmental Consequences of the Conquest of Mexico*. 1994.

Metcalf, Alida. *Go-Betweens in the History of Brazil, 1500–1600*. 2005.

Phillips, William D., and Carla Rahn Phillips. *The Worlds of Christopher Columbus*. 1993.

Restall, Matthew. *Seven Myths of the Spanish Conquest*. 2003.

Schwartz, Stuart, ed. *Tropical Babylons: Sugar and the Making of the Atlantic World, 1450–1680*. 2004.

Townsend, Camilla. *Malintzin's Choice: An Indian Woman in the Conquest of Mexico*. 2006.

Wey-Gómez, Nicolás. *Tropics of Empire: Why Columbus Sailed South to the Indies*. 2008.

Chapter 17

Scholars of precolonial Atlantic Africa have made great strides in recent years by using a blend of written, material, and oral sources to build narratives similar to those for the pre-Columbian Americas. We now know a great deal about Atlantic Africa's diverse array of chiefdoms, kingdoms, and gatherer-hunter bands.

Blackburn, Robin. *The Making of New World Slavery from the Baroque to the Modern, 1492–1800*. 1997.

Brooks, George E. *Eurafricans in Western Africa: Commerce, Social Status, Gender, and Religious Observance from the Sixteenth to the Eighteenth Century*. 2003.

Charney, Judith. *Black Rice: The African Origins of Rice Cultivation in the Americas*. 2001.

Collins, Robert O., and James M. Burns. *A History of Sub-Saharan Africa*. 2007.

Ehret, Christopher. *The Civilizations of Africa: A History to 1800*. 2002.

Heywood, Linda, and John Thornton. *Central Africans, Atlantic Creoles, and the Foundation of the Americas, 1585–1660*. 2007.

Klieman, Kairn. *"The Pygmies Were Our Compass": Bantu and Batwa in the History of West Central Africa, Early Times to ca. 1900 CE*. 2003.

Sweet, James H. *Domingos Álvares, African Healing, and the Intellectual History of the Atlantic World*. 2013.

Sweet, James H. *Recreating Africa: Culture, Kinship, and Religion in the African-Portuguese World, 1441–1770*. 2003.

Wheat, David. *Atlantic Africa and the Spanish Caribbean, 1570–1640*. 2016.

Chapter 18

Once seen as static and "despotic," the diverse polities and empires of the Middle East and South Asia are now understood to have been stunning in their complexity, dynamism, and material wealth. Scholars have recovered many new sources in local languages to give voice to numerous peoples until recently seen only through European eyes.

Alam, Muzaffar. *Writing the Mughal World: Studies on Culture and Politics*. 2011.

Andaya, Barbara Watson, and Leonard Andaya. *A History of Early Modern Southeast Asia, 1400–1830*. 2015.

Asher, Catherine B., and Cynthia Talbot. *India Before Europe*. 2006.

Barendse, R. J. *The Arabian Seas: The Indian Ocean World of the Seventeenth Century*. 2002.

Boyajian, James C. *Portuguese Trade in Asia under the Habsburgs, 1580–1640*. 2007.

Floor, Willem. *The Persian Gulf: A Political and Economic History in Five Port Cities, 1500–1730*. 2006.

Lockard, Craig. *Southeast Asia in World History*. 2009.

Matthee, Rudi. *Persia in Crisis: Safavid Decline and the Fall of Isfahan*. 2011.

Newitt, Malyn. *A History of Portuguese Overseas Expansion, 1400–1668*. 2005.

Parthesius, Robert. *Dutch Ships in Tropical Waters: The Development of the Dutch East India Company (VOC) Shipping Network in Asia, 1595–1660*. 2010.

Reid, Anthony. *A History of Southeast Asia: Critical Crossroads*. 2015.

Reid, Anthony, ed. *Southeast Asia in the Early Modern Era: Trade, Power, and Belief*. 1993.

Stein, Burton. *Vijayanagara*. 2005.

Stern, Philip J. *The Company-State: Corporate Sovereignty and the Early Modern Foundations of the British Empire in India*. 2012.

Subrahmanyam, Sanjay. *Europe's India: Words, People, Empires, 1500–1800*. 2017.

Chapter 19

The early modern period in European history has been transformed by the rise of world history, forcing scholars to resituate this dynamic and often warring region in a broader context, linking overseas expansion back to internal transformations. By including the Ottoman Empire in this narrative, we begin to see the larger dimensions of an age of regional struggle before nation-states.

Casale, Giancarlo. *The Ottoman Age of Exploration*. 2010.

Davis, Natalie Zemon. *Women on the Margins: Three Seventeenth-Century Lives*. 1995.

Faroqhi, Suraiya. *Subjects of the Sultan: Culture and Daily Life in the Ottoman Empire*. 2005.

Findlen, Paula, ed. *Early Modern Things: Objects and their Histories, 1500–1800*. 2013.

Goffman, Daniel. *The Ottomans and Early Modern Europe*. 2002.

Gruzinski, Serge. *The Eagle and the Dragon: Globalization and European Dreams of Conquest in China and America in the Sixteenth Century*. 2014.

Jamieson, Alan G. *Lords of the Sea: A History of the Barbary Corsairs*. 2012.

Kaplan, Benjamin J. *Divided by Faith: Religious Conflict and the Practice of Toleration in Early Modern Europe*. 2009.

Matar, Nabil. *Britain and Barbary, 1589–1689*. 2005.

Parker, Geoffrey. *Global Crisis: War, Climate Change and Catastrophe in the Seventeenth Century*. 2014.

Pierce, Leslie. *The Imperial Harem: Women and Sovereignty in the Ottoman Empire*. 1993.

Pomeranz, Kenneth. *The Great Divergence: China, Europe, and the Making of the Modern World Economy*. 2000.

Schwartz, Stuart B. *All Can Be Saved: Religious Tolerance and Salvation in the Iberian Atlantic World*. 2008.

Smith, Pamela, and Paula Findlen, eds. *Merchants and Marvels: Commerce, Science, and Art in Early Modern Europe*. 2002.

Chapter 20

Scholars of East and Southeast Asia have long known how important this region was in producing technical innovations and driving global trade, even as it suffered its own internal upheavals. As with Europe, the region has come to be seen as core to understanding the world's first era of genuine globalization, linked by silver, silk, porcelain, and many other commodities, if also divided by gunpowder.

Andrade, Tonio. *The Gunpowder Age: China, Military Innovation, and the Rise of the West in History.* 2017.

Andrade, Tonio. *Lost Colony: The Untold Story of China's First Great Victory over the West.* 2013.

Brewer, Carolyn. *Shamanism, Catholicism, and Gender Relations in the Colonial Philippines, 1521–1685.* 2004.

Clunas, Craig. *Pictures and Visuality in Early Modern China.* 2012.

Elvin, Mark. *The Retreat of the Elephants: An Environmental History of China.* 2006.

Engel, Barbara. *Women in Russia, 1700–2000.* 2004.

LeDonne, John. *The Grand Strategy of the Russian Empire, 1650–1831.* 2004.

Marcon, Federico. *The Knowledge of Nature and the Nature of Knowledge in Early Modern Japan.* 2017.

Poe, Marshall. *The Russian Moment in World History.* 2003.

Rafael, Vicente. *Contracting Colonialism: Translation and Christian Conversion in Tagalog Society Under Early Spanish Rule,* 2nd ed. 1993.

Seth, Michael J. *A Concise History of Korea from the Neolithic Period Through the Nineteenth Century.* 2006.

Struve, Lynn A, ed. *Voices from the Ming-Qing Cataclysm: China in Tiger's Jaws.* 1998.

Sunderland, Willard. *Taming the Wild Field: Colonization and Empire on the Russian Steppe.* 2004.

Vaporis, Constantine Nomikos. *Voices of Early Modern Japan: Contemporary Accounts of Daily Life During the Age of the Shoguns.* 2013.

Von Glahn, Richard. *Fountain of Fortune: Money and Monetary Policy in China, 1000–1700.* 1996.

Chapter 21

The early modern Americas were something new under the sun, whole continental regions claimed by distant European monarchs, yet clearly these colonies were on their own paths of social, political, and economic development. Once seen as mere dependencies with derivative cultures, the Americas before independence are now regarded as serious gravitational forces in world history as well as sites of cautionary tales of environmental transformation.

Alchon, Suzanne Austin. *A Pest in the Land: New World Epidemics in Global Perspective.* 2003.

Andrien, Kenneth. *Andean Worlds: Indigenous History, Culture, and Consciousness Under Spanish Rule.* 2001.

Brown, Vincent. *The Reaper's Garden: Death and Power in the World of Atlantic Slavery.* 2010.

Candiani, Vera. *Dreaming of Dry Land: Environmental Transformation in Colonial Mexico City.* 2014.

Demos, John. *The Heathen School: A Story of Hope and Betrayal in the Age of the Early Republic.* 2014.

Giráldez, Arturo. *The Age of Trade: The Manila Galleons and the Dawn of the Global Economy.* 2015.

Morgan, Philip, and Nicholas Canny. *The Oxford Handbook of the Atlantic World, 1450–1850.* 2013.

Norton, Mary Beth. *In the Devil's Snare: The Salem Witchcraft Crisis of 1692.* 2003.

Rediker, Marcus. *The Slave Ship: A Human History.* 2008.

Robins, Nicholas. *Mercury, Mining, and Empire: The Human and Ecological Cost of Colonial Silver Mining in the Andes.* 2011.

Rushforth, Brett. *Bonds of Alliance: Indigenous and Atlantic Slaveries in New France*. 2014.

Schwartz, Stuart B. *Sea of Storms: A History of Hurricanes in the Greater Caribbean from Columbus to Katrina*. 2016.

Seijas, Tatiana. *Asian Slaves in Colonial Mexico: Chinos to Indians*. 2015.

Smallwood, Stephanie. *Saltwater Slavery: A Middle Passage from Africa to American Diaspora*. 2008.

Tutino, John. *Making a New World: Founding Capitalism in the Bajío and Spanish North America*. 2011.

Chapter 22

The age of revolutions is rich in biographies and histories of uprisings that covered a vast area of the globe. There were both historical "winners" and "losers" not to mention dramatic change, as almost every book listed here demonstrates.

Elliott, John H. *Empires of the Atlantic World: Britain and Spain in America, 1492–1830*. 2006.

French Revolution: http://chnm.gmu.edu/revolution/

Girard, Philippe. *Toussaint Louverture: A Revolutionary Life*. 2016.

Haitian Revolution: http://www.albany.edu/~js3980/haitian-revolution.html

Hunt, Lynn. *Inventing Human Rights: A History*. 2007.

Jasanoff, Maya. *Liberty's Exiles: American Loyalists in the Revolutionary World*. 2011.

Landers, Jane G. *Atlantic Creoles in the Age of Revolutions*. 2010.

Lovejoy, Paul. *Jihad in West Africa in the Age of Revolutions*. 2017.

Lynch, John. *Simón Bolívar: A Life*. 2006.

Mack, Phyllis. *Heart Religion in the British Enlightenment: Gender and Emotion in Early Methodism*. 2008.

Massie, Robert K. *Catherine the Great: Portrait of a Woman*. 2011.

May, Cedrick. *Evangelism and Resistance in the Black Atlantic, 1760–1835*. 2008.

Napoleonic Empire: http://www.bbc.co.uk/history/historic_figures/bonaparte_napoleon.shtml

Popkin, Jeremy. *You Are All Free: The Haitian Revolution and the Abolition of Slavery*. 2010.

Qadhi, Abu Ammar Yasir. *A Critical Study of Shirk: Being a Translation and Commentary of Muhammad b. Abd al-Wahhab's Kashf al-Shubuhat*. 2002.

Rucker, Walter. *Gold Coast Diasporas: Culture, Identity, and Power*. 2015.

Shovlin, John. *The Political Economy of Virtue: Luxury, Patriotism, and the Origins of the French Revolution*. 2006.

Van Young, Eric. *The Other Rebellion: Popular Violence, Ideology, and the Mexican Struggle for Independence, 1810–1821*. 2001.

Walker, Charles. *Tupac Ameru*. 2014.

Wood, Gordon S. *Revolutionary Characters: What Made the Founders Different?* 2006.

Chapter 23

World history allows us to think differently about the Industrial Revolution, understanding it less as a radical departure and more as a burst of productivity and inventiveness taking place in many parts of the world.

Banerjee, Swapna M. *Men, Women, and Domestics: Articulating Middle-Class Identity in Colonial Bengal*. 2004.

Bello, David Anthony. *Opium and the Limits of Empire: Drug Prohibition in the Chinese Interior, 1729–1850*. 2005.

Bezis-Selfa, John. *Forging America: Ironworkers, Adventurers, and the Industrious Revolution*. 2004.

Carney, Judith A., and Richard N. Rosomoff. *In the Shadow of Slavery: Africa's Botanical Legacy in the Atlantic World*. 2009.

Clark, Gregory. *A Farewell to Alms: A Brief Economic History of the World*. 2007.

D'Costa, Anthony. *The Long March to Capitalism: Embourgeoisement, Internationalization, and Industrial Transformation in India*. 2005.

Dolan, Brian. *Wedgwood: The First Tycoon*. 2004.

Goswami, Manu. *Producing India: From Colonial Economy to National Space*. 2004.

Inikori, Joseph. *Africans and the Industrial Revolution in England: A Study in International Trade and Economic Development*. 2002.

Izzard, Sebastian. *Hiroshige/Eisen: The Sixty-Nine Stations of the Kisokaido*. 2008.

Jones, Gareth Stedman. *Karl Marx: Greatness and Illusion*. 2016.

Lowe, Lisa. *Intimate Relations across Four Continents*. 2015.

Meeker, Michael E. *A Nation of Empire: The Ottoman Legacy of Turkish Modernity*. 2002.

Platt, Stephen R. *Autumn in the Heavenly Kingdom: China, the West, and the Epic Story of the Taiping Civil War*. 2012.

Porter, Susie. *Working Women in Mexico City: Public Discourses and Material Conditions, 1879–1931*. 2003.

Public Broadcasting Service. *American Experience*, "Andrew Carnegie." http://www.pbs.org/wgbh/amex/carnegie/.

Rappaport, Erica. *A Thirst for Empire: How Tea Shaped the Modern World*. 2017.

Riello, John. *Cotton: The Fabric that Made the Modern World*. 2013.

Rocchi, Fernando. *Chimneys in the Desert: Industrialization in Argentina During the Export Boom Years*. 2006.

Sarkar, Tanika and Sumit Sarkar. *Women and Social Reform in Modern India: A Reader*. 2008.

Shepherd, Verene A. *A Maharani's Misery: Narratives of a Passage from India to the Caribbean*. 2002.

Chapter 24

Walthall and Steele's collection of primary sources gives an intimate look at nation-building in Japan, while Judson shows nations deriving from empires and the process as the work of culture and grass-roots actors.

Bay, Mia. *To Tell the Truth Freely: The Life of Ida B. Wells*. 2009.

Burbank, Jane, and Frederick Cooper. *Empires in World History: Power and the Politics of Difference*. 2010.

Carter, Marina, and Khal Torabully. *Coolitude: An Anthology of the Indian Labour Diaspora*. 2002.

Delay, Brian. *War of a Thousand Deserts: Indian Raids and the U.S.-Mexican War*. 2008.

Doyle, Dan. *The Cause of All Nations: An International History of the American Civil War*. 2015.

Feifer, George. *Breaking Open Japan: Commodore Perry, Lord Abe and the American Imperialism of 1853*. 2006.

Fenn, Elizabeth. *Encounters at the Heart of the World: A History of the Mandan People*. 2014.

Fisher, Michael. *Migration: A World History*. 2014.

Froment, Carlos. *Democracy in Latin America, 1760–1900: Civic Selfhood and Public Life in Mexico and Peru*. 2003.

Judson, Pieter M. *The Habsburg Empire: A New History*. 2016.

Lynch, John. *Argentine Caudillo: Juan Manuel de Rosas*. 2001.

Mathew, Johan. *Margins of the Market: Trafficking and Capitalism Across the Arabian Sea*. 2016.

Minawi, Mostafa. *The Ottoman Scramble for Africa: Empire and Diplomacy in the Sahara and the Hijaz*. 2016.

National Park Service: Frederick Douglass: https://www.nps.gov/frdo/learn/historyculture/frederickdouglass.htm

*Nikitenko, Alexander. *Up from Serfdom: My Childhood and Youth in Russia, 1804–1824*. Translated by Helen Saltz Jacobson. 2001.

Osborne, Myles, and Susan Kingsley Kent. *Africans and Britons in the Age of Empires, 1660–1980.* 2015.

Sahadeo, Jeff. *Russian Colonial Society in Tashkent, 1865–1923.* 2007.

Sergeev, Evgeny. *The Great Game, 1856–1907: Russo-British Relations in Central and East Asia.* 2013.

Tuna, Mustafa O. *Imperial Russia's Muslims: Islam, Empire, and European Modernity, 1788–1914.* 2015.

*Walthall, Anne and M. William Steele, eds. *Politics and Society in Japan's Meiji Restoration: A Brief History with Documents.* 2017.

*Primary source.

Chapter 25

Studies of the wars and revolutions of the early twentieth century and their global impact abound. The following selections are among the best at providing either a broad picture or an individual account.

Allawi, Ali A. *Faisal I of Iraq.* 2014.

Callahan, Michael D. *A Sacred Trust: The League of Nations and Africa, 1929–1946.* 2005.

Gerwarth, Robert and Erez Manela. *Empires at War 1911–1923.* 2014.

Gingeras, Ryan. *Mustafa Kemal Atatürk: Heir to an Empire.* 2016.

Gordon, David B. *Sun Yatsen: Seeking a Newer China.* 2009.

Hajdarpasic, Edin. *Whose Bosnia: Nationalism and Political Imagination in the Balkans, 1840–1914.* 2015.

Hart, Paul. *Emiliano Zapata.* 2018.

Hart, Peter. *Gallipoli.* 2011.

Healy, Maureen. *Vienna and the Fall of the Habsburg Empire: Total War and Everyday Life in World War I.* 2004.

Hunt, Nancy Rose. *A Nervous State: Violence, Remedies, and Reverie in Colonial Congo.* 2016.

Jones, Mark. *Founding Weimar: Violence and the German Revolution of 1918–1919.* 2016.

King, Charles. *Midnight at the Pera Palace: The Birth of Modern Istanbul.* 2014.

Paice, Edward. *World War I: The African Front.* 2011.

Pederson, Susan. *The Guardians: The League of Nations and the Crisis of Empire.* 2015.

Reynolds, Michael A. *Shattering Empires: The Clash and Collapse of the Ottoman and Russian Empires, 1908–1918.* 2011.

Romero, Luis Alberto. *A History of Argentina in the Twentieth Century.* Translated by James P. Brennan. 2002.

Scales, Rebecca. *Radio and the Politics of Sound in Interwar France, 1921–1939.* 2016.

*Wasserman, Mark. *The Mexican Revolution: A Brief History in Documents.* 2012.

Weinbaum, Alys Eve, et al. *Modern Girl Around the World: Consumption, Modernity, and Globalization.* 2008.

Williamson, Edwin. *Borges: A Life.* 2004.

*Primary source.

Chapter 26

This grim period in human history has yielded an ever-growing crop of excellent works, some of them clearly examining the worst aspects of the Great Depression and World War II and others looking at resistance, survival, and intellectual breakthroughs.

Allman, Jean, Susan Geiger, and Nakanyike Musisi, eds. *Women in African Colonial Histories.* 2002.

Browning, Christopher. *Remembering Survival: Inside a Nazi Slave Labor Camp.* 2010.

Bucur, Maria. *Heroes and Victims: Remembering War in Twentieth-Century Romania.* 2009.

Danke, Li. *Echoes of Chongqing: Women in Wartime China.* 2010.

Driscoll, Marc. *Absolute Erotic, Absolute Grotesque: The Living, Dead, and Undead in Japan's Imperialism, 1895–1945.* 2010.

Feinstein, Charles H., et al. *The World Economy Between the World Wars.* 2008.

Fyne, Robert. *Long Ago and Far Away: Hollywood and the Second World War.* 2008.

Hanebrink, Paul. *A Specter Haunting Europe: The Myth of Judeo-Bolshevism.* 2018.

Hellbeck, Jochen. *Stalingrad: The City That Defeated the Third Reich.* 2015.

Khan, Yasmin. *The Raj at War: A People's History of India's Second World War.* 2015.

Krylova, Anna. *Soviet Women in Combat: A History of Violence on the Eastern Front.* 2010.

Kushner, Barak. *The Thought War: Japanese Imperial Propaganda.* 2006.

Matera, Marc, Misty L. Bastian, and Susan Kingsley Kent. *The Women's War of 1929: Gender and Violence in Colonial Nigeria.* 2011.

Matera, Marc and Susan K. Kent. *The Global 1930s: The International Decade.* 2017.

Mitter, Rana. *Forgotten Ally: China's World War II 1937–1945.* 2013.

Naimark, Norman. *Genocide: A World History.* 2016.

*Pa, Chin. *Family.* 1931.

Slezkine, Yuri. *The House of Government: A Saga of the Russian Revolution.* 2017.

Snyder, Timothy. *Bloodlands: Europe Between Hitler and Stalin.* 2010.

Spector, Ronald H. *In the Ruins of Empire: The Japanese Surrender and the Battle for Postwar Asia.* 2007.

Tidrick, Kathryn. *Gandhi: A Political and Spiritual Life.* 2007.

Wildt, Michael. *An Uncompromising Generation: The Nazi Leadership of the Reich Security Main Office.* 2009.

St. Andrews University in Scotland provides a number of links to sources for the diplomatic history of the origins of World War II: http://www.st-andrews.ac.uk/~pv/courses/prewar/resources.html.

*Primary source.

Chapter 27

The Cold War transformed world politics amid the often violent accomplishment of decolonization. Despite the postwar world recovery, notable leaders of new nations worked to overcome poverty, illiteracy, and lingering factionalism.

Brown, Jonathan C. *Cuba's Revolutionary World.* 2017.

Burleigh, Michael. *Small Wars, Faraway Places: Global Insurrection and the Making of the Modern World, 1945–1965.* 2014.

Cullather, Nick. *Hungry World: America's Cold War Battle Against Poverty in Asia.* 2013.

Cumings, Bruce. *Korea's Place in the Sun: A Modern History.* 2005.

Elkins, Caroline. *Imperial Reckoning: The Untold Story of Britain's Gulag in Kenya.* 2005.

Feinberg, Melissa. *Curtain of Lies: The Battle over Truth in Stalinist Eastern Europe.* 2017.

Fontaine, Darcie. *Decolonizing Christianity: Religion and the End of Empire in France and Algeria, 1940–1965.* 2016.

Guha, Ramachandra. *Makers of Modern Asia*. 2014.

Halleiner, Eric. *Forgotten Foundations of Bretton Woods: International Development and the Making of the Postwar Order*. 2014.

Hong, Young-Sun. *Cold War Germany, the Third World, and the Global Humanitarian Regime*. 2015.

Jobs, Richard I. *Backpack Ambassadors: How Youth Travel Integrated Europe*. 2017.

Joseph, Peniel E. *Stokely: A Life*. 2014.

Korean War Educator: http://www.koreanwar-educator.org

Lee, Christopher J. *Making a World After Empire: The Bandung Moment and Its Political Afterlives*. 2010.

Matera, Marc. *Black London: The Imperial Metropolis and Decolonization in the Twentieth Century*. 2015.

Sanos, Sandrine. *Simone de Beauvoir: Creating a Feminist Existence in the World*. 2017.

Shepard, Todd. *Voices of Decolonization: A Brief History with Documents*. 2015.

Thomas, Martin. *Fight or Flight: Britain, France, and Their Roads from Empire*. 2013.

White, Luise. *Unpopular Sovereignty: Rhodesian Independence and African Decolonization*. 2015.

Zhou, Xun. *Forgotten Voices of Mao's Great Famine, 1958–1961*. 2014.

Chapter 28

The decades around the turn of the twenty-first century were full of events that shifted balances of economic and political power. Globalization is hotly debated, and this selection of works shows why.

Alexievich, Svetlana. *Secondhand Time: The Last of the Soviets*. 2016.

Bayly, Susan. *Asian Voices in a Post-Colonial Age: Vietnam, India and Beyond*. 2007.

Benjamin, Thomas. "A Time of Reconquest: History, the Maya Revival, and the Zapatista Rebellion." *American Historical Review*. 2000.

Fong, Mei. *One Child: The Story of China's Most Radical Experiment*. 2015.

Haass, Richard. *A World in Disarray: American Foreign Policy and the Crisis of the Old Order*. 2017.

Kandiyoti, Deniz, and Ayse Saktanber. *Fragments of Culture: The Everyday of Modern Turkey*. 2006.

Kato, M. T. *From Kung Fu to Hip Hop: Globalization, Revolution, and Popular Culture*. 2007.

Keller, Richard. *The Environment: A World History*. 2018–2019.

Khair, Tabish. *The New Xenophobia*. 2016.

Louie, Miriam Ching Yoon. *Sweatshop Warriors: Immigrant Women Workers Take on the Global Factory*. 2001.

Myers, Steven Lee. *The New Tsar: The Rise and Reign of Vladimir Putin*. 2016.

Prunier, Gérard. *Darfur: The Ambiguous Genocide*. 2005.

Roach, Stephen S. *Unbalanced: The Codependency of America and China*. 2014.

Sassen, Saskia. *Cities in a World Economy*. 2006.

Smith, Raymond A., and Patricia Siplon. *Drugs into Bodies: Global AIDS Treatment Activism*. 2006.

South Africa: http://www.info.gov.za/documents/constitution/1996/96cons2.htm

Taubman, William. *Gorbachev: His Life and Times*. 2017.

United Nations. http://www.un.org/womenwatch/. Provides ample information on women around the world and also on the UN's programs for women.

Credits

Chapter 13

Pictures from History/Bridgeman Images, p. 452; Biblioteca Monasterio del Escorial, Madrid, Spain/ Bridgeman Images, p. 458; Vollbehr Collection, Rare Book and Special Collections Division, Library of Congress, p. 462; © British Library Board/Robana/ Art Resource, p. 463; akg-images, p. 468; Pictures from History/Bridgeman Images, pg. 473; © The Metropolitan Museum of Art. Image source: Art Resource, NY, pg. 475; Bildarchiv Preussischer Kulturbesitz/Staatsbibliothek zu Berlin, Stiftung Preussicher Kulturbesitz, Berlin, Germany/Art Resource, NY, p. 477; akg-images/Gerard Degeorge, p. 481; Getty Images, p. 484;

Chapter 14

Erich Lessing/Art Resource, NY, p. 488; akg-images, p. 495; The John Work Garrett Library, The Sherican Libraries, Johns Hopkins University, p. 503; Ariadne Van Zandbergen/Alamy Stock Photo, p. 507; Topkapi Palace Museum, Istanbul, Turkey/Bridgeman Images, p. 511; Ashmolean Museum, University of Oxford, UK/Bridgeman Images, p. 512; Erich Lessing/Art Resource, p. 520.

Part 3

V&A Images, London/Art Resource, NY, p. 526.

Chapter 15

Jonathan Irish/National Geographic Creative/ Bridgeman Images, p. 530; National Museum of the American Indian, Smithsonian Institution. Catalogue Number 5/5059. Photo by Katherine Fogden, p. 534; The Granger Collection, New York, p. 539; Scala/Art Resource, NY, p. 542; Firenze, Biblioteca Medicea Laurenziana, Ms. Med. Palat. 219, f. 132v. Su concessione del MiBACT, p. 546; AP Photo/Natacha Pisarenko, p. 556; Aurélia Frey/akg-images, p. 557; NATIONAL MUSEUM OF THE AMERICAN INDIAN, SMITHSONIAN INSTITUTION

(CATALOG NUMBER 1/2132). PHOTO BY NMAI PHOTO SERVICES., p. 562.

Chapter 16

Museo Naval, Bridgeman Art Library, p. 566; The Art Archive/Science Academy Lisbon/Gianni Dagli Orti, p. 572; Courtesy of the John Carter Brown Library at Brown University, p. 579; De Historia Stirpium, 1542, Leonhard Fuchs, Iowa State University, p. 582; Courtesy of the John Carter Brown Library at Brown University, p. 587; The Granger Collection, New York, p. 588; The Hispanic Society of America Museum and Library, New York, p. 592; Courtesy of the John Carter Brown Library at Brown University, p. 596; Courtesy of the University of Oviedo Library, Spain, p. 600.

Chapter 17

Image copyright © The Metropolitan Museum of Art. Image source: Art Resource, NY, p. 604; © National Maritime Museum, London/The Image Works, p. 610; Aldo Tutino/Art Resource, NY, p. 614; Image copyright © The Metropolitan Museum of Art. Image source: Art Resource, NY, p. 616; Manoscritti Araldi/Michele Araldi. Photo: Vincenzo Negro, p. 619; Manoscritti Araldi/Michele Araldi. Photo: Vincenzo Negro, p. 626; General Collection, Beinecke Rare Book and Manuscript Library, Yale University, p. 629; © British Library Board. All Rights Reserved/Bridgeman Images, p. 633; Martin Harvey/Photolibrary/Getty Images, p. 636.

Chapter 18

V&A Images, London/Art Resource, NY, p. 640; Ms 1889. Biblioteca Casanatense, Rome, p. 647; Photo by Colin McPherson/Corbis via Getty Images, p. 649; Private Collection/Photo © Christie's Images/ Bridgeman Images, p. 658; V&A Images, London/ Art Resource, NY, p. 661; The Granger Collection, New York, p. 669; Rijksmuseum, Amsterdam, The Netherlands/Bridgeman Images, p. 671.

Chapter 19

Topkapi Palace Museum, Istanbul, Turkey/Bridgeman Images, p. 678; Ketan Gajria, p. 684; De Agostini Picture Library/A. Dagli Orti/Bridgeman Images, p. 687; CBL T 439.9 © The Trustees of the Chester Beatty Library, Dublin, p. 688; The Palace Museum, Beijing/ChinaStock, p. 698; akg-images, p. 702; akg-images/Universal Images Group, p. 707; akg-images/Hervé Champollion, p. 711; Private Collection/Bridgeman Images, p. 716.

Chapter 20

The Palace Museum, Beijing/Hu Weibiao/ChinaStock, p. 720; Tretyakov Gallery, Moscow, Russia/Bridgeman Images, p. 727; Golestan Palace, Tehran, Iran/Bridgeman Images, p. 730; De Agostini Picture Library/G. Dagli Orti/Bridgeman Images, p. 732; The Granger Collection, New York, p. 735; The Granger Collection, New York, p. 740; The Granger Collection, New York, p. 743; © RMN-Grand Palais/Art Resource, NY, p. 745; Courtesy, The Lilly Library, Indiana University, Bloomington, Indiana, p. 754.

Chapter 21

Acervo da Fundação Biblioteca Nacional - Brasil/ Archives of the National Library Foundation – Brazil, p. 758; Corsham Court, Wiltshire/Bridgeman Images, p. 764; Mark Hoberman/Corbis Documentary/Getty, p. 765; Album/Art Resource, NY, p. 768; ©Iberfoto/ The Image Works, p. 770; De Agostini Picture Library/A. Dagli Orti/Bridgeman Images, p. 773; National Maritime Museum, London/The Image Works, p. 779; Private Collection/Bridgeman Images, p. 785; ©Mary Evans/Kings College London/The Image Works, p. 792.

Part 4

©Illustrated London News Ltd/Mary Evans, p. 796.

Chapter 22

De Agostini Picture Library/M. Seemuller/ Bridgeman Images, p. 800; Private Collection/Bridgeman Images, p. 806; Hillwood Estate, Museum & Gardens, photo by Ed Owen, p. 808; The Library Company of Philadelphia, p. 814; Journée du 5 Octobre 1789/ Photo © CCI/Bridgeman Images, p. 817; Bibliothèque Nationale, Paris, France/Bridgeman Images, p. 822; Private Collection/Bridgeman Images, p. 825; akg-images, p. 830; De Agostini Picture Library/G. Dagli Orti/Bridgeman Images, p. 834.

Chapter 23

Santa Barbara Museum of Art, Gift of Dr. and Mrs. Roland A. Way, 1984.31.5, p. 838; Cotehele House, Cornwall, UK/Bridgeman Images, p. 844; Photo by William Henry Jackson/Library of Congress/Corbis/ VCG via Getty Images, p. 848; Brooklyn Museum of Art, New York, USA/Gift of Dr. and Mrs. Maurice Cottle/Bridgeman Images, p. 852; Bulletin of the Pan American Union, 42, 1916, Benson Latin American Collection, p. 855; Victoria and Albert Museum, London, p. 857; Dinodia Photos, p. 863; akg-images, p. 864; akg-images, p. 870.

Chapter 24

Art Resource, NY, p. 874; akg-images /De Agostini Picture Library, p. 881; Sovfoto, p. 884; Image Courtesy of Skinner, Inc. www.skinnerinc.com, p. 888; ©The British Library/The Image Works, p. 903; ©Art Media/Heritage/The Image Works, p. 904; akg-images, p. 906; Tetra Images/Getty Images, p. 907; National Portrait Gallery, Smithsonian Institution/Art Resource, NY, p. 910.

Chapter 25

Schalkwijk/Art Resource, NY, p. 914; Private Collection/Bridgeman Images, p. 920; Bettmann/ Corbis/Getty Images, p. 926; Walter Trier-Archiv, Konstanz, p. 928; Photo by David Pollack/Corbis via Getty Images, p. 929; De Agostini Picture Library/ A. Dagli Orti/Bridgeman Images, p. 934; Keystone-France/Gamma-Keystone via Getty Images, p. 939; The Granger Collection, New York, p. 944; Still from Zi Mei Mua, directed by Zheng Zhengqiu, p. 947; Music Division, The New York Public Library for the Performing Arts, Astor, Lenox, and Tilden Foundations, p. 951.

Chapter 26

bpk Bildagentur, Berlin/Art Resource, NY, p. 954; Schalkwijk/Art Resource, NY, p. 961; akg-images, p. 964; Bettmann/Corbis/Getty Images, p. 965; Universal History Archive/UIG / Bridgeman Images, p. 979; Bettmann/Corbis/Getty Images, p. 981; bpk Bildagentur, Berlin/Art Resource, NY p. 983; Bettmann/Corbis/Getty Images, p. 987; Kharbine-Tapabor, Paris, p. 989.

Chapter 27

©Illustrated London News Ltd/Mary Evans, p. 992; Bettmann/Corbis/Getty Images, p. 997; akg-images/ Universal Images Group, p. 1000; Commemorative cloth Nigeria, 1960/Cotton, roller-printed/Gift of Barbara Barde T01X0025/Textile Museum of Canada/Photo by Maciek Linowski, p. 1010; © CORBIS/Corbis via Getty Images, p. 1014;

akg-images/Horizons, p. 1017; Photograph courtesy of Sotheby's Picture Library, p. 1020; Bettmann/Corbis/ Getty Images, p. 1024; AP Photo/Asia-Africa Museum, HO, p. 1026.

Chapter 28

akg-images/Bildarchiv Monheim, p. 1030; akg-images/ Yvan Travert, p. 1041; Louise Gubb/The Image Works, p. 1045; Richard Nowitz/National Geographic Creative, p. 1050; REUTERS/Bazuki Muhamad BM/DY, p. 1051; RIA Novosti/The Image Works, p. 1052; NASA/Goddard Space Flight Center/Science Source, p. 1055; REUTERS/Thomas Mukoya, p. 1062; (left) Fonds Claude Lévi-Strauss. Photographies d'expéditions. Voyages au Brésil. 2 ID/Cote :NAF 28150 (246) photo n° 29 = Nambikwara. Bibliothèque nationale de France, Paris, p. 1064; (right) Stephanie Maze/Corbis Documentary/Getty Images, p. 1064.

Index

Note: Page numbers followed by *f, t, m,* or *b* refer to figures or illustrations, tables, maps, and boxes, respectively.